What's on the enclos

87
53

- Step-by-step training from proven experts
- Simulation Exercises that reinforce certification objectives
- Test Prep tools to help you prepare for the certification exam
- Electronic version of the this Study Guide
- Your link to comprehensive Online Training Resources from LearnKey

MW01226913

MCAD/MCSD Visual C#® .NET™ Certification
(Exams 70-315, 70-316, 70-320)

EXAM GUIDE

OSBORNE
P/N 0-07-222445-2

LIND, REMPEL

Copyright © 2002
The McGraw-Hill Companies, Inc.
All rights reserved.

C# is an object oriented programming language developed by Microsoft that enables developers to quickly build a wide range of applications for the .NET platform. In the C# for Developers course from LearnKey, expert instructor Jesse Liberty begins with a solid introduction to programming methods, shows you how to build applications and continues with advanced topics like class libraries, threading streams and interoperations with COM. At the conclusion of this course, you will understand how to build Windows and Web applications on .NET using C#.

Load the enclosed CD for dynamic Online instruction from LearnKey and McGraw-Hill/Osborne. Your first Session is FREE!

Special Online Discounts for Osborne Customers!

Because you purchased an Osborne Study Guide with a MediaPoint CD, you are entitled to incredible savings on LearnKey online training courses.

Save up to 60% on Online Training!

Purchase the complete course and get 12 months access to all of the online training materials including:

- **Media-rich Courseware**
- **Supplemental Articles**
- **Study Plans**
- **Labs**
- **Reference Material and more!**

This is a limited time offer so don't delay. Get started on your online training today!

For additional Online training contact LearnKey.

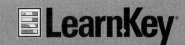

ALL · IN · ONE

MCAD/MCSD
Visual C#® .NET™
Certification

EXAM GUIDE

(Exams 70-315, 70-316, 70-320)

ABOUT THE AUTHORS

Kenneth S. Lind (MCSD, MCAD, MCSE+I, MCSE, MCP+SB, MCT, CTT+, CET) is the owner of No Problem Computers and works out of Toronto, Ontario, Canada, as an independent training consultant and author. Kenneth has over 20 years experience in software development and has developed applications using C, FORTRAN, C++, Java, VB, C#, and assembler. He left his native Sweden after receiving an engineering degree in telecommunications, a move he never regretted. He has specialized in object-oriented (OO) development and its use in Java and C++. Kenneth can be reached at KennethSLind@hotmail.com.

Marj Rempel (MCSD, MCSE, MCT, CTT+, JCP, A+, CCNA) is a computer professor for Durham College. Since attending the University of Waterloo in the dark ages of computer processing, over 25 years ago, Marj has been involved in software development for mainframe computers and—for the past 15 years—in the PC arena using C, Java, Visual Basic, and Visual C# .NET. After spending three years teaching software development in the corporate field, she recently accepted her current position as a professor and specializes in teaching computer-related subjects. Marj can be reached at MarjRempel@hotmail.com.

About the Technical Editors

James Keogh teaches courses on Java Application Development, including J2EE, at Columbia University and is a member of the Java Community Process Program. He developed the first e-commerce track at Columbia and became its first chairperson. Jim spent more than a decade developing advanced systems for major Wall Street firms. He introduced PC programming nationally in his *Popular Electronics Magazine* column in 1982, just four years after the start up of Apple Computers in a Los Altos, CA garage. He was also a team member who built one of the first Windows applications by a Wall Street firm, featured by Bill Gates in 1986. Jim is the author of 54 books and several best-selling computer books. He is also a faculty member of Saint Peter's College Graduate School, Jersey City, NJ.

Larry Chambers (B.Sc., MCSD, MCSE) is a freelance technical writer who has contributed technical expertise as an editor and writer for various books. Larry works for a large Fortune 50 financial services firm in Winnipeg, Manitoba, Canada. Before that, Larry worked with a large consulting firm that provided consulting and services for Fortune 100 companies throughout Canada. Larry has been providing consulting, management, and technical expertise in the computer industry for the last 14 years. In his spare time, you can find him on a mountain bike somewhere in the wilderness.

About LearnKey

LearnKey provides self-paced learning content and multimedia delivery solutions to enhance personal skills and business productivity. LearnKey claims the largest library of rich streaming media training content that engages learners in dynamic media-rich instruction complete with video clips, audio, full motion graphics, and animated illustrations. LearnKey can be found at www.LearnKey.com.

ALL ■ IN ■ ONE

MCAD/MCSD
Visual C#® .NET™
Certification

EXAM GUIDE

(Exams 70-315, 70-316, 70-320)

Kenneth S. Lind & Marj Rempel

McGraw-Hill/Osborne

New York • Chicago • San Francisco • Lisbon
London • Madrid • Mexico City • Milan • New Delhi
San Juan • Seoul • Singapore • Sydney • Toronto

The McGraw·Hill Companies

McGraw-Hill/Osborne
2600 Tenth Street
Berkeley, California 94710
U.S.A.

To arrange bulk purchase discounts for sales promotions, premiums, or fund-raisers, please contact **McGraw-Hill**/Osborne at the above address. For information on translations or book distributors outside the U.S.A., please see the International Contact Information page immediately following the index of this book.

MCAD/MCSD Visual C#* .NET™ Certification All-in-One Exam Guide
(Exams 70-315, 70-316, 70-320)

1234567890 DOC DOC 0198765432

Book p/n 0-07-222444-4 and CD p/n 0-07-222445-2
parts of
ISBN 0-07-222443-6

Publisher
Brandon A. Nordin

Vice President & Associate Publisher
Scott Rogers

Editorial Director
Gareth Hancock

Senior Acquisitions Editor
Nancy Maragioglio

Senior Project Editors
Betsy Manini
Jody McKenzie

Project Editor
Monika Faltiss

Acquisitions Coordinator
Jessica Wilson

Technical Editors
Jim Keogh
Larry Chambers

Copy Editor
Andy Carroll

Proofreaders
Stefany Otis
Linda Medoff
Emily Rader
Paul Medoff

Indexer
Claire Splan

Computer Designers
Tara A. Davis
Michelle Galicia
Lucie Ericksen

Illustrators
Michael Mueller
Lyssa Wald

This book was composed with Corel VENTURA™ Publisher.

DEDICATION

I dedicate this book to my son Andy
for his bravery in adversity and his love for humanity.

Kenneth S. Lind

I dedicate this book to my husband, Hans, and my son, Matthew,
both of whom display a love of life and family every day of their lives.

Marj Rempel

CONTENTS AT A GLANCE

CONTENTS

ACKNOWLEDGMENTS

It seems like just yesterday that I started to work with Nancy Maragioglio while she was with another publisher, and, as luck would have it, Nancy and I have crossed paths many times since. I would like to thank Nancy for making this book a reality. As the senior acquisitions editor, she has suffered all the plausible and implausible tales an author invents about why the schedule is slipping. Additionally, I would like to thank Gareth Hancock, the editorial director of this book.

Thanks, too, to Jessica Wilson, the acquisitions coordinator, who kept all the segments of the book flowing seamlessly between the team members who—in the end—produced this book.

Andy Carroll was the copy editor who put Swedish-English techno speech into grammatically correct English. Andy also showed a very high degree of understanding for the software development process, catching many errors that had made their way through the editing process.

The senior project editor was Betsy Manini, and without her diligent work this book would never have found its way to press.

Great thanks to Marj, my co-author and good friend, who has followed my breadcrumbs through many discussions and brought me back to the path that lead to this book. *Heja*, Marj. I also want to thank Marj's trusted thunderstorm prognosticator, Sheb the Dalmatian, that can foretell storms that are 80 miles away.

I would also like to thank my wife Dorette, my daughter Inga, and my son Anders, for not calling the men in white when I uttered incoherent rantings about C# and databases in a never-ending sequence of days and nights.

Kenneth S. Lind

The staff at McGraw-Hill has been incredible. Nancy, without you this book would never have been started or completed. How can we ever thank you for all of your support, encouragement, and understanding? Many, many thanks, and I raise my glass to you! I would also like to thank Betsy, Andy, and Jessica, without whom this book would never have found its way to the printer. Betsy, I will always remember the em-dash, eh? Andy, thanks for being more than just a copy editor. Have you ever considered tech editing?

Heja and *Hoppla* to my co-author and favorite Swede, Ken. We have spent many (and I mean *many*) hours side-by-side, making sure that this book was put together in a manner that will help you, the reader. Thanks for your patience and assistance.

I would also like to thank the members of my family who will be grateful to see me away from the keyboard for a while. Hans and Matthew—it just couldn't have been done without you. To the rest of my family—Mom, Kathy, Susan, Pat, Aunt Jean, Uncle Keith, Koby, Lauren, Brian, Jim, Clem, Paul, and Elizabeth—thank you for all of your help, support, and kind words. You'll never know how much it means to me.

Marj Rempel

INTRODUCTION

Welcome to the *MCAD/MCSD Visual C# .NET™ Certification All-in-One Exam Guide*. This book has been specifically written to help you prepare for MCSD/MCAD certifications, but also to act as an on-the job reference after your achieve your certification. You'll find many hands-on labs and exercises within these pages, and much of the code is also included on the CD-ROM as an additional help.

Because many of the concepts addressed in the exams overlap somewhat, we've taken the approach of addressing the material covered by the exams by topic rather than by individual objective. While each objective is covered in the book, we feel that by exploring the topics behind the objectives, we can provide you with a more complete background for understanding the concepts. If you prefer to study by objective, Appendix B is a mapping document that will guide you to the appropriate chapter for each of the objectives.

There are several elements used within the text to help highlight information of specific interest:

- **Exam Tips** Give you hints and information about how Microsoft approaches the topic during the exam. These are an excellent tool for reviewing right before you take the test.

- **Notes** Provide a bit more insight into various topics. While you might not need this depth of information for the exam, it is information that may prove useful on the job.

- **Hands-On Exercises** There's no replacement for hands-on experience, and these exercises are designed to give you practical experience while preparing you for the exam. Be sure to work through them to help reinforce what you're reading.

- **Questions and Answers** There are hundreds of questions in this book/CD package, along with answers and explanations. By taking advantage of these self-assessment options, you can establish areas where you may need additional study, as well as practice facing the testing scenario.

Why Certify?

Microsoft certification has a history of positive impact on career growth and salary increase. It is an accepted standard of qualification that corporations worldwide respect. With the shift toward integrated computing and the establishment of the .NET Framework, the role of the developer will gain visibility, and the MCSD and MCAD certifications will be a key differentiator for those working with the .NET technologies.

MCAD vs. MCSD

According to Microsoft, candidates for the MCAD certification credential are professionals who use Microsoft technologies to develop and maintain department-level applications, components, web or desktop clients, or back-end data services, or who work in teams developing enterprise applications.

Comparatively, candidates for the MCSD certification are lead developers who design and develop leading-edge enterprise solutions with Microsoft development tools, technologies, platforms, and the Microsoft .NET Framework.

MCSD certification encompasses the skill set of the MCAD certification, and you may wish to pursue the MCAD as a step toward MCSD certification. You may even find that MCAD matches your career interests and plans more accurately than the MCSD track. Either way, certification is a valuable asset when building your career.

MCSD Certification Requirements

Achieving the MCSD certification requires passing four core exams and one elective exam. The core exams are listed here.

 NOTE   Please observe that the italicized exam names are those which are covered within this text.

MCSD Core Exams

Solution Architecture Exam (Required)
Exam 70-300—Analyzing Requirements and Defining .NET Solution Architectures

Web Application Development Exams (One Required)
Exam 70-305—Developing and Implementing Web Applications with Microsoft Visual Basic .NET and Microsoft Visual Studio .NET
Or
Exam 70-315—Developing and Implementing Web Applications with Microsoft Visual C# .NET and Microsoft Visual Studio .NET

Windows Application Development Exams (One Required)
Exam 70-306—Developing and Implementing Windows-Based Applications with Microsoft Visual Basic .NET and Microsoft Visual Studio .NET
Or
Exam 70-316—Developing and Implementing Windows-Based Applications with Microsoft Visual C# .NET and Microsoft Visual Studio .NET

Web Services and Server Components Exams (One Required)

Exam 70-310—Developing XML Web Services and Server Components with Microsoft Visual Basic .NET and the Microsoft .NET Framework

Or

Exam 70-320—Developing XML Web Services and Server Components with Microsoft Visual C# and the Microsoft .NET Framework

In addition to the core exams, you must pass one of the following elective exams:

- **Exam 70-229**—Designing and Implementing Databases with Microsoft SQL Server 2000, Enterprise Edition

- **Exam 70-230**—Designing and Implementing Solutions with Microsoft BizTalk Server 2000 Enterprise Edition

- **Exam 70-234**—Designing and Implementing Solutions with Microsoft Commerce Server 2000

MCAD Certification Requirements

Microsoft's MCAD only requires three core exams and one elective, and permits the use of some exams as either core or elective credits.

MCAD Core Exams

Web Application Development Exams (One Required)

Exam 70-305—Developing and Implementing Web Applications with Microsoft Visual Basic .NET and Microsoft Visual Studio .NET

Or

Exam 70-315—Developing and Implementing Web Applications with Microsoft Visual C# .NET and Microsoft Visual Studio .NET

Windows Application Development Exams (One Required)

Exam 70-306—Developing and Implementing Windows-Based Applications with Microsoft Visual Basic .NET and Microsoft Visual Studio .NET

Or

Exam 70-316—Developing and Implementing Windows-Based Applications with Microsoft Visual C# .NET and Microsoft Visual Studio .NET

Web Services and Server Components Exams (One Required)
Exam 70-310—Developing XML Web Services and Server Components with Microsoft Visual Basic .NET and the Microsoft .NET Framework
Or
Exam 70-320—Developing XML Web Services and Server Components with Microsoft Visual C# and the Microsoft .NET Framework

In addition to the core exams, you must pass one of the following elective exams:

- **Exam 70-229**—Designing and Implementing Databases with Microsoft SQL Server 2000, Enterprise Edition
- **Exam 70-234**—Designing and Implementing Solutions with Microsoft Commerce Server 2000

The following may be used for elective credit if they have not been used toward core exam credit.

- Exam 70-305
- Exam 70-306
- Exam 70-310
- Exam 70-315
- Exam 70-316
- Exam 70-320

 EXAM TIP Visit www.microsoft.com to get the latest certification information. Exams are subject to change without notice, so be sure to check this site frequently as you prepare for your exam.

PART I

C#: The Language

Introduction to C# .NET and the .NET Platform

In this chapter, you will

- Learn about the .NET Framework
- Become familiar with the .NET languages
- Discover the environment surrounding C# .NET
- Compile your first C# program
- Learn the basics of the C# language
- Be introduced to object-oriented programming
- Learn to use abstraction and encapsulation
- Learn to differentiate between instance data and class data

If you have been around the programming world for a while, you may have some experience with languages such as Visual Basic, C++, or Java. These languages commonly provide desktop solutions, and over the years have had to expand their reach to include "enterprise" development. In order to accommodate the concepts of distributed programming, reusable software, and platform independence, languages were extended and programming structures were put into place. These additions include such things as Component Object Model (COM), Distributed Component Object Model (DCOM), Transaction servers and Application servers. Microsoft was quick to notice that a shift in development practices began with the introduction of Internet programming. The Internet necessitated some kind of common interface to be placed in front of the user. The software languages were struggling to provide scripted or interpreted environments that could run in a browser on every kind of platform. If you have ever had to work with plug-ins, browser incompatibility, slow scripted languages, or out-of-date runtime environments, you will understand the difficulties that developers faced over the past five years.

You will also appreciate the excitement over Microsoft's latest offering to the world— the .NET platform. This platform means different things to different people. For the world of network administrators, it means new service applications, such as Microsoft Exchange 2000 Server, Microsoft SQL 2000 Server, and the soon-to-be-released Microsoft .NET Servers.

For the development world, it means delivery of the long-awaited Visual Studio .NET and its arsenal of new and old languages, as well as the Common Language Runtime (CLR). This chapter will introduce you to the .NET platform and explore the fundamentals of the Visual C# programming language, as well as the introductory concepts of object-oriented programming (OOP). Please keep in mind that if you are an experienced OOP programmer, you may just need to skim this chapter for differences between C# and other languages, such as C++ and Java, or you may want to review the chapter as a refresher.

Whatever route you choose, there is little or nothing in this chapter that will be directly tested on the Microsoft exams. However, having said that, Microsoft assumes a working knowledge of all the concepts covered in this chapter. If you are new to OOP, you may want to spend extra time in this chapter and work outside the book a little in order to bring your skills to the level required. This book assumes that you already have an excellent grasp of the concepts that are briefly looked at in this chapter.

Overview of .NET

Before one can start talking about the C# language, it is imperative to understand the platform upon which it works. Historically, programming using Microsoft development tools has involved the traditional Windows API, a programming interface that sits between coders and the desktop. Microsoft realized that as software progressed, APIs became complicated and corrupted by a series of updates and changes. Instead of continuing to improve upon it, Microsoft chose to completely revamp the process. .NET introduced a brand-new development platform, called the .NET Framework, which brings together many old, familiar languages, and, of course, includes a new and exciting language, Microsoft C# .NET.

So, What Is .NET?

.NET is huge. Microsoft has invested a great portion of its budget to researching and developing this brand-new way of doing things. It's not just an offering to the programming world. It introduces a combined and consistent effort between operating systems, services, and programming languages. Of course, our focus will be on the .NET Framework, but in order to be conversant with the other side of .NET, here is the shortlist of elements that make up the .NET architecture:

- **A set of .NET languages that can be said to function in a common environment**   These languages all execute in a common runtime and all make use of a common library of components. Any language can be said to be .NET-compliant if it does this. As the future unfolds, you will see many languages strive to function this way and join the ever-growing list of .NET languages. Visual Studio .NET includes a group of Microsoft-built languages that conform to the .NET standard.

- **A set of services provided by the .NET Enterprise Servers**   Over the last few years, we have watched the release of a new e-mail server, Microsoft Exchange

Server; a new database server, Microsoft SQL Server; and just recently, a whole new set of servers, such as BizTalk Server and Commerce Server—all 2000 releases. These servers provide the infrastructure that will be used to host and manage .NET applications and services.

- **A distributed application service**   Increasingly, services will be accessible from the Internet, and Microsoft has been aware of this trend for a long time. As network bandwidth increases and waiting times decrease, it has become apparent that it is possible to provide real-time services through the Internet. The .NET platform makes use of XML (Extensible Markup Language) and SOAP (Simple Object Access Protocol) in order to describe and deliver data.

- **A service for .NET enabled devices**   These devices include hand-held computers, cell phones, game machines, and so on.

As you can see, .NET is more than just a development environment. However, the focus of this book will be just that. In the next sections, we will attempt to fight our way through the many acronyms and phrases that make up the usual descriptions of the .NET Framework. When we are done, we hope that you will have a new-found appreciation for the amount of time, work, and effort that went into making the .NET Framework the exciting offering that it is. You will also have a solid foundation for the topics that will be covered on the C# exams.

Application Development in .NET

Quite simply put, .NET (from a developer's perspective) is a new runtime environment packaged together with a plethora of prebuilt, ready-to-use software components. Given that, we will start talking about things like the Common Language Runtime (CLR) and the .NET Framework. The CLR is the underlying software that allows your program to run, and the .NET Framework is a library or collection of object-oriented software built for you in order to make your programming tasks easier.

Microsoft had several goals in mind when they decided to create the .NET platform:

- *An object-oriented code execution environment provides a consistent approach.* This means that whether you code for the Internet, the local desktop, or a remote, server-based distribution center, you will be accessing the same .NET runtime in order to execute your code.

- *Fully object-oriented languages are built into the .NET platform.*   Familiar languages, such as Visual Basic, have been extended and reworked to make them more object-oriented. C# is the new language that combines elements of Java and C++.

 NOTE   If you are unfamiliar with the concepts of object-oriented programming, we will explore programming with classes later in this chapter. Refer to Chapter 3 for some of the more advanced features.

- *In a world of Internet access and deepened security concerns, it is a challenge to securely execute code.* The .NET platform includes several built-in mechanisms to ensure the code conforms to specifications, such as the Common Language Specifications (CLS). Code must also be guaranteed to be "safe" when it enters the runtime environment and, conversely, the user of the code must be authorized to use the program. We will be exploring many levels of security in the coming chapters. .NET provides developers with a heightened sense of code security.

- *If you have coded using dynamic-link libraries (DLLs), you will appreciate it when we tell you that this nightmare is now over.* Developers have long been concerned with versioning DLLs, which are reusable software components whose references are stored in the Windows Registry. By versioning, we mean that these components, when upgraded, have to provide some backward compatibility as well as performing their new functions in the upgraded environment. Microsoft has eliminated these concerns by replacing the traditional DLL with assemblies. Versioning is built right into the assembly, and many versions can live together harmoniously.

An end user of application software is guaranteed, in this fast-paced technological world, to have the patience and the attention span of a hyperactive child. This is not a criticism—this is a fact. We have developed a world in which we don't want to wait for technology. To this end, the .NET Framework makes it possible to reduce the performance problems that we have experienced with languages that are scripted (VBScript, JavaScript, and the like) and languages that are interpreted at runtime (Java). As you read on in this book, you will gain an understanding of how this is accomplished and why this is such an important development.

If you are not excited yet, keep reading! We will be showing you how easy it is to create applications that can be initiated from the Internet, as well as software that interacts with the desktop in a traditional forms manner. You will be able to create practical applications right away while you are preparing to take the Microsoft C# exams.

The .NET Platform

We've mentioned the .NET platform so often that it's now time to formalize our discussion. Just what is the .NET platform? In this section, we will explore the architecture of the .NET platform, which is made up of the .NET Framework, the Common Language Specifications (CLS), the Common Language Runtime (CLR), Microsoft Intermediate Language (MSIL), and the Base Class Library (BCL). Once we've finished with that alphabet soup, we will put it all in perspective and look at how all the pieces come together to create a development platform.

The .NET Framework

The .NET Framework is made up of the Common Language Runtime, the Base Class Library, and services that allow you to create Web applications (ASP.NET) and Windows applications (Windows forms). If we explore the architecture, we can see how this is all put together.

Figure 1-1 shows the overall picture, demonstrating how the .NET languages adhere to the rules provided by the Common Language Specifications. These languages can all be used independently to create Web services, Web forms, or Windows forms, and can all be used with built-in data describers (XML) and data accessors (ADO.NET and SQL). Every component of the .NET Framework can take advantage of the large prebuilt library of classes called the Base Class Library. Once everything is put together, the code that is created is executed in the Common Language Runtime, which is similar to (but different from) the Java Virtual Machine (JVM). You can see a very large difference in just this one point—the JVM is designed to accommodate a single language (Java); but the Common Language Runtime is designed to allow any .NET-compliant language to execute its code. At the time of writing, these languages included Visual Basic .NET, C# .NET, and C++ .NET, but any language could become .NET-compliant.

The following sections will address each of the parts of the architecture. By understanding the parts, you will understand the sum of the parts—the excitement and functional power of .NET!

The CLS—Common Language Specifications

In an object-oriented environment, everything is an object. (This point is explained in this chapter and the more advanced features are explained in Chapter 3.) In a nutshell, you create a blueprint or template for an object (this is called the class file), and this class file is used to create multiple objects.

TIP Consider a wheel. You may want to create many wheels in your lifetime; but each wheel will have certain characteristics and certain functions. For example, each wheel will have a specific circumference, width, and color. Each wheel must be able to be rotated and installed on a vehicle. So now, suppose your neighbor also wants to create a wheel. Why reinvent the wheel? (Pardon the bad joke.) You can create a template and share it with others. They create the physical wheels based on your template. This is the crux of object-oriented programming—the template is the class file, and the physical wheels are the objects built from that class.

Figure 1-1
The .NET Framework architecture

VB	C++	C#	JScript	Other .NET languages
CLS: Common Language Specifications				
Web services		Web forms		Windows forms
Data and XML classes: XML, ADO.NET, SQL, etc.				
Base Class Library				
CLR: Common Language Runtime				

Once you have created an object, your object needs to communicate with many other objects. These other objects may have been created in another .NET language, but that doesn't matter, because each language adheres to the rules of the Common Language Specifications. The CLS defines such things as common variable types (this is called the Common Type System—CTS—you knew there had to be an acronym!), common visibility (when and where can you see these variables), common method specifications, and so on. See how wonderful this is! Essentially, we are now all speaking the same language. You don't have one rule describing how C# composes its objects and another rule describing how Visual Basic does the same thing. To steal a phrase, there is now "One *rule* to bind them all."

One thing to note here is that the CLS simply provides the bare-bones rules. Languages can adhere to their own subset of the specification. In this case, the actual compilers do not need to be as powerful as those that support the full CLS. It also means that a language can add to the rules; however, if those languages interoperate with CLS-compliant code, they are not fully guaranteed to work. If you are interested in looking at the specifications, check them out at http://www.microsoft.com.

The CLR—Common Language Runtime

Not to harp on the point, but did you notice the similarity in names: Common Language Runtime and Common Language Specifications? Common to both is the word "common." This is not just coincidence. The days of a language needing its own environment in which to execute its code are over. All .NET-compliant languages run in a common, managed runtime execution environment.

Let's back up a step and explore the advantages of having a common runtime environment.

- **Simplified development and integrated development with other languages** As a programmer in the not-so-distant past, you had to concern yourself with such things as components written in different languages, GUIDs, something called IUnknown, and other nightmares. With the CLR, you can rely on code that is accessed from different languages. This is a huge benefit. One coder can write one module in C++, and another can access and use it from Visual Basic.

- **Safe deployment and execution** Security has been a concern of Microsoft developers for many years. With the release of the .NET Framework, Microsoft has demonstrated that it has listened to these concerns and made security a top-level priority. As soon as a class is loaded into the CLR, security begins. Type safety is checked (Is it a legitimate type? Is it safe to use?), verification refuses to let an application access random memory locations, and credentials are checked, to name just a few of the security measures. .NET also introduces the concept of assemblies, in which all the pieces of the product are put together in a package that includes security information. We will be exploring security in great detail in this book, both for the Windows applications and Web applications.

- **Automatic object management**   C++ programmers will be relieved when they find out that the .NET languages take care of memory issues automatically. In the earlier OOP days, programmers had to consciously create memory space for their objects and then remember to destroy that object space when they were finished with the objects. If they did not take care of this, they created a "leaky" application that would eventually grab all of the system's memory resources and choke the machine. With .NET, Microsoft has followed Java's lead by making use of a garbage collector that goes through the memory heap periodically and removes those objects that are no longer in use.

- **Replacement of DLLs with versioned assemblies**   "DLL Hell" is over! Long live assemblies—.NET-packaged components. The CLR uses the version information that comes packaged in an assembly to make sure that the application will load the correct component. This was a nightmare for DLL programmers, even though COM (Component Object Model) was supposed to correct most of the problems. The issue here was when your less-than-perfect component needed upgrading. Suppose someone has an application that needs the first version of your DLL, but you have installed software that has overwritten the previous version with a newer version. All of a sudden the application will stop running, since it is no longer able to access the component that it needs. Read on in this book to learn more about assemblies and how they solve this problem.

- **Improved performance and scalability**   Performance and scalability are not new issues and, despite the hype, they will always be an issue, no matter the environment. However, Microsoft has attempted to provide you with many tools to improve the performance of applications. This book will address many of these issues and provide you with tips and tricks to continue improving performance.

This is just a short list of the advantages of the Common Language Runtime. If you are interested in more details on the .NET platform, be sure to explore the wide range of technical articles available to you through the Microsoft network.

MSIL—Microsoft Intermediate Language

So how can many different languages be brought together and executed together? Enter Microsoft Intermediate Language (MSIL) or, as it's more commonly known, Intermediate Language (IL). In its simplest terms, IL is a programming language. Yes, Virginia, there still is an assembly-type language. If you wanted to, you could write IL directly, compile it, and run it. But why would you? Microsoft has provided you with higher-level languages, such as C#, that you can use.

Let's look at the steps you follow to create, compile, and run a C# program. By exploring this, you will be able to see where the MSIL fits in and how it works with the .NET Framework.

1. Write the source code in C#.

2. Compile the source code using the C# compiler (csc.exe).

3. The compiler produces MSIL code. This code is similar to Java's byte code; however, it is not interpreted code. It is compiled code that includes just-in-time (JIT) compilation, meaning that there is a significant performance improvement over Java's byte code. Not only is there a performance improvement, but all of the .NET languages compile into MSIL code. Now, hopefully, you can see where the language interoperability comes in. The MSIL also includes metadata, which describes the types that are included in your code. This means that there is no need for type libraries or Interface Definition Language (IDL). It's all included in the metadata.

4. Before the code is executed, the MSIL must be converted into platform-specific code. The CLR includes something called a JIT compiler. The combination of the metadata and MSIL code is contained in a Portable Executable (PE) file.

5. The code is executed on a runtime host. The runtime host includes the CLR. Runtime hosts are ASP.NET, Microsoft Internet Explorer, the desktop shell, and so on.

If this is very confusing, have a look at Figure 1-2, which attempts to put the flow into a picture that explains the process. We'll go into more detail on the process of writing and running C# programs later in this chapter.

The BCL—Base Class Library

Included in the .NET Framework is the Base Class Library. The BCL is a runtime library that describes many classes that can be used in any software project. Essentially, this means that you have at your fingertips an arsenal of prebuilt blueprints to assist you in your programming effort. Remember Microsoft's goal of reducing development time? That goal is addressed in part by providing the Base Class Library.

Suppose you have to create an application that provides network communication between two computers. Your first step would be to create a socket, which is a combination of the IP address and a port number. So you would set about creating a class file (see the next section for more on creating a class file) that describes this process. In anticipation of this, Microsoft has created a Socket class within the Base Class Library. You simply

Figure 1-1
The process of creating a .NET program

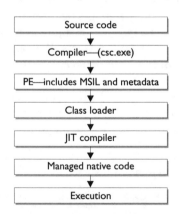

Source code

Compiler—(csc.exe)

PE—includes MSIL and metadata

Class loader

JIT compiler

Managed native code

Execution

"plug" into its functionality and use a socket rather than creating the design for one. Appendix D gives a sampling of the Class Library.

The .NET Languages

As we write this, the following languages are included in Visual Studio .NET:

- Microsoft C# .NET, the subject of this book.
- Microsoft VB .NET, the newest release of Visual Basic.
- Microsoft C++ .NET, an extended version of Visual C++ that supports the .NET Framework.
- Microsoft J++, for compatibility only. It is not upgraded to .NET.
- JScript .NET.

Microsoft C# .NET

C# (pronounced C sharp) is the latest language in the C family of languages. C# is a modern, type-safe, simple, object-oriented language that inherits its features from the C, C++, and Java languages. Java developers will feel very much at home with C#, as will C++ developers. However, both C++ and Java developers will discover that many of the shortcomings of those languages have been eliminated in C#. You will not find pointer arithmetic or memory allocations, both of which have complicated the lives of C++ programmers for years. You will also find that the creation of the executable program is not as complicated or performance-draining as it is in the Java language.

NOTE   The C# language looks like Java, but beware; there are differences that will create problems for seasoned Java developers. One item that will stand out immediately is the declaration for the `Main()` method (lowercase *m* in Java, `main()`). C#, like Java, is a case-sensitive language. You will also find that some of the familiar identifiers are spelled with a different case.

Microsoft submitted the C# language to ECMA (European Computer Manufacturers Association) for consideration as a standard, and ECMA released the standard for C# at the end of 2001. Now that C# is a public standard, other vendors can release C# compilers written against that standard. This should propel C# to the same wide use as the ANSI standards did for C++. Microsoft's implementation of the standard is called Microsoft C# .NET (referred to as C# in this book).

The remainder of this chapter will serve as an introductory overview of the C# language and of object-oriented concepts.

EXAM TIP   Remember that you are not likely to find any questions on the Microsoft exam that are directly answered in this chapter. If you are familiar with either Java or C++, you will want to skim through the rest of this chapter.

Basic C# Concepts

It has been the tradition since the first book on the C language to start any text introducing a computer language with a program that prints "Hello World!" on the screen. We will follow that tradition—here is the "Hello World!" program written in Microsoft Visual C# .NET:

```
using System;
class Hello
{
    public static int Main()
    {
        Console.WriteLine("Hello World!");
        return 0;
    }
}
```

The program can be typed into any editor (we used Notepad) and saved in a file with a `.cs` extension (`.cs` is the default file extension for C#).

To be able to run the Visual Studio .NET command-line programs (like csc.exe) you will have to have the environment properly configured. The easiest way is to start the command prompt from the batch file supplied with Visual Studio .NET, which you can find by selecting Start | Programs | Microsoft Visual Studio .NET 7.0 | Visual Studio .NET Tools | Visual Studio .NET Command Prompt. In Chapter 5, we will introduce the Visual Studio development environment, which makes your coding and testing much easier, but for the purpose of examining the details of coding, we will stick to Notepad for now. It's important to note that the C# language is case sensitive. You must type everything exactly as listed.

In order to create an executable file for the "Hello World!" program, you will have to compile the code into IL. The C# compiler will do that for you from a command line—just enter **csc.exe Hello.cs**. You may also want to work with the integrated development environment (IDE) for Visual Studio. If this is your first time working with a Visual Studio release, refer to Chapter 5 for assistance.

 NOTE   For the complete syntax of the csc program, see Appendix C.

Let's have a quick look at the five lines of code (shown previously) that display "Hello World!" in a console window. If you are familiar with C++ or Java, the program should look fairly readable, but there are some "gotchas" that you should be aware of. The first line (using System;) tells the compiler and runtime system where to search for library entries. This is very similar to the Java import keyword.

 CAUTION   The C++ `#include` statement is not the same as the C# `using` statement, since the `using` statement does not insert any code into the executable. The `#include` used in C/C++ actually reads the content of the include file into the source file.

13

In C#, everything is a class. Keep this statement in mind as you create your programs in C#. In reality, you are not creating traditional *programs*. Instead, you are creating *classes*—you'll get a complete explanation of class files in the "Object-Oriented Programming Concepts" section of this chapter. In our example, the line class `Hello` is the definition of a new class called "Hello."

Every executable program must have one and only one entry point (an entry point being the start of execution). In our program, the entry point is the third line: `public static int Main()`. The four parts of the method `Main()` will be explored later in this chapter.

In order to print "Hello World!" on the screen, we use the System libraries (which were referred to by the `using` statement). All input and output is handled through these libraries. The object that we interact with is the `Console` and the method that prints data on the console is the `WriteLine()` method. The line `Console.WriteLine("Hello World!");` calls the `WriteLine()` method of the `Console` class in the `System` library.

Congratulations! You have just written your first C# program. If only everything else were that simple! However, before we complicate things, let's examine the basic concepts of C# in more detail. Again, this is just a cursory look—we are assuming that you are quite familiar with these concepts and are just looking for an explanation of their handling within the C# language.

The `.csc` program produces an executable file (`hello.exe`) that can be run directly from the command line (see Figure 1-3).

Data Types

Data types can be of two different types—*value types* and *reference types*. Value types are used to address primitive or basic data types, such as char, int, float, and so on. Reference types encompass all other items like classes, interfaces, delegates, and arrays. These are the only types of variables available in the .NET Framework.

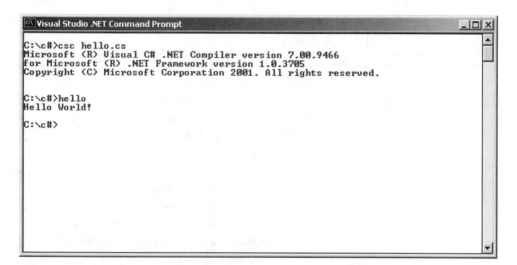

Figure 1-2   Running `hello.cs` from a command line

From our point of view as developers, value types contain data, and reference types (or objects) are accessed indirectly through a reference variable that gives a handle (dare we say "pointer") to the object. The .NET Framework provides all the data types we can use.

 NOTE All data types inherit their methods and properties from the parent class `Object`. Read on in this chapter for a description of inheritance or refer to Chapter 3 for the details of inheritance.

Primitive Types All value types are defined in the .NET Framework as primitive types. C# directly accesses the .NET base classes and the data types defined by .NET; hence, a C# `int` is a synonym for `System.Int32`, a primitive data type that defines a 32-bit signed integer. Table 1-1 contains the definition for the primitive types.

 NOTE The sizes of the primitives in Table 1-1 will be the same on all platforms. Unlike some programming languages that have variable sizes, C# primitive sizes are set by the .NET specification, not by the underlying hardware.

The character type in C# is called a `char` data type. The `char` and the `string` class both represent Unicode characters. The `char` is an unsigned 16-bit integer that can represent all the Unicode characters (65,535 distinct values). To a character value to a variable (called a char literal), several different methods can be used:

```
// as a quoted character
char c = 'B';
// as a hexadecimal value
char d = '\x0042';
// as an int with a cast
char e = (char)42;
// as a Unicode value
char f = '\u0042';
```

Table 1-1 The Primitive Data Types	Variable Type	Description
	sbyte	8-bit signed integer
	short	16-bit signed integer
	int	32-bit signed integer
	long	64-bit signed integer
	byte	8-bit unsigned integer
	ushort	16-bit unsigned integer
	uint	32-bit unsigned integer
	ulong	64-bit unsigned integer
	float	Single-precision floating-point value
	double	Double-precision floating-point value
	char	Unicode character
	decimal	Exact decimal with 28 significant digits
	bool	Boolean value

To specify a string literal, you can use one of two forms—quoted and @-quoted (also known as a "verbatim string"). A quoted string literal is enclosed in double quotes (") and can use the normal C-style escape sequences for newline (\n), tab (\t), and so on. The @-quoted string literal is similar to the quoted style except escape sequences are not processed. This makes the @-quoted literal very convenient for processing pathnames.

```
// quoted string literals
string s = "Hello World!";
string p = "c:\\winnt\\system32";
                    // note the \\ that is interpreted as a literal backslash
// @-quoted string literals
string path = @"c:\winnt\system32";     // note that escape sequences are not processed
```

Reference Types   Reference-type variables allow us to access objects. There are two parts to a reference type—the reference variable and the actual object itself. The reference is declared as the type of the object that it references, as in the following declaration of a reference (objClock) to a Clock object:

```
Clock objClock;
```

The declaration only makes the compiler aware of what kind of object the variable objClock references. The second step is to create (or instantiate) the Clock object and bind the reference to the new object. This is done by using the new keyword, which causes the constructor of the Clock class to be called, and a new object of type Clock to be placed on the memory heap:

```
objClock = new Clock();
```

 NOTE   We'll provide a more detailed discussion of object instantiation in Chapter 2.

Variables and Constants

Not to be too simplistic, but a *variable* is used as a placeholder for either a value type or a reference type. When you use variables in C#, keep in mind that like Java and C++, C# will not initialize stack (local) variables. All variables must be declared and initialized prior to using them. Value-type variables and reference-type variables are covered in more depth in Chapter 2.

A *constant* is a special type of variable storage that cannot be changed once it is defined. Any variable can be made a constant by adding the keyword const. When a variable is marked as const, it must be initialized and cannot be modified later in the application.

```
const int x = 42;      // Okay, x is now a constant with the value of 42
const int x;           // Error, a value must be provided
// const variables can be initialized from const expressions.
const int y = 3 * x;   // Okay, x is known
int m = 3;             // a normal int variable
const int z = m * x;   // Error! m is not a const
```

Startup

All C# programs must have one class definition that contains one and only one Main() method. The Main() method requires a set number of modifiers (words that change how a method will be created—public, private, and so on) to be approved by the compiler. The following declaration shows the most common declaration of the Main() method:

```
public class Button
{
    public static int Main(string[] args)
    {
        return 0;
    }
}
```

The modifiers are:

- **public** Makes the method "visible" through the whole project. This is an optional modifier.

- **static** Makes the method available without having to create the class first. More on this later in this chapter. The Main() method must be declared as static.

- **int** Specifies the data type returned from the Main() method. This data type must be declared.

- **string[] args** Specifies a string array that will hold the command-line arguments.

The Main() method can have an integer as a return value or can have the return type set to void, which indicates that no return value is expected. Typically, if you want to return an indication of program success to the operating system, you will need to have the return type coded.

The legal definitions (also called signatures) of the Main() method are as follows:

```
static void Main() {…}
static int Main() {…}
static void Main(string[] args) {…}
static int Main(string[] args) {…}
```

 TIP Java developers beware—C# does not require the class to have the same name as the application. You can also store the class under a completely different filename.

A C# program terminates when the Main() method is exited and control is returned to the environment under which the program was executed. If Main() was defined to return an int, the value returned will be used as the termination status code. If the Main() method is defined to not return any termination status code (by having the return type set to void), a termination status code of 0 is returned.

Declarations

Unlike some other languages, C# insists that all variables be declared before they are used. The declaration takes a data type and the name of the variable. An optional initial value can be included with the declaration in order to have the variable initialized and declared in one operation. The following lines declare two integer variables—foo and bar. In this case, foo is initialized to 42 and bar is simply declared:

```
int foo = 42;
int bar;
```

The declaration can contain calculations, as in the following:

```
int foo = 42;
int bar = 12;
int foobar = foo + bar;
```

Note that the following code segment will *not* compile because the variable bar is used before it is initialized:

```
int foo = 42;
int bar;
int foobar = foo + bar;
```

It is important, therefore, to make sure that all variables are initialized before you compile your code.

Arrays

Arrays are named structures that are used to store data of a particular type. For example, we can use an array to store the temperatures for each day of the month. Arrays make it easier to manipulate the data in our program.

Arrays in C# can be one-dimensional or multidimensional. If you think in terms of columns and rows, this means that you can have a single column or multiple rows and columns. In fact, your multidimensional arrays can have any number of dimensions.

Arrays are declared using the new keyword, indicating that arrays are classes in C#. The following line declares an array intArray that will hold five integer members:

```
int[]  intArray = new int[5];
```

Array indexes are zero based, giving us intArray[0] as the first element and intArray[4] as the fifth element (the last element) in the array.

The following program creates an integer array with five elements, assigns a value to each element, and then prints them out:

```
using System;
class ArrayTest
{
    public static void Main()
    {
        int[] intArray = new int[5];    // 5 elements
```

```
        // Arrays have a Length property to indicate
        // how many elements are in the Array
        for (int i=0; i<intArray.Length; i++)
        {
            intArray[i] = i;
        }
        Console.WriteLine("The Array contains:");
        for (int i=0; i<intArray.Length; i++)
        {
            Console.WriteLine("intArray[{0}] = {1}", i, intArray[i]);
        }
    }
}
```

Try to think of an array in C# as an object that contains a column of data. Each row in that column can contain a reference variable that "points" to another array. This is what gives the array the multidimensional effect. C# supports both rectangular and jagged-edged multidimensional arrays. In a rectangular multidimensional array each element refers to another array, and each referred-to array is the same length. Jagged arrays, on the other hand, contain an array of one-dimensional arrays, each of which can be a different size.

The following code shows how to declare and use a rectangular array. The statements between the brace brackets will be executed five times—j will start with the value 0 and be incremented (j++) each time through the loop until it reaches 6. This results in five iterations through the loop.

```
int[,] arryOne;  // 2 dimensional array of ints
arryOne = new int[6,6];  // create the array to 6 by 6
for (int j=0; j<6; j++)
    for (int k=0; k<6; k++)
        arryOne[j,k] = (j + k) + 42; // initialize the array

// different syntax to create a 3 by 2 array
int[,] arryTwo = new int[,] {
    {1,2},        // the first row
    {4,5},        // the second row
    {6,7}         // the third and last row
};
```

We'll be discussing arrays in more detail in Chapter 4.

Access

In order to restrict user access to data and methods in classes that we create, we can set access modifiers on the member declarations. These modifiers create an accessibility domain, which describes the boundaries where access to a member is permitted. Accessibility of members (variables, methods, classes, and so on) can be controlled by the way the member is declared.

When declaring the accessibility of a member, the following keywords are used to control access:

Modifier	Meaning
public	Access is unlimited.
protected	Access is limited to the class itself or to classes that are derived (inherited) from the class.
internal	Access is limited to the current program.
private	Access is limited to the enclosing region.
protected internal	Access is limited to this program or types derived from the class.

Scopes

The term *scope* refers to the region of a program where a named entity can be referenced directly. Scopes can be used to hide the variable and method definitions in an outer code block and to localize the use of variables. Scopes can be compared to a circle or a wall surrounding a variable, a class, or a method, for example. The circle can be of varying size, depending on how it is created. What's inside the circle can access the variable, and what's outside cannot.

Scopes can be nested, meaning that in the inner scope you can redefine a name from an outer scope. This is called *name hiding through nesting*. Scopes are defined based on the boundaries of namespaces, classes, methods, and statements. If no namespaces are declared, the scope of a named entity is the entire program text of the file. There are potential problems related to scopes that might produce unwanted compilation errors, or even worse—logical program errors. The following examples show some possible problems with scope.

In this example, j is declared outside of the method Te() but is still available inside Te() because Te() is nested in the class:

```
class Tester
{
    void Te()
    {
        j = 42;     // Valid! Te() is nested in Tester, j is declared
                    // in the class
    }
    int j = 12;
}
```

In contrast, the following example will not compile because the method Te() tries to use the class definition of the variable j and then create its own j variable.

```
class Tester
{
    int j = 0;
    void Te()
    {
        j = 12;     // Error! there is a local declaration of j later.
        int j;
        j = 12;
    }
    void Ta()
```

```
    {
        int j = (j = 42);     // Legal!
    }
    void Tu()
    {
        int k = 12, h = ++a;   // Legal!
    }
}
```

Object-Oriented Programming Concepts

It is critical that programmers using the new .NET programming languages understand completely the concepts behind the term *object oriented* (commonly written as OO). In everything that you design or code, you will be taking advantage of this style. As a matter of fact, C# programs cannot be written without first designing a class file. Although it is possible to "get by" writing code in an object-oriented environment, you should know how to properly design class files and work with the key concepts of OO, such as abstraction, encapsulation, inheritance, and polymorphism. These are not just words—they are a lifestyle in the programming world.

If you consider yourself an expert in proper class design, please skim through the rest of this chapter in order to appreciate the differences between C# and other object-oriented languages. If you are looking for a refresher in OOP, you are in the right chapter. Also, it is a given that Microsoft will expect you to be conversant in the ways of class design for the exam, so this is a great place to start. It is to your advantage to spend some time in this chapter getting comfortable with all of the concepts. For a more advanced look into object-oriented programming, you should also work through Chapter 3.

If you are a newcomer to object-oriented technology, you may want to finish reading this chapter and then invest in other material to help you understand this very important reality of today's programming. Whoever you are and whatever your background, OOP is here to stay. Entire operating systems (Windows 2000, Windows XP, and the new .NET Servers) are written using objects. If you want to explore the properties and capabilities of these objects, you will need to understand how an object asks another object for information. It's not only necessary to grasp these concepts for a Microsoft exam—it is essential to participate actively in the new object-oriented computer world.

A Brief History of Object-Oriented Programming

Traditional structured programming languages have been around for a long time and, it should be noted, they still are. In the early computer days, programmers followed a top-down approach to creating their programs. This means that a program executed from the start of the code to the bottom of the code, with the odd deviation when the program reached out to run a stored piece of code called a *function*. Functions were essentially small, one-task units of execution that a program could call multiple times and rely on to accomplish the same task each time.

The program shown in Figure 1-4 is written in C, and it demonstrates how a function can be separated from the main body of code. The function, convert, is called from

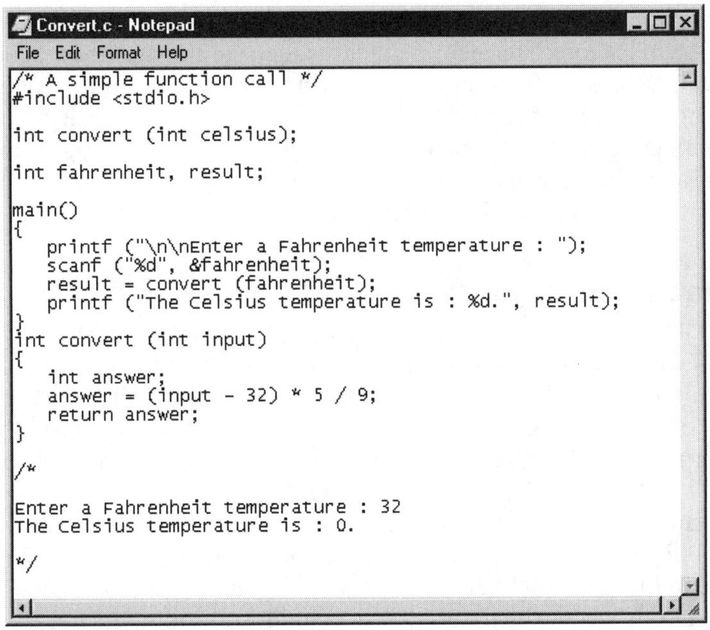

```
Convert.c - Notepad                                    _ □ ✕
File  Edit  Format  Help
/* A simple function call */
#include <stdio.h>

int convert (int celsius);

int fahrenheit, result;

main()
{
    printf ("\n\nEnter a Fahrenheit temperature : ");
    scanf ("%d", &fahrenheit);
    result = convert (fahrenheit);
    printf ("The Celsius temperature is : %d.", result);
}
int convert (int input)
{
    int answer;
    answer = (input - 32) * 5 / 9;
    return answer;
}

/*

Enter a Fahrenheit temperature : 32
The Celsius temperature is : 0.

*/
```

Figure 1-3   A traditional, structured approach to programming

the "main line" of the program to perform its duty, and it then returns the result to the main body of the program.

Now consider this scenario—you are developing a completely different application and you realize that you also need the capability of converting Fahrenheit temperatures to Celsius (and, if you are a Canadian born in the yuppie era, you need to do this all the time!). You now must spend some of your precious time either developing the code yourself or finding the code somewhere else.

Language developers realized that both of these approaches required a great investment of time and went about creating libraries of these functions. If you had to convert Celsius to Fahrenheit or vice versa, you asked that the appropriate library be added to your program, and then you could call on the function's services without coding it into your program. This was the beginning of reusable code.

In the 1980s, a group of people realized that there might be another way to approach this need to reuse code. They had the foresight to recognize that not only was it prudent to store functions in libraries, but it might be worthwhile to store attributes as well. This led to the development of object-oriented design and programming. If you are interested in learning the complete history of this fascinating topic, go right to the source. Grady Booch, Ivar Jacobson, and James Rumbaugh have authored several excellent books on the subject—the one that comes to mind is Grady Booch's *Object Oriented Analysis and Design*, Second Edition (Addison-Wesley, 1994). These three individuals are the grandfathers of OOP and demonstrated so much vision with this approach to programming that every language written now follows these concepts.

Due to the influence of early OO languages (SmallTalk, Ada, Eiffel, C++, and Java), the developers of C# took a page from the Java language and decided that everything in C# is a class. This means that every piece of code you write is found inside a class file. Structured programmers often find the transition to OOP very difficult because the style of programming is completely different and you must now think in terms of classes and objects instead of a top-down design. So, without further ado, it is time for us to explore these concepts and delve into the world of object-oriented programming.

Just What Is an Object?

In order to fully understand the concept of an *object*, allow us to paint a picture for you. Imagine that you have been given the daunting task of designing an application that will build an automobile from scratch. This particular application will be used by car manufacturers all over the world. This means that your design must be so solid and flexible that manufacturers of the Oldsmobile can build a car and manufacturers of the Volkswagen Beetle can also build a car using your application. Can you imagine coding this using a structured language? You would have to build a large library of functions, and you might find yourself duplicating large portions of your work in order to achieve the required flexibility. You might also find that you spend more time searching for functions and determining in which library they belong. You could find yourself going gray before anything of substance is actually produced.

Let's step back from this picture and paint a new, object-oriented picture. You have to be able to build an Olds as well as a Beetle. Instead of focusing on the differences between these two cars, examine the similarities. They both have wheels, steering mechanisms, seats, engines, windows, brakes, and so on. Breaking it down even further, the wheel must be able to rotate, has to be attached to the vehicle, and must provide features that grip the road—it doesn't matter whether that wheel will be on an Olds or a Beetle. We can also determine that the wheel must have a size, a color, and an air capacity.

The nouns that describe the similarities between the two vehicles (and, in reality, the similarities of every car) are the objects that we will build into our application. We can also see that these objects must be able to do things (such as rotate, grip, and attach), and these are the verbs, or functions, of our objects. Finally, the objects have characteristics or attributes (such as size, color, and capacity)—these are the properties of our object.

Imagine how powerful this is! Once we actually design and program this, anyone in the world can use our "wheel." It doesn't just have to be a car manufacturer. The people that create bicycles may be just as interested in our wheel as the developers of jumbo jets might be. All of these builders can use our design and build their own actual wheels. Each wheel has its own individual size, color, and capacity. The objects are, therefore, the physical creations from a design. Each may look totally different from one another but, essentially, they all have the same characteristics and capabilities.

To summarize, an object combines data (or properties) with its functionality (or methods). An object is a physical creation based on a design. We are repeating this to emphasize the *design* part. A *class file* is the design of the object. Just as a car manufacturer has a blueprint or a design in order to construct a wheel, so must our program have a blueprint that describes the properties and methods that make up an object. We will look at how to create a class file later in this chapter.

Before we leave this section, you also need to understand that these objects must be able to interact with each other. You have probably realized by now that you will also have to create the mechanism to which the wheel is attached. This means creating another design that contains properties and methods of its own. When done, we will effectively have two objects—one being a wheel and one a wheel mechanism. The wheel may have to "ask" the wheel mechanism to "loosen a bolt." Just as you suspected, "loosen a bolt" will be a method of the wheel mechanism. One object can request that another object perform one of its methods. This is called "sending a message" to another object. As long as the programmer has a handle for that object, the programmer can ask that object to do something that it knows how to do (perform one of its own methods).

Structs Explained

We will take a moment out from talking about classes and objects to introduce the concept of a *structure*, or *struct*. We do it in this chapter because it will be of significance in the next chapter when we discuss *types*. Historically, a struct was a means of creating a user-defined type by combining several types together. For example, you may wish to create an employee struct that has a first name, a last name, and a birth date. By combining several "fields" or types together, you have effectively created a new type that can be accessed as a single entity.

Look at the following piece of code that describes an employee `struct` using the C language:

```
struct employee
{
  char first_name[20];
  char last_name[20];
  int birthday;
} emp1;
```

Once the variable `emp1` is created, you can access any member of the structure by using the variable name, a dot, and the required field—for example, `emp1.first_name`. Notice that this closely resembles OOP, since we can include multiple properties for a single structure.

In C#, the struct continues the tradition of being a simple user-defined type. As a matter of fact, it is very similar to a class, with the following exceptions:

- A struct does not support *inheritance* (a concept explained in Chapter 3).

- A struct is a value type, not a reference type, which means that it defines a value and not an object.

- A struct is stored on the stack, not on the heap like an object. This provides for faster performance because it can be accessed directly.

NOTE   Value types and reference types were discussed in the "Data Types" section earlier in the chapter, and will be discussed further, along with details on memory management and locations, in Chapter 2.

You would use a `struct` instead of a class file if you wished to create a small and simple data type that is similar in behavior to the built-in types of C#, such as `Int`, `Char`, or `Double`.

An important distinction between the structures found in C and the structs of C# is that C# structs are allowed to have methods defined as well as properties. A typical C structure is only permitted to contain properties or fields. Consider our employee `struct`, but this time in C#:

```
public struct Employee
{
    public String firstName;
    public String lastName;
    public int birthday;
    public void SayHappyBirthday (String Name)
    {
        System.Console.WriteLine ("Happy Birthday {0}!", Name);
    }
}
```

 NOTE   Although a `struct` is allowed to contain methods, it is recommended that they do not. Consider their purpose—to form a user-defined type, or more precisely, to be a blueprint for a value. A class is a blueprint for an object and therein lies the fundamental difference.

We will explore the differences between structs and classes as we move on in this book. It is discussed here simply to complete the history of OOP.

The convert Routine Using an Object-Oriented Approach

We will now return to our original discussion of objects and classes. The following code demonstrates the Fahrenheit to Celsius application built using OOP. Don't concern yourself too much with the actual syntax and construction of the following class file; rather, explore the possibilities that are opened up by designing this code in an object-oriented fashion.

```
using System;
// First, we describe the Converter object.
// This is the class file or the blueprint for a Converter.
class Converter
{
    public int fahrenheit;   // A property of the object
    public int Convert()     // A method of the object
    {
        return ( (fahrenheit - 32) * 5 / 9);
    }
}
// Test class in order to create a Converter object
class Test
{
    static public void Main()
```

```
    {
        Converter c = new Converter();    // Build a converter object
        System.Console.Write ("Enter a Fahrenheit temperature : ");
        // Set the fahrenheit property of the converter object
        c.fahrenheit = Int32.Parse(System.Console.Read());
        // Ask the converter object to run the convert method
        System.Console.Write ("The Celsius temperature is : ");
        System.Console.WriteLine (c.Convert());
    }
}
```

This program listing demonstrates the `convert` routine using an OO approach to programming. The class `Converter` describes the object that has `fahrenheit` as its data and `Convert()` as its method. The remainder of the code listing simply creates a class file in which to create the `Converter` object (`Converter c = new Converter();`), populate its data (`c.fahrenheit = Int32.Parse(System.Console.Read());`), and request that it execute the `Convert` method (`c.Convert();`). Although the 25 lines of code may seem inefficient when compared to the 15 lines of code in Figure 1-4, you will notice that we have created a class file called `Converter` that can be reused in any program code anywhere. This is the beauty of OOP. If we were to pull the `Converter` code out of the file, put it in its own file, and combine it with a number of other utility-type classes, we would have a very functional group of classes that could be used for any project.

Although this demonstration is very simplistic and only creates a utility class (a single function not related strongly to the data of the object), perhaps you can now see how this approach extends into our car project. Our car objects are less utilitarian—a wheel is a physical object, whereas our converter is an object designed to perform a single function.

The following list summarizes the advantages of coding in an object-oriented fashion:

1. The code modules are less complex.

2. The segments of code are easily maintained.

3. Reusable code can be used to perform complex tasks.

4. It allows us to think in terms of objects, which, once mastered, makes you wonder how you ever thought any other way.

5. It provides support for inheritance and polymorphism, which we will explore in Chapter 3.

Notice that it is helpful to think of objects in terms of two major characteristics—properties and methods. In the following section, we will explore both of these parts in more detail.

Properties and Methods of an Object

Given what we discovered in the previous section, we can now safely say that we have three important OOP concepts. The first is the concept of an object, which, in effect, is a physical creation that consists of properties and methods. A *property* is an attribute, a characteristic, or the data of the object. You will also hear this referred to as the *state* of an object.

Finally, a *method* is something that the object knows how to do—a task (or function) that it can perform.

In this section, we will explore how these concepts fit into C#. Some of the mechanics (such as how you build a method, construct a property, or invoke methods) will be discussed fully in Chapters 4 and 5.

Properties

Properties are the data that describe the attributes of an object. In our wheel project, some of the properties are size, color, and capacity. When you think about your object, consider everything that describes it. These become the properties. Some of the other terms that may be used instead of "properties" include *data, attributes, fields, state,* and so on.

Inside your C# class, you define properties by simply declaring variables and perhaps attaching a default value to the property. In our example of the `Converter` class, there is a single property, `fahrenheit`, declared using `public int fahrenheit;`. This is called *instance data* because every time an object is created, that new object gets its very own copy of `fahrenheit`. If there are 100 `Converter` objects around, there are also 100 `fahrenheit` properties, each belonging to its own `Converter` object.

Notice that you must use a *handle* (or *reference variable*) to access the right object. This is demonstrated by (`c.fahrenheit`). In order to set the `fahrenheit` property, you use the variable that was created (`Converter c = new Converter();`) to "send a message" to the object that it should load the `fahrenheit` property with the value read in through the keyboard. They say that a picture is worth a thousand words. Figure 1-5 demonstrates this process.

The syntax for creating a property within a class file is as follows:

```
<field modifier> <type> <variable name> = <initial_value>;
```

The field modifier is optional and specifies where the variable can be seen from. This is called the *scope* of the field. The modifier can be new, `public`, `protected`, `internal`, `private`, `static`, or `readonly`.

The type declares whether the variable is an integer, a string, another object reference, and so on. C# is strongly typed and requires that these be legitimate types upon declaration.

The variable name is an identifier that the creator of the class declares.

Figure 1-4
Sending a
message to an
object to update
a property value

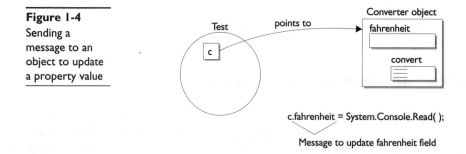

Remember our wheel? It has properties that define its size, color, and capacity. In the class file that describes a wheel, we could include the following code to define the properties:

```
public double size;
public int color;
public double capacity;
```

Every wheel that is created would have those properties as part of its data.

Methods

A *method* describes the function that an object can perform. This is a little more complicated than a property. A property is either set to some value or its value is retrieved from the object. A method is actually a section of code that is executed when called upon from the object reference.

Methods are invoked the same way that the value of an object is set. Using the handle (or reference value) of the object, you "send a message" to the object and ask it to run the method. The object then retrieves that method and executes the code found in it. By using the reference c and the dot (.) operator to send the message, c.Convert(); asks the object to which c refers to run the method Convert();. Once the method has been completed, execution returns to the calling object and the next line of code is run. The diagram in Figure 1-5, although it demonstrates the setting of a property, can be used just as easily to describe method invocations. The message is sent to the object, and the object complies by running the appropriate code.

The syntax for creating a method within a class definition is as follows:

```
<method modifier> <return type> <method name> (<formal parameter list>)
{
method execution code
}
```

The method modifier and the formal parameter list are optional components of the method signature. You must specify what type the method returns—for example, when it does its computations, what will it return to the caller of the method? It is possible for a method to return nothing, and in that case you would code a void return type.

Examine the following method in our wheel class that defines how a wheel rotates:

```
public void rotate (int NumberOfTimes)
{
    int counter = 0;
    do
    {
       // the code to actually turn the wheel
       counter++;
    } while (counter < NumberOfTimes);
    return;
}
```

Every wheel that is created would have access to this method and can execute this method when asked.

Classes—Putting It All Together

This cannot be said enough—*a class is a blueprint for an object, and an object is the physical result of using that blueprint to create something concrete.* The class file itself has a defined structure, and you will see how it is all put together in Chapter 2. For the purposes of this chapter, however, let's put everything we have learned so far into our blueprint for a wheel. We will call this class `Wheel` and include a small test engine class (called `UseTheWheel`) in the file.

```
using System;
public class Wheel
{
    public double size;
    public int color;
    public double capacity;
    public void Rotate (int NumberOfTimes)
    {
        int counter = 0;
        do {
            // this is where the code goes to turn the wheel
            counter++;
            System.Console.WriteLine ("The wheel is on rotation # {0} ", counter);
        } while (counter < NumberOfTimes);
    }
}
class UseTheWheel
{
    public static void Main()
    {
        Wheel w = new Wheel();
        w.Rotate (4);
    }
}
```

The brace bracket following the `public class Wheel` line, through to the bracket on the line before `class UseTheWheel`, encompass the definition of the `Wheel` class. Following that, we create a new class (`UseTheWheel`), which actually creates a new wheel (`Wheel w = new Wheel();`). This is called *instantiation* and it creates a new instance of the class. The variable w is the reference to the new object, and it can be used to send messages to the object (such as `w.Rotate(4);`).

When this file is compiled, it creates an executable file called `Wheel.exe`, which, when executed, starts at the `Main()` method and executes anything within its brace brackets.

Instance Data vs. Class Data

Up until now, we have dealt with properties that are described as data belonging to an object when it is created. Consider this line:

```
Wheel w = new Wheel();
```

The object referred to by the reference variable w has its own copy of `size`, `color`, and `capacity`. If we were to create a new wheel (`Wheel w1 = new Wheel();`), it would also have its own copy of `size`, `color`, and `capacity`. Suppose, though, that you have to keep some data about a wheel that is universal and constant for every wheel created. It would be a waste of space and time to create this information for every instance of a wheel. Instead we would declare the property with the modifier `static` in order to tell the compiler that the data belongs to the class and not to the object. In order to access class data, you use the class name and not the reference variable.

Consider our class file `Converter`. Instead of using the number 32 in the code, we could create static data that represents the number. This is similar to creating global constants in other programming languages. In the `Converter` class, we would add a line in the variable declarations that states:

```
static public int difference = 32;
```

In order to access this variable, we would code `Converter.difference` since the data does not belong to any one particular instance of the `Converter` class. There is a difference here between the constants of other languages and this manner of creating static data: In another language, you would not be able to change the value of `difference` because it is a constant (non-changeable). In C#, you are able to change the value because it is a variable, not a constant. If any changes are made to `difference`, all other access to the variable (as long as the class is loaded in memory) will reflect the change. See Chapter 4 for a detailed description of the class loader and memory locations.

 NOTE If you are a Visual Basic programmer, the concept of a static variable is quite different. Static, in VB, means simply, that the variable's value is retained between method calls. In C#, it means that the data belongs to the class and not to the object.

Static Methods

The `static` modifier can be applied to methods as well as properties. As a matter of fact, we have been doing just that throughout this chapter. Every time we create a class file, we have included this line:

```
public static void Main()
```

By placing `static` in the signature of the method, you are asking the compiler to consider the method as belonging to the class and not to an instance of the class (an object). When an application that contains the class is loaded, all static methods are loaded as part of the class. That is why the `Main()` method must be declared as static—in order for it to be executed, it cannot be a method that belongs to an object because those methods are only called by sending a message to the object. Class methods (or static methods) are executed independently without the assistance of an object.

So that explains why `Main()` is static, but why else would you create static methods? Consider utility functions like our `Convert()` method. It is possible to place this method in a class that simply defines static, utility methods as follows:

```
public class MyUtilities
{
    public static int convertValue = 32;
    public static int ConvertToCelsius(int Fahrenheit)
    {
        return ( (Fahrenheit - convertValue) * 5 / 9);
    }
    public static int ConvertToFahrenheit (int Celsius)
    {
        return ( (Celsius * 9 / 5) + convertValue);
    }
}
```

To get access to these static methods, you create yet another class file that contains the `Main()` method as follows:

```
public class Test
{
    public static void Main()
    {
        System.Console.WriteLine (MyUtilities.ConvertToCelsius(32));
        System.Console.WriteLine (MyUtilities.ConvertToFahrenheit(0));
    }
}
```

Notice that there is no object of the `MyUtilities` type—there is simply a call to the static method using the class name itself.

Another good reason for creating static methods would be to group together all of the static data in one place where it can quickly and efficiently be retrieved through the single method.

 NOTE   There is only ever a single copy of a static method or a static property. Static methods cannot be called from object methods without using the class name to call them.

Abstraction and Encapsulation

So far in all of our code examples, we have been using the access modifier `public` to refer to properties and methods. In a nutshell, this means that you are exposing to the world those properties and methods and allowing anyone to have access to them.

Consider the following scenario. You create a class file to describe the date as follows:

```
public class TheDate
{
    public int year;
    public int month;
```

```
public int day;
public void PrintDate ()
{
    System.Console.WriteLine ("The full date is : {0} / {1} / {2} ", year, month, day);
}
}
```

Since year, month, and day all have public access, anyone using this class can modify their values.

Examine the following code:

```
public class MyDate
{
    public static void Main()
    {
        TheDate t = new TheDate();
        t.year = 12;
        t.month = 42;
        t.day = 1242;
        t.PrintDate();
    }
}
```

Is there anything to stop someone from doing this? Of course, the output from this class is The full date is : 12 / 42 / 1242. It doesn't make sense that you would allow this to happen, and this leads us to the discussion of abstraction and encapsulation.

Abstraction

Abstraction is an object-oriented term that means to hide (or abstract) the unimportant details and expose only the necessary elements to the users of your class file. Take a moment to think of everyday abstractions. When you get into your car in the morning to go to work, you don't have to think about how the gasoline moves through the internal workings or what exactly happens when you turn the key in the ignition. These things are abstracted from you, and unless you are the manufacturer of the car, you will never have to deal with them.

The same is true of good OO software. If we were to hide the day, month, and year properties in our TheDate example, we would not have to worry about anyone messing with them.

 NOTE It would be possible to put some error checking in the code that would reduce the possibility of invalid date values being printed. Prior to printing, we could check that the date value didn't exceed 31, and so on, but imagine if every person using our TheDate class had to insert this identical validation code. Also key to this discussion is the possibility that someday, someone will decide that it is legitimate to have 42 days in a month. You would now have to assume that each user of your class would make this change. Abstraction allows you to have control over these circumstances and guarantees that the change has to be made in only one place—the original class file.

By using good abstraction in your initial code design, you will achieve the following:

- **Minimal dependency** By exposing (letting others make changes to) only the necessary elements of your class, you overcome the problem of the "small change" described in the preceding note.

- **Software is less complex** To the consumer of your class file, the interface (what they see) is greatly simplified. The complexity lies "under the hood."

- **Software is less likely to exhibit different behavior under different circumstances** By using abstraction, you are eliminating a large element of error. The author of the class file has the ultimate control over items that should not be placed in the hands of the user.

But just how do we accomplish abstraction? *Encapsulation* is the method used to enforce our abstractions.

Encapsulation

To *encapsulate* means bringing together common elements and binding them into one. To a developer, it also means controlling the visibility and accessibility of the properties of a class. Let's examine both of these qualities of encapsulation:

- **Bringing together common elements** Isn't that just what creating our class files is all about? We spend a great deal of development time determining the objects that are needed in a project and then building blueprints (class files) to describe them. Encapsulation puts the common elements into a single class file. As a matter of fact, if we follow the principles of encapsulation properly, our class file will be strongly cohesive and loosely coupled. *Strongly cohesive* means that our class has a single purpose—to describe a single entity with functionality only related to that entity. *Loosely coupled* ensures that one object is not highly dependent on the existence of another object. Each object operates independently, in effect. When you design your classes, be very cognizant of these two qualities of encapsulation and you will ensure yourself a good class design.

- **Controlling the visibility (and ultimately, the accessibility) of the properties and methods of your class** Returning to our problem of the `TheDate` class, we would now like to create a situation whereby those using the class will not "see" the `day`, `month`, and `year` properties. We accomplish this by making those fields private to the class. They are only accessible to methods within the class itself. However, we must allow their values to be set and retrieved, and we do this by providing public methods called *accessor methods* (or *getters* and *setters*).

 TIP To help deal with too much visibility of fields, all of the properties of your class file should be preceded by the `private` modifier, unless absolutely necessary. Then, for every property that needs to be edited by the user, expose (or make public) a method to get access to the property. With the exception of methods that are critical only to the class file (called *helper methods*), most of your methods will be exposed to the users of your class.

TheDate Using Good Encapsulation   Let us rewrite the TheDate class using the concepts that we have just covered. Examine the following class file:

```
public class TheDate
{
   private int year;
   private int month;
   private int day;
   public void SetDate (int d, int m, int y)
   {
      // this accessor method allows the user to change the current date value
      // place validation code here to ensure that d, m, and y are valid data
      // return error messages to the user if the data is invalid.
      year = y;
      month = m;
      day = d;
   }
   public int GetDay ()
   {
      // this accessor method allows the user to retrieve the current data value
      // you would need to create like methods for month and year
      // you could also include formatting code here if required
      return day;
   }
   public void PrintDate ()
   {
      System.Console.WriteLine ("The current day is : {0}", GetDay());
   }
}
```

Now when we use this class file, we have no opportunity to corrupt the values of the data:

```
public class MyDate
{
   public static void Main()
   {
      TheDate t = new TheDate();
      t.SetDay(1242, 12, 42);
      // at this point the method SetDay() would return an error to this
         routine since the day value is out of range
      // we would trap and correct this error (See Chapter 4 for Exception
         Handling)
      t.PrintDate();
   }
}
```

Practicing Good Abstraction and Encapsulation   As a developer committed to creating a good OO design for your software, you must always be prepared to employ abstraction and encapsulation. Here is a quick checklist of how to accomplish this:

- *Make sure that your class design employs strong cohesive behavior.*   Have you grouped together similar elements and not brought in foreign elements to the design?

- *Ensure that your class design exhibits loose coupling.*   How dependent will objects created from your class be on other objects? For example, does a Time object rely on a Date object? This is strong coupling and is not recommended in good OO design.

- *Hide all of your class data from the users of your class by declaring it with the* `private` *keyword.* Expose (make public) methods to set and get the hidden data. Within these methods, place the code that validates the input, formats the output, and so on. In other words, all data massaging should happen inside these setter and getter methods.

By following these simple practices with every class that you design, you will become a good OO developer and create reliable and less complex code.

For a more comprehensive and detailed explanation of the finer points of object-oriented programming, work through Chapter 3 on advanced OOP. In this section, we have highlighted good OO programming practices—Chapter 3 will let you see how this is all put into practice and how to use inheritance, polymorphism, overloading, and overriding.

Summary

We've come to the end of this introductory chapter. You should now feel comfortable with the concepts of C# and the .NET platform. Remember that you will not be directly questioned on any of this on the Microsoft tests. However, the information should come to you as naturally as breathing.

If this is your first exposure to OOP, try envisioning a few examples of your own. Look around you and pick out five objects that you can see. Take a piece of paper and create a class file (blueprint) for each object. Determine whether there are any relationships between these objects (inheritance) and document those. Create a class file that contains the class descriptions for all of your objects—be sure to practice encapsulation and data-hiding. If you try this exercise a number of times, you will eventually change your mindset and see everything in terms of objects. When that happens, you are well on your way to becoming an excellent OO developer!

In the rest of Part I of this book, you will be introduced to the remaining concepts of the C# programming language—variables, program structure, advanced OO, strings, exceptions, events, and the .NET development environment. Part I is in this book to assist you with the background information to the exam. Remember that you will probably not see any direct questions from Chapters 1 through 5. Part II will set you up with the information common to all three exams, and then the remaining parts are dedicated to the individual exams. Good luck with your studying!

Test Questions

1. Under which of the following environments does your program's execution code run?

    A. MSIL

    B. CLS

    C. CLR

    D. VB .NET

2. What is the compiler called that converts IL code into platform-specific code?

    A. MSIL-converter

    B. JIT

    C. JTI

    D. Metadata

3. What is the output format of the file the C# compiler produces?

    A. Byte code

    B. IL

    C. Hex dump

    D. Intel Assembler

4. Given the following program, what is the outcome when you try to compile and run it?

```
using System;
class Test
{
    public static int Main()
    {
        Console.WriteLine("Hello World!");
    }
}
```

    A. It will compile and print "Hello World!" when run.

    B. It will compile and result in a runtime error indicating that the Console is an unknown object.

    C. It will fail to compile with an "error CS0161: 'Test.Main( )': not all code paths return a value".

    D. It will fail to compile with an "error CS0161:'Test.Main( ): method cannot return an int".

5. Hiding the implementation and exposing the interface is a concept of OOP called:

    A. Polymorphism

    B. Encapsulation

    C. Overloading

    D. Static

6. Which of the following statements is true?

    A. A class is the implementation of an object.

    B. An object is the implementation of a class.

    C. A class is the instantiation of an object.

    D. An object is the instantiation of a class.

7. Which of the following is the correct way to declare the method
   `GetPayCheck()`?

   A. `public int GetPayCheck()`

   B. `private int GetPayCheck()`

   C. `private void GetPayCheck(int a)`

   D. `public void GetPayCheck(int a)`

8. Which is a definition of a static method?

   A. `public static MethodA()`

   B. `public void MethodA()`

   C. `private static MethodA()`

   D. `public static void MethodA()`

9. Which of the following languages is not part of the current .NET languages?

   A. Visual Basic

   B. C#

   C. C++

   D. FoxPro

10. In order to compile a C# program from the command line, what command
    would you use?

    A. cmd

    B. comp

    C. csc

    D. daml

Test Answers

1. **C.** Common Language Runtime

2. **B.** Just-in-time compiler

3. **B.** Intermediate Language

4. **C.** Based on the declaration, the `Main()` method needs to return an integer.

5. **B.** Encapsulation means that you make your data private and expose the
   methods.

6. **D.** When you create an object, it is called instantiation, and the class file is
   the blueprint for that object.

7. **A.** Since this is a getter method, the method will need to return the value that it retrieves, hence the return type of `int`. All getter methods should be declared as `public`.

8. **D.** The static modifier must be present as well as the return type.

9. **D.**

10. **C.**

Variables and Program Structure

In this chapter, you will

- Learn more about value-type and reference-type variables
- See the uses of boxing and unboxing
- See how objects are created and destroyed
- Learn the function of the garbage collector
- Discover the structure of a C# class file
- Get acquainted with the syntax of the C# programming language
- Learn to recognize keywords, operators, statements and blocks
- Learn to control program flow with conditional expressions and loops
- Get to understand the `using` directive and namespaces

Microsoft's .NET Framework defines the Common Type System (CTS) that specifies the universal data types used by all languages in the .NET family. The CTS defines both the data types and the rules for how the CLR declares and uses these data types. In this chapter, we will explore the CTS and the use of the different data types in C# programming, as well as the two categories of types—value types and reference types. We'll also look at the process of converting between value and reference types by boxing and unboxing. Finally we will cover how objects are constructed on the heap (the heap of memory), and how they are removed (destroyed) by the garbage collector. We will also examine the structure of class files by looking at where you should declare variables and methods, how you should use keywords and operators, how you can control the program flow, and so on.

The Microsoft exams will assume that you have a solid foundation for the information that this chapter presents. Take your time to ensure that you are comfortable with the elements in this chapter—you will more than likely not be tested on them directly, but you will need to be very fluent in their usage.

Variables

The C# language defines two types of variables that you will use for data and objects; variables can be value-type and reference-type variables. In the following sections you will explore the variable types as well as the data types they are used with.

Value-Type Variables

When you need to store numbers or characters in a program, you will most likely use value-type variables. While you could create a class for the data, we will assume for now that we are only using the basic data types.

Value-type variables are based on the primitive data types defined in the CLR. These primitive data types will always be the same on all platforms. In Table 2-1 you can see the mapping between C# and the primitive data types.

The value types are divided into integral, floating, decimal, and Boolean types. You will see the specifics for these value types in the following sections.

Integral Types

Integral types represent a whole number (for example, 42 and 491) that can be either signed or unsigned. A signed type can represent both positive and negative numbers, while an unsigned type can only represent positive numbers.

The C# language defines nine integral types: sbyte, byte, short, ushort, int, uint, long, ulong, and char. In Table 2-2 the ranges of values for the integral types are listed.

C# Variable Type	CLR Data Type	Description
sbyte	System.Sbyte	8-bit signed integer
short	System.Int16	16-bit signed integer
int	System.Int32	32-bit signed integer
long	System.Int64	64-bit signed integer
byte	System.Byte	8-bit unsigned integer
ushort	System.UInt16	16-bit unsigned integer
uint	System.UInt32	32-bit unsigned integer
ulong	System.UInt64	64-bit unsigned integer
float	System.Single	Single-precision floating-point value
double	System.Double	Double-precision floating-point value
char	System.Char	Unicode character
decimal	System.Decimal	Exact decimal with 28 significant digits
bool	System.Boolean	Boolean value

Table 2-1 The C# Versus Primitive Data Types

Type	Value Range
sbyte	Signed 8-bit integer between −129 and 127
byte	Unsigned 8-bit integer between 0 and 255
short	Signed 16-bit integer between −32,768 and 32,767
ushort	Unsigned 16-bit integer between 0 and 65,535
int	Signed 32-bit integer between −2,147,483,648 and 2,147,483,647
uint	Unsigned 32-bit integer between 0 and 4,294,967,295
long	Signed 64-bit integer between −9,223,372,036,854,775,808 and 9,223,372,036,854,775,807
ulong	Unsigned 64-bit integer between 0 and 18,446,744,073,709,551,615
char	Unsigned 16-bit integer between 0 and 65,535 representing the Unicode characters

Table 2-2   The Integral Data Types

NOTE   The Unicode character set represents all possible characters in one double-byte character. Unicode is the standard for national language support; C# uses only Unicode characters.

Floating-Point Types

Floating-point types represent signed numbers with decimal portions (for example, 3.14159 and 42.12). The C# language supports two floating-point types: float and double. The float type is represented using a 32-bit precision and the double using a 64-bit precision IEEE 754 format. The double type can represent values from approximately

$$5.0 \times 10^{-324} \quad \text{to} \quad 1.7 \times 10^{308} \quad \text{(with a precision of 15 to 16 digits)}$$

while the float can represent values from approximately

$$1.5 \times 10^{-45} \quad \text{to} \quad 3.4 \times 10^{38} \quad \text{(with a precision of 7 digits)}$$

Decimal Types

The decimal type is represented by a 128-bit (16-byte) data type that is designed for currency or financial calculations. The decimal type can represent signed values from

$$1.0 \times 10^{-28} \quad \text{to about} \quad 7.9 \times 10^{28} \quad \text{(with 28 to 29 significant digits)}$$

Calculations using the decimal type are exact to 28 or 29 digits, but never to more than 28 decimal places.

Boolean Types

The bool type represents a Boolean logical value that can have two possible values: true or false. There are no conversions possible between any other data type and bool.

 EXAM TIP   If you are used to the C and C++ languages where zero (0) normally is converted to a Boolean false, and a non-zero value to a true, you must beware. C# does not permit this kind of conversion; expect to be faced with these types of conversions in the exams.

Strings

C# has a data type that is used to store strings of Unicode characters, only it is not actually a type; rather, it's a class designed to represent the characters. The string class is immutable, meaning that once constructed, the stored string cannot be changed. If the string is modified, a new string is created, leaving the original string to be removed by the garbage collector.

When you look at the string class, you'll find that it behaves very much like a "normal" variable: the string is not instantiated (created) with the new operator as classes are; instead, the string is created the same way an int would be. Consider the following example:

```
string s;      // assign s to represent a string
string p = "Hello";  // assign p to represent a string and initialize it
                     // to Hello
s = "World!";        // assign World! to s
string strHello = p + " " + s;
                     // assign p and a space and s to the strHello string
                     // strHello now contains 'Hello World!'
```

The plus operator (+) in the preceding example performs a concatenation of the strings.

Reference-Type Variables

Reference-type variables are variables that are used to get access to objects that are used by the C# language. The reference variables are so called because they are made up of two parts: the reference and the object that the variable references. We must explore how memory is used before we can get into the details of how the reference variable is constructed, so the next section will do just that.

Memory and Variables

The first thing we need to look at when exploring variables is the memory subsystem used by the Common Language Runtime. Memory is assigned to the running program in essentially three areas: *stack*, *static*, and *heap*. You can see the three areas in Figure 2-1. The heap is all the remaining memory after the stack and static memory has been defined. For the purposes of this chapter, we will only look at the stack.

Figure 2-1
The parts of
CLR memory

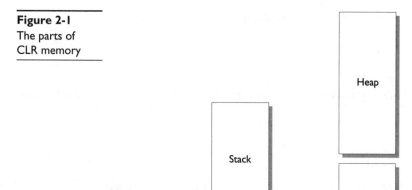

Heap

Stack

Static

The stack is an area of memory that works something like a pile of pancakes: you add pancakes to the top, and you remove them from the top (this is known as last in–first out, or LIFO). The heap and static memory is where variables and methods that must be available even if they are out of scope (not visible from the current location) are stored. For example, the Main() method is the entry point to your application, so it must be in the static area so it can be called, even if the class has not been created yet.

When you create variables, they are created in memory in one of two ways, depending on whether the variable is a value type or a reference type. In the following sections, we will look at how memory is assigned when variables are declared and used.

Variable Declarations

In C# all variables must be declared before they are used. In the declaration you must specify a data type and a name for the variable so that memory can be set aside for the variable. An optional initial value can be included with the declaration if you know what the value should be to start.

The syntax for variable declaration is as follows:

```
[scope] <data type> <variable name> [= initial value];
```

The scope determines the accessibility of the variable (public, local, private), and the default is private. The data type specifies what kind of data the variable will hold. Optionally the variable can be initialized to a specific value.

All variables must be initialized (given a value) before they are used in any calculation. If the variables are not initialized, the compilation of the program will fail. The following lines declare two integer (int) variables: foo and bar. foo is assigned the initial value 42:

```
int foo = 42;
int bar;
```

The variable declaration can contain calculations, as in the following:

```
int foo = 42;
int bar = 12;
int foobar = foo + bar;
```

The following code segment will not compile because the variable `bar` is used before it is initialized:

```
int foo = 42;
int bar;
int foobar = foo + bar;
```

In order to declare a reference-type variable, the same syntax is used:

```
string strMimico;
City objToronto = null;
object objGeneric;
```

The preceding lines create reference variables for a `string`, `City`, and `object`, respectively.
We will now look at how the declaration affects memory allocation.

Value-Type Variables on the Stack

Value-type variables are also known as stack variables because they are stored on the stack. Figure 2-2 shows the result of the following declarations.

```
Int x;
Int y = 42;
Float f = 3.14159
```

As the variables go out of scope, they are removed from the stack, ensuring the proper destruction of the variables. As the variables are created on the stack, they are not initialized—that is the responsibility of the program. The use of an uninitialized variable will result in a compiler error.

Figure 2-2
Memory map for
the declaration
of value-type
variables

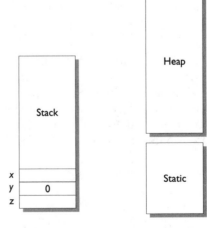

The Parts of Reference-Type Variables

Reference-type variables are made up of two parts: the reference on the stack and the object on the heap. The creation of the object and the reference to the object is commonly known as the instantiation of the object.

In order to create an object on the heap, we go through two steps, as follows:

1. Declare the variable reference.

2. Instantiate the object on the heap by calling the new operator.

The following two lines of code perform these actions:

```
City objMimico;          //Declare objMimico to be a reference to an
                         //object of City type
objMimico = new City();  //Call the constructor of the City class to return
                         //a reference that is stored in the objMimico reference
```

The two lines can be combined into one:

```
City objMimico = new City();
```

The result in memory can be seen in Figure 2-3.

Once we are done with the object, and have reassigned the reference to another object, set the reference to null, or let the reference go out of scope; the object will then be destroyed by the garbage collector. The garbage collector is explained in the "Memory Management" section, later in this chapter.

Figure 2-3
Memory layout
after the
instantiation
of an object

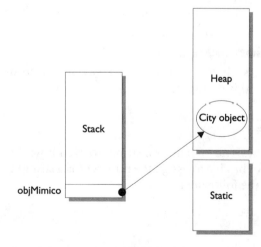

Type Conversions

The C# language is a strongly typed language—every variable must be assigned a data type and that data type cannot be changed after the declaration. One result of the strong typing in C# is that the compiler will not allow you to assign values to the wrong data type: a double value to an int, or a string value to an int, for example. However, the compiler will accept assignments that are valid, even though they might use different data types: assigning an int to a long is valid because the long is larger than the int. This type of conversion is called *implicit conversion*.

In order to convert between different types that might not be allowed without intervention, you can use *casting* (giving hints to the compiler about what to do) or use conversion functions based on the primitive types defined in the .NET Framework. In the following sections we will look at both types of conversions.

Implicit Conversions

Implicit conversions are used when a variable of a smaller data type is assigned to a larger one. The data types must be compatible for the implicit conversion to take place. In the following example, all assignments are valid and the conversions are implicit:

```
int x = 42;
short s = 12;
int y;
long l;
float f;
double d;
float const PI = 3.14159;
l = x;    // int -> long
d = PI;   // float -> double
y = s;    // short -> int
f = l;    // long -> float, not exact conversion, but valid
```

Conversion Methods

There are times when there is no direct way of converting the value from one type to another, as in this example:

```
int x;
x = System.ReadLine();
```

`System.ReadLine()` returns a string, so even if we type in a number, the compiler would still not be able to assign the number (as a string) to the int variable x. The solution is to do the following:

```
int x;
x = Int32.Parse(System.ReadLine());
```

The magic in this code is that we use one of the primitive value types as a class (Int32 is the class that defines the 32-bit signed integer that C# uses as the int data type). The numeric classes from the Common Type System all have a Parse() method that will convert the string to the respective data type. The conversion is pure magic, and one almost feels like calling out like Kim the Danish magician: "Nothing up my sleeves and Wupti! The conversion is done."

The mechanics in this conversion make use of a feature in the C# language that seamlessly allows a data type to be switched from a value type to a reference type and back. This is the boxing and unboxing process we mentioned in the introduction.

Boxing and Unboxing

As we discussed, the terms *boxing* and *unboxing* refer to the process of converting value-type variables to reference types. Boxing is the conversion from a value type to a reference type, while unboxing is the reverse conversion.

As we said before, it is almost magic, but consider what has to happen behind the scenes to box an int variable. The memory allocated at compile time to the int variable is on the stack, while the memory allocated to an object is on the heap. The box operation will take the int from the stack, copy it, and then place the copy on the heap wrapped up as an object, leaving the reference to the object on the stack. The opposite is the unboxing operation, where the value of the object is converted to an int and returned to the stack location where the variable is stored. These are rather massive changes, but C# performs them in a heartbeat, as can be seen in this example:

```
int x = 12;
object o = x;     // o is the boxed integer
int y = (int) o;  //  unbox o, the explicit (int) cast tells the compiler what to
                  // convert the object to.
```

You might well ask the question, "Why do we box and unbox in this fashion?" One reason for doing this is if you have a double that you need to pass as a parameter to a method that requires a reference (an object), and you would do the reverse when a method returns an object that represents a value.

Memory Management

One of the most important tasks of a software implementation is managing the memory resources that the application has available at runtime. If the application fails to manage the memory properly, the application will run out of memory—this condition is called a *memory leak*. Let's look at how memory management has developed through C, C++ and Java, which C# and the Common Language Runtime are derived (and inherit) from.

In the C and C++ languages, the developer is fully responsible for the allocation and de-allocation of all memory resources; the failure to de-allocate memory when it was no longer being used was one very common reason for problems with C++ programs. When an object is created (constructed) a pointer (memory address) is assigned to the object—as long as the pointer isn't changed, there is a valid reference to the object. The C and C++ languages permit pointers to be changed by adding, subtracting, or just plain changing the values, and when this happens, it is no longer possible to refer to the memory occupied by the object. Objects orphaned in this fashion can never be de-allocated, so the operating system will hold the memory until the next reboot. This de-allocation problem, among others that C++ programmers experienced, was solved with the development of the Java language.

The Java language uses a runtime environment called the Java Runtime Environment (JRE). One of the functions performed by the JRE is to automate the de-allocation of un-used memory for Java applications. Once an application sets an object's reference to an-other object (or to null) the first object (now with no references to it) will be orphaned on the heap. A part of the JRE will traverse the heap from time to time and remove all objects that do not have any valid references. This function is called the garbage collec-tor, and Java left the implementation of the garbage collector up to each implementer of the JRE, resulting in wildly varying performance between different JREs.

The C# language's management of memory is similar to Java's, with some improve-ments. For example the garbage collector is the responsibility of the CLR in C#. The stan-dard for the Common Language Runtime specifies how the garbage collector must be implemented in the .NET Framework, guaranteeing that it will perform the same way on all platforms.

Creating and Destroying Objects

Let's take a look at object creation. In the following code, the result is that the reference type e is assigned the reference to the Employee object on the heap:

```
Employee e;
e = new Employee();
```

The following things happen in this code:

- A variable, e, is declared to be a reference to an Employee object (in the first code line).
- The Employee object is constructed on the heap (in the second code line).
- The variable, e, is assigned the reference to the Employee object.

While e refers to the Employee object, the garbage collector will not affect the ob-ject. If the variable (e) is assigned to a second object, as in the following code, the origi-nal object will be orphaned. Figure 2-4 depicts this state.

```
Employee f;
f = new Employee();
e = f;                  // both e and f now refer to the same object
```

In order to ensure that the object e originally referred to is de-allocated, the garbage collector will remove the object. At least, that is the story. In reality, the garbage collector will not run until the application experiences a low memory situation, thus ensuring that the overhead of the garbage collector is not incurred during normal operation of the application.

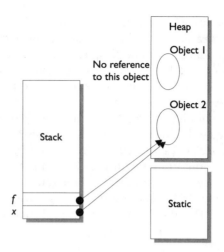

Figure 2-4
The memory
map with the
orphaned object

You can request that the garbage collector run by calling the System.GC.Collect() method, but that is not a recommended practice because the load on the system will increase with every call to Collect(). The only realistic situation in which a programmatic call to force garbage collection might be necessary is if you create and destroy a large number of objects in a loop, and you want to clean up the heap after each pass through the loop.

Cleaning Up the Objects

In the C++ environment, a developer would use a constructor to define the initialization for an object (very much as in C#) and a destructor method to clean up after the object. The C# language does not have the concept of a destructor that is guaranteed to run when the object is destroyed, nor is there normally any need for the destructor, as the garbage collector will take care of the object on the heap. There are, however, times when you'll need to close some resources (files, network connections, and the like) as the object is destroyed. C# defines two ways to do this, and both are inherited from System.Object: the Finalize() method and the Close() or Dispose() methods. The preceding three methods are designed to work as a team. In the following sections we will explore how they operate and the recommended way to use them.

Destructors and Finalizers

The Finalize() method is similar to the traditional destructor in C++. If a class has a Finalize() method defined, that method will execute before the object is destroyed, permitting you to close resources before the object is destroyed.

Unfortunately, Finalize() is not deterministic. In other words, there is no way of determining when the method will run, or the order in which Finalize() will be called for different objects. The garbage collector queues all objects that need Finalize() to run. If a lot of objects need to run Finalize(), there will be a high load on the garbage collector, which in turn results in a major degradation in application performance with no measurable positive impact on the garbage collection process.

The recommendation is to not implement a `Finalize()` method except in those cases when it is absolutely needed. The only such case would be when a class must have resources closed before the object is destroyed, and in those cases it is better to use the `Close()` and `Dispose()` methods.

In brief, while implementing the `Finalize()` method does guarantee that any resources that need to be cleaned up will be, it doesn't specify when it will be done. It is better to use a declared destructor rather than `Finalize()`. Declaring a destructor (~classname) is more in line with the C++ culture, but it still only calls the `Finalize()`, so the issue of deterministic destruction is still there.

In the following class definition, the class `Heja` is defined with a constructor (Heja(int Counter)) and a declared destructor (`~Heja()`).

```
public class Heja
{
    private int instanceNumber;      // Keep this instance number

    public Heja(int Counter)
    {
        instanceNumber = Counter;
        System.Console.WriteLine("Instance number {0} created", instanceNumber);
    }
    ~Heja()
    {   // use the destructor to make the Finalize() method execute, this is
        // enforced by the Framework
        // Perform some cleanup operations here.
        System.Console.WriteLine("Finalizing object {0}", instanceNumber);
    }
}
```

What you see in this example is the definition of a class with a constructor (code that will run when the object is created on the stack) and a declared destructor (code that will run when the object is garbage collected). The C# compiler will actually convert the declared destructor to a call to the `Finalize()` method. The `Finalize()` method is called recursively for all of the instances in the inheritance chain, from the most derived to the least derived.

The Structure of a C# Class File

Before we go into the details of the syntax and structure of C#, let's take a moment to look at the overall layout of a C# class file. Since everything is an object in C#, it follows that every file you create is made up of at least one class definition. You can combine many class definitions into a single file, but a single class cannot span multiple files.

The following example demonstrates a simple class file containing a single class definition. Take a look at this sample and notice the structure of the file. In particular, pay attention to the positioning within the file of the different types of declarations (namespace, class, and so on):

```
// StructureExample.cs
// The using statement identifies class libraries that your program uses
using System;
using Shorter = MyCompany.ProjectA.Longer;
// The namespace statement organizes related classes together
namespace MyCompany.ProjectB;
class StructureExample.cs
{
  // declare properties here
  private int prop1;
  private int prop2;
  // declare any constructors here
  public StructureExample ()
  {  ......  }
  // declare methods here
  public int MethodA ()
  {  ......  }
}
```

Namespaces and the Using Directive

Namespaces and the using keyword go hand in hand in organizing and retrieving libraries of class files. Consider the programs that we have created so far in this book. At the beginning of each program is this statement:

```
using System;
```

Without this statement, it would be necessary to precede every reference to an external class with the namespace under which it was created.

The namespace is used to organize these classes into named entities that can be referred to using a hierarchical naming convention—this is very similar to the way we store files in folders on our hard drives.

Namespaces

Namespaces group related classes and types, and they define categories in which we can include any new class that provides related functionality. By the same token, when we have need of a class in a namespace, we simply include the name of the namespace at the beginning of our source file.

Consider the following application, in which, for simplicity's sake, we have two class files. The first class provides a utility for converting temperatures from Celsius to Fahrenheit.

```
using System;
namespace MyCompany.Utilities
class ConvertToFahrenheit
{
  public int fahrenheit;     // A property of the object
  public int Convert()       // A method of the object
  {
    return ( (fahrenheit - 32) * 5 / 9);
  }
}
```

The next class file provides a utility for converting from Fahrenheit to Celsius.

```
using System;
namespace MyCompany.Utilities
class ConvertToCelsius
{
  public int celsius;      // A property of the object
  public int Convert()     // A method of the object
  {
    return ( (celsius + 32) * 9 / 5);
  }
}
```

By placing the namespace declaration in the beginning of the source file, we have identified that these classes belong to the grouping MyCompany.Utilities. Now whenever we need a utility class, we can simply look at the collection of classes in that grouping.

Here are some of the syntax rules for the namespace declaration:

- There is no semicolon at the end of the declaration.

- The qualified identifier is separated by a period (.). This is similar to a fully qualified domain name, such as www.osborne.com. As a result, this provides for a hierarchical solution. A company can group all of its home-grown classes within a particular namespace (the MyCompany namespace in these examples) and further divide classes into groups under that namespace.

- Instead of using the period (.), you can also nest namespaces as follows:

```
namespace MyCompany
{
  namespace Utilities
  {    ...
  }
}
```

- A namespace must be unique within its outer namespace (scope). MyCompany is the outer namespace in the preceding example. Utilities is an inner namespace. All namespaces at this level must be uniquely named.

- The top-level namespace (MyCompany in these examples) becomes part of the global namespace and, if used outside of your company, must be unique as a top-level namespace. Therefore, something unique about your company, like its name, would be a good top-level namespace.

 NOTE   The C# namespace declaration is very similar to the Java package statement.

The Using Directive

If you want to use shorter names within your program to identify prebuilt classes, you precede the class declaration with any number of using directives. For example, to ask that the compiler look for classes within the MyCompany.Utilities namespace grouping, add this line to the beginning of your class file:

```
using MyCompany.Utilities;
```

Alternatively, you can type the full name, which includes the namespace, when you want to call the class: MyCompany.Utilities.ConvertToCelsius.

 NOTE The using directive simply tells the compiler that it should look in the namespace for class files that are referenced in the source code. Unlike C and C++, it does not include the code in the compiled version of the program.

Coding Conventions

Computers can understand things that aren't particularly easy for people to read. By following this short list of coding conventions, you will create class files that are easy for your fellow C# programmers to read and maintain.

- Use PascalCasing for everything except method parameters and private class fields. In PascalCasing, you capitalize the first letter of each word in order to visually separate the words. An example of this is the name of our example class file—ConvertToCelsius.

- Use CamelCasing for method parameters and private class fields. In this convention, the first word in the identifier is lowercase and all subsequent words start with capital letters. An example of this is the parameter name myFirstParameter.

- Use whitespace (new lines, tabs, spaces, and so on) to separate parts of your code. C# can have any amount of whitespace in the source code. Proper use of whitespace ensures that your program is easy for others to read.

Lexical Structure

Lexical structure has to do with the way we specify comments, identifiers, constants, keywords, literals, operators, statements and expressions, and flow control in C#.

Comments

By using comments in your source code, you will provide those reading the code with the necessary background to understand your class file. There are three specific ways of commenting code.

Single-Line Comments

C# considers all text on a line following two slashes (//) to be comments (or code that will not be compiled). The following example shows that the single-line comment can either start at the beginning of a line or be placed anywhere within a line of code (but, remember, everything after the comment is ignored by the compiler).

```
Console.WriteLine ("Hello"); // this will produce a single line of output

// this is a single-line comment
```

Multiple-Line Comments

Sometimes it is necessary to tell a little story before you start a section of code. You can start a comment section by using a slash followed by an asterisk (/*) before the comment text. Type all of your comments on as many lines as necessary, and then end the section with the reverse of the two characters (*/). The compiler will ignore anything between the two delimiters. Consider this example comment:

```
/* This method will use Console class within the System namespace
   in order to run the method WriteLine() which will display the message
   on the standard output device and then cause a carriage return. */
```

XML Documentation Comments

Here is another extremely useful way of creating program documentation as you code your program. By using three slashes (///) in front of comment lines, the C# compiler (if used with a /doc option) will parse the code and generate XML documentation from the comments. This means that you can create a separate XML documentation file from the program code and view it from within a browser.

The following code segment introduces you to the concept of creating XML documentation within a class file:

```
///<summary>
///   This is an example of creating a short summary of a particular class
///   This section of code will be ignored by the compiler
///   unless the /doc switch is used.
///   Along with the /doc switch, you must specify the output .xml file
/// </summary>
```

XML documentation will be discussed more in Chapter 8.

Identifiers

An *identifier* is a name that you choose to use when you declare class names, structures, methods, variables, and so on. The rules that are applied to identifier usage come from the Unicode 3.0 standard. (Unicode is a standard, 16-bit character format for using numbers to represent every character, no matter the language or platform.) The following points must be kept in mind when creating your identifier names:

- C# is case-sensitive—myIdentifier and MyIdentifier are two different identifiers.

- An identifier must be a whole word. You cannot use whitespace in an identifier.

- An identifier must start with a letter or an underscore. It cannot start with a digit.

- An identifier cannot be the same as a keyword (see the "Keywords" section shortly in this chapter for a list).

- An identifier can contain any Unicode character, which means that you can now use international characters in your identifiers.

Here are some examples of valid identifiers:

```
Employee
CalculatePay
\u0041NeatIdentifier     // the \u0041 is Unicode for 'A'
```

The following are invalid identifiers:

```
12IsTheAnswer      // this starts with a digit
\u0027WillNotDo     // \u0027 is a formatting character in Unicode
continue          // this is a keyword
```

Constants and Read-Only Variables

By placing the keyword `const` in the declaration of a variable, you are, in effect, saying that the variable is actually non-changing, and thus is a constant. The following line of code declares a constant to represent the value of pi.

```
const double PI = 3.14159;
```

You can increase the efficiency of your program by properly using constants. The value of constants is determined at compile time and not at run time. Since the value never changes, there is no need for the extra overhead of a variable.

There is another way to create a pseudo-constant, and that is by using the `readonly` modifier on a variable. Effectively, it produces the same result—you end up with a variable that cannot change. However, the big difference between constants and `readonly` variables is that a `readonly` variable can receive its value at run time and a constant receives its value at compile time.

The following example declares a constant to hold the date March 12, 2002. That date can never change—it is compiled into the program. The second declaration is for a `readonly` variable that is initialized at run time to the current date.

```
const string TheDate = "03/09/2002";
public static readonly string TheDateRO = new DateTime().ToString();
```

Keywords

The C# programming language has 74 words that have special meanings and cannot be used in any other way. These words are called *keywords* and are listed in Table 2-3.

abstract	delegate	if	override	this
as	do	implicit	params	throw
base	double	in	private	true
bool	else	int	protectedpublic	try
break	enum	interface	readonly	typeof
byte	event	internal	ref	uint
case	explicit	is	return	ulong
catch	extern	lock	sbyte	unchecked
char	false	long	sealed	unsafe
checked	finally	namespace	short	ushort
class	fixed	new	sizeof	using
const	float	null	stackallocstatic	virtual
continue	for	object	string	void
decimal	foreach	operator	struct	while
default	goto	out	switch	

Table 2-3   C# Keywords

Literals

Inside your source code, you will regularly need to represent values of all sorts that are hard coded into the code listing. These representations are called literals. The following list identifies the literal types and the correct way to represent them.

- **Boolean literals**   There are only two Boolean literals—true and false.
- **Integer literals**   You can represent integer literals in either decimal or hexadecimal form. If an integer literal has no suffix, its type is one of int, uint, long, or ulong. By placing a suffix at the end of the literal value, you specifically state its type. For example:

    ```
    long LongValue = 1242L;
    ```

    The L in this example specifies that the value is either of type long or ulong, whichever can be used to represent the value. Check the online documentation for Visual Studio to see all the integer literal suffixes.

- **Real literals**   As with integer literals, you can represent any real number (a number with a decimal point) as a literal value. If no type suffix exists, the type is assumed to be double. By placing an F or f at the end of the literal value, you are specifically asking that it be considered as type float.

- **Character literals**   You can represent a single character using a *character literal*. The most recognized type would be a single character within single quotes, as in 'B'. However, you can also represent Unicode characters by placing a backslash in front of the Unicode number, as in '\u0012'. You can also use the escape sequence characters to represent special characters—these are listed in Table 2-4.

Table 2-4	Escape Sequence Character	Character Name
List of Escape Sequence Characters	\ '	Single quote
	\ "	Double quote
	\ \	Backslash
	\ 0	Null
	\ a	Alert
	\ b	Backspace
	\ f	Form feed
	\ n	Newline
	\ r	Carriage return
	\ t	Horizontal tab
	\ v	Vertical tab

- **String literals**   By placing text within double quotes ("text"), you create a *string literal.* You can embed any escape sequences inside the quotes and they will be treated according to their function. For example, consider this line:

```
string MyString = "This is a \t test";
```

This example will produce a line of output with a tab character between the words "a" and "test".

   If you want to eliminate that behavior, you can create a *verbatim string literal* by placing an "at" character (@) before the first double quotes. Here's the previous example modified to create a verbatim string literal"

```
@string MyString = "This is a \t test";
```

This line results in the \t being treated as part of the text. The output from this line of code would be this:

```
This is a \t test
```

- **Null literal**   In order to represent a null value, you simply type the word null. This is considered to be the null literal.

Operators

This section will deal with a few features unique to C# operators. We assume that you are familiar with C++ or Java operators and do not need a lesson in how to use them. If this is not the case, we suggest looking at the online documentation found in Visual Studio .NET and reviewing how these operators work.

   Table 2-5 lists the C# operators in order of their precedence.

Assignment Operator vs. Comparison Operator

Like the Java compiler, the C# compiler catches an error that has long caused debugging nightmares for C and C++ programmers. Have a look at the following code:

```
if (i = 42)
```

Type of Operator	Description	Operator
Primary	Member access	`object.member`
	Post-increment	`identifier++`
	Post-decrement	`identifier --`
	Constructor	`new`
	Type	`typeof`
	Size	`sizeof`
	Overflow control	`checked unchecked`
Unary	Positive	`+`
	Negative	`-`
	Not	`!`
	Bitwise complement	`~`
	Pre-increment	`++identifier`
	Pre-decrement	`--identifier`
	Type cast	`(newtype) identifier`
Arithmetic	Standard	`* / %` `+ -`
Shift	Left	`<<`
	Right	`>>`
Relational	Less than	`< or <=`
	Greater than	`> or >=`
	Type equality	`is`
Equality	Equals	`==`
	Not equals	`!=`
Logical bitwise	And	`&`
	Exclusive or	`^`
	Or	`|`
Logical	And	`&&`
	Or	`||`
Ternary	Conditional	`?:`
Assignment	Assignment	`=`
Combination		`*= /= %= += -= <<= >>=` `&= ^= |=`

Table 2-5   List of C# Operators and Order of Precedence

Under the rules of C and C++ programming, this is a legitimate piece of code. The statement means that after you assign the value of 42 to the variable, the result is checked for a Boolean `true` or `false` value. The end result is that if the assignment was successful, the condition returns a `true`, which, of course, always happens.

If the test was really meant to be against the actual value of the variable, it should have been coded as follows:

```
if (i == 42)
```

Now the desired outcome will be achieved. The program will test whether the variable equals 42, and only if this is true will it execute the next code block.

The type safety rules of the C# programming language do not allow for this implicit conversion to a Boolean value, and, therefore, the compiler will not allow this code segment:

```
if ( i = 42 )
```

Operator Shorthand

The C programming language introduced a method of writing code that was short and to the point. One of the techniques employed that can sometimes be confusing to the new programmer is the use of operator shorthand. Examine this very simple line of code:

```
y = y + 42;
```

This line causes the literal 42 to be added to the value of y, and the result to be assigned to the variable y. The shorthand version for this is as follows:

```
y += 42;
```

This means exactly the same thing as the previous line.

This shorthand technique can be used in many ways, such as the following:

```
y -= 42;   // subtract 42 from y, then assign the result to y
y *= 42;   // multiply y by 42, then assign the result to y
```

Any of the arithmetic or bitwise operators can be used this way.

The other shortcut operators are called increment and decrement operators (++ and --). These are very common and useful shortcuts, but they take some practice and knowledge of the operator precedence table to use properly. Instead of coding this operation:

```
y = y + 1;
```

You can simply code it as either y++ or ++y.

The same is true for this operation:

```
y = y - 1;
```

It can be coded as either y-- or --y.

You may be wondering at this point what determines whether the operator is at the end (*postfix*) or the beginning (*prefix*). Good question! The answer lies in the order of evaluating an expression. Consider this piece of code:

```
newValue = oldValue++;
```

This code causes the value of oldValue to be placed in newValue, and then oldValue is incremented. If oldValue contained 41, newValue would also be 41, and then oldValue would be incremented to 42.

Now look at the code written with a prefix operator:

```
newValue = ++oldValue;
```

In this case, oldValue is incremented and then assigned to newValue. Given the same initial value of oldValue, 41, this expression causes oldValue to be incremented to 42 and then assigned to newValue.

Statements and Expressions

This will be a very brief overview of statements and expressions in the C# programming language. We assume, again, that you have experience with another programming language and that this section is just a review for you. If this is not true, we suggest you become very familiar with these concepts—the Microsoft exams will assume that you are proficient in them.

Statements

A statement is something that ends with a semicolon (;) or is enclosed in a block ({ }). A very common statement is the assignment statement:

```
numberOfHours = regularHours + overTimeHours;
```

Any amount of whitespace can be found in a statement unless it is in an identifier. Sometimes it is easier to split a statement over many lines of code, since a very long statement can be hard to read and can span more than a single displayed line.

The following is a short list of statement types:

- Blocks
- Labels
- Declarations
- Expressions
- Flow control (which will be covered in the next section)

In the remainder of this section, we will briefly explore each one of these statement types.

 NOTE Leave out a semicolon, and the compiler will complain with very odd error messages. A good debugging practice is to automatically check for missing semicolons.

Blocks   A block is a section of code (or a statement) that begins with an opening brace bracket ({) and completes with a closing brace bracket (}). By placing code within a block, you are asking that the code be treated as if it were a single unit. So far, we have seen blocks that represent classes and method groupings. You can also use a block to group together code based on a certain condition, like this:

```
if ( x > 42)
{
  y = 12;
  System.Console.WriteLine ("The value of x is greater than 42");
}
```

The only way that the code within the brace brackets gets executed is if the value of x is greater than 42.

Blocks are required in order to mark the boundaries of certain structures and statements.

Labels   Labels are used to name a position in the program. The labels can be any legal identifier closed with a colon (:). Here are two examples of labels:

```
finished:
label1:
```

Declarations   A declaration is used to "declare" the existence of and the type of variables. You can simply declare a variable, like this:

```
int MyInteger;
```

Or you can declare and initialize a variable:

```
int MyInteger = 10;
```

The declaration type can be any predefined C# type, or it can be a user-defined type.

Expressions   An expression is anything that can be computed or evaluated, such as the following:

```
x > 12;
```

This expression returns a Boolean `true` if x is indeed greater than 12, and returns a `false` if x is equal to or less than 12.

Expressions include the full range of statements and operators as already discussed in this chapter. Another type of expression that has not been covered so far is the enumeration expression. Consider the following code:

```
public enum MonthsOfTheYear
{
  Jan=01, Feb, Mar, Apr, May, Jun, Jul, Aug, Sep, Oct, Nov, Dec
}
```

By coding this expression, you are creating a new type called MonthsOfTheYear, which can be used in a more intuitive way than by simply using the numerical values. Essentially, it is a user-defined integer type. When we code MonthsOfTheYear.Jan, the compiler will consider this equal to 01. The compiler will assign values to the enumeration that are incremented from Jan=01 though Feb=02 up to Dec=12. To the human eye, though, it is much more friendly than that. We understand Jan to be the first month of the year.

By using enumerations, you will make your program easier to maintain, more visually appealing, and easier to type (especially if you are using an intuitive IDE, such as Visual Studio .NET).

Flow Control

There is nothing new in this section for experienced C++ or Java programmers, but if you haven't programmed much before, you'll need to fasten your seat belt. In this section, we will very briefly describe *flow control statements*, such as if, switch, while, do, and so on.

The if Statement

All programmers need to condition the sequence of instructions in their programs by using if statements at some point. An if statement allows you to ask whether a certain condition is true, and then control the execution based on whether it is true or false.

A simple if statement looks like this:

```
if (x==42) do something here;
```

Or if you need to execute more than one statement, it will look more like this:

```
if (x == 42)
{
    do something here;
    and something here;
}
```

Notice that the brace brackets aren't always needed. It depends on whether you want to execute a single statement based on the expression being true, or multiple statements. Multiple statements must be placed within brace brackets to tell the compiler that they belong together.

You can create an if statement that executes code based on the expression evaluating to Boolean false as well:

```
if (x == 42)
{ ONE do something here; }
else
{ TWO do something else here; }
```

In this case, if x ==42 evaluates to true, the code at ONE will be executed, but the code at TWO will not. For all other values of x, the code at TWO will be executed, and the code at ONE will not. (Again, the brace brackets are only needed if the blocks contain multiple statements.)

If you wish to evaluate multiple conditions, you can use the following structure:

```
if (x == 12)
{ do something here; }
```

```
else if (x == 10)
{ do something else here;}
else if (x == 8)
{ do yet another thing here; }
else
{ if none are true, do this; }
```

This structure starts to become clumsy after two evaluations, and at that point you should consider using a `switch` statement to control the execution.

NOTE The Boolean data type is either `true` or `false` and is never an `int`. C++ programmers will particularly need to keep this in mind— C# evaluates the expression to a Boolean value. It cannot be converted to an integer.

The switch Statement

When you have many conditions to evaluate (the guideline is more than three), a much neater and more readable solution than the `if` statement is available, and that is the `switch` statement. The code in the previous example can be converted to use the `switch` statement, as follows:

```
switch (x)
{
  case 12 :
    do something here;
    break;
  case 10 :
    do something here;
    break;
  case 8 :
    do something here;
    break;
  default :
    if none are true, do this;
}
```

See how clean this looks! The execution of this statement is as follows:

1. The value of x is compared to the three case values. If one is found to be equal, execution transfers to that portion of code. Within that code block you can make declarations, make calls to methods, and do just about anything that you can do in any other block of code. Execution continues to the `break` statement and then passes to the statement following the `switch` statement.

2. If there is no matching `case` statement and there is a `default` statement, control is transferred to the `default` label.

3. If there is no matching `case` statement and no `default` statement, execution goes to the statement after the end of the `switch` statement.

Here's a list of the C#-specific rules for using the `switch` statement:

- A `switch` block consists of zero or more cases.

- The switch expression can be of these types: `sbyte`, `byte`, `short`, `ushort`, `int`, `uint`, `long`, `ulong`, `char`, `string`, or enum.
- There can only be one `default` label, and it is optional. If none of the `case` statements match the `switch` value, execution is transferred to the `default` label.
- Execution of the `switch` section is not permitted to "fall through" as is the case in C, C++, and Java. This means that you must code the `break` statement at the end of each case evaluation.
- Since execution is not permitted to fall through, you can put the `case` statements in any order.
- A case selection can have multiple labels as in the following:

```
case 12 :
case 42 :
default :
    do something here;
break;
```

NOTE Java and C++ programmers—look out for the no "fall through" rule. You will be tempted to use it, and C# will not allow it.

Loops

There are four different kinds of loops in C#: the `for` loop, the `while` loop, the do ... `while` loop, and the `foreach` loop. We will look at each one quickly and provide an example to follow. Again, there are no big surprises here.

The for Loop   If you want to execute a certain block of code a specified number of times, use a `for` loop. The syntax of the `for` loop is as follows:

```
for (control variable initial value; condition to evaluate; control variable iterator)
{
  statements
}
```

The following example shows a simple `for` loop that starts a control variable at 1, increments by 1 each time through the loop, and determines whether the control variable has reached 42 before it enters the block of the loop:

```
for (int i = 0; i < 42; i++)
{
  System.Console.WriteLine ("The value of i is : {0}", i);
}
```

The while Loop   Pardon the pun, but *while* the `for` loop is used for a known number of executions, the `while` loop is used when you want to test a condition before entering into the loop. The `while` loop is considered a pretest loop, since the condition is evaluated before the loop is executed. This allows you to stop entering the loop even once if the condition is not true.

```
int x = 49;
while (x > 42)
{
  System.Console.WriteLine ("What's 42 got to do with it?");
  x--;
}
```

 NOTE If you are really wondering where 42 comes from and why it's so predominant in this book, we recommend reading *The Hitch Hikers Guide to the Galaxy*.

Consider the difference between this while loop and the previous for loop. The loop variable for the while loop must be initialized *outside* of the loop, and, most important, changed *inside* the loop to avoid an endless loop.

The do ... while Loop   If you would prefer that the testing of the loop condition is done after executing the loop's code, you would use the post-test version of the while loop, called the do ... while loop.

```
do
{
  System.Console.WriteLine ("What's 42 got to do with it?");
  System.Console.Write ("Enter a new value for x : ");
  System.Console.ReadLine (x);
} while (x > 42);
```

We have left it up to the users to determine the next value of x, and at some point they will enter a value greater than 42.

The Jump Statements
When you want to deliberately change the order of statement execution, you can issue a jump statement, which effectively transfers program control to another section of the code. Unlike a method call, the execution does not return to the original point of departure. There are a few ways to issue jump statements: break, continue, goto, return, and throw. We will cover the throw statement in Chapter 4, and the others are covered here.

Break   You will have noticed in the switch section that each case statement ended with a break statement. The break statement causes execution to exit the enclosing block. You can break out of a switch statement or while, do, for, or foreach loops. When you issue a break statement, you send program control to the statement immediately following the end of the loop (or switch).

```
for (x = 1; x <12; x++)
{
```

```
  // do something exciting here
  if (x == 6) break;
  // do something else exciting here
}
// next statement in the code
```

Of course, this is a silly example. However, you can see that as soon as x hits the value of 6, the `break` statement will cause the execution to go to the next line after the `for` loop and, in effect, move out of the `for` loop.

Continue   Unlike the `break` statement, the `continue` statement causes execution to continue with the next iteration of the loop. This is an ideal way to bypass code if a certain condition is true.

```
for (x = 1; x <12; x++)
{
  // do something exciting here
  if (x == 6) continue;
  // do something else exciting here
}
// next statement in the code
```

In this example, when x hits the value of 6, the program control is transferred to the `for` loop control statement (and to another iteration of the `for` loop).

Goto   We can think of only one good reason to use a `goto` statement, and that is to simulate the "fall-through" behavior the `switch` statement allows in C++. The `goto` statement causes execution of the program to jump to a predefined label. This is considered "bad" programming style and can cause "spaghetti" coding, whereby the reader must jump all over the place to follow the flow.

The `goto` functionality is included in the C# language to enable implementation of those algorithms that are designed to use `goto` statements.

Return   You can use the `return` statement to exit a method of a class. When the `return` statement is invoked, it causes program execution to return to the caller of the method. If the method has a return type, you must follow the `return` keyword with the value of the return type:

```
public int MyMethod (int y)
{
  int x;
  x = y + 2;
  return x;
}
```

You could also change this to simply return the expression (y + 2;):

```
public int MyMethod (int y)
{
  return y + 2;
}
```

If the method's return type is void, then you would simply code a `return` statement with no return value.

Preprocessor Directives

Although C# does not have the same concept of preprocessor compilation as C and C++, the designers of C# continued to name these instructions *preprocessor directives*. They are simply instructions to the compiler that never get translated into commands in the executable portion of your code. Such instructions could include preventing the compiler from actually compiling certain parts of your code. You may want to do this if you have code in the program that is simply for the development process and is not intended to be shipped with the final product. For example:

```
public static int MyMethod()
{
  int x = 12;
  // do something interesting to x here
  // for development purposes, you want to see the value of x
  #if DEBUG
     System.Console.WriteLine ("Wow! The value of x is : {0}", x);
  #endif
}
```

The preprocessor directives start with the # character, the #if statement checks to see if there is a DEBUG value defined, if it is the code between the #id and #endif that will be included in the program. You need to use the `#define` command to specify that DEBUG is known. This allows you to keep the code in the source, but to test it with or without the `WriteLine` code.

For a complete reference to all the syntax and lexical rules for C#, check the online documentation for the C# programming language.

Summary

In this chapter you learned about the variables and data types used in the C# language, and how they relate to the underlying CLR and CTS. A very important topic in this chapter was the memory architecture and how the two variable types use memory. Value-type variables are stored on the stack, whereas reference-type variables are stored in two parts—the reference is on the stack and the object referenced is on the heap.

We have essentially gone through all of the syntax and rules of creating a C# program. Spend time getting comfortable with everything in this chapter by writing a few class files and creating some simple applications. As mentioned before, you will not be tested directly on any of this information; however, you must know it like the back of your hand for the exams.

It is important to follow good programming practices. By doing so, you make it easier for yourself when you have to modify code. You will also create consistent and readable code that is easy to maintain and enhance later.

The next step on the C# road is to look at inheritance and polymorphism and at some additional OO concepts in Chapter 3.

Test Questions

1. Given the following code segment, what will the value returned from the method be?

```
public int ViktorMove()
{
int x = 42;
int y = 12;
int w;
object o;

    o = x;
    w = y * (int)o;
    return w;
}
```

   A. 504

   B. 491

   C. 42

   D. Runtime error, Null Pointer exception!

2. When will the garbage collector run?

   A. Every 15 minutes.

   B. Once every day at 13:00.

   C. When the application is low on memory.

   D. Randomly based on the resource load on the system.

3. The statement that is used to replace multiple `if` statements is called:

   A. The `case` statement.

   B. The `switch` statement.

   C. The `nestedif` statement.

   D. The `#endif` statement.

4. Which of the following is not a C# keyword?

   A. `if`

   B. `delegate`

   C. `private`

   D. `implements`

5. Choose the correct method for declaring a namespace:

   A. `namespace Osborne.Chapter5`

   B. `namespace Osborne.Chapter5;`

   C. `namespace Osborne.Chapter5.MyClass`

   D. `namespace Osborne.Chapter5.MyClass;`

6. Determine the output of the following code segment:

```
int x = 42;
x++;
x += --x;
System.Console.WriteLine ("The value of x is : {0}", x);
```

   A. 84

   B. 83

   C. 86

   D. 85

Test Answers

1. **A.** Assigning 42 to an object and then multiplying with that object (cast to be an int) is valid.

2. **C.** The garbage collector will only run when the application is running short on memory.

3. **A.** The case statement is the replacement for multiple nested if statements.

4. **D.** Implements is a Visual Basic .NET keyword, not a C# keyword.

5. **B.** The namespace is not a declaration of a class, and must be terminated with a semicolon (;).

6. **D.** $x = 42 + 1 + (43 - 1) = 85$

Advanced Object-Oriented Concepts

In this chapter, you will

- Discover the use of `get` and `set` accessors
- Understand how inheritance works in C#
- Become familiar with overriding methods
- Recognize sealed and abstract classes
- Be introduced to interfaces
- Learn how to overload methods and operators

This chapter is intended to familiarize you with the advanced features of object-oriented programming (OOP). We will start with a review of the goals of *encapsulation* or *data hiding*, as it is sometimes called. This will lead us to investigate the accessor methods (`get` and `set` methods). These methods allow us to expose data in a controlled setting. Anyone who uses class files that use this technique must access the data through specialized methods, which means the programmer has full control over the way it is accessed.

The next topic in this chapter is *inheritance*. Inheritance is a relationship between two or more class files specified when a class is created. We will look at two class relationships—the "is a" relationship, where one class file is a subset of another, and the "has a" relationship, where one class file contains as its data a reference to another class. Following the discussion of inheritance, we will then look at one of the most powerful techniques that you can employ with OOP—*polymorphism*, which is how you define the class inheritance structure and then utilize the methods of all the related classes. We will also discuss creating *virtual methods* by overriding the parent class methods.

Key to the discussion of inheritance is the exploration of the `System.Object` class. Since every class file you create implicitly inherits from this class, you will need to understand its key methods and properties.

We will also explore the concept of *sealed* and *abstract* classes and how they fit into the object-oriented (OO) structure that you create. Developing a good application structure includes building interfaces, and we will look at when you need an interface and when you need an abstract class.

This chapter is all about good class design, which equates to good application design, and therefore takes advantage of object-oriented principles and concepts. By getting all of these techniques under your belt, you will find your life as an object-oriented programmer much easier.

Introduction to Advanced OO Topics

In Chapters 1 and 2, we explored a lot of the beginning principles of good object-oriented programming. A class file is developed to create a template for data and methods that can be grouped together in individual implementations (objects) of that class file. We briefly touched on the need to encapsulate data and hide the data (by making it private) from the users of the class file. Let's look at a class that will represent a user logging into an application. We may decide that we need to store information such as the person's login name, password, and so on. Here's a first draft of the class file:

```
public class LogInToken
{
  public string Name;
  public string Password;
}
```

As we discussed in Chapter 1, this is bad programming. The Name and Password values are completely accessible by anyone using this class file. Following the rules of encapsulation, we can hide the data by making the access modifier private:

```
public class LogInToken
{
  private string Name;
  private string Password;
}
```

Now we have restricted access to the Name and Password values to within the class file itself; so we need to provide a public exposed method that will allow access to the Name and Password. These are called *accessor* methods, or *setters* and *getters*. Once we have done that, we have control over how the user accesses our data.

Creating Methods to Hide Data

In the following example, we will code two methods called GetName and GetPassword. These are *exposed* methods, since they are coded as public access. These methods give the user of your class two methods to use when retrieving the data associated with an object.

```
public class LogInToken
{
  private string Name;
  private string Password;
  public string GetName()
```

```
  {
    return Name;
  }
  public string GetPassword()
  {
    return Password;
  }
}
```

Although this is an extremely simplistic example, you can imagine what would happen if your data were stored in a database. These methods would then retrieve the data from the database rather than simply returning it from the object's stored state.

Consider now what would happen if you wanted the user to be able to set the value of Name and Password:

```
public class LogInToken
{
  private string Name;
  private string Password;
  public void SetName (string newName)
  {
    Name = NewName;
  }
  public void SetPassword (string newPassword)
  {
    if (Name == "mm")
      Password = newPassword;
    else
      // throw exception that password is invalid
  }
  public string GetName()
  {
    return Name;
  }
  public string GetPassword()
  {
    return Password;
  }
  public static void Main()
  {
    LogInToken t = new LogInToken();
    t.SetName("mm");
    t.SetPassword("12");
    System.Console.WriteLine ("The new user is : {0}", t.GetName());
  }
}
```

Now we have a mechanism to control the way in which the password is set. Notice in this example that we have included validation code within the SetPassword method. If we ever need to change the logic of the validation code, we simply make the change to this one class file to change the logic for every program that sets a password with this method. Anyone using this class file will have the change reflected without any modifications to their code. This is the beauty of encapsulation. A small change is easy to manage and, for that matter, larger changes and program maintenance is also easier to manage.

Using Properties to Hide Data

The second way to control access to data within a class file is by using *properties*. Instead of creating methods that start with `Get` or `Set`, you simply make the pseudo-method "look" like the data.

```
public class LogInToken
{
  private string name;
  private string password;
  public string Name
  {
    get
  {
    return name;
    }
    set
    {
      name = value;  // C# uses the implicit parameter "value"
    }
  }
  public string Password
  {
    get
    {
      return password;
    }
    set
    {
      if (name == "mm")
        password = value;
      else
        // throw an exception here for invalid password
    }
  }
  public static void Main ()
  {
    LogInToken t = new LogInToken();
    t.Name = "mm";
    t.Password = "42";
    System.Console.WriteLine ("The new user is {0}", t.Name);
  }
}
```

 TIP Visual Basic programmers will be familiar with this technique. In VB, these methods are called public properties.

There are several things to observe in this piece of code:

- The code is clean and neat. There is no need for extra identifiers such as `GetPassword`, which can get long and awkward.

- The `get` accessor must return a value as stated in the property declaration—in this case, a `string`.

- The set accessor must return a void and uses a parameter called `value` in every case. You don't need to code the actual parameter name.

- When you use the property, you set its value through an assignment operator (`t.Name = "mm";`). There is no need to use a method as in the code in the previous section (`t.SetName("mm");`).

- You can set a read-only property by simply coding a `get` accessor. The compiler will give you a warning stating that the data "is never assigned to, and will always have its default value null."

Which method you use is a matter of personal preference. However, you will find that Microsoft leans toward the use of properties. By creating `GetPassword` and `SetPassword` methods as in the earlier examples, you are asking that the user of your class become familiar with all the methods needed to access data. When you use properties, the user simply needs to know the property names and can treat them as data instead of methods.

Inheritance

Any object-oriented programming language has some built-in mechanism to create a relationship between classes. In particular, we will be looking at a relationship that allows you to create a non-specific class file and then build on it to create classes that are more specific. Throughout this section, we will be setting up a number of classes that might be needed to represent the animals in a zoo. You could build separate class files for each type of animal in the zoo, or you could take advantage of the power of inheritance and build class relationships that allow you to do so much more with your code.

Inheritance Explained

Imagine that you are the project analyst with the company "Kim's Zoo." As part of a major project, you have been asked to design the classes that will define the animals in the zoo. In your initial design phase, you decide that you need a class file to describe a lion and a snake. The following is your first attempt at the code:

```
class Lion
{
  private int NumLegs = 4;
  private int Color = "1";   // yellow
  private int Sound = "2";   // Roar
  public void Feed (int food)
  {
    // code to feed the Lion
  }
}
class Snake
{
  private int Color = "4";   // gray
  private int Sound = "5";   // sssssss
```

```
   public void Feed (int food)
   {
     // code to feed the Snake
   }
}
```

As you look at this code, you realize that there are a lot of similarities even though the animals are very different. Wouldn't it be nice if you could just define an animal and then get more specific by providing extra details for the lion and the snake?

Fortunately, the developers of OOP had the same thought and allowed for this. Using inheritance, you can build a class file called `Animal` that defines all the general data and methods for any animal. When you are done, you can create more specific classes based on `Animal`.

Inheritance—The "is a" Relationship

When one class file inherits from another class file, it is said to have an "is a" relationship. Look at the UML (Unified Modeling Language) diagram in Figure 3-1. Notice that the top class is called `Animal`, which is a very general way to describe any of the inhabitants of the zoo. From this diagram, we see that `Lion` and `Snake` are classes that stem from the `Animal` class and have more specific data and behavior.

Now we can say that a `TimberRattler` "is a" `Rattlesnake`, which, in turn, "is a" `Snake`, which "is an" `Animal`. By virtue of the principles of inheritance, the `TimberRattler` inherits `Type` and `Rattle()` from `Rattlesnake`; `Skin` and `Slither()` from `Snake`; and `NumLegs`, `Color`, and `Sound` from `Animal`. Inheritance states that the properties and methods of the base class filter down to the derived class.

Figure 3-1

Partial inheritance structure for the zoo

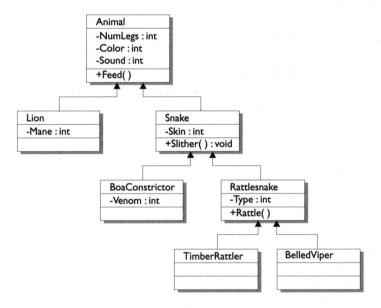

TIP There are many terms used to describe the less specific class in relation to the more specific class. The top-level class is called the *base class* (or *superclass* or *parent class*) and the inheriting class is called the *derived class* (or *subclass* or *child class*).

If we take our UML diagram for Kim's Zoo and then code the class files for Animal, Lion, and Snake, the code would look like this:

```
class Animal
{
  private int numLegs;
  private int color;
  private int sound;
  public int NumLegs
  {
    get
    {
      return numLegs;
    }
    set
    {
      numLegs = value;
    }
  }
  public int Color
  {
    get
    {
      return color;
    }
    set
    {
      color = value;
    }
  }
  public int Sound
  {
    get
    {
      return sound;
    }
    set
    {
      sound = value;
    }
  }
  public void Feed ()
  {
    System.Console.WriteLine ("Time to feed the animals");
  }
}
class Lion: Animal
{
  private int mane;
  public int Mane
  {
```

```
      get
      {
        return mane;
      }
      set
      {
        mane = value;
      }
    }
}
class Snake: Animal
{
  private int skin;
  public int Skin
  {
    get
    {
      return skin;
    }
    set
    {
      skin = value;
    }
  }
  public void Slither()
  {
      System.Console.WriteLine ("Snake slithering here");
  }
}
```

By looking at the code for the Lion class, you can see that coding inheritance is very simple. You declare the class as usual and append a colon and the base class name (: BaseClass) to the declaration. The code line class Lion: Animal means that Lion is a new class that derives from the base class Animal. Good form dictates that the colon appear directly after the derived class name.

The following rules apply to inheritance:

- The derived class inherits everything from the base class except constructors and destructors. We will look at constructors later in this section.

- When you declare the derived class, it cannot be more accessible than the base class. For instance, in our preceding example, the Lion class cannot be made public since the Animal class is not public.

- Everything declared as public or protected is inherited by the derived class. Private data or methods will not find their way into the derived class. (This is not entirely true—read on to find out more about private data.)

- You can only inherit from one class. This is called single inheritance. C++ programmers (who are accustomed to using multiple inheritance) should note that C# supports single inheritance only. However, if you need to simulate multiple inheritance, you can build interfaces (see the section on "Interfaces" later in this chapter).

Inheriting Data   In order to illustrate inheritance, we have built an entry point into the file `KimsZoo.cs` as follows:

```
public static void Main()
{
  Animal a = new Animal();
  Lion Leo = new Lion();
  Snake Viktor = new Snake();
  Viktor.NumLegs = 0;  // we can set the property of the base class
  Leo.NumLegs = 4;
  Leo.Mane = 2;
  Viktor.Skin = 4;
}
```

Each line in this piece of code demonstrates an important aspect of inheritance. Let's examine them:

- `Animal a = new Animal();`   This line creates an object of the base class type. As usual, we can access data or methods of the new object. However, we will not have access to data or methods of the `Lion` or `Snake` class. Therefore, an animal object cannot `Slither()` but it can `Feed()`.

- `Lion Leo = new Lion();`   The `Lion` object has a `Mane`, as well as everything inherited from `Animal`—`NumLegs`, `Color`, `Sound`, and `Feed()`. Since `NumLegs` is inherited, we can set the number of legs for a lion: `Leo.NumLegs = 4`.

- `Snake Viktor = new Snake();`   A `Snake` object has `Skin` and can `Slither()` and, like `Leo` inherits `NumLegs`, `Color`, `Sound`, and `Feed()`. As with `Leo`, we can set the number of legs for `Viktor` as well: `Viktor.NumLegs = 0`.

- `Viktor.Skin = 4;`   Data that is specific to the derived class can be accessed. Therefore, `Leo` can have his `Mane` set and `Viktor`'s `Skin` can be accessed: `Viktor.Skin = 4`. However, we cannot set the `Skin` property for the `Lion`. The code segment `Leo.Skin = 3` would result in a compile error, since `Skin` is particular to a `Snake` and not to a `Lion`.

Inheriting Methods   It should come as no surprise now that the methods are also inherited by the derived class. We can add the following lines to our entry-point code as follows:

```
Viktor.Feed();
Leo.Feed();
Viktor.Slither();
```

The derived classes inherit and can use the method `Feed()` as well as any methods specific to their class definition. `Slither()` is a method only available in the `Snake` class, which means that `Viktor` can `Slither()` but `Leo` cannot.

Visibility and Accessibility   As stated earlier, the only members of a base class that are inherited by the derived class are those marked with public or protected accessibility. Public accessibility makes the member visible to every class. When you modify a member of the class with the keyword protected, you limit its visibility to only classes within the namespace. If we were to modify our KimsZoo file to include namespace Zoo, any data or methods declared as protected would only be accessible from classes that are within the namespace Zoo. Private members, interestingly enough, are also inherited but not accessible, so it is as if they are not inherited. If the Animal class had a declaration of private int onlyInAnimal;, this data would not be accessible at all by any derived classes.

Let's extend our Animal class in a different manner and examine what happens with different accessibility modifiers. In the following example, we create an Animal class and extend it by creating a Dog class. Within the Animal class, there are three different data fields: numLegs, name, and color. Each has a different accessibility modifier. When we extend Animal to create the Dog class, we try to get access to each of the data fields:

```
// File DerivedExample.cs
class Animal
{
  public int numLegs;
  protected string name;
  private int color;
}
class Dog: Animal
{
  public void SetAll()
  {
    numLegs = 4;  // ok, because it is public data
    name = "Shebanik";  // ok, because it is protected data
    color = 2;  // illegal, because color is private
  }
}
class EntryPoint
{
  public static void Main()
  {
    Animal a = new Animal();
    a.numLegs = 2;
    a.name = "Animal?";  // this is illegal because name is protected
    a.color = 2;  // this is illegal since color is private
    Dog d = new Dog();
    d.SetAll();  // only one illegal is color
  }
}
```

Notice in this code that in the Dog class, we attempt to set all the data of the base class, Animal. The only line that will not compile is color = 2;. The data in the base class is private and the only way that the derived class would have access to it is if there were accessors or properties. In the Main() method, we are unable to set the name field of the Animal class (one of the compile errors noted in Figure 3-2). This is because the EntryPoint class is not related to Animal and therefore cannot see the name property. Figure 3-2 illustrates the output from compiling the preceding example.

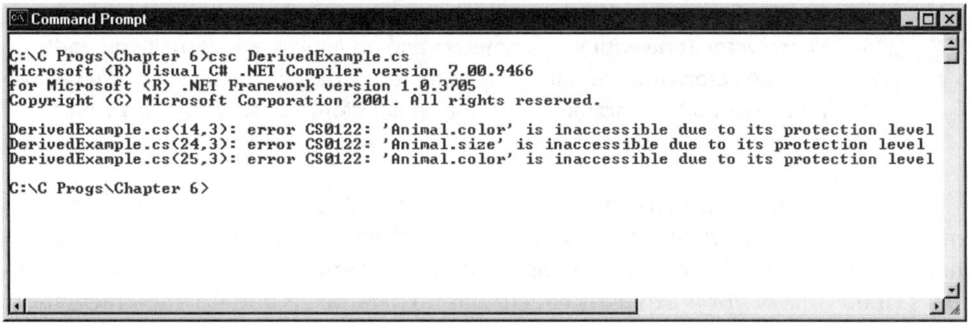

```
Command Prompt                                                          _ □ ×
C:\C Progs\Chapter 6>csc DerivedExample.cs
Microsoft (R) Visual C# .NET Compiler version 7.00.9466
for Microsoft (R) .NET Framework version 1.0.3705
Copyright (C) Microsoft Corporation 2001. All rights reserved.

DerivedExample.cs(14,3): error CS0122: 'Animal.color' is inaccessible due to its protection level
DerivedExample.cs(24,3): error CS0122: 'Animal.size' is inaccessible due to its protection level
DerivedExample.cs(25,3): error CS0122: 'Animal.color' is inaccessible due to its protection level

C:\C Progs\Chapter 6>
```

Figure 3-2   Output from compiling DerivedExample.cs

Accessibility Modifiers Revisited   We have already discussed the access modifiers as they relate to classes that are not related through inheritance. Table 3-1 is a handy reference guide to use when deciding the visibility or accessibility of data or methods between classes.

Inheritance and Constructors   As we've stated before, constructors are not inherited by derived classes. That is not to say that they are ignored, though. Consider our earlier inheritance example whereby the Dog class is derived from the Animal class. You can't create a dog without knowing all there is to know about an animal. The same is true for objects of type Dog. When the Dog object is built, there is an Animal object inside. Given that information, then, it follows that the constructor for an Animal must be called before the constructor for a Dog is called.

Accessibility Modifier	Where to Use	Visibility and Accessibility
public	Class Class data or method	Accessible everywhere. This is the default for enum members and interface members.
internal	Class Class data or method	The class or class member in one assembly is accessible only within that assembly.
protected	Class data or method	Accessible only from within itself or a derived class.
private	Class data or method	Accessible only from within itself. This is the default modifier for class data or methods.
protected internal	Class data or method	Accessible from within itself, to derived classes, and to classes within the same assembly.

Table 3-1   Accessibility and Visibility Modifiers

NOTE Remember, if a constructor is not coded, C# provides a default constructor (one with no parameters and no implementation). If you code a constructor, you are telling C# to forget its default constructor. Therefore, if you want a "no parameter, no implementation" constructor, you would have to code it as well.

The bottom line is this: There must be a constructor. You either code it or C# provides one for you. If you code one, C# will not provide one for you. Remember that you can have multiple constructors, each having a different parameter list. The one that C# provides (if no constructor is explicitly coded) has no parameters and no implementation. But if you code a constructor—any constructor—then you must code the no-parameter constructor if you need it.

If there is no constructor provided in the base class, C# calls its default constructor before calling the default constructor of the derived class. Let's look at a simple example:

```
public class Animal
{
  public Animal()
  {
    System.Console.WriteLine ("Constructor with no parameters");
  }
  public Animal (int i)
  {
    System.Console.WriteLine ("Constructor with an integer parameter");
  }
}
class Dog: Animal
{
  public Dog()
  {
    System.Console.WriteLine ("Dog constructor with no parameters");
  }
  public Dog (int j)
  {
    System.Console.WriteLine ("Dog constructor with an integer parameter");
  }
}
class EntryPoint
{
  public static void Main()
  {
    Animal a = new Animal();
    Animal a1 = new Animal(12);
    Dog d = new Dog();
    Dog d1 = new Dog(12);
  }
}
```

Let's examine the sequence of events:

1. When the line `Animal a = new Animal();` is called, the parent constructor with no parameters (`public Animal()`) is called.

2. When the line `Animal a1 = new Animal(12);` is called, the parent constructor with an integer parameter (`public Animal (int i)`) is called.

3. The next line `Dog d = new Dog();` calls the parent constructor (`public Animal()`) with no parameters and then the derived constructor (`public Dog()`) with no parameters.

4. The line `Dog d1 = new Dog(12);` causes the parent constructor (`public Animal(int i)`) to be called, and then the `Dog` constructor (`public Dog (int j)`) is executed.

The output from the `EntryPoint` class is shown in Figure 3-3.

Notice, in this example, that we have more than one constructor for each of the classes. This is called *overloading* the constructors and is a concept that we will deal with in the "Overloading" section, later in the chapter.

 TIP If you are confused as to why the second-last line of output is from the no-args parent constructor, consider that you must explicitly call a particular base constructor if you want one other than the default. For example, in order to explicitly call the constructor with an integer parameter, you must code `base (12);` in the `Dog` constructor.

Figure 3-3
Output from executing Constructor.cs

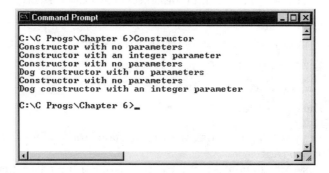

The "has a" Relationship

The other class relationship within OOP that we need to examine is the "has a" relationship. Simply put, it means that one class uses as its data an instance of another class. For example, think of a car and its parts. A car "has a" steering wheel and "has an" engine. These could all be separate classes that make the whole object, as follows:

```
class SteeringWheel
  {
  // the data and methods of a steering wheel
  }
class Engine
  {
  // the data and methods of an engine
  }
class Car
  {
  SteeringWheel s;
  Engine e;
  // the rest of the data and methods specific to the car
  }
```

Any class file that has instances of other classes as its data is considered to be part of the "has a" relationship.

System.Object—The GrandDaddy of Them All

Every class inherits from the top base class—System.Object. Even if you declare that your class inherits from another class, as in our example class Dog: Animal, your derived class ultimately inherits from System.Object. Let's examine the sequence of events:

1. The call is made to build the object—Dog d = new Dog();.

2. The parent constructor, public Animal() is called first.

3. It, in turn, calls its parent constructor—public Object().

4. The constructor for Object is executed.

5. The constructor for Animal is executed.

6. The constructor for Dog is executed.

As you can see, it is important to understand the methods that are inherited from System.Object.

The first thing to note is that the constructor is a "no parameter, no implementation" constructor. So, if you were worried about what actually happens in Step 4, you can relax. The only thing that happens is that an object of type Object is built. There is no data associated with System.Object.

However, there are some methods that will concern you. These methods should become second nature to you, and it's quite possible that Microsoft will test your knowledge of them.

The Equals( ) Method   You can use the Equals() method when you want to test the equality of two objects. This particular method compares the *instances* of two objects and not the *reference variable*. The following code segment demonstrates a comparison of the reference variable and then a comparison of the objects.

```
Animal a = new Animal();
Animal a1 = a;
Animal a2 = new Animal();
if (a == a1)  // the equals operator compares the reference variables
  System.Console.WriteLine ("The references are equal");
if (a.Equals(a2))
  System.Console.WriteLine ("The objects are equal");
else
  System.Console.WriteLine ("The objects are not equal");
```

In this example, we create three references to Animal objects. In the second line, however, the reference variable a1 is simply assigned to the object created in the first line. This means that both a and a1 are referring to the same object.

In the comparison line (a == a1), we are testing the equality of the reference variables, which are identical. However, the intent of the second test line (a.Equals(a2)) is to test the data of the two objects for equality. This brings up an interesting point. In the implementation of the Equals() method in the class Object, the comparison is called a "shallow" comparison, in that it only tests whether the reference variables are equal. If you think about it, it would be impossible for the creators of the Object class to anticipate all the different kinds of data that other classes would contain.

You should override the behavior of the base class Object if you want a "deep" comparison of object data. We will be discussing how to override base class methods in the "Method Overriding" section shortly; but, briefly, *overriding* a method means that you want to change the actual implementation of an inherited method. In this case, you would test the data members for equality rather than testing the reference variables. The advantage of this technique is that anyone using your class could compare the data of two objects and rely on the test method name to be called Equals().

There are two implementations of the Equals() method in the Object class. Their syntax is as follows:

```
public virtual bool Equals(object obj)
public virtual bool Equals(object objA, object objB)
```

When you use the second version, you can send two object references to the Equals() method and the comparison routine will test whether the two objects refer to the same object. Of course, you could override this behavior in derived classes also.

TIP   You may be wondering why there are two different implementations of this method when they are really doing the same thing. The reason is that you now have two ways of working with the method: a.Equals(b) or Object.Equals(a, b). It's up to you which you choose.

The ToString( ) Method   The method public virtual string ToString() returns a string representation of the object to the caller of the method. Its default behavior is to return an "English" or locale-specific string that contains the fully qualified name of the type of the object. The following example returns Zoo.Snake, which is the name of the class of the object prefixed with the namespace:

```
Snake sss = new Snake();
System.Console.WriteLine (sss.ToString());
```

While this might be of considerable use when debugging a program, you may want to override its behavior in order to give users of your class a method that will return a string representation of the data of the object. Even though we haven't had a formal discussion of overriding methods, look at the next piece of code and notice how the method ToString() has taken on a new task by returning data rather than the object name. Please ignore the fact that we have not followed good data encapsulation principles—this is meant as a demonstration only.

```
namespace Zoo
{
using System;
class Animal
{
  public string name;
}
class Snake:Animal
{
  public override string ToString()
  {
    return name;
  }
}
public class TestString
{
  public static void Main()
  {
    Snake sss = new Snake();
    sss.name="Viktor";
    System.Console.WriteLine (sss.ToString());
  }
}
}
```

In this example, we have told the compiler that we would like the inherited method, ToString(), to return the name of the Snake object. If you run this piece of code, you will see that instead of returning Zoo.Snake, the code sss.ToString() will now return Viktor.

Other Methods in System.Object   You should experiment with the other methods that are included in the class System.Object and become comfortable with the implementation of them. In particular, whenever you override the Equals()

method, you should also override the `GetHashCode()` method. If you don't, you may find that the hash codes (unique numbers that identify objects) are unequal. Refer to Appendix D for a full listing of the methods available in `System.Object`.

Polymorphism

Although the word *polymorphism* sometimes brings fear to the minds of beginning OOP programmers, it is really a simple concept that has far-reaching and powerful implications within the world of object-oriented class design and development. Basically, polymorphism is the ability of the reference variable of a derived class type to be treated as if it were a reference to the base class. This allows us to generically refer to objects of a more specific type.

Consider the animals in our Zoo example. Each one of them has to be fed. The manner in which the food is digested is not really important when we talk generically about feeding the animals. All we know is that we have to feed the animals, and when we send the message to "feed," we trust that the specific implementations will behave properly. When we write programs, it means that we can concern ourselves with what we know (the base class knows how to "feed") and rely on the actual object to perform correctly.

There are two very important benefits to polymorphism:

- We can group several different objects that have the same base class together and treat them the same way. This means, in our Zoo example, that we could create a collection of animals and enumerate them without caring about the individual type of each animal.

- Similarly, we can now take a group of animals and feed them. Polymorphic behavior says that at run time, the compiler will look at the real type of the object and execute the method (overridden) in that specific object's code. Now when we say `anyAnimal.Feed()` and `anyAnimal` refers to a `Lion`, the execution runtime will request that the method `Feed()` from the `Lion` class be run.

Tied in with the concept of polymorphism is the ability to override the behavior of base-class methods. In this section, we will explore these concepts and use code listings to demonstrate the power involved here.

Method Overriding

Simply put, *method overriding* is the ability to override the behavior of the base class. For instance, if the base class's `Feed()` method simply places food in a container, you may want to override it in the derived class to change the way it is placed in the container. Feeding a lion is very different from feeding a snake (although having never done either, we'll have to assume the truth of that statement).

Using the new Keyword to Override Methods

Let's look at the feed method for all three classes in the following example. We have overridden the base class's Feed() method in the derived classes by placing the keyword new in front of the declaration of the method name.

```
class Animal
{
  public void Feed()
  {
    System.Console.WriteLine ("An animal is fed here.");
  }
}
class Lion: Animal
{
  new public void Feed()
  {
    System.Console.WriteLine ("A Lion is fed here.");
  }
}
class Snake: Animal
{
  new public void Feed()
  {
    System.Console.WriteLine ("A Snake is fed here.");
  }
}
class Test
{
  public static void Main()
  {
    Animal a = new Animal();
    a.Feed();  // "An animal is fed here."
    Lion Leo = new Lion();
    Leo.Feed();  // "A Lion is fed here."
    Snake Viktor = new Snake();
    Viktor.Feed();  // "A Snake is fed here."
  }
}
```

Running this application produces the following output:

```
An animal is fed here.
A Lion is fed here.
A Snake is fed here.
```

The code listing is perfectly acceptable any time you have a reference to the derived class. However, it is possible that you may only want to have a reference to the base class (even though the actual object is of the derived class type) and this is where the power of polymorphism takes over.

Remember we decided that we might want to feed all the animals in the zoo. Perhaps we have read all the animal records from a database and are now getting ready to feed them. When we read them consecutively from the database, we don't know what kind of animal we are getting each time, so we simply store them in an Animal array. However, when we process them for feeding, we would like the runtime to figure out the actual object type of each and feed them according to the specific overridden implementation.

Hold on to your hats. The next section will explain this aspect of polymorphism in code segments. The point of this section, though, is to demonstrate that you can use the new keyword to override method behavior; to do so, though, you must have a reference variable of the overridden type.

Before we move on, let's see what happens when we try to create an array of animals and then feed them. Assume the classes `Animal`, `Snake`, and `Lion` are as described earlier in the chapter.

```
class Test
{
  public static void Main()
  {
    Animal[] animals = new Animal[2];  // declare an Animal array
    animals[0] = new Lion();  // Add specific animals
    animals[1] = new Snake();
    for (int i = 0; i < 2; i++)
      animals[i].Feed();  // Feed the animals
  }
}
```

Unfortunately, the output shows that the preceding code doesn't do what we want. Instead, because we only have references to animals, the runtime will only run the `Feed()` method from the `Animal` class. The output is as follows:

```
An animal is fed here.
An animal is fed here.
```

What has actually happened here is that the `Feed()` method is bound to the animals at compile time. This is called *early binding*. There is no chance to examine the actual type of animal before feeding it. We would like the compiler to not bind the method and allow the runtime to bind it instead. That is called *late binding* and is used to create polymorphic methods.

Using the virtual and override Keywords to Override Methods

In order to overcome the problem outlined in the previous section, we use two keywords, `virtual` and `override`. The `virtual` keyword is used on the base-class method and indicates that the method can be overridden. The `override` keyword is used on the derived-class method. It means that we intend to change the behavior of the method that is inherited. Let's look at the polymorphic recreation of our earlier example:

```
class Animal
{
  virtual public void Feed()
  {
    System.Console.WriteLine ("An animal is fed here.");
  }
}
class Lion: Animal
{
  override public void Feed()
  {
    System.Console.WriteLine ("A Lion is fed here.");
```

```
    }
}
class Snake: Animal
{
  override public void Feed()
  {
    System.Console.WriteLine ("A Snake is fed here.");  }
}
class Test
{
  public static void Main()
  {
    Animal a = new Animal();
    a.Feed();  // "An animal is fed here."
    Lion Leo = new Lion();
    Leo.Feed();  // "A Lion is fed here."
    Snake Viktor = new Snake();
    Viktor.Feed();  // "A Snake is fed here."
  }
}
```

Now we get the behavior we want:

```
A Lion is fed here.
A Snake is fed here.
```

What is actually happening here? By declaring that the Feed() method in the Animal class is virtual, we are asking that the compiler not bind the method implementation to the object. The compiler will then generate code that will check the actual object's type at run time. When the program is executed, the runtime environment will look for the appropriate override method and run that code.

Hopefully you have realized the power of this concept as well as the potential performance issues around it. In our particular case, we only have two animals. Think about a zoo with hundreds of animals—every iteration through the for loop will cause the runtime to evaluate the object's type and pull in the appropriate method. This could cause performance problems, which is why it is very important that you determine whether or not a method should be polymorphic. There are good reasons to leave the keyword virtual off your method declaration (when you don't need the polymorphic behavior).

 NOTE If you are a Java programmer, you may see the logic in virtual methods. Java programmers are forced to always have virtual methods. C# allows you to decide which methods should be virtual and which should not be virtual.

Rules of Overriding
Keep the following rules in mind when you override methods:

- You can only override identical inherited virtual methods.

- The overriding method must have the same access modifier, the same return type, and the same parameters as the method being overridden. In essence, the method signatures must be identical.
- An override is automatically considered virtual.
- You cannot declare an override as `static` or `private`.

Using Sealed

There will be times when you decide that there will never be a need for a particular class to be extended. As a matter of fact, you may want to deliberately force your users not to create derived classes. In our Zoo example, perhaps you have a method that locks the cages (think back on *Jurassic Park* scenarios). There is no way you want anyone to be able to override that behavior—in your zoo, a locked cage is a locked cage. It doesn't matter what animal is in the cage. There is a simple way to accomplish this—you simply *seal* the class or the method using the keyword `sealed`.

You can tell the compiler that a class is sealed, and then no one can extend it. There will never be a class derived from it.

```
sealed class TestFinal
{
  private int SomeData;
  public void SomeMethod()
  {
  }
}
class ExtendFinal: TestFinal
{
}
```

In this example, the `ExtendFinal` class definition will fail at compile time. The message looks something like this:

```
'ExtendFinal' : cannot inherit from Sealed class TestFinal
```

A method can also be sealed, and in that case, no one can override it.

```
class Test
{
  private int someData;
  public sealed override void SomeMethod()
  {
  }
}
class TestIt: Test
{
  public override void SomeMethod()
  {
  }
}
```

In this case, the method `SomeMethod()` cannot be overridden any further. The compiler will complain in the `TestIt` class that it "cannot override inherited member."

NOTE Java programmers will recognize this as the keyword `final`.

Don't be confused by the fact that the override is placed on the first class definition. It does not make any sense to create a method that is sealed in a base class. If you don't want it overridden, don't put the `virtual` keyword on it. In reality, `sealed` for methods should only be used further down the inheritance chain, where you want the overriding to stop.

Abstract Classes

In contrast to sealed classes, where derived classes will never exist, an *abstract* class is one where derived classes *must* exist. When you have a class that contains methods that have no implementation (i.e. abstract methods), the class is said to be abstract as well. An abstract method is simply a shell or place-marker for a method that will be defined later in a derived class. The intention of abstract methods is to force every derivation of the class to implement those methods. If a derived class does not implement an abstract method, then that class must also be declared as abstract.

NOTE C++ programmers will recognize abstract classes as pure virtual methods.

In our Zoo example, it might be wise to make a `CleanCage()` method abstract, since we really don't know the implementation of cleaning the cage of a particular animal. In that case, our code would look like this:

```
abstract class Animal
{
  // data declarations
  abstract public bool CleanCage(int numTools);
  // remaining method declarations
}
class Snake
{
  public bool CleanCage (int numTools)
  {
    // implement the CleanCage method here
  }
}
```

Notice that when you declare the abstract method, you provide no brace brackets and simply end the declaration with a semicolon (;).

Here is a list of rules concerning the abstract modifier:

- You cannot create an instance of an abstract class. For instance, the code Animal a = new Animal(); would not compile, since the Animal class is abstract.

- If you have one or more abstract methods inside a class, the class itself must be declared abstract as well.

- An abstract class cannot be sealed. This makes sense because the two terms are distinctly opposite—to seal a class is to say that it cannot be subclassed; to make a class abstract is to say that it must be subclassed.

- If a derived class does not implement the abstract methods from the base class, the derived class must also be declared abstract.

So why would you declare a class abstract? It's actually a very powerful class hierarchy design tool since you can provide the structure for something that is not very specific—just like our Animal class. You will never create an Animal object; but you will create Lions and Snakes. The other advantage is that you are moving the code to where it actually belongs. This helps you locate program logic problems.

Interfaces

When the methods of a class are all abstract, you can create an *interface*. An interface is a contract (not a base class) that states that you must provide the implementation of the methods that are declared. You declare an interface by using the interface keyword as shown in the following code:

```
interface IFeedable
{
  void FillContainer();
  void Feed();
}
```

In order to use this interface, you must declare your class in the same way that you declare a class inheriting from any other object—public class Animal: IFeedable.

It is important to note here that an interface is very different from a base class. An interface is implemented, not extended. This means that the methods declared in the interface must be implemented within the class. Follow this list of rules when using interfaces:

- It is common to place an "I" in front of your interface name, such as IFeedable.

- A class can implement multiple interfaces. For example:

```
class Animal: IFeedable, IWashable
```

- An interface cannot contain data declarations. However, you can declare properties:

```
int amountOfFood
{
   get;
   set;
}
```

- All method declarations are public within an interface. This is the default access modifier, which means you can omit the modifier in the declaration. As a matter of fact, if you code a modifier like `protected`, `private`, or even `public`, you will get a compiler error.

- There can be no implementation code within an interface. It is simply a class that declares a list of methods. Each method declaration must end with a semicolon.

- The class implementing the interface must provide implementation details:

```
class Animal: IFeedable
{
   void FillContainer()
   {
     // provide the code here to fill the container
   }
   void Feed()
   {
     // provide the code here to feed the animal
   }
}
```

Why Use Interfaces?

At this point, it might be confusing as to when you should use an interface and when you should use an abstract class.

In the purest terms, an abstract class is a base class and is therefore part of the inheritance scheme. An interface is really *not* related to inheritance, in that we can use a given interface in two projects that are not related in terms of inheritance.

In our Zoo, we have an interface called IFeedable. We can use IFeedable in our Zoo project and then use it in another project that has nothing to do with the Zoo. You might have a restaurant project that needs to feed people—IFeedable might work there. Unless you know some of my friends, there is no direct inheritance relationship between zoo animals and human beings. What's to stop us from using this interface in another project? We might have an application that simulates the work within a hospital and, surprisingly enough, the patients must be fed. If the interface is designed correctly, you should be able to reuse it in different applications, which can't be done with abstract classes. Abstract classes form part of the inheritance scheme; interfaces do not.

 TIP An interface can be derived from another interface, meaning that you can create an inheritance scheme from interfaces.

Although the preceding explanation is the best rationale for outlining the difference between abstract classes and interfaces, there is another reason for choosing one over the other. If you recall when we first started talking about inheritance, we mentioned that you could only inherit from a single class—we called this *single inheritance*. By using interfaces, you can simulate multiple inheritance.

The following list should help you distinguish between abstract classes and interfaces.

- Neither one can be instantiated—an object cannot be created from either.

- Neither one can be sealed—they are not final implementations.

- There is no implementation in an interface; but an abstract class may contain some concrete methods.

- All methods in an interface are public, but you can declare non-public methods in an abstract class.

- An interface can extend another interface.

- An abstract class may be an extension of a non-abstract class.

Extending Interfaces

An interface can inherit from another interface. You may wish to add more functionality to the interface and keep the original less-specific interface as it is. This follows the principles of inheritance that we have covered so far and should come as no surprise. In our `IFeedable` example, we could decide to create derived interfaces for `ISnakeFeedable` and `ILionFeedable`. Let's look at one of these:

```
interface ISnakeFeedable: IFeedable
{
  void FeedSnake();
}
```

In our Zoo example, we can now implement either `IFeedable` or `ISnakeFeedable`, whichever is appropriate for the work we are doing. Keep in mind, however, that any class implementing `ISnakeFeedable` must implement `FeedSnake()`, `FillContainer()`, and `Feed()`. By virtue of the contract, you must implement the derived interface methods as well as the base interface.

There is a lot more to interfaces than is described in this chapter. As we move into Parts III and IV of this book, you will come to appreciate the many uses of interfaces.

Overloading

Although it is arguably not a concept related to inheritance (or even object-oriented programming), it is a good idea to discuss overloading methods and operators at this point. We have skirted around the issues up to now, so it's time that we formalized the discussion.

When you want a particular method to accept different parameters in different cases, you can overload the method. As a matter of interest, many of the methods you have been using so far in this book are overloaded. Consider the method `WriteLine()` from the `System.Console` class. You may want to print a string one time and an integer another time. You may also want to print the data of an object. Wouldn't it be awful if you had to memorize a method for each one of these different ways of printing? Fortunately, you don't have to. The `WriteLine()` method is overloaded as follows:

```
public static void WriteLine ();
public static void WriteLine (int);
public static void WriteLine (char);
public static void WriteLine (object);
```

This is actually a subset of the `WriteLine()` methods in the `System.Console` class. There are 18 overloaded methods available to help you. You can create as many overloaded method definitions as you like—there is no practical limit.

You may have noticed the primary difference between each one of these method declarations—the parameters are different. This is one of the rules of using overloaded methods. They must declare different parameter lists, and *different* is defined as follows:

- Different parameters, such as void `MyMethod (int)` and void `MyMethod(char)`
- Different number of parameters, such as void `MyMethod (char, int)`
- Different order of parameters, such as void `MyMethod (int, char)`

One other note to make here is that the return type doesn't make a difference. That is to say that the following two methods are considered the same and not overloaded:

```
void MyMethod(int)
float MyMethod(int)
```

However, the preceding code would cause a compiler error, since the return types are different but the rest of the method signature is not.

Constructors can be overloaded as well. As we've seen before in code, it may be necessary to initialize an object differently under different circumstances. To illustrate this, think of an `Employee` class. There are times when you instantiate the `Employee` object and you know the employee's name and start date; but there may be times when you only know the employee's name.

```
class Employee
{
  // data declarations
  public Employee(string name)
  {
    // assign the passed name to the data field
  }
  public Employee (string name, int start)
  {
    // assign the passed name and start to the data fields
  }
}
```

When you instantiate an employee using `Employee e = new Employee ("Matthew")`; the first constructor will be called. When you code `Employee e = new Employee ("Matthew", 020325)`; the second constructor executes.

You can also force a call to a specific constructor from a derived class. The following code demonstrates the `SalaryEmployee` class, a subclass of `Employee`. We force the call to the correct constructor by using the keyword `base`.

```
class SalaryEmployee
{
  // data declarations
  public SalaryEmployee(string name): base (name)
  {
    // forces the call to the single parameter parent constructor
  }
  public SalaryEmployee (string name, int start): base (name, start)
  {
    // forces the call to the double parameter parent constructor
  }
}
```

TIP Be cautious Java programmers. It doesn't work exactly the same way for base-class constructor calls.

Notice the syntax around calling the base-class constructor. It is done in the same line as the derived-class constructor declaration.

As a point of interest, the `base` keyword can be used to call any method of the parent class.

NOTE This will be new to C++ programmers, but Java programmers have been using the `super` keyword.

Summary

We've come a long way in this chapter, and hopefully your appetite has been whetted for more. This has been an introduction to the advanced OOP concepts and, if you want to know more about the topic, spend some time inside Microsoft's MSDN and the Microsoft C# Language Specifications. It's very important to use inheritance and polymorphism properly. As a good analyst once said, "You need to spend 80 percent of your time on analysis and design and then only 20 percent of your time on actual coding." There is no truer statement. Good class design is as important as the actual code itself. Spend some time looking at the big picture and your time investment will pay off in the future.

Test Questions

1. Given the following code, what will the compiler do?

```
class Test1
{
  sealed abstract void MyMethod1A()
  {
    System.Console.WriteLine ("This is MyMethod1");
  }
}
```

A. The code will compile properly.

B. The class visibility is incorrect.

C. `System.Console.WriteLine` is specified incorrectly.

D. `MyMethod1()` is not properly declared.

2. Which line causes a compile error in the following code?

```
1. interface Test2
2. {
3.   int Int2;
4.   void Method2A(int);
5.   string Method2B ();
6.   int Method2C(int, int);
7.   int Method2A(char);
8. }
```

A. Line 3

B. Line 4

C. Line 5

D. Line 7

3. What is the outcome of compiling this program?

```
1 public class Test3
2 {
3   void Method3A ()
4   {
5     System.Console.WriteLine ("In Method3A");
6   }
7 }
8 class Test3a: Test3
9 {
10   void Method3B ()
11   {
12     Method3A();
13   }
14 }
15 class Test3b
16 {
17   public static void Main()
18   {
19     Test3a a = new Test3a();
20     a.Method3B();
21   }
22 }
```

A. It compiles successfully.

B. Lines 12 and 20 are in error.

C. Line 12 is an error.

D. Line 20 is the error.

4. What will happen on line 24?

```
1 class Test4
2 {
3  int test4a;
4  string test4b;
5  float test4c;
6  virtual public void Test4D ()
7  {
8     System.Console.WriteLine("Hello");
9  }
10 }
11 class Test4a: Test4
12 {
13  override public void Test4D ()
14  {
15     System.Console.WriteLine ("Goodbye");
16  }
17 }
18 class Test4b
19 {
20  public static void Main()
21  {
22     Test4a t = new Test4a();
23     Test4 t1 = t;
24     t.Test4D();
25  }
26 }
```

A. The compiler finds an error.

B. A runtime error occurs.

C. It prints "Goodbye."

D. It prints "Hello."

5. What is the result of the following code?

```
class Test5
{
  public Test5 ( )
  {
     System.Console.WriteLine ("Test5 1");
  }
  public Test5 (int num)
  {
     System.Console.WriteLine ("Test5 2");
  }
}
class Test5a
{
  public Test5a (): base(5)
  {
  }
```

```
        public Test5a(int numb): base()
        {
        }
}
class Test5b
{
    public static void Main()
    {
        Test5a t = new Test5a(12);
    }
}
```

A. It prints "Test5 1."

B. It prints "Test5 2."

C. It does not compile.

D. It does not run.

Test Answers

1. **D.** You cannot specify `sealed` and `abstract` in the same declaration.

2. **A.** Line 3 declares a field/data, which is illegal in an interface.

3. **B.** Line 12 cannot access Method3A and line 20 cannot access Method3B.

4. **C.** It prints "Goodbye" via polymorphic behavior.

5. **A.** The derived class constructor that takes an integer makes a call to the empty parameter base constructor that prints "Test5 1."

Strings, Exceptions, and Events

In this chapter, you will

- Learn about the `string` class
- Explore arrays
- Manipulate collections
- Learn the purpose of exception handling
- Be introduced to the `System.Exception` class
- Get acquainted with `try` and `catch` blocks
- Learn how to use the `finally` statement
- Create your own exception classes
- Get to understand the event-handling mechanism in the .NET Framework

The information in this chapter is included for background. If you already understand the subjects listed, you can go on to Chapter 5 and the Visual Studio .NET development environment.

This chapter will explain three concepts that are used throughout the .NET development environment. We'll look at the `string` class and how to use it, along with collections and arrays. We will also look at the concept of exception handling, which takes care of those pesky runtime errors. The final topic in this chapter is the event-handling environment in the .NET Framework.

The String Class

The C# language uses the string data type as if it were a primitive data type, but it is really a very functional data type that has no relation to any of the primitives. The string data type is a C# keyword that refers to the `System.String` class. The `System.String` class is not the only class in the .NET Framework that provides string-related functionality, however. We will start by investigating the `System.String` class, we will also look at the `System.Text` and `System.Text.RegularExpressions` namespaces. The `System.Text.StringBuilder` class that is used to build strings, as well as the `Console.Write` and `Console.WriteLine` to format strings are introduced. We will also touch on regular expressions, which are used to manipulate strings.

System.String

The System.String class is the class most commonly used to represent strings. The class stores a string and provides a large number of operations that can be performed on that string. Unlike other classes, System.String has its own keyword and syntax to make it simple to create and manipulate string data. The string keyword is used when referring to the System.String class. We do not create strings using the new keyword—we declare them as if they were primitives.

The following example shows how strings are created, and how more string data is appended to them:

```
string str;      //Declare the string
str = "No man is an island"; //Assign a string of characters to str
str += ", wrote John Donne"; //concatenate to the original string
string r = str + "!"; //create a new string from the old
```

An instance of a string is said to be *immutable* because its value cannot be modified once it has been created. Methods that appear to modify a string actually return a new string containing the modification. In the third line of the preceding example, the string str is "modified" by concatenating some additional data, but what actually happens is that a new string is created and the reference str is assigned that new instance. The old string will be cleaned out by the garbage collector.

There are a lot of members in the string class that are used to manipulate strings; Table 4-1 lists the common members.

Member	Description
Chars	Gets the character at a specified character position in this instance
Clone	Returns a reference to this instance of String
Compare	Compares two specified string objects
Concat	Concatenates one or more instances of string, or the string representations of the values of one or more instances of Object
Copy	Creates a new instance of String with the same value as a specified string
CopyTo	Copies a specified number of characters from a specified position in this instance to a specified position in an array of Unicode characters
EndsWith	Determines whether the end of this instance matches the specified string
Equals	Determines whether two string objects have the same value (overridden)
Format	Replaces each format specification in a specified string with the textual equivalent of a corresponding object's value
GetEnumerator	Retrieves an object that can iterate through the individual characters in this instance
GetHashCode	Returns the hash code for this instance
GetType	Gets the Type of the current instance

Table 4-1   Members of System.String

Member	Description
GetTypeCode	Returns the TypeCode for class String
IndexOf	Reports the index of the first occurrence of a string, or of one or more characters, within this instance
IndexOfAny	Reports the index of the first occurrence in this instance of any character in a specified array of Unicode characters
Insert	Inserts a specified instance of string at a specified index position in this instance
Intern	Retrieves the system's reference to the specified string
IsInterned	Retrieves a reference to a specified string
Join	Concatenates a specified separator string between each element of a specified string array, yielding a single concatenated string
LastIndexOf	Reports the index position of the last occurrence of a specified Unicode character or string within this instance
LastIndexOfAny	Reports the index position of the last occurrence in this instance of one or more characters specified in a Unicode array
Length	Gets the number of characters in this instance
PadLeft	Right-aligns the characters in this instance, padding on the left with spaces or a specified Unicode character for a specified total length
PadRight	Left-aligns the characters in this string, padding on the right with spaces or a specified Unicode character, for a specified total length
Remove	Deletes a specified number of characters from this instance, beginning at a specified position
Replace	Replaces all occurrences of a specified Unicode character or string in this instance with another specified Unicode character or string
Split	Identifies the substrings in this instance that are delimited by one or more characters specified in an array, and then places the substrings into a string array
StartsWith	Determines whether the beginning of this instance matches the specified string
Substring	Retrieves a substring from this instance
ToCharArray	Copies the characters in this instance to a Unicode character array
ToLower	Returns a copy of this string in lowercase
ToString	Converts the value of this instance to a string
ToUpper	Returns a copy of this string in uppercase
Trim	Removes all occurrences of a set of specified characters from the beginning and end of this instance
TrimEnd	Removes all occurrences of a set of characters specified in a Unicode character array from the end of this instance
TrimStart	Removes all occurrences of a set of characters specified in a Unicode character array from the beginning of this instance

Table 4-1   Members of System.String *(continued)*

String Building

As you learned in the previous section, strings are immutable objects, meaning that a string cannot be modified; instead we get an entirely new string when we modify the original. Consider the following lines of code:

```
string strOne = "This is the first string's data";
strOne += " and this is the second part!";
```

The result of these two lines is that we have a `string` object on the heap containing "This is the first string's data", and the reference on the stack (`strOne`) is assigned to the `string` object. After the second line of code, there is a change: the original `string` object is still on the heap, and it is unchanged. A new `string` object has been created containing "This is the first string's data and this is the second part!". The reference (`strOne`) is now assigned to the new `string` object, and the first `string` object will be cleared away by the garbage collector.

Immutable strings are very efficient when it comes to manipulating strings of known length, but they suffer when the length of the string changes. For example, let's take our earlier code and perform that old children's cipher on the text by shifting every letter two characters back in the alphabet; *e* becomes *c*, and so on. For example, "Hello World" will be turned into "Fcjjm Umpjb".

```
// String.cs
using System;

public class MainClass
{
  public static void Main()
  {
    string strHello = "Hello World!";
    for (int i = (int)'a'; i<=(int)'z'; i++)
    {
      char chOld = (char)i;
      char chNew = (char)(i-2);
      strHello = strHello.Replace(chOld, chNew);
    }
    for (int i = (int)'A'; i<=(int)'Z'; i++)
    {
      char chOld = (char)i;
      char chNew = (char)(i-2);
      strHello = strHello.Replace(chOld, chNew);
    }
    Console.WriteLine("Child version: /n" + strHello);
  }
}
```

This program produces a large number of new `string` objects because each time we call the `Replace()` method, a new object will be constructed. This example highlights the need for another string-like class—the `System.Text.StringBuilder` class.

The `System.Text.StringBuilder` class produces a mutable object whose memory allocation we can control by adding and removing space from the object. Let's start by rewriting the preceding example using the `System.Text.StringBuilder` class:

```
// StringBuilder.cs
using System;
using System.Text;

public class MainClass
{
  public static void Main()
  {
    StringBuilder strHello = new StringBuilder("Hello World!", 30);
    for (int i = (int)'a'; i<=(int)'z'; i++)
    {
      char chOld = (char)i;
      char chNew = (char)(i-2);
      strHello = strHello.Replace(chOld, chNew);
    }
    for (int i = (int)'A'; i<=(int)'Z'; i++)
    {
      char chOld = (char)i;
      char chNew = (char)(i-2);
      strHello = strHello.Replace(chOld, chNew);
    }
    Console.WriteLine("Child version: /n" + strHello.ToString());
  }
}
```

With some very small changes, we have altered the processing to create only one object—the `StringBuilder` object—constructed by using the `new` keyword and specifying an initial length of 30 characters.

You will normally use the `StringBuilder` class to perform string manipulations on strings that are used for display purposes. Table 4-2 lists the members of the `StringBuilder` class.

Member	Description
Append	Appends the `string` representation of a specified object to the end of this instance
Capacity	Gets or sets the maximum number of characters that can be contained in the memory allocated by the current instance
Chars	Gets or sets the character at the specified character position in this instance
EnsureCapacity	Ensures that the capacity of this instance of `StringBuilder` is at least the specified value
Equals	Returns a value indicating whether this instance is equal to a specified object
GetHashCode	Serves as a hash function for a particular type, suitable for use in hashing algorithms and data structures like a hash table
GetType	Gets the `Type` of the current instance
Insert	Inserts the string representation of a specified object into this instance at a specified character position (this is an overloaded method)
Length	Gets or sets the length of this instance
MaxCapacity	Gets the maximum capacity of this instance
Remove	Removes the specified range of characters from this instance
Replace	Replaces all occurrences of a specified character or string in this instance with another specified character or string
ToString	Converts a `StringBuilder` to a string

Table 4-2 The Members of the `StringBuilder` Class

String Formatting

The output of strings or any data onto the screen sometimes produces unwanted effects or, indeed, almost incomprehensible effects. Take the formatting of dates as an example. Dates are formatted differently in different countries (and sometimes in different parts of a country). In the United States, the date 02/10/02 would translate to February 10, 2002, while in Canada it could mean October 2, 2002—that difference alone makes the date format problematic. The date format used in a specific location is part of that location's *locale* (sometimes called *culture*), and taking advantage of the locale and making applications truly international is the topic of Chapter 7—for now we simply need to understand that there is an issue to be addressed.

C# has the ability to use the client's locale to present the date in the right format for that user. Similar issues apply to currency ($, €, or SKR) as well as how the boundary between the integral and decimal part of a number is marked—in the English-speaking world, the period (3.141592653) is almost always used to mark the separation, while in the French, Spanish-speaking, and Swedish cultures the comma (3,141592653) is used.

In the next example, we will print out a formatted string with some numbers in it to demonstrate how number formatting is controlled by using formatting qualifiers.

```
// StringFormat.cs
using System;

public class MainClass
{
    public static void Main()
    {
        double PI = 3.14159;
        int i = 42;

        Console.WriteLine("The double is {0,10:E} and the int contains {1}", PI, i);
    }
}
```

The output from this program can be seen in Figure 4-1. The formatting inserted in the string is used to make the numbers print in a predetermined way: {0,10:E} specifies that the first (zero-based) parameter following the formatting string will be printed in a field of 10 characters using scientific format. The second format, {1}, takes the second parameter and prints it using the default settings.

Arrays

The *array* is one of the most common concepts used when storing a series of data points, either in a one-dimensional or multidimensional format. C# implements arrays as a class, and the arrays can hold data of one type (such as int, double, long, and so on). It also lets you create arrays of any number of dimensions.

You were already introduced to arrays in Chapter 2, and here we are going to look more closely at the Array class and see how we can take advantage of it.

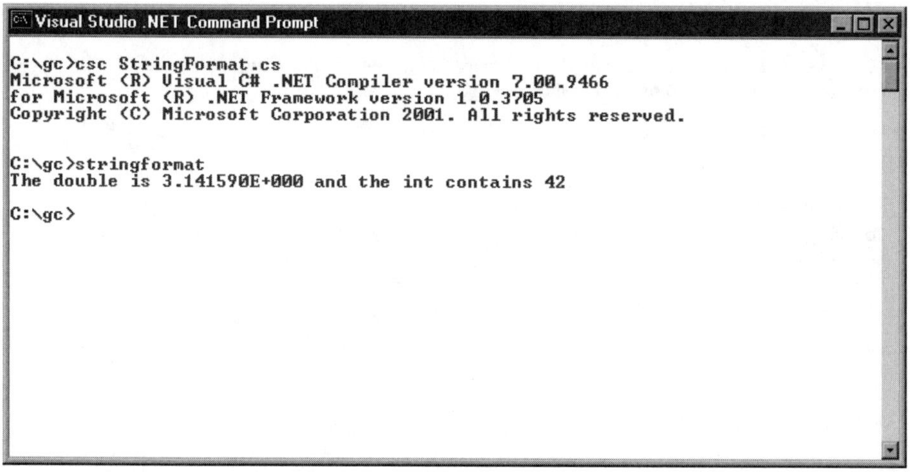

Figure 4-1 The output of the string formatting program

The System.Array Class

The array in C# uses the `System.Array` class, which provides many members to manipulate the resulting array, as well as the option to create multidimensional arrays. Table 4-3 lists the members of the `Array` class.

The following example uses some of the methods and properties from Table 4-3 to show their use:

```
// Array.cs
using System;
class ArrayTest
{
  static public void Main()
  {
    // Declare some arrays
    int[] Ints;
    Ints = new int[10]; //create an int array with 10 members
    for (int i=0; i<Ints.Length; i++)
    {
      Ints[i] = i;
    }
    int[] Instr = new int[10];
    //Copy Ints to Instr
    Array.Copy( Ints, Ints.GetLowerBound(0), Instr,
       Instr.GetLowerBound(0), 10 );
    // Reverse the content of Instr
    Array.Reverse(Instr);

    Console.Write("The initial Array has the following members : ");
    for (int i=0; i < Ints.Length;i++)
    {
```

```
      Console.Write(Ints[i]);
    }
    Console.Write("\n\nThe reverse Array has the following members : ");
    for (int i=0; i < Instr.Length;i++)
    {
      Console.Write(Instr[i]);
    }
    //Sort the Instr Array
    Array.Sort(Instr);
    Console.Write("\n\nThe reverse sorted Array has the following members : ");
    for (int i=0; i < Instr.Length;i++)
    {
      Console.Write(Instr[i]);
    }
  }
}
```

Member	Description
Clear	Sets a range of elements in the array to zero, to false, or to a null reference, depending on the element type
Clone	Creates a shallow copy of the array—a shallow copy will only copy the values or references that are in the original array, not the physical objects
Copy	Copies a section of one array to another array and performs type casting and boxing as required
CopyTo	Copies all the elements of the current one-dimensional array to the specified one-dimensional array starting at the specified destination array index
Equals	Determines whether two Object instances are equal
GetLength	Gets the number of elements in the specified dimension of the array
GetLowerBound	Gets the lower bound of the specified dimension in the array
GetType	Gets the Type of the current instance
GetUpperBound	Gets the upper bound of the specified dimension in the array
GetValue	Gets the value of the specified element in the current array
IndexOf	Returns the index of the first occurrence of a value in a one-dimensional array or in a portion of the array
Initialize	Initializes every element of the value-type array by calling the default constructor of the value type
IsFixedSize	Gets a value indicating whether the array has a fixed size
IsReadOnly	Gets a value indicating whether the array is read-only
Length	Gets the total number of elements in all the dimensions of the array
Rank	Gets the rank (number of dimensions) of the array
Reverse	Reverses the order of the elements in a one-dimensional array or in a portion of the array
Sort	Sorts the elements in one-dimensional array objects
ToString	Returns a string that represents the current Object

Table 4-3   The Members of the System.Array Class

In the preceding program you can see the use of `Reverse` and `Sort`. The output will be as follows:

```
The initial Array has the following members : 0123456789
The reverse Array has the following members : 9876543210
The reverse sorted Array has the following members : 0123456789
```

Collections

A different way of storing items is to use the OO concept of a *collection*, which you were introduced to in Chapter 3. We will now look at the support for this OO concept in C#.

A collection is defined as a set of similarly typed objects that are grouped together, similar to an array, but built to store objects. The .NET Framework support for collections is provided through the `System.Collections` namespace. Table 4-4 lists the collections defined in that namespace.

Class	Description
ArrayList	Implements the `IList` interface using an array whose size is dynamically increased as required
BitArray	Manages a compact array of bit values, which are represented as Booleans, where `true` indicates that the bit is on (1), and `false` indicates the bit is off (0)
CaseInsensitiveComparer	Compares two objects for equivalence, ignoring the case of strings
CaseInsensitiveHashCodeProvider	Supplies a hash code for an object, using a hashing algorithm that ignores the case of strings
CollectionBase	Provides the abstract base class for a strongly typed collection
Comparer	Compares two objects for equivalence, where string comparisons are case-sensitive
DictionaryBase	Provides the abstract base class for a strongly typed collection of key-and-value pairs
Hashtable	Represents a collection of key-and-value pairs that are organized based on the hash code of the key
Queue	Represents a first-in, first-out collection of objects
ReadOnlyCollectionBase	Provides the abstract base class for a strongly typed read-only collection
SortedList	Represents a collection of key-and-value pairs that are sorted by the keys and are accessible by key and by index
Stack	Represents a simple last-in, first-out collection of objects

Table 4-4 The Classes in the `System.Collections` Namespace

The following example illustrates the use of the `SortedList` class to store string objects:

```csharp
using System;
using System.Collections;
public class ExampleSortedList
{

    public static void Main()
    {

        // Creates and initializes a new SortedList.
        SortedList slOne = new SortedList();
        slOne.Add("First", "Hello");
        slOne.Add("Second", "World");
        slOne.Add("Third", "!");

        // Displays the properties and values of the SortedList.
        Console.WriteLine( "slOne" );
        Console.WriteLine( "  Count:     {0}", slOne.Count );
        Console.WriteLine( "  Capacity: {0}", slOne.Capacity );
        Console.WriteLine( "  Keys and Values:" );
        WriteKeysAndValues( slOne );
    }
    public static void WriteKeysAndValues( SortedList sList )
    {
        Console.WriteLine( "\t-KEY-\t-VALUE-" );
        for ( int i = 0; i < sList.Count; i++ )
        {
            Console.WriteLine( "\t{0}:\t{1}", sList.GetKey(i), sList.GetByIndex(i) );
        }
        Console.WriteLine();
    }
}
```

The output from the preceding example code is as follows:

```
slOne
  Count:     3
  Capacity: 16
  Keys and Values:
        -KEY-    -VALUE-
        First:  Hello
        Second: World
        Third:  !
```

Overview of Exception Handling

If you consider any application, you can probably think of a number of things that can go wrong with it. Suppose you ask the user to enter a number into your program, and then you store that number in an integer variable—it's possible that the user will give you a number that exceeds the boundaries of the integer type. Another possibility is that a user gives your program a filename to work with, and when the program looks for the file, it can't be found. These types of errors are unavoidable; they happen frequently and must be dealt with properly.

Note that we are not talking about errors that can and should be avoided. You don't want to write complicated exception handling for an error such as division by zero, which you shouldn't let happen. Along the same lines, there is no point in "handling" an error that occurs because your program tried to add an element to an array beyond the array boundaries. These are program bugs, and they should be fixed before the program is considered complete. Don't make the mistake of creating error-handling routines for these kinds of errors.

An *exception handler* is a piece of code that handles the first kind of error—those that cannot be avoided. When a program is asked to look for a file that is not there, the program code that looks for files causes an exception object to be "thrown." This means that it creates an object (in this case, an object of type FileNotFoundException) and then searches for code that will deal with the error. If it doesn't find the code in the current method, program execution returns to the caller of the method and searches there. This search continues (in a process called *unwinding the call stack*) until either the error is handled or the Main() method is entered. If the error flows back through all the calling methods and is not handled anywhere (including in Main()), the error is "caught" by the .NET runtime. This is not good news, since it means that the user of your program will be presented with a dialog box that essentially says your program bombed out.

By using the techniques described in this chapter for handling errors, you will achieve the following:

- Take advantage of an OO approach. One of the goals of OOP is to have loosely coupled objects, meaning that one object should not rely heavily on another object. By decoupling the logic of the program from the logic of error handling, you will achieve good OO design.

- Make use of an object to describe or explain an error. You can create your own exception objects from class files that you build. These objects can have properties that describe the error and methods that will display meaningful messages.

- Eliminate duplicate code. Very often, we must code the same thing over and over again, in order to achieve proper error handling. By placing all of the code in a single object, we are able to *write once, use many times*, another OOP goal.

Throwing and Catching Exceptions

The process of creating a new error object when a particular condition occurs is called *throwing* an exception. For example, upon dividing by zero, the CLR causes an exception object (of type System.DivideByZeroException) to be thrown and then looks for a *handler* (code that *catches* the exception). In the following example, there is no handler to catch the error, so the CLR displays the dialog box shown in Figure 4-2 to the user of the program, and then causes the program to end.

```csharp
public class DivideByZero
{
  public static void Main()
  {
    int x = 0;
    int y = 10;
    int z = y / x;
    System.Console.WriteLine ("We'll never get here in the code.");
  }
}
```

Coding to Handle Errors and Exceptions

There are three types of code blocks that you can use to test, catch, and handle runtime errors:

- **`try` block**   This tells the CLR that we know an exception might occur in the code.

- **`catch` block**   This is the block of code that tells the CLR what to do if a specific exception has occurred.

- **`finally` block**   This is the last piece of code to be executed, whether an exception occurred or not.

Before we examine each of these blocks in detail, take a moment to look at the following sequence of events that will take us through the steps of how the exception handling flows:

1. Program execution enters a `try` block. Each line of code is executed. If no error occurs, control is transferred to the nearest `finally` block (Step 4 in this list). If no `finally` block exists, execution continues on the instruction following the last `catch` block.

2. If an error occurs, the CLR creates an object to represent the error and transfers execution control to the `catch` blocks. Each `catch` block is examined, in

Figure 4-2

The dialog box presented to the user before the program closes

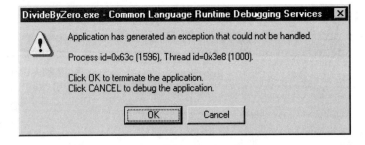

order of appearance. If a catch block is found that deals with the error object, the code within that block is executed and control is then transferred to the finally block (step 4 in this list).

3. If no catch block is found that handles the error object, the CLR passes the error object to the caller of the current method. The process described in step 2 continues in the caller method. Again, if no catch block is found, the error is passed back until it reaches the Main() method. Once in Main(), the error is either "caught" or it causes the program to terminate prematurely and it displays a dialog box like the one shown earlier in Figure 4-2.

4. The finally block is executed. Notice that we do not mention any conditions on this block of code executing. This is because you are guaranteed (unless some abnormal abort like a power failure or a kernel abort occurs) that the finally block of code will run, whether there was an error or not.

In the following sections, we will examine the use of the try and catch blocks and then look at the benefits of coding a good finally block. We will also explore the System.Exception class and its children in order to understand the types of exceptions that may occur.

The try ... catch Block

If you suspect that your code may cause an exception to be thrown, you can first place that code within a try block. True to its name, it tells the compiler to try the code and, if an error occurs, exit from the block and check for a catch block that handles the error. If we recode our DivideByZero example and use a try block, we can handle the error without the user getting involved at all.

```
public class DivideByZeroHandled
{
  public static void Main()
  {
    try
    {
      int x = 0;
      int y = 10;
      int z = y / x;
      System.Console.WriteLine ("We'll never get here in the code.");
    } catch (System.Exception e)
    {
      System.Console.WriteLine ("We caught an error!");
      // write code to handle the error here
    }
    System.Console.WriteLine ("We will now get to the end of the code!");
  }
}
```

Here we've told the CLR to try to execute the code in the try block. Of course, we know that the division by zero will cause an error. The CLR will then create an object to represent the error. Later in this chapter, we will deal with the types of objects that it creates; however, notice that, in this case, we have asked the CLR to catch System. Exception objects. This is the parent class of all exception objects, and by using it within our catch block, we are assured that any exception will be caught.

Once the CLR has created the object, it transfers program control to the code following the end brace after the try block. It then searches through the catch blocks (in this case, there's only one, but there could be many for different types of exceptions) until it finds one that has the appropriate type of the exception as its parameter. The code within the catch block is then executed. Remember that without the try and catch blocks, the CLR throws the exception object and then, because it was not handled, creates an error dialog box and aborts the program.

The output from the preceding example will be as follows:

```
We caught an error!
We will now get to the end of the code!
```

The program did not abort in this instance. Rather, it is allowed to continue since, in effect, we have "handled" the error. However, regardless of whether you follow this approach or allow the CLR to terminate the program, the line after the attempted divide-by-zero will never execute.

We mentioned earlier that the stack will unwind if the method containing the error does not handle the error. The following simple example demonstrates this using our DivideByZero code:

```
using System;
public class StackTest
{
  public static void Main ()
  {
    try
    {
      MethodA();
    } catch (DivideByZeroException d) {
      System.Console.WriteLine ("Catching the appropriate exception");
    } catch (Exception e) {
      System.Console.WriteLine ("Here we are in Main()");
    } finally {
      System.Console.WriteLine ("This code will always execute");
    }
  }
  public static void MethodA()
  {
    // this method simply calls MethodB
    MethodB();
  }
  public static void MethodB()
  {
    int x = 0;
    int y = 12;
    int z = y / x;  // LINE WITH THE ERROR
    System.Console.WriteLine ("We never get here");
  }
}
```

Keep this `StackTest` class file in your sights while we look at several issues that it introduces.

The first issue is that the actual code that causes the error (displayed in bold) is not enclosed in a `try` block directly. Instead, it has been called by a method that was called by a method that was enclosed in a `try` block. When the line shown in bold is executed, the CLR looks for exception handling in `MethodB()`. Of course, none is found, so it unwinds the call stack looking back at `MethodA()` for a `catch` block, and then to `Main()` where it finds the `catch`.

The next thing that you might notice about this code is that there are two `catch` blocks in Main(). You may want to have the anticipated error caught (`System. DivideByZeroException`) and then provide a default catch for any unanticipated errors. You can code as many catches as you like, as long as you follow these rules:

- Order your `catch` blocks by the specificity of the exception that is handled. This means that if you know a `System.DivideByZeroException` could happen, code it first. In our example, if the `catch` blocks were in the reverse order, the `System.Exception` block would be executed and our specific handling of the division by zero ignored. Only one `catch` block will execute, and control then passes to the `finally` block, if one is coded.

- You can place a general `catch` at the end of the `catch` blocks as follows:

```
} catch
    {   // write some very general code here }
```

In this case, no actual object is caught, but the general `catch` block allows you to handle completely unanticipated type exceptions. The compiler will enforce the rule that this block *must* be at the end of the `catch` blocks.

- You cannot catch the same type of exception twice. For example, there cannot be two `catch` blocks that start with:

```
} catch (DivideByZeroException d) {
```

- You cannot catch an exception of a type derived from the class of an object from a previous `catch`. For example, if there was a class `System.DivideIntegersByZeroException` that was a subclass of `System.DivideByZeroException`, you could not code a `catch` block for the subclass after the parent class, since one derives from the other.

The finally Block

The C# programming language allows you to execute code after a `try` block regardless of whether there was an exception thrown. You accomplish this by coding a `finally` block. C# guarantees that this code will execute even if attempts to side-step the block are coded (such as `break`, `continue`, `return`, or `goto` statements). This is a very useful concept.

Sometimes, you will want to end a program if an exception occurs. Take the example of trying to open a file that cannot be found. That may be the key that stops the execution of the program. By coding a `finally` block after the `catch` that handles the exception, you have a chance to release any system resources that have been used, and you can perform any necessary cleanup routines before exiting the program.

In our previous `StackTest` example, we have coded a `finally` block, so the program produces the following output:

```
Catching the appropriate exception
This code will always execute
```

Even if the highlighted line were changed as follows (which would not cause the exception to be thrown), the `finally` block will execute:

```
int z = y / 2;
```

In that case the output would be as follows:

```
We never get here
This code will always execute
```

You may find the `finally` block useful for avoiding duplicate code. Suppose many exceptions could occur within a particular `try` block. You would need `catch` blocks coded for each type of exception, and perhaps, as a final piece of code, a routine that must be executed regardless of which exception happens. Without the `finally` block, you would have to code the segment in each `catch` block. Fortunately, you don't have to do this—just code it once in the `finally` block.

Throwing Exceptions

As a final note to this discussion, there may be times when you decide it is necessary to cause an exception that can then be put through the normal handling routines. You do this by using the `throw` keyword.

In the following code example, we ask the user for an integer between 12 and 42. The user normally accommodates us by providing a value in that range. But occasionally a value less than 12 or greater than 42 escapes from the user's fingers. We can deal with this by throwing an exception object that will handle the error.

```
using System;
public class UserInputTest
{
  public static void Main ()
  {
    try
    {
      int x;
      Console.Write ("Enter an integer between 12 and 42 : ");
      x = Int32.Parse (Console.ReadLine());
      if (x > 42)
        throw new GreaterThan42Exception(); //home-grown exception
      else if (x < 12)
        throw new LessThan12Exception(); // home-grown exception
    } catch (GreaterThan42Exception g) {
      Console.WriteLine ("You entered a value greater than 42");
    } catch (LessThan12Exception l) {
      Console.WriteLine ("You entered a value less than 12");
    } catch (Exception e) {
      Console.WriteLine (e.Message);
```

```
   }
 }
 class GreaterThan42Exception : Exception
 {
   // put some specific code here
 }
 class LessThan12Exception : Exception
 {
   // put some specific code here
 }
}
```

The highlighted lines will cause the exceptions `GreaterThan42Exception()` or `LessThan12Exception()` to be thrown, and then execution control moves to the `catch` blocks where the exception can be handled. Remember the goal of this type of coding—you have separated the exception-handling logic from the business logic of the program, thereby accomplishing the decoupling goal of OOP.

.NET Framework Class Library Exceptions

The folks that brought you the .NET languages have anticipated a number of common exceptions and provided prebuilt classes for you to use in your programs. These exist in the Base Class Library (or, as it is also known, the .NET Framework Class Library). We will briefly look at the `System.Exception` class; for more information on the BCL and exceptions see Appendix D.

 EXAM TIP All exceptions inherit from `System.Exception`. If you want to catch all the exceptions from a `try` block, catch `System.Exception`.

System.Exception The `System.Exception` class is the parent class of all exceptions. All other exceptions, whether they are prebuilt or home-grown (your own exception classes), should derive from `System.Exception`. It's a good idea to become familiar with the properties and methods of this class, since any classes built will inherit these properties and methods. Here are some of the properties:

- **Message** retrieves a message that describes the exception.
- **Source** gets or sets the name of the object that caused the exception.
- **StackTrace** allows you to display the call stack at the time of the exception. This way you can chase back through the method calls to determine the sequence of execution.
- **TargetSite** retrieves the methods that threw the exception.
- **InnerException** gets the `Exception` instance that caused the current exception.

The best way to become familiar with these properties and to explore the methods that are either inherited by `System.Object` or are new to `System.Exception` and thereby are inherited by all other exceptions is to review the .NET Framework Class Library documentation.

Creating Your Own Exceptions

When you design your business logic, you will find certain error conditions that will regularly arise. Errors such as "Not enough money to withdraw", "No such customer", and so on, can be handled very nicely using the same approach that we have been discussing in this chapter. Create your own exception classes, and throw the exception object when the error occurs.

There are a few things that you should do when you create your own exception class:

- Inherit from `System.Exception`. As you can see in the previous section, you may want to create your exceptions under `ApplicationException`.

- Override the constructor of the base class. In particular, you may want to set the error message properly. The base class has been constructed as a bare-bones class—you will need to override its behavior.

- Name your class file with a descriptive error name. For example, if you are creating an exception class to describe the error condition "No such customer", call your exception class `NoSuchCustomerFoundException`. You will be following the good example set by the Microsoft engineers.

The following class file definition illustrates a simple exception class:

```
public class NoSuchCustomerFoundException : ApplicationException
{
    public NoSuchCustomerFoundException (string Message)
      : base (@"Customer Not Found. The customer you have requested
                cannot be found in the database. Try again, please")
    {
    }
}
```

This is a very simple example, but it does give you an idea of what you need to do to create your own exception class. The next step entails throwing this exception when a customer is not found. Presumably, your logic will go out to the database, search for the customer, and return with the result of the search. If the customer was not found, you would code the following line:

```
throw new NoSuchCustomerFoundException ();
```

The `catch` block would deal with the logic that pertains to an invalid customer request.

Event Handling

Event handling is the area of programming that has given procedural developers the biggest problem over the years—what is an *event* and how it is handled? The first item on our agenda must be the definition of an event. The examples commonly used to describe event handling are based on the concept of a cup object, and we have found that this type of example, rather than a code-based example, makes the topic easier to comprehend.

When we use the term *event*, we are referring to something that is an object considered important to communicate to the world. For example, imagine a coffee-travel-mug object: the specific object we have is blue in color with a black lid. The object has two methods, drink() and spill(); two parameters, noSpill (closes the lid) and level (indicates how much coffee there is in the cup). This can be a very common, everyday travel mug, or it can be a software object that emulates a travel mug—either way we can interact with the mug object.

Here is our task: We want to make sure we can refill the mug object as soon as it is empty, so we need to perform a loop asking "is it empty?" that reads the level parameter every so many seconds. When the level indicates that the mug is empty, the mug should be refilled. We could have produced a procedural software structure similar to this pseudo-code.

```
do while (true)
{
  if (mug.level <= 0)
  {
    refill(mug)
  }
}
```

This type of looping structure was the mainstay of the procedural world; we used to draw lovely flowcharts so we would know the flow of execution through the application. This type of processing is synchronous, with everything happening in a predetermined order, and only in that order. In our travel mug example, the end result of all that checking would be that coffee most likely would be removed from the daily food list—it is too much work for the person checking the level in the mug.

The natural question is whether there is a better way, and fortunately there is. The event model gives us the ability to have two or more objects communicating with each other asynchronously.

We will bestow our travel mug with two events. For now we will just define an *event* as something that is important to the object, and in this case we will create the empty event and the full event. The mug will cause the empty event when the mug is empty and the full event when the mug is close to overflowing. To take advantage of this new better travel-mug model, we need to do one extra thing—we need to tell the mug that we would like to be told when these events take place. This request is a registration of interest. We give the mug a sticky note that says "Tell me when the empty event happens" and gives an address where we can be contacted. Now we can go about our day doing what we do best, and when the mug is empty we will get a message from the mug telling us that it is empty.

This process is performed in the .NET environment every time we use an event. Actually this is the processing that took place in previous versions of the Windows operating system, as well. In the software world, we call the event routing a *callback*. The receiver of the event registers an address that should be called when the event *fires* (happens). The code that is called when the event fires is called the *event handler*.

Now let's have a look at how we perform event handling in the .NET environment: we use a delegate to connect the event with the code that will handle the event.

Delegates

Previous languages in the C family use the concept of the *function pointer;* every function occupies a block of memory, and the starting address is the function pointer. Being able to refer to a function by its memory address (pointer) is very powerful, but it is also fraught with dangers: if a pointer changes, the call to the location of the pointer will most likely run code that will crash the application, or even the operating system. The design of the C# language intentionally removed the ability to use pointers and perform pointer operations that C and C++ permitted and that led to many difficult-to-locate bugs. Instead, the C# designers created the equivalent of the function pointer in a type-safe OO way: they created the *delegate*.

Here's the one-sentence definition of a delegate: The delegate object encapsulates a reference to a method.

Let's look at how you declare and instantiate a `delegate`. The first step is to declare the `delegate`, defining the return data type as well as the parameters. The following code defines a couple of delegates:

```
// declare a delegate for a method that takes a single
// parameter of type string and has a void return type
delegate void MyDelegate1(string s);

// declare a delegate for a method that takes three parameters
// of type double, double, int and returns an int.
delegate int MyDelegate2(double d, double d1, int i);
```

Once the delegate is declared, we can instantiate it, as in the following code segment:

```
// Instantiate the delegate with a static method
// MyClass.Method1 must have this signature for the delegate to work:
// public static void Method1(string s)
MyDelegate1 k = new MyDelegate1(MyClass.Method1);

// Instantiate a delegate with an instance method
// The signature of the method must be:
// public int Method2(double d, double d, int i);
MyClass m = new MyClass();
MyDelegate2 p = new MyDelegate2(m.Method2);
```

When we have the delegate declared and instantiated, we need to call it. The following code segment shows how to call a delegate.

```
// call Method1 through the delegate
k("Hello Delegate World");

// call Method2 through the delegate
int a = p(3.14159, 12.0003, 42);
```

Let's have a look at a more complete example. Let's build a console application that will print assorted things for us and then call these methods through delegates.

```
using System;
namespace Deleg
{
  class Class1
  {
    delegate void MyprtString(string s);
    delegate int MyprtNumbers(double d, double d1, int i);

    static void Main(string[] args)
    {
      MyprtString a = new MyprtString(MyClass.prtString);
      MyClass m = new MyClass();

      MyprtNumbers o = new MyprtNumbers(m.prtNumbers);

      Console.WriteLine(o(3.14159, 12.003, 42));
      a("Jones");
    }
  }
  class MyClass
  {
    public static void prtString(string s)
    {
      Console.WriteLine("Hello " + s +"!");
    }
    public int prtNumbers(double d, double d1, int i)
    {
      double x;
      x = d * d1;
      return (x < 12 ? 42 : i);
    }
  }
}
```

The two delegates, `MyprtString` and `MyprtNumbers`, are declared and instantiated to encapsulate references (pointers) to the two methods in `MyClass`. When we execute the program, it results in the following output:

```
42
Hello Jones!
```

In the examples we have worked with thus far, the delegate performed a single coupling between the caller and the method. Such a delegate is known as a *single delegate*. What would happen if the invocation of the delegate resulted in multiple methods being called? There are several things that would need to be considered. For example, the delegate would need to keep a list of all the methods that need to be called, and some mechanism to add and remove methods from the delegates list would also be needed. A delegate with multiple methods listed is called a *multicast delegate*.

Multicast delegates are derived from the System.MulticastDelegate class. All the delegates have an invocation list with all the references that are to be called when the delegate is invoked. The `MulticastDelegate` class has two static methods that are used to add and remove references from the invocation list: the `Combine` and `Remove` methods. The

Combine method returns a `delegate` object with an invocation list that is the concatenation of the two `delegate` objects that were combined. The `Remove` method returns a `delegate` object with an invocation list that is the original minus the reference to be removed. The C# compiler will base all delegates that have a void return type on the `MulticastDelegate` class.

The following example simplifies the concept of delegates, and in particular multicast delegates. We will build some multicast delegates and exercise them.

```csharp
using System;
namespace MultiDelegate
{
  public delegate void PetDelegate();
  class Application
  {
    static void Main(string[] args)
    {
      // instantiate the pet objects
      Dog dog = new Dog();
      Snake snake = new Snake();

      PetDelegate a, b, c, d;

      // assign the delegates
      a = new PetDelegate(dog.Bark);
      b = new PetDelegate(snake.Hiss);

      // combine a and b as c
      c = (PetDelegate)Delegate.Combine(a, b);

      // invoke c(), the result should be that the two methods are called
      c();

      Console.Write("\n\n");
      // combine c and a into d
      d = (PetDelegate)Delegate.Combine(c, a);

      // invoke d(), the result should be that three methods are invoked
      d();
    }
  }
  public class Dog
  {
    public void Bark()
    {
      Console.WriteLine("WOOF");
    }
  }
  public class Snake
  {
    public void Hiss()
    {
      Console.WriteLine("Sssssssssssssss");
    }
  }
}
```

The output from this example follows, and you can see that there are two groups of invocations (c() and d()). When we call c() we get two lines of output, but when we call d() we get three lines.

```
WOOF
Ssssssssssssssss
```

```
WOOF
Ssssssssssssssss
WOOF
```

Microsoft has overloaded some operators in the C# language to make working with delegates easier. We can use the plus sign (+) or the += operator rather than using the Combine() method directly. Similarly, the minus sign (-) and the -= has been overloaded to give us the Remove() functionality. Using this syntax, we can rewrite the previous example as in the following code segment.

```
// combine a and b into c
c = a + b;
...
// combine c and a into d
d = c + a;

// remove a from c
c = c - a;

// or we can use the += and -= operators
c += a;
c += b'

d += c;
d -= a;
```

Events

Now that we've defined the delegates, we can look at how we declare, connect to, and raise events. This is what we have learned so far:

- We have a class that will raise an event.
- We have code in a second class that will respond to the event by running the code of the handler.

We now need a technique for connecting the event with the handler so we don't have to continually keep checking for the event. That connection is the delegate described in the previous section.

The first step in event processing is to declare the event and the delegate that will be used to register clients to the event. The following code segment shows how that is done.

```
// declare the delegate for the event
public delegate void TravelMugEmptyEventHandler();

public class Mug
{
  // declare the TravelMugEmpty event
  public static event TravelMugEmptyEventHandler TravelMugEmpty;
  // …
}
```

When we declare a delegate for a method with a void return type, the delegate will be compiled as a MulticastDelegate by the C# compiler, and Combine and Remove methods are added for members from the invocation list. The client accesses those methods with the overloaded operators += and -=.

The client code contains the method to handle the event, as well as the code to connect the method to the event. The client code to use the TravelMugEmpty event will look like this:

```
// The client's event-handling method
private void FillMug()
{
  mug.Refill();
}

// initialization code to connect to the event handler
Mug.TravelMugEmpty += new TravelMugEmptyEventHandler(FillMug);
```

Once the object that has declared the event is ready to raise (or fire) the event, it can use the event both as a class attribute and as a method. In our example, the TravelMugEmpty event can be tested to see if it is not null—the event attribute will be null only if there are no registered event handlers. If there are registered event handlers, we raise the event by calling the event method TravelMugEmpty(), as can be seen in this code segment:

```
// raise the TravelMugEmpty event if there are any connected event handlers
if (TravelMugEmpty != null) TravelMugEmpty();
```

Let's recap the event handling:

- The class that is defining the event will declare the delegate and the event.

- The client will define the event-handling method and connect to the event.

- The class that defined the event tests to see if there are any clients registered, and raises the event as needed.

Summary

In this chapter, we have looked at how to work with character strings in the form of `System.String` classes as well as `System.Text.StringBuilder` classes, and we looked at where each can be used. We also discussed arrays and the utility methods available for manipulating array data. We also looked at collections. There are a large number of collections that can be built using the collection support in C#—there is a special operator (foreach) that simplifies the way you can go through a collection from the start to the end very efficiently.

We also looked at the techniques of error handling. Creating applications that handle error conditions successfully is not rocket science. You simply need to understand when the exception might occur and code your `catch` blocks accordingly. You will also have to consider what kind of user-application errors could occur, and then build your custom exception class library.

Finally we discussed delegates and events, and how to declare them.

The next chapter will introduce the graphical environment that can be used when working with C# in Visual Studio .NET.

Test Questions

1. Given the following code segment, what is the content of the string s in line 4?

```
1 string s = "Hello";
2 string r;
3 r = s;
4 r += " World!";
```

   A. "Hello World!"

   B. "Hello"

   C. Nothing, it is garbage collected

   D. The code will not compile

2. Which of the following array declarations will produce a compiler error?

   A. `int[] Integers = new int[] (1,2,3,4,5,6,7,8,9,0};`

   B. `int[] Integers = new int[42];`

   C. `int[] Integers = {1,2,3,4,5,6,7,8,9,0};`

   D. `int I = 4;`
      `int[] Integers = new int[I] {1,2,3,4};`

3. In the following code, what will be printed by the `Console.WriteLine()` method?

```
string[] str = {"Hello", "!", "World"};
Array.Reverse(str);
Console.WriteLine(str[0]);
```

A. "!"

B. "Hello"

C. "olleH"

D. "World"

4. In the following code, what will be printed by the `Console.WriteLine()` method?

```
string[] str = {"Hello", "!", "World"};
Array.Sort(str);
Console.WriteLine(str[0]);
```

A. "!"

B. "Hello"

C. "olleH"

D. "Hello World !"

5. What is the outcome of the following code?

```
01 public void MethodB ()
02 {
03    int [] MyInts = new int [2];
04    try
05    {
06      for ( int i = 0; i < 3; i++)
07      {
08        MyInts[i] = i;
09      }
10    } catch (System.Exception e)
11    {
12      System.Console.WriteLine ("Some error occurred");
13    }
14 }
```

A. The code will not compile because there is an incorrect `catch` block.

B. The code will not compile because of an error on line 6.

C. The code will compile and displays "Some error occurred".

D. The code will compile and will abort upon execution.

6. What is the outcome of the following code?

```
01 public void MethodB ()
02 {
03    int [] MyInts = new int [2];
04    try
05    {
06      for ( int i = 0; i < 3; i++)
07      {
08        MyInts[i] = i;
09      }
10    } finally
11    {
12      System.Console.WriteLine ("This is executed");
13    }
14 }
```

A. The code will not compile because there is a missing `catch` block.

B. The code will compile and abort upon execution.

C. The code will compile and displays "This is executed".

D. The code will compile and will abort upon execution and then display "This is executed".

7. You need to define a delegate for the following method:

```
public class Class1
{
  public static int Method42(int i)
  {
    return i*42;
  }
}
```

How is the delegate for `Method42()` declared?

A. `delegate Class1.Method42;`

B. `delegate int Met42(int i);`

C. `delegate void Method42(string s);`

D. `delegate int Class1.Method42(int i);`

8. What kind of delegate will be created for the following method?

```
public void Method12(object sender, System.EventArgs e)
{
  ...
}
```

A. Single delegate

B. Event delegate

C. Multicast delegate

D. Proxy delegate

9. The following code segment creates an event handler. What text must be inserted in place of **<<replace text here>>** for the event to work?

```
// declare the delegate for the event
public delegate void SendFaxEventHandler();

public class Fax
{
  // declare the SendFax event
  public <<replace text here>> event SendFaxHandler SendFax;
  // …
}
```

A. void

B. delegate

C. Combine

D. static

10. You are building an event handler for the SendFax event from the sFax component, and you have written the following code. When you test the event handler, you find that it never runs. What code must you add to your application to make the event execute in response to the SendFax event?

```
private void Send_Fax()
{
   Console.WriteLine("Fax is sent!");
}
```

A. public delegate SendFax(Send_Fax);

B. this.sFax.SendFax += new SendFaxHandler(this.Send_Fax);

C. public event SendFax(Send_Fax);

D. this.sFax.SendFax =+ new SendFaxHandler(this.Send_Fax);

Test Answers

1. **B.** Through all the processing the content of s never changes.

2. **D.** The array constructor cannot take an explicit size parameter as well as initialization.

3. **D.** The output is the first string in the array, the array was reversed so the output is "World".

4. **A.** The output is the first string in the array, the array was sorted so the output is "!".

5. **C.** The array has size 2, we try to access index 0, 1, and 2. There will be an exception when we try to access index 2, resulting in an exception, the catch block will sink the exception, then the finally block will execute.

6. **D.** The array has size 2, we try to access index 0, 1, and 2. There will be an exception when we try to access index 2, resulting in an exception, then the finally block will execute.

7. **B.** The delegate should have the same signature as the method it will encapsulate, except the name must be unique in the scope.

8. **C.** Any delegate that is declared as public void is a multicast delegate.

9. **D.** Events must be declared as static.

10. **B.** The delegate must be registered, the += operator performs that action.

Visual Studio .NET Development Environment

In this chapter, you will

- Be introduced to the new integrated development environment in Visual Studio .NET
- Get acquainted with the Start page
- Discover the different kinds of projects that can be created
- Learn to build projects
- Get to know the various tools inside VS .NET
- Learn to move around the VS .NET interface

Although most of the sample code we have presented thus far has been entered into a simple text editor and tested through a command prompt, there is a whole other world waiting for you in Visual Studio .NET. If you are accustomed to using VS6, you will be pleasantly surprised and grateful for the amount of work that has gone into providing you with an integrated development environment (IDE) that will make your job much easier. If this is your first introduction to Visual Studio, you will come to appreciate how quickly you can put together applications, and you will learn how to use some of the tools that are contained within the interface.

Please remember as you read through this chapter that it is an introduction to the Visual Studio .NET environment. This is a vast subject that could easily fill a separate book. However, we have provided enough information here to get you started using this valuable resource.

You should also be aware that you will probably not be tested on your knowledge of the Visual Studio IDE. This chapter has been added to our book in order to give you an alternative to using Notepad as your editor. You will also find that Windows and Web development is made much easier by using the IDE.

What is Visual Studio .NET?

In order to build a project that contains many class files, other resources, and programs from different languages, you need an environment that has been developed to pull all of these files together. That is what Visual Studio .NET does for you. Essentially, it's a fully integrated development environment. It was created to allow you to write your code, test it, debug it, and package it into an assembly so that the time to market is as short as possible.

As well as providing an extremely intuitive code editor, here are some of the advantages of using Visual Studio .NET as your development environment:

- You can write, compile, test, and debug programs, all from within the same graphical interface.

- An extensive help facility is located inside the program. You can get access to MSDN (Microsoft Solution Developer Network), online information, and many other help routines.

- You can build Web applications, Windows forms, XML Web services, and so on, all from the same environment. Select File | New Project from the menu system to see a list of the different types of projects that can be created within the IDE.

- Of course, the IDE supports the .NET Framework, which is essential to development within .NET.

- The edit and debug tools are extensive and extremely helpful.

- The IDE install includes sample applications that will help you develop better enterprise solutions.

This list may sound like a commercial or a paid endorsement of Visual Studio .NET, but rest assured that it is not. The IDE is simply a very exciting environment in which to code. If you have been around programming long enough, you know of the days when you coded in something much less than Notepad, compiled in an awkward way, and then waited for the program to crash in order to begin your debugging process, which might involve chasing hexadecimal core dumps around looking for the contents of a single variable. Those days are gone. Visual Studio .NET lets you move your mouse around the code while it is running to determine the contents of a variable. You can watch expressions and see when they evaluate to a particular result. For more on the debugging capabilities of Visual Studio .NET, please refer to Chapter 9.

Let's start by looking at the various parts of the VS .NET interface, and then work our way through the plethora of tools and techniques available to the C# developer.

The Start Page

After you install Visual Studio .NET and launch the program for the first time, you will be presented with a page called "Start" (see Figure 5-1). Although the temptation is to simply close this page and move into the development interface, you should take a few

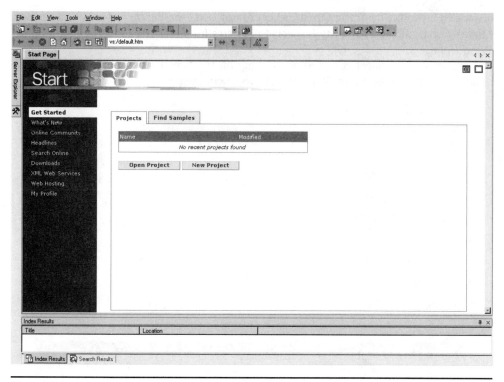

Figure 5-1   The Visual Studio .NET Start page

moments to look at the information and resources presented on this page. You can close the Start page and retrieve it at any time by selecting Help from the menu system and then Show Start Page.

We will look at the Get Started, Online Community, and Downloads pages, all of which are accessed from the Start page. Be sure to explore the other pages, though, and click your way through the many resources that can help you develop great applications.

Get Started

The Get Started page (shown in Figure 5-1) is the first page that you see as you open Visual Studio (unless you decide to turn off the Start Page option). Two tabs are visible—one for working with your projects, and the other for finding sample code. Under the Projects tab, you can select an existing project from the recent project list. You can also open a project from the Open Project dialog box (see Figure 5-2). As you can see, Microsoft has allowed for a My Projects folder similar to the My Documents folder for Windows users.

Starting a new project is as easy as clicking on the New Project button. You will be asked to select a project template from the following list:

- Windows Application
- Class Library
- Windows Control Library
- ASP.NET Web Application
- ASP.NET Web Service
- Web Control Library
- Console Application
- Windows Service
- Empty Project
- Empty Web Project

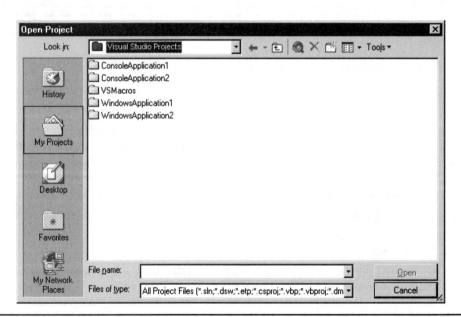

Figure 5-2   The Open Project dialog box

We will be discussing these different kinds of projects in the next section.

If you examine Figure 5-3, you will see that you can select the type of project, as well. Since we are interested in Visual C# .NET, our choice is likely to be clear; however, VS .NET will allow you to create a project using any language from the list.

The Find Samples tab on the Get Started page (see Figure 5-1) allows you to enter keywords or types into a search box. Visual Studio will then search through the MSDN and online help for samples and documentation that is pertinent to your search. Figure 5-4 illustrates a search for "controls" types and the resulting samples. You can see some of the links that will lead you to sample code.

Online Community

Another very useful page is the Online Community page. From it you can explore third-party code development as well as coding and application examples. There are four tabs on the page (see Figure 5-5) that will let you find an appropriate newsgroup to join, talk to the experts, or search a component catalog. (The Component Catalog tab provides third-party component solutions that can be used in your applications.) The

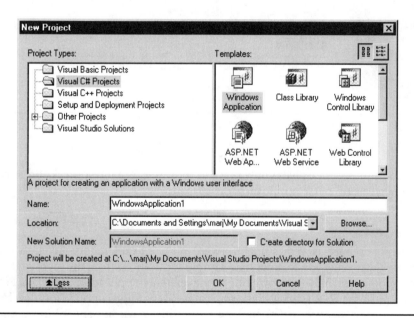

Figure 5-3 The New Project dialog box

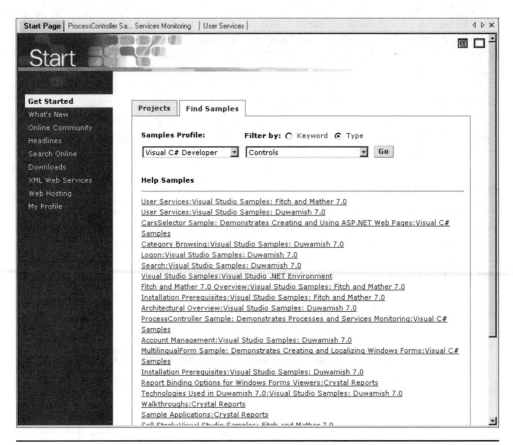

Figure 5-4   The Find Samples tab of the Get Started page

Online Community page gives you a place to look at external resources and to become part of a large group of C# application developers.

Downloads

The Downloads page is very straightforward and self-explanatory. It is an excellent resource that will allow you to download sample applications from the Internet. If you are a Java developer, you may recognize one of the reference applications, The Java Pet Store. It is a blueprint for J2EE (Java 2 Platform, Enterprise Edition) application development that explains best practices when creating a multi-tier environment solution. Microsoft has written the same application using C# and the Microsoft .NET Framework.

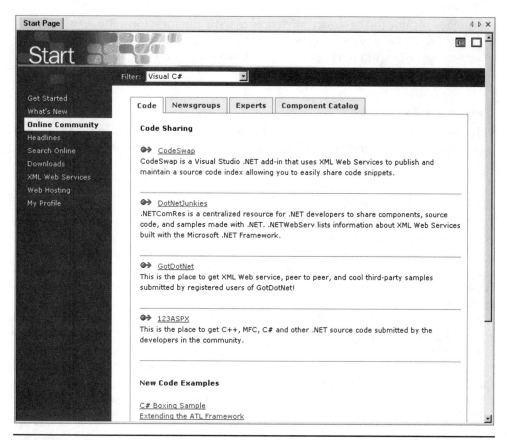

Figure 5-5   Online Community

Microsoft's claim to fame for the .NET solution is that it is up to 28 times faster than the J2EE benchmark times with less than half the code. It's pretty amazing to have all of these resources at your fingertips. On this page, you will also find many free downloads that, again, can be invaluable to your development team.

Projects

One of the many advantages of using the Visual Studio .NET development interface is the ability to create a new application based upon a template of common application types. Up until this point in the book, we have been creating single-purpose class files, coding them in Notepad, and then compiling and executing them from the command line. Every time you start up a new program, you must code all the necessary using statements, include the necessary references to .NET libraries, form the new class with the appropriate brace brackets, and so on. Imagine having the option to select from a list of application types and having the outline of your program be created for you. Well, that's a *project*.

Types of Projects

Visual Studio .NET allows you to select from many preexisting templates (and you can even create your own template and add it to the list). You first saw the project types in Figure 5-3. Table 5-1 identifies the purpose of each project type.

Creating a Project

By selecting one of the project types described in Table 5-1, you are asking Visual Studio .NET to create a project for you. The project, by default, will contain all the necessary code and references that a project of that type will need. In Figure 5-6, you can see the template for a console application. By default, its name is `ConsoleApplication#` (where the # is incremented according to the number of `ConsoleApplication` files in the directory).

Notice that a shell of a class file has been created for you. The system assumes that you will need the `System` namespace and has added the appropriate `using` statement. It has also generated the documentation comments for you, as well as the entry point, `Main()`.

There are a number of exciting new features in Visual Studio .NET, and the first you should notice is the expansion bar running down the left side of the code window. This is a handy feature that allows you to close a particular section of code and look at an outline

Project Type	Usage
Windows Application	To build a Windows application. (See Part IV of this book for Windows applications.)
Class Library	To create class files that can be added to the library of class files.
Windows Control Library	To create controls for use in Windows applications (see Part IV).
ASP.NET Web Application	To create an application with a Web user interface (see Part III).
ASP.NET Web Service	To create XML Web services that can be used from other applications (see Part III).
Web Control Library	To create controls for use in Web applications (see Part III).
Console Application	To create an application that can be run from the command prompt.
Windows Service	To create a service that runs in the background of the Windows operating system.
Empty Project	There is no actual template for this. You start from scratch.
Empty Web Project	Same as before—start from scratch.
New Project in Existing Folder	To bring in code from a previous application not built in Visual Studio .NET.

Table 5-1 List of Project Types in Visual Studio .NET

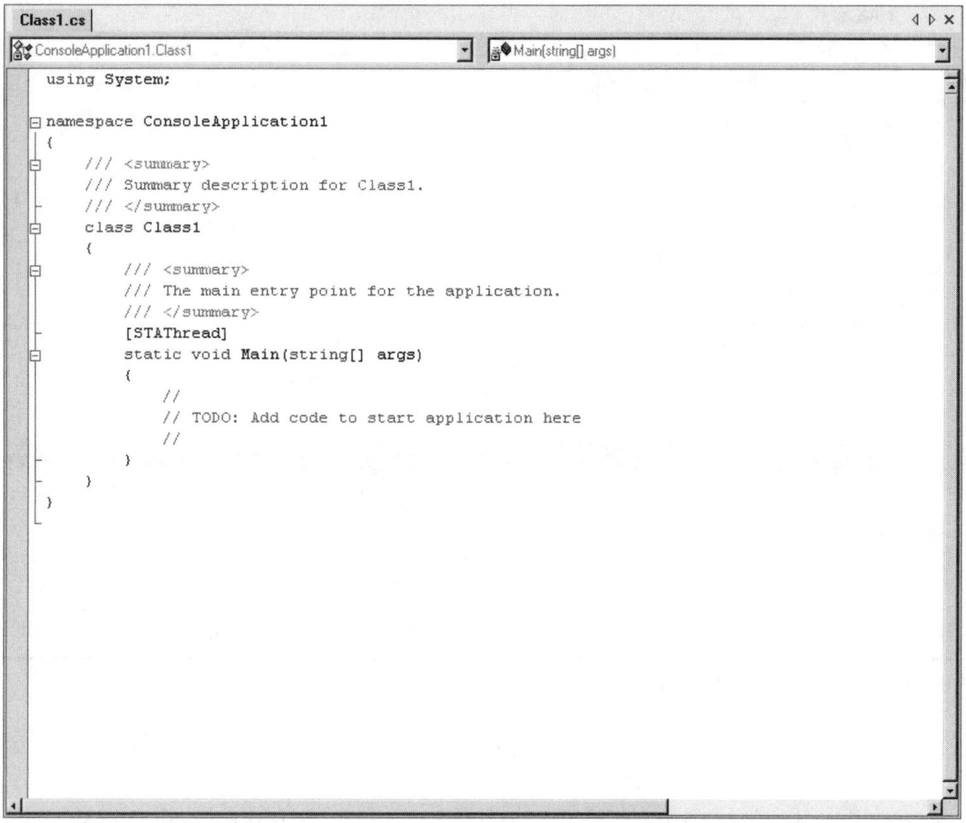

```
Class1.cs                                                                    ◄ ▷ ×
ConsoleApplication1.Class1                        ▼    Main(string[] args)           ▼
    using System;

  namespace ConsoleApplication1
  {
      /// <summary>
      /// Summary description for Class1.
      /// </summary>
      class Class1
      {
          /// <summary>
          /// The main entry point for the application.
          /// </summary>
          [STAThread]
          static void Main(string[] args)
          {
              //
              // TODO: Add code to start application here
              //
          }
      }
  }
```

Figure 5-6   A new console application

version to get an idea of where everything is. We will be covering the interface, itself, in the next sections; but you might want to take a minute and move around the windows.

Building the Project

To build your project (or compile and run it), you simply need to press F5. You can do this for the class file in Figure 5-6, but there will be no output since it's only a shell of a program. However, by pressing F5, you will see a couple of important things. First, Visual Studio .NET pulls together all the necessary compile instructions for a console application and then compiles it. If there are compile errors, you will see them in a newly opened Output window at the bottom of the screen. In Figure 5-7, you can see the "Hello World!" program with the void keyword taken off the Main() declaration, which, as you know, is an illegal method declaration (no return type). When we press F5, the compiler runs and then displays the error in the output window.

If we add the void keyword to the Main() declaration, this program will now compile and execute. However, when it runs, it opens a command window or a shell, displays "Hello World!", and then closes the shell. If you are not very fast, you will miss the

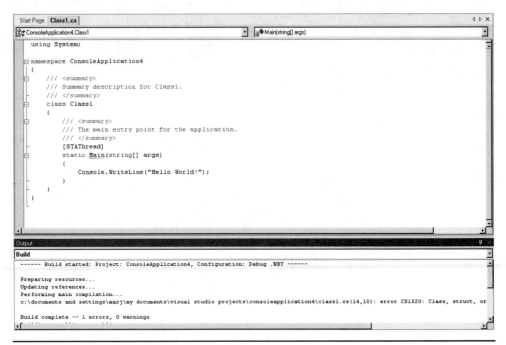

```
Start Page  Class1.cs                                                              ◁ ▷ ×
ConsoleApplication4.Class1                          ▼    Main(string[] args)          ▼
    using System;

    namespace ConsoleApplication4
    {
        /// <summary>
        /// Summary description for Class1.
        /// </summary>
        class Class1
        {
            /// <summary>
            /// The main entry point for the application.
            /// </summary>
            [STAThread]
            static Main(string[] args)
            {
                Console.WriteLine("Hello World!");
            }
        }
    }


Output                                                                              ╄ ×
Build                                                                                 ▼
------ Build started: Project: ConsoleApplication4, Configuration: Debug .NET ------

Preparing resources...
Updating references...
Performing main compilation...
c:\documents and settings\marj\my documents\visual studio projects\consoleapplication4\class1.cs(14,10): error CS1520: Class, struct, or

Build complete -- 1 errors, 0 warnings
```

Figure 5-7   A compiled program with an error

screen output. There are two ways to avoid this scenario. One way is to add an extra out-put line, `Console.ReadLine()`, which will force the output device to pause for input from the keyboard. The other, most acceptable way is to build your project by pressing CTRL-F5. This causes the shell to remain on the screen and gives you an opportunity to observe the console output, which will show "Hello World!" followed by "Press any key to continue" on the next line.

Grouping Projects into Solutions

A *solution* is a grouping of projects put together into a single package. You could conceivably have many different types of projects make up a solution. Observe the setup in Figure 5-8. You can see that to the right side of the code window is something called the Solution Explorer. This is similar to Windows Explorer, which shows all your computer's folders and files. Solution Explorer lists all the elements that make up your solution.

You can see all of the elements that make up the solution by examining the Solution Explorer. In Figure 5-8, there are two projects—one called `ConsoleApplication4` (what a creative name we've chosen!), and the other equally creatively named `ConsoleApplication5`. Not only are the two projects listed there, but all the references within the projects are also listed. Notice that the References folder holds three

Figure 5-8

A solution

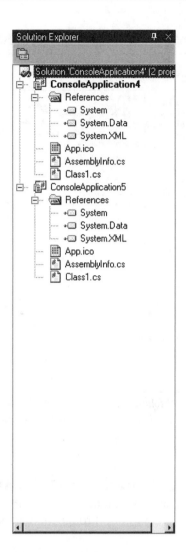

namespaces—System, System.Data, and System.XML. This is the default reference setting for a new console application.

TIP   VB developers—you will recognize a *solution* as a *project group*.

You can set the properties of your new solution by right-clicking on the solution name and selecting Properties from the drop-down list. You will get a dialog box similar to the one shown in Figure 5-9, where you can set the startup project, project dependencies, location of debug files, and configuration properties. Be sure to set the appropriate startup project if you have a solution with multiple projects.

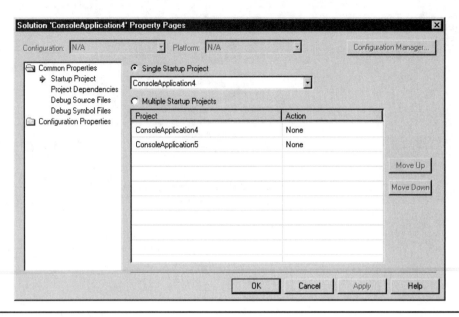

Figure 5-9   Solution properties

    NOTE   A *solution* is a grouping of all the related projects that make up a *software application*. A *project* is a grouping of all the related files and resources that make an *assembly*.

Customizing Visual Studio .NET

There will be times that you want to change the look of the Visual Studio interface. You can do this in two different ways—through the Start page or from the Options dialog box.

Customizing with the Start Page

When you select My Profile from the Start page, you will be presented with the My Profile page shown in Figure 5-10. This page allows you to customize the interface in certain ways and then save the settings to a particular profile.

From the existing profile list, you can choose to be a Visual C# developer or a developer in any other Visual Studio language. You can select your keyboard scheme, window layout, help filter, and even whether the Start page is displayed at startup. Each profile will present you with a screen modified for that particular language or feature. If you so desired, you could set the Visual Studio .NET environment to look like the previous release of VS—Visual Studio 6—although you would then fight to gain back the advanced features of the new .NET IDE.

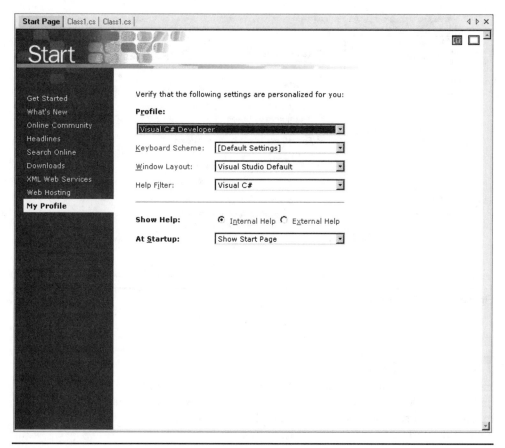

Figure 5-10   The My Profile page

Customizing with the Options Dialog Box

If you want to do some in-depth customization, you can choose Tools | Options from the menu system. You will see the dialog box shown in Figure 5-11.

This dialog box gives you an opportunity to select the different fonts and colors for displayed elements of the IDE. You can also set or release automatic features, such as IntelliSense. IntelliSense is a handy feature that assists you as you code in the IDE—it provides such tools as List Members, a drop-down list of methods belonging to the object you are referencing; Parameter Info, which lists the parameters of a method and the order in which they are coded; Quick Info, which displays the actual declaration of any identifier; a Complete Word tool; and Automatic Brace Matching, which determines whether you have completed your brace brackets properly. If you want to display line numbers in your code, you can also choose to set this option. These are just a few of the items that can be set in the Options dialog box. It's not a bad idea to spend some time here in order to make the development environment as comfortable as possible for you, the developer.

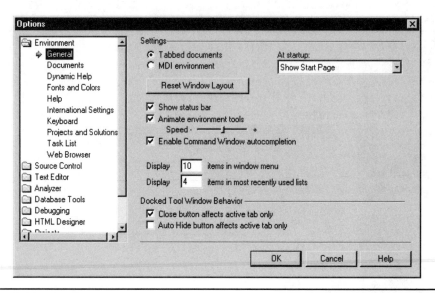

Figure 5-11   The Options dialog box

The Interface

It's now time to look at the actual IDE itself and look through the various explorers, design and code windows, as well as the numerous tools available for use. Keep in mind that this is a cursory overview of what's in the IDE, and experimentation is your best bet before you start into some heavy-duty coding.

Explorers

Visual Studio .NET comes with a number of "explorer-type" windows that can be constantly displayed, tucked away for quick access, or simply removed from the page display. If you look at the environment setup in Figure 5-12, you can see that there are three different explorers visible on the page.

    TIP   You can toggle the display of explorer windows through the View menu.

Are you still looking for the third explorer window? Check the far right side of the screen—tucked away is the Properties Explorer. This is a very convenient feature of Visual Studio .NET. By clicking on the little thumbtack in the title bar of the explorer window, you can ask VS to "hide" the window and just leave enough of a display so that you know it is there. If you move your mouse to the right of the screen, the explorer window reappears.

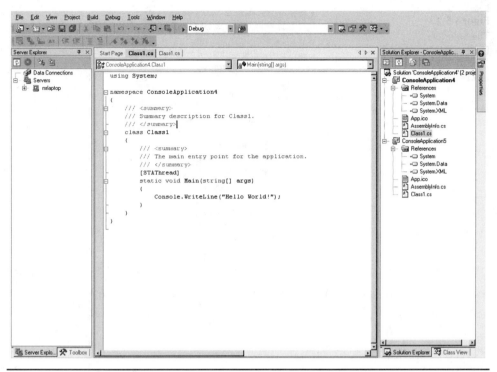

Figure 5-12   Explorer windows

Server Explorer

Server Explorer is an exciting addition to the development environment. If you want a list of connected servers, you can select to view the Server Explorer, and it will list any server that you have asked to be connected to your development environment. This will give you a chance to link database servers so you can have access to the actual database according to your permissions. One of the advantages of this setup is that the database connection properties and pages don't interfere with your code pages and are off to the right or left of the full development environment.

Solution Explorer

We have seen Solution Explorer in Figure 5-8, and it is shown specifically in Figure 5-13. Any of the explorer windows will operate in the same way as this one. You can right-click on most of the elements within the window to get a drop-down menu, from which you can select relevant activities. You will find the property pages on this menu, and from there you can set the properties of the selected item. The Solution Explorer allows you to set the properties of the solution or of any of the individual projects found in the solution.

Notice in Figure 5-13 that we have finally changed the names of the solution, the projects within, and even the class files within the project. This is done by right-clicking and selecting Rename from the drop-down menu. You will find that you'll use the main

Figure 5-13
The Solution
Explorer

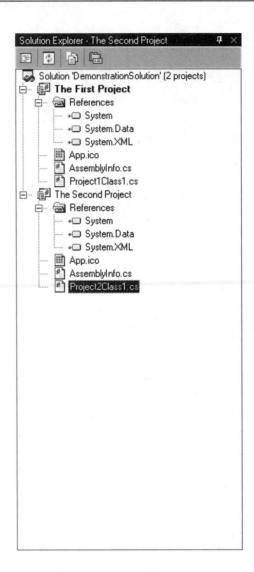

menu system infrequently if you get used to right-clicking and using the drop-down menus for each item.

Properties Explorer

Here is one of the explorer windows that you will find invaluable if you are creating Windows or Web projects. In Figure 5-14 you will see the standard startup environment for a new Windows project. To the right is the Properties Explorer.

If you select any component on the form (or even the form itself), you will see a list of the properties available, and you can change them through the Properties Explorer. If you are creating a Windows form, you will probably find that this explorer needs to be

Figure 5-14
The Properties
Explorer

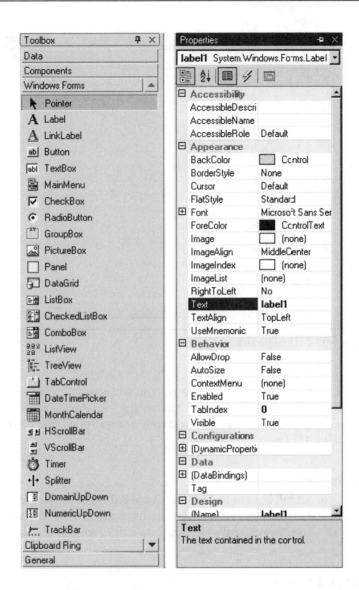

open along with the form itself. You can organize the Properties Explorer window to display the elements in alphabetical order or by category.

Task List

The Task List is a handy tool for keeping yourself organized. You can add your own tasks to the list simply by clicking where it says "Click here to add a new task" (see Figure 5-15). A task can be anything to remind you that something needs to be completed, added, changed, and so on. You can then order your tasks by priority.

You will also find that certain tasks may be added dynamically to the Task List windows. As you are debugging an application, for example, some tasks will be added to

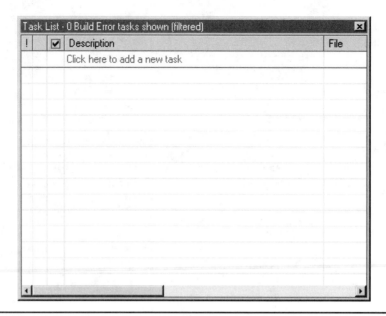

Figure 5-15   The Task List

mark the errors that were encountered. You will also find the Task List to be a great tool if you are doing group development and using Visual SourceSafe. Everyone on the team can see the current task list and add to it or remove items. It's almost like a built-in project "to-do" list.

Tools

In order to get full benefit from using Visual Studio .NET, you must understand how to use the various tools that are included in the product. These include the Object Browser, Help, the Class Viewer, and so on. In this section, we will briefly explore some of these features.

Object Browser

So just what do you do when you know the library and class that you need, but you are not sure what methods and data are exposed to you (or available to use)? This is where the Class Viewer comes into play. This handy and convenient tool should be at every developer's fingertips. You can see all the .NET classes from the Object Browser.

TIP   VB developers, this is not the Object Browser of Visual Basic 6. In order to see COM components, you need to ask for the OLEView tool.

From the menu system, you can select View | Other Windows | Object Browser to open the Object Browser window. In Figure 5-16, you can see that we have opened the base assembly, `mscorlib`, and drilled down into the `System` namespace and the `Exception` class.

To the left, in the Objects pane, you can see the assemblies, the namespaces, and the individual classes. Each class lists its base classes and interfaces, and as soon as you click on the class you want to see, the right side of the window displays the exposed members of the class.

To the right, in the Members Of pane in Figure 5-16, you can see the associated members of the class `Exception`. Notice that we have chosen the `StackTrace` field to illustrate that the bottom pane of the window displays the help associated with the field. In this case it tells us that `StackTrace` is used to get a string representation of the frames on the call stack at the time the current exception was thrown.

Help

Everyone needs a little help from their friends, and your friend today is Microsoft. They have packed so much Help into Visual Studio .NET that sometimes you can be overwhelmed as to where to go for help. Explore the Help menu for the different kinds of Help available. You can use Dynamic Help and receive a window like Figure 5-17.

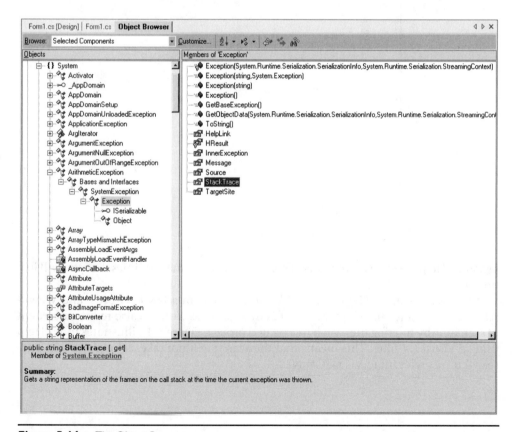

Figure 5-16   The Object Browser

Figure 5-17

The Dynamic
Help window

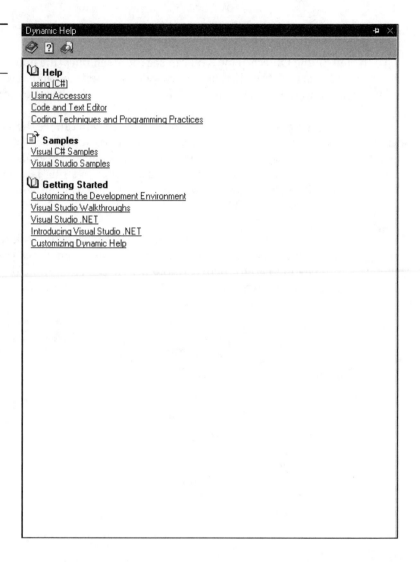

Dynamic Help is expensive in terms of resources, so there may be times that you will just turn it off.

If you ask for Index Help, you will be able to type in a few keywords, and VS will search the Help files and display a list of pertinent topics. You can also reduce the extent of searching by filtering the search to a related project. Figure 5-18 illustrates Index Help using a Visual C# filter. This means that the search will not take as long and will only search topics relevant to Visual C# .NET.

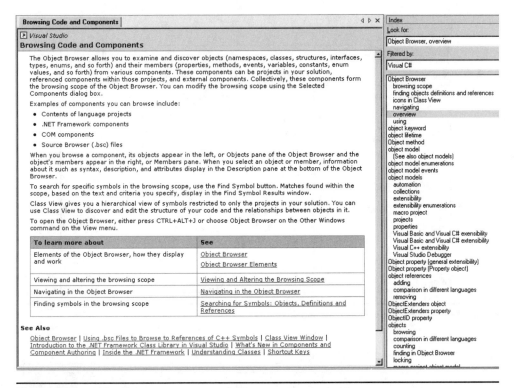

Figure 5-18   Index Help

Class Viewer

Here's a handy tool hidden in the recesses of the Visual Studio installation. From the command prompt, type in **WinCV** in order to access the Class Viewer. As with the Object Browser, you can explore the Base Class library through a graphical interface. You will start with a screen similar to Figure 5-19.

We have chosen to explore the Array class, so we enter the word **Array** in the Searching For box and after pressing Enter are presented with the results of the search (see Figure 5-20). By clicking on the desired class in the left Search Results pane (in our case, Array), we see in the right Selected Class pane all the method and data signatures from the actual class file. This is a quick glance at the class, and it lets you see what is available in the class and how to use it.

So why would you use this over the Object Browser? The Class Viewer allows you to search through all the classes in the .NET library, whereas the Object Browser only shows the assemblies that you have added (or that are added by default) to your solution. Notice that you access the Class Viewer from outside of the Visual Studio environment. If you want to see everything, you will need to use the Class Viewer.

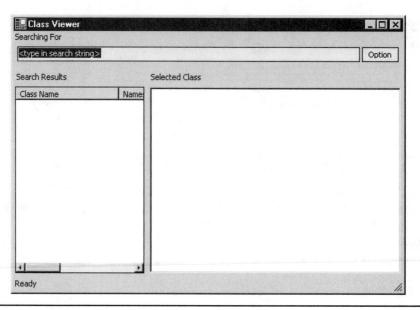

Figure 5-19   Class Viewer search window

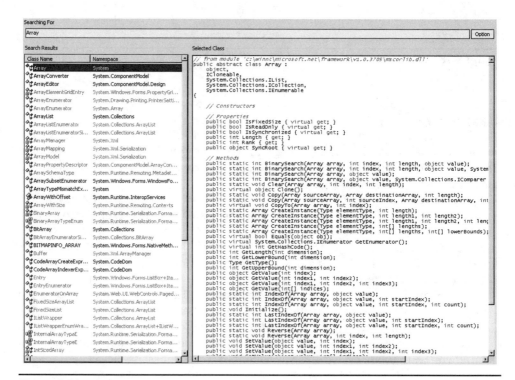

Figure 5-20   Class Viewer Results

Other Highlights of Visual Studio .NET

Visual Studio .NET has a built-in Web browser that will allow you to test and display your Web pages directly within Visual Studio. You simply choose View | Web Browser | Show Browser from the menu. Once open, the browser acts like a normal Web browser with all the functions available. You can even store favorites inside VS .NET, itself, and access them at any time by choosing View | Other Windows | Favorites from the menu.

You can create XML schemas, datasets, and documents from within Visual Studio .NET by choosing the XML Editor. This handy tool allows you to open an XML file, edit it, and then select Create Schema, among other things.

If you spend some time in the documentation, you will see two names repeated over and over again—"Duwamish" and "Fitch and Mather." These are fictitious enterprise companies that Microsoft has created to demonstrate enterprise solutions using .NET platforms. Duwamish is a book-selling e-commerce application that demonstrates best practices in enterprise architecture. Fitch and Mather is a brokerage firm implementing enterprise heterogeneous distributed transactions. If you are fortunate enough to be the lead project analyst on your team, you may find that by scouring these documents, you will learn excellent practices for scalability, extensibility, and performance.

Summary

Although you will not be tested directly on your knowledge of Visual Studio .NET, it is always a good idea to become familiar with the development environment. You can save yourself a tremendous number of hours by taking advantage of the collection of tools and features that are incorporated into the IDE.

You are ready now to delve into the exams. The next part of this book, Part II, will take you through the common elements of both exams. For instance, no matter which exam you take, you will need to understand the basics of data access using C#. In Chapter 10, you will do just that. You're on the journey now to getting ready for the Microsoft exams—good luck!

Test Questions

1. You want to see all the methods of a particular class that you are using in your application. Which tool would you use?

   A. Class Viewer

   B. Object Browser

   C. Class Explorer

   D. Object Explorer

2. You want to change the color of the text in the code window. Which menu item would you select?

A. View | Options

B. Tools | Customize

C. View | Customize

D. Tools | Options

3. Which key combination will allow you to compile your console application and leave the console window open?

A. CTRL-F5

B. ALT-F5

C. F5

D. SHIFT-F5

4. To create a class file that can be added to a library, you would select which project type?

A. ASP.NET Web Application

B. Class Library

C. Console Application

D. Web Control Library

Test Answers

1. B. Since the class is in your application, you don't need to use the Class Viewer.

2. D.

3. A.

4. B.

PART II

The C# Exams: Common Elements

Assemblies

6

In this chapter, you will

- Create and modify a .NET assembly
- Create and implement satellite assemblies
- Create resource-only assemblies

The assembly in the .NET Framework is the solution to a number of problems that have plagued the Windows developer for some time. The problem even has a name—*DLL Hell*—that describes the problems we get into when the Registry entry for a DLL (dynamic-link library) or the DLL itself gets altered, deleted, or just mismatched. These problems have been solved by the assembly, and in this chapter we will explore what assemblies are and how we work with them.

The .NET Assembly

In the Microsoft development world before the .NET Framework, there was a problem that faced developers and administrators alike: the DLL Hell. This term describes the situation that can and does occur when we develop component-based applications. Most applications are divided between multiple physical files: an executable (.exe file) plus multiple DLL files. In order for an application to make use of the components, the DLLs must register themselves in the computer's Registry. If one DLL alters another's registration, you have a broken reference; if the physical file is overwritten, you have a broken reference.

One possible solution for these problems is to store all of an application's files in a private folder, and that usually works. However, if the component you need is in a system library (part of the operating system), there could be other issues: If the DLL is replaced when the operating system is updated, you have a potential version problem, and there is no mechanism in the Registry to support multiple versions, nor to request a specific version.

The solution to this dilemma is to stop using the central computer's Registry, and to let all files carry information about themselves as part of the file, including version information, and to separate an application's local components from the system's global components. This is what was done with assemblies in the .NET Framework.

Microsoft has defined the *assembly* and its role in .NET in the following terms: In the .NET Framework an assembly is the physical unit that can be executed, deployed, versioned, and secured. All .NET Framework applications contain one or more assemblies.

Versioning

The .NET Framework assists you by providing a number of features to ensure proper versioning between components in an application:

- The .NET infrastructure enforces versioning rules so that an application that needs version 1.1.1.1 will not end up getting version 1.0.0.0.

- The versioning rules can be specified between the assemblies that are part of the application.

- Shared assemblies are signed with a strong name (which includes a public key, a simple name, a version, and a culture). Assemblies that are not shared do not require strong names.

- The .NET Framework permits different versions of the same assembly to execute at the same time.

The versioning is maintained in the assembly, as well as the signatures of all public methods, and metadata for the assembly is stored in the manifest (the manifest is the fingerprint of the assembly). The versioning rules that can be applied for an application allow the developer and the administrator to specify what version of an assembly should be used.

Deployment

Assemblies can be deployed using three different methods: the Microsoft Installer (MSI) deployment, a CAB (cabinet archive) file, or the XCOPY deployment. The XCOPY deployment is very interesting because all you need to do is use the system command xcopy to copy the assembly into the application directory—the assembly holds all the information about itself in the manifest. For more information on the deployment of web applications, see Chapter 17; for Windows applications, see Chapter 24; and for XML web services, see Chapter 28.

The XCOPY deployment will only work when you deploy to a private assembly that is stored together with the application. For shared assemblies that are available to all applications on the computer, you need to register the assembly with the GAC (Global Assembly Cache). The registration with the GAC results in a uniquely named folder being created and the assembly files being copied into that folder. The GAC is then updated with the name and version of the folder.

Uninstalling a private assembly is as easy as deleting the assembly, but uninstalling a shared assembly requires that the assembly be uninstalled from the GAC.

Deployment of applications and assemblies will be discussed in different parts of the book. For web applications see Chapter 17, for Windows applications see Chapter 23, and for web services see Chapter 30.

Security

One of the problems that can occur with program files is that they get corrupted, modified, or replaced with the wrong version. Windows 2000 introduced a security model for system components (operating system libraries) that has been extended through the .NET Framework security model to include assemblies. The application code is secured against damage or misuse by other application code.

The security model is based on the following:

- Type safety verifies that the code is only accessing data it is allowed to access.
- Code signing prevents tampering with the assembly by other software or indeed hackers.
- Data encryption protects data in storage and transmission.
- Code-access security is based on a policy that ensures the code is not accessing data or features it does not have permission to.
- Role-based security extends Windows security by mapping users into roles with permissions in the assembly.
- Isolated storage uses a virtual file system for data storage. The storage is separated into virtual sections based on the assembly and user.

What Is in the Assembly?

The assembly contains MSIL code (from the compilation of your code), resources, and the metadata (which is data that describes the assembly). The metadata defines the following, among other things:

- Type information for the methods and public members in the assembly
- The name of the assembly
- Version information
- Strong-name information
- Culture that defines the client's language and cultural preferences; for more information see Chapter 7.
- A list of the files in the assembly
- A list of referenced assemblies

The assembly is the file that is stored on the disk. As part of that file the metadata defines all the aspects of the assembly, and the manifest is the part of the metadata that defines the assembly and its properties. The PE (Portable Executable) file contains metadata, as do all assemblies.

Working with a .NET Assembly

In this section we will look at creating and modifying .NET assemblies. You will meet up with some command-line utilities as well as a graphical tool you can use to disassemble assemblies and executable code. One reason for disassembling the code is to learn more about how the source code is compiled into MSIL. We will start by creating a resource assembly and look at how we can work with the tools to manage those assemblies.

The tool used to view the content of an assembly is the MSIL Disassembler (Microsoft Intermediate Language) and to examine any managed module, including any *.exe, *.dll, and *.netmodule. The syntax for running the MSIL Disassembler is as follows:

```
ildasm [options] filename [options]
```

To see a short version of the documentation for the ildasm utility use the /? option as in this example:

```
C:\gc>ildasm /?
Microsoft (R) .NET Framework IL Disassembler.  Version 1.0.3705.0
Copyright (C) Microsoft Corporation 1998-2001. All rights reserved.

Usage: ildasm [options] <file_name> [options]

...
Example:  ildasm /tok /byt myfile.exe /out=myfile.il
```

Figure 6-1 shows the display for the string.exe program, while Figure 6-2 shows the manifest for that file.

The exam will focus on the creation of satellite and resource assemblies. *Resource assemblies* are assemblies that contain strings, icons, images, and so on, and the resource assembly acts as a central storage of the resources for the application. *Satellite assemblies* are resource assemblies that are created to match a particular language and culture, such as U.S. English.

Figure 6-1
The MSIL
disassembler

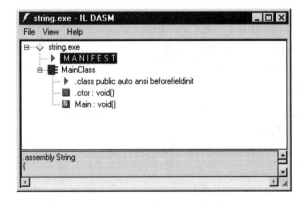

```
/ MANIFEST                                                                 _ □ X
.assembly extern mscorlib
{
  .publickeytoken = (B7 7A 5C 56 19 34 E0 89 )              // .z\U.4..
  .ver 1:0:3300:0
}
.assembly String
{
  // --- The following custom attribute is added automatically, do not uncomment -------
  //   .custom instance void [mscorlib]System.Diagnostics.DebuggableAttribute::.ctor(bool,
  //                                                            bool) = ( 01 00 00 01 00 00 )
  .hash algorithm 0x00008004
  .ver 0:0:0:0
}
.module String.exe
// MVID: {480E78E0-9BE2-42D9-A504-095FBF834959}
.imagebase 0x00400000
.subsystem 0x00000003
.file alignment 512
.corflags 0x00000001
// Image base: 0x03100000
```

Figure 6-2   The manifest of the string.exe PE file

There are many types of files that are involved when building .NET assemblies:

- Source code resides in files with the file extension `.cs`.

- Managed modules are the compiled IL versions of the source code. The extension of the file that is built when making a module from source files is `.netmodule`.

- Assemblies are either DLLs or `.exe` files containing managed modules, resources, and metadata.

Assemblies can be either single-file assemblies that contain the manifest, metadata, and the module, or multi-file assemblies where the manifest is part of one of the files in the assembly, or indeed is its own file. Using multi-file assemblies will assist us when we want to deploy them over a network, because the download speed will improve.

 EXAM TIP   Use multi-file assemblies to optimize the download speed of your assemblies.

Creating and Modifying a .NET Assembly

An assembly can be built using the tools supplied with Visual Studio .NET or with the language compilers (such as `csc.exe`) and linkers (such as `al.exe`) supplied with the .NET Framework. We will use the command-line tools in this chapter to build the assemblies.

When you build assemblies, you must build them either as *private* or *strongly named* assemblies (strongly named assemblies are needed for shared deployment).

The simplest assembly to build is the private assembly; all the files for the private assembly are deployed in the folder for the application. Private assemblies are not shared with other applications and are not added to the GAC.

The examples in this chapter will work with the following source files that will print "Hello World!" on the console for us:

```
Hello.cs
namespace HelloWorld
{
  using System;
  public class Hello
  {
    string strHello = "Hello World!";
    public Hello()
    {
      // empty constructor
    }

    public void SayHello()
    {
      Console.WriteLine(strHello);
    }
  }
}
```

The following is the Heja.cs source file:

```
Heja.cs
using System;
using HelloWorld;
namespace HelloAssembly
{
  public class Heja
  {
    public static void Main()
    {
      Hello hej;
      hej = new Hello();
      hej.SayHello();
    }
  }
}
```

Setting the /target:module compiler command-line switch will produce a module that can be used to create a multi-file assembly. The following example builds the Hello.netmodule file:

```
csc /target:module Hello.cs
```

To reference another module to be included in the assembly use the /addmodule switch to make the type information available:

```
csc /addmodule:Hello.netmodule /t:module Heja.cs
```

Once this command has been run, the `Heja.netmodule` will be created. To finally link the modules together, you use the `al.exe` utility (the Assembly Linker), as in this example:

```
al Heja.netmodule Hello.netmodule /main:HejaAssembly.Heja.Main
   /t:exe /out:Hello.exe
```

This command produces the `Hello.exe` output file from the two modules. The `/main` option tells the linker where to find the `Main` method for the application. Note that the options are case-sensitive.

Strongly Named Assemblies and GAC

In order to be able to install an assembly in the GAC, it must be a strongly named assembly. The following steps are involved in creating a strongly named assembly:

1. Create a strong-name key file using the Strong Name tool (`sn.exe`) as in this example:

   ```
   sn -k HelloKey.snk
   ```

2. Add assembly attributes to one of the source files referencing the strong-name key file. The following example adds the `AssemblyKeyFile` and `AssemblyVersion` attributes to the `Hello.cs` source file.

   ```
   using System.Reflection;
   [assembly: AssemblyKeyFile("HejaKey.snk")]
   [assembly: AssemblyVersion("12.1.42.0")]

   namespace HelloWorld
   {
     using System;
     public class Hello
     {
       string strHello = "Hello World!";
       public Hello()
       {
         // empty constructor
       }

       public void SayHello()
       {
         Console.WriteLine(strHello);
       }
     }
   }
   ```

3. Compile the library using the csc compiler. Use the `/t:library` switch to create a DLL, as in this command:

   ```
   csc /t:library Hello.cs
   ```

4. Install the module in the GAC using the `gacutil.exe` utility, as is shown here:

   ```
   gacutil -i Hello.dll
   Microsoft (R) .NET Global Assembly Cache Utility.  Version 1.0.3705.0
   ```

```
Copyright (C) Microsoft Corporation 1998-2001. All rights reserved.

Assembly successfully added to the cache
```

The -i switch installs the assembly, -l lists all the installed assemblies in the GAC, and -u uninstalls an assembly.

Creating and Implementing Satellite Assemblies

When you plan to localize your application (make the application customizable for different languages and cultures), you can write culture-neutral code (code that uses resources from an assembly rather than hard-coding the resources in the program) and distribute the localized modules in separate assemblies called *satellite assemblies*. The culture is made part of the assembly's identity, as is the version. When the application searches for the proper assembly to load, that information will be used as the basis for the assembly-binding selection performed by the binding manager. The binding selection is performed at run time when the client's locale and culture is known—the selection will pick the proper assembly (or best fit). For more information on localizing applications see Chapter 7.

The object model for the assembly is the hub-and-spoke model where the main assembly (the culture- neutral or default assembly) is the hub and the culture-specific satellite assemblies are the spokes. This means you can deploy the application with the default culture first, and then incrementally add cultures. The locale is a setting that is defined on the client computer and specifies a culture that indicates the language that is spoken (English, for example) and a subculture that identifies the country the client is in (such as the United States). The locale defines the measurement system (metric or imperial) and number and date-formatting rules.

When you create the resources that will make up the satellite assembly, you should work with the naming convention suggested by Microsoft. It uses a culture/subculture string to indicate the locale; for example, for the English culture in Canada, the identifier would be en-CA, while the English culture in the United States would be en-US. When creating the resource files, the filename will be in this format:

```
<resource_name>.<culture_identifier>.resource
```

For example, a resource file with strings specific to the English culture might have any of the following names, depending on whether the resource is English-language neutral or specific to a culture:

```
strings.en.resource
strings.en-JM.resource
strings.en-US.resource
```

To create the satellite assemblies, you will use the al.exe utility (Assembly Linker) to link your resource file to an assembly, as shown in this example:

```
al /t:library /embed:strings.en.resources /culture:en /out:MyApp.resources.dll
```

The /t option will direct al to build a library, and the /embed option identifies the file to be linked.

Summary

In this chapter, you have seen how to create assemblies and satellite assemblies using the command-line utilities csc and al. The assemblies are the cornerstones for the .NET Framework, and are the reason it can avoid the DLL Hell. One very important use of assemblies is satellite assemblies that are used to store culture-specific resources, letting the resource manager select the appropriate culture for the client's locale.

This ability to localize applications will be further explored in the next chapter.

Test Questions

1. What is the name given to the type of assembly that contains localized resources?

   A. Spoke

   B. Hub

   C. Sputnik

   D. Satellite

2. What is the correct name for a resource file with images for the English culture, in the United States subculture?

   A. `images.US-en.resources`

   B. `images.en-US.resources`

   C. `resources.images.en-US`

   D. `images.en-US.dll`

3. What is the minimum number of assemblies a .NET application can have?

   A. 0

   B. 1

   C. 2

   D. 3

4. How is the metadata for an assembly stored?

   A. In the Registry.

   B. In `.ini` files.

   C. As XML in the manifest.

   D. As a Type Library (`.tlb`) file.

5. What tool is used to manage the assemblies in the Global Assembly Cache?

   A. gacmgr.exe

   B. gacutil.exe

   C. gassy.exe

   D. al.exe

Test Answers

   1. D.

   2. B.

   3. B.

   4. C.

   5. B.

Resources
and Localization

In this chapter, you will
- Implement localizability for the user interface
- Convert existing encodings
- Implement right-to-left and left-to-right mirroring
- Prepare culture-specific formatting

Localization is rapidly becoming a central part of application development, not only for building applications that can be used in different languages, but that also accurately mirror the local culture of the client. Localization becomes paramount when you think of web sites that will potentially be used by clients from all the corners of the world.

Localization is the process of writing software that is able to sense the user's locale and change its behavior based on that information. The user can change his or her locale by making changes to the Regional Settings in the control panel.

The term *culture* refers to a combination of parameters and methods that allow a program to adjust to the geographical location of the user. For example, the program can correctly display the currency of a region and print it in the proper location (for example, $42.00 for the United States and Canada; 42,00 kr for Sweden). The culture also contains information on how to display dates and numbers.

One part of localization is the use of strings in the language of the region. In this chapter you will learn how to use strings from many different cultures to write as generic a program as possible. This will allow you the freedom to define the strings and resources used in a program in a central store that can be maintained for multiple languages and locales.

All applications contain resources that can be centralized for better management, such as the string literals used for labels and button controls. The .NET Framework draws on the ancestry of Windows to provide resources for strings, images, icons, and custom resources.

String Resources

String resources are language-specific strings that are made available to a program so that the resource manager can find the properly localized string to use when the application is executed on the user's computer. Using string resources enables you to write code that has no string literals in it—the literals are defined in either text files or XML-formatted resource files.

We will start with our old friend, the Hello World program, and localize it.

```
Using System;
class Hello
{
  public static void Main()
  {
    Console.WriteLine("Welcome to the Hello Program");
    Console.WriteLine("\n\nHello World!");
    Console.WriteLine("\n\nSee you Later");
  }
}
```

This program will always display the same thing, irrespective of where in the world it is executed. To make the program display in German, we would have to create a new version for Germany, and yet another version for any other language that might be needed. This is an almost impossible situation to manage.

The way to start on the road towards localization is to move the strings out from the program and store them in a separate file. In our example, the file will be named `strings.txt`, and it is located in the same directory as the source file for the program. It has this content:

```
txtGreeting = Welcome to the Hello Program
txtBye = See you soon.
txtHello = Hello World!
```

This text file is not directly usable by itself—it needs to be compiled, and the tool that is used to compile resource files is the `resgen` utility. To create a resource file from the `strings.txt` file that can be embedded in an assembly, use the following command:

```
resgen strings.txt
```

The result is a new file named `strings.resources` that can be used in our program.

We also need to make some changes to our program to be able to use the new resource file. First we need to add some namespaces to support localization:

```
using System.Globalization;
using System.Resources;
```

`System.Globalization` adds the support for culture-related information, while `System.Resources` adds the support for resources, and most importantly, the Resource Manager.

Once we have the namespaces added, we can proceed to get a reference to the Resource Manager. The Resource Manager is a rather heavy resource for the application, so you should take care to only create one. The common technique is to create the Resource Manager as a static member of the class—the code looks like this:

```
static ResourceManager rm = new ResourceManager("strings",
                                Assembly.GetExecutingAssembly());
```

 EXAM TIP The name of the resource in the `ResourceManager` constructor is case-sensitive: "string" is different from "String".

Now we are ready to use the strings in the string resource file. We do that by using the `GetString()` method of the Resource Manager:

```
Console.WriteLine(rm.GetString("txtHello"));
```

The final program will be as follows. The `CultureInfo` object is used to retrieve the current culture with this statement:

```
CultureInfo ci = Thread.CurrentThread.CurrentCulture;
```

The current thread of our program uses the culture of the operating system for the UI (user interface) culture, the current culture is what the user has configured in the Regional Settings. To make the current thread's UI culture the same as the current culture, we use this statement:

```
Thread.CurrentThread.CurrentUICulture = gh.ci;
```

We also changed the name of the class to `GlobalHello` to indicate the global nature of the program, and the file is now called `HelloGlobalWorld.cs`. Here's the revised program:

```
using System;
using System.Globalization;
using System.Resources;
using System.Reflection;
using System.Threading;
class GlobalHello {
  // create the resource manager once only, it is resource heavy
  static ResourceManager rm = new ResourceManager("strings",
                                Assembly.GetExecutingAssembly());
  // create a culture information object
  CultureInfo ci = Thread.CurrentThread.CurrentCulture;
  public static void Main()
  {
    GlobalHello gh = new GlobalHello();
    // ensure the current thread is using the culture
    Thread.CurrentThread.CurrentUICulture = gh.ci;
    // Display a welcome
    Console.WriteLine(rm.GetString("txtGreeting"));
    Console.Write("\n\n");
    // say hello world
```

```
        Console.WriteLine(rm.GetString("txtHello"));
        Console.Write("\n\n");
        // say bye
        Console.WriteLine(rm.GetString("txtBye"));
    }
}
```

To compile the program use the `csc` compiler with the `/res:` switch to indicate the default (fallback) resource to use:

```
csc /res:strings.resources HelloGlobalWorld.cs
```

When you run the program, it will display the following:

```
C:\gc\global\demo>HelloGlobalWorld
Welcome to the Hello Program

Hello World!

See you soon.
```

If you go in now and change your Regional Setting in the control panel to French, and you run the program again, there will not be any change to the output—there are no French resources defined for the program yet. That's what we need to do next.

To define language-specific resources, you will need to create a subdirectory under the directory where the executable is located. For the French language, you use the two-letter code from the RFC 1766 hierarchy to name the directory for French as `fr`; other language codes are `en` for English, `de` for German, `sv` for Swedish, and so on. The electronic documentation that comes along with Visual Studio .NET contains a complete listing of the codes.

Once the directory is created, you need to create a language-specific string resource file in the new directory. The following is an example of a language-specific string resource:

```
txtGreeting = Bienvenue bonjour au programme
txtBye = Voyez-vous plus tard.
txtHello = Bonjour Monde!
```

In order to make the resource available, you must compile it into a resource file (as we did earlier for the English version) and then create a satellite assembly (for a refresher on assemblies, see Chapter 6). It is important to remember that the naming of the file is critical, and it is case-sensitive. The resource file we used as the fallback was called `strings.txt`, so we will call the French version `strings.fr.txt`. When we compile it using the `resgen` utility, the resulting resource will be called `strings.fr.resources`.

To create the satellite assembly, you need to use the assembly-building utility, `al`, as follows:

```
al /t:lib /culture:fr /embed:strings.fr.resources
   /out:HelloGlobalWorld.resources.dll
```

Remember that the commands are case-sensitive; the output file must have the same name as the program (`HelloGlobalWorld`) and must end with `resources.dll`.

The result is that there is an assembly in the `fr` directory. Now use the Regional Settings applet in the control panel to change your region to "French (France)" as in Figure 7-1, and run the program. The result is as follows:

```
C:\gc\global\demo>HelloGlobalWorld
Bienvenue bonjour au programme

Bonjour Monde!

Voyez-vous plus tard.
```

The language has changed to the language of the client's Regional Settings.

Localized Formatting

Once the strings are localized, we need to look at the formatting of data such as currency, numbers, and the date and time. The localization of these items is done through the boxing (conversion to objects) of the data.

As an example, the following code segment will create an `int` variable that is then printed using the boxing of the `int` to an `Int32`, on which we can call the `ToString`

Figure 7-1

The Regional Options dialog box

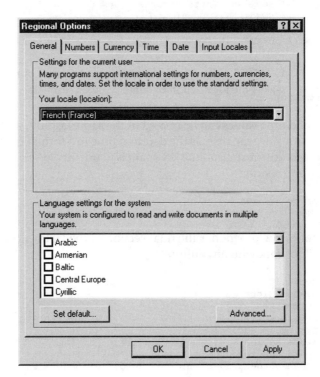

method (for a refresher in boxing and unboxing see Chapter 2). The formatting string passed to the method specifies how the data is to be formatted:

```
int i = 420000000;
Console.WriteLine(" " + i.ToString("N"));
```

The resulting display depends on the client's locale, as shown in the following examples:

```
420 000 000,00     // French
420.000.000,00     // German
420,000,000.00     // English
```

The boxing technique is an elegant way of ensuring that the client's locale is honored. The same technique can be used with other data types, like `double` and `long`. The special treatment of currency formatting takes the currency sign and position (pre or post) into consideration, as well as the representation of the decimal and thousands separator. The following code segment will display the `double` 42.00 as currency using the client's locale:

```
double d = 42.00;
Console.WriteLine(" " + d.ToString("C"));
```

The resulting output will be as follows:

```
$42.00     // English (United States)
42,00 kr   // Swedish (Sweden)
L. 42      // Italian (Italy)
42.00 DM   // German (Germany)
```

EXAM TIP The boxing operation, and the use of the `ToString()` method makes the localization of numeric dates seamless.

Date and time values can be treated in the same fashion, and by taking advantage of the formatting, we can display the date and time in a format familiar to the user. The following code does just that—the key again is to use the `ToString()` method to perform the localized action:

```
DateTime dt = DateTime.Now;
Console.WriteLine(" " + dt.ToString("F"));
```

The following program is the final version of the HelloGlobalWorld program that is localized to work with any culture:

```
using System;
using System.Globalization;
using System.Resources;
using System.Reflection;
using System.Threading;
class GlobalHello {
    // create the resource manager once only, it is resource heavy
    static ResourceManager rm = new ResourceManager("strings",
```

```
                            Assembly.GetExecutingAssembly());
  // create a culture information object
  CultureInfo ci = Thread.CurrentThread.CurrentCulture;
 public static void Main()
  {
    GlobalHello gh = new GlobalHello();
    // ensure the current thread is using the culture
    Thread.CurrentThread.CurrentUICulture = gh.ci;
    // Display a welcome
    Console.WriteLine(rm.GetString("txtGreeting"));
    Console.Write("\n\n");
    // say hello world
    Console.WriteLine(rm.GetString("txtHello"));
    Console.Write("\n\n");
    // print out some numbers using the culture
    // assign the value 420000000 to a variable and display it
    int i = 420000000;
    Console.Write("{0} " + rm.GetString("txtNumber"), i);
    Console.WriteLine(" " + i.ToString("N"));
    // print out 42.00 of the default currency for the culture
    double d = 42.00;
    Console.Write("{0} " + rm.GetString("txtCurrency"), d);
    Console.WriteLine(" " + d.ToString("C"));
    // print out todays date and week day using the culture
    DateTime dt = DateTime.Now;
    Console.Write(rm.GetString("txtDate"));
    Console.WriteLine(" " + dt.ToString("F"));
    // say bye
    Console.WriteLine(rm.GetString("txtBye"));
  }
}
```

The string resource that is used would look like this:

```
txtGreeting = Welcome to the Hello Program
txtBye = See you soon.
txtHello = Hello World!
txtNumber = written in localized format is:
txtCurrency = written using the localized currency:
txtDate = Today is:
```

Running this program with the regional setting for English would produce this output:

```
C:\gc\global\demo>HelloGlobalWorld
Welcome to the Hello Program

Hello World!

420000000 written in localized format is: 420,000,000.00
42 written using the localized currency: $42.00
Today is: Tuesday, March 26, 2002 7:53:31 PM

See you soon.
```

All the strings in this program are localized. There are no string literals used in the code, nor are the numeric values displayed without using the formatting of the `ToString()` method.

Implementing Right-to-Left Mirroring and Encoding

For locales that use a right-to-left script direction, you will have to implement the proper interface for direction, which is done by setting the RightToLeft property to RightToLeft.Yes for all the controls and forms in the application. The controls on a form all inherit the RightToLeft property of the form. In Figure 7-2 you can see the property set to Yes, and that the form's caption has moved to the right side of the window bar.

When working with ASP.NET pages, you must also work with RightToLeft script direction as well as allow the UTF-8 encoding (Unicode characters encoded using UCS Transformation Format, 8-bit form) to be used to send Unicode characters to the client.

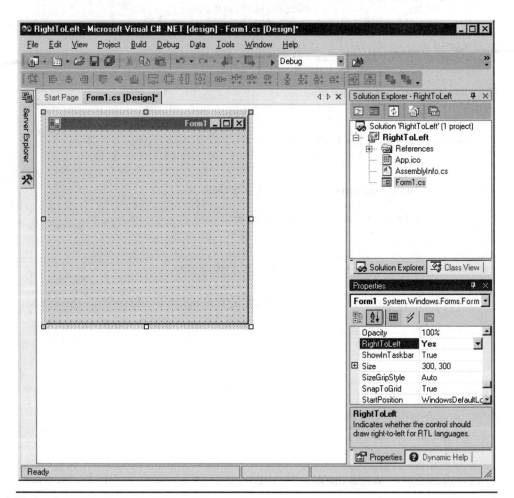

Figure 7-2   Setting the RightToLeft property

There are two UTF encodings available: UTF-7, which encodes 2-byte wide Unicode characters in 7-bit characters for the original US-ASCII e-mail systems, and UTF-8, which encodes Unicode characters as two 8-bit characters for transmission over the network. ASP.NET uses Unicode internally, and by including the following directive at the top of the ASP.NET page, UTF-8 will be returned to the client:

```
<%@Page Language="C#" ResponseEncoding="UTF-8"%>
```

To set the script direction, the element that needs the direction specified must have the `dir` attribute set to `rtl`, as in the following Hebrew text inserted in the `div` element:

הכללים המופיעים ברשיונות השונים ואין בה כדי למצות את כל כללי הרישוי. השתדלנו לכלול את כללי הרישוי העיקריים, אשר לגביהם פנו אלינו

Best Practices

Localization is a State of Mind; it has to be designed into the application from the beginning. There are some things that must be done to successfully implement a localized application, and the following list highlights the most important rules:

- Never use string literals in the code.
- Never set static string values to any interface elements in a form.
- Always build the default (fallback) string resource first, and then add additional locales as needed.
- Always set the string values for the form and controls from the string resource.
- When adding locales, store them in subdirectories that are named after the locale.

The resources can be stored in satellite assemblies, as we have seen in this chapter, or they can be added to a strongly-named assembly that is added to the GAC. The naming of the resources is very important. The Resource Manager uses the names to find the requested locale: the format is `<name>.<locale>.txt` for the strings, `<name>.<locale>.resources` for the resource, and finally `<application>.re-sources.dll` for the assembly. The Resource Manager is very unforgiving when it comes to errors in the resources. Any error will be ignored, and the Resource Manager will use the fallback (default) without any indication of the error having occurred.

Summary

In this chapter you were introduced to the world of localization, and you used string resources to turn our Hello World program into something that works all over the world. You were also introduced to the `RightToLeft` script direction, as well as the encoding needed to send 16-bit Unicode characters over the 8-bit Internet by using the UTF-8 encoding.

The need for localization will only grow as we continue towards a more integrated world where software, and especially the Internet, will be global products working in the culture of the client.

The next step in preparing for the C# exams is to look at how our code can be used to generate its own documentation in XML format.

Test Questions

1. What is the code for the German language?

   A. ge

   B. gb

   C. de

   D. dk

2. What namespace contains the `ResourceManager` class?

   A. System.Localization

   B. System.Resources

   C. System.Globalization

   D. System.Threading

3. What is the process called that converts a primitive to a class?

   A. Primary

   B. Boxing

   C. Conversion

   D. Encoding

4. Which of the following code segments will correctly display the string resource `txtHello`? (All objects are correctly created.)

    A. `Console.Write(rm.ToString("txtHello");`

    B. `Console.WriteLine(rm.Strings("txtHello");`

    C. `Console.Write(txtHello.ToString("s");`

    D. `Console.Write(rm.GetString("txtHello"));`

5. What does the following command do?

    `csc /res:strings.resources HelloGlobalWorld.cs`

    A. Builds only the `HelloGlobalWorld` program.

    B. Builds the `HelloGlobalWorld` and links the fallback resource.

    C. Creates an assembly for the `HelloGlobalWorld` program.

    D. Creates a name resolution report for the `HelloGlobalWorld` program.

6. When localizing a web application, you find that you need to encode Unicode characters that are sent to the client. What attribute would you set?

    A. ResponseEncoding="UTF-8"

    B. Encoding="UTF-8"

    C. ResponseCode="UTF-8"

    D. EncodedResponse="UTF-8"

7. What happens when the Resource Manager fails to find the localized resource for a locale?

    A. It uses the closest locale.

    B. It throws an exception.

    C. Nothing, the resource will be blank.

    D. It uses the fallback resource.

8. What namespace contains the `CultureInfo` class?

    A. System.Localization

    B. System.Resources

    C. System.Globalization

    D. System.Threading

9. Do you have to produce all the locale-specific assemblies before deploying the application?

    A. Yes, the assemblies must be present for the final compile of the application.

    B. Yes, the fallback manifest must be built from all the satellite assemblies.

    C. Yes, the .NET Framework must update the registry with all the information at deployment.

    D. No, the satellite assemblies can be deployed at will after initial deployment.

10. In the following code segment, what is the significance of the "Strings" literal?

```
static ResourceManager rm = new ResourceManager("Strings",
                                Assembly.GetExecutingAssembly());
```

   A. Arbitrary name for the assembly.

   B. The base name of the resource to be loaded.

   C. The base name of the assembly to be loaded.

   D. Alias for the Resource Manager.

11. Where in the object model is the information relating to the date format stored for a specific locale?

   A. ResourceManager

   B. CultureInfo

   C. LocalFormat

   D. Reflection

12. Your application is called AccountingOne.exe. What must the name of the French string resource be?

   A. AccountingOne.resources.dll

   B. strings.resources

   C. strings.fr.resources.dll

   D. strings.fr.resources

13. What does the attribute dir="rtf" stand for?

   A. The direction of RTF files.

   B. The encoding of RTF files.

   C. The direction for the display of characters.

   D. A directory listing of all RTF files.

14. Your application is called AccountingOne.exe. What must the name of the satellite assemblies be?

   A. Accountingone.resources.dll

   B. accounting.Resources.dll

   C. AccountingOne.resources.dll

   D. Accounting.resources.dll

Test Answers

1. C.
2. B.
3. B.
4. D.
5. B.
6. A.
7. D.
8. C.
9. D.
10. B.
11. B.
12. D.
13. C.
14. C.

XML and C# Documentation

In this chapter, you will

- Be introduced to Extensible Markup Language (XML)
- Learn to create a well-formed XML document
- Discover how XML is used to create C# documentation

This is another topic that could fill an entire book. Extensible Markup Language (XML) is an exciting new addition to the list of markup languages, and it redefines the way we transfer data. We will take a brief look at XML and apply that information to the type of documentation that you can create in your C# programs by using documentation comments.

Although the exam may not contain any specific questions on creating C# documentation, it will expect that you understand XML. To that end, this chapter will deal with the basics of the XML language, including the rules for creating a well-formed XML document. This information will be revisited in Chapter 11, where you will find out how XML fits into the big picture. So let's move on and discover the newest standard for exchanging data—Extensible Markup Language.

Introduction to XML

In the olden days of computers (which, as you know, in most cases means yesterday), data exchange over the network and between applications happened in two ways. You either created a binary file that included formatting code for a specific application (such as a Word document) or you produced a straight text file that could be read by any text editor (such as Notepad). (Technically, of course, these are both binary files—but a document that includes formatting code cannot be read by a straight text editor.) The advantage of a binary file is that the formatting code is in binary, which makes it faster for a computer to interpret; thus a Word document opens quickly once it reads the formatting information (which we could call *metadata,* or data about data). However, we are limited to sending such data only to those applications that understand the metadata.

Enter SGML—Standard Generalized Markup Language. This was the first attempt to create a format that allows a document to be self-describing. In other words, the text is "marked up" with metadata that describes the formatting of the text. One of the most popular extensions of SGML is HTML—Hypertext Markup Language—which is used to produce formatted documents within a browser program. However, as we'll see in the next section, HTML is simply a way to format data. What if we want to create and store data?

Typically, we use a database to store data, and any program requesting information from the database must understand how to ask the database for the information. In other words, you need to understand the schema or the way the data is described. XML is self-describing in that you create the schema along with the actual data. This is a very exciting technique that opens the doors for many possibilities, and we will explore them in this chapter.

What Is XML?

XML is a standard that was created in order to represent data in an easily readable, self-defining, and structured approach. It is a markup language that uses tags to define the structure of the data that is included in the document. There are many advantages to using XML over the more traditional data storage and retrieval methods:

- It's a standard—every application that follows the standard is capable of parsing the XML data.

- It's extensible—there are no limits, because *you* define the markup tags.

- It's an open technology—no one vendor "owns" XML.

- It's interoperable—let's face it, this is one of the most desirable qualities of data in today's world. If we can read the information from any application, we have eliminated a very large concern of the past. Consider the different operating systems (Windows, Unix, Linux, Mac, ...), hardware (PCs, mainframes, hand-held computers, ...), transfer protocols, and so on. Interoperability is the desired outcome of any new technology, and XML is interoperable.

- It's text-based—you don't need a fancy application to read it. As a matter of fact, it is readable by the human eye, which is another goal of XML.

- It's easily transferred over a network—this is a big advantage. We want our information to be produced visually for us, quickly and efficiently. XML accomplishes this and more. The load on servers is now greatly reduced because a client-side application (browser) or script can do a lot of the parsing of the data and the formatting of it. Servers are now freed up to do the more intensive work of storing and retrieving the data, rather than formatting it for data transfer.

There are some disadvantages to using XML, but they are being more easily overcome as the industry swings towards its use. For example, one drawback that may have come to mind already is that while we might describe an employee record using XML in one fashion; you may choose to define it in another fashion. In that case, many different documents could wind up defining the same thing. In order to overcome this potential confusion, the industry has started to produce *vocabularies*, or industry-standard ways to describe recurring data. This allows you to produce software that is more compatible with other software. Because the industry has not settled on all of the standards, XML still exhibits some nonstandard behavior, but you can expect this to disappear as time moves on.

HTML vs. XML

Although both XML and HTML are markup languages, their use is quite different. If you can keep their purposes separated, you will have conquered the difference between XML and HTML:

- The purpose of HTML is to display data.
- The purpose of XML is to exchange data.

HTML

HTML is used to format data and render it in a web browser or other application that translates HTML. There is a fixed set of tags within HTML that have been defined so that there is a standard way of presenting the data.

Let's look at an HTML file and then see how it is rendered in a web browser.

```
<html>
<body>
<h1 align="center"><i><b>My HTML Page</b></i></h1>
<div align="center">
  <center>
  <table border="1" width="55%">
    <tr>
      <td width="16%" align="center"><i><b>Student ID</b></i></td>
      <td width="17%" align="center"><i><b>First Name</b></i></td>
      <td width="15%" align="center"><i><b>Last Name</b></i></td>
      <td width="39%" align="center"><i><b>Program of Study</b></i></td>
    </tr>
    <tr>
      <td width="16%">123456</td>
      <td width="17%">Matthew</td>
      <td width="15%">Rempel</td>
      <td width="39%">Software Engineering</td>
    </tr>
    <tr>
      <td width="16%">234567</td>
      <td width="17%">Geoff</td>
      <td width="15%">Hamilton</td>
      <td width="39%">Mining Engineering</td>
    </tr>
    <tr>
      <td width="16%">345678</td>
      <td width="17%">Koby</td>
      <td width="15%">Waldron</td>
      <td width="39%">Business Administration</td>
    </tr>
    <tr>
      <td width="16%">456789</td>
      <td width="17%">Lauren </td>
      <td width="15%">Waldron</td>
```

```
        <td width="39%">Bachelor of Education</td>
      </tr>
    </table>
    </center>
</div>
</body>
</html>
```

Notice that the file is divided into tag sections—<html> is the top-level tag, followed by <body> and the rest. Each section is completed when you end it with a backslash tag—such as </html>. Since a browser understands these predefined tags, you can open the HTML file in any browser (see Figure 8-1). Notice that this web page contains data elements—Student ID, First Name, Last Name, and Program of Study. However, the data is simply contained in tags that describe how it is presented visually. There is nothing that actually describes the data itself.

XML

Now let's look at the same data formatted using XML tags. XML has no predefined set of tags to describe the student data we have presented in the HTML example. We describe this data ourselves in XML. Notice in the following code example that there is nothing to specify how the data is presented to the "viewer."

```
<?xml version="1.0" ?>
<students>
  <student>
    <id>123456</id>
    <firstname>Matthew</firstname>
    <lastname>Rempel</lastname>
    <program>Software Engineering</program>
  </student>
  <student>
    <id>234567</id>
    <firstname>Geoff</firstname>
    <lastname>Hamilton</lastname>
    <program>Mining Engineering</program>
  </student>
  <student>
    <id>345678</id>
    <firstname>Koby</firstname>
    <lastname>Waldron</lastname>
    <program>Business Administration</program>
  </student>
  <student>
    <id>456789</id>
    <firstname>Lauren</firstname>
    <lastname>Waldron</lastname>
    <program>Bachelor of Education</program>
  </student>
</students>
```

Notice that this entire file is dedicated to simply describing the data. We will discuss the various tags and how you create a well-formed document later in this chapter. For now, just observe the code and the output as rendered in an XML-parser program, which in this case is Internet Explorer 6 (see Figure 8-2).

Figure 8-1

An HTML file opened in Internet Explorer

My HTML Page

Student ID	First Name	Last Name	Program of Study
123456	Matthew	Rempel	Software Engineering
234567	Geoff	Hamilton	Mining Engineering
345678	Koby	Waldron	Business Administration
456789	Lauren	Waldron	Bachelor of Education

Figure 8-2

An XML file opened in Internet Explorer

```xml
<?xml version="1.0" ?>
- <students>
  - <student>
      <id>123456</id>
      <firstname>Matthew</firstname>
      <lastname>Rempel</lastname>
      <program>Software Engineering</program>
    </student>
  - <student>
      <id>234567</id>
      <firstname>Geoff</firstname>
      <lastname>Hamilton</lastname>
      <program>Mining Engineering</program>
    </student>
  - <student>
      <id>345678</id>
      <firstname>Koby</firstname>
      <lastname>Waldron</lastname>
      <program>Business Administration</program>
    </student>
  - <student>
      <id>456789</id>
      <firstname>Lauren</firstname>
      <lastname>Waldron</lastname>
      <program>Bachelor of Education</program>
    </student>
  </students>
```

If we want to display this XML file, we can use tools that render the XML into a presentation format, such as the following:

- Microsoft Internet Explorer 6
- XSLT—Extensible Stylesheet Language Transformations
- CSS—cascading style sheets

At this point, however, we are not too interested in displaying the data—if you are interested in either XSLT or CSS, grab a book on XML rendering. Rather, we need to understand how the data is described and what constitutes a well-formed XML document. We will discuss the rules of a well-formed XML document later in this chapter.

Why Use XML?

As you can see, HTML and XML are very different. As a matter of fact, they actually complement each other. While XML is focused primarily on the data itself, HTML can be used to present the information.

Let's think of some of the applications that can make use of XML. In order to exchange information between programs and operating systems, you need an interoperable method of transferring the data. XML provides this functionality. Documents can be written in XML and then transformed using presentation software. Companies can send data to each other using a standard, readable format. One company can transmit an invoice to another using XML definitions, and the receiving company can easily parse the document and render it. Say goodbye to fax machines, photocopiers, and even the post office!

Creating an XML Document

An XML document is made up of the following parts:

- **XML declaration and processing instructions**   A document starts with a declaration of the version of XML along with some encoding information. Following that declaration, you can include any number of processing instructions. You may want to tell the XML-parser application to use a particular style sheet for presenting the data.
- **Comments**   You can insert any number of comments into an XML document.
- **Elements**   An element is a piece of data—we will explore elements in greater detail later in this chapter.
- **Attributes**   An attribute is an additional piece of information associated with an element.

In the next few sections, we will briefly look at each of these and then examine the rules for creating a well-formed XML document.

XML Declaration and Processing Instructions

Although it is not necessary to include an *XML declaration* in your document, it is a good idea to do so. It helps identify to the reader of your document the type of XML used, the character set, and whether there are other files necessary to enhance the document.

The XML declaration looks like this:

```
<?xml version="1.0" encoding="UTR-16" standalone="yes"?>
```

The declaration starts with `<?` and ends with `?>`. If you include a declaration, it must be at the beginning of the file, and you must code the version. Everything else is optional. Notice that the values are enclosed in double quotation marks. You can use either double or single quotes, but they must match. The `encoding` entry specifies the character set that is used. This could be ASCII (American Standard Code for Information Interchange), which allows for 256 characters, Unicode 8 or 16 (UTF-8, UTF-16), which allows for a far greater number of characters and provides international characters, or it could simply be Windows if you built the file in Notepad. The `standalone` entry specifies whether there are other files required to render the document.

In order to embed application-specific instructions into the XML, you must provide *processing instructions*. An example of this would be to include an instruction that tells the document to apply a particular style sheet to the data:

```
<?xml-stylesheet type="text/xsl" href="mystylesheet.xsl"?>
```

This line tells the XML-parser program that when it reads the data, it can format it for output according to the specifications of the style sheet.

Comments

Any number of comments can be included in an XML document. Comments, of course, provide detailed information to the reader of the file, but no information to the actual document itself. As a matter of fact, comments may not even be passed on to the application parsing the document.

A comment starts with `<!--` and ends with `-->`, like this:

```
<!--Here is an example of a comment-->
```

Elements

We are now at the crux of the matter. *Elements* are the most common type of markup that you will see in an XML document. Elements are used to describe the data and formulate the hierarchy of the data itself.

You use a tag to define data elements. In between the start tag, `<element_name>`, and the end tag, `</element_name>`, is the actual text or data that belongs to the element. In our student example, we define a student's first name as follows:

```
<firstname>Matthew</firstname>
```

Because data can be hierarchical in nature, we can create nested elements. A student has a student ID, a first name, a last name, and a program:

```
<student>
  <id>345678</id>
  <firstname>Koby</firstname>
  <lastname>Waldron</lastname>
  <program>Business Administration</program>
</student>
```

In this example, there are four sub-elements nested within the top-level element, `student`. We can further nest by defining a collection of `students`:

```
<students>
  <student>
    <!--Student elements go here -->
  </student>
  <student>
    <!--Next student here -->
  </student>
</students>
```

Eventually, your design will include a single top-level element. This is called the *root element*. As you will see in the rules of a well-formed document, you can only have a single root element. All other elements are children of the root element.

When designing the structure of elements, you should follow these simple rules:

- Every start tag must have a corresponding end tag.
- There can only be one root element.
- XML is case sensitive; therefore, `Student` is a different element from `student`.
- You cannot overlap tags. In other words, using the preceding example, the `<student>` tag must be closed off before the `<students>` tag is closed.

Attributes

Elements can make use of *attributes*, which are names matched with values that belong to an element. We could redefine our student as follows:

```
<student id="123456" >
  <firstname>Lauren</firstname>
  <lastname>Waldron</lastname>
  <program>Business Administration</program>
</student>
```

In this case, `<id>` is an attribute that further describes the element `<student>`. The value of the attribute must be enclosed in quotation marks (either double quotes or single quotes).

A Well-Formed XML Document

Yes, Virginia, there are rules. If a document is said to be a "well-formed XML document," this means that it adheres to the syntax rules for XML. These are the rules:

- There must be matching opening and closing tags.

- XML is case-sensitive, so naming must be consistent.

- There can only be one root element.

- All other elements are children of the root element.

- You cannot have repeating attributes for a single element.

- All attribute values must be enclosed in quotations. It doesn't matter if they are double or single quotations; they just have to match.

Well-formed means that the document complies with the XML specifications. A document can also be considered a *valid* document. In that case, it must conform to either a DTD (document type definition) or an XML schema.

> **NOTE**   DTDs are XML documents that exist within the XML file or outside of it. A DTD defines the rules for how the document is structured, what elements are included, the kinds of data, and any default values.

There are several things to consider when deciding whether to use an XML schema or a DTD. A DTD is not extensible, and there can only be one for each document. The syntax of DTD is not XML, and the data typing is very weak. An XML schema *is* XML, which means that all of the advantages of using XML are also inherited by the XML schema.

> **NOTE**   An XML schema is made up of data types and structures and defines the structure of the XML document.

Having said all of that, a valid XML document adheres to the rules laid down in either the DTD or the schema. Your XML document will fit into one of these categories:

- **An invalid document**   One that doesn't follow the tag rules

- **A well-formed document**   One that follows the tag rules but has no DTD or schema

- **A valid document**   One that follows the tag rules and the rules defined in the DTD or schema

We have now looked at the very large topic of creating and using XML documents. The next thing to do is discuss XML documentation using special comments within your C# program code.

XML Documentation in C#

A Java program can generate HTML documentation from special documentation comments inside the program itself. Microsoft Visual C# .NET has followed this example and embellished it by creating XML documentation from the comments instead of straight HTML. As we have already seen in this chapter, you can take such XML data and use it in any way, shape, or form you want. That's the beauty of XML.

XML Documentation Tags

All comments in C# that are to be treated as documentation comments begin with three forward slashes (/ / /). These comments must preface a user-defined type—a class definition, structure, enum, method, and so on. Unlike Java, the C# compiler will generate the XML file if you include the /doc switch. There is no separate utility to generate the documentation.

Figure 8-3 illustrates a simple program with documentation comments inserted. When we compile the source code, we use the compiler and the /doc switch:

```
csc MyXMLExample.cs /doc:MyXMLExample.xml
```

Figure 8-4 shows the XML file that is created.

Table 8-1 lists the common tags you can include in your documentation code to add more descriptive items to the final XML file. If your XML comments don't produce a well-formed XML document, the C# compiler will return an error.

XML Comments and Visual Studio .NET

Although you really don't need to know too much about Visual Studio .NET for the exams, it warrants discussing here how valuable the IDE is for creating and managing XML

```
 1   using System;
 2   /// <summary>
 3   /// This class demonstrates using documentation comments to create XML documentation
 4   /// </summary>
 5   public class MyXMLExample
 6   {
 7       /// <summary>
 8       /// MyInt is used to hold some integer value.
 9       /// </summary>
10       public int MyInt;
11       /// <summary>
12       /// MyString is used to hold string data.
13       /// </summary>
14       public string MyString;
15       /// <summary>
16       /// MyMethod will take a single parameter and return it back
17       /// </summary>
18       /// <param name="i"></param>
19       /// <returns></returns>
20       public int MyMethod (int i)
21       {
22           return i;
23       }
24   }
25
```

Figure 8-3   A C# class file with documentation comments

```
<?xml version="1.0" ?>
- <doc>
  - <assembly>
      <name>MyXMLExample</name>
    </assembly>
  - <members>
    - <member name="T:MyXMLExample">
        <summary>This class demonstrates using documentation comments to create XML
          documentation</summary>
      </member>
    - <member name="F:MyXMLExample.MyInt">
        <summary>MyInt is used to hold some integer value.</summary>
      </member>
    - <member name="F:MyXMLExample.MyString">
        <summary>MyString is used to hold string data.</summary>
      </member>
    - <member name="M:MyXMLExample.MyMethod(System.Int32)">
        <summary>MyMethod will take a single parameter and return it back</summary>
        <param name="i" />
        <returns />
      </member>
    </members>
  </doc>
```

Figure 8-4   XML documentation file generated from documentation comments

Documentation Tag	Description
`<c>`	Includes code in the text; for example, `<c>string s = "hello";</c>`
`<code>`	Includes multiple lines of code in the text
`<example>`	Documents a code example
`<exception>`	Causes compiler to check that this matches an exception that can be thrown
`<include>`	Includes documentation from another file
`<list>`	Inserts a list into the documentation file
`<param>`	Describes the parameters of a method; the compiler will check that it matches the parameters of the method
`<paramref>`	Marks a parameter
`<permission>`	Identifies access permissions
`<remarks>`	Includes a description
`<returns>`	Marks the return value of a member
`<see>`	Gives a cross reference to a related item
`<seealso>`	Gives a "see also" section
`<summary>`	Provides an executive summary of the member
`<value>`	Describes a property; this is also used by IntelliSense in order to display additional information about a member

Table 8-1   C# Documentation Tags

comments. The first thing to notice is how friendly the interface is when you want to enter a documentation comment. As soon as you type the three slashes (///), the program will return an extensive number of lines, which will assist with your documentation (see Figure 8-5). Notice how handy this is. Visual Studio has inserted the summary lines as well as the param and returns tags. We just have to fill in the blanks.

Another excellent feature of Visual Studio .NET is the option to have the XML documentation rendered in an HTML file. By selecting Tools | Build Comment Web Pages from the menu, you will be presented with the Build Comment Web Pages dialog box, as shown in Figure 8-6.

Fill in the location for the HTML file, and Visual Studio will create the HTML for you. In your project directory, you will find a new directory that will contain all the files needed to render a documentation page (see Figure 8-7). You can move through the links and see that the comments that were added to our C# source file have now been transformed into XML. Then, by using the Visual Studio .NET Comment tool they have been rendered into HTML and can be opened and viewed in any browser or from within the IDE itself.

Isn't this just unbelievably exciting? The days of programmers sweating over documentation are over. You only have to add these comments as you go, and you have a brilliant piece of documentation when you are done. You don't have to use the Visual Studio .NET tools to render the HTML—you can use an XSL (Extensible Stylesheet Language) file to accomplish the same thing. Here are the steps:

1. Create your C# source file with the documentation comments.

2. Compile it with the C# compiler and the /doc switch.

3. Take the generated XML file, and together with an XSL file, run them through an XSLT processor.

4. You will now have the final HTML documentation in the style you prefer.

Figure 8-5
Visual Studio
.NET IntelliSense

```
/// <summary>
///
/// </summary>
/// <param name="s"></param>
/// <returns></returns>
public string MySecondMethod (string s)
{
    return s;
}
```

PART II

Figure 8-6
The Build
Comment Web
Pages dialog box

MyXMLExample Class

This class demonstrates using documentation comments to create XML documentation

Access: Public

Base Classes: Object

Members	Description
MyInt	MyInt is used to hold some integer value.
MyString	MyString is used to hold string data.
MyMethod	MyMethod will take a single parameter and return it back
MySecondMethod	MySecondMethod

Figure 8-7   The HTML documentation page

Summary

This chapter has introduced you to a lot of new topics surrounding XML. As we have suggested before, if you are completely new to XML, you would be wise to catch up on this technology by reading through documentation focused on XML. It's a data-exchange format that you don't want to miss. Although the exam will probably not test you directly on your knowledge of XML, you will need to understand its uses in your applications. Be sure to check in with Part III of this book on ASP.NET to explore more of the uses of XML. You may also find that the Microsoft exams ask you one or two questions on the documentation comments.

Test Questions

1. Which command will cause an XML file to be generated from documentation comments?

   A. `csc MyClass.cs /doc:MyClass.cs`

   B. `cscd MyClass.cs /doc:MyClass.xml`

   C. `cscd MyClass.cs /doc:MyClass.cs`

   D. `csc MyClass.cs /doc:MyClass.xml`

2. Which line causes the following XML to be not well-formed?

   ```
   <VideoList>
   <tape>
   <name>XML is cool!</name>
   </VideoList>
   </tape>
   ```

   A. `<tape>`

   B. `</VideoList>`

   C. `</tape>`

   D. `<name>XML is cool!</name>`

3. Which XML rule does the following break?

   ```
   <employees>
   <Employee>
   <name>Kenneth S. Lind</name>
   </Employee>
   <employee>
   <name>Marj Rempel
   </employee>
   </employees>
   ```

   A. There must be a single root element.

   B. There must be matching opening and closing tags.

   C. XML is case-sensitive.

   D. All attributes must be in quotes.

4. Which XML rule does the following break?

```
<employees>
<employee>
<name id=123>Kenneth S. Lind</name>
</employee>
<employee>
<name id=456>Marj Rempel</name>
</employee>
</employees>
```

    A. There must be a single root element.

    B. There must be matching opening and closing tags.

    C. XML is case-sensitive.

    D. All attributes must be in quotes.

5. Visual Studio .NET provides a tool to generate HTML from the XML documentation file. It is found where?

    A. Tools | Generate XML

    B. Tools | Generate HTML

    C. Tools | Build Comment Pages

    D. Tools | Build Comment Web Pages

6. Which XML line(s) generates an employee attribute?

    A. `<employee name="Ken">`

    B. `<employee attribute name="Ken">`

    C. `<employee Name='Ken'>`

    D. `<employee attribute Name='Ken'>`

7. Which of the following lines is an XML declaration?

    A. `<xml version="1.0">`

    B. `?xml version="1.0"?`

    C. `<?xml version-1.0?>`

    D. `<?xml version="1.0"?>`

8. Why will the following XML code not be rendered by a browser?

```
<name>
<lastname>Dowdy</lastname>
<firstname>Howdy</firstname>
</lastname>
```

    A. The browser is not specified.

    B. The root element is missing.

    C. The root element is not closed properly.

    D. The firstname element is incorrect.

9. Assess the following XML. Which answer correctly describes the code?

```
<addresses>
<listing>
<name>
<lastname>Dowdy</lastname>
<firstname>Howdy</firstname>
</name>
<address>
<street>123 Anywhere St</street>
<city>MyCity</city>
</address>
</listing>
</addresses>
```

A. The `name` element is described incorrectly.

B. The `address` element is described incorrectly.

C. The `addresses` root element is described incorrectly.

D. Nothing—this is well-formed XML.

10. Which of the following documentation comments is correct?

A. `/// summary This is a summary comment summary`

B. `/// <summary> This is a summary comment </summary>`

C. `/// <summary> This is a summary comment`

D. `/// summary This is a summary comment`

Test Answers

1. D.

2. B. This line needs to be at the end.

3. B. There must be matching opening and closing tags: `<name>Marj Rempel`

4. D.

5. D.

6. A and C. You can use double or single quotes.

7. D.

8. C.

9. D.

10. B.

Debugging and Testing

In this chapter, you will

- Be introduced to the debugging capabilities of the .NET SDK
- Configure the debugging environment
- Learn how to create and apply debugging code
- Learn to use breakpoints and watches
- Get acquainted with creating unit test plans
- Learn how to implement tracing
- Become familiar with trace listeners and trace switches
- Display trace output

This chapter comes to you straight from the objectives of both Microsoft exams—70-315 "Developing and Implementing Web Applications with Microsoft Visual C# .NET and Microsoft Visual Studio .NET" and 70-316 "Developing and Implementing Windows-Based Applications with Microsoft Visual C# .NET and Microsoft Visual Studio .NET." Whether you are developing for the Web or for Windows, you must know how to configure your development environment to take full advantage of the debugging techniques available. There are so many tools available that you need to identify those that work best for you, and then become expert with them. By working through this chapter, you will learn how to use each tool, make the determination for yourself as to which ones are the most effective for your purposes, and then use them effectively to take full advantage of their potential.

Once you learn how to remove the logic "bugs" from your application, you need to understand how to test it successfully. A well-tested program saves a lot of time in the long run—we've all experienced the dreaded "application error" and want to avoid it at all costs. In order to avoid them, you need to plan the testing cycle and then implement your plan. In this chapter, you will be introduced to a "unit test plan" and then you will see how it fits into the bigger testing picture. You will also learn to use trace listeners inside your code to assist your testing. You can be sure that Microsoft will test you on your understanding of this chapter as well as your expertise in the field of testing and debugging. You'll want to be sure to try the code in this chapter and put it through each of the debugging tools. Have fun—we're going to break things now!

Debugging Your Application

Before you begin to test your application, you will have many opportunities to exhibit your skills as a program debugger. Debugging is the technique of removing the *bugs* or errors from your program. There are many different kinds of bugs that can occur, but we can categorize most of them into two types:

- **Syntax errors**   A syntax error is a violation of the programming language rules. These types of errors will either be caught by the development environment or will be reported by the compiler as terminal errors.

- **Logic errors**   A logic error is when the program doesn't do what you set out to ask it to do. You will discover these errors when you run your program.

In this chapter, we will be concentrating on the second type of error—logic errors—since syntax errors must be cleaned up before your program will compile. Logic errors, left unchecked, will result in the user receiving the screen at some point (see the following illustration), which is obviously an undesirable situation. By employing good debugging techniques and following excellent testing routines, you can avoid having your users ever see this screen.

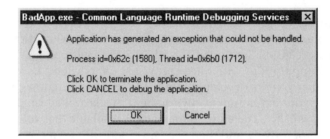

In order to illustrate good debugging techniques, we will be working with code for a buggy application that you'll see in the next section. We will investigate this application using the command-line debugger (CorDbg) and the graphical debugger (DbgCLR).

 TIP   It is safe to assume that Microsoft will expect you to be familiar with both of these debugging programs on both of the C# exams.

We will also spend time looking at the different tools available to you through the graphical debugger.

The Buggy Application

The following application has been created specifically to demonstrate good debugging practices. The program has been designed to create a random number matrix of a size specified by the command-line arguments. Once the two-dimensional array has been created, the user is asked to input a number between 1 and 100, and the program looks in the array to see if it is there. If it is, the user receives a confirmation message—if not, a condolences message. The user is allowed to try any number of times.

```
using System;
public class BuggyApp
{
  public static void Main (string [] args)
  {
    int Columns = Int32.Parse(args[0]);
    int Rows = Int32.Parse(args[1]);
    int MyNumber;
    int gotIt = 0;
    string Answer = "yes";
    MyArray a = new MyArray ();
    a.BuildMatrix(Columns, Rows);
    // for testing purposes, we print the array
    for (int i = 0; i < Columns; i++)
      for (int j = 0; j < Rows; j++)
        Console.WriteLine (a.x[i,j]);
    while (Answer == "yes")
    {
      Console.Write ("Please enter a number between 1 and 100 : ");
      MyNumber = Int32.Parse(Console.ReadLine());
      for (int i = 0; i < Columns; i++)
      {
        for (int j = 0; j < Rows; j++)
        {
          if (MyNumber == a.x[i, j])
          {
            Console.WriteLine ("You got it!");
            gotIt = 1;
            break;
          }
        }
      }
      if (gotIt == 0)
        Console.WriteLine ("Sorry, that's not it!");
      gotIt = 0;
      Console.WriteLine ("Want to play again?");
      Answer = Console.ReadLine();
    }
  }
}
public class MyArray
{
  public int [,] x;
  public void BuildMatrix (int columns, int rows)
  {
    int j, k = 0;
    x = new int [columns, rows];
    Random randomNumber = new Random();
    for (j = 0; j < columns; j++)
      x[j,k] = randomNumber.Next(1, 100);
    for (k = 0; k < rows; k++)
      x [j,k] = randomNumber.Next (1, 100);
  }
}
```

If you run the program the way it exists right now, you will receive an application error similar to the one in Figure 9-1. Once you terminate the program by clicking OK in the runtime error dialog box, you can see the type of error reported to you on the command line:

```
Unhandled Exception: System.IndexOutOfRangeException: Index was outside the bounds
of the array.
    at MyArray.BuildMatrix(Int32 columns, Int32 rows)
    at BadApp.Main(String[] args)
```

Notice the format of this error message. You can see the type of exception object that was thrown (`System.IndexOutOfRangeException`), a description of the exception, as well as the call stack. Right away, we can tell that the program was executing the `BuildMatrix()` method of the `MyArray` class, which was called from the `Main()` method of the `BuggyApp` class.

Two Debuggers—CorDbg and DbgCLR

`CorDbg.exe` is a command-line debugger, which may be preferred over the Windows debugger, `DbgCLR.exe`, depending on the type of application building method you are using. Which one you use is up to you, the developer. For example, if you are building a Windows-based application, you may want to always use the Visual Studio .NET IDE because of its convenience and easy access to Windows controls. In that case, you will be using the GUI debugger `DbgCLR.exe`. Other times, you will be programming, compiling, and testing through the command line (as we have so far in this book), and then you will use the command-line debugger, `CorDbg.exe`. We will look at each one of these separately in the next few sections of this chapter.

CorDbg.exe—Using the Command-Line Debugger

As part of the .NET Framework Software Development Kit, you will have access to the command-line debugger—`CorDbg.exe`. This is not a utility that will compile your program; rather, it steps you through your application code and allows you to make enquiries

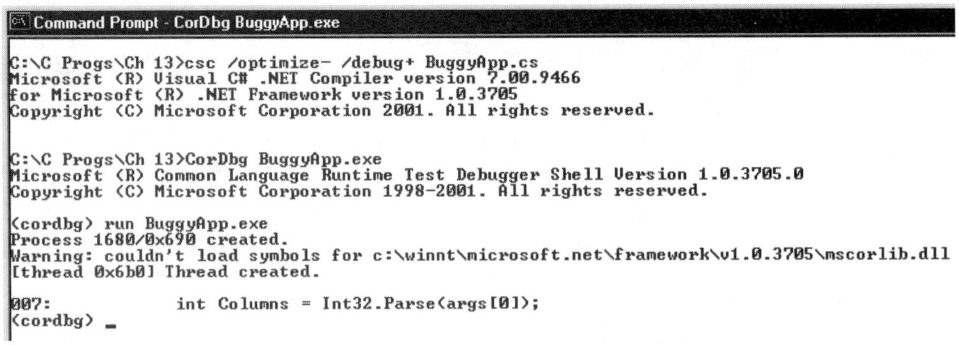

Figure 9-1 Using `CorDbg.exe`

as it progresses. Since it is not a compiler, you need to compile your program using the /debug switch. Recall from Chapter 1 that C# source code compiles into MSIL (Microsoft Intermediate Language) and then creates native code (code to run under the operating system). The debugging process is the reverse of that—it will take native code, map it back to MSIL, and then take the MSIL and map it back to source code. In order for the debugger to accomplish this, it needs to create the mapping information during the compilation of the program. Thus, you need to compile with the /debug switch.

At the command prompt, type the following to set up debugging for BuggyApp.cs:

```
csc /optimize- /debug+
```

This will turn off code optimization and turn on the debugger, and therefore map the debugging information. Optimization allows you to specify areas that will be compacted in the final code output. We will deal with these options as they arise in Parts III, IV, and V.

When you run our buggy application using the command-line debugger (CorDbg BuggyApp.exe), you will receive the screen you see in Figure 9-2. Notice that once the program is run through the debugger, it creates the program thread and then stops on line 007. This is the first executable line in our code.

```
C:\C Progs\Ch 13>CorDbg BuggyApp.exe
Microsoft (R) Common Language Runtime Test Debugger Shell Version 1.0.3705.0
Copyright (C) Microsoft Corporation 1998-2001. All rights reserved.

(cordbg) run BuggyApp.exe
Process 1680/0x690 created.
Warning: couldn't load symbols for c:\winnt\microsoft.net\framework\v1.0.3705\mscorlib.dll
[thread 0x6b0] Thread created.

007:              int Columns = Int32.Parse(args[0]);
(cordbg) ?
Usage: ? [<command> ...]
Displays debugger command descriptions. If no arguments
are passed, a list of debugger commands is displayed. If
one or more command arguments is provided, descriptions
are displayed for the specified commands. The ? command
is an alias for the help command.

The following commands are available:

ap[pdomainenum]    Display appdomains/assemblies/modules in the current process
a[ttach]           Attach to a running process
as[sociatesource]  Associate a source file with a breakpoint or stack frame
b[reak]            Set or display breakpoints
conn[ect]          Connect to a remote device
cont               Continue the current process
ca[tch]            Stop on exception, thread, and/or load events
dis[assemble]      Display native or IL disassembled instructions
del[ete]           Remove one or more breakpoints
du[mp]             Dump the contents of memory
d[own]             Navigate down from the current stack frame pointer
de[tach]           Detach from the current process
ex[it]             Kill the current process and exit the debugger
f[unceval]         Function evaluation
g[o]               Continue the current process
h[elp]             Display debugger command descriptions
i[n]               Step into the next source line
ig[nore]           Ignore exception, thread, and/or load events
k[ill]             Kill the current process
l[ist]             Display loaded modules, classes, or global functions
m[ode]             Display/modify various debugger modes
ns[ingle]          Step over the next native or IL instruction
n[ext]             Step over the next source line
news[tr]           Create a new string via function evaluation
newobjnc           Create a new object via function evaluation, no constructor
newo[bj]           Create a new object via function evaluation
o[ut]              Step out of the current function
pro[cessenum]      Display all managed processes running on the system
p[rint]            Print variables (locals, args, statics, etc.)
pa[th]             Set or display the source file search path
```

Figure 9-2   CorDbg commands

```
wt                        Track native instruction count and display call tree
wr[itememory]             Write memory to target process
w[here]                   Display a stack trace for the current thread
x                         Display symbols matching a given pattern

<cordbg> w
Thread 0x6b0 Current State:Normal
0)* BuggyApp!BuggyApp::Main +0048 in C:\C Progs\Ch 13\BuggyApp.cs:7
                args=(0x00ba18b8) array with dims=[0]

<cordbg> i
First chance exception generated: (0x00ba19e4) <System.IndexOutOfRangeException>
Unhandled exception generated: (0x00ba19e4) <System.IndexOutOfRangeException>
   _className=<null>
   _exceptionMethod=<null>
   _exceptionMethodString=<null>
   _message=(0x00ba783c) "Index was outside the bounds of the array."
   _innerException=<null>
   _helpURL=<null>
   _stackTrace=(0x00ba78a4) array with dims=[12]
   _stackTraceString=<null>
   _remoteStackTraceString=<null>
   _remoteStackIndex=0x00000000
   _HResult=0x80131508
   _source=<null>
   _xptrs=0x00000000
   _xcode=0xe0434f4d

Thread 0x6b0 R --- Exception filter ---

<cordbg> _
```

Figure 9-3   Stepping into the code

 NOTE   In Figure 9-1, we are receiving a warning message about the debugger not being able to load symbols—this is simply because we are not using the debug version of the CLR. You can ignore this message for now.

You can now query for information, step through the code, set a breakpoint, print variables, and so on. Type a question mark (**?**) at the <cordbg> prompt to see a list of commands (Figure 9-2).

Since we are interested in seeing exactly where our program crashed, we now step into the code by typing **i** at the <cordbg> prompt—this will open the Application Exception window. When you close the window, you will see that the exception generated is the System.IndexOutOfRangeException exception (see Figure 9-3).

By employing this debugging technique, we are able to identify the exception to the exact line. Now we can go back into the debugger and ask it some questions about what was happening just prior to the exception. For example, you can inquire as to the value of the visible variables by typing **p** at the <cordbg> prompt. This will list the current variables along with their values.

As we delve deeper into this exception, it becomes apparent that the problem was caused by accessing the args array. As a matter of fact, it looks like we've forgotten to include the command-line parameters when we executed the program.

After correcting this problem and rerunning the program, we now receive a new exception:

```
Unhandled Exception : System.IndexOutOfRangeException: Index was outside the
    bounds of the array.
   at MyArray.BuildMatrix(Int32 columns, Int32 rows) in <path>\BuggyApp.cs:line 53
   at BuggyApp.Main(String[] args) in <path>\BuggyApp.cs:line 13
```

Notice the extra information that we receive by using the BuggyApp.exe that was created with the debugger information. We now have the offending line number from both the calling method and the called method.

After correcting line 13 and running the debugger with the command-line parameters (CorDbg BuggyApp.exe 10 9), we can now step through the code to see exactly what is happening. Look at Figure 9-4 to see the executable code transformed into source code (assembly code). You can see from this figure that the power in this method of debugging is the detail of the results.

Experiment with some of the commands that you can use in the debugger. The more useful commands are as follows:

- **l[ist]** Typing the letter l (for *list*) lists the modules, classes, and global functions that are currently loaded.

- **p[rint]** prints the current variables.

- **b[reakpoint]** <line number> sets a breakpoint at the specified line number. See the "Breakpoints" section for more information.

- **sh <number>** shows the preceding <number> lines of code.

TIP Use the <compilation debug="true"/> setting in the application's (or computer's) .config file to accomplish debugging when using codebehind pages in ASP.NET.

```
C:\C Progs\Ch 13>cordbg BuggyApp.exe 10 9
Microsoft (R) Common Language Runtime Test Debugger Shell Version 1.0.3705.0
Copyright (C) Microsoft Corporation 1998-2001. All rights reserved.

(cordbg) run BuggyApp.exe 10 9
Process 1344/0x540 created.
Warning: couldn't load symbols for c:\winnt\microsoft.net\framework\v1.0.3705\mscorlib.dll
[thread 0x690] Thread created.

007:             int Columns = Int32.Parse(args[0]);
(cordbg) i

[0008] push      0
(cordbg) i

[000a] mov       ecx,edi
(cordbg) i

[000c] mov       edx,7
(cordbg) i

[0011] call      dword ptr ds:[02D92748h]
(cordbg) i

[0014] mov       ecx,dword ptr [ebp+8]
(cordbg) i

[0017] call      dword ptr ds:[02D937A0h]
(cordbg) i

[000d] test      edi,edi
(cordbg) i

[000f] je        0000003C
(cordbg) i

[004b] call      dword ptr ds:[02D937E4h]
(cordbg) i

[0009] call      dword ptr ds:[02D9665Ch]
(cordbg)
```

Figure 9-4   Step-by-step debugging code

DbgCLR.exe—Using the CLR Debugger

If you do not have Visual Studio .NET installed on your system, you may prefer to run the GUI debugger, which is called DbgCLR.exe. It is located in the \Microsoft Visual Studio .NET\FrameworkSDK\GuiDebug folder. This debugger gives you a common Windows interface (see Figure 9-5) that you may find easier to use than the straight command line.

However, if you do have Visual Studio .NET installed, you will want to use the full graphical interface utilities that come with the program.

Using the Visual Studio .NET Debugging Capabilities

Many people prefer the command-line debugger employed in the previous section since they have full control over the debugging process at the command line. However, if you are like some of us, you will appreciate the same capabilities in a graphical interface. Built right into Visual Studio .NET is a full suite of debugging tools. In this section, we will explore some of the more popular (and more than likely, exam-worthy) topics.

Breakpoints

One of the techniques that you will use often is called a *breakpoint*. In a nutshell, a breakpoint is a marked spot in the code. When the runtime encounters this spot, it will stop execution and allow the developer to examine what is happening. You can set a break-

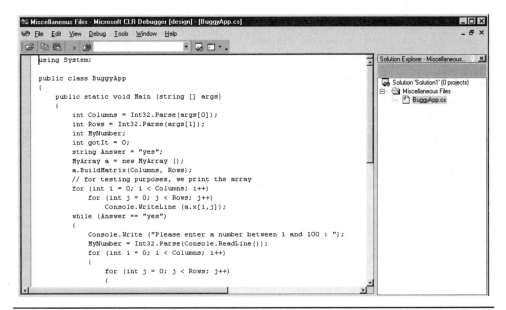

Figure 9-5   Using DbgCLR.exe

point in your code by selecting a line of code and choosing Insert Breakpoint from the right-click menu.

> **NOTE** There are a number of ways to set a breakpoint for a line. Perhaps the easiest is to click in the gray margin portion of the GUI—this will automatically set the breakpoint for that line (shown in Figure 9-6).

We have modified our example code in order to avoid having command-line parameters, we have inserted two lines at the start of the `Main()` method, and we have modified the assignment lines for `Columns` and `Rows`.

```
Console.WriteLine ("Enter the number of columns : ");
int Columns = Int32.Parse(Console.ReadLine());
Console.WriteLine ("Enter the number of rows : ");
int Rows = Int32.Parse(Console.ReadLine());
```

In order to have the runtime stop on your breakpoint line, you must choose Start (F5) from the Debug menu and not CTRL-F5 (Start without debugging). After you are asked for the number of columns and rows, execution will continue until it hits line 54, where the breakpoint is encountered (Figure 9-6).

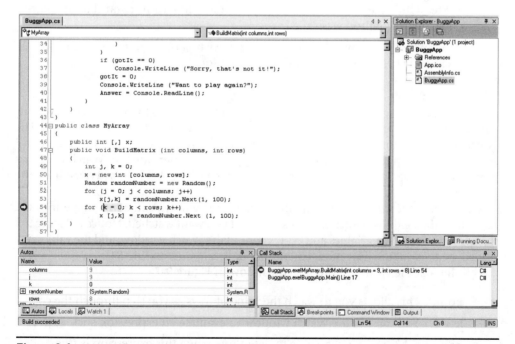

Figure 9-6   Using a breakpoint in the code

You will notice by looking at this figure that the breakpoint is, in fact, on line 54 (observe the arrow in the left margin). Look around the screen, and you will see a lot of other help available:

- By placing your mouse pointer on any variable, you can see its value. Try placing it on the `rows` variable in line 54 and you will see `[parameter] int rows = 8`.

- At the bottom of the screen, you will see other windows that we will describe in the coming sections—the Call Stack, Locals, This, Immediate, and Watch windows.

- You can click on the Debug menu to see the options available at this point:

  - **Continue** Continues execution.

  - **Step into** Steps into the current method or (if there is no method) continues with the next line of execution. Essentially, this is the option to choose if you want to see step-by-step execution.

  - **Step Over** Steps over the current method, which will execute the method, and returns to the calling method. Again, if there is no current method, control will pass to the next executable line of code. Choose this option if you are not interested in stepping through a current method but you want to see the step-by-step execution of everything else.

  - **Step Out** Steps out of the current method and returns control to the place where the method was called.

- You can also insert new breakpoints, clear existing breakpoints, or simply disable the breakpoints and continue execution.

Watch Window

Another valuable tool to use when debugging an application is the Watch window. This window is available when you are in break mode (stepping through the code). The Watch window allows you to "watch" variables, expressions, and so on. Figure 9-7 shows a Watch window added to our buggy application. There are four Watch windows available for use, and you can add them by selecting Debug | Windows | Watch from the menu system.

When the Watch window is initially opened, it is empty. You simply type into the name field the fields, variables or expressions that you want watched. Notice in Figure 9-7 that we have included variables and expressions in the Watch window, and the values displayed are those at the time of execution (at our breakpoint on line 54).

Let's look at the entries in the Watch window in Figure 9-7:

- **rows** This allows you to watch the value of rows as you step through the code.

- **k + 1** You can ask the Watch window to evaluate an expression such as this.

- **rows == 12** You will be able to determine when this expression is true.

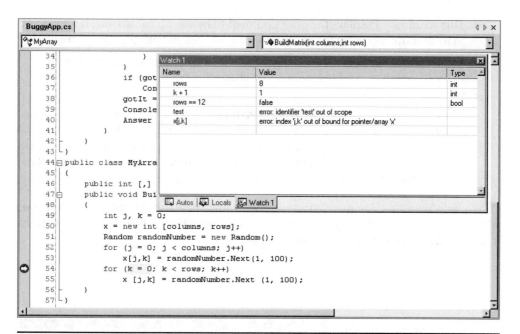

Figure 9-7   The Watch window

- **test**   This entry tells you that this is a variable that is not in scope at the time. Although this is a fake variable in our example, it could be that you thought it would be in scope, and its "out of scope" property is a clue to you.

- **x[j,k]**   This entry tells you that the index is out of bounds, and this is the source of our error.

Further debugging would lead us to examine the variables j and k, as well as the loop structure in this section of code. You have probably realized by now that the two for loops are causing the problem in the code. By employing all of these methods of debugging, you can isolate the problem and discover its source much more quickly.

Other Windows

There are a number of other windows to help you with your debugging. Figure 9-8 shows some of these windows, which include the following:

- **Locals window**   Displays the names and values of all the variables that are in scope.

- **Call Stack window**   Displays the program's method call stack. This is a valuable tool that will let you see the exact sequence of method calls so far.

- **This window**   Displays the object pointed to by the `this` variable. It allows you to look at the members of the object that is associated with the current method.

- **Immediate window**   Allows you to ask the runtime questions, change the value of variables, and test against the changed values. Notice the changed value of `j` in Figure 9-8.

- **Autos window**   Allows you to see variables and their values when the current statement runs and when the previous statement runs. Note that the current statement is the statement to which the breakpoint is attached. This means that the values you see are the values of the next statement to be executed as well as the statement just executed.

You will see in the Debug | Windows menu that there are several other debugging windows available, including Threads, Modules, Disassembly, Registers, and Memory. Typically, these are used for much larger applications.

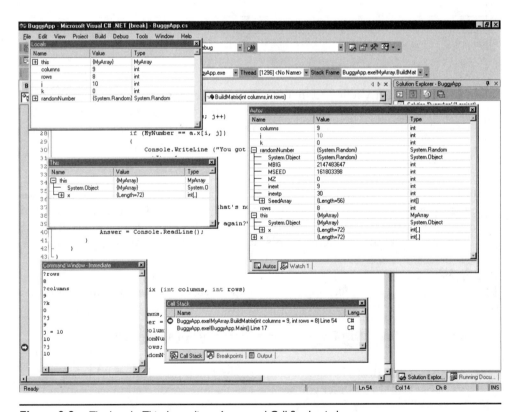

Figure 9-8   The Locals, This, Immediate, Autos, and Call Stack windows

.NET Diagnostics

There is yet another way to debug your application, and that is by using some of the classes in the `System.Diagnostics` namespace. True to its name, this namespace contains classes that allow you to communicate with the system Event Log (`EventLog`), with classes that monitor the system processes (`Process`), and with classes that deal with performance issues (`PerformanceCounter`). However, for our purposes, we will examine two of the other classes contained in the namespace—Debug and Trace.

The `Debug` and `Trace` classes enable you to debug your application and to trace the execution of your program, respectively. By adding these classes and some of their methods to your source code, you will be able to determine what is happening in your application within a development environment (`Debug`) or while the program is in production (`Trace`).

 TIP If you are doing your development in Visual Studio .NET, you will find that, by default, `Trace` is enabled, which means that the code is generated for any of the trace methods. If you create a debug build, `Debug` is also enabled.

The Debug Class

Let's step up a simple example of creating debugging statements within your program code. Take a look at the code listing in Figure 9-9. We have added debugging code to the beginning of the program. The first thing done (in lines 11 and 12) is that the output of the Debug statement is redirected to the console window. By default, it will appear in

```
BuggyApp.cs                                                        ◁ ▷ ✕
BuggyApp                              ▾   Main()                           ▾
    1   #define DEBUG
    2
    3 ⊟ using System;
    4 │ using System.Diagnostics;
    5 └
    6 ⊟ public class BuggyApp
    7 │ {
    8 ⊟     public static void Main ()
    9       {
   10           // set up the location for the debugging output
   11           TextWriterTraceListener t = new TextWriterTraceListener(Console.Out);
   12           Debug.Listeners.Add (t);
   13
   14           // output the debug information - this can be anywhere in your code
   15           Debug.WriteLine ("We are at the beginning of Main");
   16
   17           Console.WriteLine ("Enter the number of columns : ");
   18           int Columns = Int32.Parse(Console.ReadLine());
   19           Console.WriteLine ("Enter the number of rows : ");
   20           int Rows = Int32.Parse(Console.ReadLine());
   21           int MyNumber;
   22           int gotIt = 0;
   23           string Answer = "yes";
   24           MyArray a = new MyArray ();
```

Figure 9-9   Adding debugging code to your program

the output windows, which may not help you as you execute the program. You could decide to redirect this output to a debug file, as well, by following the same practice.

From this point on, you can use the Debug.WriteLine statement to output any debugging information you wish. The output of this program is shown in the next illustration.

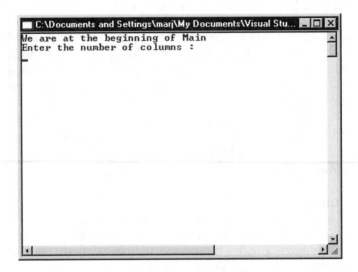

There are two ways of enabling the debugging (other than those previously mentioned within Visual Studio .NET)—you can add the DEBUG directive (as shown at the top of the code in Figure 9-9) or you can enable it through the command line with this command:

```
csc /d:DEBUG BuggyApp.cs
```

The Debug class has several methods and properties available for use:

- **Assert()** Checks for a specified condition and then displays a dialog box if false (see Figure 9-10).
- **Write()** Writes the debugging information to the trace listeners (which can redirect the default console output) without causing a carriage return.
- **WriteIf()** Checks for a true condition before writing the debugging information.
- **WriteLine()** Does the same thing as Write(), except it causes a carriage return after writing.
- **WriteLineIf()** Does the same thing as WriteIf(), except it causes a carriage return after writing.

Figure 9-10 demonstrates a very simplistic example of using Assert() and WriteIf(). Notice the output from the program in Figure 9-11.

```
Assert Method   Class1.cs
SimpleDebug                                              Main(string[] args)
1  using System;
2  using System.Diagnostics;
3      class SimpleDebug
4      {
5          static void Main(string[] args)
6          {
7              int x = 4;
8              Debug.Assert (x==0, "This is an example of an assertion");
9              Debug.WriteLineIf (x==0, "This is an example of WriteLineIf");
10         }
11     }
12
```

Figure 9-10   Using the Debug class

To enable debugging for ASP.NET, follow these steps:

- For a single page, add <@ Page Debug = "true"%>.
- For an application, add the following to web.Config:

```
<configuration>
  <system.web>
    <compilation debug="true" />
  </system.web>
</configuration>
```

Implementing Tracing

Tracing can provide valuable feedback on a running, "live" application. It allows you to enable diagnostic tracing that has low overhead for the executing program. You will see in the next few sections how you can add trace switches to the application and thereby control the level of tracing. You will also see how to add trace listeners to the program to control the destination output of the message.

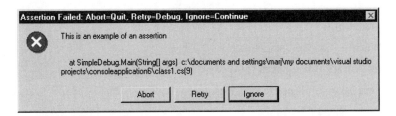

Figure 9-11   Output from the program in Figure 9-10

Imagine the power of creating an environment that reports on its progress, its errors, and its warnings. It's easy to think of Windows applications that do just this. If you look into the Event Log of Windows 2000, you will see a lot of valuable program and service information. By implementing tracing, you are providing this same functionality for your application. In a large, multi-tier application, this information could be critical to the system analyst.

If you examine the .NET documentation, you will find that the members of the `Trace` class are identical to the `Debug` class. Microsoft intends that you use the `Debug` class during your debug builds and the `Trace` class for all builds.

 EXAM TIP Remember that `Debug` code will not be added to anything except debug builds. Therefore, your execution code will be free of `Debug` statements.

`Trace` code, on the other hand, is intended for runtime execution code, so, by default, tracing is enabled within the Visual Studio .NET development environment. To enable it otherwise, you add `#define TRACE` to your code or add the `/d: trace` switch to the command-line compile.

 TIP You want to ensure that good tracing code is added to a production application. By using trace switches, you control how much actual tracing is done.

In the past, tracing caused a lot of output overhead. Consider the example of an application with tracing enabled that outputs to a trace log file every time a particular field is accessed. The output file could become enormous, depending on the usage. By ensuring that you follow good tracing practices, as defined in the next section, and that you employ trace switches carefully, you will provide administration with valuable output information about your application.

Adding Trace Switches   As we have mentioned, tracing can cause an exorbitant amount of output if not controlled properly. As a result, Microsoft developed a `TraceSwitch` class in the `System.Diagnostics` namespace to let you dynamically set the level of tracing. There are five tracing levels:

- **0** None
- **1** Errors only
- **2** Warnings as well as errors
- **3** Information messages (and warnings and errors)
- **4** Verbose—as its name suggests, everything

TIP You can use the `TraceLevel` enumeration to replace the numbers with words—`Off`, `Error`, `Warning`, `Info`, and `Verbose`.

In order to set the switches, you must edit the XML configuration file of your application (`<program name>.EXE.Config`) as follows:

```
<configuration>
  <system.diagnostics>
    <switches>
      <add name="Switch1" value="Error" />
      <add name="Switch2" value="Warning" />
    </switches>
  </system.diagnostics>
</configuration>
```

Within your program, you must also create the `TraceSwitch` object using the same name as in the configuration file (`Switch1` and `Switch2` in the previous example). This is how the two pieces fit together:

```
TraceSwitch ts = new TraceSwitch ("Switch1", "This is just a description
parameter");
```

Notice that the constructor of the `TraceSwitch` class takes as its first parameter the actual name of the switch. This must match the name used in the configuration file. The second parameter of the constructor is simply a description for documentation purposes.

Once the switch object is created, you can use it to provide tracing output. The next code snippet is for demonstration purposes and checks the setting of the switch and conditionally outputs a message:

```
Trace.WriteLineIf (ts.TraceError, "Tracing for errors is set");
```

All the methods that we looked at in the `Debug` class are also available in the `Trace` class, so you can use the `WriteLineIf()` method to check for a condition and then output a message if the condition is true.

 NOTE Although you can use the `Assert()` method of the `Trace` class, you may want to avoid it since it produces a message box. This may not be a good idea in the middle of a production environment.

Adding Trace Listeners You control the destination of tracing messages by using trace listeners, which are classes that receive the output of tracing. The following list gives you three examples of built-in classes that capture trace output:

- **DefaultTraceListener** Output will go to any attached .NET debugger or to the `OutputDebugString` (see MSDN documentation for a description of this class).

- **TextWriterTraceListener** Output will be directed to a text file or `System.Console.Out` (the console) depending on the parameter you send to the constructor.

- **EventLogTraceListener** Output will be directed to the event log.

Both the `Debug` and `Trace` classes have as a property `Listeners`, which is a collection of `TraceListener` objects. If you want to use any other output besides the default, `DefaultTraceListener`, you must set the possible tracing output devices by adding `TraceListener` objects to your code. To add an `EventLogTraceListener` to the collection, enter the following:

```
Trace.Listeners.Add (new EventLogTraceListener ( <eventlog> );
```

The following code demonstrates the use of a `TextWriterTraceListener`. The example will create an output file and add it to the `Listeners` collection.

```
Stream outputFile = File.Create ("TraceFile.txt");
// Add a new text writer to the trace listener collection
TextWriterTraceListener tl = new TextWriterTraceListener (outputFile);
Trace.Listeners.Add (tl);
// Write tracing information to the file
Trace.Write ("This line will be placed in the TraceFile.txt file");
```

You should carefully plan where you place `Trace` code in your program. Recall that the output is generated during the run life phase of the application. Consider the following:

- Where are you likely to need program information?
- What kind of information is valuable to a performance analyst?
- What kind of information will assist with application errors that might occur (although your intent is not to have these happen)?
- What information is critical (must be written out)?

By using tracing effectively, you will be able to provide valuable information during the execution of your application. The following steps summarize the process:

1. Add code to your program that will instantiate and initialize the necessary `TraceListeners`.

2. Add code to your program that will instantiate and initialize the necessary `TraceSwitches`.

3. Write your trace messages.

4. In your configuration file, configure the trace switches.

Trace Output in ASP.NET   By setting page-level tracing in ASP.NET,

```
(<%@ Page Trace="true"%>)
```

you can set up debugging statements to print directly to the page's output. The page exposes a property of the `Trace` class called `System.Web.TraceContext`, which captures execution details about a web request. You can then use this to write out trace information using the standard `Trace.Write()` methods.

TIP   Trace output can be set conditionally through the `Trace="true"` or `Trace="false"` statements.

Application tracing is set within the `web.Config` file. This will allow you to set tracing across multiple pages, rather than just for one as with page-level tracing. The output details will be written to the trace viewer application, `trace.axd`. This is an HTTP handler that you can use to view the details of the trace.

Debugging an ASP.NET Application

This section will demonstrate the additional steps required to set up debugging for ASP.NET applications. Of course, in Visual Studio .NET, you can utilize any of the tools that we have discussed so far.

The following steps must be taken in order to debug an ASP.NET application:

1. Start the application by navigating to the `default.aspx` page.

2. Attach to the debugger program—`DbgCLR.exe`.

3. ASP.NET is a system process, and you will need to attach the debugger to the process.

    a. In the Tools menu, select Debug Processes.

    b. Check the Show System Processes check box in the Processes dialog box (see Figure 9-12).

    c. In the Available Processes list, select `aspnet_wp.exe`, which is the ASP.NET system process.

    d. Click Attach.

4. You can now open your aspx and cs files and set breakpoints as needed.

5. Return to the browser and refresh your page. You will then be placed back into the debugger program and will be able to view the windows available—Locals, Watch, and so on.

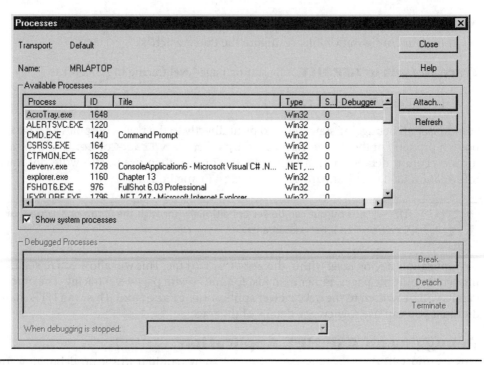

Figure 9-12   Debugging an ASP.NET application

Testing Your Application

What we have been discussing so far are methods to look for errors, present informational messages, and so on, either while your program is in a debug build or in production. Another important area of concern is that of testing your application. When we speak of testing in this context, we are not referring to the testing that catches program bugs, per se, but rather the testing that checks the types of input that can be expected and observes its results. In this section, we will be looking at the purpose of testing and then will move into creating a test plan for your application.

 EXAM TIP   One of the objectives of both Microsoft C# exams is to "Create a unit test plan." Be sure to pay particular attention to that section.

Purpose of Testing

When you present a software package to the public for its consumption, you need to be particularly sure that the quality is top-notch. In order to ensure that, you'll want to employ good testing techniques prior to releasing your software.

There are several advantages of good testing:

- **Reduced cost of development**   You will have anticipated the type of testing as you move along in the process. By leaving the testing until the end of the project, you risk an enormous amount of time overhead.

- **Good market product**   The testing that you do will ensure that your code does what it promises. Your customers will look forward to dealing with you again.

- **Less maintenance time**   Because you have anticipated most of the situations that can occur, you will reduce the amount of time spent on maintaining the application.

The testing process does not start when the code is written and ready for market. Good testing means that you initiated the process from the very start of development. In order to accomplish this, you will need to create a testing plan that is viable and workable. As a suggestion, we will be showing you a *unit test plan* that has had proven success in the testing field for many years.

 EXAM TIP   Microsoft's expectation on the exam is that you are aware of this type of test planning and understand its implementation.

Developing a Test Plan

In the course of developing your test plan, you will outline the entire test process and identify the test data. Over the years, testing has been part of the final process just prior to product release. Essentially, the steps went something like this:

- Analyze requirements
- Create designs and specifications
- Create the code
- Test the application
- Release

Unfortunately, this approach places most of the valuable testing at the end of the process. This means that expensive mistakes are found at the end, and not during the development cycle. As an alternative, a new approach called *unit testing* has emerged. This process follows these steps:

- Develop a unit or module of the entire application
- Test the unit
- Refine the unit
- Add another unit or module
- Continue the cycle

The advantages of this process are many. As you move through unit testing, you will discover hidden traps and problems and fix them before they become costly mistakes that may hold up the entire project. You are also following a modular approach to application development, which lends itself to the many advantages of object-oriented development. Rather than trying to test an entire project, which may seem very overwhelming, you have reduced the burden to testing individual modules and thereby increased the odds of finding small bugs or problems.

Unit Testing

As its name suggests, unit testing is the process of breaking a larger piece or application into smaller pieces or units. The goal is to isolate the unit from the whole and test it on its own without interference from other units. In this manner, each unit is tested alone and then integrated back into the larger application. The key to the success of this approach is that the unit tests are written before the actual coding is done.

Don't ignore the power of unit testing. This is not simply a process that means you make your code do what it is supposed to do. It is a revolutionary way of thinking—you now not only think about how to code your unit, but you pre-think the testing involved. When you start to code, you know the tests that the code will be put through.

In the next section, we will outline a sample unit-testing process. For the purposes of the developer, it may be as easy as writing two separate programs that will simulate the overall testing:

- **The driver**   This program will act as a module that makes calls to the unit being tested.
- **The stub**   The stub will simulate the called module or unit.

These testing modules can be reused when changes are introduced and will always exhibit the same predictable behavior. In this manner, you will have a ready-made test engine for that particular unit.

Creating a Unit Test Plan

The following sample plan will illustrate the power of unit testing. By spending the extra minutes that it takes to set this properly, you will realize an enormous time-saving on the other end when the application is put together. In this world of very short TTM (time to market) intervals, this is absolutely crucial.

We will be using the following piece of code to illustrate the sample plan. The code segment requests that the user input a value, examines the value, and based on its contents, executes separate routines (which, by the way, would need their own unit testing).

```
public void TestValue (int valueToTest)
{
  Console.Write ("Select your choice : ");
  int result = Int32.Parse(Console.ReadLine());
  try
  {
    switch (result)
```

```
   {
     case 1 :
        // break to another unit
     case 2:
        // break to another unit
     default :
   } catch (YouChosePoorly e)
   {
     // deal with the exception here
   }
}
```

In the first section of the plan, you need to document the objective of the code module. This means providing a brief statement as to the purpose of the module—in this case, that it receives a parameter, and based on the value, executes the appropriate routine. This part of the plan should also relate the inputs and the outputs of the module and possibly provide a logic flow diagram if the scope of the unit is rather large.

Next you would provide a listing of the test cases that should be used to make sure that the code is reliable and is responding the way it should. Test cases should contain data that will make the program break, make the program select from the choice list, or cause the exception object to be created:

- **Positive Test cases**   These cases produce valid results. Number each test case and specify what it is intended to show.

- **Negative Test cases**   These cases will involve incorrect data formats, missing data, and otherwise invalid input. As a developer, you should list the possible inputs that can be received and sort the positive outcomes from the negative outcomes.

- **Exception Test cases**   The data involved here will cause the exception object to be thrown.

The next step is to introduce the outside influences to your module of code. For instance, what external classes are needed to make your code work? Where is the data likely to have originated?

You can list the tools that can be used in the test plan. You may find utilities or programs that will facilitate the testing process or provide input into the testing process. Also useful at this stage is documenting your driver and stub classes and suggesting the testing environment—are you testing on Windows 2000 Professional? Is it a Web-based test? Etc.

Provide any further details about the unit test. You may want to suggest the location of your test data, provide any future considerations, and so on. This gives you an opportunity to list anything that may not be within the parameters of the four previous sections.

This is a vast subject for which there is much documentation. You can research the topic through articles or books. You will see many conflicting methods and techniques for creating a unit test. Your best bet is to research the standard itself, 1008-1987 IEEE Standard for Software Unit Testing, which can be found at http://www.ieee.org.

Summary

In this chapter, we examined the exam objectives surrounding debugging and testing. We looked at implementing tracing within your application. Microsoft will test you on your knowledge of adding trace listeners and trace switches to your code. Be sure to pay particular attention to that section and run some tests of your own. We also investigated the .NET IDE and looked at how to configure the debugging environment. You want to be sure that you understand the difference between the different windows available for debugging purposes. Examine the Watch, Locals, This, Immediate, and Autos windows, as well as the Call Stack window. It is recommended that you test the two debuggers, CorDbg.exe and DbgCLR.exe.

We also went through the process of creating a unit test plan. You will need to understand this method of testing, whereby a full application is separated into modules or units and each is tested individually. The next step is integration testing. This involves putting the pieces of the puzzle back together in order to test their interoperability. Integration testing is beyond the scope of this book.

In the next chapter, we will look at basic data access using C#.

Test Questions

1. You have been asked to debug a Web-based ASP.NET application. For some reason, the debugging information is not presented. What could be missing?

   A. `<%@ Page Debug="true" %>`

   B. `<%@ Application Debug="true" %>`

   C. `<%@ Page Trace="true" %>`

   D. `<%@ Application Trace="true" %>`

2. You want to examine and change the value of a variable in your C# application. You are developing using Visual Studio .NET. What window will allow you to change the value during execution?

   A. Locals window

   B. Call Stack window

   C. Immediate window

   D. Watch window

3. You want to compile a console-based program at the command line. What is the correct syntax of the command-line compiler that will allow you to see debugging information?

   A. `csc /b:debug MyApp.cs`

   B. `csc /d:debug MyApp.cs`

   C. `csc MyApp.cs /b:debug`

   D. `csc MyApp.cs /d:debug`

4. Trace switches can be set using which class?

   A. `System.Diagnostics.Trace`

   B. `System.Diagnostics.DefaultTraceListener`

   C. `System.Diagnostics.TraceSwitches`

   D. `System.Diagnostics.TraceSwitch`

5. The correct syntax for adding a trace listener to the `Listeners` collection is:

   A. `TraceListeners.Add (new`
      `TextWriterTraceListener("myfile.txt");`

   B. `Trace.Listeners.Add (new`
      `TextWriterTraceListener("myfile.txt");`

   C. `Trace.Add (new TraceListener ("myfile.txt");`

   D. `TraceListener.Add (new TraceListener("myfile.txt");`

6. To debug an ASP.NET application, you need to attach to which process?

   A. `aspnet.exe`

   B. `asp.net.exe`

   C. `aspnet_debug.exe`

   D. `aspnet_wp.exe`

7. How would you create a breakpoint in your code within Visual Studio .NET?

   A. Press F9.

   B. Right-click in the margin and select Insert Breakpoint.

   C. Choose Debug | New Breakpoint from the menu system.

   D. All of the above.

   E. None of the above.

Test Answers

1. A.

2. C. The Immediate window allows you to set the value of variables during execution.

3. C.

4. C.

5. B.

6. D.

7. D.

CHAPTER 10

Basic Data-Access Techniques

In this chapter, you will
- Access and manipulate data from a Microsoft SQL Server database
- Learn to create and use ad hoc queries and stored procedures
- Access and manipulate data from a data store
- Use XML techniques with ADO.NET
- Handle data errors

In this chapter you will be introduced to Microsoft's newest data-access technology: ADO.NET and the objects that make it tick. Microsoft has placed a very heavy emphasis on the data-access components in all their language exams, including the Visual Basic and the Visual C++ exams. For that reason, we will divide the data-access information into three parts. This chapter will address a number of subjects that set the ground rules for accessing data, including examples of how to use the ADO.NET objects, and basic SQL syntax for retrieving and modifying data. Chapter 16 will deal with the web-specific data-access operations, Chapter 20 will handle the Windows application-specific issues and Chapter 29 will focus on data usage for the XML services.

In this chapter, we will first look at the basics of ADO.NET, accessing data (using SQL), and connecting to data providers. Then we'll look at how this is all done from C#.

ADO.NET

ADO.NET is a group of classes that are used to access data, and it is at the center of the .NET Framework. As these classes are part of the .NET Framework, they also make use of the CTS and CLR and common XML support.

One of the purposes of the ADO.NET classes is to provide an architecture for building scalable robust enterprise applications, without adding too much overhead. ADO.NET does this by providing an application architecture that provides recordsets that are disconnected from the data store, which is a natural for multi-tier Application models. Because XML is the language that ADO.NET uses to move data between components, and

XML can be used as a data source as well as for data output, it is safe to say that ADO.NET is very tightly coupled to XML.

In this section we will look at the benefits of ADO.NET, and the object model provided by ADO.NET, which supports applications from the smallest to the largest enterprise systems.

Application Models

In the realm of software engineering, there are a number of ways to describe how an application is structured, from an architectural point of view—these are called *models*. The most common model used by Microsoft, both in its literature as well as by its consulting service is called the *services model* and it is based on the theory that every application can be broken down into three distinct services: *Presentation Service*, *Business Service*, and *Data Service*. Table 10-1 outlines which tasks belong in each service.

 EXAM TIP The exam will test your understanding of the three services in the services model, not the software design of the services.

How these services are combined into an application architecture determines the Application model, and each has benefits and disadvantages. The model can be one of four special types: 1-tier, 2-tier, 3-tier, or n-tier. Figure 10-1 shows a graphical view of the Application models.

One-Tier

This is the traditional mainframe model; the three services are physically located in one computer. The 1-tier model can also be used to describe a single computer with all services being used by one single user. (See Figure 10-1.)

Service	Description
Presentation	The Presentation Service is responsible for drawing (rendering) the user interface (UI). It will request data from the Business Service and send updates or new data to the Business Service to be forwarded to the Data Service. The Presentation Service is commonly an application that runs on the client computer. For example, the web page displaying the corporate phone list is a Presentation Service, as is the C# Windows Form application displaying the same information to users on the local network.
Business	The Business Service is responsible for ensuring that the data and processing meets the requirements of the business (enforcing business rules). An example of a business rule would be "Don't ship goods to a customer who has an overdue account." Some business rules are very changeable, and can be modified almost on a daily basis. This is one of the challenges of the system architect who must identify the business rules and correctly place them within the architecture.
Data	The Data Service is the encapsulation of the data source, allowing the Business Service access to any data without the Business Service having to know how that data is stored. This service is the realm of ADO.NET.

Table 10-1   Services in the Service Model

Figure 10-1
The single-tier
Application
model

Presentation
Business logic
Data storage

I-Tier Model

One-Tier Advantages   Because all the services are in one place, this type of application is fairly simple to develop.

One-Tier Disadvantages   Any update to any of the services will interfere with the other services and the application as a whole. This type of application is typically totally rebuilt when even a small change is needed.

Two-Tier
This is the classic client/server model as it was introduced to offload the Presentation and sometimes the Business Services from the mainframe. The two-tier model usually involves one computer for the client and a central server that is shared among clients. See Figure 10-2 depicting the Intelligent Client model and Figure 10-3 that shows the Intelligent Server model.

Two-Tier Advantages   Some of the services are separated. If designed properly, changes will be trivial when requirements change.

Two-Tier Disadvantages   This model is not very scalable if the client contains some of the business rules; even if the business rules are all on the server, there are still scalability issues. This model also requires more hands-on management, costing more to maintain than other models.

Three-Tier
In this model, the services are each in their own layer or tier, and the business rules are in a new middle tier. See Figure 10-4.

Figure 10-2
Intelligent Client
2-tier Application
model

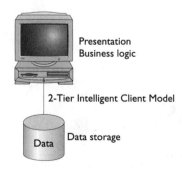

Presentation
Business logic

2-Tier Intelligent Client Model

Data   Data storage

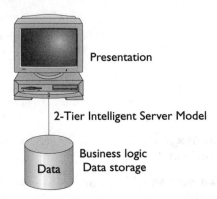

Figure 10-3
Intelligent Server
2-tier Application
model

Presentation

2-Tier Intelligent Server Model

Business logic
Data storage

Data

Three-Tier Advantages   This model separates the functions of the services into tiers, providing a "thin client" that is separated from the Business and Data Services.

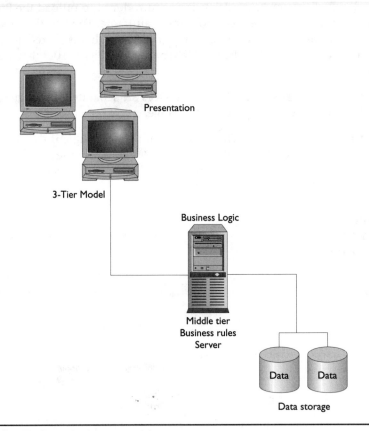

Presentation

3-Tier Model

Business Logic

Middle tier
Business rules
Server

Data   Data

Data storage

Figure 10-4   The 3-tier Application model

Three-Tier Disadvantages   Security is a concern, and scalability is not as good as in the n-tier model. This model is complex to manage.

n-Tier

This model is the neural network of Application models. The Business and Data Services are spread out among numerous systems that provide a scalable environment. See Figure 10-5.

n-Tier Advantages   This model makes it possible for different applications on different platforms and operating systems to interact with both the data and the user.

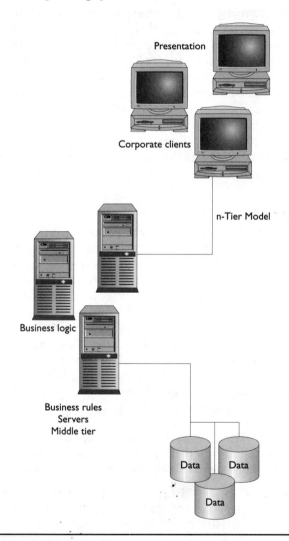

Presentation

Corporate clients

n-Tier Model

Business logic

Business rules
Servers
Middle tier

Data   Data

Data

Figure 10-5   The n-tier Application model

n-Tier Disadvantages   Security is a concern. The database security must be defined in terms of applications, rather than user access. The business components must have security rules defined to ensure that the components aren't misused.

n-Tier Web   The services are spread among multiple servers. The Presentation Service is provided by the Internet server (web server), while Business and Data Services are provided by the same servers as in the n-tier model. See Figure 10-6.

n-Tier Web Advantages   There is no client-deployment cost; all the client needs is a web browser. Only the web server will need to be updated.

n-Tier Web Disadvantages   There are security issues, as in the n-tier architecture.
We refer to security as a disadvantage for the 3-tier and n-tier models. The concern is that the user must authenticate to a middle-tier component that then performs the actions of the user using a common security login (a common *context*). If the common context is compromised, the application is open to anyone who has access to the broken security login. There is also an additional management burden on the security administrator—the administrator must maintain the user authentication to the middle tier and the application authentication to the database server.
ADO.NET can be used in all these models, even though it has been designed specifically to be the data-access solution to the 3-tier and n-tier models. In the next section, we will look at the parts of ADO.NET.

ADO.NET Architecture

ADO.NET has evolved from DAO (Data Access Objects), VBSQL (Visual Basic SQL), RDO (Remote Data Objects), and ADO (ActiveX Data Objects), but it does not share the same programming model, even though most of the functionality is the same. The different data-access technologies represent the history of how Microsoft has supported database developers over the different versions of development tools and operating systems. DAO was introduced with VB 3 to support Access development, VBSQL was a technology that allowed VB programmers to access SQL Server data, RDO provided for disconnected recordsets, and ADO gave us COM and data.
Microsoft defines ADO.NET as being "A set of classes for working with data." In other words the ADO.NET "package" is an object model that helps us work with data: any data, from anywhere, using any storage technology.
These are some of the advantages of ADO.NET:

- **Interoperability**   The language used to transfer data between the data source and the in-memory copy of the data is the standard XML document, which allows seamless data interoperability between dissimilar systems.

- **Maintainability**   ADO.NET maintains local in-memory caches of the data, making it possible to spread the application logic between many tiers in an n-tier application. This makes the application more scalable.

- **Programmability**   ADO.NET is based on the .NET Framework, which uses strongly typed data types. Strongly typed data makes the source code more concise and less prone to "undocumented features" (bugs).

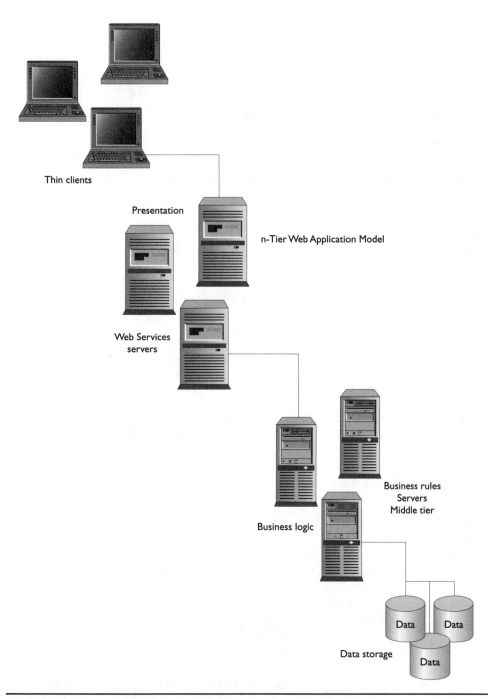

Thin clients

Presentation

n-Tier Web Application Model

Web Services
servers

Business rules
Servers
Middle tier

Business logic

Data storage

Figure 10-6   The n-tier web Application model

- **Performance**   Because ADO.NET is strongly typed, it also helps you avoid data conversions that can be costly to the performance of the application.

- **Scalability**   ADO.NET encourages programmers to minimize resource use by maintaining a local in-memory copy (cache) of the data, enabling you to disconnect from the data source, and by doing so avoid keeping database locks and connections open between calls.

To use ADO.NET, you need to use its related namespaces, listed in Table 10-2.

 EXAM TIP   Commit these namespaces to memory. They will be needed.

The Object Model

The object model of ADO.NET contains two major components: the `DataSet` classes and the .NET `data provider` classes.

The `DataSet` class manages data storage in a disconnected in-memory cache. The `DataSet` class is totally independent of the underlying data source. This way the application can use all the features of the `DataSet` regardless of where the data came from (SQL Server, Access, Oracle, DB/2, and so on).

A .NET `data provider` class is specific to the type of data source—.NET data-provider classes are custom built for particular data sources. The .NET `data provider` classes can include the ability to connect to, retrieve data from, modify data in, and update data sources.

The DataSet Class   The `DataSet` is a collection of `DataTable` objects that represents the underlying data. A `DataSet` has one or more tables associated with it. The tables are accessed through a `Tables` property that refers to a collection of `DataTable` objects in the `DataSet`. If the tables have relationships between them, those relationships are available through the `Relations` property, which refers to a collection of

Namespace	Description
`System.Data`	Contains the core classes of ADO.NET, including the classes that enable disconnected data (such as the `DataSet` class).
`System.Data.Common`	Contains utility classes and interfaces that the data providers inherit and implement.
`System.Data.SqlClient`	Contains the SQL Server .NET data provider.
`System.Data.OleDb`	Contains the OLE-DB .NET data provider.
`System.Data.SqlTypes`	Contains classes and structures that encapsulate the native SQL Server data types. This is a type-safe faster alternative to native data types.
`System.Xml`	Contains the support for the XML standard, including classes for processing and encapsulating an XML document (such as the `XmlDataDocument` class).

Table 10-2   ADO.NET Namespaces

DataRelation objects in the DataSet. By using the DataRelation object, you can join two tables together to programmatically read the data in a parent/child relationship.

Let's look at the DataTable object and the collections that hold information on the data in the table and the cache. Table 10-3 contains information on the most important collections.

A DataSet can be bound to most controls in a Windows Form or a Web Form (data binding is the process by which a control is automatically synchronized with the DataSet). The data binding provides the underlying services needed to build data forms easily.

.NET Data Providers   The ADO.NET classes contain .NET data providers that encapsulate a connection to a data source and the functionality to read, change, and update data in the data source. The .NET data providers are designed to be lightweight and include a minimal abstraction layer between the data source and your code. Microsoft supplies three .NET data providers for you to use, as listed in Table 10-4.

There are four objects in each of the .NET data providers, as listed here (the prefix replacing the Xxx for each of these objects is specific to the provider):

- XxxConnection (for example, SqlConnection or OleDbConnection)
- XxxCommand (for example, SqlCommand or OleDbCommand)
- XxxDataReader (for example, SqlDataReader or OleDbDataReader)
- XxxDataAdapter (for example, SqlDataAdapter or OleDbDataAdapter)

Collection	Object in Collection	Description
Columns	DataColumn	The DataColumn object contains data that describes the data in the column (metadata), such as the column name, the data type, whether the column can be NULL, and so on.
Rows	DataRow	DataRow encapsulates a row of data in the table. The DataRow object also includes the original row data before any changes were made.
Constraints	Constraint	Constraint is an abstract class. It represents the constraint on one or more DataColumn objects. The collection can use any derived class or the two concrete subclasses: UniqueConstraint and ForeignKeyConstraint.
ChildRelations	DataRelation	DataRelation objects are used to represent relationships between columns in different tables. Use a DataRelation object to link (join) two tables on the primary and foreign keys.

Table 10-3   Collections in the DataTable Object

Data Provider	Description
SQL Server .NET	This is an optimized provider for use with Microsoft SQL Server 7.0 or higher databases.
OLE-DB .NET	This is the provider for all OLE-DB provider connections; you can use this .NET data provider for connections to Oracle, DB/2, Informix, and Access. This is actually the .NET data provider that sits on top of any OLE-DB provider.
ODBC .NET	The ODBC .NET data provider is available as a download from Microsoft at msdn.Microsoft.com/downloads. ODBC is legacy support from the .NET Framework.

Table 10-4   The .NET Data Providers

Table 10-5 provides a description of the objects.

 EXAM TIP   The different providers and the products they service will be tested in the exam.

The XxxDataAdapter lets you manage the disconnected nature of the ADO.NET environment by acting as the manager of the XxxConnection and DataSet objects. You use the XxxDataAdapter to populate the DataSet and to update the data source with any changes that have been made to the DataSet.

Some objects also have child objects associated with them. For example, the XxxConnection object has an XxxTransaction object and an XxxError object that expose underlying functionality.

Object	Description
XxxConnection	The XxxConnection object is used to encapsulate the connection between the code and a specific data source.
XxxCommand	XxxCommand objects are used to execute commands on the data source. In the case of SQL Server, the SqlCommand is used to execute a stored procedure on the server.
XxxDataReader	The XxxDataReader provides a forward-only read-only data stream from the data source. You can access the data stream through the ExecuteReader method of the XxxCommand object. The xxxCommand object is usually the result of an SQL SELECT statement or a stored procedure call.
XxxDataAdapter	The XxxDataAdapter provides the services to connect a DataSet to an XxxCommand. It populates the DataSet and resolves any updates with the data source.

Table 10-5   The Objects of the .NET Data Provider

XML and ADO.NET

Over the last couple of years, the XML standard has emerged as the most important standard ever. It provides for the exchange of data, and most importantly, the metadata, between components. ADO.NET is tightly incorporated with XML. Both the object model and the services have XML at their core rather than as an add-on. With ADO.NET, you can easily convert from relational data to XML and back again.

XML is text-based, making it instantly portable and universal. It is an open extensible standard that can be used for many different purposes. The following list identifies just some of the things you can do with XML support in ADO.NET:

- Read data from an XML document.

- Fill a `DataSet` with data from an XML document.

- Create an XML schema for the data in a `DataSet`, and then use the XML schema to write the data as XML.

- Use the XML schema to programmatically treat the XML document as a `DataSet`.

The most exciting fact about XML is that it is the standard format for exchanging data between dissimilar environments. XML is the basis for B2B (business-to-business) e-commerce and is rapidly replacing proprietary protocols for data exchange.

 EXAM TIP   XML is such an important technology for the .NET Framework that you can expect XML to be part of many exam questions.

Data-Access Basics

Before we get into the details of using ADO.NET, we should take a look at the basics of data access, namely at SQL (structured query language) and transactions. The ADO.NET environment uses the standard ANSI92 SQL language for DML (data modification language). DML is the three commands that modifies data in SQL (`INSERT`, `UPDATE`, and `DELTE`), and it exposes the transaction model of the underlying data source, making it possible to take advantage of those database managers that provide transactions.

SQL

SQL is a language, even though Microsoft calls their database server SQL Server, and in this section we will look at the DML elements of the language (`SELECT`, `INSERT`, `UPDATE`, and `DELETE`) that are used to manipulate data stored in a Relational Database Manager system (RDBMS). We will start with the `SELECT` statement, which returns information from a database, and then look at how to modify the content of the tables in a database by using `INSERT`, `UPDATE`, and `DELETE` statements.

All our examples will use the Northwind Traders sample database that is supplied by Microsoft as part of Access, SQL Server 7.0, and SQL Server 2000.

 EXAM TIP The SQL statements will be used in many different questions. It is very important to have mastery over the SQL language.

SELECT

You use SELECT statements to retrieve data from tables in a database. The SELECT statement is the basic command for querying the database. In the statement, you specify the columns and tables you want data from, and you can optionally specify conditions and sorting instructions. The full syntax for the SELECT statement is rather complex; we will look at a shorter syntax listing with the most commonly used options:

```
SELECT [ALL | DISTINCT] select_list
FROM table_source
[ WHERE search_condition ]
[ ORDER BY order_expression [ ASC | DESC ] ]
```

The columns to be returned are listed in the select_list parameter. Use a comma to separate the column names or use the column wildcard character (*) to select all columns in the table. The ALL argument specifies that all rows in the table_source should be returned, even if there are duplicate rows. The DISTINCT argument removes all duplicates in the returned data. ALL is the default.

The FROM clause specifies the tables that the columns will be returned from. The FROM clause is mandatory, and you must provide at least one table name.

The following example returns all the staff from the Northwind Trading database (the query is executed against an SQL Server 2000 database):

```
/* Retrieve the First Name, Last Name, City and Country
   for all the staff */
USE Northwind
SELECT FirstName, LastName, City, Country
FROM Employees
```

The preceding SELECT statement produced the following result:

FirstName	LastName	City	Country
Nancy	Davolio	Seattle	USA
Andrew	Fuller	Tacoma	USA
Janet	Leverling	Kirkland	USA
Margaret	Peacock	Redmond	USA
Steven	Buchanan	London	UK
Michael	Suyama	London	UK
Robert	King	London	UK
Laura	Callahan	Seattle	USA
Anne	Dodsworth	London	UK

The SELECT statement returned all the rows in the table. If you only want the staff working in London, you can include a WHERE clause. The WHERE clause limits the number of rows that are returned to those that match the criterion supplied as part of the statement. Our SELECT statement looks like this with the new WHERE clause:

```
/* Retrieve the First Name, Last Name, City and Country
   for all the staff that live in London*/
USE Northwind
SELECT FirstName, LastName, City, Country
FROM Employees
WHERE City = 'London'
```

The result of this SELECT statement is as follows:

```
FirstName   LastName               City              Country
----------  -------------------    ---------------   ---------------
Steven      Buchanan               London            UK
Michael     Suyama                 London            UK
Robert      King                   London            UK
Anne        Dodsworth              London            UK
```

The WHERE clause can compare columns against literal values using the logical operators listed in Table 10-6. String literals in SQL are enclosed in single quotes (').

The WHERE clause has some additional tricks we can take advantage of. For example, to search for records where we only know part of the data in a column, we can use the

Logical Operator	Description	Sample and Explanation
=	Equality	WHERE City = 'London' Returns all records where the City is London.
<	Less than	WHERE Day < 21 Returns all records where Day is less than 21.
>	Greater than	WHERE Day > 5 Returns all records where Day is greater than 5.
<=	Less than or equal	WHERE Day <= 21 Returns all records where Day is less than or equal to 21.
>=	Greater than or equal	WHERE Day >= 5 Returns all records where Day is greater than or equal to 5.
!=	Not	WHERE City != 'London' Returns all records where the City is not London.
AND	And	WHERE Day > 5 AND Day < 21 Returns all records where the Day is between 5 and 21; note that records where Day is 5 or 21 are not returned.
OR	Or	WHERE Day < 5 OR Day > 21 Returns all records where Day is less than 5 or greater than 21.

Table 10-6 Comparisons Using the WHERE Clause

LIKE argument, which lets us write string search patterns. The following example shows how to use the LIKE argument in a search for all records where the FirstName column starts with 'An':

```
/* Retrieve the First Name, Last Name, City and Country
   for all the staff that have
   First Names that start with 'An'*/
USE Northwind
SELECT FirstName, LastName, City, Country
FROM Employees
WHERE FirstName LIKE 'An%'
```

The percent sign (%) is the wildcard character that is used with all string and character comparisons in the SQL language, so 'An%' translates to any string that starts with "An". If you are looking for a substring, you can use multiple percent signs.

 TIP   Remember that character literals in SQL must be enclosed with single quotes.

The result of the preceding query is that only records that match the LIKE argument are returned:

FirstName	LastName	City	Country
Andrew	Fuller	Tacoma	USA
Anne	Dodsworth	London	UK

In our next example, we want to list all employees that have "ll" in their last names:

```
/* Retrieve the First Name, Last Name, City and Country
   for all the staff that have
   First Names that start with 'An'*/
USE Northwind
SELECT FirstName, LastName, City, Country
FROM Employees
WHERE LastName LIKE '%ll%'
```

This query results in the following output:

FirstName	LastName	City	Country
Andrew	Fuller	Tacoma	USA
Laura	Callahan	Seattle	USA

The other clause we haven't looked at yet is the ORDER BY clause. If you look back at the first result we received in this section, when we selected all the staff, you will find that it is not sorted on any of the columns, and it seems to be returned in a random order. If we go back again and run the same query, we might get our results in the same order, but more likely we will not. Unless we specify an order, there is no guarantee as to what order the data will be returned in.

The ORDER BY clause lets us request that the result be returned in specific sorted order. The following example requests that the result be sorted on the LastName column:

```
/* Retrieve the First Name, Last Name, City and Country
   for all the staff and
   sort on the LastName column*/
USE Northwind
SELECT FirstName, LastName, City, Country
FROM Employees
ORDER BY LastName
```

The preceding query returns the following result:

```
FirstName   LastName               City              Country
----------  ---------------------  ---------------   ---------------
Steven      Buchanan               London            UK
Laura       Callahan               Seattle           USA
Nancy       Davolio                Seattle           USA
Anne        Dodsworth              London            UK
Andrew      Fuller                 Tacoma            USA
Robert      King                   London            UK
Janet       Leverling              Kirkland          USA
Margaret    Peacock                Redmond           USA
Michael     Suyama                 London            UK
```

You can combine these SELECT clauses as you need them. Here are some recommendations for working with SELECT statements:

- Never use the column name wildcard (*) in the SELECT statement; list all the columns you need instead.
- Always include a WHERE clause to limit the number of rows returned.
- If you need the data sorted, use the ORDER BY clause.

JOIN   You will often need to combine data from two or more tables, and the JOIN clause allows you to perform this task. JOIN statements are used to query any number of tables and return a single result set that contains merged data from these tables. Joins are a central part of relational database theory and are used in the real world to implement relations between entities in a normalized data model.

There are three types of joins in SQL: *inner joins*, *outer joins*, and *cross joins*. These joins are described in Table 10-7.

The syntax for an inner join is as follows:

```
SELECT select_list
FROM first_table_name
[INNER] JOIN join_table_name
ON join_condition
```

The ON keyword defines the comparison that must be true for the inner join to return the row. The INNER keyword is optional, as it is the default join in the ANSI92 SQL standard.

Join Type	Description
Inner join	The inner join combines tables based on the equality comparison of data values in common columns in the two tables. Only rows that match the comparison are returned in the result set.
Outer join	The outer join combines rows from two tables based on the equality comparison of data values in common columns in the tables. The outer join returns all matching rows plus all the unmatched rows from one of the tables. The LEFT OUTER JOIN returns all the rows from the table that is named first, plus all the rows in the last named table that match the comparison. The RIGHT OUTER JOIN returns all the rows from the table that is named last, plus all rows from the first table that match the comparison.
Cross join	A cross join produces a Cartesian product of the rows in both tables—it returns all possible combinations of rows. You do not specify any condition, as no comparison is used. The cross join is used to generate test data for databases.

Table 10-7 The Different Join Types

Let's look at an example. Figure 10-7 shows the relationships between three tables. The relationship is set up to enable us to join the three tables together. The EmployeeID column is used to connect the Employees and EmployeeTerritories tables, and the TerritoryID column is used to connect the EmployeeTerritories and Territories tables.

If we needed to query this database and return TerritoryDescription, FirstName, and LastName for an employee with a last name of Buchanan, we could use the following query:

```
USE Northwind
SELECT TerritoryDescription, FirstName, LastName
FROM Employees
JOIN EmployeeTerritories
ON Employees.EmployeeID = EmployeeTerritories.EmployeeID
JOIN Territories
ON EmployeeTerritories.TerritoryID = Territories.TerritoryID
WHERE LastName = 'Buchanan'
```

This query will return all records for employees named Buchanan where there is an entry for a territory.

```
TerritoryDescription                      FirstName  LastName
------------------------------------      ---------- --------------------
Providence                                Steven     Buchanan
Morristown                                Steven     Buchanan
Edison                                    Steven     Buchanan
New York                                  Steven     Buchanan
New York                                  Steven     Buchanan
Mellvile                                  Steven     Buchanan
Fairport                                  Steven     Buchanan
```

Let us take a look at what happened. The SELECT line specifies the columns that we need; notice that we used the name of the column from the Territories table without

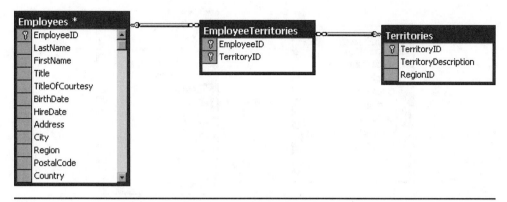

Figure 10-7 Table relationships for an inner join example

specifying what table it came from. As long as the column names are unique we do not have to specify the table name as well. In the FROM clause we added the JOIN clause to specify that we want the tables on either side of the JOIN clause to be connected. The ON statement sets the rules of the connection; in our case, we want the Employees table joined to the EmployeeTerritories table using the EmployeeID column in both tables.

When there are columns in two tables that have the same name, we use a syntax that specifies the table and the column names in a dotted format: `table.column` (for example, `Employees.EmployeeID`). You must use this format in the ON clause unless the two columns have unique names.

Finally we join the Territories table to the result of the first JOIN. This results in the preceding output. The default behavior of the JOIN clause is to return all records that match the ON clause from the two tables, and this is known as an inner join.

 EXAM TIP Remember the syntax for the JOIN operation, and remember that the inner join is the default JOIN.

In the next example, we will use aliasing to make the code easier to read. Figure 10-8 shows the model for the example. We want a query that returns the CategoryName, ProductName, and Supplier for the beverages category, and we want to sort the output on the ProductName. The following query performs that task:

```
USE Northwind
SELECT CategoryName, ProductName, CompanyName
FROM Categories c
JOIN Products p
ON c.CategoryID = p.CategoryID
JOIN Suppliers s
ON p.SupplierID = s.SupplierID
WHERE CategoryName = 'Beverages'
ORDER BY ProductName
```

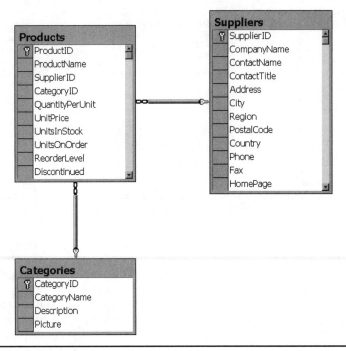

Figure 10-8 Table relationships for an aliasing example

The biggest difference between this example and the previous one is that we used aliases to identify the tables. The following code segment defines c as the alias for the Categories table and p as the alias for the Products table:

```
FROM Categories c
JOIN Products p
```

We can now use c and p to refer to the tables, simplifying the query.

The result of the preceding query is as follows:

```
CategoryName   ProductName                 CompanyName
-------------  --------------------------  -------------------------------
Beverages      Chai                        Exotic Liquids
Beverages      Chang                       Exotic Liquids
Beverages      Chartreuse verte            Aux joyeux ecclésiastiques
Beverages      Côte de Blaye               Aux joyeux ecclésiastiques
Beverages      Guaraná Fantástica          Refrescos Americanas LTDA
Beverages      Ipoh Coffee                 Leka Trading
Beverages      Lakkalikööri                Karkki Oy
Beverages      Laughing Lumberjack Lager   Bigfoot Breweries
Beverages      Outback Lager               Pavlova, Ltd.
Beverages      Rhönbräu Klosterbier        Plutzer Lebensmittelgroßmärkte AG
Beverages      Sasquatch Ale               Bigfoot Breweries
Beverages      Steeleye Stout              Bigfoot Breweries
```

INSERT

There are a number of different ways of inserting data into tables in a database. We will look at how to insert one row with new column values, and how to create a new table based on a query.

The INSERT statement is the fastest way of adding new data to the database. The syntax for the INSERT statement is as follows:

```
INSERT [INTO] table_name [(column1, column2, …, column)]
VALUES (value1, value2, …, value3)
```

The column list following the table_name allows you to specify the order in which data is inserted. If the column list is not used, the values must be listed in the column order of the table.

For example, to insert a new employee in the Employees table, you could use the following statement:

```
USE Northwind
INSERT Employees (FirstName, LastName)
VALUES ('Robert', 'Burns')
```

 TIP The column list of the INSERT statement is optional. If it is not used, the order of the values in the VALUE clause must match the column order of the table.

To insert data from a query into an existing table, you can use the INSERT ... SELECT statement. The syntax is as follows:

```
INSERT table_name
SELECT select_list
FROM table_source
[WHERE condition]
```

The result set from the SELECT statement will be added to the table_name table. There are some rules that you need to consider when using this technique:

- The data type of the columns in the result set should match the data types of the columns in the table.
- The result set must have data for all required columns in the destination table.

The following example takes all our employees and adds them to the Customers table so our staff can also be our customers. We will build the CustomerID column data by taking the first three characters from the first name and the first two characters from the last name and concatenating them. The employee's first name is used as the contact name, and the last name as the company name.

```
USE Northwind
INSERT Customers
  SELECT substring(FirstName, 1, 3) + substring(LastName, 1, 2),
```

```
         LastName, FirstName, Title, Address, City,
         Region, PostalCode, Country, HomePhone, NULL
FROM Employees
```

To create a new table from the query, you use this syntax:

```
SELECT select_list
INTO new_table
FROM table_source
[WHERE condition]
```

The `new_table` can be either a local temporary table (`#table_name`), global temporary table (`##table_name`), or a permanent table (`table_name`). One pound sign (#) indicates a local table that will be available as long as the session that created it is open; two pound signs (##) is a globally available table that will exist until it is no longer used in any session. In order to be able to create a permanent table, the administrator of the database must have enabled `SELECT INTO`.

The `select_list` is commonly used to alias column names to new names for the new table. The `AS` keyword is used to change the name of a column. In the following example, we will retrieve the pricelist from the Products table and save the product and the price in a new table. We will also calculate a 25 percent sales tax on the price.

```
USE Northwind
SELECT ProductName AS Product
     , UnitPrice AS Price
     , (UnitPrice * 0.25) AS SalesTax
     , UnitPrice + (UnitPrice * 0.25) AS NewPrice
  INTO #SalesTaxTable
FROM Products
```

The preceding example created a new local table named #SalesTaxTable. To query the new table you could execute this query:

```
USE Northwind
SELECT *
FROM #SalesTaxTable
```

The partial result set is seen here:

```
Product                      Price         SalesTax         NewPrice
---------------------------- -----------   --------------   ---------
Chai                         18.0000       4.500000         22.500000
Chang                        19.0000       4.750000         23.750000
Aniseed Syrup                10.0000       2.500000         12.500000
Chef Anton's Cajun Seasoning 22.0000       5.500000         27.500000
...
(77 row(s) affected)
```

UPDATE

You can use the `UPDATE` statement to make changes to one or more rows at a time. The syntax for the `UPDATE` statement is as follows:

```
UPDATE table_name
  SET column_name = expression, …
  [WHERE condition]
```

As you use the UPDATE statement, you should be aware of some rules and recommendations:

- Use the WHERE condition to control which rows are updated; if you don't use a WHERE condition, every row in the table is updated.
- Use the SET keyword to specify the new value for a column in the row.
- The UPDATE statement will only work on one table at a time.

If we wanted to increase the unit price for the products that were supplied by New Orleans Cajun Delights (SupplierID = 2) by 25 percent, we could use the following:

```
USE Northwind
UPDATE Products
  SET UnitPrice = UnitPrice * 1.25
  WHERE SupplierID = 2
```

 TIP Always include a WHERE clause in the UPDATE statement.

DELETE

Use the DELETE statement to remove rows from a table. The DELETE statement has the following syntax:

```
DELETE table_name
  [WHERE condition]
```

If you issue the DELETE statement without a WHERE clause, the statement will remove all the rows in the table.

To remove rows representing products that were shipped before November 1, 2001, you could use this code:

```
USE Northwind
DELETE Orders
  WHERE shippeddate < '11/1/2001'
```

 TIP Always include a WHERE clause in the DELETE statement.

ACID Rules (Transactions)

When you work with data on central database servers, there are two main areas of concern: allowing multiple users access to the same data in a safe way, and guaranteeing that any data modification performed will maintain the integrity of the data. To attempt to solve both these issues, we use *transactions*.

A transaction is a group of related operations that either succeed or fail as one unit—the transaction either will *commit* or *roll back*, respectively. In order for a transaction to commit, all parts of the transaction must succeed. Transactions provide all-or-nothing processing.

A popular example of a transaction is the ATM (automatic teller machine) where you might transfer $100.00 from your checking account to your savings account. You can reasonably expect that the $100.00 was transferred, or if something went wrong with the ATM or the banking system, that the money would still be in the checking account. The transfer either takes place (commits), or if there is a problem (any problem) with the transfer, the accounts are returned to the original state (the transaction rolls back).

A transaction is tested against its *ACID* properties, named for the four key concepts of a transaction (atomicity, consistency, isolation, and durability):

- **Atomicity**   A transaction is said to be atomic when it is one unit of work containing many steps; it will execute exactly one time and it will either commit or roll back.

- **Consistency**   A transaction maintains the integrity (consistency) of the data when the transaction either commits or rolls back; in this case, there is never any chance of undefined states after the transaction executes.

- **Isolation**   A transaction is isolated from all other transactions on the system, making the process look as if it is the only transaction running. This isolation guarantees that no transaction will ever be able to "see" intermediate values from any other transaction (meaning there are no *dirty reads*).

- **Durability**   A transaction that commits is guaranteed to have its values persist even if the system crashes directly after the transaction commits.

The ACID properties ensure predictable behavior and the all-or-nothing nature of a transaction. A database system that does not provide transactions or can't meet the ACID properties is considered unsuitable for anything beyond personal use.

In SQL you can control transactions using the transaction control statements shown in Table 10-8. They can be used as part of any SQL process.

Table 10-8 SQL Transaction Control Statements	Statement	Description
	BEGIN TRANSACTION	Starts the transaction; all statements after the BEGIN TRANSACTION statement are part of the transaction.
	COMMIT TRANSACTION	Ends the transaction, indicating success; all processing will be persisted in the database.
	ROLLBACK TRANSACTION	Ends the transaction, indicating failure; all processing will be rolled back to the state it was in when the transaction started.

The following example uses the traditional bank example—we are going to move $100.00 from one account to another. This example will not execute against the Northwind database.

```
BEGIN TRANSACTION
INSERT INTO BankAccount (AccountNUM, Amount, Type)
  VALUES (424242, 100, 'debit')
INSERT INTO BankAccount (AccountNUM, Amount, Type)
  VALUES (121212, 100, 'credit')
IF (@@ERROR > 0) ROLLBACK TRANSACTION
  ELSE COMMIT TRANSACTION
```

There are two data-modification statements in this example that insert debit and credit rows in the specific accounts. If there are any errors during this processing, the global @@ERROR variable will be set to a non-zero value. A non-zero value will cause a rollback, otherwise we commit.

EXAM TIP   Transactions are focused on the connection to the database.

Connecting to a Data Provider

In order to connect to a data source, we need the libraries (providers or drivers) that are designed to work with a particular data source. The .NET data providers supplied by Microsoft as part of the .NET Framework are the SQL Server .NET data provider and the OLE-DB .NET data provider. Microsoft has also made the ODBC .NET data provider available as a download from the MSDN download site.

Selecting the right data provider should be a straightforward process and is based on the type of the data source and the available connectivity for that source. In Table 10-9 you can see the providers and the data sources they can be used with.

Table 10-9 Data Provider Selection	Data Provider	Data Source
	SQL Server .NET data provider	Microsoft SQL Server 7.0 or higher
	OLE DB .NET data provider	Microsoft SQL Server 6.5 or older Oracle Microsoft Access Any database where you have an OLE-DB provider
	ODBC .NET data provider	Oracle Microsoft Access Any database where you have an ODBC driver as the only access method

Database Security

Depending on the provider chosen, you will have to specify the security credentials for the connection in different formats. Each database vendor has its own security design. As we are dealing with Microsoft-centered information, we will only cover the specifics for the current model of SQL Server.

SQL Server uses one of two types of security—Windows Authentication or SQL Server Authentication:

- Windows Authentication uses the user's login credentials from the Windows Active Directory to authenticate against the database server. The resulting connection is called a *trusted* connection because SQL Server trusted the Windows credentials to be safe.

- SQL Server Authentication requires the user to log in to SQL Server with an additional username and password. The resulting connection is called an *untrusted* connection because SQL Server did not trust anyone but itself to provide the authentication.

When the server is configured, the administrator can enable either Windows Authentication or Mixed Mode, which adds the SQL Server Authentication.

Depending on the type of application you are writing and the type of client that will use the application, there can be reasons to use either method to authenticate. Windows Authentication is the preferred method when all clients are in the same company and you are building an internal application. SQL Server Authentication is normally used when building Web Services, or when you have non-Windows clients using the application.

Connection Strings

In order to connect to a data source, you need to build a connection string that will define the context of the connection. The parameters of the connection string will differ somewhat depending on the data provider and are listed in Table 10-10.

Connections

The .NET data providers give us the three connection classes: `SqlConnection` (for use with SQL Server 7.0 or higher), `OleDbConnection` (for use with data sources through OLE-DB providers), and `OdbcConnection` (for use with legacy ODBC drivers).

Let's look at a few example connection strings and connections for a number of different data sources. Suppose we want to make a connection to an SQL Server 2000 data provider with the following parameters:

- Server name is Hjalmar
- Database name is Marvin
- Security is set to Mixed Mode
- Username is "sa"

- Password is "42"

- Timeout is 1 minute (60 seconds)

The following code will make the connection.

```
// The following code segment defines the connection string
// We will use SQL Server .NET Data Provider
string strCn;
strCn = "User ID=sa;Password=42;Initial Catalog=Marvin;";
strCn = strCn + "Data Source=Hjalmar;Connection TimeOut=60;";
// now we define the connection object and open the connection
SqlConnection sqlCn = new SqlConnection(strCn);
sqlCn.Open();
```

The next example will connect to the Access 2000 database

c:\data\Marvin.mdb

Here's the code:

```
// The following code segment defines the connection string
// We will use an OLE DB .NET Data Provider
string strCn;
strCn = "Provider=Microsoft.Access;Initial Catalog=c:\data\Marvin.mdb;";
OleDbConnection oleCn = new OleDbConnection(strCn);
oleCn.Open();
```

Finally we'll connect to the following SQL Server 6.5 data provider:

- Server name = SalesServer03

- Database name = Pubs

- Security = Windows Security

Parameter	Description
Provider	The Provider property is used to specify the OLE-DB provider to use; this property is only used with the OLE DB .NET data provider.
Connection Timeout	The number of seconds to wait for a server to reply; 15 seconds is the default.
Initial Catalog	The name of the database to connect to.
Data Source	The name (or address) of the database server to connect to.
User ID	The username if connecting using SQL Server Authentication.
Password	The password to use if connecting using SQL Server Authentication.
Trusted Connection	True or False; specifies whether the connection is going to be encrypted.
Persist Security Information	Specifies whether sensitive security information is to be resent if a connection is reopened. The default is False; changing this property to True can be a security risk.

Table 10-10   Connection String Parameters

Here's the code:

```
// The following code segment defines the connection string
// We will use the OLE DB .NET Data Provider
string strCn;
strCn = "Provider=SQLOLEDB.1;Data Source=SalesServer03;Initial catalog=Pubs;";
OleDbConnection oleCn = new OleDbConnection(strCn);
oleCn.Open();
```

Closing the Connection

After we are finished with a connection, we should close it down by calling the `Close()` method of the connection object, like this:

```
sqlCn.Close();
```

It is permissible to let the connection object go out of scope and have the garbage collector deal with it, but that would leave the connection active on the data source until the garbage collector runs. However, that would destroy any scalability dreams we had for this application, so it is important to manage the connections to keep the load on the server as low as possible.

The `Close()` method closes down the connection to the data source, but it will not release any memory object, like the connection object itself. To remove the object from memory, you can call the `Dispose()` method of the object:

```
sqlCn.Dispose();
```

The following code segment shows the flow of creating and disposing of objects:

```
string strCn;
strCn = "Provider=SQLOLEDB.1;Data Source=SalesServer03;Initial catalog=Pubs;";
OleDbConnection oleCn = new OleDbConnection(strCn);
oleCn.Open();
// perform some database operations

// Close the connection to the data source
oleCn.Close();
// remove the connection object
oleCn.Dispose();
// set the reference to Null
oleCn = Null;
```

TIP Always clean up the connections to save on connection resources; otherwise the connection will tie up resources until the garbage collector runs.

Connection Pooling

Data providers have the ability to do *connection pooling*. Connection pooling is the mechanism of keeping connections open and reusing one unused connection for more than one connection attempt. In order for connection pooling to happen, the connection strings for the connections must be identical, and connection pooling must be enabled for the connection. The default is that all connections are enabled for connection pooling.

The benefit of connection pooling is that our applications scale better against the data source. The resource cost of creating and closing connections is a limiting factor for how many concurrent connections a data source can handle, and by pooling the connections, the number of processes that can access the data source is increased, without increasing the number of connections.

The key to making connection pooling possible is having connection strings that are absolutely identical, including the security settings; if the strings are identical, the provider creates a pool. When a connection is attempted in a pool and there is an unused connection, it will be used; if there are no available unused connections, a new connection is created and added to the pool.

The connection string can contain a number of parameters that are used to control the behavior of connection pooling. These parameters are listed in Table 10-11.

Error Handling

Whenever you access resources that are remote from your application, such as a data source, you must include error handling to ensure that unhandled errors never reach the user. In Chapter 7 you were introduced to exception handling using the `try ... catch ... finally` structure; we will use that exception handling here.

Parameter	Description	Default
Connection Lifetime	When a connection is returned to the pool, this parameter is compared to the creation time of the connection. If the connection has been active longer than the parameter allows, it is destroyed. The default of 0 translates to unlimited lifetime.	0
Connection Reset	If this is set to True, the connection is reset to its initial context when removed from the pool.	True
Enlist	When this is set to True, the pool controller will automatically join a transaction if one is present.	True
Max Pool Size	This parameter specifies the maximum number of connections that are allowed in the pool.	100
Min Pool Size	This parameter specifies the minimum number of connections in the pool.	0
Pooling	This parameter turns connection pooling on (True) or off (False).	True

Table 10-11   Connection String Parameters for Connection Pooling

Let's start with an example that highlights how we want to use exception handling to control connection processing.

```
OdbcConnection odbcCn = new OdbcConnection(
            "DSN=MS Access Database;DBQ=c:\\data\\Marvin.mdb;" );
try
{
  odbcCn.Open()
  // perform some data processing
}
catch( XcpNullRef e )
{
  Console.WriteLine("Failed to create the connection object!");
}

catch( Xcp e)
{
  Console.WriteLine(Xcp.ToString());
}
finally
{
  odbcCn.Close();
  odbcCn.Dispose();
  odbccn = Null;
}
```

The `try` block contains all the database operations we need to perform. If we fail to create the connection object, the first `catch` block will execute. Any other error will be handled by the second handler, and finally we close the database.

 TIP In real life, the code that deals with potential database errors will always be longer than the code that performs the action.

You need to define `catch` blocks for all the possible exceptions that can be thrown in your data-access application. Handle the exceptions or throw them up the calling chain until they are handled, but never let an unhandled exception reach the end user.

The data source can raise events to inform the user of potentially important information, and each data source will have different messages. The `SqlConnection` has an `InfoMessage` event that we can use to get access to these messages. The `SqlException` class contains the exception that is thrown when SQL Server returns an error or a warning. The `SqlException` class always contains at least one instance of `SqlError`. By using the severity level of the `SqlError` object, you can determine how big a problem the server has, and what has happened to the connection. Table 10-12 lists the severity properties.

The `SqlException` object holds a collection of `SqlError` objects. To work with them, you can use code similar to the following sample:

```
foreach (SqlClient.SqlError serr in e.Errors)
{
  Console.WriteLine(serr.Message);
}
```

Severity	Description	Result
1–10	Information messages	The connection remains open
11–16	User-generated errors	User corrects data entries and resubmits
17–19	Hardware or software errors	Connection remains open; there might be problems with some statements
20–25	Fatal hardware or software errors	The connection is closed; the user must reopen the connection to continue working

Table 10-12   Severity Levels in SQL Server Messages

The Command Object

You may have been wondering when we finally would get to the data—now that we have our groundwork in place, we are there. In this section you will see how to create a command object that encapsulates an SQL statement. The command object then uses an existing connection to perform the requested operation. For example, the following code segment creates a command based on a connection:

```
SqlCommand cmCategories = new SqlCommand("SELECT * FROM Categories", sqlCn);
```

The command object has a number of properties and methods that are used to manipulate the object. Table 10-13 lists the members of the command object.

The command object contains a parameters collection that can be used when calling stored procedures on the database server (a stored procedure is a database object that is used as a function). Suppose we have been given the following specifications for the stored procedure: the name is GetProcCat, @CatID is an int as an input, @CatName

Member	Description
CommandText	The text that defines the command object
CommandType	The type of the command, either command text (generic), SQL statements, stored procedure, or undefined; the undefined type indicates to the command object that the command type is unknown
Connection	The connection to use for this command object
ExecuteNonQuery	Executes the command that performs some data processing; returns the number of rows affected
ExecuteReader	Executes the command, returning a rowset
ExecuteScalar	Executes the command, returning a single value
ExecuteXmlReader	Executes the command, returning an XML result
Parameters	If the CommandType is a stored procedure, the Parameters collection can hold the parameters for the command

Table 10-13   The Members of the Command Object

is a `string` of Unicode characters as output, and the stored procedure returns an `int` as a return value. The following code creates the parameters for a command object:

```
// create the command object
SqlCommand sqlCom = new SqlCommand();
sqlCom.Connection = sqlCn;
sqlCom.CommandType = StoredProcedure;
sqlCom.CommandText = "GetProcCat";

// add parameters to the sqlCom command object

SqlParameter p1, p2, p3;
p1 = new SqlParameter("@RETURN_VALUE", SqlDbType.Int, 4);
p1.Direction = ParameterDirection.ReturnValue;p2 =
    new SqlParameter("@CatID", SqlDbType.Int, 4);
p2.Direction = ParameterDirection.Input;
p3 = new SqlParameter("@CatName", SqlDbType.Nchar, 15);
p3.Direction = ParameterDirection.OutPut;
// Add the parameters to the collection
sqlCom.Parameters.Add(p1);
sqlCom.Parameters.Add(p2);
sqlCom.Parameters.Add(p3);

// At this time we can execute the command object
```

In this example, we created the parameters and added them to the collection in the command object. The direction of the parameter is set with the assignment to the Direction parameter. Before we can execute the command object, we need to look at the specification of the stored procedure to see what is returned from the stored procedure. If the command object is not configured to accept return values we will not be able to retrieve those values. For us to access these return values we must use a different execute method.

The following example executes the command and assigns the output to a variable:

```
// assign the value we will look for in the @CatID parameter
sqlCom.Parameters("@CatID").Value = 42;
sqlCn.Open();       // open the connection
sqlCom.ExecuteNonQuery();
sqlCn.Close();      // close the collection

// print out the values
Console.WriteLine(sqlCom.Parameters("@CatName").Value);
Console.WriteLine(sqlCom.Parameters("@RETURN_VALUE").Value;
```

The preceding command was executed with the ExecuteNonQuery method.

In the next example we will use a command object that returns a single value (a scalar).

```
// Create the command object
SqlCommand sc = new SqlCommand("SELECT COUNT(*) FROM Customers", sqlCn);
int qty;
// execute the command
qty = Ctype(sc.ExecuteScalar(), Integer);
```

When we need to get rows back from a command object, we use the `DataReader` object to represent the returned rows. The `ExecuteReader` method returns a `DataReader` object that can be used to access the row data with strongly typed methods. The next example uses the `SqlDataReader` object to access a table:

```
// create the command object
SqlCommand sc = new SqlCommand(
                "SELECT FirstName, LastName FROM Employees", sqlCn);
sqlCn.Open();
SqlDataReader sqlDr;
sqlDr = sc.ExecuteReader(CommandBehavior.CloseConnection);
// The reader will close the connection when done
// now iterate through the DataReader
do while (sqlDr.Read())
{
  Console.WriteLine(sqlDr.GetString(0) + " " + sqlDr.GetString(1));
}
sqlDr.Close();
```

We are now able to get and display data from our data sources. This is only part of the story, though. The next section will explore the `DataSet` and the related objects that give us the in-memory cache of data.

The DataSet Object

The `DataSet` object in ADO.NET represents data in a local in-memory cache and provides the functions to access the data independent of where the data originated. The `DataSet` is a disconnected representation of the data that does not have to be connected to the data source for the data to be available.

The `DataSet` stores data much like data is stored in a table, with rows and columns. `DataSet` objects can even have constraints and relationships defined. The `DataSet` uses the `DataTable` collection to represent the tables; a `DataTable` represents one table of in-memory data, and it uses the `DataColumn` collection to represent the columns of the `DataTable`.

The data in the `DataSet` is represented in a relational view regardless of the origin of the data. The data can optionally be represented as an XML formatted document, and we will look at the XML representation later in this chapter.

To create a `DataSet`, you must create a reference for the object and give it a name, as in the following example:

```
DataSet dsNw = new DataSet("Northwind");
```

This line creates a new `DataSet` that we called `Northwind` using dsNw as the variable name.

`DataTable` objects are added to the `DataSet` object's `Tables` collection by using the `Add` method of the collection:

```
DataTable dtEmployees =dsNw.Tables.Add("Employee");
```

Finally, we can add the columns to the `DataTable` object's `Columns` collection and define what the `DataTable` will look like:

```
DataColumn colEmployeeID = dtEmployees.Columns.Add("EmployeeID");
colEmployeeID.DataType = System.Int32;
colEmployeeID.AllowDBNull = false;  // not null
colEmployeeID.Unique = true;  // enforce unique entries

DataColumn colLastName = dtEmployees.Columns.Add("LastName");
colLastName.DataType = System.String;
colLastName.Unique = false;
DataColumn colFirstName = dtEmployees.Columns.Add("FirstName");
colFirstName.DataType = System.String;
colFirstName.Unique = false;
```

After the structure of the `DataTable` has been defined, you can start adding data to the `DataSet` by creating `DataRow` objects for the data:

```
DataRow dr = dtEmployees.NewRow();
dr("EmployeeID") = 42;
dr("LastName") = "Smith";
dr("FirstName") = "Bob";
dtEmployees.Rows.Add(dr);
```

The preceding five lines of code could also be written as one line:

```
dtEmployees.Rows.Add(new Object() {42, "Smith", "Bob"});
```

By using the `Object()` class, we can create new rows in one step rather than five. The order of the column data must be the same as it was defined in `DataRow`.

ADO.NET and XML

ADO.NET uses XML (Extensible Markup Language) to manage and move data from and to a data source and the dataset objects. In this section we will look at the `XmlDataDocument` object and how to read and write a dataset into an XML document.

By using XML, we can view data both as an XML document and as a relational set of tables. This dual personality of XML makes it a very powerful technology when moving data between objects. There is one potential problem with these transfers though; if the sender and receiver are using different data structures, the receiver will get bad data. The solution to this potential problem is to use a schema to define the layout of the data, as well as the data types. The current standard for the schema is the XSD (Extensible Schema Definition) that allows both parties in the transfer to certify that the XML data is consistent with what they expect.

 EXAM TIP We can't state too strongly the fact that XML is central to all data movement in ADO.NET.

Loading XML into a DataSet

The `DataSet` object has a `ReadXml` method that is used to read data into the `DataSet` from an XML file. The `ReadXml` method can read XML documents from `Stream`, `File`, `TextReader`, and `XmlReader` sources. The syntax for the `ReadXml` method is as follows:

```
ReadXml(Stream | FileName | TextReader | XmlReader, XmlReadMode)
```

The `XmlReadMode` parameter can be any of the values listed in Table 10-14.

The following code example loads a schema into the `DataSet` and then loads the XML documents:

```
private void ReadXml()
{
  try
  {
    DataSet xmlDataS = new DataSet();
    // read in the schema
    xmlDataS.ReadXmlSchema("Order.xsd");

    // read in the data using the loaded schema
    xmlDataS.ReadXml("Order.xml", XmlReadMode.IgnoreSchema);
  }
  catch(Exception e)
  {
    Console.WriteLine("Exception: " + e.ToString());
  }
}
```

XmlReadMode Value	Description
`Auto`	Examines the XML document and selects the action accordingly from these choices: If the `DataSet` already has a schema, or the document contains an inline schema, it sets `XmlReadMode` to `ReadSchema`. If the `DataSet` does not already have a schema and the document does not contain an inline schema, it sets `XmlReadMode` to `InferSchema`. The use of an `XmlReadMode` of Auto does not give the best performance; specifying a mode will always be better. Auto is the default value.
`DiffGram`	Reads a `DiffGram` (a format that contains both the original and the current values of the data) applying changes from the `DiffGram` to the `DataSet`.
`Fragment`	Reads XML documents, such as those generated by executing FOR XML queries against an instance of SQL Server. When `XmlReadMode` is set to Fragment, the default namespace is read as the inline schema.
`IgnoreSchema`	Ignores any inline schema and reads data into the existing `DataSet` schema. If any data does not match the existing schema, it is discarded (including data from differing namespaces defined for the `DataSet`).

Table 10-14 `XmlReadMode` Values

XmlReadMode Value	Description
InferSchema	Ignores any inline schema, and instead infers schema from the data and loads the data. If the DataSet already contains a schema, the current schema is extended by adding new tables or adding columns to existing tables. An exception is thrown if the inferred table already exists but has a different namespace, or if any of the inferred columns conflict with existing columns.
ReadSchema	Reads any inline schema and loads the data. If the DataSet already contains a schema, new tables may be added to the schema, but an exception is thrown if any tables in the inline schema already exist in the DataSet.

Table 10-14 XmlReadMode Values *(continued)*

The resulting DataSet (xmlDataS) now holds the content of the Order.xml file and the schema is set by Order.xsd. Any data that does not match the Order.xsd schema will be discarded.

In the next example, we will read the XML data and the inline schema of the document:

```
private void ReadXmlandSchema()
{
  try
  {
    DataSet xmlDataS = new DataSet();

    // read in the Order.xml document using the inline schema of the file.
    xmlDataS.ReadXml("Order.xml", XmlReadMode.ReadSchema);
  }
  catch(Exception e)
  {
    Console.WriteLine("Exception: " + e.ToString());
  }
}
```

The ReadSchema mode will read the inline schema from the XML document; the schema and the data are then loaded into the DataSet.

Writing XML from a DataSet

A DataSet can be created based on the processing needs of the application, resulting in a schema that may be rather complex. There are good reasons for saving (*persisting*) that schema for future processing in your application. The DataSet object provides two methods for reading and writing the schema: WriteXmlSchema and ReadXmlSchema.

The *schema* of a `DataSet` can be written to a file, `Stream`, `TextWriter`, or `XmlWriter`. This is the syntax for the `WriteXmlSchema` method:

```
WriteXmlSchema(FileName | Stream | TextWriter | XmlWriter)
```

 EXAM TIP The schema is usually reused during a read operation when the data is to be imported into another application.

In the following example, we will write out the schema resulting from a `ReadXml` call with the mode set to `ReadSchema`:

```
private void WriteSchema()
{
  try
  {
    DataSet xmlDataS = new DataSet();

    // read in the Order.xml document using the inline schema of the file.
    xmlDataS.ReadXml("Order.xml", XmlReadMode.ReadSchema);

    // save the schema to a file
    xmlDataS.WriteXmlSchema("Order.xsd");
  }
  catch(Exception e)
  {
    Console.WriteLine("Exception: " + e.ToString());
  }
}
```

After the preceding method executes, the schema of the `Order.xml` document is written into the `Order.xsd` file, which can be used in further processing.

To save the *data* from a `DataSet`, we use the `WriteXml` method, which can save to either a file, `Stream`, `TextWriter`, or `XmlWriter`. The syntax is as follows:

```
WriteXml(FileName | Stream | TextWriter | XmlWriter, XmlWriteMode)
```

The `XmlWriteMode` parameter specifies how the schema of the `DataSet` should be dealt with. Table 10-15 details the values.

Table 10-15	`XmlWriteMode` **Value**	**Description**
XmlWriteMode Values	IgnoreSchema	The output is an XML file containing the data from the `DataSet`; no schema information is generated.
	WriteSchema	The output is an XML file containing the data from the `DataSet` and the inline schema.
	DiffGram	The output is an XML file in the `DiffGram` format containing both the original and current values for the data.

In the following example, we will write the data and inline schema from the `DataSet` to an XML document file.

```
private void WriteSchema()
{
  try
  {
    DataSet xmlDataS = new DataSet();

    // read in the Order.xml document using the inline schema of the file.
    xmlDataS.ReadXml("Order.xml", XmlReadMode.ReadSchema);

    // save the data and the schema to a file
    xmlDataS.WriteXml("Orders.xml", XmlWriteMode.WriteSchema);
  }
  catch(Exception e)
  {
    Console.WriteLine("Exception: " + e.ToString());
  }
}
```

The resulting file (`Orders.xml`) contains the inline schema of the `DataSet` and the data.

Using the XmlDataDocument Object

The `XmlDataDocument` is based on the standard Document Object Model (DOM) that gives you the power to load, manipulate, and save XML documents through code. The `XmlDataDocument` object can be used to represent the same data as the `DataSet` can. The difference between the two representations is the structure; a `DataSet` is represented as a relational structure, while the `XmlDataDocument` represents the data as a hierarchical structure. The `XmlDataDocument` exposes a database as an XML DOM tree of nodes, giving you the power to treat any data as if it were an XML document.

There are a number of reasons to use the `XmlDataDocument`:

- The `XmlDataDocument` gives you the ability to work with any data by using the Document Object Model (DOM).

- An `XmlDataDocument` can be synchronized with a `DataSet` so that any changes in one will be reflected in the other.

- When an XML document is loaded into an `XmlDataDocument`, the schema is preserved; the `DataSet` does not preserve the entire schema, only the parts that are used in that particular `DataSet`.

The `XmlDataDocument` can be created from an existing `DataSet` object to provide two ways to manipulate the same data. The following code snippet shows how to instantiate the `XmlDataDocument`:

```
XmlDataDocument xmlDoc;
xmlDoc = new XmlDataDocument(theDataSet);
```

The result is that the xmlDoc document now represents a hierarchical view of the relational data in theDataSet.

The reverse, providing a relational view of hierarchical data, can be performed by using the Load method of the XmlDataDocument object. These are the steps involved:

1. Create and populate a DataSet with schema.

2. Create and synchronize an XmlDataDocument with the DataSet.

3. Load the XML data into the XmlDataDocument object.

The following code segment illustrates these steps.

```
// declare the variables
DataSet theDS;
XmlDataDocument theDoc;

// instantiate the DataSet and load the schema
theDS = new DataSet();
theDS.ReadXmlSchema("Order.xsd");

// instantiate the XmlDataDocument and synchronize with theDS
theDoc = new XmlDataDocument(theDS);

// load the XML data into the XmlDataDocument object
theDoc.Load("order.xml");
```

The result of the preceding segment is that the two objects (theDS and theDoc) are synchronized and theDS provides the relational view of the hierarchical data in theDoc.

 EXAM TIP   One important feature of the XmlDataDocument is the ability to apply an Extensible Stylesheet Language Transformation (XSLT) style sheet to the document. XSLT is used to change the XML document, either for presentation or to provide a different schema for the data. The steps involved are to load the XML data into the XmlDataDocument and then apply the XSLT document in order to perform the transformation. The XmlDataDocument object has a number of methods that assist in the transformation of the document. The Load() method is used to load an XSLT document, and the Transform() method is used to perform the transformation.

Using the DataAdapter to Access Existing Data

The DataAdapter classes provide the connection between a data source and the DataSet defining the methods to read and write data. The DataAdapter classes contain a number of methods used to work with the data as well as the data connection that is used to fill a DataSet object with data from the table. The focus of the DataAdapter is a single DataTable object in the DataSet, and a single RowSet from an SQL statement or stored procedure.

There are two primary DataAdapters:

- OleDbDataAdapter   Use this adapter with any data source that can be accessed through an OLE-DB provider.
- SqlDataAdapter   Use this adapter to access Microsoft SQL Server 7.0 or higher.

The DataAdapter classes expose some properties that are used to configure the operation of the adapter, and they are listed in Table 10-16.

The SQL statement that are stored in the properties can be an SQL sentence or a stored procedure call; the properties are used to define the behavior of the DataAdapter. When you create a DataAdapter, you do not have to create all four commands—to create a read-only DataAdapter, only the SelectCommand is needed; if inserts are required, define the InsertCommand; and so on.

The DataAdapter classes also expose some methods used to work with the data, as listed in Table 10-17.

Creating the DataAdapter

The DataAdapter can be created as a specific adapter for a connection, or as you will see later in this section, as a generic adapter used to load data into a DataSet. In order to create a new DataAdapter, use the following steps:

1. Add the System.Data.SqlClient namespace to your source file.
2. Declare and instantiate a DataAdapter object.
3. Declare and instantiate a connection object.
4. Declare and instantiate a command object.
5. Assign the command object to the SelectCommand property.

Table 10-16	Property	Description
Properties of the DataAdapter Classes	SelectCommand	The SQL statement used to populate the DataSet
	InsertCommand	The SQL statement used to insert new data into the data source
	UpdateCommand	The SQL statement used to update the data source
	DeleteCommand	The SQL statement used to delete rows from the data source

Method	Description
Fill	Uses the SelectCommand to retrieve data from the data source and populate the DataSet
Update	Uses the UpdateCommand to edit the data in the data source
GetChange	Creates a new DataSet that contains the changes made to a DataSet
Merge	Merges two DataSet objects, commonly used in middle-tier applications to include client data changes into the database

Table 10-17 Methods of the DataAdapter Classes

The following code segment performs these steps using the SqlDataAdapter:

```
// reference the namespace
using System.Data.SqlClient;

// declare and instantiate the DataAdapter
SqlDataAdapter sqlDa = new SqlDataAdapter();

// declare and instantiate the connection
SqlConnection cnNw;
string strCn = "data source=(local);initial catalog=Northwind;" +
               "user id=sa;";
cnNw = new SqlConnection(strCn);

// declare and instantiate the command
SqlCommand cmNw;
cmNw = new SqlCommand("SELECT * FROM Employees", cnNw);

// assign the command to the Adapters SelectCommand
sqlDa.SelectCommand = cmNw;
```

In the preceding example, the SelectCommand was created using a SELECT statement; you can, however, bind the command object to a stored procedure. The following code segment shows that technique:

```
// reference the namespace
using System.Data.SqlClient;

// declare and instantiate the DataAdapter
SqlDataAdapter sqlDa = new SqlDataAdapter();

// declare and instantiate the connection
SqlConnection cnNw;
string strCn = "data source=(local);initial catalog=Northwind;" +
               "user id=sa;";
```

```
cnNw = new SqlConnection(strCn);

// declare and instantiate the command
SqlCommand cmNw;
cmNw = new SqlCommand();
cmNw.Connection = cnNw;
cmNw.CommandType = CommandType.StoredProcedure;
cmNw.CommandText = "GetEmployees";

// assign the command to the Adapters SelectCommand
sqlDa.SelectCommand = cmNw;
```

A `DataSet` can be defined and populated from a `DataAdapter` by creating a `DataTable` and using the `Fill` method of the `DataSet` to perform the load. The following example creates a `DataTable` (called `Employees`) and populates it:

```
// declare and instantiate the DataSet
DataSet dsEmp = new DataSet();
dsEmp.Tables.Add(new DataTable("Employees"));

// Fill the DataTable using the cnNw connection
dsEmp.Fill(cnNw, "Employees");
```

The `DataTable` enforces all constraints defined for it during the `Fill` operation. To streamline the operation, you should turn off constraint checking by calling the `BeginLoadData()` method before the `Fill` call, and `EndLoadData()` after the operation. To do so, the last line in the preceding example would be replaced with the following:

```
// Fill the DataTable using the cnNw connection
// turn off constraint checking
dsEmp.Tables[0].BeginLoadData();
dsEmp.Fill(cnNw, "Employees");
// turn on constraint checking
dsEmp.Tables[0].EndLoadData();
```

To fill a `DataSet` from a `DataAdapter` using the commands of the adapter, use the following code:

```
dsEmp.Employees.BeginLoadData();
sqlDa.Fill(dsEmp.Employees);
dsEmp.Employees.EndLoadData();
```

Updating the Data Source

The `DataTable` object contains a collection of `DataRow` objects, and these `DataRow` objects have a `RowState` property that indicates the state of the row: whether it has been changed, inserted, or updated. The values for the `RowState` property are listed in Table 10-18.

The `DataSet` also maintains two copies of the row: the original as it was populated from the data source, and the current version as it appears in the `DataSet`. By having these values available together with the `RowState` property, you have full control over

RowState Value	Description
DataRowState.Added	The row has been added since the last call to the AcceptChanges() method.
DataRowState.Deleted	The row has been deleted since the last call to the AcceptChanges() method.
DataRowState.Detatched	The row is created, but has not yet been added to the DataRow collection in the DataSet.
DataRowState.Modified	The row has been modified since the last call to the AcceptChanges() method.
DataRowState.Unchanged	The row has not been modified since the last call to the AcceptChanges() method.

Table 10-18   RowState Values

the data modifications. To accept all the changes you call the AcceptChanges() method.

In order to access either the original or the current version of the data as it is maintained by the DataSet, you have access to the DataRowVersion.Current and DataRowVersion.Original parameters. This allows you to compare and base decisions on the way the data has changed.

Resolving Conflicts

Whenever we use disconnected DataSets, there is a potential for conflict when the data in the DataSet is saved back to the data source. The conflicts are caused by the fact that ADO.NET is using optimistic locking, meaning that the locks in the database are released as soon as the create operation of the DataSet is completed, letting other applications access and modify the data. You need to be aware that conflicts can (and will) occur, and how to resolve them.

The DataSet, DataTable, and DataRow objects each have a HasErrors property that you can use to determine the success of your data updates, and to find out if there were any conflicts.

To resolve conflicts, you can adopt a couple of strategies: *last one wins* ensures that all conflicts will be won by the client that performed the last modification, and a business rule involves the client in the resolution of any conflicts. Conflict resolution must be designed based on the requirements of the application—the business rule can be a component that tries to resolve the conflict automatically, based on the rules defined for the transaction, but in most cases the final arbiter will be an administrator or the user.

The following code segment shows a method for working with the HasErrors property:

```
// try the update, check for any exceptions and deal with the
// conflicts that might be there
try
{
```

```
      daEmp.Update(dsEmp);
}
catch(System.Exception e)
{
// arrive here if there are errors
// first check the DataAdapter, then the tables, rows and columns
  if(dsEmp.HasErrors)
  {
    foreach(DataTable table in dsEmp.Tables)
    {
      if(table.HasErrors)
      {
        foreach(DataRow row in table.Rows)
        {
          if(row.HasErrors)
          {
            Console.WriteLine("Row: {0} has {1}",
                               row["EmployeeID"], row.RowError);
            foreach(DataColumn col in row.GetColumnsInError())
            {
              Console.WriteLine("{0} Error in this column", column.ColumnName);
            }
            // clear the error and reject the changes
            // i.e. make the current view the same as the original
            row.ClearErrors();
            row.RejectChanges();
          }
        }
      }
    }
  }
}
```

 NOTE The DataAdapter will also be used in Chapters 22 and 25, which deal with the Web and Windows Forms.

Summary

In this chapter, you were exposed to the core concepts of one of the largest topic areas to be covered in the exam. Additional Web and Windows-based information will be presented in greater detail later in the book, but we've established our groundwork here.

Data is the root of all applications, and the ways you access data determines the success of your application. You were exposed to the ADO.NET concepts and the object models that make it possible to treat data in the same way irrespective of where it originated. The connection object encapsulates the data source to the point where we no longer need to know the specifics of the vendor's implementation. The DataSet makes the data available in a disconnected table, and it has moved the data architecture forward by leaps and bounds.

Because this topic is so large, it is important that you practice using the ADO.NET environment as much as you can to ensure you have a firm grasp of the topics we covered here.

The next chapter will introduce you to the class library that lies at the bottom of the C# language and the .NET Framework.

Test Questions

1. What does the following SQL statement return, assuming that all tables and column names are correct?

```
SELECT FirstName, StreetAddress
FROM Employees
JOIN AddressBook
ON Employees.EmpID = AddressBook.EmpID
```

   A. Nothing, the JOIN syntax is wrong.

   B. All the records from the Employees table, and only the matching ones from the StreetAddress table.

   C. All the records from the StreetAddress table, and only the matching records from the Employees table.

   D. Only the matching records from the two tables.

2. What is a transaction?

   A. A banking term.

   B. A concept used to describe a step in the business process.

   C. A combination of DML steps that must succeed or the data is returned to its initial state.

   D. A combination of DDL steps that must succeed or the data is returned to its initial state.

3. What object is used to encapsulate a data source?

   A. XxxConnection

   B. XxxCommand

   C. XxxDataAdapter

   D. DataSet

4. What object is used to encapsulate a rowset?

   A. DataSet

   B. DataAdapter

   C. DataRowSet

   D. DataTable

5. What property is used on the `DataTable` to indicate a conflict after an update?

   A. `HasConflict`

   B. `HasError`

   C. `HasCollision`

   D. `HasDataError`

6. What is a `DiffGram`?

   A. An XML file containing both the original and current values for the data.

   B. An XML file containing the difference between original and current data.

   C. A `DataSet` loaded with two XML files, resulting in the difference being current.

   D. A `DataSet` loaded with an XML file and the original values from the data source.

7. How is the data represented in an `XmlDataDocument`?

   A. Relational

   B. Flat

   C. Hierarchical

   D. Tabular

8. When would you not use the `OleDbConnection` object?

   A. To connect to an SQL 7.0 database.

   B. To connect to a DB/2 database.

   C. To connect to an Access database.

   D. To connect to an SQL 6.5 database.

9. What connection is used in ADO.NET to connect to an SQL Server 6.0?

   A. Use the `OleDbConnection` class.

   B. Upgrade the server to SQL 7.0 and use the `OleDbConnection` class.

   C. Upgrade the server to SQL 2000 and use the `OdbcConnection` class.

   D. Upgrade the server to SQL 6.5 and use the `SqlConnection` class.

10. On what object is the transaction in ADO.NET focused on?

    A. The command object

    B. The `DataSet` object

    C. The connection object

    D. The `DataAdapter` object

11. What is the SQL argument that sorts the data returned by an SQL SELECT statement?

    A. GROUP BY

    B. SORT BY

    C. SORTED

    D. ORDER BY

12. What combination of methods are used to improve the speed of the `Fill()` method of the `DataAdapter`?

    A. `BeginFillData()` and `EndFillData()`

    B. `StartFillData()` and `EndFillData()`

    C. `BeginLoadData()` and `EndLoadData()`

    D. `StartLoadData()` and `EndLoadData()`

13. The following SQL INSERT statement fails. What is the most probable reason for the failure?

    ```
    INSERT INTO Employees VALUES (42,'Bob','Carol', 12)
    ```

    A. Syntax error in the INSERT statement.

    B. The columns in the Employees table are not in the indicated order (`int, char, char, int`).

    C. The Employees database does not have a default table defined.

    D. The SELECT INTO permission is not set.

14. In the following code, what is the result of compilation?

    ```
    using System;
    using System.Data;
    using System.Xml;

    class question14
    {
      public static void Main()
      {
        DataSet dsNw = new DataSet();
        string strCn = "data source=(local);user id=sa;" +
                       "initial catalog=northwind;";
        SqlConnection cnNw = new SqlConnection(strCn);
        string strSQL = "SELECT * FROM Employees";
        SqlDataAdapter daNw = new SqlDataAdapter(strSQL, cnNw);
        daNw.Fill(dsNw, "Employees");
        XmlDataDocument doc = new XmlDataDocument(dsNw);
        doc.Save(Console.Out);
      }
    }
    ```

    A. No errors

    B. One error

C. Two errors.

D. Three errors.

15. What is the result of the following SQL statement?

```
USE Northwind
DELETE Employees
```

A. The Employees table is emptied.

B. The current record is deleted.

C. Syntax error, the USE command is wrong.

D. The Employee database in the Northwind server is deleted.

Test Answers

1. **D.** The syntax is correct so all the matching rows will be returned.

2. **C.** Transaction work with DML (INSERT, UPDATE, DELETE) statements.

3. **A.** The XxxConnection defines how the application will connect and authenticate to the data source.

4. **D.** The DataTable represents a rowset.

5. **B.** The DataTable object uses HasError to indicate conflicts.

6. **A.** DiffGrams are XML documents.

7. **C.**

8. **A.** The SqlDbConnection object is used with Microsoft SQL Server 7.0 and higher.

9. **A.** The SqlDbConnection object is used with Microsoft SQL Server 7.0 and higher.

10. **C.** Transactions are focused on the connection.

11. **D.**

12. **C.**

13. **B.** INSERT statements must match the data types of the inserted columns.

14. **D.** The namespace System.Data.SqlClient is missing resulting in an error on the definition of cnNw and dawn, as well as an error when dawn.Fill() is called.

15. **A.** The lack of a WHERE clause empties the table.

PART III

Exam 70-315: Developing and Implementing Web Applications

Welcome to the Internet and ASP.NET

In this chapter, you will

- Discover the Internet standards
- Delve into the protocols used on the Internet
- Explore XML
- Master the Internet architecture
- Learn about the ASP.NET object architecture

Active Server Pages (ASP) was released in 1996 by Microsoft to act as the interface for web application development centered on their Internet Information Server (IIS). The release of ASP and IIS 3.0 brought a new era for web developers around the world. The ASP object model was programmed with scripted languages like VBScript and ECMAScript (JavaScript).

Scripting of web sites introduced a very convoluted application that was hard to maintain and to scale—this was one of the potential problems in the ASP architecture. With the release of the ASP.NET object model, Microsoft has based their web server architecture on the .NET Framework, which means we can program web applications with any mixture of the .NET languages (C#, C++, J#, JavaScript, and VB .NET from Microsoft), including the third-party Cobol.NET that will be released for the .NET Framework.

In this chapter, you will be introduced to the basics of ASP.NET and we will define the acronyms and look at the technology that will be used throughout this part of the book. We will also create a first web application to display "Hello World!" in the browser. So without any more delays we'll start the journey towards ASP.NET with a visit to the Internet.

The Internet: Its Standards

When the Internet came into being many computer generations ago, it was based on a couple of concepts: TCP/IP for the network protocol, and some simple protocols like HTTP (Hypertext Transfer Protocol) for the connections between web servers and web browsers. In the intervening years, the Internet has benefited from standardization of many of the protocols and processes that run on it. Some of those standards have been included in the core of what Microsoft refers to as ASP.NET. There are a couple of standards maintained by W3C (the World Wide Web Consortium) that are keystones in the ASP.NET architecture—standards like HTTP, XML (Extensible Markup Language), SOAP (Simple Object Access Protocol), and so on.

Before the Internet, there were oracles who predicted that the TCP/IP protocol suite would not survive into the modern world of computers. It was felt that the standardization based on a community process called Request For Comments (RFC) would not be good enough for the future. The community process gives "voting" rights to a large number of interested experts that can add to, vote on, and comment on the proposals (RFCs). That was then, this is now, and the de facto standard for all computing is TCP/IP. You cannot even install a Microsoft Windows 2000 Active Directory infrastructure without it. As a matter of fact, the strength of the Internet is the RFC-based standards. All successful standards have included some form of the RFC process. All RFCs are publicly available through a number of web sites; the Internet Engineering Task Force site (www.ietf.org/rfc.html) is one of many resources for RFCs.

There are a number of standards bodies that control the different standards and conduct meetings to move the standards forward. The W3C is the body that standardizes protocols used on the Internet, such as HTML, HTTP, XHTML, SOAP, and XML. You can find the W3C web page at www.w3c.org. A second important standards organization is the European Computer Manufacturers Association (ECMA), found at www.ecma.ch. ECMA is an organization that has standardized computer languages for use on the Internet. The standard scripting language for all Internet scripting is ECMAScript—a scripting language that is based in part on JavaScript. The .NET Framework's Common Language Runtime (CLR) and C# are both standards under the ECMA umbrella.

In the rest of this section, we will look at the protocols that make up the Internet from TCP/IP to XML.

The TCP/IP Protocols

At the core of the Internet there is a standard made up of a multitude of protocols—that standard is TCP/IP (Transmission Control Protocol/Internet Protocol). TCP/IP started out as a set of protocols designed to let the generals in the U.S. Armed Forces connect their four computers together in a fashion that was as robust as possible without being too big. The protocol suite that was designed became TCP/IP. The network designers used the protocols to provide MILNET, which initially connected the military computers and ultimately was developed into the Internet today.

The standard protocols that make up TCP/IP consist of one protocol for guaranteed traffic delivery (TCP), one protocol for very fast non-guaranteed delivery (UDP), as well as protocols for resolving the address of a given computer from a name (DNS). You will have noticed by now that in the protocol world acronyms rule. Every college or university computer program always has one mandatory course on the acronyms. We will not go that far, but we must define some of these names.

TCP—the Connection-Oriented Protocol

The Transmission Control Protocol (TCP) is one of the core protocols on the Internet; it is a connection-oriented protocol that gives us guaranteed delivery of our data. TCP works very much in the same way as a phone conversation:

1. Dial the number.

2. Request that the person you wish to talk with come to the phone.

3. Introduce yourself.

4. Carry out the conversation.

5. Hang up when you're done.

The key parts of the list can be found in steps 1 through 3—they are called the three-way handshake, involving calling a number, identifying the other party, and identifying yourself. The TCP protocol does exactly that. As part of the three-way handshake, the two computers will configure the parameters they will use to acknowledge data receipt.

All web-related network traffic uses TCP as its transport protocol.

UDP—the Connectionless Protocol

The connectionless protocol works more like the post office. You drop your message in a mailbox, but you do not know when, or even if, the message is delivered. The User Datagram Protocol (UDP) is used for data transfer that must use the lowest possible number of resources. The quality control is left to the application rather than the network. UDP is not used by any web applications; it is mostly used by the administration programs for the Internet that let the routers communicate with each other as well as provide the backbone for network monitoring.

Ports

When you connect to a computer on the Internet, you supply the address of the computer you're trying to connect with. This is the same as when you call a courier to deliver a package to someone in an office, and you give the courier the address of the office. Suppose you want to send a letter via a courier to Greg at 1190 George Street in Mimico; this is an office building with eight floors. If that is all the information we give our intrepid courier, he will have to randomly go through the building looking for Greg.

Computers are analogous to business offices; the computer has many applications (employees) that perform different tasks. If we connected using only the address of the computer, we would have to search through all the applications looking for the one we were trying to connect to, which is very inefficient. The solution is to give each application a number (like an employee cubicle number) that can be used to identify the application. When we want to connect, we pass this number along, making the process of finding the application on the computer seamless.

These numbers are commonly called *ports*, and there are 65,536 possible port numbers. To make the port numbers more functional, the first 1,024 ports are defined for use with specific applications (they are called *well-known ports*). For example, one such port is port 80, the port universally used by all web servers. When you try to connect to a web server, the browser will by default try to connect on port 80.

HTML

Hypertext Markup Language (HTML) saw the light of day as part of a much larger standard (Standard Generalized Markup Language, SGML) in 1986. HTML was not used for web pages until the early 1990s but has become a standard by itself since then.

The HTML language defines how various elements on a web page are to be interpreted by the web browser and rendered (displayed). A web browser does not have to understand all the possible elements that are defined in the standard, but if the browser finds an unknown element, it must ignore it. This rule makes it possible for different versions of HTML to be used in different documents—if a new element is added to the standard, all older browsers will ignore the element, while browsers designed for the new version will properly display the element.

Pages that are to be sent to a browser follow a predefined layout, as you can see in the following examples (and in Table 11-1). Elements in HTML consist of an opening and a closing tag surrounding the element. For example, a TITLE tag would be entered like this:

```
<TITLE>An Example Title</TITLE>
```

The element tags are enclosed with angle brackets (< and >), with the slash (/) indicating that the second of the two is a closing tag.

The following HTML document will display the text "Hello HTML World!" in any browser:

```
<HTML>
<HEAD>
  <TITLE>The Hello World Page</TITLE>
</HEAD>
  <BODY>
    <H1>Hello HTML World!</H1>
  </BODY>
</HTML>
```

The elements in this script are listed in Table 11-1.

HTTP

The Hypertext Transfer Protocol is at the heart of the Internet. This is the protocol that gives us the ability to send information seamlessly between web browsers and web servers. HTTP defines how a browser requests a web page and how the server responds to that request.

The standard defines two messages that are used for the communication. The GET message is what the browser uses to request a page, and the POST message is what the server uses to respond to the browser. On the surface, this looks straightforward—the browser

	HTML Element	Description
Table 11-1 The Basic HTML Elements	\<HTML\>	The root element in an HTML page must be the HTML element. It tells the browser to expect the document to contain HTML elements.
	\<HEAD\>	The HEAD element is used to contain information about the page. For instance, the title of a page would be contained in a HEAD element. This element is optional, but if it is used, it must be the first entry after the HTML element.
	\<TITLE\>	The TITLE element defines the text that will be displayed in the title bar of the browser.
	\<BODY\>	The BODY element defines the part of the page that will be displayed. Anything in the BODY element will be interpreted to be displayed.
	\<H1\>	The H1 element identifies the first heading level, and it specifies that the text in the element should be displayed with the largest, boldest font possible. The HTML standard defines headings from H1 through to H6.

sends a GET message and the server sends a POST message. As you will see, however, the browser can also send POST messages that are interpreted as requests by the server.

An HTTP GET message is a maximum of 1,024 characters in length, and it contains the name and path of the document requested on the server. In addition, it should include the browser's model and version, operating system version, screen resolution, username ("anonymous" if not known), and a host of other information about the browser environment.

The POST message has a header that is a maximum of 1,024 characters in length, plus an unlimited body size. POST messages are used to return requested items from the server to the browser, and are also used by FORM elements that are used by the browser to group fields together to return information to the server.

 EXAM TIP   The authors of the exams assume that you have a firm knowledge of HTML, especially the TABLE and FORM elements.

The header in a POST message is virtually the same as for the GET message. The POST message can be used to send any type of data in the body of the message. The type parameter in the header specifies what the data is so the receiver can handle it properly.

XML

When it comes to standards, they don't come any cooler than XML. XML is based on the same standard as HTML (SGML), and it uses the familiar HTML syntax. You will have encountered XML in Chapter 8 already; the following discussion serves as a refresher.

One feature of XML is that it is both human and machine readable. The way XML is structured into a text document makes it possible for a user to read the document and glean information from it, while the structure of the XML document makes it readable from any program, including most modern web browsers. XML is extensible and open, so there are no limits to the kinds of elements that can be added to an XML document—if you need something new, just add it.

There are really only six basic rules that a well-formed XML document must follow:

- There must be one and only one root element.
- There must be opening and closing tags for every element.
- XML is case-sensitive; the tags for an element must be in the same case.
- Elements can be nested, but they must be nested properly. The following example shows proper nesting:

```
<A>
    <B>
    …
    </B>
</A>
```

- Attributes must have their data enclosed in quotes.
- Attributes are not allowed to be repeated.

Given that the only requirement of a well-formed XML document is that it must follow these six rules, we could create many different documents to describe the same information. This would cause problems for businesses if customers sent in their XML orders in various formats. The solution to this quandary as you saw in Chapter 8 is to use a *grammar* or *schema*. Using an XML schema, we can guarantee that the XML documents all have the same structure. The XML schema defines the layout of the XML document, the names of the elements, the data types for those elements, and how the elements are related to each other.

 EXAM TIP The use of XML in virtually all configuration files means that you will be presented with XML documents in a large number of questions. Make sure you are familiar with how to read XML documents.

Internet Architecture

The Internet is a client/server architecture, where the client (browser) requests services from the server (web server). This architecture is at the center of the popularity explosion we have seen for the Internet. It is the place where we get our news, buy our groceries, and plan our travel, just to mention some of the many things that are possible because the Internet is built around the client/server model.

There are a couple of different ways a Web Server and Browser client can interact using the models that are used with the Internet, and they will be detailed in the following sections. The Internet models use different locations to perform the execution of programs (for example, in the client browser or at the server), as well as defining how the data that is presented to the client is stored (static in premade web pages or dynamically as a result of the client's request for information).

Static Web Pages—the Beginning

The most prolific web architecture is based on the static web page. This page does not change when it is sent from the hard drive of the server to the browser. A static page is usually manually typed into a file with the .htm or .html extension, and the exact content and layout of the web page is determined when you save the file.

As an example, let's create a static web page that greets the client (browser) in multiple languages. Because we do not know what language the client uses, we will use as many languages as we know. By writing the following HTML code and saving it as Greeting.htm, you will create a page that produces the output shown in Figure 11-1.

```
<html>
<head>
  <title>The Greeting Page</title>
</head>
<body>
  <h1>Welcome</h1>
  <h1>Välkommen</h1>
  <h1>Willkommen</h1>
  <h1>Bienvenu</h1>
  <h1>Bienvenido</h1>
  <hr>
  <br>
  <p>Welcome to our International page
</body>
</html>
```

Every time this page is loaded in the client's browser, it will display the same information; it is static. The content of the page was determined before the request for the page was made—it was determined when the page was saved to the disk.

So how does the HTML page get to the client's browser from the hard drive of the web server? The following steps outline the process, which is shown in Figure 11-2:

1. The user requests the page through the browser, and the request is sent to the web server.

2. The web server finds the page on its hard drive, and packages it up as a response.

3. The web server returns the response to the client browser.

4. The browser receives the response, processes the HTML code, and displays the page.

Figure 11-1
Displaying a static
web page

The static page was the model for many web sites, some of which were very innovative in providing changing content—these interesting web sites resulted from the hard work of the webmasters who managed the pages and updated them on an ongoing basis. One problem with static pages is just that; it takes a large effort to keep the pages updated as information changes.

Another challenge of static pages is that they give us no way of personalizing the page based on the users' preferences or their previous browsing history. The static page is written before the client requests it, so there is no possibility of making changes based on the actual conditions when the page is used.

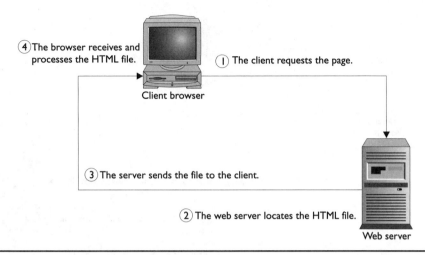

Figure 11-2   The process of serving a static web page

All browsers can display the HTML code that makes up a static web page. However, with static pages there is no way to secure the code, so it will always be available to anyone who wants to see it and copy it.

There are two ways to work around the limitations of the static web page—we will explore both techniques in the following sections.

Dynamic Web Pages—the Client Story

One architecture that emerged in the quest for more dynamic and responsive web pages used the client's browser to process the dynamic behavior of the web pages. This client-side scripting model involves the web server sending HTML and scripting code (JavaScript, VBScript, and so on) to the client browser.

When the client's browser requests a page that contains scripting instructions, there are two common ways of providing the information to the client. In the first, the web server sends one HTML file in response to the client's request. If the scripting code is stored in a separate file, the web server will combine the static (HTML) portion with the script file and return the combination to the client. A second technique that may be more common in the Microsoft IIS world is to combine the scripts and the HTML in advance, so that the file requested already contains both.

When the browser receives the response from the web server, it will process the file and display the page, this time with the dynamic scripts added in. The model is shown in Figure 11-3.

Our step-by-step model for delivering the page to the browser has now changed to include five steps:

1. The user requests the page through the browser, and the request is sent to the web server.

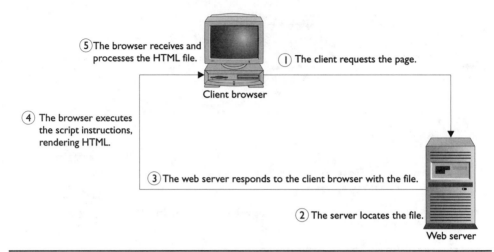

Figure 11-3   The process of serving a web page to a dynamic client

2. The web server finds the page on its hard drive, plus the server might also have to locate the file with the scripts, and it packages up the response.

3. The web server returns the response to the client browser.

4. The browser receives and executes the scrip instructions and renders (returns) HTML for display.

5. The browser processes the HTML code and displays the page.

While the client-side model was very innovative a number of years ago, there is a problem with it in that different browser vendors have totally different support for the scripting and the architecture of the browser (known as the DOM—Document Object Model). In addition, the scripts must be sent down to the client to be executed, resulting in a larger page size and longer download times. And if the script needs to access server resources, such as databases, it is the client that must connect and manipulate the resource, which again is not very efficient. There is possibly an even more serious problem in that the script code is clearly available in the client's browser, creating a security problem.

The result of these limitations is that the client-side model has fallen out of favor with web site developers. The current web site architecture is to use the server to run scripts to create the HTML that the browser will then display, as we will see in the next section.

Dynamic Web Pages—the Server Story

The server-side web site model is based on the ability of the server to perform processing on the data that is being sent to the client. The file the client asks for contains HTML and scripting instructions, and the server converts this mix of display instructions (HTML) and processing instructions (written using scripting languages such as JavaScript or VBScript) into the HTML code that is sent to the client. Our delivery model now has an additional step for the server to route the page through the processing. We no longer do that processing on the client:

1. The user requests the page through the browser, and the request is sent to the web server.

2. The web server finds the page on its hard drive.

3. The web server routes the file with processing instructions to a part of the server that will perform the processing.

4. The web server returns the HTML response to the client browser.

5. The browser receives the response, processes the HTML code, and displays the page.

This process is shown in Figure 11-4.

The benefits for developers are enormous: all code can be developed for a known environment (the server) rather than for whatever the client system is using, the code is secure because it never leaves the server, and only the resulting dynamic HTML is returned to the client. This model is the base for the older ASP and now the ASP.NET architecture.

The main benefit of this model is that what is sent to the browser to be displayed is not created until after the client requests the page—this produces a dynamic page. The following example contains one possible way of creating a Greeting page that displays the time at the server when the page is requested by the client.

```
<html>
<head>
  <title>The Greeting Page</title>
</head>
<body>
  <h1>Welcome</h1>
  <h1>Välkommen</h1>
  <h1>Willkommen</h1>
  <h1>Bienvenu</h1>
  <h1>Bienvenido</h1>
  <hr>
  <br>
  <p>Welcome to our International page
  <p>The time here in the Dynamic WebLand is:  <%=Time()%>
</body>
</html>
```

The file is saved on the web server using the name Greeting.asp. The <% and %> tag delimiters tell the server process that the content of the element is a script to be executed. The =Time() script returns the current time on the server. Saving the file with an extension of .asp tells the server to send the file to the process that handles .asp files rather than to return the file without processing.

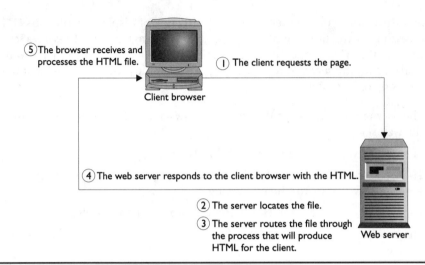

Figure 11-4   The process of serving a dynamic web page from the server.

The preceding example used the ASP scripting model, and we will get back to this example later in the chapter to see how we can develop the page using ASP.NET. First, though, we must look at the technologies in use.

The Internet Technologies

Looking back at the discussion we had earlier about the standards that drive the Internet, it is understandable to think that all is rosy—new standards are released and everyone implements them at once. Unfortunately, the Information Systems world doesn't change at the drop of a hat. The term *legacy* conveys the idea that there are older standards still being used. The challenge to us as developers is to find the most suitable technologies from the current standards that will solve the problem we are developing our application for, while trying to support as many legacy systems as we can in order to make our application available to as many systems as possible.

Client-Side Technologies

There are a number of technologies in use on the client side that we need to look at. The client-side technologies were developed to solve problems and, in some cases, to be "different" than a competitor.

VBScript

Microsoft developed a scripted version of the popular Visual Basic language, VBScript, which was introduced in Internet Explorer 3.0. The VBScript language is not case sensitive, making it the language of choice for VB developers. It is a direct competitor to JavaScript. VBScript has one serious drawback: it is only available in Microsoft browsers, making it of limited use on the client.

JavaScript

JavaScript was originally known as LiveScript when Netscape developed it for use on their web server and browser; the language was released in the Netscape 2 browser. The scripting language is based on the C family of languages, and the name was changed from LiveScript to JavaScript when Sun Microsystems joined forces with Netscape. The base of JavaScript is the C-style syntax (which Java uses, as well), and as a language it is more in line with classical development languages. In addition, the standard script language is ECMAScript, which is virtually the same as JavaScript.

Java Applets

Java is a name that describes a number of different technologies; it is among others a language, a runtime environment, and a deployment environment. Java was originally developed as a language that would solve some of the problems found in developing applications in C++. Java is firmly in the C family of languages, but is also an object-oriented language. Java applets are small components that require a container to execute, and the most common container is a web browser.

Both Microsoft Internet Explorer and Netscape Navigator implement the runtime environment for Java applets (Java Virtual Machine—JVM), giving you a wide range of browsers that support this technology. Java has not become the cure-all technology that it was expected to be by some industry experts, but it is still a language that has growing support in the web-development community.

ActiveX Controls

The ActiveX control is a Microsoft technology that is very much dependent on the Windows platform for its use. The ActiveX controls are usually written in C++, but can also be developed using VB. The technology is limited to use in Internet Explorer and so has gone out of vogue. Netscape Navigator can use ActiveX controls with an add-on, but if we have to make the user install specific software to work with our site, there will be a large number of users who will not install the add-on and therefore will not be able to take advantage of our pages. For these reasons, ActiveX controls have fallen into the legacy category.

Server-Side Technologies

The server-side technologies are add-ons to the server software. They process the requested file before it is returned to the client, and they produce HTML as their output. The aim is to be able to dynamically build the HTML responses using a technology that does not need to be installed on the client, making the design as browser neutral as possible. The first server-side technology was CGI, and the most current is ASP.NET.

CGI

The Common Gateway Interface (CGI) has been used on web sites for quite some time; it is one of the most widely used technologies for creating dynamic content sites. CGI uses a script to execute a program on the server, and that program can then perform the tasks that are needed to build the response.

The most common language that is used for scripting with CGI is Perl. CGI is the mechanism that makes a specific program run; it is not the architecture for the web site, as ASP or ASP.NET are. Perl is the language used to provide the dynamic behavior of the CGI application.

Some issues with using CGI are that the CGI environment almost forces the developer to use languages like C, C++, and Perl (languages with strong string-manipulation functionality), and even though these languages are very powerful, they are also the languages that have the longest learning curve in the industry. CGI development also requires extra power on the server to be able to support a given load in multi-user environments because the CGI process must run separately from the web server.

CGI, with its history of having been around when the Internet was young, has aged well and is still very popular with many large web sites. The CGI technology's ability to operate on virtually any platform will ensure its popularity for quite some time.

ASP

Active Server Pages (ASP) are built using either VBScript or JavaScript, and they have access to the same services as a Windows application, including ADO (ActiveX Data Objects) for database access, SMTP (Simple Mail Transfer Protocol) for e-mail, and the entire COM (Component Object Model) structure used in the Windows environment. ASP is now a legacy technology and is commonly called *classic ASP*.

ASP is implemented through a dynamic-link library (asp.dll) that is called by the IIS server when an .asp page is requested from the server. When ASP was released, it made it possible for developers in the Windows family of servers to start developing dynamic web sites, and although the ASP technology has some very good features, it also has some that make developers cringe. Speed is one—every time a page is loaded, the script must be processed through the asp.dll component. Being limited to scripted languages for development is another problem.

JSP

Java Server Pages (JSP) is a technology that lets you leverage your Java knowledge by combining HTML and Java code to build a dynamic response from the server. The JSP technology is available for almost all web servers, including IIS, giving the panacea of platform independence for the code.

PHP

PHP is an acronym with two meanings—the original meaning was Personal Home Pages, and the acronym currently translates to PHP Hypertext Preprocessor (that sought-after acronym within an acronym). PHP is similar to ASP in architecture and is built using a scripting language reminiscent of C and Perl. PHP is open source and is available for many different platforms.

ColdFusion

ColdFusion is a commercial product that can be added to any web server. It uses its own HTML-like extensions to produce the server-side dynamic response.

ASP.NET

Finally! We have now made it to the topic of this part of the book, ASP.NET, Microsoft's newest and most powerful web-server technology designed to create dynamic server-side pages. ASP.NET is implemented as a server component (`aspnet_isapi.dll`) that uses the .NET Framework to perform all the processing for the dynamic page. The rest of Part III will deal with the specifics of ASP.NET, starting in the next section, where you will discover what ASP.NET is and start learning how to control it.

ASP.NET

ASP.NET is distributed by Microsoft as part of the .NET Framework, which is made available as a free download from the Microsoft download site. In addition to ASP.NET, the .NET Framework also contains the runtime environment for all the .NET languages (Visual C# .NET, Visual C++ .NET, Visual Basic .NET, and JScript .NET). This runtime environment includes the compilers as well as the base class library.

In our investigation of this environment, we will start with a quick "Hello Web World!" web application.

Hello Web World!

For this exercise, you will need to set up your computer for use with ASP.NET. We will make the assumption that you have successfully installed Windows 2000 with IIS 5.0 and Visual Studio .NET.

The first step is to test the installation of IIS and learn how to access web pages on the local computer. To do so, you will need to connect to IIS through Internet Explorer. The following steps detail that test:

1. Open Internet Explorer.

2. Enter **http://localhost** in the Address bar, and press ENTER.

3. The result should be a default page from the web server.

 NOTE The special computer name `localhost` is defined as the computer it is used on—it is an alias for your computer. The special IP address 127.0.0.1 is also defined to be the local computer.

Step two is to create a directory to store your web pages. This new directory will be located in the default root directory for IIS, which is the directory you will access when you type http://localhost. The new directory you are creating will be a subdirectory of the root directory, so you can access this directory by using http://localhost/csw. The name csw stands for C Sharp Windows and is a name we made up for this book.

Here's how to create the new directory:

1. Open a "Visual Studio .NET Command Prompt" window by selecting Start | Programs | Microsoft Visual Studio .NET | Visual Studio .NET Tools | Visual Studio .NET Command Prompt).

2. Navigate to the c:\InetPub\WWWRoot directory by entering **cd\ InetPub\WWWRoot**.

3. Create a new directory called csw by entering **md csw**.

 NOTE We will refer to the "Visual Studio .NET Command Prompt" window as the command prompt from now on.

Now that we have a directory, we can create our first ASP.NET program. At the command prompt, change the directory to the one you created (csw). Then, at the command prompt, open a new file with the Notepad editor by entering **notepad HelloOne.aspx**, and confirm that Notepad should create a new file.

Now you can enter the following ASP.NET code in the editor. The line numbers are for reference only; they are not to be entered in the program:

```
1.  <script language="c#" runat="server">
2.    void Page_Load()
3.    {
4.      lblTime.Text = "Hello Web World! The time here is " +
5.                     DateTime.Now.Hour.ToString() + ":" +
6.                     DateTime.Now.Minute.ToString();
7.    }
8.  </script>
9.  <html>
10. <head><title>The Punctual Web Server</title></head>
11.   <body>
12.     <h1>Welcome</h1>
13.     Here in ASP.NET Server Land the current time is:
14.     <asp:label id="lblTime" runat="server" />
15.   </body>
16. </html>
```

Save the page from Notepad, and view the page in Internet Explorer by typing the address into the address bar: **http://localhost/csw/HelloOne.aspx**. The code produces the display in Figure 11-5.

The first code line tells the ASP.NET environment that the program in this file should execute (runat) at the server, and that the language of the file is C#:

```
<script language="c#" runat="server">
```

The code in line 2 is the code that will run when the page loads.

Figure 11-5
The display from
the first ASP.NET
program

Lines 4, 5, and 6 are actually the same line split over three physical lines; we did that to make the line fit on the page while still being readable. The line sets the content of a label to the hello message and then adds the current time: the method call `DateTime.Now.Hour.ToString()` returns a string (converted by `ToString()`) representing the current hour, and the plus (+) operator concatenates the strings together to create a string with the hour and minute of the current time.

Between lines 9 and 16 we have a normal HTML document, except for line 14, which uses the new ASP.NET capability to run a control on the server and render it on the client using standard HTML code. Line 14 creates a label control on the server (`runat="server"`), sets the ID so we can refer to it by name as we did in line 4, and it is identified as an ASP.NET control (`asp:`).

Congratulations, you have created your first ASP.NET application (that's a big word for one page of code, but it does something, so we call it an application). Now you can move on to learning more about the object model used in ASP.NET. The next section will take you into the exciting world of the five ASP.NET objects that make the whole thing rock.

Before we go on, though, first a note about your choice of editor. You can use your favorite text editor for creating this code. We use the Notepad editor because it is part of the operating system. The reason for allowing this choice of editor is so that we can focus on the code and the object model rather than on the Visual Studio .NET IDE. The Visual Studio .NET IDE will be used for some of the form-building exercises and debugging sessions to explore the debugging technology, but we will use Notepad as the editor whenever possible.

The Object Model of ASP.NET

In this section you will explore the heart of ASP.NET—the five objects that are possibly the most important part of ASP.NET. These objects are listed in Table 11-2.

The objects of ASP.NET are the heart of the system; they are used to control the application and the session, making it possible to build *stateful* applications. A stateful application is one that remembers (stores) client data while the client goes away to do something different—such as go to another site to check for some information, or drink a cup of coffee.

The issue of state is one that pits developer ease against the "S" word, *scalability*. A scalable system is a software system that can be expanded (scaled) to support more clients by merely adding hardware. This book is not the place for a big scalability discussion, but you need to know about keeping state, so the "S" word must be introduced. Keeping state information on the server consumes server resources and in turn lowers scalability because we are limiting growth by rapidly using up the resources. Keeping the state information on the client will use more network resources to send the information back and forth to the server, also resulting in a lowered scalability. The weighing of resource usage and state is very important when designing an application.

All the classes that are used to build the ASP.NET objects are in the `System.Web` namespace. For example, the `Response` object is an instance of the `System.`

ASP.NET Object	Description
Request	Gives the program access to the information from the client requesting the web page.
Response	Encapsulates the data returned to the client.
Session	Manages the data (state) of one user connected to the web server. The `Session` object is used to store data that must be available while the client is connected.
Application	Provides the central definition of the entire web application, and is usually used to store global data.
Server	Provides system utilities and information at the server level.

Table 11-2   The ASP.NET Objects

Web.HttpResponse class. We refer to it as the Response object because the instance of the HttpResponse class is referenced through the Response property of the Page object.

When a file with the .aspx extension such as ThePage.aspx is requested from the web server, it will be represented as a class called ASP.ThePage_aspx, and from this class an object by the same name will be instantiated. The ASP.ThePage_aspx class inherits from System.Web.UI.Page, which has the references to the ASP.NET objects. Figure 11-6 shows this relationship.

The Page object provides a number of properties that contain references to objects, among them Request, Response, and Session. We will start by looking at the Request Object. The Server and Application objects will also be described.

Now we'll look at the objects and how they are used.

The Request Object

When a web client (a browser) requests a web page from a web server, the server collects the client's HTTP request in the ASP.NET Request object. The information that is encapsulated in the Request object includes details about the client system, including the operating system, browser version, language preferences, form data from the client, and so on. The information is a gold mine for the web server—it can glean information from the Request object to be able to customize the output to meet the user's system configuration and language preference.

We do not have to gather all this information from the user by asking the user to fill in forms manually. The entire HTTP request is packaged into a single object that in essence holds the client's ID and wishes, effectively saying "This is who I am, and this is my request from you." Some properties in the Request object are listed in Table 11-3.

Figure 11-6
The relationship between the .aspx page and the ASP.NET objects

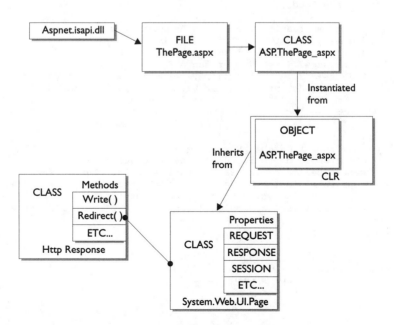

Property	Description
ApplicationPath	Contains the folder on the server that the requested page lives in (such as /csw).
Browser	Holds a reference to the Browser object that gives us information about the client's web browser and what features it has.
Cookies	Provides access to the cookies that the client has from a previous visit to this page. A cookie is a small amount of data the web server has sent to the client that identifies the client to a web page in our site. When the client returns to the page where the web server sent the client browser a cookie, the browser will add that cookie to the request.
QueryString	Gives access to the parameters passed along with a GET request.
Url	Contains the complete address requested by the client (such as http://nopserver.nopcomp.com/csw/HelloOne.aspx).
UserHostAddress	Returns the IP address of the client's computer (such as 10.0.0.102).
UserHostName	Returns the hostname of the client's computer (such as hjalmar.nopcomp.com).
UserLanguage	Returns the language settings that the client browser has been configured to use.

Table 11-3   Some Request Object Properties

The following example will use some of the properties to list the browser information from the client's browser.

```
<%@ Page Language="c#" %>
<script Language="C#" runat="server">
  void Page_Load()
  {
    HttpBrowserCapabilities bc = Request.Browser;
    lblMessage.Text   = "Type = " + bc.Type;
    lblMessage1.Text  = "Name = " + bc.Browser;
    lblMessage2.Text  = "Version = " + bc.Version;
    lblMessage3.Text  = "Major Version = " + bc.MajorVersion;
    lblMessage4.Text  = "Minor Version = " + bc.MinorVersion;
  }
</script>
<html>
  <body>
    <h1>Browser Capabilities</h1>
    <asp:Label id="lblMessage" runat="server" Text=""/><br/>
    <asp:Label id="lblMessage1" runat="server" Text=""/><br/>
    <asp:Label id="lblMessage2" runat="server" Text=""/><br/>
    <asp:Label id="lblMessage3" runat="server" Text=""/><br/>
    <asp:Label id="lblMessage4" runat="server" Text=""/><br/>
  </body>
</html>
```

This code is designed to run when the page is loaded (when the Page_Load() event handler runs) and to create labels as server-side components that are populated with information from the Request object.

The lines like the following define a label:

```
<asp:Label id="lblMessage" runat="server" Text=""/><br/>
```

The label is an ASP.NET object (asp:Label) that is server based (runat="server"), and that has the ID of lblMessage. Server-based controls will create standard HTML code that is returned to the browser—this way we do not have to create different code for different browsers that support different capabilities.

The code that displays the information looks like this:

```
lblMessage.Text    = "Type = " + bc.Type;
```

The Text property of the lblMessage label is assigned the value of the bc.Type property.

The Response Object

We use the Response object to control what is sent back to the client and when it is sent through. The Response object allows us to send HTML, XML, or any of the file types defined for use with HTTP.

Just as the Request object encapsulated the HTTP request from the client browser, the Response object encapsulates the HTTP response that our web server sends back to the client as a result of the request. The Response object is an instance of the HttpResponse class, and the methods and properties provided through the HttpResponse class include Write() and Buffer. Table 11-4 lists the methods and properties of the Response object.

Buffering is a technique that is used to provide for better performance. When we return data from the web server to the client, buffering is controlled through the Response object. The Response object buffers the data we send back to the client, collecting it and sending it all at once, so that the network is used more efficiently. The Response object has a buffer that holds the data as it is being generated for the client. The normal behavior of the Response object is to hold all the buffered data until the page is finished executing. We have control over how the buffer behaves through the properties and methods of the Response object.

 NOTE Buffering works like the vehicles on a freeway: one car can transport 5 passengers while we can transport 60 passengers in a bus. It would be less efficient to transport just one passenger in a bus—the bus uses more resources (gas, tires, and the like). The same is true for the TCP/IP protocols. If we send one character at the time back to the client, we will spend more resources on the overheads than if we can return larger amounts of data at one time.

Method/Property	Description
Buffer	The Buffer property is used to turn on or off the buffer feature of the Response object. The default value is True; meaning that the buffer is turned on. If you set the Buffer property to False, the buffer will be turned off and the data will be sent to the browser as the Response object receives it.
Close()	The Close() method closes the connection to the client.
ContentType	This property lets us read or set the type of data that is sent through the Response object. The content type is described using one of the MIME types that are supported by HTTP. MIME (Multipurpose Internet Mail Extensions) is a standard way of identifying the data currently being sent—browsers use this content type to determine how to deal with the data. HTML code is identified as "text/html", XSL (Extensible Stylesheet Language) is "text/xsl", and GIF images are "image/gif". There are a large number of MIME types, but most browsers only use a handful.
Cookies	The Cookies parameter is used to set (return) a cookie to the client browser.
End()	The End() method sends all data in the buffer to the client and closes the connection. You cannot add any more data to the buffer after the End() call.
Flush()	You use the Flush() method to empty the buffer and send all data to the client. After flushing the buffer, you can still continue adding HTML data to the buffer.
IsClientConnected	This property returns a value indicating whether or not the client is still connected. This property is used before starting anything long-running on the server, just to be sure there is someone out there waiting for the data.
Redirect()	This method lets you send the client to a new web page. One of the rules about the Redirect() method is that no HTML is allowed to be sent to the browser prior to the call to Redirect().
Write()	This method is the workhorse of the Response object. The Write() method sends a string to the buffer. You will probably use this method more than any other in the Response object.

Table 11-4   Some Common Methods and Properties of the Response Object

The following example uses the Response object and the buffer to return data to the client. The first example will write some characters to the browser using buffering; you will see that the entire screen will be drawn in one operation:

```
<%@ Page Language="c#" %>
<html>
  <body>
    <%
```

```
      int i = 0;
      do
      {
        Response.Write("   ");
        i++;
      } while (i < 2000);
    %>
  </body>
<html>
```

This program uses a code block between the two tags <% and %>, and this code will write 2000 Euro symbols in the browser using the buffer. We use a do ... while loop to generate the characters.

In the next example, we will turn off the buffering. Notice how the display is drawn one character at the time.

```
<%@ Page Language="c#" %>
<html>
  <body>
    <%
      int i = 0;
      Response.Buffer = false;
      do
      {
        Response.Write(" @ ");
        i++;
      } while (i < 2000);
    %>
  </body>
<html>
```

In this example, we turned off the buffering by setting the Response.Buffer property to False—the display will be in steps. The effect might be more pronounced on slower servers.

The Server Object

When our program needs to interact with the web server to create server-based objects or find out about any error messages the web server has experienced, it can use the Server object. The Server object represents the actual web server. The Server object is made available through the Page object in the same way as the Request and Response objects were. The Server object is based on the HttpServerUtility class. The functionality that is provided through the Server object is based on a set of general tools that are useful when building ASP.NET applications.

Table 11-5 lists the most common methods and properties of the Server object.

State or No State

The traditional Internet model is one where clients and servers operate in a stateless mode, meaning that the server never remembers the client once it has disconnected

Method/Property	Description
ClearError()	Clears the current error (exception).
CreateObject()	Creates a server-based COM object.
GetLastError()	Returns the previous error (exception).
Transfer()	Stops processing the current page and loads the page transferred to.
UrlDecode()	Converts an encoded URL to a normal string. For example, if we received "great+%26+small+%26+creatures" from the client, the UrlDecode() method would convert it into the string "great & small & creatures".
UrlEncode()	Converts a string to follow the rules of web addresses. When you want to pass a string to the server in the URL (web address), you need to convert the string. If you want to use the URL "heja.aspx?query=great & small & creatures", there will be an error because "?", "&", and spaces are illegal in URLs. The UrlEncode() method converts all the illegal characters to the quoted (encoded) versions. A part of the preceding string becomes "great+%26+small+%26+creatures". Spaces are quoted as "+" and "&" as "%26".

Table 11-5   Members of the Server Object

from the server. However, there are many very good reasons why you want to remember the client, or to keep state:

- **State**   An application that maintains state will remember (or persist) the data defining the client, such as the name, e-mail address, customer number, phone number, and so on. Keeping state has a price tag—we must store the data somewhere and possibly send and receive extra data across the network.

- **Stateless**   A stateless application never remembers anything about the client. There is no overhead associated with storing data.

One common debate among web developers is where to store the shopping cart in an e-mall: on the client or on the server? ASP.NET gives you a large number of solutions that will help you maintain state in your web application, either by storing the information on the server in the objects provided for this purpose (the Application and Session objects) or on the client using cookies.

State is the common term for any data defining an object, so we can refer to state as anything that is part of the application or the client session. When we refer to application state, we mean data that is globally used in the entire application, while session state refers to data that is focused on one user (one session). The following list should give you some ideas of what we mean by the term state:

- The string that contains the company addresses and phone information of the web site's company is application state.

- Database connection settings are application state.
- The shopping cart is session state.
- The customer ID is session state.

The following two sections will explore application and session state through the ASP.NET objects we use to keep that state.

The Application Object

The Page object contains a property that is a reference to an object of the HttpApplicationState class. We refer to it as the Application object.

To use the Application object to store data like the address of our company, we would use the following code:

```
Application["Address"] = "42 North Galaxy Road";
```

This line creates a variable in the Application object that is given the name Address and assigned the value "42 North Galaxy Road". Once the variable is created, we can access it through code similar to this:

```
Response.Write(Application["Address"]);
```

The following example is made up from two pages that must be opened one after the other (we will solve that inconvenience later in this section). The first page is called SetApplication.aspx.

```
<%@ Page Language="c#" %>
<html>
  <body>
    <% Application["Address"] = "42 North Galaxy Road";
       Application["Source"] = "SetApplication.aspx"; %>
    <h1>Thank you for setting the Application State for our Address</h1>
  </body>
</html>
```

The second page is called GetApplication.aspx:

```
<%@ Page Language="c#" %>
<html>
  <body>
    <h1>We are located at: <br />
    <% Response.Write(Application["Address"]); %><br /><br />
    The source of this information is :
    <% Response.Write(Application["Source"]); %><br /><br />
    Thank you for getting the Application State for our Address</h1>
  </body>
</html>
```

The preceding example uses a page to set the `Address` variable in the `Application` object and a second page to read the information.

 EXAM TIP   Note that the two pages communicated with each other through the `Application` object.

The common procedure for initiating the `Application` object's variables is to use the `global.asax` file; it is the entry point to the web application and is the common location for initialization code. The equivalent `global.asax` code is seen in the following example:

```
<script language="c#" runat="server">
  void Application_OnStart()
  {
    Application["Address"] = "42 North Galaxy Road";
    Application["Source"] = "global.asax";
  }
</script>
```

The code we entered is in the `Application_OnStart()` event handler, so this code will be executed as soon as the application starts.

The variables created in the `Application` object are visible through the entire application and can be used by all the pages that are part of the application. However, this can lead to problems if two or more pages try to change the same variable at the same time—one page might want to write the same data that the second page wants to read. The question becomes what data we will read? The original data? The data after the change? Or perhaps some intermediate "dirty" data? This problem is easily handled by *locking* the `Application` object during modifications.

The `Application` object has two methods that perform this locking action: the `Lock()` and `UnLock()` methods, shown in this example:

```
Application.Lock();
Application["Variable"] = "10";
Application.UnLock();
```

The `Lock()` method is a blocking call. It will wait for access to the lock before returning to the program, ensuring that changes are not permitted from more than one process at a time. After modifying the data, you call the `UnLock()` method to let other pages access the data.

Application state should be used to store global data that is frequently used. There is a danger with using too many `Application` object variables because the object is stored in memory and gets larger with each item stored in it. If the `Application` object is heavily used, you should consider using the `web.config` file instead. The `web.config` file is used to configure the web application without actually storing the data in the `Application` object. For more information on the `web.config` file, see Chapter 17.

The Session Object

When a client connects to our web server, the connection will be encapsulated in the `Session` object—the `Page` object's `Session` property is a reference to an object of the `HttpSessionState` class. A *session* is defined as one visit to a web site: it starts when the client connects, and it ends when the client has not visited a page for a certain time period. (The default is 20 minutes.)

You will use the `Session` object to store client-specific data, such as the following:

- A shopping cart with the items the user has selected while browsing through your e-mall.
- Custom settings for the client.
- Client preferences (language, formatting, and the like).
- Personalization data (name, address, e-mail address, phone, and so on).

You assign values to `Session` variables the same way you did with the `Application` variables. To set the `Name` variable to "Garfield O'Reilly", you would use the following statement:

```
Session["Name"] = "Garfield O'Reilly";
```

To read the variable, you would use this line:

```
string Who = Session["Name"];
```

The `Session` object has a number of methods and properties that are useful in working with the clients session with the web server. Table 11-6 lists the most commonly used members.

Session variables are visible only to pages opened in the session, which means there will never be more than one user modifying any values, so we do not need to lock the session object for changes.

The `Session` object is used to store variables related to each session on the web server. The default timeout setting for the `Session` object's lifetime is 20 minutes; if you have a large number of visitors, you will want to lower the timeout value so the server will drop the unused Session objects earlier.

Method/Property	Description
Clear()	Clears all values from session state.
Count	Gets the number of items in the session-state collection.
SessionID	Gets the unique session ID used to identify the session.
Timeout	Gets and sets the time-out period (in minutes) allowed between requests before the session-state provider terminates the session.

Table 11-6   The Commonly Used Members of the `Session` Object

Summary

In this chapter, you have learned about the Internet standards and the different architectures used to build web sites for the Internet over the years. You explored client-side and server-side execution while taking a look at ASP.NET.

The most important portion of this chapter for the exam is the ASP.NET object model. You can expect a number of questions that refer to the objects in the model and how to use them. As a matter of fact, the objects are so important that we will revisit them a number of times in this part of the book.

Now you have enough information to start working with the ASP.NET pages. In the next chapter you will explore the ASP.NET page with a focus on Web Forms and server controls.

Test Questions

1. What definition correctly defines a label server control with the name set to `lblHoop`?

   A. `<asp:Label name="lblHoop" runat="server" />`

   B. `<Label id="lblHoop" runat="server" />`

   C. `<asp:label id="lblHoop" runat="server" />`

   D. `<server label name="lblHoop" runat="asp" />`

2. What ASP.NET object encapsulates the user's data as it is sent from a form in a page?

   A. The `Session` object.

   B. The `Application` object.

   C. The `Response` object.

   D. The `Request` object.

   E. The `Server` object.

3. What important standard is used to connect client browsers with web servers?

   A. HTTP

   B. TCP/IP

   C. ASP.NET

   D. HTML

4. What ASP.NET object is used to get information about the web servers hostname?

   A. The `Session` object.

   B. The `Application` object.

    C. The `Response` object.

    D. The `Request` object.

    E. The `Server` object.

5. When writing server-side code, what marks are used to indicate the code block?

    A. `<% %>`

    B. `<!-- -->`

    C. `<@ language="c#" @>`

    D. `<asp:script runat="server" />`

6. What computer language is installed with the .NET Framework, by default?

    A. JavaScript

    B. QuickBasic

    C. C

    D. LiveScript

7. What is the name of the process the browser uses to find the address of a web server?

    A. DMZ

    B. DNS

    C. Active Directory

    D. Database lookup

8. How many rules are there regarding a well-formed XML document?

    A. Nine

    B. Three

    C. Six

    D. Two

9. What line in the following XML document will generate an error?

```
1 <?xml version="1.0">
2 <employees>
3   <employee>
4     <name>Bob Andcarrol</Name>
5   </employee>
6   <employee>
7     <Name>Robert Burns</Name>
8   </employee>
9 </employees>
```

    A. 6

    B. 4

C. 1

D. There is no error.

10. What language is the standard web script language ECMAScript based on?

A. JavaScript

B. Java

C. Perl

D. Jscript

11. What is the behavior of a web browser when it receives an invalid element?

A. The web browser will display the element in raw form.

B. The web browser will send a report to the webmaster detailing the error by using the `Request` object.

C. The web browser will report the error, letting you debug the page.

D. The browser will ignore the invalid section.

12. What ASP.NET object encapsulates the state of the client and the browser?

A. The `Session` object.

B. The `Application` object.

C. The `Response` object.

D. The `Request` object.

E. The `Server` object.

13. What object would you use if you needed to support Netscape Navigator and Microsoft Internet Explorer?

A. ActiveX control

B. Intrinsic controls

C. XML

D. Java applet

14. What method(s) must be used with the `Application` object to ensure that only one process accesses a variable at a time?

A. `Synchronize()`

B. `Lock()` and `UnLock()`

C. `Lock()` and `Unlock()`

D. `SingleUse()`

15. What ASP.NET object encapsulates the web site?

A. The `Session` object.

B. The `Application` object.

    C. The `Response` object.

    D. The `Request` object.

    E. The `Server` object.

Test Answers

1. C.

2. D.

3. B.

4. E.

5. A.

6. A.

7. B.

8. C.

9. B. The opening and closing elements, <name> and </Name>, do not match; XML is case-sensitive.

10. A.

11. D.

12. A.

13. D.

14. B.

15. B.

CHAPTER 12

Web Forms: Client-Side Programs

In this chapter, you will

- Create ASP.NET pages
- Add and set directives on ASP.NET pages
- Separate user interface resources from business logic
- Add HTML server controls to ASP.NET pages
- Set properties on controls
- Add HTML code to ASP.NET pages
- Set styles on ASP.NET pages by using cascading style sheets
- Incorporate existing code into ASP.NET pages

We've now reached the part of the book where you will be able to build your first functional web site. We spent some time in the previous chapter on handcrafting a single page, but now we are going to use the power of Visual Studio .NET (VS .NET). The exam will test your knowledge of how to create ASP.NET pages and customize them with the controls provided in ASP.NET, and we will cover those topics here. In this chapter we will build an address book application that can be accessed using a browser, and this application will incorporate the new server controls that were introduced with ASP.NET.

Introduction to Web Forms

So far in this book, you have handcrafted the web sites you created. Now we will look at the graphical tools that are part of VS .NET. You were introduced to the integrated development environment in Chapter 5, and we'll use it here as we look closely at how to create a skeleton web application, and at the files that make up the application.

ASP.NET pages are designed to use controls and features that are almost as powerful as the ones used with Windows Forms, and so they are called *Web Forms*. This gives us great control over what data is presented to the client and how.

The Web Form uses a server-side object model that allows you to create very functional controls that will execute on the server and that are rendered as HTML on the client. The statement that directs the server to handle the controls, rather than the client, is the `runat="server"` statement. In the following code segment, you can also see the `<script>` tag—it defines a script block that will execute on the web server.

```
<script language="c#" runat="server">
    // the server-side program goes here
</script>
```

Because this code will execute at the server, there are a number of languages that can be used to develop the code, C# being one.

On the other hand, if the `runat` attribute is missing from the script tag, the default behavior is for the script to execute on the client. The client can only use two scripting languages, VBScript and JavaScript, and the object model for controls and elements is different as well. The object model for the browser is based on the DOM (Document Object Model) and is implemented differently in each browser, as opposed to the model for ASP.NET, which sends browser-neutral HTML that will work similarly in any browser. The reason for using client-side scripts is that some specific processing is better handled on the client, such as building menus. The following code segment shows how a client-side code block is constructed:

```
<script language="javascript">
    // client-side code goes here
</script>
```

ASP.NET Web Forms are processed so that anything that is not a server-side program will be sent through to the client as HTML. Indeed, the following one-line page will work:

```
Hello World!
```

You can build all your Web Forms by hand, rather than by using the IDE, and possibly gain some speed and reduce their size by doing so, but the real power of web development is that you can build powerful applications using the RAD (Rapid Application Development) tools in Visual Studio .NET.

Building Your First Web Form

To build a Web Form, you need to start Visual Studio .NET by selecting Start | Programs | Microsoft Visual Studio .NET and then clicking on Microsoft Visual Studio .NET. From the Start Page, select New Project, which will display the New Project dialog box, shown in the following illustration.

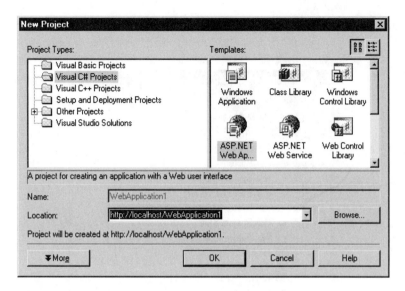

To create the project, you need to do three things in this dialog box:

1. Select the ASP.NET Web Application template.
2. Enter a server name and an application name in the Location field.
3. Click OK.

NOTE The server name must identify an IIS 5.0 (or higher) web server that has been configured for developing ASP.NET Web Forms.

Once you have clicked OK, Visual Studio will create the files that represent the solution (the project) you are building. The files are located at the web server in the directory you indicated in the Location field and a copy is kept in a local cache maintained by

Visual Studio .NET. The files that are created can be seen in the Solution Explorer shown here.

 EXAM TIP The name given to the application will be part of the URL used to access the application. For example, the `WebApplication1` application on the host `localhost` will be accessed through the URL `http://localhost/WebApplication1`.

The New Project dialog box starts a process that sets up the following items:

- A new solution, with the name you assigned in the dialog box (`WebApplication1` in our example), encapsulating the C# web application (`WebApplication1`).

- The `AssemblyInfo.cs` C# source, which contains the standard description for the assembly source file that is the codebehind module.

- The `Global.aspx` file, which is used to hold global information and event handlers for initializing the application as well as application information.

- The `WebApplication.disco` file, which will be used to describe any web services, thus enabling dynamic discovery of those web services. By using the `.disco` file, the client can dynamically find a web service at run time, rather than having to bind to a specific server at design time.

- The `Web.config` file, which contains the configuration information for the application.

- The WebForm1.aspx file, which is the first ASP.NET page in the web application.

The Solution Explorer also displays the References item, which lists the namespaces that are referenced in the solution. The term *solution* is used to describe the final application that you are building—the solution can contain multiple projects that together form that application. To edit any one of these files, you can just double-click on the file to open it in the appropriate editor.

The .aspx files in our solution can be viewed in two different ways: in Design or HTML view. The Design view can be seen in Figure 12-1.

The text shown in the Design view is a reminder to you about the different layout modes available. The default is *grid layout* (shown in Figure 12-1), in which the components added to the form will be positioned using a grid with *x* and *y* coordinates. The other option is *flow layout*, in which components are added starting at the top left of the form the same way text is presented in a document. To change the layout setting of the form, change the pageLayout property of the document.

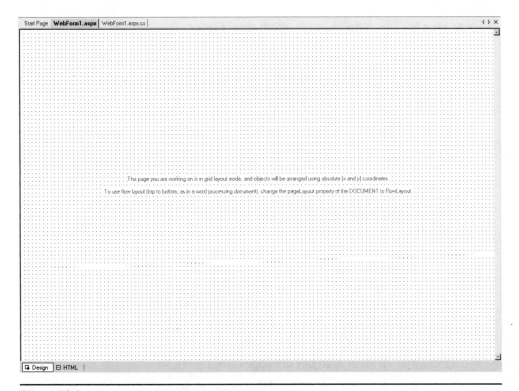

Figure 12-1   Design view for an .aspx file

Selecting the HTML view from the tabs in the bottom left of the editor will display the HTML code that is used to lay out the document for the client. The following listing shows an example:

```
<%@ Page language="c#" Codebehind="WebForm1.aspx.cs" AutoEventWireup="false"
                      Inherits="WebApplication1.WebForm1" %>
<!DOCTYPE HTML PUBLIC "-//W3C//DTD HTML 4.0 Transitional//EN" >
<html>
   <head>
      <title>WebForm1</title>
      <meta name="GENERATOR" Content="Microsoft Visual Studio 7.0">
      <meta name="CODE_LANGUAGE" Content="C#">
      <meta name="vs_defaultClientScript" content="JavaScript">
      <meta name="vs_targetSchema"
                  content="http://schemas.microsoft.com/intellisense/ie5">
   </head>
   <body MS_POSITIONING="GridLayout">
      <form id="Form1" method="post" runat="server">
      </form>
   </body>
</html>
```

There are a few points to be made about this HTML code:

- The @ Page directive has the following attributes:
  - The language="c#" attributes specifies that the C# language will be used on the page.
  - The Codebehind="WebForm1.aspx.cs" attribute names the file that will hold the C# code to be executed on the server for the Web Form.
  - The AutoEventWireup="false" attribute is used to disable a call to the Page_Load() event handler. You have to perform this initialization yourself. Setting the attribute to True will automatically wire the OnPageLoad event to the Page_Load() event handler. (One reason you might choose to leave this attribute set to False is to gain better control of what initialization takes place.)
  - The Inherits="WebApplication1.WebForm1" attribute specifies the class file from which the .aspx file is derived.
- The <!DOCTYPE> element contains the document type definition (DTD) for the HTML language.
- The <meta> elements set the information about the development environment and the client-browser assumptions.
- The <body> element specifies the page layout.
- The <form> element defines the HTML form for this ASP.NET Web Form.

These page directives for the ASP.NET page can be set by right-clicking the page and clicking the Properties menu item.

The Web Form consists of two views, as you have seen: the HTML view that is the graphical layout, and the programmatic view that shows the code that will remain on the server to be called every time the Web Form is called by a client. The codebehind module is the C# source code that is stored in the `WebForm1.aspx.cs` file; this file is left behind on the server and is what actually makes the Web Form programmable. To view the codebehind module, right-click on the Web Form file in the Solution Explorer and select View Code.

The code in the codebehind module can be broken up into two parts—the listing of the namespaces and the declaration of the Web Form class that defines the behavior of the Web Form. Here is the first part:

```
using System;
using System.Collections;
using System.ComponentModel;
using System.Data;
using System.Drawing;
using System.Web;
using System.Web.SessionState;
using System.Web.UI;
using System.Web.UI.WebControls;
using System.Web.UI.HtmlControls;

namespace WebApplication1
{
```

The first part of the codebehind module is the definition of the references that are used in the Web Form and the namespace declaration for the application.

The next part of the code defines `WebForm1` as the base class for the `.aspx` page. The class is based on the `System.Web.UI.Page` class. The code following the `#region` directive is added to support the initialization of the page.

```
public class WebForm1 : System.Web.UI.Page
{
  private void Page_Load(object sender, System.EventArgs e)
  {
    // Put user code to initialize the page here
  }

  #region Web Form Designer generated code
  override protected void OnInit(EventArgs e)
  {
    InitializeComponent();
    base.OnInit(e);
  }

  private void InitializeComponent()
  {
    this.Load += new System.EventHandler(this.Page_Load);
  }
  #endregion
}
```

The `OnInit()` event handler is called when the page is initialized. The default behavior is for the handler to call `InitializeComponent()` and the base class `OnInit()` event handler. The `InitializeComponent()` method performs one task by default, and that is to register the `Page_Load()` event handler for the `Load` event. This code must be added because the `AutoEventWireup` attribute was set to False, which means you must perform the registrations manually.

To run the application, select Debug | Start (or press F5). The resulting empty page in the browser is not all that interesting, but we will start adding components to it in the next section.

Adding Controls to a Form

There are four types of controls that can be added to your ASP.NET pages:

- **HTML server controls**   These controls are very much like the standard HTML elements normally used in HTML pages. They expose properties and events that can be used programmatically.

- **Web server controls**   These controls are scripted on the server to encapsulate the most common HTML controls, but also to give access to enhanced controls that are made up from multiple HTML controls, like the `Calendar` control.

- **Validation controls**   These controls implement validation logic so you can test the user's input against patterns, values, or ranges of values.

- **Custom and user controls**   These controls are created as Web Forms and you can embed them in other Web Forms. Custom controls are excellent for frequently reused components.

In the following sections, we will look at how to use the different types of controls.

To add controls to a Web Form, you need to use the Toolbox that is part of the VS .NET environment. The Toolbox is by default hidden along the left edge of the Visual Studio .NET IDE—to make it visible, position the mouse pointer over the word Toolbox at the left edge of the screen, as shown in Figure 12-2. If you want the Toolbox to stay on the screen at all times, click the push pin in the top-right corner of the Toolbox, as shown in Figure 12-3.

The various controls in the Toolbox are selected by clicking on them, so to select the HTML controls, click on the button labeled HTML.

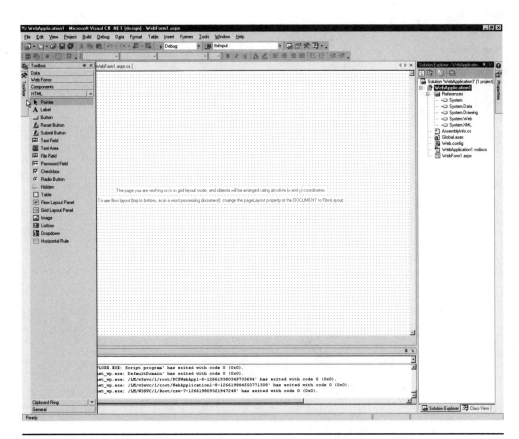

Figure 12-2   The Toolbox tab

HTML Server Controls

The HTML controls that are used from the toolbox are the general elements that are
defined in the HTML standard. Some of the controls included in VS .NET are listed in
Table 12-1.

Figure 12-3
The Toolbox
push pin

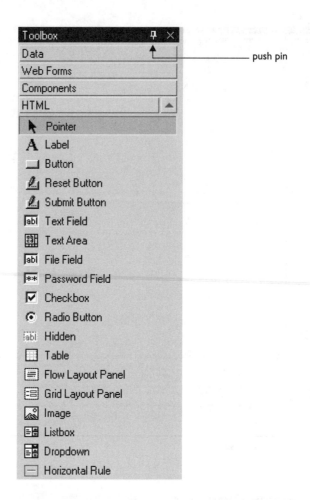

push pin

VS .NET HTML Controls	Description
Label	Displays textual information that cannot be edited by the user.
Button	Presents a clickable control that allows for user interaction.
Reset Button	Presents special controls used in forms to interact with the server.
Submit Button	The reset button clears the form and the submit button sends the information in the form to the server.
Text Field	Creates a single-line text field for input or display. This control is commonly used to give the user the ability to enter and edit information.
Text Area	Defines multiple-line text areas used mostly for free text information, for example a description field. This control is commonly used to give the user the ability to enter and edit information.

Table 12-1   Some of the HTML Controls in the Visual Studio .NET Toolbox

VS .NET HTML Controls	Description
File Field	Creates a file upload object with a text box and a browse button.
Password Field	Creates a field that hides the information entered in the field by replacing it with a selectable character. For example, if the asterisk character (*) is used and the field contains the word "secret," the display would contain six asterisks: ******.
Checkbox	Represents a True/False Boolean value. The graphical representation is a box that can have three visual states: empty, checked, and grayed out (indicating an invalid condition).
Radio Button	Allows users to select between mutually exclusive values. The key to using radio buttons is to keep the number of values to a reasonable range; 5 values is functional while 25 is not. For larger numbers of mutually exclusive values, you should use a Drop-down control.
Hidden	Creates a control that is logically on the page and can contain data, but that is not displayed. The most common use for the Hidden control is to transmit state information about a form or page.
Table	Creates a table, which is commonly used to lay out forms and pages, though the new layout panels will reduce the use of tables. This is the most versatile control in the entire HTML family of controls.
Flow Layout Panel	Provides an area in the page that follows the flow layout.
Grid Layout Panel	Provides an area in the page that follows the grid layout.
Image	Puts pictures on the page. This control accepts a number of image file formats, .gif and .jpg being the most common.
Listbox	Displays a window with many choices; the user can select from one or more options.
Dropdown	Provides a large number of selections in a very small control. It displays one field with the selected value, but can display a list of values when the selection button is clicked. The control can have many names, such as combo control or select control.

Table 12-1   Some of the HTML Controls in the Visual Studio .NET Toolbox *(continued)*

PART III

To add any control from the Toolbox to a Web Form, you can use either of two techniques:

- Double-click the control to get a default-sized control on the form.

- Select the control and draw the control on the form.

Adding HTML Controls

Let's continue working with the `WebApplication1` form you created in a previous section—add two text fields and a button as shown in Figure 12-4. The HTML definition of the controls can be viewed in the HTML editor for the Web Form, as shown in Figure 12-5.

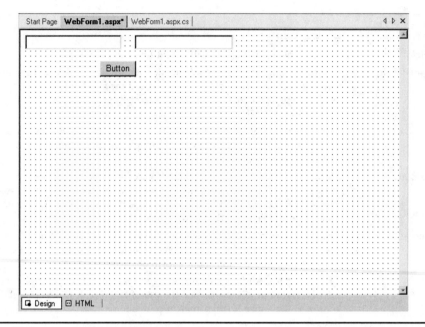

Figure 12-4 Web Form with HTML controls

```
Page  WebForm1.aspx*  WebForm1.aspx.cs
t Objects & Events                                              ▼  (No Events)
 1  <%@ Page language="c#" Codebehind="WebForm1.aspx.cs" AutoEventWireup="false" Inherits="WebApplication1.WebForm1" %>
 2  <!DOCTYPE HTML PUBLIC "-//W3C//DTD HTML 4.0 Transitional//EN" >
 3  <HTML>
 4    <HEAD>
 5      <title>WebForm1</title>
 6      <meta content="Microsoft Visual Studio 7.0" name="GENERATOR">
 7      <meta content="C#" name="CODE_LANGUAGE">
 8      <meta content="JavaScript" name="vs_defaultClientScript">
 9      <meta content="http://schemas.microsoft.com/intellisense/ie5" name="vs_targetSchema">
10    </HEAD>
11    <body MS_POSITIONING="GridLayout">
12      <form id="Form1" method="post" runat="server">
13        <INPUT style="Z-INDEX: 101; LEFT: 8px; POSITION: absolute; TOP: 8px" type="text">
14        <INPUT style="Z-INDEX: 103; LEFT: 128px; POSITION: absolute; TOP: 48px" type="button" value="Button">
15        <INPUT style="Z-INDEX: 102; LEFT: 184px; POSITION: absolute; TOP: 8px" type="text"></form>
16    </body>
17  </HTML>
18
```

Figure 12-5 The HTML code for the controls

The code added to the form looks like this:

```
<INPUT style="Z-INDEX: 101; LEFT: 8px; POSITION: absolute; TOP: 8px" type="text">
```

Where the attributes are set for absolute positioning, the control will have position values based on the top-left corner of the Web Form. After the control has been added to the form it does not, however, have any name properties set, so we need to attend to that. The properties are set through the Properties Explorer in the IDE, shown in Figure 12-6.

The HTML controls allow you to develop traditional client-side dynamic HTML applications. The power of ASP.NET, however, lies in how you can use server-side controls for better cross-platform availability, and, in many cases, better performance. The next section will delve into the server-side controls.

Figure 12-6
The Properties
Explorer

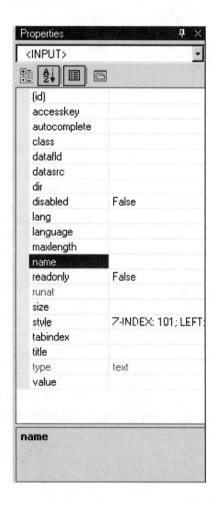

PART III

Web Server Controls

ASP.NET server controls are rendered using standard HTML in the client's browser, making the controls functional in almost any browser version. Server controls are very close to HTML controls, but you program them using C# and the object model you have become used to through your C# experience. The server controls are found in the Toolbox under the Web Forms section, as shown in Figure 12-7.

 NOTE You must be in Design view in order to see the Web Forms section of the Toolbox.

Some of the web server controls are encapsulated standard HTML controls, while others are totally new. Table 12-2 lists some of the server controls.

To declare a server control, you use an XML-style element to define the control, and that element must follow the XML rules, even though it's not technically XML. It is a good rule to always follow the XML rules.

Web Server Control	Description
Label	Displays textual information. The user cannot edit the text. Use the Text property to change the content of the Label control.
TextBox	Creates a single-line text box for the input and display of text. It is commonly used to allow the user to enter and edit information.
Button	Creates a clickable control for user interaction.
HyperLink	Encapsulates a hyperlink.
DropDownList	Displays one field with the selected value and a list of alternative values when the selection button is clicked.
ListBox	Displays a window with many choices. The client can select from one or more options.
CheckBox	Represents a True/False Boolean value. The check box has three visual states: empty, checked, and grayed (indicating an invalid condition).
CheckBoxList	Creates a collection of check boxes that are treated as one item. The control functions similarly to other list controls.
RadioButton	Allows the user to select between mutually exclusive values.
RadioButtonList	Creates a collection of RadioButton controls that are treated as one object.
Image	Puts pictures on the page. This control accepts a number of image file formats, with .gif and .jpg being the most common.
Panel	Creates a container for other controls.
PlaceHolder	Allows dynamic control creation at run time.

Table 12-2 Some of the Web Server Controls

Figure 12-7
The web server
controls

The web server control definition is entered into the `<Form>` section of the `.aspx` file; it uses this general format:

```
<asp:SC runat="server" attributes="value">Content</asp:SC>
```

 EXAM TIP   Learn the basic form for the ASP.NET server control element, especially that `runat="server"` must be included.

The `SC` is the name of the server control, and the attribute to the element is one or more of the attributes specified for the control, such as the `name` attribute. Note the XML end tag that must be included. Note also that the web server control definition is case-sensitive. The `runat="server"` attribute is mandatory; if it is forgotten, the control will not display.

 EXAM TIP   Remember the six rules of XML we looked at in Chapter 8. There must be one and only one root element, XML is case- sensitive, elements must be properly nested, elements must have opening and closing tags, attributes cannot be repeated, and attribute values must be enclosed in quotes.

Adding Buttons and Labels

Let's start a new ASP.NET Web Application project to test some of these controls. Create a project called `WebApplication2` and locate it at the `localhost`. After the application has been created, the majority of the code for the Web Form is created by the wizard; to add some functionality add the bold code to the `WebForm1.aspx` file:

```
<%@ Page language="c#" Codebehind="WebForm1.aspx.cs" AutoEventWireup="false"
                        Inherits="WebApplication2.WebForm1" %>
<!DOCTYPE HTML PUBLIC "-//W3C//DTD HTML 4.0 Transitional//EN" >
<html>
  <head>
    <title>WebForm1</title>
...
  </head>
  <body MS_POSITIONING="GridLayout">
    <form id="Form1" method="post" runat="server">
      <asp:Label Runat="server" ID="lblHello"/><br/>
      <asp:Button Runat="server" ID="btnHello" Text="Say Hello"/><br/>
    </form>
  </body>
</html>
```

When you switch back to Design view, you will see the controls that have been added to the form, as shown in the following illustration.

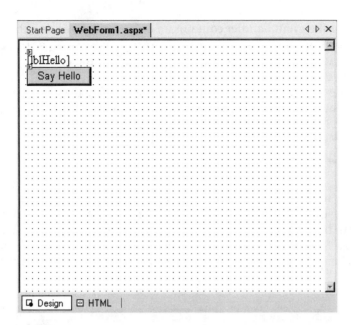

There were some changes in the codebehind module that was generated by the wizard; these changes we added when the two web server controls were added to the Web Form. When you open the `WebForm1.aspx.cs` file (by right-clicking in the form and selecting the View Code option) you can see that two protected members were added to the `WebForm1` class:

```
public class WebForm1 : System.Web.UI.Page
{
  protected System.Web.UI.WebControls.Label lblHello;
  protected System.Web.UI.WebControls.Button btnHello;
...
```

Any control you add to the form will automatically become a member of the class hierarchy of the form that is represented in the codebehind module. This is a benefit for the C# developer because you can use the Web Form class that is defined in the codebehind module to design the behavior for the web server controls and ultimately the application.

For example, to make the application display something in the label when you click the button, add the following code to the `WebForm1.aspx.cs` file. The code can be typed into the code module directly, or if you double-click on the button in Design view, you will be taken directly to the event handler for the click event.

```
private void btnHello_Click(object sender, System.EventArgs e)
{
}
```

The method for the event handler contains an object called `sender` that can be used to access the button object, and a variable (e) that passes a `System.EventArgs` structure. This structure can be used by the originator of the event to pass additional information to the handler.

To add some functionality to the form, you can modify the click event handler by adding the following code to set the content of the label to "Hello Web World!"

```
private void btnHello_Click(object sender, System.EventArgs e)
{
   lblHello.Text = "Hello Web World!";
}
```

You are now ready to test the application. To run it, you need to compile the application and request the `WebForm1.aspx` from the web server. In Visual Studio .NET, those steps can be completed by pressing F5, which is the equivalent of the menu command Debug | Start. When you press F5, you should see your form displayed in the browser. Clicking on the Say Hello button results in the display of your first web form, shown here.

One other thing happened automatically behind the scenes to make the click event from the button connect to the `btnHello_Click()` event handler in the codebehind module. That piece of magic is handled by one line of code that was inserted into the `InitializeComponent()` method in the `WebForm1` class:

```
private void InitializeComponent()
{
   this.btnHello.Click += new System.EventHandler(this.btnHello_Click);
   this.Load += new System.EventHandler(this.Page_Load);
}
```

The preceding bold line registers the event handler `this.btnHello_Click` to the `this.btnHello.Click` event. The default behavior for buttons is to automatically call the event handler when the click event takes place, thus calling the codebehind module. Other controls do not automatically cause the call-back to the server; the events in those cases are cached and are handled when the call finally goes back to the server.

Adding Drop-Down Lists

The next example will build on the previous one by adding a `DropDownList` control that lists "Hello World!" in different languages so that we can select the text that will be displayed in the label. The first step is to add a `DropDownList` control to the form by adding the bold line of code to the `WebForm1.aspx` file.

```
...
<form id="Form1" method="post" runat="server">
  <asp:Label Runat="server" ID="lblHello" /><br>
  <asp:Button Runat="server" ID="btnHello" Text="Say Hello" /><br>
  <asp:DropDownList id="cmbHello" runat="server"></asp:DropDownList><br/>
</form>
...
```

You then have to create a variable that can hold the string data that will be used to print the "Hello World!" message in the label. This is done by adding a private variable to the class definition and setting the initial value to "Hello World!" You also need to change the click event handler for the button to use the private string variable just defined. The following code shows those parts of the `WebForm1.aspx.cs` file.

```
...
public class WebForm1 : System.Web.UI.Page
{
  private string strHello = "Hello World!";
...
  private void btnHello_Click(object sender, System.EventArgs e)
  {
    lblHello.Text = strHello;
  }
...
```

The web page should work at this point, so go ahead and test it. Note that the `DropDownList` control is displayed, but there are no values inserted in it. We will now look at two ways to populate a control in the `List` family, such as the `DropDownList` control.

The first method is used when the list is static and is not expected to change during the life of the web page. The `Items` property represents a collection of `ListItem` objects; each `ListItem` object will appear as an entry in the drop-down list. Select the `DropDownList` control in Design view and select the `Items` property in the Properties Explorer, as shown in Figure 12-8. By clicking on the ellipsis in the `Items` property line

PART III

Figure 12-8
The Items
properties

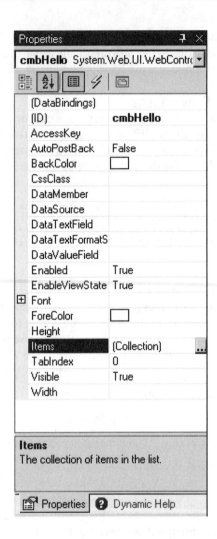

you will be able to open the ListItem Collection Editor dialog box (shown in the following illustration), which will allow you to add list items to the DropDownList control.

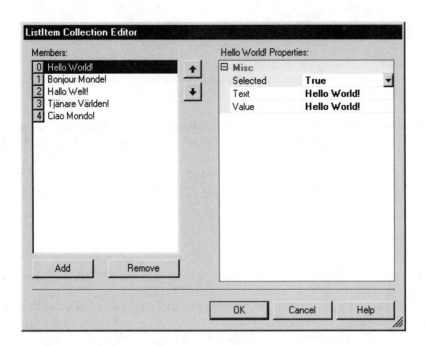

Items can be added to the control by clicking the Add button and filling in the fields as shown. The order of the entries can be changed by selecting a member and clicking the up or down arrows, and the default value can be defined by setting the `Selected` property for the default value to True.

If you run the form now, the list is populated, but there is no change to the string displayed in the `Label`, regardless of the selection you make in the `DropDownList`. To tie the `DropDownList` to the `Label`, you must implement an event handler for the `SelectedIndexChanged` event of the `DropDownList` control. The easiest way to create the event handler is to double-click the `DropDownList` control in Design view—this causes the following code to be added to the codebehind module.

```
...
private void InitializeComponent()
{
    this.btnHello.Click += new System.EventHandler(this.btnHello_Click);
    this.cmbHello.SelectedIndexChanged += new
```

```
                    System.EventHandler(this.cmbHello_SelectedIndexChanged);
    this.Load += new System.EventHandler(this.Page_Load);
}
...
private void cmbHello_SelectedIndexChanged(object sender, System.EventArgs e)
{
}
```

The event handler has now been created, as has the binding between the control and the event. Now you can update the string (strHello) that the Label displays when the selection changes in the DropDownList.

The way you retrieve the selected value in the DropDownList is by using the Text property of the SelectedItem property, as in this code:

```
private void cmbHello_SelectedIndexChanged(object sender, System.EventArgs e)
{
    strHello = cmbHello.SelectedItem.Text;
}
```

Once you have made these changes, save the application and run it (F5) to see how well it works. The resulting form should look similar to Figure 12-9.

There is a second way of populating a list control, and that is to do it dynamically with programming code. To demonstrate this, we will remove the static entries in the Items property and instead write a method to add the strings. The following method will add entries to the Items collection of ListItem objects.

```
...
private void populateList()
{
    cmbHello.Items.Add("Hello World!");
    cmbHello.Items.Add("Bonjour Monde!");
    cmbHello.Items.Add("Halo Welt!");
    cmbHello.Items.Add("Tjänare Världen!");
    cmbHello.Items.Add("Ciao Mondo!");
    cmbHello.SelectedIndex=0;
}
```

The last line in the preceding code sets the default value to the first value in the list (it uses a zero-based index).

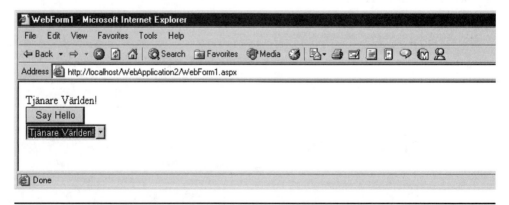

Figure 12-9   The application with the DropDownList control

In order to populate the control's `Items` collection when the page is loaded you need to call this method when the form is displayed; you add a call to the method in the `OnInit()` method.

```
...
override protected void OnInit(EventArgs e)
{
  InitializeComponent();
  populateList();
  base.OnInit(e);
}
```

When you run this application now, it will operate just as the previous version did, but you have now taken programmatic control of the `DropDownList` contents and can dynamically extend your application with little or no coding changes (see the following illustration).

After you have run the application a few times, you might decide that it is a waste of steps to first select the text and then have to click on the button—why not eliminate the clicking of the button? Indeed, you can change the behavior of the application.

To make a selection in the `DropDownList` box trigger the update of the label, you can include the update code in the `SelectedIndexChanged` event handler. Just add this line to handler:

```
lblHello.Text = strHello;
```

If you run the application now, you will notice that there is no change to the label until you click the button—this is the default way events are handled. Remember that the event code is running on the server, based on the codebehind module. In order for the event to be transmitted to the server (codebehind module) the client must initiate a postback sequence. The postback sends the form data to the server; by default, the `Button` (and all components that inherit from the `Button`) is the only control that will start the postback, and all other events that were created at the client are cached and transmitted the next time there is a postback.

It's easy to add the behavior that triggers a postback to the `Drop DownList` (or any other control) by adding the `AutoPostBack="true"` attribute to the definition of the control:

```
<asp:dropdownlist id=cmbHello runat="server" AutoPostBack="True"/>
```

The default is for the event to be handled when the server is called by a control that sends a postback, but you can control which object sends that postback message by setting the `AutoPostBack` attribute of a control to True. When you run the application, you will now have the behavior you expected from the application.

We will revisit these controls later in this chapter, but first we need to have a look at the validation controls.

Validation Controls

There is an old adage in computer science: garbage in = garbage out. We'll look here at one thing you can do to validate the data before it is processed, to make sure garbage doesn't get in. This validation can never verify that the data is absolutely correct—that type of data validation must be performed closer to the data source, where the data is used. The ASP.NET validation controls simply validate that the data is in the correct range or style. Table 12-3 lists the controls that are available.

Adding Validation Controls

The best way to learn about the controls is to use them in a solution, so we will start a new project. Call the project `WebApplication3` and use `localhost` as the server.

Control	Description
RequiredFieldValidator	Used to verify that the user has entered data into the field.
CompareValidator	Compares the value entered to a specified value. This validating control uses two properties: Operator and ValueToCompare to define the validation. Operator can be set to Equal, GreaterThan, GreaterThanEqual, LessThan, LessThanEqual, NotEqual, or DataTypeCheck. The ValueToCompare property contains the value to compare against.
RangeValidator	Validates the control based on a range of acceptable values.
RegularExpressionValidator	Validates the control against the regular expression in ValidationExpression.
CustomValidator	Uses the ClientValidationFunction property to set the client-side function that will be used for validation. This means that you need to write the code in a scripting language and not in C#.

Table 12-3   The Validation Controls

After the project is created, open up WebForm1 in HTML view and add the following ASP.NET lines to the form:

```
...
<form id="Form1" method="post" runat="server">
  <asp:Label ID="lblFName" Runat="server">First Name</asp:Label>
  <asp:TextBox ID="txtFName" Runat="server" Width="170px" />
  <asp:RequiredFieldValidator ID="valFName" Runat="server"
                              ErrorMessage="You must enter a First Name"
                              ControlToValidate="txtFName"
                              Display="Dynamic" />
  <br>
  <br>
  <asp:Button ID="btnSend" Runat="server" Text="Click Me!" />
  <br>
  <br>
  <asp:Label ID="lblDisplay" Runat="server" />
</form>
...
```

PART III

Then add a click event handler for the button (double-click the button in Design View) as follows:

```
private void btnSend_Click(object sender, System.EventArgs e)
{
  lblDisplay.Text=txtFName.Text;
}
```

When you run the application and click the Click Me button without entering a first name in the TextBox control, the display looks like this:

The RequiredFieldValidator uses a number of attributes to control its behavior. The more important ones are the ErrorMessage, which specifies the message to be displayed when the validation fails; ControlToValidate, which specifies the control to bind the validator to; and Display, which specifies the behavior of the validator (None means it is hidden, Dynamic sets it to be visible when needed, and Static makes it visible all the time).

If you set the Display attribute to None, the validator will not display any messages. This setting is normally used when the form has a ValidationSummary control that will display the messages from all the validators on the page at one time.

By changing the code in the form to match the following code, you can take advantage of the ValidationSummary control.

```
...
<form id="Form1" method="post" runat="server">
  <asp:Label ID="lblFName" Runat="server">First Name</asp:Label>
  <asp:TextBox ID="txtFName" Runat="server" Width="170px" />
  <asp:RequiredFieldValidator ID="valFName" Runat="server"
                              ErrorMessage="You must enter a First Name"
                              ControlToValidate="txtFName"
                              Display="None" />
  <br>
  <br>
  <asp:Button ID="btnSend" Runat="server" Text="Click Me!" />
  <br>
  <br>
  <asp:Label ID="lblDisplay" Runat="server" />
  <br />
```

```
<asp:ValidationSummary ID="validationSummary" Runat="server"
                        HeaderText="Before you submit your request:"/>
</form>
```

Save the project and run the application. The display will look like what you see here.

Now you can start adding some of the other validator controls to see how they operate. Let's add a `CompareValidator` as well as a `RangeValidator` to our form, along with two `TextBox` controls—one for age, and the other for salary. The range for the accepted age will be from 1 to 125 years, and the salary must be positive. The following code will create that form:

```
...
<form id="Form1" method="post" runat="server">
  <asp:Label ID="lblFName" Runat="server">First Name</asp:Label>
  <asp:TextBox ID="txtFName" Runat="server" Width="170px" />
  <asp:RequiredFieldValidator ID="valFName" Runat="server"
                        ErrorMessage="You must enter a First Name"
                        ControlToValidate="txtFName" Display="None" />
  <br>
  <asp:Label ID="lblAge" Runat="server">Age</asp:Label>
  <asp:TextBox ID="txtAge" Runat="server" Width="80px"/>
  <asp:RangeValidator ID="rangeValidator" Runat="server"
```

```
                              ErrorMessage="Your age must be from 1 to 125 years"
                              ControlToValidate="txtAge"
                              MinimumValue="1" MaximumValue="125" Display="None"/>
        <br>
        <asp:Label ID="lblSalary" Runat="server">Salary</asp:Label>
        <asp:TextBox ID="txtSalary" Runat="server" Width="120px" />
        <asp:CompareValidator ID="compareValidator" Runat="server"
                              ErrorMessage="Your salary must be positive"
                              ControlToValidate="txtSalary"
                              Operator="GreaterThan"
                              ValueToCompare="0" Display="None"/>
        <br>
        <asp:Button ID="btnSend" Runat="server" Text="Click Me!" />
        <br>
        <br>
        <asp:Label ID="lblDisplay" Runat="server" />
        <br>
        <asp:ValidationSummary ID="validationSummary" Runat="server"
                              HeaderText="Before you submit your request:"/>
</form>
```

The final result can be seen here.

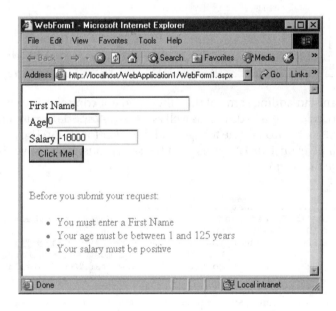

Make use of the validation controls to ensure the data collected from the client is within the right ranges and that fields that should have entries do indeed have them. The `RegularExpressionValidator` uses the regular expressions that Unix and Perl developers are used to; these expressions are very powerful string-manipulation statements and are beyond the scope of the book.

The `CustomValidator` control uses a client-side script to validate the content of the control. Unfortunately, you cannot use C# on the client's browser.

 EXAM TIP The `CustomValidator` control uses client-side script languages such as VBScript or JScript to validate the control.

Custom and User Controls

The reality of the web developer's world is that there is always a need for more powerful controls than those supplied with the environment. To solve that problem, you have user controls and custom controls. User controls allow the developer to take an existing ASP.NET page and turn it into a control, very much like the scriptlets in ASP 3.0. Custom controls are a control type that mimic the ActiveX controls of previous versions of Visual Studio—custom controls allow you to combine many controls into one logical control that is then used in the web application. The creation and use of user and custom controls are detailed in Chapter 14.

Creating an Address Book Web Form

In this section, we will build the beginning of a form for an address book that will be carried through a number of chapters in this part of the book. These are the requirements for the application:

- It should display an easy-to-read listing of addresses.
- It should allow addresses to be added, deleted, and edited.
- It should contain name, address, phone, e-mail, web address, birthday, and anniversary date information.
- It should be secure, though initial working models do not have to meet this requirement.
- It should store the data in a database, for better performance.

The application uses a form to display information about the entries in the database of addresses, but that "database" will be a static routine until we reach the data connectivity discussion in Chapter 16.

The first step in building the address book application is to start a new project. Call the application `AddressBook` and use the `localhost` server, as shown next.

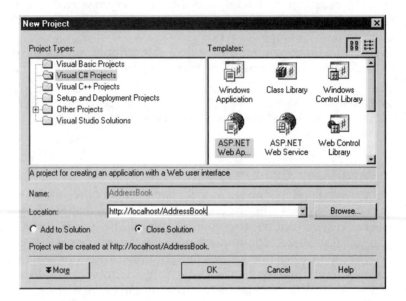

The interface will be utilitarian for now, and will consist of 26 buttons labeled from A to Z. The names of the buttons should be `btnA` through to `btnZ`. Place the buttons as shown in Figure 12-10.

The next thing you need is a list box to display the names in the address book when the alphabet buttons are clicked. For example, clicking the H button (`btnH`) should display names that start with the letter H. In the first version of this application, that data will be hard-coded into the click event handlers for the buttons.

First add a `ListBox` control, name it `lstAddress`, and position it as shown in Figure 12-11.

To populate the `ListBox` control, we will use a trick and have one click event handler service all 26 alphabet buttons. In order to connect an event with an event handler a reference to the event handler is added to the collection of handlers that are registered to the event. . The code is similar to the following segment, where the name of the event handler in this case is `setList()`, located in the `InitializeComponent()` method. This code line registers the event handler for the `btnA` control.

```
this.btnA.Click += new System.EventHandler(this.setList);
```

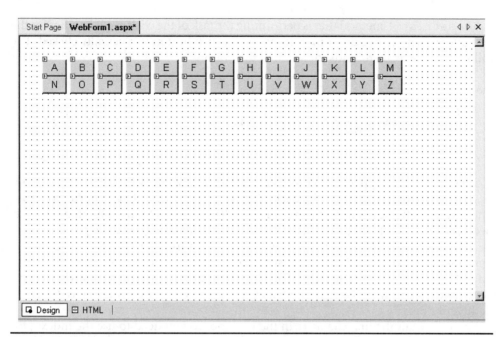

Figure 12-10   Adding the alphabet buttons to the application

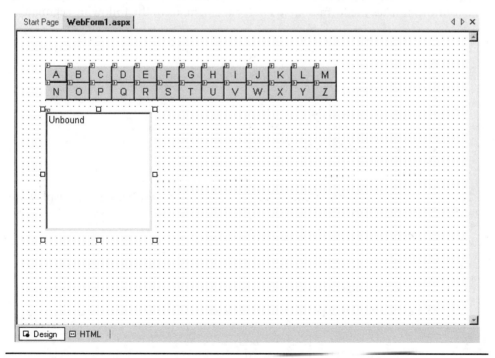

Figure 12-11   Adding the List control to the application

The setList() method that is performing the task of the click event handler for the 26 buttons uses the sender object to find out which button was actually clicked. The following code segment finds the value of the button:

```
private void setList(object sender, System.EventArgs e)
{
  string x;
  System.Web.UI.WebControls.Button y = (System.Web.UI.WebControls.Button) sender;
  x =  y.Text;
  getName(x[0] );
}
```

Let's see what is happening in this code. You want to set the value of the Text property of the button that created the click event so you can send that character to a routine that will retrieve the names (getName()). The string (x) is used for that purpose. Because the object that will trigger the event handler is of type System.Web.UI.WebControls.Button, you can create a variable (y) of that type and assign the sender object to y, casting the sender to be of type System.Web.UI.WebControls.Button. The end result of that line is that y now is a Button, so you can read the Text property of y and get access to the string that is displayed in the Button.

You only want the first character in the string, so you need to use the indexer for the string x to get the first letter (string[0]) and pass it to the getName() method. The getName() method is implemented to populate the ListBox control with static data for now. It takes the form of a switch statement, as in the following segment:

```
private void getName(char a)
{
  clearList();
  switch (a)
  {
  case 'A':
     lstAddress.Items.Add("Adams, Jim");
     lstAddress.Items.Add("Adams, Ken");
...
     lstAddress.Items.Add("Adams, William");
     break;
...
```

The clearList() method empties the ListBox control before you display any new data. It has this format:

```
private void clearList()
{
  int x;
  x = lstAddress.Items.Count;
  for(int i = 0;i < x;i++)
  {
    lstAddress.Items.Remove(lstAddress.Items[0]);
  }
...
```

The `clearList()` method will iterate through the ListBox control, deleting all the entries. The `for` loop will execute until `lstAddress.Items.Count` items are removed—it always removes the first item in the list, and the list contracts when the entries are removed. The `lstAddress.Items.Add()` method adds entries in the `ListItem` collection referred to by the `Items` property of the ListBox control.

The complete listing of the `InitializeComponent()`, `setList()`, `clearList()`, and `getName()` methods are found here:

```
private void InitializeComponent()
{
  this.btnA.Click += new System.EventHandler(this.setList);
  this.btnB.Click += new System.EventHandler(this.setList);
  ...
  this.btnZ.Click += new System.EventHandler(this.setList);
  this.lstAddress.SelectedIndexChanged +=
      new System.EventHandler(this.lstAddress_SelectedIndexChanged);
  this.Load += new System.EventHandler(this.Page_Load);
}



private void setList(object sender, System.EventArgs e)
{
  string x;

  System.Web.UI.WebControls.Button y = (System.Web.UI.WebControls.Button) sender;
  x = y.Text;
  getName(x[0] );
}



private void clearList()
{
  int x;
  x = lstAddress.Items.Count;
  for(int i = 0;i < x;i++)
  {
    lstAddress.Items.Remove(lstAddress.Items[0]);
  }
}

private void getName(char a)
{
  clearList();
  switch (a)
  {
    case 'A':
      lstAddress.Items.Add("Adams, Jim");
      lstAddress.Items.Add("Adams, Ken");
  ...
      lstAddress.Items.Add("Adams, William");
      break;
  ...
```

```
    case 'Z':
      lstAddress.Items.Add("Zoro, Jim");
      lstAddress.Items.Add("Zoro, Ken");
...
      lstAddress.Items.Add("Zoro, William");
      break;
  }
}
```

The listing for the `setName()` method has been truncated, as it is just a repetitious listing of names. After these controls and methods are created, you can test the application. Figure 12-12 shows the form after the H button has been clicked.

The next step is to add some fields to display the name and additional information for the entries in the address book. Start by adding labels and text boxes to the form, as shown in Figure 12-13. The names and `Text` properties of the controls are listed in Table 12-4.

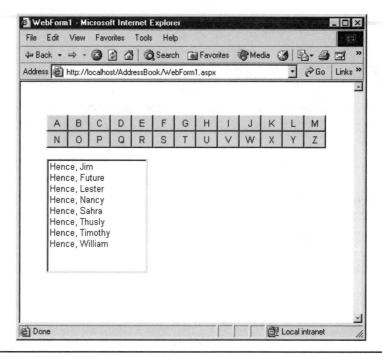

Figure 12-12   The Interface after the addition of the alphabetic buttons

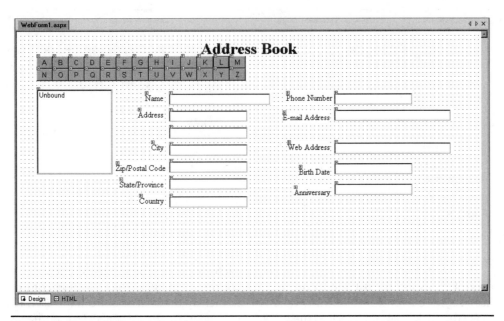

Figure 12-13   The expanded interface

Component	Name	Text Value
asp:Label	LblName	Name
asp:Label	LblAddress	Address
asp:Label	LblCity	City
asp:Label	LblProvince	State/Province
asp:Label	lblPostalCode	Zip/Postal Code
asp:Label	LblCountry	Country
asp:Label	lblPhoneNumber	Phone Number
asp:Label	LblEmail	E-mail Address
asp:Label	LblURL	Web Address
asp:Label	lblBirthdate	Birth Date
asp:Label	lblAnniversary	Anniversary
asp:TextBox	TxtName	

Table 12-4   The User Interface Controls for the Address Book

Component	Name	Text Value
asp:TextBox	TxtAddress1	
asp:TextBox	TxtAddress2	
asp:TextBox	TxtCity	
asp:TextBox	TxtProvince	
asp:TextBox	txtPostalCode	
asp:TextBox	TxtCountry	
asp:TextBox	txtPhoneNumber	
asp:TextBox	TxtEmail	
asp:TextBox	TxtURL	
asp:TextBox	txtBirthDate	
asp:TextBox	txtAnniversary	

Table 12-4   The User Interface Controls for the Address Book *(continued)*

Once the interface is built, you need to populate the form. You can use the ListBox control to display the list and let the user select from the names. The ListBox control has a SelectedIndexChanged event that can pick up the selections from the user. To make the click event postback to the server, you need to set the AutomaticPostBack attribute of the ListBox control to True. The definition of the ListBox control will then look like this:

```
<asp:ListBox id="lstAddress" runat="server" Width="152px" Height="176px"
        AutoPostBack="True"></asp:ListBox>
```

Now you can write the event handler for the ListBox control by double-clicking on the control in Design view. The SelectedIndexChanged event handler and the getAddress() method are listed in the following code segment.

```
private void lstAddress_SelectedIndexChanged(object sender, System.EventArgs e)
{
  txtName.Text=lstAddress.SelectedItem.Text;
  getAddress();
}

private void getAddress()
{
  txtAddress1.Text = "42 Galaxy Blvd.";
  txtAddress2.Text = "Suite 12";
  txtCity.Text  = "Toronto";
  txtProvince.Text = "ON";
  txtPostalCode.Text = "H0H 0H0";
  txtCountry.Text = "Canada";
  txtPhoneNumber.Text = "(416) 555-5555";
  txtEmail.Text = "fingal.olsson@hotmail.com";
  txtBirthDate.Text = "12/12/1942";
  txtAnniversary.Text = "7/12/1966";
}
```

Finally, you need to make one more change to the application to make it functional with the fictitious data. In the `clearList()` method, you need to clear the `TextBox` controls so the client is presented with a clean screen for the next query—the new version of `clearList()` is listed here:

```
private void clearList()
{
  int x;
  x = lstAddress.Items.Count;
  for(int i = 0;i < x;i++)
  {
    lstAddress.Items.Remove(lstAddress.Items[0]);
  }
  txtAddress1.Text = "";
...
  txtAnniversary.Text = "";
}
```

Now you can test the application to see that the `ListBox` is properly populated when you click one of the letter buttons and that the data for the user is displayed when the name is selected in the `ListBox`. The application can be seen in Figure 12-14.

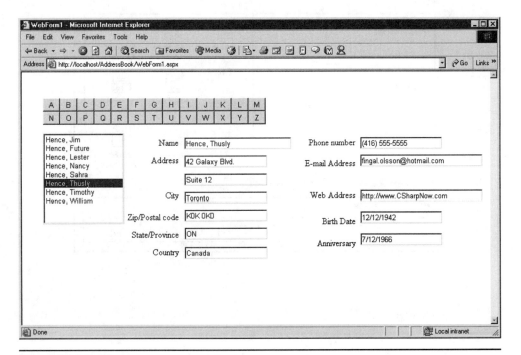

Figure 12-14 The `AddressBook` application

To make the application a little more pleasing to the eye, you can add a header and use a cascading style sheet (CSS) to set the properties for the elements in the form. To add the header, you can add some HTML code to the top of the <BODY> tag, as shown in the following code segment:

```
<body MS_POSITIONING="GridLayout">
  <h1 align="center">Address Book</h1>
  <form id="Form1" method="post" runat="server">
...
```

Now you can add styles to the file. (Before you do, though, save the project to ensure you have a stable version to go back to if something goes wrong.) The first step in applying a cascading style sheet is to build the style for the page by adding a style sheet to the project.

To add items to the project, right-click on the project in the Solution Explorer or select Project | Add Item to open the Add New Item dialog box shown in the following illustration. Select Style Sheet in the Templates pane, and give the style sheet a name. Then click Open.

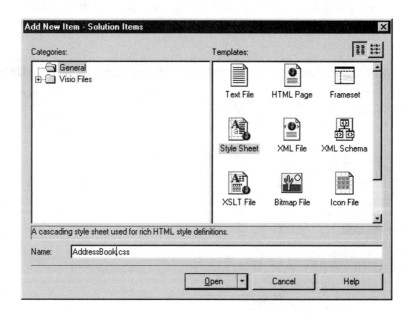

The CSS editor will open, as shown in Figure 12-15. The left part of the editor shows the different items that have styles associated with them. To change the style for a `Label` control, you need to add the element to the style pane. In order to add the control to the style pane you use the Add Style Rule dialog box (shown in the following illustration). To open the Add Style Rule dialog box, right-click in the right pane and select Add Style Rule. After adding the style click OK to close the dialog box. The illustration shows the Add Style Rule dialog box with a `Label` element added.

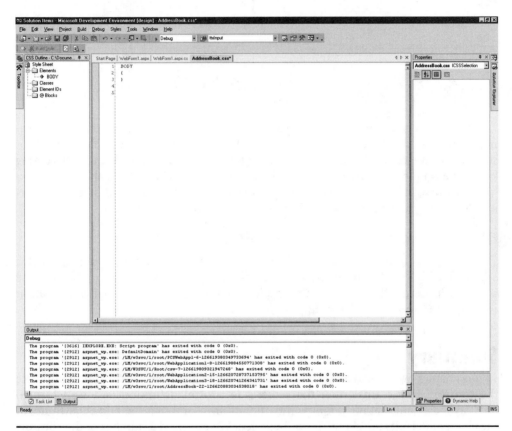

Figure 12-15   The CSS editor

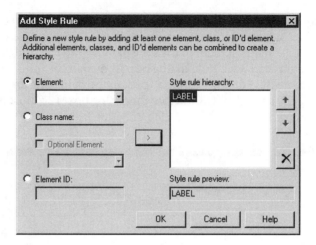

Now the specifics for the element can be changed by right-clicking the Label element and selecting Build Style to open the Style Builder dialog box, in the CSS Editor shown in Figure 12-16. The different styles for the element can be set through this dialog box. For example, the font and color styles are commonly changed for the elements.

Once the style sheet is created, you can add it to the document by adding the following HTML code in the <HEAD> section of the .aspx file:

```
<LINK REL="STYLESHEET" TYPE="text/css" HREF="AddressBook.css">
```

The address book application is now fairly functional, even though the color scheme is a bit loud (we returned it to normal for the printers of this book), and there is very little useful information in the application yet. We will return to the application in Chapter 16 to add database support.

Summary

In this chapter, we looked at the ASP.NET Web Form and how to add and manipulate the controls. You learned that the server-side control definition is a well formed XML-style element that must follow the rules of XML, and that the runat attribute of the element defaults to "client" if not included. We exercised a number of the controls that are included in ASP.NET to learn how they behave when used with different browsers. We also started to look at event handling in ASP.NET, as well as how to have one event handler deal with multiple controls. The address book application you started to build uses some of the common controls that are found in real live web pages. This application will be used again when we look at database connectivity in Chapter 16.

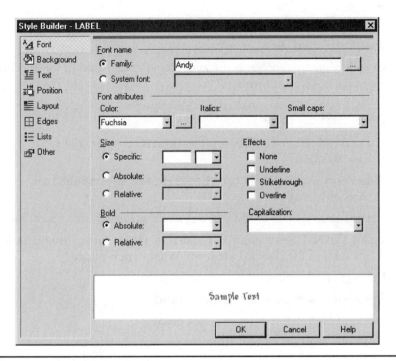

Figure 12-16   The Style Builder dialog box

The 70-315 exam is likely to test your knowledge on how to dynamically add controls to the Web Form as well as how to dynamically create event handlers.

Test Questions

1. When working with ASP.NET server controls, it is important to use the right event handlers to capture the event for the application to function properly. What event would you use to capture the selection of a new item in a `DropDownList` control?

   A. The `Click` event.

   B. The `SelectionChanged` event.

    C. The `SelectedIndexChanged` event.

    D. The `ChangedSelection` event.

2. What code segment represents the event handler registration for the click event of the `btnA Button` control?

    A. `this.btnA.Click.Register(new System.EventHandler`
       `(this.setList));`

    B. `this.btnA.Click.Add(new System.EventHandler`
       `(this.setList));`

    C. `this.btnA.ClickEvent += new System.EventHandler`
       `(this.setList);`

    D. `this.btnA.Click += new System.EventHandler(this.setList);`

3. When an ASP.NET server control is added to a Web Form, Visual Studio .NET adds one item to the class for the form. What item is added?

    A. The event registration.

    B. A protected class member for the control.

    C. A default event handler for the click event.

    D. A default class that inherits from the control's base class.

4. When a browser requests an `.aspx` file and the file is displayed, what is actually returned to the browser from the server?

    A. HTML

    B. XML

    C. ASPX

    D. ASP

5. What is the function of the `CustomValidator`?

    A. It allows for custom C# client-side code to validate entries in a control.

    B. It allows for a custom mixture of validator controls to use one central control for the display of messages.

    C. It uses scripted client-side code to validate the entry in a control.

    D. It uses server-side code to validate the entry in a control.

6. What attribute must be set on a validator control for the validation to work?

    A. `Validate`

    B. `ValidateControl`

    C. `ControlToBind`

    D. `ControlToValidate`

7. The `Items` property of a `ListBox` is a reference to what kind of object?

   A. `Item`

   B. `ListItem`

   C. `String`

   D. Index value

8. What is the use of the `WebForm.aspx.cs` file?

   A. Holds the HTML code for the form.

   B. Holds the control configuration for the form.

   C. Holds the C# code for the codebehind module.

   D. Holds the C# code that will be translated into HTML on the client.

9. Given an ASP.NET Web Form called `WebForm1`, what class does the `WebForm1` class inherit from by default?

   A. `System.Web.Form`

   B. `System.Web.GUI.Page`

   C. `System.Web.UI.Page`

   D. `System.Web.UI.Form`

10. What layout mode is the default when a new Web Form is created?

    A. `GridBagLayout`

    B. `GridLayout`

    C. `FlowLayout`

    D. `FormLayout`

11. When does the `DropDownListBox` control reload its list?

    A. Every time the server-side codebehind module is called.

    B. Every 2 minutes by default.

    C. When the user clicks on an entry in the control.

    D. Never.

12. What is the `Web.config` file used for?

    A. To store the global information and variable definitions for the application.

    B. Configures the time that the server-side codebehind module is called.

    C. To configure the web server.

    D. To configure the web browser.

13. What happens if an ASP.NET server control with event-handling routines is missing the `runat="server"` attribute from its definition?

    A. The control will operate as usual; the default is `runat="server"`.

    B. The control will revert to being a client-side control and function as such.

    C. The control will not function; the default is `runat="client"`.

    D. The compilation of the application will fail.

14. What happens if an ASP.NET server control with no event-handling routines is missing the `runat="server"` attribute from its definition?

    A. The control will operate as usual; the default is `runat="server"`.

    B. The control will revert to being a client-side control and function as such.

    C. The control will not function; the default is `runat="client"`.

    D. The compilation of the application will fail.

15. After capturing the `SelectedIndexChanged` event for a `ListBox` control, you find that the event handler doesn't execute. What could the problem be?

    A. The `AutoEventWireup` attribute is set to False.

    B. The `AutomaticPostBack` attribute is set to False.

    C. The codebehind module is not properly compiled.

    D. The `ListBox` must be defined `WithEvents`.

Test Answers

    1. C.

    2. D.

    3. B.

    4. A.

    5. C.

    6. D.

    7. B.

    8. C.

    9. C.

    10. B.

    11. A.

    12. A.

    13. D.

    14. C.

    15. B.

Server-Side Programs and Postback Operations

In this chapter, you will

- Separate user-interface resources from business logic
- Use and edit `Response`, `Request`, `Session`, `Server`, and `Application` objects
- Retrieve values from the properties of intrinsic objects
- Set values on the properties of intrinsic objects
- Use intrinsic objects to perform operations
- Instantiate and invoke a web service
- Instantiate and invoke a COM or COM+ component
- Instantiate and invoke a .NET component
- Call native functions by using platform invoke
- Manage data during postback events

Using server-side programming allows us to separate the business logic from the presentation services and makes it possible to create reusable objects. As you will remember from Chapter 10, the Presentation Service is responsible for displaying the information, while the Business Service handles the "logic," the rules for how the data that is stored in the Data Service will be used. In this chapter, we will look at the objects in the ASP.NET object model and at how you can manipulate that model through Visual Studio .NET. We will then look at the Web Services and how to use them, as well as the COM technology.

One compelling reason for locating business logic in a separate service layer is scalability. Scalability is the ability of a software package to be used by increasing numbers of users simultaneously, simply by adding more hardware to the application rather than rewriting the software. The major factor that limits the number of concurrent clients that can access a common application is the hardware and the network that makes the service available to the clients. The decision to place a particular process in the middle tier (the business layer) is based on whether the process is of general use in the application and whether it is frequently changed.

One of the challenges that relate to scalability deals with how to store information about the user and the context of the user's connection to the web server. We will outline how to use the postback process to maintain this information.

We will end with an overview of some additional server-side issues.

The power of the web server and the new Internet protocols are awesome. They make it possible for us to create and use server-side services, which process user requests on a central server, and offer them through web servers rather than through object request brokers (ORBs) that require proprietary protocols and possibly proprietary operating system and hardware solutions. The most common ORB in the Microsoft world is Microsoft Transaction Server, and it was the solution to distributed computing in the previous version of Visual Studio. The real power of the new Internet standards is that dissimilar software systems now can communicate with each other, so without further ado, let's visit the server side.

The ASP.NET Object Model

The objects in the ASP.NET object model were introduced in Chapter 11. They are the `Request`, `Response`, `Server`, `Application`, and `Session` objects. You are now going to meet the rest of what makes up ASP.NET and learn how to maintain state for the duration of a user's connection or the life of the application. In the following sections we will look at the namespaces used in ASP.NET and the `Page` class that abstracts the web page. We will also look at ways of remembering both the user's information (state) and the applications (global state).

ASP.NET Namespaces

The namespaces that are mostly used with ASP.NET development are listed in Table 13-1, along with a brief description of each. The number of namespaces in the .NET Framework is large, and this table lists but a small fraction of all the namespaces. You will need to import additional namespaces for other functionality that you require in the application.

 EXAM TIP Remember that the `System.Web` namespace is automatically included in all ASP.NET web pages, even if it is not listed in the source file.

We will focus our efforts in this chapter on the `System.Web` and `System.Web.UI` namespaces, and the objects those namespaces provide for our support.

The Page Class

Behind every great page there is a `Page` class; actually there is a `Page` class behind all pages, great or not. The `Page` class is the magic that makes it possible to create the type of web applications we are capable of.

Namespace	Description
System.Web	This is the most important namespace for any ASP.NET web page or application. The System.Web namespace is automatically imported into any .aspx file run on the server. This namespace holds the functionality we will use in our applications.
System.Web.UI	The classes that represent the server controls are provided in this namespace. For example, the controls we used in Chapter 12 are provided from this namespace.
System.Diagnostics	The general rule of all development is that "If anything can go wrong, it will" (Murphy's Law), but as you know, Murphy was a pessimist and he did not have access to the System.Diagnostics namespace that provides support for diagnosing problems with your pages.
System.Data	This namespace will give us data access. It and the classes it provides are so important that we will spend all of Chapter 16 on them.
System.Globalization	When we want to build web applications that are localized based on the language and culture of the user, we need the System.Globalization namespace.
System.XML	Last but not least, the XML support for .NET is in this namespace where a lot of very interesting XML support classes are located.

Table 13-1   The Basic Namespaces Used with ASP.NET

The Page class provides the framework for all web pages that will be constructed on the server—all web pages will inherit from the Page class indirectly through other abstractions. The processing of the web page on the IIS server actually creates an object representing our web page that indirectly inherits from the Page class.

The following events happen when a client requests your ASP.NET page from the IIS server:

1. A client requests an ASP.NET page on your server (such as MyPage.aspx).

2. IIS sends the request to the ASP.NET module (aspnet_isapi.dll).

3. The ASP.NET module incorporates the .aspx file in the ASP namespace, making a new class, ASP.mypage_aspx. This file inherits from System.Web.UI.Page.

4. The class is instantiated in CLR, and a rendering method is called to return HTML to the ASP.NET module that will, in turn, return the HTML to the client's browser through IIS.

Because the new class that `aspnet_isapi.dll` creates is in a new namespace and inherits from the `Page` class (`System.Web.UI.Page`) we have access to a number of methods and properties that make it possible to write very precise server-side programs. Table 13-2 lists the properties, Table 13-3 the methods, and Table 13-4 the events available from the `Page` class.

The members listed in Tables 13-2, 13-3, and 13-4 are added to your page and are part of the `Page` object that represents the page to the ASP.NET module. ASP.NET gives us all this power to work with. The `Page` object holds properties that are populated with the data received in the `Request` object; these properties hold information about, among other things, the client's browser type and version. The browser information is

Property	Description
Application	Holds a reference to the `Application` object for the current web request.
ClientTarget	Gets or sets a value that allows you to override automatic detection of browser capabilities. This property can be used to specify how a page renders for particular browser clients.
EnableViewState	Gets or sets a value indicating whether the page maintains its view state, and the view state of any server controls it contains, when the current page request ends.
ErrorPage	Gets or sets the error page to which the requesting browser is redirected in the event of an unhandled page exception.
IsPostBack	Gets a value indicating whether the page is being loaded in response to a client postback, or if it is being loaded and accessed for the first time. Postback refers to the operation of sending form data from the client to the server.
IsValid	Gets a value indicating whether page validation succeeded.
Page	Holds a reference to the `Page` instance that contains the server control.
Request	Holds a reference to the `HttpRequest` object for the requested page.
Response	Holds a reference to the `HttpResponse` object associated with the `Page` instance. This object allows you to send HTTP response data to a client and contains information about that response.
Server	Holds a reference to the `Server` object, which is an instance of the `HttpServerUtility` class.
Session	Holds a reference to the current `Session` object provided by ASP.NET.
Trace	Gets the `TraceContext` object for the current web request.
User	Gets information about the user making the page request.
Visible	Gets or sets a value indicating whether the `Page` object is rendered.

Table 13-2   Public Properties of the `Page` Class

Method	Description
DataBind()	Binds a data source to the invoked server control and all its child controls.
FindControl()	Searches the current naming container for the specified server control.
GetPostBackEventReference()	Obtains a reference to a client-side script function that causes, when invoked, the server to postback to the page.
GetType()	Gets the Type of the current instance.
GetTypeHashCode()	Retrieves a hash code that the Page object generated at run time. This hash code is unique to the Page object's control hierarchy.
HasControls()	Determines whether the server control contains any child controls.
LoadControl()	Obtains a UserControl object from a user control file.
ToString()	Returns a string that represents the current object.

Table 13-3   Public Methods of the Page Class

Event	Description
AbortTransaction	Occurs when a user aborts a transaction.
CommitTransaction	Occurs when a transaction completes (inherited from TemplateControl).
DataBinding	Occurs when the server control binds to a data source.
Disposed	Occurs when a server control is released from memory, which is the last stage of the server control lifecycle when an ASP.NET page is requested.
Error	Occurs when an unhandled exception is thrown (inherited from TemplateControl).
Init	Occurs when the server control is initialized, which is the first step in its lifecycle.
Load	Occurs when the server control is loaded into the Page object.
PreRender	Occurs when the server control is about to render (convert to HTML) for its containing Page object.
Unload	Occurs when the server control is unloaded from memory.

Table 13-4   Public Events of the Page Class

used to customize the rendered HTML that is returned to the user through the Re-sponse object. See Chapter 11 for a refresher on the five ASP.NET objects. By using the properties and methods of the Page object, you can, for example, query (and modify) the browser type and version stored in the Page object in order to render the best possible web page on the client, as well as redirect the user to custom pages, keep state (data that is remembered between visits) for the user, and so on. We will highlight some of those techniques in this section.

To demonstrate how a server-side program is constructed, let's build a web page that has a navigation system based on a DropDownList control. To build the project, start Visual Studio .NET, create a project on the localhost server, and call the project WebNav, as shown here.

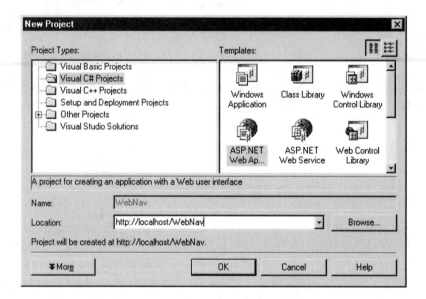

In the new project, add one Label control (lblNavigate) and set the Text property to "Navigate To:". Also, add a DropDownList control (cmbNavigate) as in Figure 13-1.

In order to populate the DropDownList control with the URLs that users can navigate to, you need to add some code to the Page_Load() event handler, as listed here:

```
private void Page_Load(object sender, System.EventArgs e)
{
  cmbNavigate.Items.Add("http://www.CSharpNow.com");
  cmbNavigate.Items.Add("http://www.osborne.com");
  cmbNavigate.Items.Add("http://www.emarj.com");
}
```

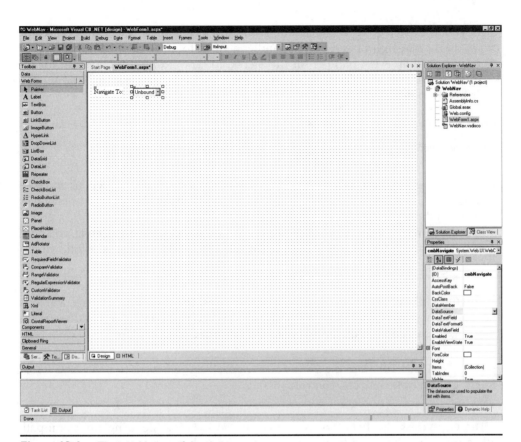

Figure 13-1   The initial layout of the project

To run the application, you press the F5 key. The resulting web page displayed in the browser should look like Figure 13-2. Use the `DropDownList` control to see the different addresses, and select an address to see what the result is.

Figure 13-2   The resulting web page

As you will see, there is no action taken when a URL is selected because the DropDownList control has no event handler defined for it. To add that functionality, we need to add an event handler for the SelectedIndexChanged() event for the DropDownList control: double-click on the control in design view, and add the following code to the event handler:

```
private void cmbNavigate_SelectedIndexChanged(object sender, System.EventArgs e)
{
    Response.Redirect(cmbNavigate.SelectedItem.Text);
}
```

The Response object, as you will recall from Chapter 11, is what gives us access to the Redirect() method. The Redirect() method tells the browser to open a new location on the Web.

In order to make the DropDownList control send the request to the server, you need to set the AutoPostBack attribute of the control to True with code like the following:

```
<asp:DropDownList AutoPostBack=True id="cmbNavigate" runat="server"/>
```

Run the application and test the different addresses. The resulting web page will look the same as in Figure 13-2, but it will now work. When you select a new address in the DropDownList control, the browser will be redirected to that address.

 EXAM TIP Use the SelectedIndexChanged event to trap events from DropDownList controls.

The Page class also helps when we need to work with a file using a physical path rather than the virtual path that is used for the web server. For example, the file ReadMe.txt that is located in the root of the WebNav application has the virtual path of /WebNav/ReadMe.txt, but depending on the configuration of the web server, the physical location of the file cannot be gleaned from the virtual path. The MapPath() method of the Page class will translate the virtual name to the physical path so we can use file-based I/O to read or write to physical drives.

The following example will read in a file called ReadMe.txt that is located in the root of the WebNav application and send it to the client browser for display. There are some additional elements to deal with in this example: how to perform file I/O and how to connect streams from source to sink (consumer) to make the data flow.

To read and write files, we use the System.IO namespace, so we must add that to our codebehind module first. In order to open and read a file, we need to call some stream methods that will open the file for us—we need a StreamReader as shown here:

```
StreamReader sr = new StreamReader(MapPath("ReadMe.txt"));
```

The `MapPath()` method is used to turn `ReadMe.txt` into the physical path for the file in the filesystem. Once we have the stream open, we can start reading the text file, line by line, through the `ReadLine()` method.

We will create an ASP.NET application called `ReadWeb` with `Button` (`cmdClick`) and `ListBox` (`lstBox`) controls on the form. The code is shown here:

```
...
using System.IO;
namespace ReadWeb
{
  public class WebForm1 : System.Web.UI.Page
  {
...
    private void cmdClick_Click(object sender, System.EventArgs e)
    {
      StreamReader sr = new StreamReader(MapPath("ReadMe.txt"));
      string nextLine;
      while ((nextLine = sr.ReadLine()) != null)
      {
        lstBox.Items.Add(nextLine);
      }
      sr.Close();
    }
  }
}
```

When you run this program by pressing F5 you will be presented with a web page that has a `ListBox` control containing all the lines from the `ReadMe.txt` file.

 EXAM TIP It is imperative that you know the five ASP.NET objects: `Request`, `Response`, `Session`, `Application`, and `Server`, and what they do.

We are now ready to start working with the objects exposed by the `Page` class. First, however, we are going to look at how to manage application and session state.

State Management

The issue of keeping state—remembering the user's data between visits to the site—is one of resources. The information consumes some resource, such as memory, disk space, or even network bandwidth, either on the server, network, or client computer. The decision to keep state must be an informed decision, not lightly taken. There must be some benefit for the client and for you in order to spend resources on remembering the user's information.

We dealt with the mechanics of keeping state in Chapter 11, so we will only touch on the issue of state here.

Application State

The *application*, as it relates to state, is defined as the entire collection of all the data, code, and users using the application. The Application object makes it possible to view the entire collection through one object. Each web site has one and only one Application object, so using it to store global information is logical. There are two types of global information commonly kept: information that relates to the data sources needed for the application and static information that the application as a whole needs to access.

 EXAM TIP   Any information that is needed throughout the entire application and that is not client specific is a candidate to be stored in the Application object.

Session State

Session state is client specific and contains information that is used during one connection (session) between the client and the web application. Session state is where you would keep the user's shopping cart, as well as the login information the user supplied upon initially connecting to the site.

We will begin our look at session state with cookies and their usefulness.

Cookies   The cookie is a small file that the web server stores on the client's computer in a directory defined by the browser's configuration. The cookie is used to store client-side session state. You would use cookies to hold much the same type of information you would use session variables (stored in the Session object on the web server) for:

- **User preferences**   This allows you to give the user the "warm and fuzzy" feeling of a custom experience.

- **User recognition**   Once users sign in, the cookie lets the application remember them so the users don't have to log in every time.

- **Window tracking**   You can keep track of pop-up windows so you don't pop up the same window all the time.

The process of writing a cookie to a user's computer starts on the web server when you add the cookie to the Response object's Cookies collection. The cookie is sent to the client's browser, which stores it on the client's hard drive. Later, when the client returns to your web site, the browser will send the cookie back. ASP.NET makes the cookie available for processing through the Request object.

To look at how cookies work, let's create an application that uses a cookie to remember what we had selected the last time we were on the site. For this application we will create a WebCookie application on the localhost. The following illustration shows this application being created.

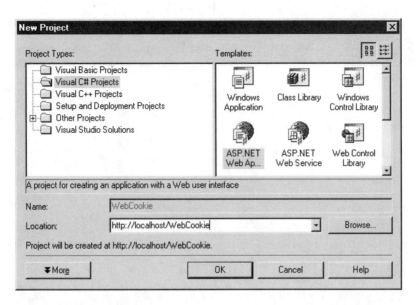

We need to add a `Panel` and call it `panOut` and a `RadioButtonList` named `rbutList` as shown in Figure 13-3. The `RadioButtonList` is created statically by adding members to the `RadioButtonList.Items` collection as can be seen in in the next illustration.

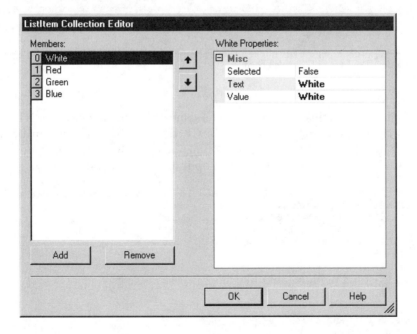

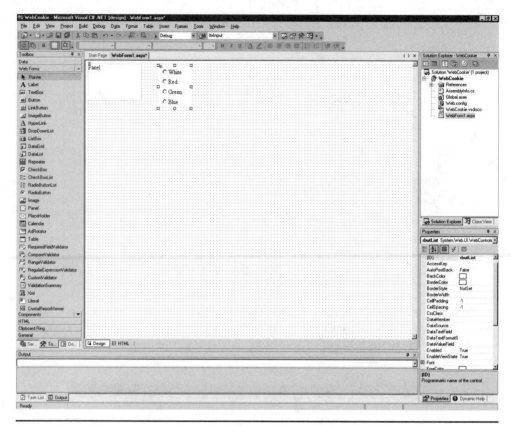

Figure 13-3 The layout of the Web Form

The first version of this application needs some code added to both the HTML document as well as the codebehind module (the C# code module where the functionality of the web page is defined) to give it some functionality. The following code segments must be added to the HTML code for the application to function properly:

```
<asp:RadioButtonList AutoPostBack="True" id="rbutList"runat="server">
  <asp:ListItem Value="White">White</asp:ListItem>
  <asp:ListItem Value="Red">Red</asp:ListItem>
  <asp:ListItem Value="Green">Green</asp:ListItem>
  <asp:ListItem Value="Blue">Blue</asp:ListItem>
</asp:RadioButtonList>
```

The codebehind module looks like this:

```
using System;
using System.Collections;
using System.ComponentModel;
using System.Data;
```

Chapter 13: Server-Side Programs and Postback Operations

```
using System.Drawing;
using System.Web;
using System.Web.SessionState;
using System.Web.UI;
using System.Web.UI.WebControls;
using System.Web.UI.HtmlControls;

namespace WebCookie
{
  public class WebForm1 : System.Web.UI.Page
  {
    protected System.Web.UI.WebControls.Panel panOut;
    protected System.Web.UI.WebControls.RadioButtonList rbutList;

    private void Page_Load(object sender, System.EventArgs e)
    {
      // Put user code to initialize the page here
      if (!(IsPostBack))
      {
        rbutList.SelectedIndex = 0;
      }
    }
...
    private void rbutList_SelectedIndexChanged(object sender, System.EventArgs e)
    {
      switch (rbutList.SelectedItem.Value)
      {
        case("Blue"):
          panOut.BackColor= Color.Blue;
          break;
        case "Red":
          panOut.BackColor = Color.Red;
          break;
        case "Green":
          panOut.BackColor = Color.Green;
          break;
        default:
          panOut.BackColor = Color.White;
          break;
      }
    }
  }
}
```

The following line in the `Page_Load()` event handler sets the default color for the `Panel`.

```
rbutList.SelectedIndex = 0;
```

The switch statement in the `SelectedIndexChanged()` event handler sets the color according to the selection of the user. Every time the user returns to the page, the color of the `Panel` is always set to the initial color white. The resulting application can be seen in Figure 13-4.

Wouldn't it be nice if we could remember the user's color selection? We can by adding some code to the `rbutList_SelectedIndexChanged()` and the `Page_Load()` event handlers. The following code segments show that change.

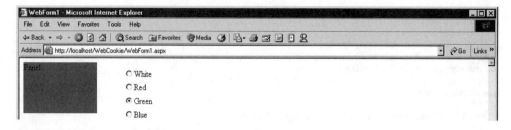

Figure 13-4   The WebColor application

First we need to write out a cookie to the client when there has been a change in the color selection:

```
private void rbutList_SelectedIndexChanged(Object sender, System.EventArgs e)
{
  switch (rbutList.SelectedItem.Value)
  {
    case("Blue"):
      panOut.BackColor= Color.Blue;
      break;
    case "Red":
      panOut.BackColor = Color.Red;
      break;
    case "Green":
      panOut.BackColor = Color.Green;
      break;
    default:
      panOut.BackColor = Color.White;
      break;
  }
  HttpCookie panCookie = new HttpCookie("BackColour");
  panCookie.Value = rbutList.SelectedItem.Value;
  Response.Cookies.Add(panCookie);
}
```

The addition of the cookie to the Response object's Cookies collection effectively sends the cookie to the client. After we run the application, we can look for the cookie in the cookies directory, which in our case is in the C:\Documents and Settings\<user name>\Cookies directory (we are using Windows 2000).

The code changes needed to use the cookie are added to the PageLoad() event handler as shown here:

```
private void Page_Load(object sender, System.EventArgs e)
{
  // Put user code to initialize the page here
  Response.Cache.SetExpires(DateTime.Now);
  if (!(IsPostBack))
  {
    switch (Request.Cookies["BackColour"].Value)
    {
      case("Blue"):
        rbutList.SelectedIndex = 3;
        break;
      case "Red":
        rbutList.SelectedIndex = 1;
        break;
      case "Green":
        rbutList.SelectedIndex = 2;
        break;
      default:
        rbutList.SelectedIndex = 0;
        break;
    }
  }
}
```

The `Request.Cookies["BackColour"].Value` statement reads the cookie we saved the last time the client visited our web site and applies it to the color of the `Panel`.

Session Variables   The session variables are used to store information that will not be saved for longer than the session is active (the default limit is 20 minutes of inactivity). Common uses for the session variables are to store the user's login name and password so they can be accessed centrally during the execution of the application. As you saw in Chapter 11, session variables can also be used for storing shopping carts, although there is a problem if the user logs in one day, selects some items, and goes away and returns the next day. If we store the shopping cart in session variables, the cart will be gone when the user returns. There are a number of solutions to the shopping-cart dilemma; for instance, we can store the shopping cart in a database server, or we can keep it on the client's computer. The deciding factors will be the application architecture and the needs of the application.

EXAM TIP   Information that is specific to a single client is a good candidate to be stored as a session variable, or, if you need a longer lifetime for the information, as a cookie.

We will look at an example that consists of a login form that saves the user's name and password in two session variables and then redirects the user to the main page of the application. We will start the project as usual, naming the application `WebLogin`, and putting it on the `localhost` server, as shown here.

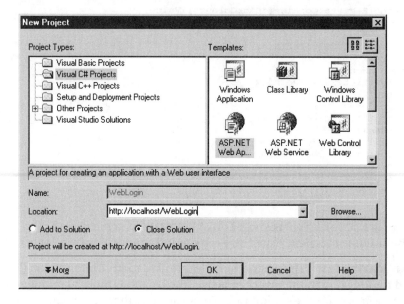

The form shown in Figure 13-5 uses two `TextBox` controls, two `Button` controls, and two `Labels` that have their properties set as listed in Table 13-5.

We now need to write some code to save the login name and password in session variables if the user clicks OK, and to clear the text boxes if the user clicks Cancel. The following two event handlers perform that task:

```
private void btnOK_Click(object sender, System.EventArgs e)
{
  // save the login and password
  Session["Login"] = Request.Form["txtLoginName"];
  Session["Password"] = Request.Form["txtPassword"];
}
private void btnCancel_Click(object sender, System.EventArgs e)
{
  txtLoginName.Text = "";
  txtPassword.Text = "";
}
```

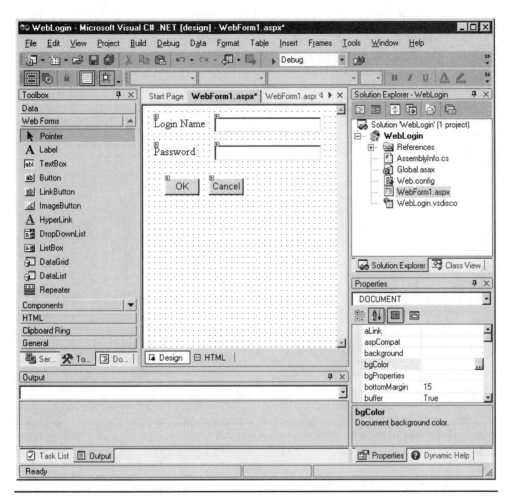

Figure 13-5   The login form for the WebLogin application

To be able to redirect the user to another page, we need first to create a new page. Name the page WebPage42.aspx and put something unique on the page so you will know the page when you see it. You can see our web page in Figure 13-6.

Control	Name	Text
Label	lblLoginName	Login Name
Label	lblPassword	Password
TextBox	txtLoginName	
TextBox	txtPassword	
Button	BtnOK	OK
Button	btnCancel	Cancel

Table 13-5   Properties for the Controls in the WebLogin Application

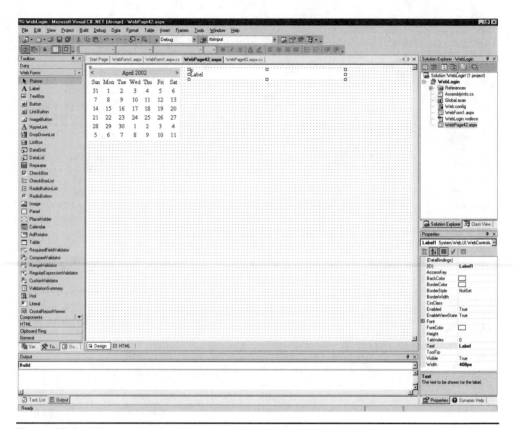

Figure 13-6   The second page of the `WebLogin` application

Add the following code to the `Page_Load()` event handler of the `WebPage42`
`.aspx` file so we can see the session variable at work:

```
private void Page_Load(object sender, System.EventArgs e)
{
  // Put user code to initialize the page here
  Label1.Text = "Welcome to our site " + Session["Login"];
}
```

Now go back to the `btnOK_Click()` event handler in the `WebForm1.aspx` (HTML)
file, and add the code to redirect the user to `WebPage42.aspx`:

```
private void btnOK_Click(object sender, System.EventArgs e)
{
  // save the login and password
  Session["Login"] = Request.Form["txtLoginName"];
  Session["Password"] = Request.Form["txtPassword"];
  Response.Redirect("WebPage42.aspx");
}
```

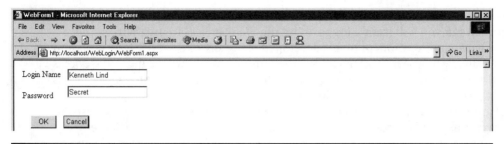

Figure 13-7   The login form

Run the application, and given the input in Figure 13-7, the final result should be as shown in Figure 13-8.

Remember to always consider the purpose of the variable when it comes to using either cookies or session variables, and you should also try to avoid keeping state if at all possible. Keeping state and providing scalability are diametrical opposites.

The next section of this chapter will take us into the Web Services world of ASP.NET, where you will learn how to use a web service.

Web Services

One of the ASP.NET technologies that has generated lots of interest is Web Services. In most industry magazines Web Services will be referred to as the "greatest thing to happen to computing." But what are they? And do you need to know the technology of Web Services to pass the two C# exams?

The answer to the second question is no, you don't need to understand the technology—you need to know how to use the services that a web service performs, but not how to develop one. The answer to the first question must be tempered by the previous

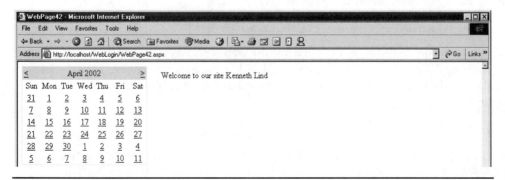

Figure 13-8   The redirected form

answer. We are not going to delve too deeply into the technology of the Web Services in this chapter, but you will learn enough about the Web Services to use them.

A *web service* is a component that is developed using any of the .NET languages and is made available for use from a web server. The component that will be the web service is accessed using the standard protocols, HTTP, XML, and SOAP (Simple Object Access Protocol); we will look at them later in this section.

XML came into its own with the introduction of .NET. It is the data format used to send everything between components in the enterprise architecture. XML's strength is that it encapsulates the data as well as the structure that is being sent. That way the receiver can use the data even if it is a totally different system from the originator of the data. In 2002 BEA, IBM, Hewlett-Packard, and Microsoft (among others) founded an organization called the Web Services Interoperability Organization (WS-I) that will take the standards further and create a uniform environment.

The Simple Object Access Protocol (SOAP) is the protocol that enables all the different components to communicate using XML to carry the data. SOAP is a software protocol that can be used by any underlying technology to deliver the calls and messages. We can use SOAP with HTTP, SMTP, or message queue technology.

Enough about the standards. You'll need to remember their acronyms, but that is true for any new technology. Let's build a web service and then put it to use.

How to Write a Web Service

A web service is made up of four separate parts:

- The processing directive
- The namespaces
- The public class
- Methods that are web-callable

The web service will be assembled in a file with the extension `.asmx`.

The processing directive defines the file as a web service:

```
<%@ WebService Language="language" Class="classname" %>
```

The `Language` attribute indicates the language the web service is written in, while the `Class` attribute defines the class that is encapsulated in the web service.

You also need to add the namespace in order to have support for the web service architecture:

```
using System.Web.Services;
```

The name of the public class that is defined in the `.asmx` file will be the name of the web service and should be the same as the name defined in the `Class` attribute in the processing directive.

The last item that makes up a web service is the methods that are marked as web methods. These methods are said to form the public interface of the web service. When you start building your Web Services, you can include more than one WebMethod in the same .asmx file.

To define a method as a web method, you need to insert a declaration before the method in question:

```
[WebMethod]
public double CtoF(double Celsius)
```

The WebMethod declaration can take attributes by itself to modify the behavior of the method.

Let's build a temperature-conversion web service to convert from degrees Celsius to degrees Fahrenheit and back. We'll call the service TemperatureConversion, and we will start by building the project on the localhost server, as shown here.

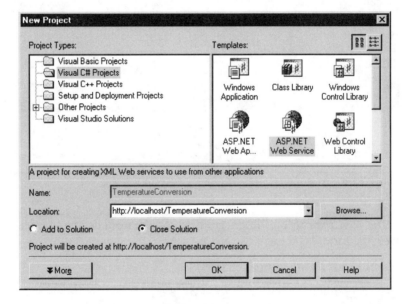

After the project is built, we end up with a view of the project as in Figure 13-9. Because we are building a web service, there will be no Design view of the project, and as you notice, the file is named TemperatureConversion.asmx.cs to indicate that it is a web service.

The text in the middle of the display prompts us to drag objects from the Toolbox or the Solution Explorer onto the view to add the object to the service. You can also click on the link for the project's source module, as shown in Figure 13-10.

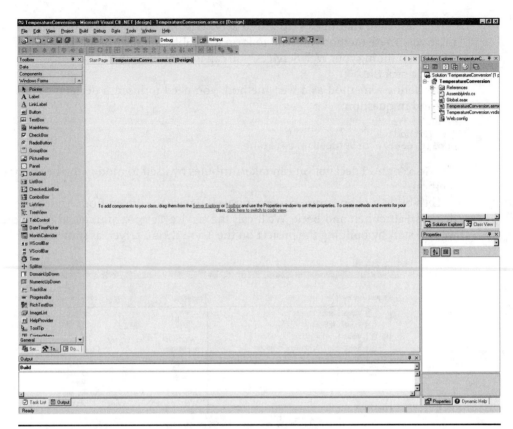

Figure 13-9 The `TemperatureConversion.asmx.cs` file

The service we are building is going to convert from degree Celsius to Fahrenheit and back; the formulas we will use are

Celsius = (Fahrenheit − 32)*5/9

Fahrenheit = (Celsius * 9/5) + 32

These conversions are done by two web methods named `CtoF` and `FtoC`, shown in the following code segment:

```
[WebMethod]
public double CtoF(double Celsius)
{
  return (Celsius * 9/5)+ 32;
}

[WebMethod]
public double FtoC(double Fahrenheit)
{
  return (Fahrenheit - 32)*5/9;
}
```

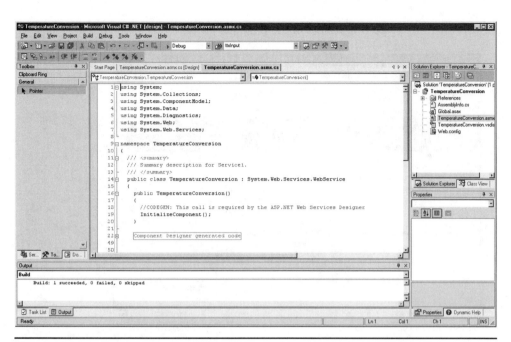

Figure 13-10   The source module

To test the web service, press F5 to start the component on the server. The default output from a web service started in this fashion can be seen in the following illustration—the service is presented and the two web methods are listed as hyperlinks.

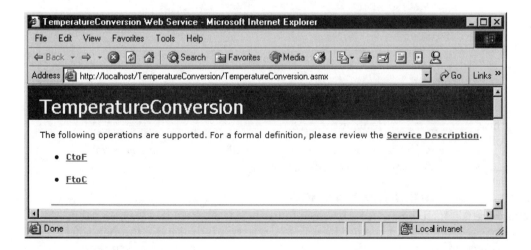

Clicking on the CtoF hyperlink results in the page shown here.

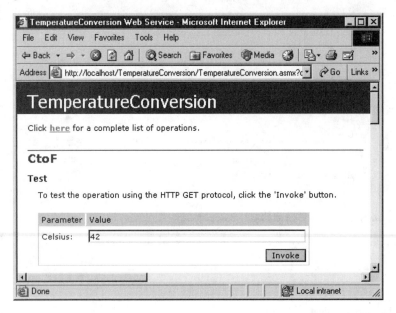

Entering a value in Celsius and clicking the Invoke button results in the XML output shown next. The different XML documents that are displayed in the web page document is the way to call the web service from another client.

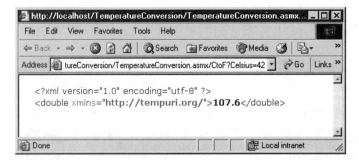

EXAM TIP Even though you will not be expected to build a web service in the exams, you can expect to be presented with questions containing web service information as part of the question.

How to Consume a Web Service

A web service is not all that useful if we need to use it in the convoluted way we did in the previous section. Instead, we need a way to get access to the service through software. This section will take you through the steps needed to consume a web service. Microsoft uses the term *consume* to mean *connect to and use* in the context of Web Services, so we will use the same terminology in this chapter.

The first step in consuming a web service is to create an interface for the client application so that it can communicate with the web methods in the service. This interface is called a proxy, and it communicates with the web service on behalf of the client application. The proxy resides on the client once it is created.

The proxy is created by compiling a Web Service Description Language (WSDL) file that will create the map needed for the `WebMethod` calls and how the client calls them. The client calls the web methods in the proxy, which in turn make the call to the web service. The network and protocol settings and addressing is the responsibility of the proxy, as is the management of the WSDL. The proxy abstracts the web service so that it looks like a local service to the client.

Here is the sequence of events when a client uses a web service:

1. The client executes a method in the proxy.

2. The proxy handles the call by first encapsulating the call in a packet that includes any required parameters for the call.

3. The proxy sends the packet to the web service using the protocol defined in the WSDL file that built the proxy.

4. The web service receives the packet and extracts the call with the parameters, executes the `WebMethod`, and formulates a return packet for the client.

5. The web service returns the packet to the proxy.

6. The packet is received by the proxy and the return data is extracted.

7. The client receives the data from the proxy.

The proxy will use XML to encapsulate the data and calls as they are sent over the network—the underlying protocol is immaterial.

The next task is to build the proxy, the proxy will be build into a run-time library that has the .dll extension. The steps involved start by creating the C# source code file from the web service followed by compiling that source in to a run-time library.

We are going to set up a run-time library for the `TemperatureConversion` web service in the previous section.

We are going to perform the tasks from a command prompt, so the first thing to do is start the Visual Studio .NET command prompt. Then, at the command prompt, use the cd (change directory) command to go to the directory where the `Tempera tureConversion.asmx` file is stored. In our case, that is `C:\Inetpub\wwwroot\ TemperatureConversion`.

Next you need to execute the following command from the command prompt:

```
>wsdl /l:cs /o:TemperatureConversionProxy.cs
http://localhost/TemperatureConversion/TemperatureConversion.asmx?WSDL
    /n:TempConvService
```

The output from the command should look like this:

```
Microsoft (R) Web Services Description Language Utility
[Microsoft (R) .NET Framework, Version 1.0.3705.0]
Copyright (C) Microsoft Corporation 1998-2001. All rights reserved.

Writing file 'TemperatureConversionProxy.cs'.
```

To compile the proxy code, we use the `csc.exe` compiler. This will build the runtime library:

```
>csc /out:TempConvProxy.dll /t:library /r:system.web.dll, system.dll,
system.xml.dll, system.web.services.dll, system.data.dll
TemperatureConversionProxy.cs
```

The output from the preceding command should look like this:

```
Microsoft (R) Visual C# .NET Compiler version 7.00.9466
for Microsoft (R) .NET Framework version 1.0.3705
Copyright (C) Microsoft Corporation 2001. All rights reserved.
```

Now you need to create a root directory for the application at `C:\InetPub\WWWRoot\TempConv`, and you'll need a bin directory in that root directory:

```
C:\Inetpub\wwwroot>md TempConv
C:\Inetpub\wwwroot>md TempConv\bin
```

Copy the newly created `TempConvProxy.dll` to the bin directory, and then create an application in the root (`C:\InetPub\WWWRoot\TempConv`) as `Temperature.aspx` using the following code:

```
<%@ Page Language="c#" Debug="true" %>
<%@ Import namespace="TempConvService" %>
<script Language="c#" runat="server">
private void CDtoFD(object sender, EventArgs e)
{
  TempConvService.TemperatureConversion tc =
        new TempConvService.TemperatureConversion();
  lblOutF.Text = System.Convert.ToString(tc.CtoF(System.Convert.ToDouble(txtTemp.Text)));
  lblOutF.Text = lblOutF.Text + " F";
}
private void FDtoCD(object sender, EventArgs e)
{
  TempConvService.TemperatureConversion tc =
        new TempConvService.TemperatureConversion();
  lblOutC.Text = System.Convert.ToString(tc.FtoC(System.Convert.ToDouble(txtTemp.Text)));
  lblOutC.Text = lblOutC.Text + " C";
}
</script>
<html>
  <body>
    <form id="Form1" method="post" runat="server">
      <asp:TextBox id="txtTemp" runat="server"/><br/>
      <asp:Button id="Button1" runat="server" Text="Convert to Fahrenheit" OnClick="CDtoFD"/>
      <asp:Label id="lblOutF" runat="server"/><br/>
      <asp:Button id="Button2" runat="server" Text="Convert to Celsius" OnClick="FDtoCD"/>
      <asp:Label id="lblOutC" runat="server"/><br/>
    </form>
  </body>
</html>
```

The bold lines in the preceding code are the important ones. The directive in the second line will cause the search for the `TempConvService`, starting in the local bin directory. Three lines further along, the web service is instantiated, so we can call the web methods in the service. Save and run the application by pressing F5; the resulting display is seen in Figure 13-11.

 EXAM TIP The application must be able to find the proxy. The local bin directory is the default location where the application will search for libraries.

What made our example work is the way we created the proxy and then placed it in the bin directory of the application. The bin directory that is located in the root of the application is the default location where the web service will look for run-time libraries and assemblies. If you want to move the application to a different web server you would move the proxy to that web server and leave the web service on the original server. In order to create a proxy for a web service that is located on a different web server from the one where it will be consumed you will need to create a new WSDL file specifying the web server where the web service is running. For example, to use the web service on the server named `kensnabben.nopcomp.com` we would run the WSDL command as follows:

```
>wsdl /l:cs /o:TemperatureConversionProxy.cs
http://kensnabben.nopcomp.com/TemperatureConversion/TemperatureConversion.asmx?WSDL
/n:TempConvService
```

Giving the fully qualified URL for the web service is one way of linking the web service with the client, and it is all very well when you are writing a web service to run on your own computers. However, if you want to use the service from other businesses or vendors, you'll want to use UDDI (Universal Description, Discovery, and Integration) to make a dynamic web service structure. UDDI is an industry standard that is supported by Microsoft and IBM, among others.

 EXAM TIP The exam includes questions with code segments that may use many different techniques—you will need to know the C# language to glean the right answer.

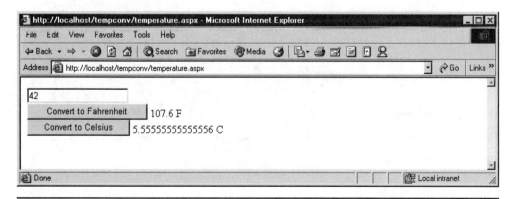

Figure 13-11 Consuming the web service

COM Interoperability

Even though Microsoft considers the .NET environment to be the latest and greatest in software engineering, and in a perfect world everyone would immediately switch from their current software environment to the .NET Framework, we don't live in a perfect world. Companies that have developed their enterprise applications around the COM and COM+ technologies will keep using the software they have invested in for quite some time. In this section, we will look at the interoperability between COM and .NET.

The first thing to look at is the Add Reference dialog box in the VS .NET IDE (see Figure 13-12). This dialog box gives us the ability to add and remove references to objects that are part of the project.

To open the Add Reference dialog box, select Project | Add Reference. The dialog box has three tabs for different types of objects: the .NET tab is for .NET assemblies, the COM tab is where we will import COM components into our project (see Figure 13-13), and the Projects tab lists all the projects that are referenced in the current project.

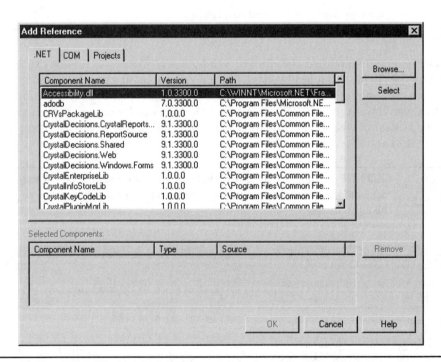

Figure 13-12   The .NET tab of the Add Reference dialog box

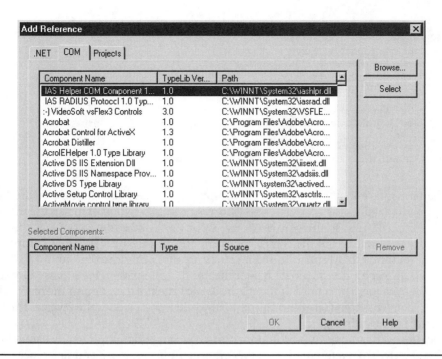

Figure 13-13 The COM tab of the Add Reference dialog box

Clicking the Browse button in the Add Reference dialog box displays the Select Component dialog box, where you can select a COM component to interoperate with, as shown in Figure 13-14. Once the component is selected and you click Open, the component is added to the reference list in the Add Reference dialog box, as shown in Figure 13-15.

Now that the reference for the component has been added to the project, you can use it in your C# code. Visual Studio .NET has created a namespace for the component and added the classes from the COM component into that namespace. You can use the COM components in the same way you use native C# objects: by setting a reference, and instantiating and invoking the component's classes.

The following code segment uses the temperature-conversion COM component TConv that we added in the Add Reference dialog box.

```
private void Button1_Click(object sender, System.EventArgs e)
{
  TConv.CConverterClass tc;
```

```
      tc = new TConv.CConverterClass();
      double d;
      d = Convert.ToDouble(TextBox1.Text);
      Label1.Text = Convert.ToString(tc.FtoC(ref d));
}
private void Button2_Click(object sender, System.EventArgs e)
{
   TConv.CConverterClass tc;
   tc = new TConv.CConverterClass();
   double d;
   d = Convert.ToDouble(TextBox1.Text);
   Label2.Text = Convert.ToString(tc.CtoF(ref d));
}
```

The namespace that was used for the wrapper is `TConv`, and the class in the COM component that does the conversions is `CConverter`. The wrapper makes that into the `CConverterClass`, so the type is `TConv.CConverterClass`.

We use the methods of the class to perform our processing. The COM component has two methods that return `double` values: `CtoF(ref double)` and `FtoC(ref double)`. The `ref double` data type indicates that the parameter is passed by reference, not by value. The names of the methods indicate the direction of the conversion, `CtoF()` converts from Celsius to Fahrenheit, while `FtoC()` does the reverse. The final converter is shown in Figure 13-16.

The process of adding COM components to a web page is simplified by using the Visual Studio .NET. To reference the COM component through the Add Reference dialog

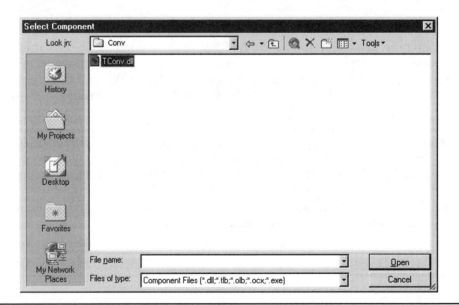

Figure 13-14   Browsing for a COM component

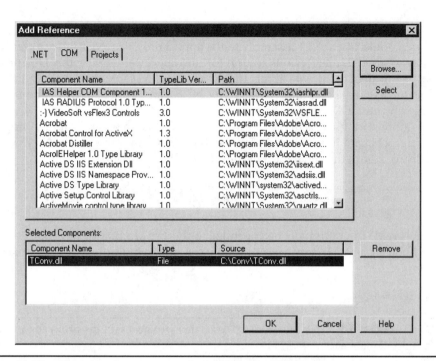

Figure 13-15   The selected component in the Add Reference dialog box

box, two tasks are performed: it generates the .NET proxy for the COM component, and it puts a copy of the component in the project directory.

The .NET proxy that is generated by Visual Studio .NET is technically called the Runtime Callable Wrapper (RCW); it is the part that makes the component self-describing.

Figure 13-16   The temperature converter application

This means it wraps the COM component in a layer of XML, called the *manifest,* so the component looks like a .NET assembly to the application. The .NET proxy differs from the proxy we used in the previous section to consume a web service; the .NET proxy is the .NET equivalent to the type library that was used in the COM model; the .NET proxy contains the data type mapping between the .NET Framework data types and the data types used by the COM component.

The utility tool that actually creates the proxy is the Type Library Importer (TlbImp.exe), and it is included with the .NET SDK. You can execute TlbImp.exe manually to control the generation of the .NET proxy.

```
The assembly version must be specified as: Major.Minor.Build.Revision.
Multiple reference assemblies can be specified by using the /reference option
multiple times.
```

A resource ID can optionally be appended to the TypeLibName (MyModule.dll) when importing a type library from a module containing multiple type libraries. Here's an example:

```
TlbImp MyModule.dll\1
```

EXAM TIP   Use the TlbImp.exe utility to generate the proxy for a COM component.

On the surface it looks like the generation of the .NET proxy has hidden the imported COM component (with all its problems) behind the RCW; that is not the case. The COM component is still the component that needs to perform the work. COM components that are used by .NET applications still have to be deployed in the same careful and meticulous way as always—they must even be registered using the regsvr32.exe utility like this:

```
regsvr32 tconv.dll
```

EXAM TIP   The regsvr32.exe is only used to register COM components in the Registry. COM components used by .NET applications must be registered in the Registry.

Platform Invoke

There are times when you'll need to get access to functionality that is in libraries or applications that are considered *unmanaged code.* One example is any calls you make to the Win32 API.

In the .NET Framework, the term *unsafe code* refers to code that has been marked as an unsafe code block. The code in such a block can use the entire palette of features that are not normally allowed in C#, such as pointers—they can be used if you turn off the language's safety checking. Code segments in C# can be marked as unsafe by setting attributes for those sections; however, the default is for code to be marked as safe. Unsafe code is still managed by the .NET environment.

Unmanaged code is code that is run outside the .NET environment. .NET has no control over the garbage collection or the security of the code.

Platform invoke (`pinvoke`) is the functionality provided by the CLR to enable managed code to call unmanaged native DLL entry points—one example of a native dynamic link library is a library that is compiled from languages such as C to be part of the operating system. An entry point is the address of the function. The most common use of `pinvoke` is to call Win32 API methods to extend the application; these API methods are in libraries like `user32.dll`, `gdi32.dll`, and `kernel32.dll`. The `pinvoke` functionality resides in the `System.Runtime.InteropServices` namespace, which must be imported for `pinvoke` to work.

The API method being called is defined using attributes to indicate what library the method is in. Consider the following code segment:

```
using System.Runtime.InteropServices;
...
[DllImport("user32.dll")]
public static extern int MessageBoxW(int Modal,
                                     string Message,
                                     string Caption,
                                     int Options);
```

The preceding segment has exposed (or imported) the API method `MessageBoxW` from `user32.dll`. If we look up the signature for the method, we find that it is as follows:

```
WINUSERAPI int WINAPI MessageBoxW (HWND hWnd, LPCWSTR lpText,
                                   LPWCWSTR lpCaption, UINT uType);
```

The `MessageBoxW()` method is the Unicode version of the `MessageBox()` method.

Once the method has been imported, we can call it by using the signature of the method as in the following code segment:

```
MessageBoxW(0, "Hello World!", "The Pinvoke Hello Program", 0);
```

The result of the call can be seen in the `MessageBoxW`, here.

If you need to rename the methods in the imported libraries, you use a different version of the Dll Import attribute, as shown in the following sample:

```
[DllImport("user32.dll", EntryPoint = "MessageBoxW")]
public static extern int InfoBox(int Modal, string Message, string Caption,
                                 int Options);
```

The WIN32 API uses a very terse style for some of its methods names, and you might want to use something that fits the naming convention of your project. Or you might have a name conflict between the imported method and an existing method.

Although it looks very beneficial to use pinvoke to get to platform-dependent functionality, it is platform dependent, and one of the major selling points for .NET is the platform independence built into the system. Use pinvoke sparingly, and only after solid planning. One reason for using pinvoke is to get direct access to operating- system functionality that is too slow or cumbersome to access through the .NET Framework.

NOTE Remember, the platform invoke bypasses the platform independence we want to achieve.

ASP.NET and Events

In earlier chapters in this part of the book, we used controls in Web Forms and wrote event-handling code for them. Now we will look at how the event is wired to actually perform the actions we need.

The following code segment is the default codebehind module for an ASP.NET web application:

```
using System;
using System.Collections;
using System.ComponentModel;
using System.Data;
using System.Drawing;
using System.Web;
using System.Web.SessionState;
using System.Web.UI;
using System.Web.UI.WebControls;
using System.Web.UI.HtmlControls;

namespace Events
{
  public class WebForm1 : System.Web.UI.Page
  {
    private void Page_Load(object sender, System.EventArgs e)
    {
      // Put user code to initialize the page here
    }
```

```
        #region Web Form Designer generated code
        override protected void OnInit(EventArgs e)
        {
          InitializeComponent();
          base.OnInit(e);
        }
        private void InitializeComponent()
        {
          this.Load += new System.EventHandler(this.Page_Load);
        }
        #endregion
    }
}
```

The important method, InitializeComponent(), has been highlighted in the code. It is called from the OnInit() event handler that will be called at the start of every ASP.NET web page. By default, the only event handler that is registered is the Page_Load() event handler, and that is where we should write the startup code for the page.

When we add components to the form, a protected member variable is created to hold the control variable. The following is the declaration for a Button control:

```
protected System.Web.UI.WebControls.Button Button1;
```

In order to handle the events from the control, there must be entries in the InitializeComponent() method to register the event handler. Their registration entries can be entered manually, or we can let Visual Studio .NET perform the registration for us. In the case of the Button control, the most common event to be handled is the Click event, and to request that Visual Studio .NET add the event handler for us, we need to double-click the control in Design view. The following is the code that is added to the codebehind module:

```
// the event handler registration in InitializeComponent()
this.Button1.Click += new System.EventHandler(this.Button1_Click);
...
// the event handler that Visual Studio .NET creates
private void Button1_Click(object sender, System.EventArgs e)
{
}
```

The event-handler registration is very flexible, and it gives us the control we need over how events are handled. We can use one event handler for a large number of controls to truly centralize our code, as we did with the 26 Button controls in the address book application in Chapter 12.

You can double-click on any control in Design view to add the most common event handlers. Other handlers will need to be added manually, defining the event handler first and then registering the event handler. The code in the codebehind module that executes in response to the event will not execute immediately, nor will it execute on the client—it will execute on the server, and only when the postback event occurs.

The Postback Event

The server-centric Web Form needs some way to communicate events and data back to the server from the client. The way that is handled with ASP.NET web pages is with the *postback*, which returns the data and any events that might have happened on the client since the last postback to the server. The benefit behind sending the data from the client to the web server is that between calls to the server we can maintain the information contained in the form on the server. In traditional forms, if we switch away from a form and then return, we need to reenter all the information again. The postback process ensures that we maintain the state of the form between calls.

The following example will show the difference between a traditional HTML form and an ASP.NET web form. The HTML form is built with the following HTML code:

```
<html>
<head>
  <title>HTML Form</title>
</head>
<body>
  <form method="post">
    What is your favorite sport?<br/>
    <br/>
    <input type="radio" value="Football" name="sport">Football<br/>
    <input type="radio" value="Hockey" name="sport">Hockey<br/>
    <input type="radio" value="Soccer" name="sport">Soccer<br/>
    <input type="radio" value="Baseball" name="sport">Baseball<br/>
    <input type="radio" value="Rugby" name="sport">Rugby<br/>
    <input type="submit" value="Send selection"
              onclick="alert('You have clicked the submit button!')">
  </form>
</body>
</html>
```

We saved this file in the root of our web server (C:\inetpub\wwwroot\) and called the file htmlform.htm. Opening the form in the browser allows you to make a selection for your favorite sport, as shown in Figure 13-17. After you click Send Selection, the form clears and appears as in Figure 13-18. The form cleared as we submitted the data to the server. This happens because the data is sent to the server and the original page is redrawn; at no point in this process is any state being saved.

Now we will look at the equivalent form using ASP.NET and postback. The following ASP.NET page (htmlform.aspx) will display the same form as the HTML version does, but the state is preserved as we submit the form to the server.

```
<html>
<head>
  <title>HTML Form</title>
</head>
<body>
  <form runat="server">
```

```
      What is your favorite sport?<br/>
      <br/>
      <asp:radiobuttonlist id="sport" runat="server">
        <asp:listitem id="Football" value="Football" runat="server" />
        <asp:listitem id="Hockey" value="Hockey" runat="server" />
        <asp:listitem id="Soccer" value="Soccer" runat="server" />
        <asp:listitem id="Baseball" value="Baseball" runat="server" />
        <asp:listitem id="Rugby" value="Rugby" runat="server" />
      </asp:radiobuttonlist>
      <input type="submit" value="Send selection">
    </form>
  </body>
</html>
```

The resulting display can be seen in Figure 13-19. After selecting a sport and clicking the button, we still have our selection in the display, showing that the state of the form has been remembered.

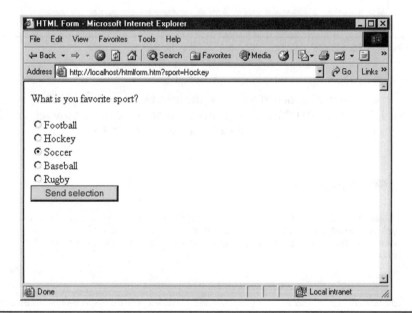

Figure 13-17   The `htmlform.htm` page with a selection

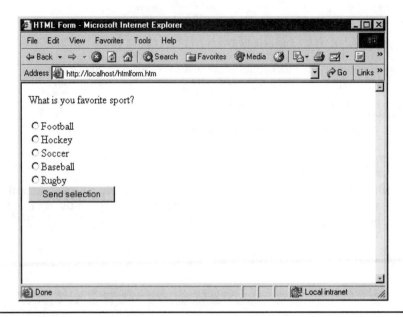

Figure 13-18   The `htmlform.htm` page after sending the data

To understand what happened and how the selection was remembered, we need to look at the HTML code that the ASP.NET process sent to the client browser. The following listing is the resulting HTML for the display in Figure 13-19.

```
<html>
<head>
  <title>HTML Form</title>
</head>
<body>
  <form name="_ctl0" method="post" action="htmlform.aspx" id="_ctl0">
    <input type="hidden" name="__VIEWSTATE"
    value="dDwyMDE0NTgwNzI1Ozs+rR+xbfriVGiHInW3uHd11uisuj4=" />
  What is your favorite sport?<br/>
  <br/>
  <table id="sport" border="0">
    <tr>
      <td><input id="sport_0" type="radio" name="sport" value="Football" />
          <label for="sport_0">Football</label></td>
    </tr><tr>
      <td><input id="sport_1" type="radio" name="sport" value="Hockey" />
          <label for="sport_1">Hockey</label></td>
    </tr><tr>
      <td><input id="sport_2" type="radio" name="sport" value="Soccer"
```

```
                checked="checked" />
        <label for="sport_2">Soccer</label></td>
   </tr><tr>
     <td><input id="sport_3" type="radio" name="sport" value="Baseball" />
        <label for="sport_3">Baseball</label></td>
   </tr><tr>
     <td><input id="sport_4" type="radio" name="sport" value="Rugby" />
        <label for="sport_4">Rugby</label></td>
   </tr>
</table>
   <input type="submit" value="Send selection">
  </form>
</body>
</html>
```

As you can see, the `radiobuttonlist` from the `htmlform.aspx` listing was turned into a table with standard HTML `radio input` elements.

The highlighted portions of the HTML code are what make ASP.NET's postback work. The hidden control with the name `__VIEWSTATE` and the binary value `"dDwyMDE0NTgwNzI1Ozs+rR+xbfriVGiHInW3uHd11uisuj4="` is the key. The value of the `__VIEWSTATE` control is the binary representation (hash) of the form, and it is the comparison between the original version of the form, as represented by the

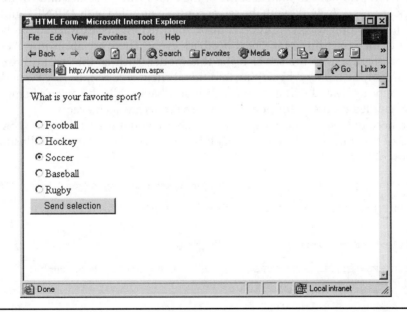

Figure 13-19   The ASP.NET form

binary string, and the current form, as represented by the values of the controls. That gives ASP.NET the ability to maintain the state of the form.

There is one other postback issue to look at, and it focuses on the `Page_Load()` event handler of the Web Form, which will be called for every postback. We normally reset the form in the `Page_Load()` event handler, but resetting the form rather than persisting the state would defeat our purposes. However, there is one property of the `Page` object that is available to us and can prevent this problem. We can test whether the `IsPostBack` property is True or False, as shown in the following code segment:

```
private void Page_Load(object sender, System.EventArgs e)
{
    // Test if this is a postback event
    if (!IsPostBack)
    {
        // Put user code to initialize the page here
        // any subsequent visits to this page will result in
        // that this block will be bypassed
    }
}
```

Now that we have looked at how postback maintains the data for a form between server calls we will need to look at some of the issues with postback and controls. The postback process only works with the server controls supplied with ASP.NET, and it is by default initiated only by the `Button` control. All other events are queued on the client and sent to the server during the next postback event. There are also some events that cannot be processed by the server using this model, such as the `MouseOver` event, which can only be handled by writing traditional client-side scripts. Any event that will be called repeatedly and will need immediate feedback while the page is being viewed must be handled on the client side. The mouse events are such events.

If you need to have a control trigger the postback, you must set the `AutoPostBack` attribute of the control to True (the default is False). The following code illustrates the use of `AutoPostBack`:

```
<%@ Page language="c#" Codebehind="WebForm1.aspx.cs" AutoEventWireup="false"
Inherits="AddressBook.WebForm1" %>
<!DOCTYPE HTML PUBLIC "-//W3C//DTD HTML 4.0 Transitional//EN" >
<HTML>
  <HEAD>
    <title>WebForm1</title>
...
    <LINK REL="STYLESHEET" TYPE="text/css" HREF="AddressBook.css">
  </HEAD>
  <body MS_POSITIONING="GridLayout">
    <h1 align="center">Address Book</h1>
    <br>
    <form id="Form1" method="post" runat="server">
      <asp:ListBox id="lstAddress" AutoPostBack="True"></asp:ListBox>
    </form>
  </body>
</html>
```

Be very careful with the use of `AutoPostBack`. There is additional overhead associated with the postback process, and raising the `AutoPostBack` event from numerous components will adversely affect the application. The state of the page or the view is controlled by setting the `EnableViewState` attribute for the control, or for the entire page. If you have controls on the form that do not need to have their state maintained by the postback process, you should mark those controls' `EnableViewState` properties to False (the default is True). When you set the `EnableViewState` property to False, the control will not participate in the postback event:

```
<asp:label EnableViewState="False" runat="server"/>
```

If you want to disable view state for an entire page, set the @ Page directive's `EnableViewState` attribute to False, as in this example:

```
<@ Page EnableViewState="False">
```

Summary

This chapter has taken you through the server-side neighborhood of .NET, from the ASP.NET objects (`Request`, `Response`, `Session`, `Application`, `Server`), through web services and COM components, to the waters of platform invoke. The amount of space devoted to these topics in the chapter reflects their relative importance on the exam. The topic of Web Services is not "supposed" to be in the exam, but we feel that it is still a topic that might show up, so be prepared to know the basics about how to build a web service.

You might expect combination questions that use information from this chapter to set the background for another question.

Test Questions

1. What must be done before you can consume a web service?

   A. Build a proxy library by using the `TblImp.exe` utility.

   B. Build a proxy library by using the `Disc.exe` utility.

   C. Build a proxy library by using the `csc.exe` utility.

   D. Build a proxy library by using the `wsdl.exe` utility.

2. You need to use the web service `TempConvService`. Where should you place the proxy file?

   A. In the lib directory off the root directory of the application.

   B. In the root directory of the application.

   C. In the bin directory off the root directory of the application.

   D. In the bin directory of .NET Framework.

3. You need to use the web service `TempConvService`. What page directives correctly expose the web service?

   A. `<%@ Page Language="c#" Debug="true" %>`
      `<%@ Import = "TempConvService" %>`

   B. `<%@ Page Language="c#" Debug="true" %>`
      `<%@ Import namespace="TempConvService" %>`

   C. `<%@ Page Language="c#" Debug="true" %>`
      `<%@ Import ProxyNameSpace="TempConvService" %>`

   D. `<%@ Page Language="c#" Debug="true" %>`
      `<%@ Import namespace="bin/TempConvService" %>`

4. You need to call a function that is located in a library named `MyLibrary.dll`, and this is the function signature:

   ```
   int MyFunc(int intAction, int intOption, uint uValue)
   ```

   You also need to rename the function to `Func42` to avoid name conflicts in the application. Which code segment will correctly make the function available to your application?

   A. `[DllImport("MyLibrary.dll")]`
      `public static extern int Func42 (int intAction, int intOption, int uValue);`

   B. `[DllImport("MyLibrary.dll", EntryPoint = "Func42")]`
      `public static extern int Func42 (int intAction, int intOption, uint uValue);`

   C. `[DllImport("MyLibrary.dll")]`
      `public static extern int MyFunc() = Func42();`

   D. `[DllImport("MyLibrary.dll", EntryPoint = "MyFunc")]`
      `public static extern int Func42 (int intAction, int intOption, uint uValue);`

5. You need to call a method located in a web service named `TService` that has been correctly registered in your application. The method is in the class `Tconv` and is named `CtoF()` with the following signature:

   ```
   int CtoF(double dd)
   ```

   What code segment correctly calls the `CtoF()` method?

   A. `TService.Tconv tc = new TService.Tconv;`
      `int x = tc.CtoF(42.12);`

   B. `TService tc = new TService();`
      `Int x = tc.CtoF(42.12);`

   C. `TService.Tconv tc = new TService.Tconv();`
      `x = tc.CtoF(42.12);`

D. `TService.Tconv tc = new TService.Tconv();`
   `int x = tc.CtoF(42.12);`

6. You have been given the task of designing a web service to expose the data that is stored in a database on the server. In order to successfully build the Web Services, you need to import some namespaces. What is the minimum namespace you need to import?

A. `System.Web`

B. `System.WebServices`

C. `System.Web.Services`

D. `System.Web.ServiceModel`

7. You have designed an event for the class you are working on, and the event is declared as follows:

```
// declare the delegate for the event
public delegate int MugEmptyHandler(int RefillVolume);
// declare the event
public static event MugEmptyHandler OnMugEmpty;
```

When you try to register the event in the client code by using the following line, you receive a syntax error:

```
this.OnMugEmpty += new MugEmptyHandler(this.Mug_Empty);
```

You need to make the `OnMugEmpty` event functional. What will you do?

A. Change the declaration of the event to indicate the parameter.

B. Change the declaration of the event to indicate the return type.

C. Change the declaration of the delegate to have no parameters.

D. Change the declaration of the delegate to have a void return type.

8. You are building an event handler for the `SendFax` event from the `sFax` component, and you have written the following code:

```
private void Send_Fax()
{
  Console.WriteLine("Fax is sent");
}
```

When you test the event handler, you find that it never runs. What code must be added to your application to make the event execute in response to the `SendFax` event?

A. `public delegate SendFax(Send_Fax);`

B. `this.sFax.SendFax += new SendFaxHandler(this.Send_Fax);`

C. `public event SendFax(Send_Fax);`

D. `this.sFax.SendFax =+ new SendFaxHandler(this.Send_Fax);`

9. Your manager has asked you to describe what you would use application variables for. What statement best describes the use of application variables?

   A. Application variables are used to keep state for each connected user.

   B. Application variables are used to keep state for the web site.

   C. Application variables are used to keep state for all the applications on the server.

   D. Application variables are used to keep state for all application objects in the web site.

10. You are using Visual Studio .NET to set up a reference to a COM component, but the reference operation fails. What is one possible solution?

    A. Register the COM component with .NET using `TlbImp.exe`.

    B. Register the COM component using `wsdl.exe`.

    C. Move the COM component to the bin directory of the application.

    D. Register the COM component in the Registry using `Regsvr32.exe`.

11. What information do you need to have in order to successfully reference a web service using the Add Reference dialog box?

    A. The URI for the web service's `.asmx` file.

    B. The URL for the web service's `.asmx` file.

    C. The URL for the web service's `disco` file.

    D. The URI for the web service's `disco` file.

12. You have defined some web service methods, but when you test the web service, you do not have the methods available. The web service is defined as follows:

```
[WebMethod]
private void email(string to, string[] message, int option)
{
...
}
```

What will you do to solve the problem?

    A. Replace the attribute with `[WebServiceMethod]`.

    B. Make the method `public`.

    C. Change the `string[]` to an object array.

    D. Change the return type to `int`.

13. You find that after running the following command-line commands from the root directory of your web site that the web service is not available:

```
>wsdl /l:cs /o:Address.cs http://localhost/Address/Address.asmx?WSDL
/n:AddressService
>csc /out:AddressProxy.dll /t:library /r:system.web.dll, system.dll,
system.xml.dll, system.web.services.dll, system.data.dll Address.cs
```

What will you do to make the web service available with the least amount of code and work?

A. Run the following command:

```
regsvr32 /.NET AddressProxy.dll
```

B. Rerun the `csc` command specifying `/o:bin/AddressProxy.dll`.

C. Rebuild the `AddressProxy.dll` file using the `/AutoPost` option.

D. Rebuild your application after adding the reference to the web service.

14. You have designed a web form that has one `listbox` control. You have implemented the `SelectedIndexChanged` event handler, and you have verified that all required declarations are in place and that the event handler is registered. During testing of the form, you find that the event does not execute. What is the most efficient way to make the event execute?

A. Set the `AutoPostBack` attribute of the `listbox` control to False.

B. Set the `AutoPostBack` attribute of the `@ Page` directive to True.

C. Set the `AutoPostBack` attribute of the `listbox` control to True.

D. Change from the `listbox` control to the `DropDownList` control.

Test Answers

1. D.

2. C.

3. B. The namespace of the web service must be imported.

4. D. The entry point must be the name in the library; the signature is what C# will use.

5. D. The fully qualified method name is `TService.Tconv.CtoF()`, and the return variable must be declared.

6. C.

7. D. Multicast delegates must be declared with a void return type.

8. B. The event must be registered.

9. **B.**

10. **D.** The COM component must be registered in the Registry before it is available in Visual Studio .NET.

11. **B.**

12. **B.**

13. **B.** The proxy file should be put in the bin directory.

14. **C.**

Server Controls in ASP.NET

In this chapter, you will

- Add web server controls, HTML server controls, user controls, and HTML code to ASP.NET pages
- Create custom controls and user controls
- Load controls dynamically

Now that we have defined the event and postback architecture of the Web Form, we can start looking at some of the more exciting components that are included with ASP.NET. In this chapter you will learn about the different server controls and how they are rendered as HTML to the client, and how ASP.NET is taking care to render HTML that will work different platforms by carefully using only the lowest common denominator standards for each browser.

We will also work with user controls and build our own special controls to simplify the processing of data and centralize the functionality for a group of controls.

Working with ASP Controls

The building blocks of our Web Forms are the controls that give us the ability to display data to the user, as well as enabling the user to interact with the application. There are a couple of families of controls available for use in ASP.NET Web Forms: there are the traditional HTML controls that can be used as is, with no further involvement from the server, and there are the intrinsic HTML controls that use a server control to encapsulate the HTML control (rich controls), giving us a richer object model to work with.

In the ASP.NET environment we have validation controls that we can use to validate the data from the user, and we looked at the use of these controls in Chapter 12. What this section will add to the control pallet is the use of the so-called *rich controls*. These are controls with no direct HTML counterpart—they are combinations of different intrinsic controls that form a functional unit.

ASP.NET automatically senses the browser version and manufacturer used by the client, and it renders the server controls properly for that browser. This means you do not have to produce a "least common denominator" version of your site or have multiple versions for different browsers. For example, we do not have to produce one version of our web site for each browser on the market; ASP.NET provides support to generate HTML that is browser specific taking care not to send HTML elements that are not supported in the browser. In some cases the generated HTML code is the same as is the case with the ListBox control that would be rendered in the same fashion by both Netscape and Internet Explorer, while the Calendar control would be rendered totally different between the different browsers.

Your Web Forms can be configured to meet a lowest-common-denominator browser by changing the setting for TargetSchema on the document object, as shown in Figure 14-1. You would change this setting to the lowest browser version that you must support; Internet Explorer 5 is the default for this property. Set this property based on the expected client base—if the site will be used on the Internet, you could set it to a version 4 browser; for an intranet you could set a very specific, high-version browser.

Figure 14-1

Changing the
TargetSchema
for the
Web Form

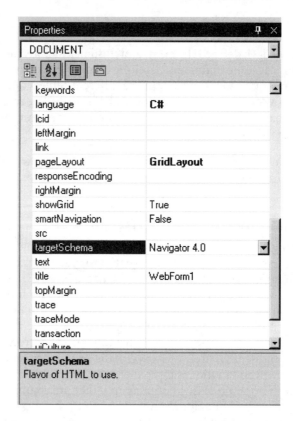

Base Properties of Server Controls

All the server controls have a common set of base properties, in addition to their specific properties. The base properties are used to control the look and feel of the control. Table 14-1 lists the more commonly used base properties and outlines their use.

These are just a few of the properties that are available to us in Visual Studio .NET. Although there are more properties than some browsers can support, the .NET Framework will render the control based on the target browser, ensuring that the page will look okay in any browser.

The following Label control uses some of the properties for the control:

```
<asp:Label id="Label1" runat="server" Height="80px" Width="320px"
        BackColor="DodgerBlue" BorderStyle="Ridge" BorderWidth="6px"
        Font-Names="Kristen ITC" Font-Size="XX-Large" >
Hello World!</asp:Label>
```

The Label control is actually rendered as an HTML span for both Netscape and Internet Explorer. The HTML for Internet Explorer looks like this:

```
<span id="Label1" style="background-color:DodgerBlue; border-width:6px;
        border-style:Ridge; font-family:Kristen ITC; font-size:XX-Large;
        height:80px; width:320px; LEFT: 10px; POSITION: absolute; TOP: 15px">
Hello World!</span>
```

Property	Description
BackColor	Sets the background color of the control. This property can be set to any of the color constants in the .NET Framework's Color structure property, such as DodgerBlue, AntiqueWhite, or to hexadecimal literal values like #C8C8C8 (gray).
BorderWidth	Sets the width of the control's border, in pixels.
Enabled	Determines whether or not the control is available for user interaction. If this property is set to False, the control will be grayed out and the control will not process any event until the Enabled property has been set to True.
Font	Controls the appearance of the text in the control. This property has a number of subproperties, such as Size, which specifies the size of the font; Name, which specifies the name of the font; and Bold, which can be set to True or False to make the font bold or not.
ForeColor	Determines the color of the text in the control.
Height	Sets the height of the control.
ToolTip	Specifies the text to be displayed beside the control when the user keeps the mouse pointer near the control. This property is one of the ways we can use to actually teach our users how to use our web site.
Visible	Determines whether the control is visible (True) or hidden (False). Use this property to hide controls that are not initially needed, and then display them based on the user's selections.
Width	Sets the width of the control.

Table 14-1 The Most Commonly Used Base Properties for Server Controls

The HTML rendered for the Netscape browser is tailored for that browser's special abilities:

```
<span id="Label1" style="LEFT: 10px; POSITION: absolute; TOP: 15px">
    <font face="Kristen ITC" size="7">
      Hello World!
    </font>
</span>
```

The power of writing one code module that will work with most browsers is immense; we can focus on the development task rather than on the minute differences between the browsers.

 EXAM TIP The .NET Framework renders the server control based on the user's browser.

HTML Server Controls

Here we will have a look at the intrinsic controls, also known as ASP Server Controls, that are encapsulations of the standard HTML controls, listed in Table 14-2. These controls are mostly rendered using the equivalent underlying HTML element.

Server Control	HTML Equivalent	Description
Button	Button	This is the common command button. It uses the `Click` event to communicate with the application.
CheckBox	Checkbox	`CheckBox` is the control you will use for Yes or No selections.
DropDownList	Select	`DropDownList` is used for making a selection from many different values.
Hyperlink	Anchor	The `Hyperlink` is used as a button, but the display is an `Anchor`.
Image	Img	`Image` is used to display a picture.
Label	span	`Label` is used to display descriptive text as well as read-only information.
ListBox	select	This is a control that allows the user to select an item in a list. The `ListBox` control can optionally allow multiple selections.
Panel	div	The `Panel` gives us an area in the page that can be used to group controls and treat them as one.
RadioButton	Option	`RadioButton` is used for mutually exclusive selections.
Table	table	This control is used to create an HTML table.
TableCell	td	This is a cell in a table.
TableRow	tr	This is a row in a table.
TextBox	text	This is the control to use when the user needs to enter information on the web page. The control will be rendered as a text input control.

Table 14-2 The Intrinsic Server Controls

We covered event handling and registration in detail in Chapter 11, and we'll see it put to use in the following example. In this example you will build a Web Form where you will see the code that connects a control with its event handler. Start a new Visual C# project, select an ASP.NET Web Application template, call the project `Button1` on the `localhost` server.

After the project is created open the HTML view of the web page. We will use a server control to insert an element in the HTML part of the Web Form file (`.aspx`) as we've done for the `Button` control in the following line of HTML code:

```
<asp:Button id="TheButton" runat="server" />
```

The `Button` control can have events connected to it, and there are two possible ways of performing that linking: either by registering an event handler in the `InitializeComponent()` method that will run when the Web Form is initially created, or by adding the attribute to the control when it is defined. The following code line defines the event handler in the `Button` definition:

```
<asp:Button id="TheButton" runat="server" OnClick="buttonClick" />
```

The event handler for the `Click` event is defined as `buttonClick()`. `OnClick` is the keyword that tells ASP.NET that we are talking about the `Click` event.

Expand the code display and locate the `InitializeComponent()` method. The code to register the event will look like this:

```
this.TheButton.Click += new System.EventHandler(this.button_Click);
```

After we have added the button and wired the event handling for it, we need to look at a new control that is used to group other controls in the web page.

One very useful server control is the `Panel`, which gives us the ability to handle groups of controls in the same way by using common code for the controls rather than writing individual event handlers. In this next example we will use a number of different controls to create a converter application that will convert from km/h to mph. We will work through the Visual Studio .NET IDE to build an application named `Panel1` on the `localhost` server. The user interface of the application is created as in Figure 14-2.

To place all the controls, we used the following code for the HTML portion of the form:

```
<%@ Page language="c#" Codebehind="WebForm1.aspx.cs" AutoEventWireup="false"
Inherits="Panel1.WebForm1" %>

<!DOCTYPE HTML PUBLIC "-//W3C//DTD HTML 4.0 Transitional//EN" >
<HTML>
  <HEAD>
    <title>WebForm1</title>
...
  </HEAD>
  <body MS_POSITIONING="GridLayout">
    <h1>The speed converter</h1>
    <form id="Form1" method="post" runat="server">
      <asp:Panel
        id="Panel1" runat="server" Width="352px" Height="56px"
        BackColor="Silver" BorderStyle="Ridge" BorderWidth="4px"> 
```

```
        <asp:Label id="Label1" runat="server" Width="24px">mph</asp:Label>
        <asp:TextBox id="TextBox1" runat="server" Width="112px"></asp:TextBox>
        <asp:Label id="Label2" runat="server">km/h</asp:Label>
        <asp:TextBox id="TextBox2" runat="server" Width="112px"></asp:TextBox>
    </asp:Panel>
    <asp:Button id="Button1" runat="server" Text="Convert"></asp:Button>
  </form>
 </body>
</HTML>
```

The bold code in the preceding listing shows how the Panel control encapsulates the other controls that are in the panel. Note that the spaces that are inserted are there to aid in the layout of the panel so the controls will be spaced out rather than bunched up.

The processing for the converter is configured to use the Click event from the button to convert from mph to km/h. The event handler for the button in the codebehind module will look like this:

```
private void Button1_Click(object sender, System.EventArgs e)
{
    TextBox2.Text = Convert.ToString(Convert.ToDouble(TextBox1.Text) * 1.6);
}
```

Figure 14-3 shows the application in action.

The important part of this exercise was not to build a speed converter, but rather to look at the Panel control. The ASP.NET process converts the Panel server component into a div HTML element that will be displayed using the client browser.

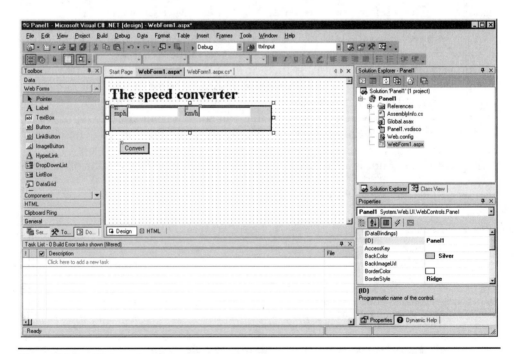

Figure 14-2   The user interface of the speed converter

Figure 14-3
The finished
speed converter

 EXAM TIP The Label controls are rendered as spans. The Panel is rendered as a div. A page using either Label or Panel controls will display well in most browsers.

Web Server Controls

The second type of server controls is the rich controls. These are controls that have no direct counterpart in HTML, and they are rendered using groups of standard controls, varying depending on the browser. Table 14-3 lists the rich controls and describes their usage.

These controls add functionality that is implemented by JavaScript client-side code and standard HTML elements. As an example, we will look more closely at the AdRotator control, which displays images as an ad banner. The images can be of any file type that can be displayed in a browser, such as .gif, .jpg, and so on. The image can be clickable so the user will be taken to a predetermined site for each image. What images are displayed and how they behave is determined by an XML document that is created using an Ad Rotator template, which we will look at shortly.

As an example, we will build a web page that uses the AdRotator control to display "Hello World" messages in different languages each time the page is redisplayed. For this example, the images can be created using any graphics program, as long as the dimensions of the different images are the same. We created five .gif files that we put in a folder called images in the root of the application. On our server, the folder is located at c:\inetpub\wwwroot\Rotator\images.

To start the project, create a new application named Rotator on the localhost server. Add an AdRotator control to the Web Form as shown in Figure 14-4.

To add the images to the project, you need to create a new folder in the project called Images and add the five .gif files to the folder. To create the new folder, right-click on

Rich Control	Description
AdRotator	This control will display a different image each time the page is redisplayed by the postback process.
Calendar	This control displays a one-month calendar that can be customized and used in any situation where a date display is needed.
CheckBoxList	This is a grouping of CheckBox controls that forms a list, which can be dynamically created from databases. The list is programmatically accessible through the ID of the list.
ImageButton	This control has a clickable image that may have coordinates for image map functionality.
LinkButton	This is a button displayed as a hyperlink.
RadioButtonList	This is a grouping of RadioButton controls that will behave as mutually exclusive controls. The entire list is accessible through the ID of the list.

Table 14-3   Rich Controls

the project name (Rotator) in the Project Explorer, and select Add | New Folder from the context menu, as shown in Figure 14-5.

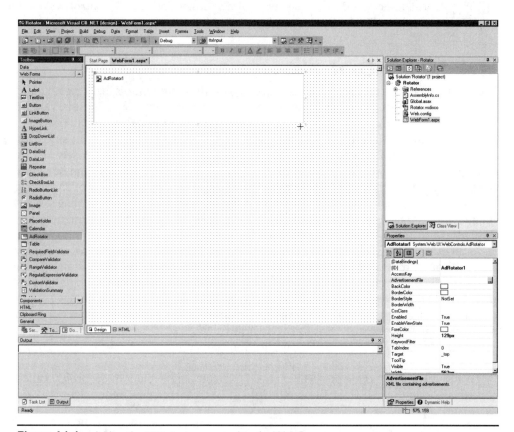

Figure 14-4   Adding the AdRotator control to the Web Form

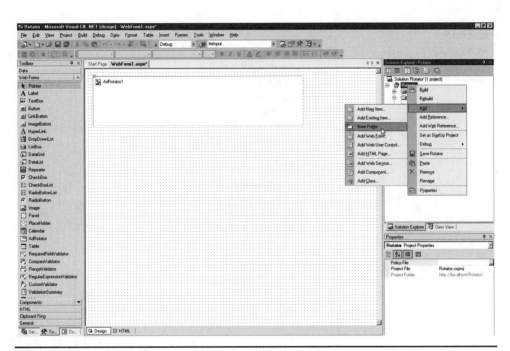

Figure 14-5   Adding a folder to the project

Now you can add the images to the new folder by either dragging them there from My Computer, or by right-clicking on the project name in the Project Explorer, selecting Add | Add Existing Items from the context menu, and browsing for the images. The final result should look something like what is shown in Figure 14-6.

The `AdRotator` has an `AdvertisementFile` property that determines the images to be displayed, as well as the text version of the image for those browsers that cannot (or will not) display graphics. The format of the `AdvertisementFile` is based on the Ad Rotator template. Table 14-4 enumerates the parameters for the `AdvertisementFile` property.

Our example is built around a web application that has five images called `ad1.gif`, `ad2.gif`, `ad3.gif`, `ad4.gif`, and `ad5.gif`. The web pages that the images are referring to are created using the names `HTMLPage1.htm`, `HTMLPage2.htm`, `HTMLPage3.htm`, `HTMLPage4.htm` and `HTMLPage5.htm` (you can find the images and HTML pages in the Chapter 14 folder on the CD).

The `AdvertisementFile` is an XML document that we need to create for the `AdRotator`. Follow these steps to create the `AdvertisementFile`:

1. Add an XML file to the project by selecting Project | Add New Item.

2. Select XML File from the Templates window, and name it `Rotator.xml`. After the file is created, the XML Editor will open.

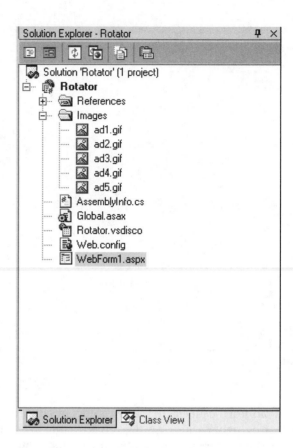

Figure 14-6
The Rotator project with the Images folder

3. Set the TargetSchema property for the XML file to Ad Rotator Schedule File, as shown in Figure 14-7. Selecting the TargetSchema adds a root element of <Advertisements> to the file.

Parameter	Description
ImageUrl	Specifies the URL of the image to be displayed.
NavigateUrl	Specifies the URL to redirect the user to when the image is clicked.
AlternateText	Contains the text to be displayed if the browser cannot display graphics.
Keyword	Identifies the category of the ad, allowing filtering of ads.
Impressions	Contains a numeric value that is used to specify how likely it is that this ad will be displayed. The sum of all Impressions values must not exceed 2,048,000,000 − 1 (2,047,999,999). This is a technical limit.

Table 14-4   The Parameters for the AdvertisementFile Property

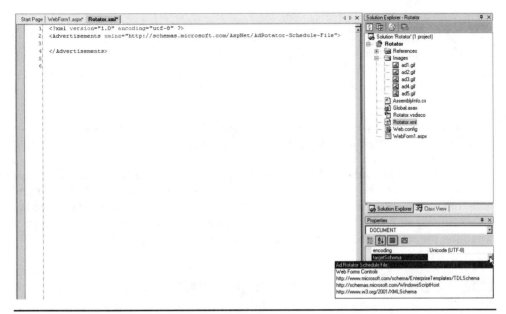

Figure 14-7   Setting the `TargetSchema` property

4. Add an `<Ad>` element as a child element to the `<Advertisements>` element in XML file. The properties for each image are inserted in the `<Ad>` element.

5. To add the items from the Project Explorer, drag and drop the items into the XML editor. Drag the image into the `<Ad>` node, as well as the HTML page that corresponds to the image.

6. Add the rest of the five ads to the XML file.

When the file is completed, it should look like the following code:

```
<?xml version="1.0" encoding="utf-8" ?>
<Advertisements
    xmlns="http://schemas.microsoft.com/AspNet/AdRotator-Schedule-File">
<Ad>
  <ImageUrl>Images/ad1.gif</ImageUrl>
  <NavigateUrl>http://localhost/Rotator/HTMLPage1.htm</NavigateUrl>
  <AlternateText>The AD1.GIF</AlternateText>
  <Keyword>Test</Keyword>
  <Impressions>10</Impressions>
</Ad>
<Ad>
```

```
    <ImageUrl>Images/ad2.gif</ImageUrl>
    <NavigateUrl>http://localhost/Rotator/HTMLPage2.htm</NavigateUrl>
    <AlternateText>The AD2.GIF</AlternateText>
    <Keyword>Test</Keyword>
    <Impressions>10</Impressions>
</Ad>
...
</Advertisements>
```

To add the XML `AdvertisementFile` to the `AdRotator` control, browse for it by
clicking on the ellipsis (three dots) next to the `AdvertisementFile` property, select
the `Rotator.xml` file, and click OK.

Save all the files, and then run the application by pressing the F5 key. Click the
browser's refresh button and notice how the banner changes; click on the banner and
note that the browser displays the HTML page. The `AdRotator` control is rendered as
an anchor tag with an image forming the clickable area. The same rendering happens
when the file is displayed in a Netscape browser or Internet Explorer.

User Controls and Custom Controls

When we need to use the same controls in many different forms, it becomes tricky to
keep them all updated to have the same functionality while also repairing any unsched-
uled features (a.k.a. bugs) in the code. There are two technologies that we can employ to
build reusable controls that can be treated as components: user controls and custom
controls. *User controls* are scripted server controls—really converted ASP.NET pages. *Custom controls* are compiled into .NET assemblies that can be used wherever a control is
needed.

We will start by looking at user controls; custom controls will be discussed later in
this section.

Building and Using a User Control

A user control is a Web Form that has been converted into a reusable component that
can be used by different Web Forms. If you use a grouping of controls in many different
Web Forms, such as a voting control, you can build one user control that can be used in
all the Web Forms. First let's look at how we can build a user control from scratch.

In this example you will build a user control that combines a `Calendar` control and
a `TextBox` to form one control. To create the user control, start a new project on the
`localhost` server and call it `UserTest`. Once the project has been created, add the user
control by selecting Project | Add New Item. This displays the Add New Item dialog box—
select the Web User Control template, and call the file `WUCUser.ascx`, as shown here.

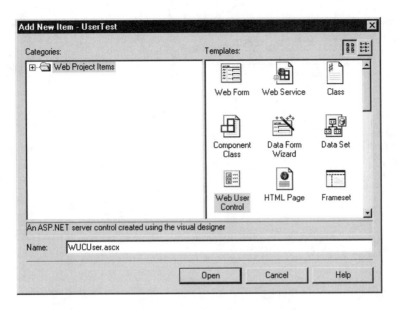

The files that are added to the project are similar to the files that make up a Web Form: there is the form file (.ascx) and the codebehind file (.ascx.cs). You'll need to add some controls to the user control so it will perform some function, so add a Calendar and a TextBox control to the form, as shown in Figure 14-8.

The HTML code for the user control should be as follows:

```
<%@ Control Language="c#" AutoEventWireup="false"
          Codebehind="WUCUser.ascx.cs" Inherits="UserTest.WUCUser"
          TargetSchema="http://schemas.microsoft.com/intellisense/ie5"%>
  <P>
    <asp:Calendar id="Calendar1" runat="server"></asp:Calendar>
  </P>
  <P>
    <asp:TextBox id="TextBox1" runat="server" Width="248px"></asp:TextBox>
  </P>
```

To be able to use the user control in our Web Form, we need to add a <%@ Register %> directive to the WebForm1.aspx file. The directive should look like this:

```
<%@ Register TagPrefix="WUC" TagName="UserControl1" Src="WUCUser.ascx" %>
```

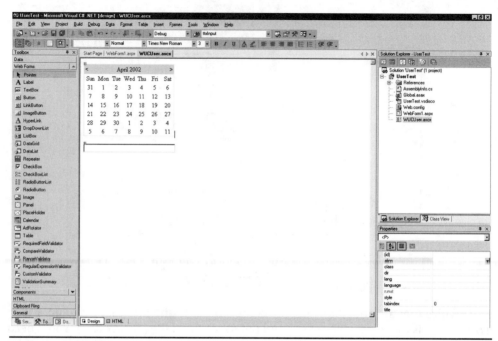

Figure 14-8 The WUCUser control

The Register directive lets us specify how we will refer to the user control, and the `TagPrefix` and `TagName` are taken together to form the name of the element, `<WUC:UserControl1 />`, that we will use in the form to display the control.

The HTML listing for `WebForm1.aspx` follows, with the additions in bold.

```
<%@ Register TagPrefix="WUC" TagName="UserControl1" Src="WUCUser.ascx" %>
<%@ Page language="c#" Codebehind="WebForm1.aspx.cs" AutoEventWireup="false"
        Inherits="UserTest.WebForm1" %>
<!DOCTYPE HTML PUBLIC "-//W3C//DTD HTML 4.0 Transitional//EN" >
<html>
  <head>
    <title>WebForm1</title>
...
  </head>
  <body MS_POSITIONING="GridLayout">
    <form id="Form1" method="post" runat="server">
      <WUC:UserControl1 runat="server" id="theUserControl" />
    </form>
  </body>
</html>
```

In the preceding code segment, the reference to the user control sets the control's ID to `theUserControl`:

```
<WUC:UserControl1 runat="server" id="theUserControl" />
```

In order to use the ID, we need a variable that is declared in the codebehind module for the Web Form (`WebForm1.aspx.cs`). The following code segment shows the manual addition we need to make to `WebForm1.aspx.cs` for the code to compile, with the addition in bold.

```
using System;
using System.Collections;
using System.ComponentModel;
using System.Data;
using System.Drawing;
using System.Web;
using System.Web.SessionState;
using System.Web.UI;
using System.Web.UI.WebControls;
using System.Web.UI.HtmlControls;

namespace UserTest
{
  public class WebForm1 : System.Web.UI.Page
  {
    protected WUCUser theUserControl;
    private void Page_Load(object sender, System.EventArgs e)
    {
      // Put user code to initialize the page here
    }

    #region Web Form Designer generated code
      ...
    #endregion
  }
}
```

The project can now be executed (F5) to reveal the `Calendar` control and the `TextBox` control. There is, however, no functionality in the user control yet. You can click on the dates as much as you want, but nothing will happen. To add functionality, you need to add some code to the user control, namely in the `SelectionChanged` event of the `Calendar` control so there will be feedback when the date is changed in the control.

To add the event handler, double-click the `Calendar` control in the `WUCUser.ascx` file's Design view. The final code in the codebehind file (`WUCUser.ascx.cs`) should look like this:

```
private void InitializeComponent()
{
  this.Calendar1.SelectionChanged += new System.EventHandler
                              (this.Calendar1_SelectionChanged);
  this.Load += new System.EventHandler(this.Page_Load);
}
private void Calendar1_SelectionChanged(object sender, System.EventArgs e)
{
  TextBox1.Text = Calendar1.SelectedDate.ToString();
}
```

The event registration and handler makes the application a little more functional. When you run the application now, you can click on a date and the `TextBox` will display the date that was clicked on, as you can see in the following illustration.

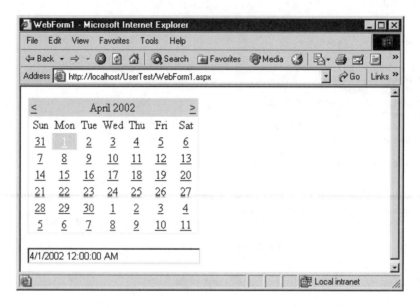

Although user controls are a step in the right direction, they are still essentially scripted ASP.NET forms that are used as subforms in another Web Form. The more powerful, but also somewhat more complex, custom controls are our next topic.

Building and Using a Custom Control

Custom controls are one notch up from user controls in that they are compiled into assemblies that can easily be deployed with the web site, or installed in the Global Assembly Cache (GAC) and be available to all applications on that server. Custom controls are built-in files with the extension `.ascx`.

The difference between custom controls and user controls starts with the fact that the `.ascx` file does not have a user interface (UI) built by using the drag and drop functions of Visual Studio .NET. Rather, the UI is designed in code as part of the custom control, and thus you have full control over what is returned to the client browser at all times. You build custom controls by inheriting from an existing control to build a derived custom control, or you can inherit from `System.Web.UI.WebControls` to build a full custom control.

The different types of custom controls are used in the same way as the user controls: by adding a `<%@ Register %>` directive to the top of the Web Form. The assembly that contains the custom control should be added to the bin directory in the root of the web application or to the GAC so that the application can find the assembly.

EXAM TIP The custom control must be added to the bin directory of the web site or to the GAC for it to be usable by the web site.

The following directive defines a `TagPrefix` of `WCC`, a `Namespace` of `WCCustomWebContols`, and an `Assembly` name of `WCCustomWebControls`:

```
<%@ Register TagName="WCC" Namespace="WCCustomWebContols"
        Assembly="WCCustomWebContols" %>
```

Once we have moved the assembly to the bin directory and added the Register directive to the page, we can add the custom control to the Web Form by adding a line like the following:

```
<WCC:DateControl runat="server" id="theDateControl" />
```

The next thing we have to look at is how to build these compiled custom controls that can be reused between projects. The example will take you through the building of a custom control that acts as a text area. We will build the example using Visual Studio .NET.

Start by creating a custom control project from the Web Control Library template, and name it `CusControl1`. The project wizard builds a default control that you can start your developments with—the project is runnable, but you need to provide the code to use the control.

As you work on the control, you will also need a way of testing it. There are a couple of ways of doing this: you can create a second project that uses the control, or you could add a web application project to the custom control solution. In this example, we will use the second technique of adding a web application project. To add the project to a solution, select File | New, and in the New Project dialog box select the ASP.NET Web Application template—ensure that the Add To Solution option is selected.

If you left everything set to the defaults, you would end up with the two projects in different areas on the hard drive, and you'd have to copy the custom control's assembly to the web application's bin directory every time you recompiled the custom control. To make the development easier, set the properties for the custom control project to send the output to the bin directory in the web application. To do so, follow these steps:

1. Open the Properties dialog box for the custom control by right-clicking on the project (`CusControl1`) in the Solution Explorer of the custom control project.

2. Expand the Configurations Properties folder and select the Build items to find the Output Path.

3. Set the Output Path to the location of the web application's bin directory. In our case that is `c:\Inetpub\wwwroot\CustControlTest\bin`. Make sure you click the ellipsis (…) to enter the path.

4. In the Configuration dropdown control select All Configurations.

Once this is done, the assembly that contains the custom control will be written into the bin directory of the web application, which is the location where the application will search for assemblies. Setting the Configuration Properties to All Configurations means that the Output Path will be used both for release and debug builds.

The next step is to make the web application the startup project. You do this by right-clicking on the `CustControlTest` project and selecting Set as Startup Project from the context menu.

Now you can add the following two lines to the web application's HTML view. The registration of the Custom Control assembly and namespace makes the control available to the web application:

```
<%@ Register TagPrefix="WCC" Namespace="CusControl1" Assembly="CusControl1" %>
<%@ Page language="c#" Codebehind="WebForm1.aspx.cs" AutoEventWireup="false"
Inherits="CustControlTest.WebForm1" %>
<!DOCTYPE HTML PUBLIC "-//W3C//DTD HTML 4.0 Transitional//EN" >
<html>
  <head>
    <title>WebForm1</title>
...
  </head>
  <body MS_POSITIONING="GridLayout">
    <form id="Form1" method="post" runat="server">
      <WCC:WebCustomControl1 runat="server" Text="The World's Greatest" />
    </form>
  </body>
</html>
```

The first highlighted line makes the custom control available to the application by registering the `TagPrefix`, `Namespace`, and `Assembly`. The application will search for the assemblies starting in the bin directory.

Now we can run the application by pressing F5. The resulting display is shown next.

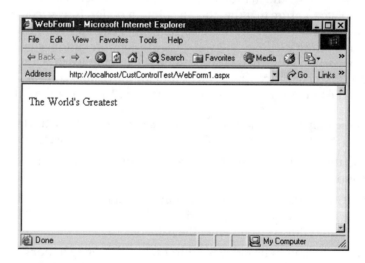

If you have run this application, you will probably be wondering why there is an error displayed in the Design view of the Web Form, even though the control is working when you execute the application. The problem has to do with the application not knowing about the custom control at design time. It only looks for the assembly at run time, so what we need to do is add a reference to the control in our Web Form project.

To do so, right-click on the References folder of the web application project. Under the .NET tab, select browse, and select the assembly to be added as shown in the following illustration. Click Open and then OK to add the custom control to the project. Rerun the application, and the error in the Design view should be gone and the control should be visible instead. A second benefit that comes from adding the reference to the control is that you can now use it in the codebehind module as well.

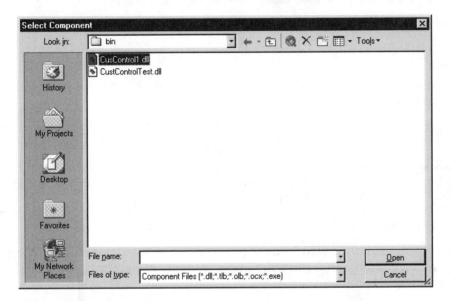

Now that we have created and used a custom control, we will look a little closer at what the custom control is, and why this stock implementation that is supplied with Visual Studio .NET is behaving like a Label control. Here's the codebehind module for the custom control:

```
using System;
using System.Web.UI;
using System.Web.UI.WebControls;
using System.ComponentModel;

namespace CusControl1
{
    [DefaultProperty("Text"),
     ToolboxData("<{0}:WebCustomControl1 runat=server></{0}:WebCustomControl1>")]
    public class WebCustomControl1 : System.Web.UI.WebControls.WebControl
    {
        private string text;
```

PART III

```
[Bindable(true), Category("Appearance"), DefaultValue("")]
public string Text
{
  get
  {
    return text;
  }
  set
  {
    text = value;
  }
}
protected override void Render(HtmlTextWriter output)
{
  output.Write(Text);
}
  }
}
```

The bold sections of the code define the behavior of this control. For example, look at the first attribute:

```
[DefaultProperty("Text"),
 ToolboxData("<{0}:WebCustomControl1 runat=server></{0}:WebCustomControl1>")]
```

This specifies that the control will have a default property (Text) and it specifies the data for the Toolbox. In the definition for the default property we find this attribute that defines the behavior of the property:

```
[Bindable(true), Category("Appearance"), DefaultValue("")]
```

The property can be bound to data, will be located in the Appearance tab in the property page for the control, and the default value is an empty string. The last bold line in this segment is this one:

```
protected override void Render(HtmlTextWriter output)
```

This is where the drawing code for the control is located. You need to override the Ren-der method for all your custom controls to define how the UI portion of the control will function.

Suppose, for instance, we want a control that reverses the string saved in the Text property when it is written to the display. In that case, we could change the Render method as follows:

```
protected override void Render(HtmlTextWriter output)
{
for (int x=Text.Length-1; x > 0; x--)
  {
    output.Write(Text[x]);
  }
}
```

Using the `System.Draw` namespace, you can perform direct drawing in the control, and you have full control over the way the control is rendered.

EXAM TIP   The `Render` method must be overridden in custom controls.

Dynamic Control Creation

There will be many times when you do not know how many controls will be needed in a form. In instances where the user can select progressive disclosure (when the amount of data is increased based on the user's request) designing *dynamic* control structures that can be added at run time is recommended. These dynamic controls must be added to a container control for them to be part of the Web Form; the container control will either be the `PlaceHolder` control or the `Panel` control. Either has the ability to add `Controls` collections dynamically.

EXAM TIP   Dynamic controls are added to existing controls that can contain collections of controls, such as `PlaceHolder` and `Panel` controls.

In this example, we will create a Web Form with a `PlaceHolder` control that allows us to add additional `TextBox` controls to a form, depending on the selection from a `DropDownList` control. To get started, create a new project on the `localhost` and call it `DynCntr`. Then add a `PlaceHolder` control to the project, as well as a `Label` and a `DropDownList` control. The layout of the final form is shown in next.

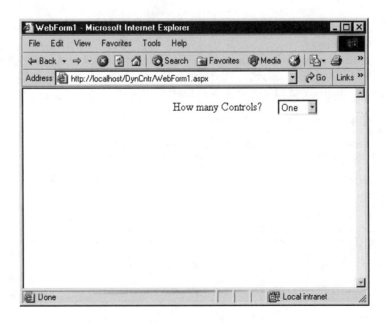

The HTML rendition of the Web Form must be configured with some special handling to make the `SelectedIndexChanged` event trigger a `postback` event. The `Label` control, as well as the `DropDownList` control, need some static text added. The following code listing shows the HTML for the Web Form:

```
<%@ Page language="c#" Codebehind="WebForm1.aspx.cs"
        AutoEventWireup="false" Inherits="DynCntr.WebForm1" %>
<!DOCTYPE HTML PUBLIC "-//W3C//DTD HTML 4.0 Transitional//EN" >
<HTML>
  <HEAD>
    <title>WebForm1</title>
    ...
  </HEAD>
  <body MS_POSITIONING="GridLayout">
    <form id="Form1" method="post" runat="server">
      <asp:DropDownList id="DropDownList1" AutoPostBack="True"
        style="Z-INDEX: 101; LEFT: 368px; POSITION: absolute; TOP: 16px"
        runat="server">
          <asp:ListItem Value="1">One</asp:ListItem>
          <asp:ListItem Value="2">Two</asp:ListItem>
          <asp:ListItem Value="3">Three</asp:ListItem>
          <asp:ListItem Value="4">Four</asp:ListItem>
          <asp:ListItem Value="5">Five</asp:ListItem>
          <asp:ListItem Value="6">Six</asp:ListItem>
          <asp:ListItem Value="7">Seven</asp:ListItem>
      </asp:DropDownList>
      <asp:Label id="Label1"
          style="Z-INDEX: 102; LEFT: 216px; POSITION: absolute; TOP: 16px"
          runat="server" Width="136px">How many Controls?</asp:Label>
      <asp:PlaceHolder id="PlaceHolder1" runat="server"></asp:PlaceHolder>
    </form>
  </body>
</HTML>
```

The bold sections in the preceding code were added after the controls were positioned using the Design view.

The dynamic behavior for the application comes from the `SelectedIndexChanged` event handler for the `DropDownList` control. The following code segment shows how you can add controls dynamically to a Web Form:

```
private void DropDownList1_SelectedIndexChanged(object sender, System.EventArgs e)
{
  // convert the value of the control to an integer
  int i = Convert.ToInt32(DropDownList1.SelectedItem.Value) - 1;

  // loop as many times as the user selected and add TextBox controls
  for (int x = 0; x <= i; x++)
  {
    TextBox txtB = new TextBox();
    txtB.ID = "Text" + x.ToString();
    txtB.Text = "Text" + x.ToString();
    PlaceHolder1.Controls.Add(txtB);
    PlaceHolder1.Controls.Add(new LiteralControl("<br/>"));
  }
}
```

The `PlaceHolder` control, as well as the `Panel` control, exposes a `Controls` property that refers to a collection of controls. We can manipulate the controls through that collection. The power of dynamic control creation comes into its own when we build data-driven applications that have widely varying needs for each form, and we want to minimize code duplication and maximize object reuse. The final application is seen in the following illustration, where three controls are selected.

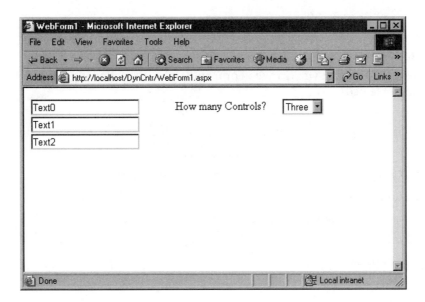

Summary

In this chapter, you have seen a number of techniques used to present controls to the user, ranging from the HTML control through server controls and user controls to custom controls. The important thing is knowing the different control families and how to properly add them to an application. Dynamic control creation will also assist you in building powerful applications, and Microsoft always asks some questions on how the dynamic creation is performed.

Now you are ready to learn how to make an application responsive and to make the user interface usable by many different groups of users. That's in the next chapter.

Test Questions

1. What HTML element is the `asp:Label` control rendered as when the target is Internet Explorer?

   A. `<label>`

   B. `<span>`

    C. `<div>`

    D. `<table>`

2. What HTML element is the `asp:Label` control rendered as when the target is Netscape Communicator?

    A. `<label>`

    B. `<span>`

    C. `<div>`

    D. `<table>`

3. What is the result when a Web Form containing the following line is compiled and executed?

```
<asp:Button id="theButton" onClick="theEvent" />
```

    A. The button control is created; `theEvent` is the `Click` event handler.

    B. Compiler error, the control must be set to `runat="server"`.

    C. Compiler error; `onClick` is not a valid attribute.

    D. Runtime exception; the control must be set to `runat="server"`.

4. What HTML element is the `asp:panel` control rendered as?

    A. `<span>`

    B. `<table>`

    C. `<div>`

    D. `<p>`

5. How do you specify the parameters for the ads in the `AdRotator` control?

    A. By programmatically setting the properties.

    B. By using an initialization file in `.xml` format.

    C. By using an initialization file in `.txt` format.

    D. By using an initialization file in `.ini` format.

6. What of the following best describes a user control?

    A. A collection of server controls gathered in a web file with the `<%@ Control %>` directive.

    B. A collection of controls that are compiled into an assembly.

    C. A control that is built from multiple user-defined COM-based controls.

    D. A simple lightweight control that can display text only.

7. Which of the following is valid after adding the following directive to a Web Form?

```
<%@ Register TagPrefix="WWW" TagName"WWWControl" Src="WWWControl1.ascx" %>
```

    A. `<WWW:WWWControl1 id="theControl" runat="server" />`

    B. `<asp:WWWControl id="theControl" runat="server" />`

    C. `<WWW:WWWControl id="WWWContr" runat="server" />`

    D. `<asp:WWWControl1 id="WWWContr" runat="server" />`

  8. You have correctly added the `<%@ Register %>` directive and the user-control definition in the `<asp:Form>` tag, but when you run the application it fails. What is the most likely cause of the failure?

    A. The protected class variable for the control is missing from the codebehind module.

    B. The event registration is not performed; you must manually add it to the `InitializeComponent` event handler.

    C. There must be a call to the control's constructor in the `Page_load()` method.

    D. The control must be added to the Web Form's `Controls` collection.

  9. After building a custom control, you test it by adding an ASP.NET web application to the solution. You add a correct `<%@ Register %>` directive and a proper declaration of the control in the `<asp:Form>` tag to the Web Form, but when you execute the application you get an error. What is the most likely reason for the problem?

    A. The custom control must be compiled first.

    B. The web application must have a reference to the control.

    C. The custom control must be registered with Windows first.

    D. The assembly from the custom control is not in the application's bin directory.

 10. You have successfully created a custom control and a web application project to test the control. The application runs with no problems, but when you look at the Design view of the Web Form, the control is displayed using an error display. What is the most efficient way to resolve the error display?

    A. Move the control to the web application's bin directory, and recompile the application.

    B. Add a reference to the control to the web application.

    C. Change the `Bindable` attribute for the `Default` property in the control to have a value of True.

    D. Manually enter the 128-bit GUID for the control in the application's configuration file.

 11. What method must be overridden in a custom control?

    A. The `Paint()` method.

    B. The `Control_Build()` method.

    C. The `Render()` method.

    D. The default constructor.

12. Your manager has asked you if ASP.NET can be used with dynamic control creation, and if it requires any extra software to make dynamic controls possible. What would you answer your manager?

    A. Yes, dynamic controls are possible using the standard control containers from ASP.NET.

    B. No, dynamic controls are not possible in ASP.NET.

    C. Yes, dynamic controls are possible in ASP.NET using a third-party assembly.

    D. Yes, dynamic controls are possible in ASP.NET by using the Web Services.

Test Answers

    1. B.

    2. B.

    3. D.

    4. C.

    5. B.

    6. A.

    7. C.

    8. A.

    9. D.

    10. B.

    11. C.

    12. A.

Web Forms and User Interface

In this chapter, you will

- Implement right-to-left and left-to-right mirroring of User Interface elements
- Prepare culture-specific formatting
- Localize the user interface
- Implement navigation tools for the user interface
- Validate user input
- Implement error handling in the user interface
- Configure custom error pages
- Implement `global.aspx`, application, page-level, and page-event error handling
- Implement online user assistance

The Importance of the User Interface

First impressions count, and that's never truer than when applied to the user interface (UI) of an application. If the user finds the UI hard to navigate or confusing, the user will always dislike the application, and no amount of change or redesign will bring that user back as a supporter.

The best way to avoid UI problems is to follow some basic rules when designing the UI. These rules reflect a variety of concerns:

- **Put the user in control** The user wants to be the one initiating an action, so the application should be as responsive and interactive as possible. After the user selects an action, that action should be easy to cancel.

- **Personalize the application** Save the state of the user and the application so that when the user returns, the application will be in the same state. This is especially important if the application allows the user to change colors or layouts.

- **Let the user manipulate the objects**   Let the user directly manipulate the objects that are used in the application using ToolTips and shortcut keys. Use very clear object models and metaphors.

- **Be consistent**   Be consistent in the use of colors, layout, and tools for controlling the application. Do not use different metaphors within an application; for example, don't use the recycling bin to perform a hard delete (with no way of retrieving the item from the bin) in one part of the application and then as a true recycling bin (from which you can get back deleted items) in another part of the same application.

- **Keep it simple**   Simplify the layout of the form so the information is presented clearly in an uncluttered way. Use progressive disclosure to let the user drill deeper into the information at their own pace.

- **Make sure the application is forgiving**   Always give the user a way out from any situation they might have ended up in by their selections. For instance, if the user selects the command to delete the entire database, make sure there is at least one chance to reconsider that command before performing the deletion. You might even create an undelete function for those kinds of dead-end operations. Forgiveness also means that you should supply meaningful default values to minimize errors, and if an error occurs, the error-handling process should return the user to a meaningful place in the application with an explanation of the error.

- **Provide feedback**   Keep the user informed about what is happening in the application. If something will take time, communicate the progress of the process to the user. Never leave the user hanging, wondering what happened, wondering whether the system broke or the network disconnected. Always communicate, but do not use modal message boxes (alerts) that require action from the user; instead, use labels or status areas on the form to keep the user informed.

- **Pay attention to visual design**   Get a graphic designer to design the physical layout of the forms to ensure that the form clearly conveys the information without being confusing or overwhelming.

- **Provide user assistance**   Build documentation and help functions into the application. The assistance should be as topical as possible to help the user learn while using your application.

- **Provide localization**   Let the user view and use the application using the culture of the user's locale. This way, numbers will be displayed in the user's format, as will the string resources created for the application.

The UI rules are many, and they are open to debate. The preceding points are based on the UI rules published by Microsoft for application developers. The MSDN (Microsoft Developer Network) has references for many UI design rules, but even so, there are times when the developer can, and will, break the rules in order to present some specific information in a more effective way. In the following sections, we will look at the specifics of UI design as it relates to the 70-315 exam.

Localization

In Chapter 7, we introduced localization and used manual techniques to create the default (fallback) as well as the specific language resources. The Resource Manager will locate the appropriate resource assembly based on the client's settings; and if there is no resource for a particular locale, the Resource Manager will use the *fallback locale*, which is the locale that the web site was created with. The fallback locale is also called the *default locale*. The resource assembly for the fallback locale is located in the bin directory, while additional locales are added in subdirectories of the bin directory.

 EXAM TIP   The fallback locale is the locale that will be used when there are no resources for the user's locale.

Let's take a look at how you can use a resource to build a localized ASP.NET application. To begin this example, create an application called `Locale` on the `localhost` server.

Instead of creating the resources manually, and adding satellite assemblies to the bin directory as we did in Chapter 7, we'll look at how to use the resource editor in Visual Studio .NET to create the resources for a couple of languages. We happen to speak English, Swedish, German, and French between us, so those are the languages we will use, as well as some culture-specific resources.

The International Organization for Standardization (ISO) has issued definitions of two-letter abbreviations to identify languages and countries. The following list contains just a small sample of the language codes; for a complete listing, see the MSDN library.

en	English
fr	French
de	German (Deutch)
sv	Swedish (Svenska)
sw	Swahili

Languages like English, French, German, and Swedish are used in many different countries throughout the world, so the countries are referred to by the country codes. The following list gives the country codes for a few countries:

UK	United Kingdom
US	United States of America
CA	Canada
SE	Sweden
SF	Finland (Suomi-Finland)

PART III

DE	Germany
AT	Austria

Now that you've seen the codes, let's put the languages and countries together into *cultures*. The culture defines the language, data formats, calendar format, and so on, and it consists of the combination of the language and the country codes. The "en-UK" culture code is for English in the United Kingdom, and "sv-SE" is Swedish in Sweden, whereas "sv-SF" is Swedish in Finland. These codes are important when we build the resource files—the name of the resource file will contain the culture code, and the compiler will build the assembly for the resources by using the culture codes.

When you create a resource file for the localized application, that file will have a name format based on this pattern:

```
<resource>.<culture>.resx
```

The `culture` is either the language code (if the resource is valid for all cultures that use that language) or the culture code. The `resource` is the type of resource you are working with, and it will be `string` for strings, `icon` for icons, and so on. There is one very specific resource file that has the name `<resource>.resx`. This file defines the default or fallback resource, and it is the resource that will be used if there is no culture that matches the user's settings.

Getting back to the example project, we are going to create resources for the default (en), French France (fr-FR), English Canada (en-CA), and Swedish (sv) cultures. There are four steps in creating a resource file for a project:

1. Add a resource file to the project. Select Project | Add New Item. In the Template list, select the Assembly Resource File template, enter the name for the `.resx` file, and create the resource. The file will be added to the project, and the XML Designer will open.

2. Select Data in the Data Tables pane.

3. Position the cursor in the Name column of the empty row in the Data pane, and enter the appropriate information. To enter a new row, click in the Name column for the new row. Note that the type and mimetype information is not used with strings; it is only used with objects.

4. Save the `.resx` file.

First, you need to create the default resource. Follow steps 1 through 4, giving the resource the name `strings.resx` and entering the information found in Table 15-1. The result should look like what you see in Figure 15-1.

Table 15-1 Data for the Default String Resource	Name	Value
	txtWelcome	Welcome to the localized Application.
	txtClick	Please click me.
	txtHello	Hello Localized World.

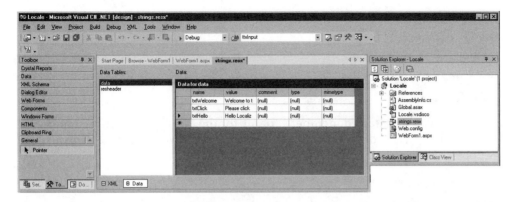

Figure 15-1 The XML Designer with the default resource strings

 TIP Use the most common language for the default resource.

Now you can repeat steps 1 through 4, using the data in Table 15-2. Once you're done, save the four resource files.

 NOTE You can enter the accented characters by using the charmap.exe application.

After you have created the resource files, you need to create the code necessary for the application to access the resources. To do so, open the codebehind module, and import the System.Globalization and System.Resources namespaces. The import

Filename	Name	Value
strings.en-CA.regx	TxtWelcome	Welcome to the ASP.NET application eh.
strings.fr-FR.regx	TxtWelcome	Bienvenue à m'application localisée!
strings.fr-FR.regx	TxtClick	Cliquetez ici!
strings.fr-FR.regx	TxtHello	Allô localisé monde!
strings.sv.regx	TxtWelcome	Välkommen till vår ASP.NET applikation
strings.sv.regx	TxtClick	Var snäll ock klicka här
strings.sv.regx	TxtHello	Hej på dig, lokaliserade Värld

Table 15-2 The Additional Resource Files

entries should be placed before the namespace declaration, as in the following code segment:

```
using System.Resources;
using System.Globalization;

namespace Locale
```

Now declare a protected member variable for the ResourceManager at the beginning of the class definition for the project, as shown next. (We'll discuss the ResourceManager class a bit later in this section.)

```
public class WebForm1 : System.Web.UI.Page
{
  protected ResourceManager locRM;
...
}
```

Finally, add the instantiation code for the ResourceManager object in the Page_Load() method of the codebehind module, as in this code segment:

```
LocRM = new ResourceManager("Locale.strings", typeof(WebForm1).Assembly);
```

At this point, you can start using the application. Add the following lines of code inside the form element of the HTML document, and you will have access to the localized strings.

```
<form id="Form1" method="post" runat="server">
  <h1><%=locRM.GetString("txtWelcome")%></h1>
</form>
```

Running the application results in the display shown in Figure 15-2 (assuming an English locale). It demonstrates that it has access to the strings through the ResourceManager object. If you want to use the strings in the codebehind module, however, you need to first change the current thread to use the client's locale. We'll continue with this example and look at how to change the current thread's locale and how to programmatically set the text by using controls.

Now you will change the current thread's locale to reflect the client settings, and then display localized information in the Web Form. The codebehind module is executed on the server while the client is running on a different computer; this process will synchronize the two.

The first thing to do is create a button and a label in our Web Form, in Design view, and then clear the default content of the Text property for the Button and Label controls. You will also need to import the System.Threading namespace by inserting the following line at the beginning of the codebehind module:

```
using System.Threading;
```

In order to set the locale for the current thread at the server, we need to use the locale setting from the client. To do so, the CurrentUICulture of the current thread on the

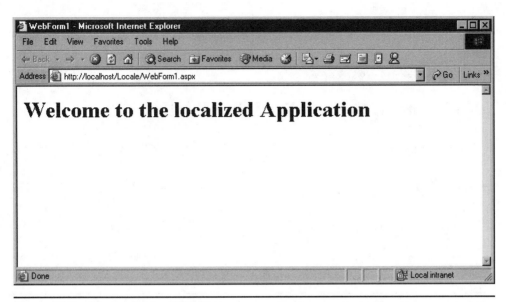

Figure 15-2   The first localized display

server must be set to the locale setting for the client that is available in the Request object's UserLanguages collection. The following two lines will perform that task and must be inserted at the beginning of the Page_Load() method:

```
Thread.CurrentThread.CurrentCulture =
            CultureInfo.CreateSpecificCulture(Request.UserLanguages[0]);
Thread.CurrentThread.CurrentUICulture =
            new CultureInfo(Request.UserLanguages[0]);
```

Then, in the codebehind module, add the following line of code to the end of the Page_Load() method:

```
Button1.Text = locRM.GetString("txtClick");
```

Finally, you'll need to create an event handler for the click event of the Button1 control. The event handler should look like this:

```
private void Button1_Click(object sender, System.EventArgs e)
{
  Label1.Text = locRM.GetString("txtHello");
}
```

Once you're done, save the project and then build it by selecting Build | Build Locale. Run the project by pressing the F5 key. After you click the button, the display should be as shown in Figure 15-3, assuming that the client is set to English.

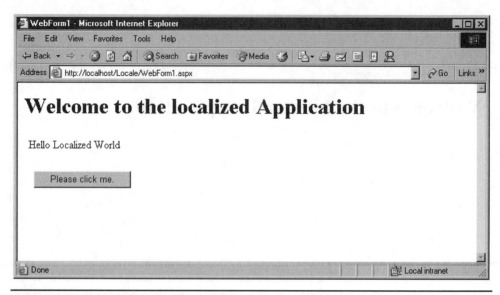

Figure 15-3   The locale application, using the English language

To test the application, you need to change the locale for your computer. The locale is controlled by the Control Panel's Regional Settings. Select English (Canada) and notice that the welcome message has changed, but all the other strings are the same as they were for the English locale. That only the items defined for English (Canada) changed and all others stayed the same is an example of the fallback resource where we used the existing content from the default (`strings.resx`) resource for all resources that were not defined in the specific English-Canadian resource. Figure 15-4 shows the display using Swedish as the locale.

The `ResourceManager` class is what makes this seamless change between locales possible. The following section will look at how the `ResourceManager` class works.

The Resource Manager Class

The first thing we need to look at is how the resource files are compiled into one assembly. The name of the resource file is the key to how Visual Studio .NET handles the compilation—as we stated earlier, the format of the filename is `<resource>.<culture>.resx.`. The `<culture>` portion of the filename is used to build a hierarchy for languages and countries, and the file that has no `<culture>` in the name is the default or fallback culture.

The `ResourceManager` class is what makes localization a convenient exercise rather than a chore. It gives us access to resources and provides the fallback when a resource does not exist. When the `ResourceManager` object is instantiated from the class, we provide information to it regarding the root name for the assembly created

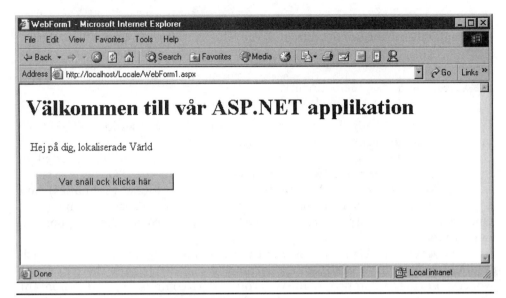

Figure 15-4   The display using the Swedish locale

when the resource was compiled (in the example in the previous section, the root is `Locale.strings`) and the main assembly for the resource. In that example, we instantiated the `ResourceManager` using the following line:

```
locRM = new ResourceManager("Locale.strings", typeof(WebForm1).Assembly);
```

Any call to the methods of the `ResourceManager` will now use the assembly located in the bin directory in the root of the application. The additional satellite assemblies for the different cultures are to be compiled into assemblies that use names that include the locale.

To retrieve a resource from a resource assembly, you need to call methods like `GetString()` on the `ResourceManager` object. For example, to retrieve the resource stored under the name `txtWelcome` and assign it to a header on the page, you could use the following code:

```
<%=locRM.GetString("txtWelcome")%>
```

The culture that the `ResourceManager` works with is the current culture of the thread that is executing. To ensure you use the culture of the client rather than the culture of the server, you need to ensure that you change to the culture according to the client.

In the following example, we will use the `Request` object's `UserLanguages` collection and select the first language in that collection by using `Request`

.UserLanguages[0] as the parameter; this will change the culture and the UI culture (for graphical elements) of the current thread. The following two lines will do this:

```
Thread.CurrentThread.CurrentCulture =
            CultureInfo.CreateSpecificCulture(Request.UserLanguages[0]);
Thread.CurrentThread.CurrentUICulture =
            new CultureInfo(Request.UserLanguages[0]);
```

Once the culture is changed on the thread, that particular user's session will be configured to use the culture of the user's computer.

One final note on localization: the namespaces that need to be imported are `System.Globalization` (which provides support for the ISO locale system), `System.Resources` (which provides support for resource assemblies), and `System.Threads` (which provides support for the threads you need to manipulate). Once imported, they will give access to all the features you need in order to support a localized application.

Whenever you build applications whose users' cultures may use different writing directions for text, you'll need to use a special property of the Web Form. The .NET Framework exposes the `dir` property of the Web Form, which controls the text direction. This property is inherited by all server controls. The `dir` property can be set to "ltr" (left to right) or "rtl" (right to left)—"ltr" is the default.

The final version of the example HTML module in this section is listed here.

```
<%@ Page language="c#" Codebehind="WebForm1.aspx.cs"
        AutoEventWireup="false" Inherits="Locale.WebForm1" %>
<!DOCTYPE HTML PUBLIC "-//W3C//DTD HTML 4.0 Transitional//EN" >
<HTML>
  <HEAD>
    <title>WebForm1</title>
...
  </HEAD>
  <body MS_POSITIONING="GridLayout">
    <form id="Form1" method="post" runat="server">
      <h1><%=locRM.GetString("txtWelcome")%></h1>
      <asp:Label id="Label1" runat="server" accessKey="L"></asp:Label>
      <asp:Button id="Button1" runat="server"></asp:Button>
    </form>
  </body>
</HTML>
```

The codebehind module for the localization example is as follows:

```
using System;
using System.Collections;
using System.ComponentModel;
using System.Data;
using System.Drawing;
using System.Web;
using System.Web.SessionState;
using System.Web.UI;
using System.Web.UI.WebControls;
using System.Web.UI.HtmlControls;
using System.Resources;
```

```
using System.Globalization;
using System.Threading;

namespace Locale
{
  public class WebForm1 : System.Web.UI.Page
  {
    protected System.Web.UI.WebControls.Label Label1;
    protected System.Web.UI.WebControls.Button Button1;
    protected ResourceManager locRM;
    private void Page_Load(object sender, System.EventArgs e)
    {
      Thread.CurrentThread.CurrentCulture =
            CultureInfo.CreateSpecificCulture(Request.UserLanguages[0]);
      Thread.CurrentThread.CurrentUICulture =
            new CultureInfo(Request.UserLanguages[0]);

      locRM = new ResourceManager("Locale.strings", typeof(WebForm1).Assembly);
      Button1.Text = locRM.GetString("txtClick");
    }
    override protected void OnInit(EventArgs e)
    {
      InitializeComponent();
      base.OnInit(e);
    }

    private void InitializeComponent()
    {
      this.Button1.Click += new System.EventHandler(this.Button1_Click);
      this.Load += new System.EventHandler(this.Page_Load);
    }
    private void Button1_Click(object sender, System.EventArgs e)
    {
      Label1.Text = locRM.GetString("txtHello");
    }
  }
}
```

 EXAM TIP The UI thread must be changed to use the current culture of the client. The Resource Manager will retrieve the resource based on the thread's current culture.

Now that we have looked at how you can localize a Web Form, we will continue with the other issues of the UI, starting with page navigation.

Page Navigation

When you build a form with multiple controls, you should make navigating the form as easy as possible, to the point of implementing the same shortcut-key scheme used in most Windows applications. Shortcut keys allow users to jump to a location or click a button by typing an ALT key sequence. The TAB key is used to move from control to control in a logical pattern. In this section, we will look at how to implement this type of navigation

Controls that receive input from the user's keyboard have *focus*. Only one control at a time can have focus in a web Form. If a control can have focus, that control can also be accessed using a shortcut key by setting the `AccessKey` property for the control. In Figure 15-5 you can see the properties for a `Button` control, and the `AccessKey` property is set to F, indicating that the button can be clicked by the key sequence ALT-F.

When you set the `AccessKey` property for a control, you should make sure that the user knows the shortcut-key sequence by adding a label with the information. You can either include instructions in the label, or you could underline the character that is set to the access key.

The tab order of the form is set by setting the `TabIndex` of the controls. For example, on a form where you have 10 `TextBox` controls that are to be tabbed through from control 1 to 10, you would set the `TabIndex` of control 1 to 1, control 2 to 2, and so on to control 10, which would have its `TabIndex` set to 10.

Designing the tab order correctly is of paramount importance for the proper functioning of the form. Set the `TabIndex` on all controls, and test to ensure that the resulting feel is correct for the application.

Figure 15-5
Setting the
`AccessKey`
property

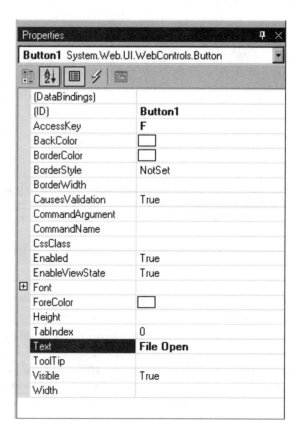

PART III

Validation Revisited

In Chapter 12, we looked at the validation controls from the code point of view. These validation controls allow us to validate user input. Now we will build a small form using the IDE so you can see the ease with which we can build quite complicated forms.

Before you validate the data in the control, however, you need to make sure the user knows what information is needed in the fields of the form. And as usual, there are two possible solutions. The first is to add labels to the form identifying the information needed, and the second is to create ToolTips that will pop up when the user hovers the mouse pointer over the field. Including labels of instructional text on the form makes the form look very cluttered and hard to understand. The ToolTip method is a very streamlined way of communicating with the user.

Every control has the ability to use ToolTips, and they can be set both at design and run time. ToolTips are implemented by adding the informative text to the `ToolTip` property of the control. Once you have indicated in the ToolTips what you expect the user to enter, you can proceed to validate the information received (or to trap missing entries) by adding validating controls to the form.

In this section, we will build an example application in which users will enter their name, e-mail address, and password into a Web Form. To start off, create a project called `ValidationExample` and use the `localhost` server.

The Web Form should look like the one shown in Figure 15-6 when the fields are added—you will need to add four labels, four text boxes, and a button. The labels are there to give the basic data requirements, and they have default IDs. The text boxes should have their properties set as listed in Table 15-3. You can use the Format | Align menu to line up the controls with either the left or right edge.
For the `txtPassword` and `txtPasswordRepeat` controls, set the `TextMode` property to `Password` to hide the entered characters.

At this point, there is no validation on the form. To add it, you need to use the validation controls in the Toolbox. For this example, you should validate that a name is entered, that the e-mail address is correctly formed, and that the two entries for the password are equal.

The validation controls should be placed to the right of the controls they validate. Add the `RequiredFieldValidator` control from the Toolbox, and set the properties according to Table 15-4.

Control	ID	ToolTip
TextBox	txtName	Enter your full name.
TextBox	txtEmail	Enter your e-mail address as name@domain.xxx.
TextBox	txtPassword	Enter your password.
TextBox	txtPasswordRepeat	Re-enter your password.
Button	btnSubmit	Click to submit information. (Note: Set the `Text` property to "Submit".)

Table 15-3 The Properties for the Web Form

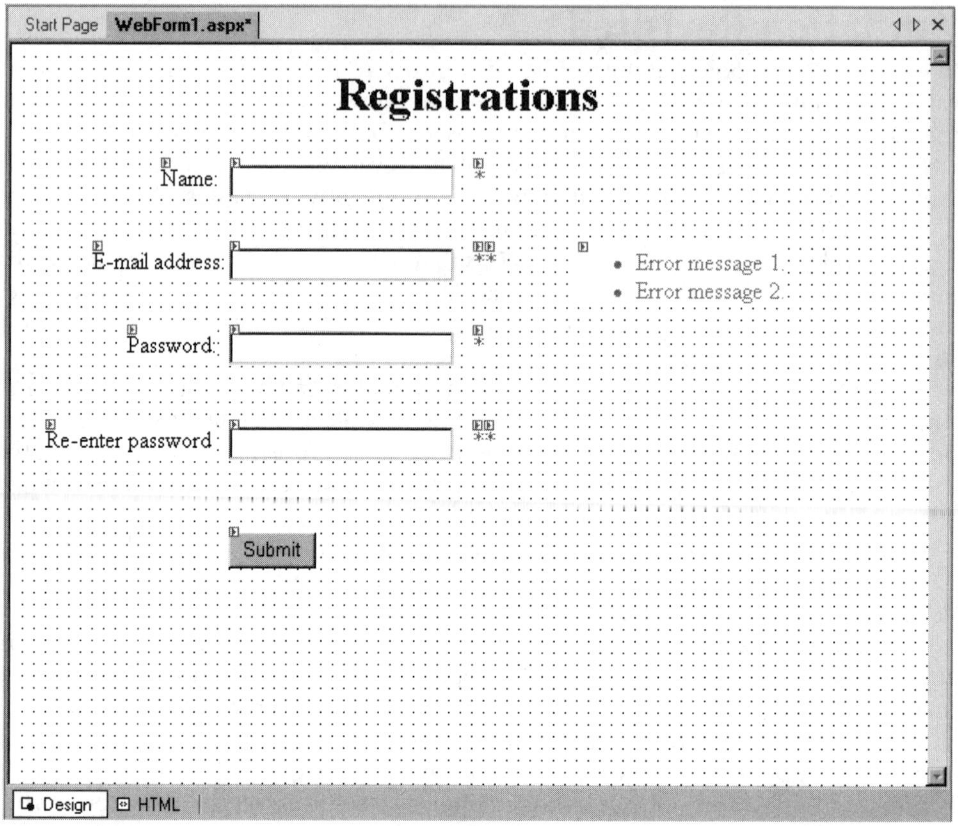

Figure 15-6 The finished `ValidationExample` form

After adding the `RequiredFieldValidator` controls, you can run the application by pressing the F5 key. Check that you are forced to enter data in every field. Note,

ID	ControlToValidate	Text	ErrorMessage
valName	txtName	*	Your name is required.
valEmail	TxtEmail	*	The e-mail address is required.
valPassword	TxtPassword	*	You must enter a password.
valPasswordRepeat	txtPasswordRepeat	*	Re-enter the password for verification.

Table 15-4 The Properties for the Validation Controls

Property	Value
(ID)	valEmail1
ControlToValidate	txtEmail
ErrorMessage	E-mail address must be in the format name@domain.xxx.
Text	*
ValidationExpression	(Select Internet E-mail Address from the list. The property will be set to the regular expression that validates an Internet e-mail address.)

Table 15-5   Properties for the `RegularExpressionValidator` Control

however, that there is no validation that the e-mail address is correctly formed, nor does the application test that the password entries match.

In order to validate the format of the e-mail address, you can use a `RegularExpression Validator` control. Start by adding a `RegularExpressionValidator` to the right of the `valEmail` control. Set the properties for the validation control as listed in Table 15-5.

The validation of the two password fields will be handled by a `CompareValidator` control. To set this up, drag a new `CompareValidator` control to the right of the `valPasswordRepeat` control, and set the properties as in Table 15-6.

You can now save and test the form (F5). As you can see, the red asterisk (*) indicates that there are errors or missing information in the fields; so while this application is very functional, you still do not see the error messages you entered into the validation controls. To display the error messages, you can use a `ValidationSummary` control that will take all the error outputs from the validation controls and display them in a bulleted list. To do so, simply drag a `ValidationSummary` control to the right of the current controls on the form. That's all! You can change the look of the summary by changing the font and the style of the list, but the wiring is already done. Figure 15-7 shows the application with a malformed e-mail address.

Property	Value
(ID)	valPasswordRepeat1
ControlToCompare	txtPassword
ControlToValidate	txtPasswordRepeat
Display	Dynamic
ErrorMessage	The passwords do not match.
Operator	Equal
Text	*

Table 15-6   Properties for the `CompareValidator`

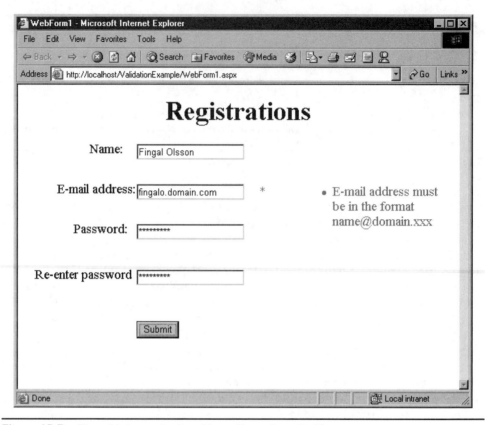

Figure 15-7 The validation application with a malformed e-mail address

Some of the HTML code for the validation example is listed here. We have not repeated all the controls in this sample—for the full code listing, see the Chapter 15 directory on the CD.

```
<%@ Page language="c#" Codebehind="WebForm1.aspx.cs" AutoEventWireup="false"
Inherits="ValidationExample.WebForm1" %>
<!DOCTYPE HTML PUBLIC "-//W3C//DTD HTML 4.0 Transitional//EN" >
<HTML>
  <HEAD>
    <title>WebForm1</title>
...
  </HEAD>
  <body MS_POSITIONING="GridLayout">
    <center><h1>Registrations</h1></center><br>
    <form id="Form1" method="post" runat="server">
      <asp:Label
        id="Label1" style="Z-INDEX: 101; LEFT: 104px; POSITION: absolute;
        TOP: 80px" runat="server" ToolTip="Enter your full name">Name:
      </asp:Label>
```

```
<asp:RequiredFieldValidator
    id="valPasswordRepeat" style="Z-INDEX: 116; LEFT: 320px;
    POSITION: absolute; TOP: 256px" runat="server"
    ErrorMessage="Re-enter the password for verification"
    ControlToValidate="txtPasswordRepeat">*
</asp:RequiredFieldValidator>
<asp:TextBox
    id="txtPasswordRepeat" style="Z-INDEX: 108; LEFT: 152px;
    POSITION: absolute; TOP: 256px" runat="server" TextMode="Password"
    ToolTip="Re-enter your password" tabIndex="4">
</asp:TextBox>
...
<asp:Button
    id="btnSubmit" style="Z-INDEX: 109; LEFT: 152px; POSITION: absolute;
    TOP: 328px" runat="server" ToolTip="Click to submit information"
    Text="Submit">
</asp:Button>
...
<asp:TextBox
    id="txtEmail" style="Z-INDEX: 106; LEFT: 152px; POSITION: absolute;
    TOP: 136px" runat="server"
    ToolTip="Enter your email address as name@domain.xxx"
    tabIndex="2">
</asp:TextBox>
<asp:RegularExpressionValidator
    id="valEmail1" style="Z-INDEX: 112; LEFT: 328px; POSITION: absolute;
    TOP: 136px" runat="server"
    ErrorMessage="Email address must be in the format name@domain.xxx"
    ControlToValidate="txtEmail"
    ValidationExpression="\w+([-+.]\w+)*@\w+([-.]\w+)*\.\w+([-.]\w+)*">*
</asp:RegularExpressionValidator>
...
<asp:ValidationSummary
    id="valSummary" style="Z-INDEX: 114; LEFT: 392px; POSITION: absolute;
    TOP: 136px" runat="server">
</asp:ValidationSummary>
    </form>
  </body>
</HTML>
```

Error Handling

Have you ever written code that does not run? Code that inadvertently included optional features (a.k.a. bugs) that you did not intend to be in the application? As a developer, you know that errors are in the nature of software. In Chapter 4, we looked at exception handling; and in Chapter 9, we covered the art of debugging.

In this section, we will look at how to gracefully inform the user when things happen that you did not intend, or that result from missing resources, such as a database server being offline or a network router being down. These types of runtime errors were not anticipated when the application was designed, and you must deal with them.

One of the most annoying errors we have seen is when connecting to a site, and after a long period the screen displays information that we do not have permission to access: "MSOLEDBSQL.1;Data Source=Coporate1;Initial Catalog=Findata; User id=sa;Password=;". As users, we should never be given that information—if we were less than ethical, that would be enough information to start a data-theft attempt. On the other hand, if the user is not a computer professional, the information is very confusing and doesn't allow the user to gracefully exit from the page.

The errors in an application can be classified into three broad groups: syntax errors, logical errors, and system errors.

- **Syntax errors**   These are the result of typing and spelling mistakes and of using objects in assemblies that are not referenced in the web application (no checking at design time). Syntax errors are found when the application will not compile, and they are usually trivial to repair.

- **Logical errors**   These are usually hard to find. They are rooted in the logic of the program and can be the result of bad input data that wasn't validated, or they can be the result of the processing making an erroneous assumption, resulting in incorrect output. To solve logical errors, you need to use tracing and other general debugging techniques, as covered in Chapter 9.

- **System errors**   These are the errors that you cannot foresee. They are usually generated by ASP.NET and can be caused by missing resources or general failures in ASP.NET or even in the Common Language Runtime. We'll focus on this type of errors in this chapter because the way we trace in a web application is different from the general debugging techniques that were covered in Chapter 9.

Custom Error Pages

The default error pages displayed from a web server can be rather cryptic; in this section, we will look at techniques to customize those error pages. The first technique we will look at sends the user a custom error page with pertinent information for the error that occurred. In order to change the default error page behavior to display a customized page, you need to make an entry in the Web application's configuration file (Web .config) in the customErrors element, as shown in the following code segment:

```
<configuration>
  <system.web>
    <customErrors defaultRedirect="TheErrorPage.aspx" mode="On"/>
  <system.web>
</configuration>
```

To edit the Web.config file, double-click on it in the Solution Explorer. The default Web.config file that is generated in Visual Studio .NET contains many more configuration entries than customErrors—we will look at those entries in Chapter 17.

The attributes for the customErrors element are listed in Table 15-7.

Now that you have the application displaying a customized error page, you need to create that error page. The page in this example is named TheErrorPage.aspx, and it is added to the project by selecting Project | Add Webform.

Attribute	Description
defaultRedirect	Holds the URL for the page the user will be redirected to for all errors that have no `<error>` element inside the `customErrors` element.
mode	Specifies when the redirected error page should be used. The browser that is used controls how the error messages are displayed; the browser running on the local development server will by default receive the detailed error page, while any remote client will receive a short error page. The `mode` attribute can be set to On, Off, or RemoteOnly to change that behavior. When set to On, the custom error page is sent to both local and remote clients; Off turns off the custom redirections; RemoteOnly sends the custom page to remote clients, while the local client gets the detailed error page from ASP.NET.
`<error>`	Identifies optional child elements that describe the redirection page for specific errors. The `<error>` element has two attributes: `statusCode`, which is the HTTP status code that the error will respond to, and `redirect`, which is the URL of the error page the user will be redirected to.

Table 15-7 Attributes for the `customErrors` Element

 EXAM TIP The value for the `mode` attribute is case sensitive.

The error page should give the user the nontechnical information about the error and direct the user how to recover from or retry the operation that failed. Figure 15-8 shows one possible error page with some feedback for the user.

The `customErrors` element gives us full control over all the error pages we might need to build for our application. For example, the "403 Forbidden," "404 Not Found," and "500 Internal Server Error" errors could be mapped to custom error pages using the following entry in the `Web.config` configuration file.

```
<configuration>
  <system.web>
    <customErrors defaultRedirect="TheErrorPage.aspx" mode="On">
      <error statusCode="403" redirect="ServerSupport.aspx"/>
      <error statusCode="404" redirect="NotFoundError.aspx"/>
      <error statusCode="500" redirect="NoAccess.aspx"/>
    </customErrors>
  </system.web>
</configuration>
```

You can configure custom error pages for all the defined HTML error codes by adding one entry for each code. If an error occurs that does not match the error codes, the user will be redirected to the `defaultRedirect` page.

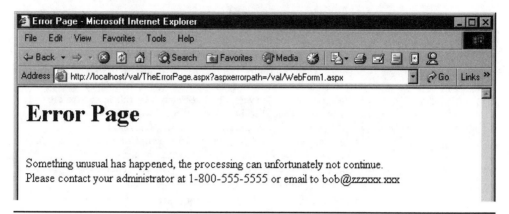

Figure 15-8   One error page

Page_Error()

When unhandled errors occur, they can be trapped on the page by implementing the `Page_Error()` method. The `Page_Error()` method is called when the `Error` event is raised by the `Page` object. An example of the use of the `Page_Error()` method can be seen in the following code segment:

```
private void Page_Error(object sender, System.EventArgs e)
{
  string str = "<font face=Arial color=black>"
           + "<h4>" + Request.Url.ToString() + "</h4>"
           + "<pre><font color=black>"
           + Server.GetLastError().ToString()
           + "</pre></font></font>";
  Response.Write(str);
  Response.Flush();
  Server.ClearError();   // Clear the error to ensure it does not bubble
}
```

The event handler must be registered in the `InitializeComponent()` method, as in the following code segment:

```
private void InitializeComponent()
{
  this.Load += new System.EventHandler(this.Page_Load);
  this.Error += new System.EventHandler(this.Page_Error);
}
```

Event Log

Windows has a very valuable feature in the Event Log. This feature can be used to save tracking information from your application that can then be viewed by the administrator of the server to find if there have been any errors that need to be resolved. The Event

Log consists of multiple physical logs that are viewed through the Event Viewer. To open the Event Viewer, select Start | Programs | Administrative Tools | Event Viewer.

The Event Log has three default views: System Log, Security Log, and Application Log. Some servers might have more logs, depending on the installed products. The System.Diagnostics namespace provides the classes that write to the Event Log.

You can write events into the log for every possible reason, but that would fill the log with lots of messages that might not be important. In the web application, however, there is an Application_Error() method that will execute when there are unhandled errors in any of the pages of the application, and these are the errors you should be sure to add to the log.

The Application_Error() method is defined in the global configuration file for the application, global.asax. It is one of many features of the global.asax file, and you will learn more about this file in Chapter 17.

In order to write information to the Event Log, start by importing the System.Diagnostics namespace into the global.asax file. The code for the Application_Error() method can be seen in the following code segment:

```
...
using System.Diagnostics;
...
protected void Application_Error(Object sender, EventArgs e)
{
  // Create the message to be stored in the Applications Log
  string strMessage = "\nURL:\n http://localhost/" + Request.Path
          + "\nMESSAGE:\n " + Server.GetLastError().Message
          + "\nSTACK TRACE:\n" + Server.GetLastError().StackTrace;
  Server.ClearError();

  //Check if the event log exists, if not create it
  string strLogName = "Application";
  if (!EventLog.SourceExists(strLogName))
  {
    EventLog.CreateEventSource(strLogName,strLogName);
  }

  // Create the Log object and insert the message
  EventLog logAppl = new EventLog();
  logAppl.Source = strLogName;
  logAppl.WriteEntry(strMessage, EventLogEntryType.Error);
}
```

 NOTE The \n sequence used in the strings in the preceding code segment is the escape sequence for a newline character. Its use will make the message more readable.

In the code example, you need to build a message entry to be added to the Application Log, and that needs to be followed by a check to see if the log is already created on the computer—if not, you need to create it using this line:

```
EventLog.CreateEventSource(strLogName,strLogName);
```

The final step is to write the entry to the Event Log by using the `WriteEntry()` method of the `EventLog` object. The text you include in the message should be descriptive, and use as full a description as possible. The Windows operating system adds a stock header to the Event Log entry, which can be seen in Figure 15-9.

Page-Level Tracing

To debug ASP.NET applications, and in particular, debug client user interfaces, you need to make use of the *tracing* facility. This facility has greatly improved the debugging services compared to what was available for the ASP environment. ASP debugging was not the most developer-friendly activity to undertake—debugging was a chore, and trying to get information from the running system entailed creating code that looked like this:

```
if (DEBUG == true)
{
  Response.Write("x = " + pointX + ", y = " + pointy);
}
```

The value of the global variable `DEBUG` determined what the output would be. Then we had to thread through the code to locate the problem spot, which was not very much

Figure 15-9

The message
written into
the Event Log

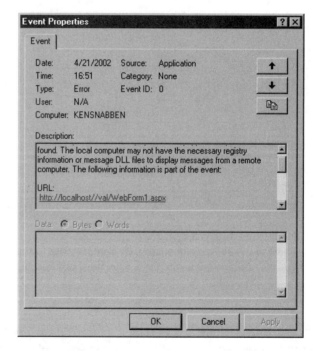

fun. And if you forgot to set DEBUG to False, the debug information ended up on the client systems.

EXAM TIP If you are given the option to use global DEBUG variables and `Response.Write()` calls, you know they are referring to the previous version and that these are wrong answers.

In ASP.NET, we have a new way of debugging our applications. Tracing does away with the hard-coded DEBUG testing, and the consequent runtime errors that make it even harder to get a page working properly. The trace feature provides a large number of information points for the page, including performance data, server variables, and any messages the developer has added to the page.

To use page-level tracing, you need to add one page directive at the top of the web page to inform ASP.NET that you require tracing information for that page. This is the directive:

```
<%@ Page Trace="true" %>
```

EXAM TIP The `Trace` directive overrides the trace setting for the application in the `Web.config` file.

In order to look at what is returned from the trace feature, we built a Web Form. The following code is all that is needed:

```
<%@ Page language="c#" Codebehind="WebForm1.aspx.cs"
        AutoEventWireup="false" Inherits="Tracer.WebForm1" trace="True"%>
<!DOCTYPE HTML PUBLIC "-//W3C//DTD HTML 4.0 Transitional//EN" >
<HTML>
  <HEAD>
    <title>WebForm1</title>
...
  </HEAD>
  <body MS_POSITIONING="GridLayout">
    <form id="Form1" method="post" runat="server">
      <asp:TextBox id="TextBox1" runat="server"></asp:TextBox>
      <asp:Button id="Button1" runat="server" Text="Button"></asp:Button>
      <br/><br/><br/>
    </form>
  </body>
</HTML>
```

Create this application, and then save and build it. Run it by pressing F5, and after a short delay you will be presented with the information shown in Figure 15-10.

The end result of turning on tracing is that the web server produces the normal content of the Web Form (the TextBox and Button) plus a large number of sections that give us information about the page and the processes on that page. The sections in the trace output are listed in Table 15-8.

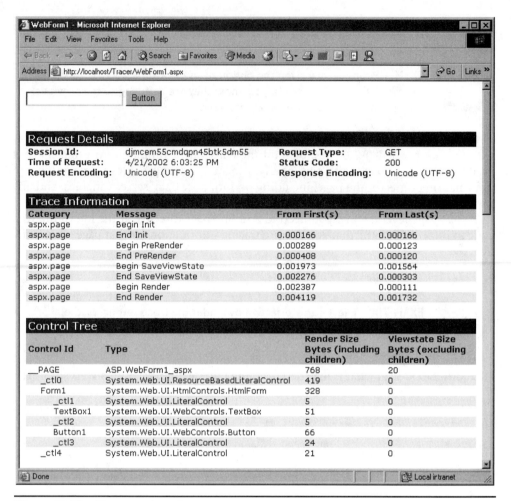

Figure 15-10   The output from the trace

Now that you've seen the sections of the trace output, we need to look at how to insert messages into the trace log. There are two methods that can be used to insert custom messages into the Trace Information section.

```
Trace.Write();
Trace.Warn();
```

Section	Description
Request Details	This section deals with the client's request for the page, and includes information such as the session ID for the current session, the request type (GET or POST), the date and time of the request, and the encoding of the request and response.
Trace Information	This is the section where trace information, as well as any messages we added to the page, will be presented. The display can be used to determine the performance of the server for this page request, as well as to see the order of the page generation.
Control Tree	This section displays the inheritance of the controls on the page (Page is the root), as well as the control IDs, type, and size of the view state.
Cookies Collection	This section contains information about the cookies collection that is attached to the web page.
Headers Collection	This section lists the different headers that the client sent to the server as part of the request for the page.
Server Variables	This section is where the different variables available through the Server object are displayed.

Table 15-8   The Sections of the Trace Output

Both methods insert information into the log, but the `Trace.Warn()` method inserts messages in red, while `Trace.Write()` inserts messages in black.

Expanding on the previous example, we will implement an event handler for the click event of the `Button` control. The following code will write information into the Trace Information section:

```
private void Button1_Click(object sender, System.EventArgs e)
{
  // We will insert some information into the trace log when the Button is clicked
  int i = 42;
  Trace.Write("TestCategory","i is initialized to " + i.ToString());
  if (12 < 42)
  {
    Trace.Warn("ErrorCategory", "Attempt to change the universal answer!");
  }
}
```

The resulting output from this code segment is shown in Figure 15-11, which displays the Trace Information section of the trace output.

Page-level tracing is very powerful, and all you need to do is set the trace page directive to True for the trace to be generated, or to False to turn off the trace. The trace option

Trace Information			
Category	**Message**	**From First(s)**	**From Last(s)**
aspx.page	Begin Init		
aspx.page	End Init	0.000209	0.000209
aspx.page	Begin LoadViewState	0.000330	0.000121
aspx.page	End LoadViewState	0.000885	0.000555
aspx.page	Begin ProcessPostData	0.000994	0.000109
aspx.page	End ProcessPostData	0.002187	0.001194
aspx.page	Begin ProcessPostData Second Try	0.002312	0.000125
aspx.page	End ProcessPostData Second Try	0.002411	0.000099
aspx.page	Begin Raise ChangedEvents	0.002504	0.000093
aspx.page	End Raise ChangedEvents	0.002600	0.000096
aspx.page	Begin Raise PostBackEvent	0.002694	0.000094
TestCategory	i is initialized to 42	0.004239	0.001545
ErrorCategory	Attempt to change the universal answer!	0.004747	0.000508
aspx.page	End Raise PostBackEvent	0.029399	0.024652
aspx.page	Begin PreRender	0.029598	0.000199
aspx.page	End PreRender	0.029725	0.000127
aspx.page	Begin SaveViewState	0.030782	0.001056
aspx.page	End SaveViewState	0.031127	0.000346
aspx.page	Begin Render	0.031233	0.000106
aspx.page	End Render	0.033035	0.001802

Figure 15-11   Output from the page-level trace

can be controlled on the application level through the Web.config configuration file
for the application. By setting the enabled attribute of the <trace> element, you can
turn on and off tracing. The following segment from the Web.config file illustrates the
setting:

```
<configuration>
  <system.web>
    <trace enabled="true" requestLimit="10" pageOutput="false"
          traceMode="SortByTime" localOnly="true"/>
  </system.web>
</configuration>
```

The attributes for the <trace> element are used to control how tracing will be configured for the web site. The attributes are described in Table 15-9.

EXAM TIP   In order to get tracing only when testing from the web server,
set the localOnly attribute to True.

Attribute	Description
enabled	Determines whether tracing is on by default on the site
requestLimit	Sets the total number of trace requests to keep for offline viewing
pageOutput	Specifies whether the trace should be output on the screen as well as kept for offline viewing
traceMode	Determines the order of the output
localOnly	Determines whether only requests from http://localhost should be traced

Table 15-9   The Attributes of the `<trace>` Element

In the previous example, we used tracing at the page level: all the tracing information is presented as part of the page. There is a second option on how to present the trace output by enabling application-level tracing: you need to remove the trace page directive and add the `<trace>` element to the `Web.config` file. With the `<trace>` element's attributes set to `enabled="true"` and `pageOutput="false"`, the tracing is still taking place, but the output is stored on the web site and can be made available through the `Trace.axd` handler. In Figure 15-12 you can see the resulting `Trace.axd` output.

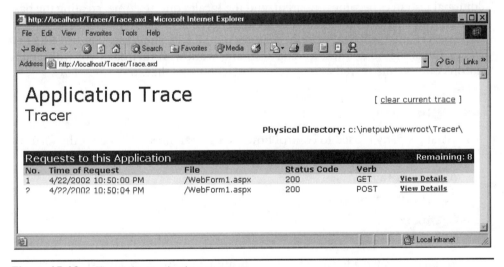

Figure 15-12   The application-level trace output

Summary

In this chapter, we have looked at a number of topics that center on the user and the user interface. Although it is easy to say that localization is the most important aspect of this chapter, there are equally compelling arguments that the honor belongs to error handling, or to validation. We think they are equally important. Using validation to ensure that the data received from the user has the right format is only prudent, as is the use of error handling to communicate any problem to the user. Building a localized application will cost some extra development time up front, but the payback will easily offset that cost in the end.

The topics of validation and error communication fall under the heading of human engineering. Always test your design on a target group to make sure that the layout and communications elements are clear and that the design isn't cluttered.

There is one element of localization that we have not touched on in this book, mainly because it is a topic that is not included in the exam. The use of resources increases object reuse and lowers the likelihood of problems with the application. It also lowers the overall cost of development. The resources are defined and created at the beginning of the project, and then are reused through the application.

The approach to localization commonly used is to create the resources for the default locale (fallback), and use that locale for the initial application release. As the need for additional resources becomes apparent, add the locales one at a time, creating the base language resources first, and adding cultures as needed.

The next chapter will deal with the features in ASP.NET and Visual Studio .NET that gives us the ability to connect to databases and work with that data. We will see the built-in components as well as hand-coded ADO.NET applications.

Test Questions

1. What property is used to control how the user can press ALT-F to set the focus to a control?

   A. `AccessKey`

   B. `ControlOrder`

   C. `TabOrder`

   D. `TraceOrder`

2. You have created a localized web application that supports English, French, German, and Spanish. After building the resource files, you code all the strings to come through the `ResourceManager.GetString()` method. You test the application by using the browser on your development computer, and as you switch languages in the Regional Settings, everything functions as expected. After deploying the application, you receive a message from a client saying that the application does not change when the client accesses it with a computer configured to use the French locale. You need to fix the application. What will you do?

A. Rebuild the resource assembly.

B. Add code to change the current thread's culture to the user's culture.

C. Add code to change the location of the resource assembly.

D. Instruct the user to upgrade to a newer browser.

3. What is used to validate complex string patterns like an e-mail address?

A. Extended expressions.

B. Regular expressions.

C. Irregular expressions.

D. Basic expressions.

4. What is the default language for the fallback culture?

A. English.

B. Swedish.

C. User's setting.

D. Neutral.

5. What namespace is needed for Event Log support?

A. `System.Event`

B. `System.Diagnostics`

C. `System.EventLog`

D. `System.Diagnostics.Event`

6. What property controls whether the text in a `TextBox` control is displayed in clear text or as a collection of * characters?

A. `PasswordCharacter`

B. `Hide`

C. `Encrypt`

D. `TextMode`

7. You need to customize the error messages from your web application. What file will you modify to customize the error messages?

A. `Web.config`

B. `Error.config`

C. `Application.config`

D. `global.asax`

8. What property is set in order to display the text in reverse flow order?

A. `rtl`

B. `ltr`

C. dir

D. reverse

9. You have configured custom error pages for your application. When you test the pages from a co-worker's computer, they display properly, but when displayed in your browser on the development computer, they display incorrectly. What will you do to correct the display of the error pages on your computer?

   A. Install Internet Explorer 6.0.

   B. Change the mode attribute to localhost in the Web.config file.

   C. Change the mode attribute to RemoteOnly in the Web.config file.

   D. Change the mode attribute to On in the Web.config file.

10. After adding messages to the trace log, you need to locate the output. What section contains the messages a developer has added to the trace log?

    A. Trace Information.

    B. Control Tree.

    C. Cookies.

    D. Headers Collection.

    E. Server Variables.

11. What file would you modify to implement application-wide error processing for all unhandled errors?

    A. Web.config

    B. Error.config

    C. Application.config

    D. global.asax

12. What property is used to control the order in which the controls are accessed?

    A. AccessKey

    B. ControlOrder

    C. TabIndex

    D. TraceOrder

13. How do you enable tracing?

    A. Set the Trace property of the Web Form to True.

    B. Set the Trace property of the Server object to True.

    C. Set the Session variable Trace to True.

    D. Set the Applications variable Trace to True.

14. What control is used to validate that two fields are equal?

    A. `RequiredFieldValidator`

    B. `RegularExpressionValidator`

    C. `CompareValidator`

    D. The `equals()` method of the field.

15. What method is used to insert a highlighted entry in the trace output?

    A. `Trace.Write()`

    B. `Trace.HighLight()`

    C. `Trace.Error()`

    D. `Trace.Warn()`

Test Answers

    1. A.

    2. B.

    3. B.

    4. D.

    5. B.

    6. D.

    7. A.

    8. C.

    9. D.

   10. A.

   11. D.

   12. C.

   13. A.

   14. C.

   15. D.

Consuming and Manipulating Data from Data Sources

In this chapter, you will

- Learn to consume and manipulate data
- Access and manipulate data from a Microsoft SQL Server database
- Access and manipulate data from a data store
- Handle data errors
- Display and update data
- Transform and filter data
- Bind data to the user interface

In Chapter 10, you were introduced to the ADO.NET object model and learned how to use it to create `DataSet` and `DataAdapter` objects. In this chapter, we are going to have a look at the process involved in getting data from a Microsoft SQL Server with error checking in a web application displaying the data using some of the data-bound controls we have at our disposal through ASP.NET.

To access data through ASP.NET, we use the ADO.NET objects: `xxxConnection`, `xxxDataAdapter`, and `DataSet`. In Chapter 10, we looked at some of those objects and at how we could use them to connect to and use databases. These different ADO.NET objects come in three individual groupings based on the technology that is used to connect to and communicate with the database. The `xxxConnection` and `xxxDataAdapter` objects are implemented as technology-specific objects that are identified through the prefix to the class name that will replace the xxx in the names. Objects that start with the "sql" prefix are specifically tuned to work with Microsoft SQL; Server version 7 or higher; those with the "oleDb" prefix work with OLE DB providers, and the last group, with the prefix "odbc" (for use with ODBC), is not supplied with ADO.NET—the ODBC objects must be downloaded from Microsoft directly.

EXAM TIP   Remember that the `sqlConnection`, `sqlDataAdapter`, and `sqlCommand` objects are specific for Microsoft SQL Server version 7 or higher. For all other database systems, use the `oleDbConnection`, `oleDbDataAdapter`, and `oleDbCommand` objects. Only use the ODBC objects for systems that do not have OLE DB support.

We will first look at how to use the Visual Studio .NET facilities to add these objects to a form and configure them through the wizards that are supplied with the IDE. Then we will work with data from the database directly, through code, without making use of the wizards.

All examples in this chapter use the Address database that is built especially for this chapter. Please see the folder for Chapter 10 on the CD that accompanies this book for instructions on how to install the database on your system.

Visual Studio .NET Support for Data

The Visual Studio .NET IDE provides ADO.NET objects that can be dragged from the Toolbox and dropped onto the form. In the following illustration, you can see the default objects that support Microsoft SQL Server and OLE DB providers—the `DataSet` object works with either of the database technologies. To use one of the objects, you need to drag it onto the form where it will reside as an icon at the base of the form in Design view.

The best way to learn how to use the objects and wizards supplied with Visual Studio .NET is to use the wizards to work with the objects, so we'll work through a couple of example projects.

Using a DataGrid Server Control

As an example, we will create a Web Form that uses a `DataGrid` server control to display data from the Address database. To start the example, create a new project with these steps:

1. On the Start Page of Visual Studio .NET, click New Project, or select File | New | Project from the menus. The New Project dialog box will be displayed.

2. Select Visual C# Projects in the Project Type pane of the New Project dialog box.

3. Select ASP.NET Web Application in the Templates pane.

4. Enter the URL for the new application into the Location field. Use the `localhost` web server, and call the application `AddressOne`.

The completed New Project dialog box can be seen in Figure 16-1.

Once the project is created, you can create and configure the `DataSet` that will be used to populate the `DataGrid` control that will display the data as a spreadsheet. We will use the Data Adapter Configuration Wizard, which will ask some questions and then configure the DataAdapter to access the data. Follow these steps:

1. Open the Data tab in the Toolbox.

2. Drag a `sqlDataAdapter` object onto the form.

Figure 16-1

The start of the AddressOne application

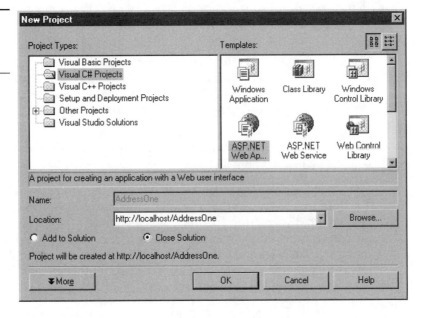

3. The Data Adapter Configuration Wizard will start, as shown here. Click Next to proceed.

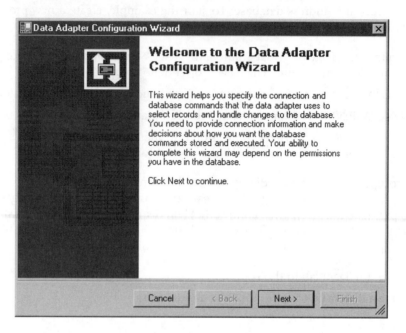

4. In the next wizard screen, click on New Connection to open the Data Link Properties dialog box.

5. In the Data Link Properties dialog box, expand the Select or Enter a Server Name combo box and select your server name from the list. Select the option to Use a Specific User Name and Password, and enter **sa** as the user name and leave the password blank. In the Select a Database File or Database Name combo box, expand and select the Address database. The finished dialog box is shown in Figure 16-2.

6. Test the connection by clicking the Test Connection button. Always test the connection to make sure it works.

7. Click Next to go to the third screen of the wizard.

8. The third screen gives you the choice of entering a SELECT statement that will be used directly, entering a SELECT statement that will be converted to a stored procedure, or selecting a stored procedure to use. Stored procedures are written in the SQL language and are stored in the database—we will look at these features later on in this chapter. Select the Use SQL Statements option, and click Next to continue to the next screen.

Figure 16-2

The completed
Data Link
Properties
dialog box

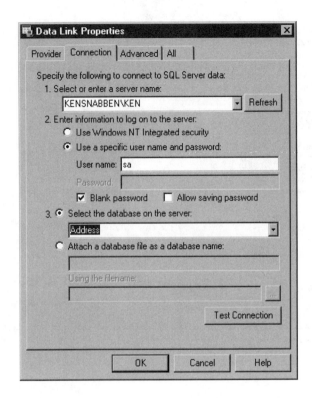

9. Enter the following SQL statement in the text area:

```
SELECT TOP 15 FirstName, LastName, EmailAddress
FROM Users
```

10. Click Next to see the queries the wizard will generate for you.

11. Click Finish to create the DataAdapter.

The Data Adapter Configuration Wizard created the two objects that can be seen at the bottom of the Web Form shown in Figure 16-3. The default names for the objects are `sqlDataAdapter1` and `sqlConnection1`.

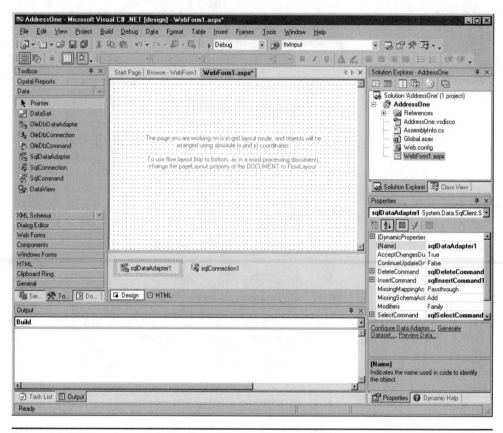

Figure 16-3 The project with the ADO.NET objects

The next step is to generate the `DataSet` from the DataAdapter that you just created. Here's how to do it:

1. Right-click on `sqlDataAdapter1` and select Generate DataSet, or select Data | Generate DataSet menus.

2. In the Generate Dataset dialog box, enter **dsUsers** as the new name for the `DataSet` (as shown next).

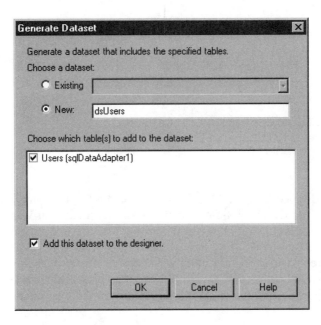

3. Select the Add This Dataset to the Designer check box to create a class that wraps the `DataSet`.

4. Click OK to generate the `DataSet`.

Visual Studio .NET generates the `DataSet` class (`dsUsers`) and a schema that defines the `DataSet` (`dsUsers.xsd`). You can view the schema in the Solution Explorer. To see the schema's dependent file, you will need to click on the Show All Files toolbar button. The wizard also added the new `DataSet` class (`dsUsers1`) to the form.

The data components are now completely configured. All you need now is to add the `DataGrid` to the form and add some code to complete the example. Follow these steps:

1. Select the Web Forms tab in the toolbox, and drag a `DataGrid` server control onto the Web Form.

2. Right-click the `DataGrid` control and select Auto Format. Look at the color schemes and select a suitable one (we selected Colorful 3).

3. In the Properties window for the `DataGrid` control, select the `DataSource` property, and select dsUsers1 as the data source.

4. Set the `DataMember` property of the `DataGrid` to Users.

Setting the `DataSource` and `DataMember` properties effectively binds the control to the `DataSet`. There is one more step to be performed before the application will run, and that is to add some code to the form:

1. Open the Web Form's codebehind module by double-clicking on the form.

PART III

2. Change the Page_Load event handler to match the following:

```
private void Page_Load(object sender, System.EventArgs e)
{
  if ( !IsPostBack )
  {
    sqlDataAdapter1.Fill(dsUsers1);
    DataGrid1.DataBind();
  }
}
```

In the preceding code, the Fill() method of the DataAdapter will populate the DataSet from the database, based on the SQL statement that was defined for the DataAdapter. The DataBind() method of the DataGrid control refreshes and updates the control.

To test the web page, save and run it by pressing F5. The end result should be similar to what is shown in Figure 16-4. This results in a very presentable and functional application that will display a table of information from the Address database.

Creating and Using Stored Procedures

As we promised earlier, we will now look at the different options for specifying what data you want to retrieve from the database. The third screen in the Data Adapter Configuration Wizard gave you the option to use a SELECT statement to retrieve the data, to build a stored procedure from the SELECT statement, or to specify a stored procedure already in existence in the database. In the previous example, we simply used a SELECT statement.

A stored procedure is built from Transact-SQL statements (the language of Microsoft SQL Server) and stored in the database for reuse. Stored procedures are like methods in a database—they can receive parameters and then return values to the caller. There are a number of reasons for using stored procedures:

- Stored procedures are stored in the procedure cache of the database server, resulting in faster execution if the stored procedure is called repeatedly.

- Stored procedures are used to centralize the data-access logic on the server.

- Stored procedures will minimize the use of the network for large queries.

In the next example, you will see how to use a stored procedure rather than an SQL statement to retrieve the data. Here is how you do that:

1. Open the Data tab in the Toolbox.

2. Drag a sqlDataAdapter object onto the form.

3. The Data Adapter Configuration Wizard will start. Click Next to proceed.

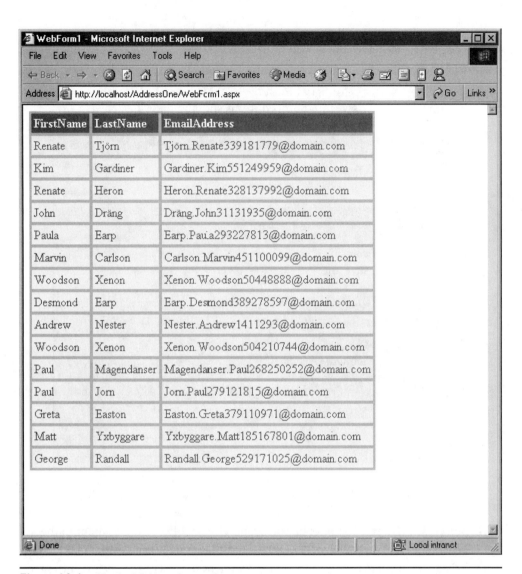

Figure 16-4   The final AddressOne application

4. In the next wizard screen, click on New Connection to open the Data Link Properties dialog box.

5. In the Data Link Properties dialog box, expand the Select or Enter a Server Name combo box and select your server name from the list. Select the option to Use a Specific User Name and Password, and enter **sa** as the user name and leave the password blank. In the Select a Database File or Database Name combo box, expand and select the Address database. The finished dialog box is shown in Figure 16-4.

6. Test the connection by clicking the Test Connection button. Always test the connection to make sure it works.

7. Click Next to go to the third screen of the wizard.

8. In the Data Adapter Configuration Wizard's third screen, select the second option to create a new stored procedure, as shown here. Click Next.

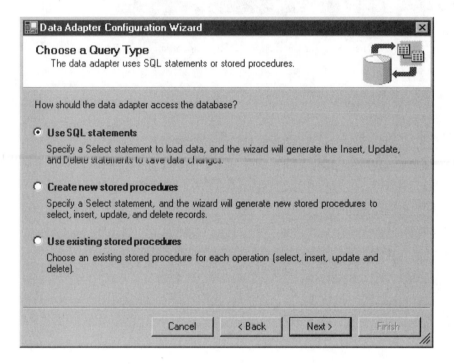

9. In the Generate the Stored Procedure screen, click on the Query Builder button.

10. Select the Addresses, PhoneNumbers, and Users tables, and add them to the Query Builder. Close the Add Table dialog box.

11. Select FirstName, LastName, and EmailAddress in the Users table by putting a checkmark in the checkbox beside the field name. (See Figure 16-5.)

12. Select Address1, City, Province, PostalCode, and Country from the Addresses table.

13. Select PhoneType and PhoneNumber from the PhoneNumbers table.

14. Right-click anywhere inside the Query Builder and select Run. Ensure that data is returned from the query.

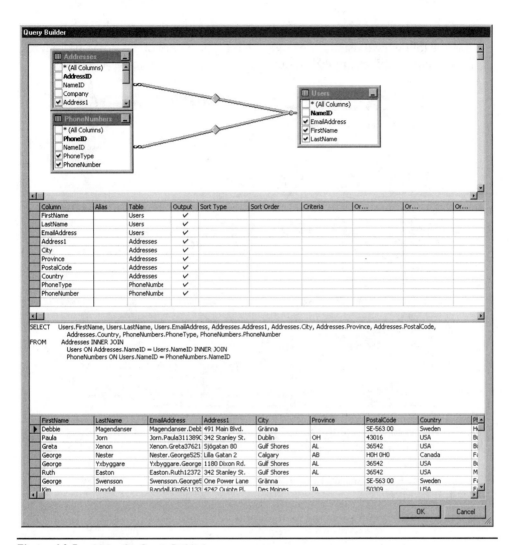

Figure 16-5 Using the Query Builder

15. Click OK to exit the Query Builder. The final query when you return from the Query Builder should look like this:

```
SELECT
    Users.FirstName, Users.LastName, Users.EmailAddress,
Addresses.Address1,
    Addresses.City, Addresses.Province, Addresses.PostalCode,
    Addresses.Country, PhoneNumbers.PhoneType, PhoneNumbers.PhoneNumber
FROM Addresses INNER JOIN Users ON Addresses.NameID = Users.NameID
            INNER JOIN PhoneNumbers ON Users.NameID =
                PhoneNumbers.NameID
```

16. Click Next, and the Create Stored Procedure screen will be displayed, as shown in the following illustration. You can change the names of the stored procedures here, but for this example, leave the default names of the stored procedures.

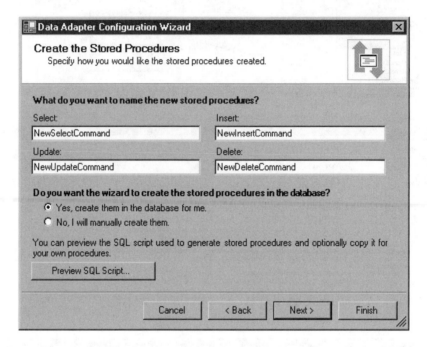

17. Click Next to generate the stored procedures. The warnings you will see are normal when the SELECT statement is based on a JOIN. The wizard cannot produce INSERT, UPDATE, or DELETE stored procedures from a JOIN statement—those stored procedures must be created by the database administrator.

18. Click Finish to complete the Data Adapter Configuration Wizard.

The procedure from this point on is the same as for the previous example. Create a DataSet from the DataAdapter, bind the DataSet to the DataGrid control, and test it.

When you are using a database that already has existing stored procedures, you can select Use Existing Stored Procedures from the Data Adapter Configuration Wizard's third screen. Figure 16-6 shows the resulting screen, from which the stored procedures can be selected.

The previous two examples built a Web Form using the DataGrid server control and the objects supplied from Visual Studio .NET. Now we will look at how you can build a form that lets you bind a DataSet to a group of controls and implement navigation and editing in the interface.

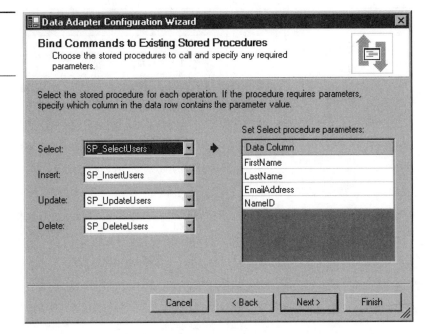

Figure 16-6
Using existing
stored
procedures

Data Binding

In the previous sections, we used *data binding* between a DataSet and the DataGrid
control, but now we will take a closer look. Data binding is a negotiated handshake
between a control and the DataSet. If the DataSet is updated from the server, the
control is updated; and conversely, if the data in the control is changed, the DataSet
is notified about that change. Data binding can be implemented both at design time
and at run time by setting the properties of the controls.

To bind a control to a data source, you use the DataBindings property, as shown in
Figure 16-7. Click on the ellipsis button (...) beside the DataBindings property to
open the Data Bindings dialog box shown in Figure 16-8. This dialog box is used to bind
data to any of the properties of a control, either by using a simple binding and providing
formatting as shown in Figure 16-8, or by specifying a custom binding expression, as
shown in Figure 16-9.

When you enter a binding expression in the Custom Binding Expression field, you
will describe the binding using the DataBinder object's Eval method (this is a static
method). As parameters, the method takes the name of the DataSet, a string that describes the data member, and a formatting string. In the example in Figure 16-9, the
DataSet name is dataSet11, the data member is "Tables[SP_SelectUsers]

Figure 16-7
The
`DataBindings`
property

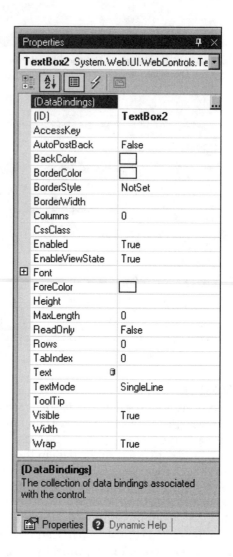

".DefaultView.[0].LastName", and the formatting string is "{0}". The preceding data member translates as follows:

- The member table in the `Tables` collection defined by the name `SP_SelectUsers`.

- The `DefaultView` that defines the columns of the returned data.

- The first (zero-based) rowset. The term *rowset* is used to describe the rows of data that the table object represents.

- The `LastName` column in that rowset.

Figure 16-8

The Data Bindings dialog box

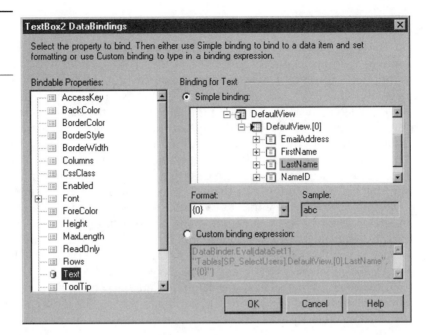

By using a custom binding expression, you can specify virtually any data binding. Any part of the user interface can be bound to data in this fashion, making it possible to configure the UI from a data source.

Figure 16-9

The Data Bindings dialog box with a custom binding expression

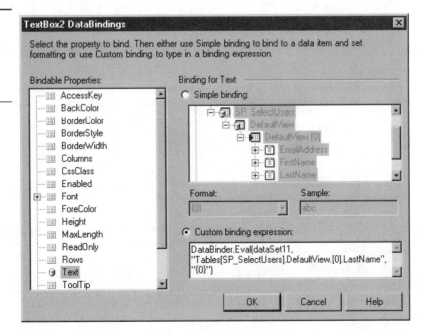

Error Handling

So far, we have omitted the error-handling code in this chapter to keep the code listings more focused on the use of ADO.NET in Web Forms, rather than on error-handling techniques. However, database access can create problems for a web site because the database will, in most cases, be located on a database server that is remote from the web server. When there are connection problems between the database server and the web server, ADO.NET will fail with an exception, and if you don't catch the exception, it will bubble through to the `Page` object and terminate the processing of your Web Form. This is not the best behavior for any application. You should always enclose your database access code in `try ... catch` blocks to ensure that you handle any errors in such a way that you can communicate the condition to the user in plain language.

In Chapter 4, you were introduced to the exception-handling structures used in C# programs. The `try ... catch ... finally` structure gives you a controlled way of executing statements in a `try` block and, if there are any exceptions, to match up the proper `catch` block to deal with the exception. The `finally` block will always execute irrespective of whether `try` or `catch` blocks completed.

The exceptions that relate to the database, and that can be raised in an ADO.NET application, are located in the `System.Data` namespace. The most common exceptions are listed in Table 16-1.

Exception	Description
SqlException	This is the general exception class for an SQL managed provider.
OleDbException	This is the general exception class for an OLE DB managed provider.
ODBCException	This is the general exception class for the ODBC managed provider.
DataException	This is the base class for most other exceptions in the System.Data namespace.
ConstraintException	This exception is raised when a constraint has been violated.
DBConcurrencyException	This exception is raised when an attempt to write to the database is detected while the database is being updated by another client.
DuplicatedNameException	This exception is raised when an attempt is made to define an object in the database with a name that already exists.
ReadOnlyException	This exception is thrown when an attempt is made to modify read-only data.
NoNullAllowedException	This exception is raised when an attempt is made to insert data into a table without supplying data for a column that is set to not allow NULL values.
SyntaxErrorException	This exception is raised when an SQL statement with syntax errors is passed to the provider.

Table 16-1   ADO.NET Exceptions Related to Databases

The ADO.NET exceptions are hierarchal, with `System.Data.DataException` as the base class—all the other exceptions inherit from it. That means that you can build a structure in your exception handling that treats special exceptions in a custom way, or you can write a catch-all type of exception-handling structure.

The following code segment illustrates the hierarchical nature of the exceptions—only the first `catch` statement that matches the exception will be executed.

```
try
{
  // do something with the database
}
catch (ConstraintException e)
{
  // handle the ConstraintException
}
catch (ReadOnlyException e)
{
  // handle the ReadOnlyException
}
catch (DataException e)
{
  // handle any other exceptions
}
finally
{
  // this code will always run, put the close statements here
}
```

 NOTE   The exception class is always called e; this has become the convention.

The exception processing proceeds from the top down through the `catch` statement. If a base exception class is higher in the listing than a child exception class, the child exception will never be caught.

 EXAM TIP   The `DataException` is the base exception for all the ADO.NET exceptions.

You will see this structure in use in the rest of this chapter as we start to use data sources programmatically in the Web Forms.

Accessing Data Programmatically

Even though we can quickly build a Web Form with very little coding, the end result will, in most cases, be an application that we still want to tune and control a bit more. This can be done by using the ADO.NET objects directly in code. In this section, we will look closer at how we can work with databases programmatically.

First, Table 16-2 gives a refresher of the objects from Chapter 10 and what they are used for. The prefix *xxx* used in the table identifies the three object variations for the three managed data providers—SQL, OLE DB, and ODBC. The prefixes are `sql`, `oleDb`, and `odbc`.

 EXAM TIP   Remember that the SQL managed provider only works with Microsoft SQL Server 7 and above.

Connecting to a Data Source

To connect to a data source, we need to select the appropriate managed provider. For the rest of this chapter, we will assume (as does Microsoft) that we are using Microsoft SQL Server 2000 as the data source.

When you create the connection object, you need to supply a connection string that defines, among other things, the name of the database and how you authenticate. A sample connection string looks like this:

```
data source=KENSNABBEN; initial catalog=Address; user id=sren;
password="123";
```

The `data source` parameter defines the server name, the `initial catalog` is the name of the database you want to connect to, the `user id` is the name you want to connect as, and the `password` is the password for the user id.

The connection string can be built by hand, or you can use the Data Link Properties dialog box (shown earlier in Figure 16-2) to build it. If you use the Data Link dialog box, the connection string will be saved by Visual Studio .NET so you can retrieve the string easily in other projects. The Data Link dialog box was described in the "Using a DataGrid Server Control" section, earlier in this chapter.

Object	Description
`xxxConnection`	Defines the way we find and authenticate with a data source.
`xxxDataAdapter`	Defines four commands that are used to `SELECT`, `INSERT`, `UPDATE`, and `DELETE` data from the data source. The `DataAdapter` is commonly used to create a `DataSet` that is then used for data processing.
`xxxCommand`	Creates an object that defines an SQL statement or a stored procedure that will be reused throughout the application.
`DataSet`	Provides a disconnected representation of the data. It contains multiple tables that can be edited, displayed, or used.
`xxxDataReader`	Provides a connected, read-only, forward-only way of manipulating the data.

Table 16-2   The .NET Data Provider Objects

The recommended procedure for creating a connection to a data source is as follows:

- Create a global string to hold the connection string, and use the `Application` object to store the string. This way, if the string needs to be changed, you only need to perform the change once; and because all connections to a particular database use the same string, the Connection Manager can take advantage of connection pooling.

- Create the connection as a local object, and explicitly destroy the connection when it is no longer needed. If the procedure where the object was created goes out of scope, the connection should be destroyed by the garbage collector. That will not happen directly, nor can it be predicted—the connection will be active until the garbage collector runs. The connections that are held open on the database server will effectively limit the performance of the server.

The following code segment illustrates how to connect to a database. In this example, the connection is made to the Address database on a Microsoft SQL Server 2000 using the name KENSNABBEN.

```
...
string strSQL = "user id=sa;password;initial catalog=Address;" +
                "data source=KENSNABBEN";
SqlConnection addressConnection = new SqlConnection(strSQL);
try
{
  addressConnection.Open();

  // perform the data processing
  ...
}
catch (SqlException e)
{
  // we will get here if the connection failed to open
  // process the error by, for example, throwing an exception to the caller
  // to try another connection.
}
finally
{
  // close the connection and set the reference to null
  addressConnection.Close();
  addressConnection = null;
}
```

 EXAM TIP Instantiate the `Connection` object outside the `try` structure, perform all operations that can have failures inside the `try` block, and close everything in the `finally` block.

Creating and Configuring a Command Object

The next step is to create a Command object. The CreateCommand() method of the Connection object does that. The following line shows how to create the object:

```
sqlCommand addressCommand = addressConnection.CreateCommand();
```

The Command object needs to have some properties set to be able to retrieve the data from the data source. We will use a stored procedure (SP_SelectUsers) to read the data. The CommandText property defines the text of the SELECT statement or the stored procedure, and the CommandType property declares what the content of the CommandText property is. The choices are listed in Table 16-3.

The following code lines declare and configure the Command object to run the SP_SelectUsers stored procedure on the database.

```
addressCommand.CommandText = "SP_SelectUsers";
addressCommand.CommandType = CommandType.StoredProcedure;
```

Populate the DataSet with the Data from the Command

Now we can create a SqlDataAdapter to represent the data from the command. The SqlDataAdapter is used to connect data sources and DataSet objects. You build it by passing the command to the constructor of the DataAdapter, like this:

```
SqlDataAdapter addressAdapter = new SqlDataAdapter(addressCommand);
```

The next step is to create the DataSet and associate it with the DataAdapter:

```
DataSet addressSet = new DataSet();
addressAdapter.Fill(addressSet, "Addresses");
```

Once you have access to the DataSet, you can bind it to some of the controls on the Web Form. For this code example, the form has a DataGrid control called DataGrid1. To bind the data to this control, you need to add the following code to the Web Form:

```
// Bind to a DataGrid.
DataGrid1.DataSource = addressSet;
DataGrid1.DataBind();
```

CommandText Property	Description
Test	Indicates that the content of CommandText is a text command, and there will be no optimization of the command. This is the default.
StoredProcedure	Declares that the CommandText property contains the name of a stored procedure. The command will optimize the use of the cache on the server, if possible.
TableDirect	Indicates that the CommandText property holds the name of a table in the database that will be returned by the command.

Table 16-3   Settings for the CommandText Property

The Completed Web Form

The entire application consists of one form with a `Button` control named `Button1` and a `DataGrid` control named `DataGrid1`. The following code is the `WebForm1.aspx.cs` file that defines the codebehind module for the application. The code presented in bold has been added from the previous code samples.

```csharp
using System;
using System.Collections;
using System.ComponentModel;
using System.Data;
using System.Data.SqlClient;
using System.Drawing;
using System.Web;
using System.Web.SessionState;
using System.Web.UI;
using System.Web.UI.WebControls;
using System.Web.UI.HtmlControls;

namespace WebData7
{
  /// <summary>
  /// Summary description for WebForm1.
  /// </summary>
  public class WebForm1 : System.Web.UI.Page
  {
    protected System.Web.UI.WebControls.Button Button1;
    protected SqlConnection addressConnection;
    protected SqlCommand addressCommand;
    protected SqlDataAdapter addressAdapter;
    protected DataSet addressSet;
    protected System.Web.UI.WebControls.DataGrid DataGrid1;

    private void Page_Load(object sender, System.EventArgs e)
    {
      // Put user code to initialize the page here
    }
...
    private void Button1_Click(object sender, System.EventArgs e)
    {
      string strSQL = "user id=sa;initial catalog=Address;" +
                   "data source=KENSNABBEN";
      addressConnection = new SqlConnection(strSQL);
      try
      {
        addressConnection.Open();

        // perform the data processing
        addressCommand = addressConnection.CreateCommand();
        addressCommand.CommandText = "SP_SelectUsers";
        addressCommand.CommandType = CommandType.StoredProcedure;
        addressAdapter = new SqlDataAdapter(addressCommand);
        addressSet = new DataSet();
        addressAdapter.Fill(addressSet, "Addresses");

        // Bind to a DataGrid.
        DataGrid1.DataSource = addressSet;
        DataGrid1.DataBind();
```

PART III

```
        }
        catch (SqlException ex)
        {
          // we will get here if the connection failed to open
          // process the error by for example throwing an exception to the caller
          // to try another connection.
          Response.Write(ex.ToString);
         }
        finally
        {
          // close the connection and set the reference to null
          addressConnection.Close();
          addressConnection = null;
        }
      }
    }
}
```

Building a Data Form

The data-bound form is one of the common forms you will build—it is a form that displays detailed information about a record in a database. The form can be read-only, or it can be used for data entry and editing, as well.

In this section, we will build a form that displays information about an entry in the Address database and that allows us to modify the information. We will implement the form as a data entry form.

Creating the SQL Statement

The first thing to consider when building a data form is the SQL statement that will be used to select the data. In this example, we want to build SQL sentences to retrieve the user's name and e-mail information. We will use a second SQL sentence to view the user's address information.

The following SQL statement will retrieve the user's name and e-mail address:

```
SELECT NameID, FirstName, LastName, EmailAddress FROM Users;
```

To select the address information for the user, we will use the following SQL sentence:

```
SELECT Address1, Address2, City, Province, PostalCode, Country, NameID
FROM Addresses
```

Building the Form

To start building the application, we need to create a project, and Figure 16-10 shows the settings for the project. Call the ASP.NET web application AddressForm, and use the localhost server.

Figure 16-10
Starting the
`AddressForm`
project

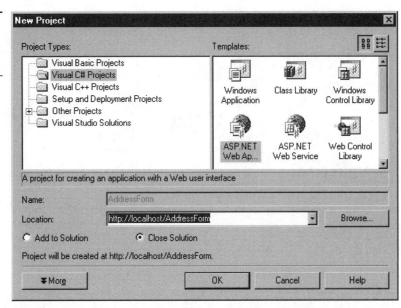

The form we will build is shown in Figure 16-11. Rename the form as `Address.aspx`. The properties for the controls are listed in the following code segment that was generated when the controls were added to the Web Form.

```
<%@ Page language="c#" Codebehind="WebForm1.aspx.cs"
                    AutoEventWireup="false"
                    Inherits="AddressForm.WebForm1" %>
<!DOCTYPE HTML PUBLIC "-//W3C//DTD HTML 4.0 Transitional//EN" >
<HTML>
  <HEAD>
    <title>Address Listing</title>
    <meta name="GENERATOR" Content="Microsoft Visual Studio 7.0">
    <meta name="CODE_LANGUAGE" Content="C#">
    <meta name="vs_defaultClientScript" content="JavaScript">
    <meta name="vs_targetSchema"
              content="http://schemas.microsoft.com/intellisense/ie5">
  </HEAD>
<body MS_POSITIONING="GridLayout">
  <form id="Form1" method="post" runat="server">
    <asp:TextBox id="txtFirstName" style="Z-INDEX: 101; LEFT: 8px;
              POSITION: absolute; TOP: 32px"
              runat="server"></asp:TextBox>
    <asp:TextBox id="txtCountry" style="Z-INDEX: 108; LEFT: 8px;
              POSITION: absolute; TOP: 256px" runat="server">
    </asp:TextBox>
    <asp:TextBox id=txtCity style="Z-INDEX: 114; LEFT: 8px;
              POSITION: absolute; TOP: 192px" runat="server">
```

```
            </asp:TextBox>
            <asp:TextBox id="txtPostalCode" style="Z-INDEX: 107; LEFT: 8px;
                    POSITION: absolute; TOP: 224px" runat="server">
            </asp:TextBox>
            <asp:TextBox id="txtProvince" style="Z-INDEX: 106; LEFT: 8px;
                    POSITION: absolute; TOP: 192px" runat="server">
            </asp:TextBox>
            <asp:TextBox id="txtAddress2" style="Z-INDEX: 105; LEFT: 8px;
                    POSITION: absolute; TOP: 160px" runat="server">
            </asp:TextBox>
            <asp:TextBox id="txtAddress1" style="Z-INDEX: 104; LEFT: 8px;
                    POSITION: absolute; TOP: 128px" runat="server">
            </asp:TextBox>
            <asp:TextBox id="txtEmailAddress" style="Z-INDEX: 103; LEFT: 8px;
                    POSITION: absolute; TOP: 64px" runat="server">
            </asp:TextBox>
            <asp:TextBox id="txtLastName" style="Z-INDEX: 102; LEFT: 168px;
                    POSITION: absolute; TOP: 32px" runat="server">
            </asp:TextBox>
        </form>
    </body>
</HTML>
```

Next you need to add an `SqlDataAdapter` to the form. To do so, open the Data tab in the Toolbox, and drag the `sqlDataAdapter` onto the form. The Data Adapter Configuration Wizard will start, and in the second screen of the wizard, select the same connection you used in the "Connecting to a Data Source" section, earlier in the chapter (use the Address database and connect as `user id = sa`).

Figure 16-11
The data form

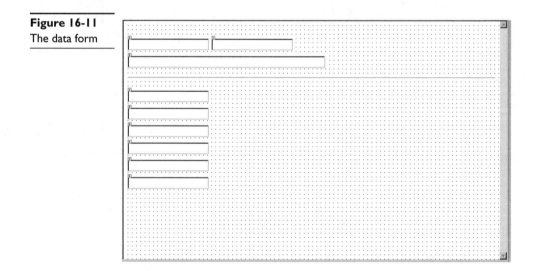

In the third wizard screen, choose to use an SQL statement. The following illustration shows the statement that should be used.

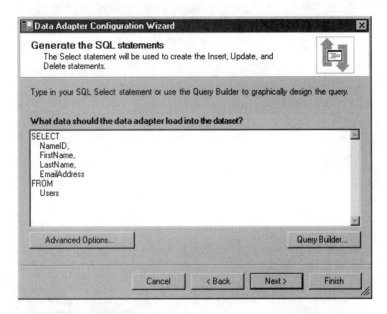

Click Finish to generate the DataAdapter. Select Data | Generate DataSet, and name the DataSet as usersDS (as shown here).

Create a second `sqlDataAdapter` using the SQL statement shown next.

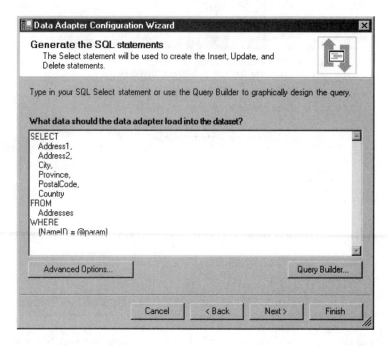

Generate the `DataSet` from `sqlDataAdtapter2` and combine it with the `usersDS` generated earlier, as shown here.

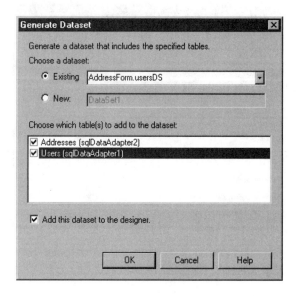

Now you need to bind the data from `usersDS` to the controls on the form. To perform the data binding, follow these steps:

1. Select Design view for the Web Form.

2. Select the `txtFirstName` control.

3. In the properties of the control, select the `DataBindings` setting and click the ellipsis button (...). The DataBindings dialog box will open.

4. In the Simple Binding box, expand `usersDS.Users.DefaultView` `.DefaultView[0]` to display the fields. Select the `FirstName` field.

5. Select the default formatting for the field, as shown here.

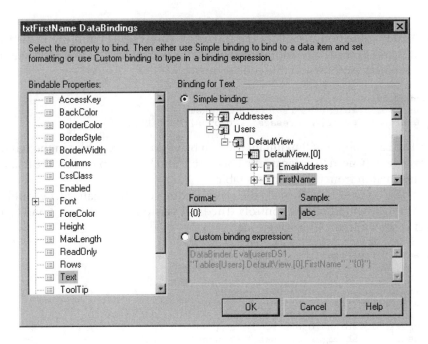

6. Click OK

Repeat the preceding steps for all the text box controls on the form, using the information in Table 16-4.

To actually populate the controls, we need some extra code in the `Page_Load` event handler for the Web Form. First, we need to populate the `DataSet` by calling the `Fill()` method on the two DataAdapter objects, as shown here:

```
sqlDataAdapter1.Fill(usersDS1, "Users");
sqlDataAdapter2.Fill(usersDS1, "Addresses");
```

Table 16-4	Control	Table	Field
The Settings for the Data Binding	txtFirstName	Users	FirstName
	txtLastName	Users	LastName
	txtEmailAddress	Users	EmailAddress
	txtAddress1	Addresses	Address1
	txtAddress2	Addresses	Address2
	txtCity	Addresses	City
	txtProvince	Addresses	Province
	txtPostalCode	Addresses	PostalCode
	txtCountry	Addresses	Country

The Fill() method populates the DataSet (usersDS1) and the named table. The next step is to create a relationship between the two tables. For this, we create a Relations object, as shown in this code segment:

```
usersDS1.Relations.Add("UserAddress",
    usersDS1.Tables["Users"].Columns["NameID"],
    usersDS1.Tables["Addresses"].Columns["NameID"]);
```

The Relations object will maintain the join between the two tables in the DataSet. This way, we only need to navigate the Users table and be able to retrieve the related address information from the Addresses table.

Once the DataSet is created, the data binding can be finalized by calling the DataBind() method on the controls. The final version of the Page_Load() event handler is shown in the following code.

```
private void Page_Load(object sender, System.EventArgs e)
{
  // Put user code to initialize the page here
  sqlDataAdapter1.Fill(usersDS1, "Users");
  sqlDataAdapter2.Fill(usersDS1, "Addresses");
  usersDS1.Relations.Add("UserAddress",
      usersDS1.Tables["Users"].Columns["NameID"],
      usersDS1.Tables["Addresses"].Columns["NameID"]);
  txtFirstName.DataBind();
  txtLastName.DataBind();
  txtEmailAddress.DataBind();
  txtAddress1.DataBind();
  txtAddress2.DataBind();
  txtCity.DataBind();
  txtProvince.DataBind();
  txtPostalCode.DataBind();
  txtCountry.DataBind();
}
```

The final Web Form is shown in Figure 16-12.

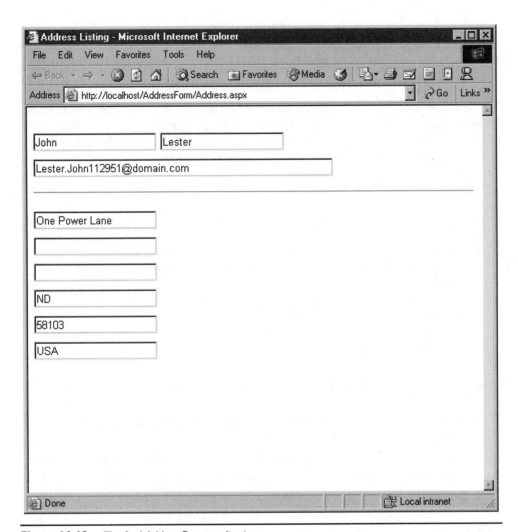

Figure 16-12 The final AddressForm application

EXAM TIP The steps for binding controls to data are to use the `Fill()` method to populate the `DataSet`, and then call the `DataBind()` method on the controls that are bound to the data source.

Retrieving Real-Time Data

In Chapter 12, we built an address book application that retrieved static information hard-coded into a `switch` statement. Now we will retrieve that data in real time through a `sqlDataReader`.

Open up the AddressBook application from Chapter 12, or if you need a clean starter for this exercise, copy the AddressBook folder from the Chapter16 folder on the accompanying CD-ROM. The folder must be copied into the root folder of the web server, c:\InetPub\wwwroot. Open the project by double-clicking on the `AddressBook .csproj` file in the AddressBook folder. If you are prompted to save the `AddressBook.sln` file when you save the project, accept the suggested location and name of the file.

The modifications that are needed to bind the application to a database are as follows:

1. In the codebehind module (`WebForm1.aspx.cs`) delete the entire `switch` statement from the `getName()` method. The resulting method should look like this:

```
private void getName(char a)
{
    clearList();
}
```

2. Import the `System.Data` and `System.Data.SqlClient` namespaces to the code module.

3. Declare an `SqlConnection` object as a local variable in the `getName()` method, and name it `addrCN`.

4. Declare a `SqlCommand` object as a local variable in the `getName()` method, and name it `addrCom`.

5. Declare a `sqlDataReader` object as a local variable in the `getName()` method, and name it `addrDR`.

6. Declare a string, call it `strSQL`, and make it a local variable in the `getName()` method. Initialize the `strSQL` string to the connection string for the database:

```
string strSQL = "user id=sa;initial catalog=Address;" +
                "data source=KENSNABBEN";
```

7. Declare a string, call it `strCom`, and make it a local variable in the `getName()` method. Initialize the `strCom` string to the following SQL statement:

```
string strCom = "SELECT FirstName, LastName, NameID from Users
WHERE LastName LIKE "; .
```

8. Instantiate the connection using the `strSQL` string.

9. Open the connection inside a `try...catch ... finally` block.

10. Declare a string called `strCom1` that is the concatenation of `strCom` and the character that is the parameter to the method:

```
strCom1 = strCom + "'" + a + "%'"
```

The purpose is to create an SQL string that is delimited by single quotes and has the SQL wildcard character (`%`).

11. Instantiate the `addrCom` object using the `strCom1` string and the `addrCN` connection.

12. Create the `sqlDataReader` by calling the `ExecuteReader()` method of the `addrCom` object.

13. Create a `while` loop that evaluates the `addrDR.Read()` method to get the next row of data.

14. In the loop, use the `Add()` method of the `ListItems` collection of the `lstAddress` ListBox control to insert a `ListItem` that concatenates the `FirstName` and `LastName` of the data row. Use the `NameID` as the value of the `ListItem`:

```
new ListItem(addrDR.GetString(0)+ " " +
addrDR.GetString(1), addrDR.GetInt32(2).ToString())
```

15. Close all the objects in the `finally` block.

The code for the `getName()` method should look like the following.

```
private void getName(char a)
{
  clearList();
  SqlConnection addrCN;
  SqlCommand addrCom;
  SqlDataReader addrDR;
  string strSQL = "user id=sa;initial catalog=Address;" +
  "data source=KENSNABBEN";
  string strCom =
      "SELECT FirstName, LastName, NameID from Users WHERE LastName
                                              LIKE ";
  addrCN = new SqlConnection(strSQL);
  try
  {
    addrCN.Open();
    string strCom1 = strCom + "'" + a + "%'";
    addrCom = new SqlCommand(strCom1, addrCN);
    addrDR = addrCom.ExecuteReader();
    // The data population commands will go here.
    while (addrDR.Read())
```

```
        {
          lstAddress.Items.Add(new ListItem(addrDR.GetString(0)+ " " +
                             addrDR.GetString(1),
                             addrDR.GetInt32(2).ToString()));
        }
      }
        catch (DataException ex)
      {
        Response.Write(ex.ToString);
      }
      finally
      {
        addrDR.Close();
        addrCN.Close();
        addrDR = null;
        addrCom = null;
        addrCN = null;
      }
```

The project can now be executed by pressing F5. The window shown in Figure 16-13 appears. When you select one of the alphabet buttons, the content of the list box changes. At present, the same address is used for all names, as you can see if you select some names in the list box. We will attend to that next.

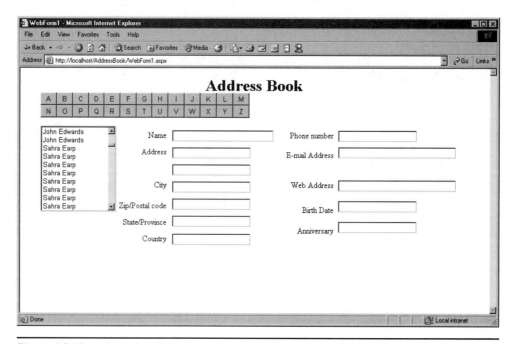

Figure 16-13   The Address Book application

Looking Up the Address Info

The final piece of the AddressBook application to attend to is looking up the address and phone number of a name when the name is selected in the list box. When we use two `sqlDataReader` objects with one connection, as we do in this example, we must close the first one before creating the second. Connections can only have one `xxxDataReader` object defined at one time.

Follow these steps:

1. Delete the `getAddress()` method.

2. Delete the call to `getAddress()` in the `lstAddress_SelectedIndexChanged()` event handler.

3. Declare an `int` variable in `lstAddress_SelectedIndexChanged()`, and call it `intIndex`.

4. Initialize the `intIndex` variable to the value from the `SelectedItem` `lstAddress` control. Use the `Int32.Parse()` method to convert the `string` into an `int`. This value will be used to retrieve the additional information for the selected name.

5. Declare one `SqlConnection` object, two `SqlCommand` objects, and two `SqlDataReader` objects. Call them `addrCN`, `addrCom`, `phoneCom`, `addrDR`, and `phoneDR`, respectively.

6. Declare a `string` and call it `strSQL`. Initialize `strSQL` to the connection string for the database:

```
string strSQL = "user id=sa;initial catalog=Address;" +
                "data source=KENSNABBEN";
```

7. Declare a `string` and call it `strCom`. Initialize the `strCom` string to the following SQL statement:

```
string strCom = "SELECT Address1, Address2, City, Province,
PostalCode, Country from Addresses WHERE NameID = " +
intIndex;
```

8. Declare a `string` and call it `strCom1`. Initialize `strCom1` to the following SQL statement:

```
string strCom1 = "SELECT PhoneNumber FROM PhoneNumbers WHERE
NameID = " + intIndex + " AND Type = 'Home'";
```

9. Instantiate the connection using the `strSQL` string.

10. Open the connection inside a `try ...catch ... finally` block.

11. Instantiate the `addrCom` object using the `strCom` string and the `addrCN` connection.

12. Instantiate the `phoneCom` object using the `strCom1` string and the `addrCN` connection.

13. Create the `sqlDataReader` by calling the `ExecuteReader()` method of the `addrCom` object.

14. Call the `Read()` method of the `sqlDataReader`.

15. Populate the text boxes with the data returned from the `sqlDataReader`.

16. Close the `addrDR` `sqlDataReader`.

17. Create the `sqlDataReader` by calling the `ExecuteReader()` method of the `phoneCom` object.

18. Call the `Read()` method of the `sqlDataReader`.

19. Populate the phone number text box from the `sqlDataReader`.

20. Close the `sqlDataReader`.

The final code for the `lstAddress_SelectedIndexChanged()` event handler should look like the following code segment.

```
private void lstAddress_SelectedIndexChanged(object sender,
System.EventArgs e)
{
  txtName.Text=lstAddress.SelectedItem.Text;
  int lstIndex = Int32.Parse(lstAddress.SelectedItem.Value);
  SqlConnection addrCN;
  SqlCommand addrCom;
  SqlCommand phoneCom;
  SqlDataReader addrDR;
  SqlDataReader phoneDR;
  string strSQL = "user id=sa;initial catalog=Address;" +
                  "data source=KENSNABBEN\\KEN";
  string strCom =
   "SELECT Address1, Address2, City, Province, PostalCode, Country " +
       "FROM Addresses WHERE NameID = " + intIndex;
  string strCom1 =
   "SELECT PhoneNumber FROM PhoneNumbers WHERE NameID = " + intIndex +
       "AND Type = 'Home'";
  addrCN = new SqlConnection(strSQL);
  try
  {
    addrCN.Open();
    addrCom = new SqlCommand(strCom, addrCN);
    phoneCom = new SqlCommand(strCom1, addrCN);
    addrDR = addrCom.ExecuteReader();
    addrDR.Read();

    // The data population commands will go here.
    txtAddress1.Text = addrDR.GetString(0);
    txtAddress2.Text = addrDR.GetString(1);
    txtCity.Text  = addrDR.GetString(2);
    txtProvince.Text = addrDR.GetString(3);
```

```
      txtPostalCode.Text = addrDR.GetString(4);
      txtCountry.Text = addrDR.GetString(5);
      addrDR.Close();
      phoneDR = phoneCom.ExecuteReader();
      phoneDR.Read();
      txtPhoneNumber.Text = phoneDR.GetString(0);
      phoneDR.Close();
   }
   catch (DataException ex)
   {
      Response.Write(ex.ToString());
   }
   finally
   {
      addrCN.Close();
      phoneDR = null;
      addrDR = null;
      addrCom = null;
      addrCN = null;
   }
}
```

The final application is shown in Figure 16-14.

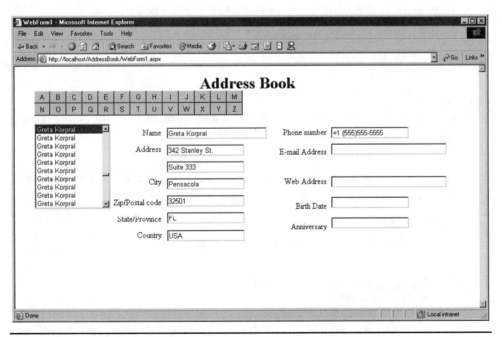

Figure 16-14   The final AddressBook application

Summary

This chapter has worked with a number of objects from ADO.NET that provide connectivity between data sources and web applications. The basis for working with all data sources is the Connection object that abstracts the potential network and database technology so you do not have to have minute knowledge of how to build the connection. Once the connection is in place, the `DataAdapter` helps to build the SQL statements needed to build the `DataSet` objects that bind to such server controls as the `DataGrid`. The `DataSet` is a disconnected object, so once the `DataSet` is populated, the connection to the data source can be removed, making for less load on the server. The `xxxDataReader` is the connected version—it maintains the connection to the data source through the whole process.

One thing to remember for the exam is that the SQL .NET Data Provider objects are used for Microsoft SQL Server 7 or higher, and that the OLE DB .NET Data Provider objects are used for any data source that has an OLE DB provider (but not for Microsoft SQL Server). Also, the `try... catch... finally` structure is tested in the exam.

Test Questions

1. What is the SQL equivalent of the `DataSet` relation object?

   A. XOR JOIN

   B. CROSS JOIN

   C. OUTER JOIN

   D. INNER JOIN

2. Why should you close all database objects and set them to NULL before leaving the method where the objects were created?

   A. To ensure that the object's destructors are called.

   B. To ensure that the connection to the database is closed as soon as possible.

   C. To ensure that the objects can be reused.

   D. Good coding practice.

3. What is the purpose of the following code segment?

```
if ( !IsPostBack )
{
    sqlDataAdapter1.Fill(dsUsers1);
    DataGrid1.DataBind();
}
```

   A. To populate the `DataAdapter` the first time the web page is displayed.

   B. To populate the `DataSet` every time the web page is displayed.

   C. To populate the `DataAdapter` every time the web page is displayed.

   D. To populate the `DataSet` the first time the web page is displayed.

4. Where are stored procedures saved?

   A. The GAC.

   B. The web server.

   C. The database server.

   D. The central store.

5. What is the root exception for the ADO.NET objects?

   A. DataException

   B. ADOException

   C. Exception

   D. DBException

6. What best describes the xxxDataReader?

   A. A disconnected collection of tables.

   B. A manager that manages the connection to a data source, using four SQL statements.

   C. A connected, read-only, forward-only representation of the data source.

   D. The component that encapsulates the database driver.

7. You are the developer of a Web Form, and you need to display data from a Microsoft SQL Server 6.5 in a DataGrid on your form. What DataAdapter is the most appropriate?

   A. sqlDataAdapter

   B. oleDbDataAdapter

   C. odbcDataAdapter

   D. adoDataAdapter

8. What is the purpose of the last string ("{0}") in the following code segment?

   ```
   DataBinder.Eval(dS1, "Tables[SP_SelUsers].DefaultView.[0].LastName", "{0}");
   ```

   A. It is the formatting string for the bound data.

   B. It is the default value that will be used when the data is NULL.

   C. It is the parameter sent to the stored procedure SP_SelUsers.

   D. It is the placeholder for a DataBinding object.

9. What is the correct namespace for use with the SQL .NET Data Provider objects?

   A. System.SQL

   B. System.Data.SqlConnections

   C. System.Data.SqlClient

   D. System.SqlConections

10. What is the correct statement to use for declaring that an xxxCommand object is used with a table?

   A. aCmd.CommandType = CommandType.Table;

   B. aCmd.CommandType = Table;

   C. aCmd.CommandType = "Table";

   D. aCmd.CommandType = "CommandType.Table";

11. How many sqlDataReader objects can be open on one Connection at one time?

   A. 4

   B. 3

   C. 2

   D. 1

12. What is the SQL wildcard character?

   A. *

   B. %

   C. &

   D. @

13. You need to connect to a Microsoft SQL Server version 6.5. What Connection object is the best choice?

   A. sqlConnection

   B. oleDbConnection

   C. ODBCConnection

   D. You must upgrade; there is no connection object for this database.

14. You are using the try... catch block seen in the following code segment, but no exceptions are ever caught by the catch block. What is the problem?

```
sqlConnection cn =new sqlConnection(strSQL);
sqlDataSet ds;
try
{
  cn.Open();
  //perform the data processing steps
...
}catch(OleDbException e){
...
}
```

   A. The exception class is wrong; it should be SqlErrors.

   B. The exception class is wrong; it should be SqlSyntaxExceptions.

   C. The exception class is wrong; it should be SqlExceptions.

   D. The exception class is wrong; it should be SQLExcptions.

15. You are designing a Web Form that needs to have data available for as long as eight hours at a time. Your manager has raised some concern that the database server will be unable to provide services to a large number of connected users. What object in the ADO.NET architecture will you bring to your manager's attention as a possible solution?

   A. SQL disconnected recordsets.

   B. `oleDbDataReader`

   C. `ODBCRecordSet`

   D. `oleDbDataSet`

Test Answers

   1. D.
   2. B.
   3. D.
   4. C.
   5. A.
   6. C.
   7. B.
   8. A.
   9. C.
   10. A.
   11. D.
   12. B.
   13. B.
   14. C.
   15. D.

Making the Web Application Available to Our Users

In this chapter, you will

- Plan the deployment of a web application
- Create a setup program that will install or uninstall a web application
- Deploy a web application
- Add assemblies to the Global Assembly Cache
- Maintain and support a web application
- Optimize the performance of a web application by implementing caching
- Configure security for a web application
- Install and configure a web server and the Microsoft FrontPage Server Extensions

The final step after designing and developing your Web Forms and web application is to complete your ASP.NET web application by deploying the application to the production server that is going to respond to the client requests. The term *deploy* is used to encompass the optimization and configuration of the web application, the planning of how and what to install on the production server, and the installation of the web application on the production server.

The deployment process also includes configuration of the web application by setting up the security for the web application as well as optimizing the response time for the web application by configuring Cache objects. The configuration of the web application is performed by modifying the content of the web applications configuration file. The configuration settings are stored in text files that must be organized to support and secure the ASP.NET web application. The deployment questions of the exam focus on the configuration files.

The last topic in the chapter is the issue of installing and configuring the IIS web server and FrontPage extensions. These topics are not exactly in the developer realm, but they are listed as potential areas that can be queried in the exam.

Deploying a Web Application

In this section, we will look at the four steps that are part of the deployment of an ASP.NET web application. The following steps are part of all deployments:

- Caching and performance—configuring the `Cache` object
- Configuring the web application—optimizing the configuration files
- Securing the web application—edit the configuration
- Deploying the web application—selecting and copying the files for deployment to the production server

The planning for deployment centers around performance and security, and it is driven by the need to achieve good performance (good response time) and the security policy in place at the site. We will start with the performance issues.

Caching and Improving Performance

The performance of an ASP.NET web application is most easily increased by using the ASP.NET `Cache` object. ASP.NET offers two types of caches: the `Cache` object that is used to cache items such as the result of a computation, and the output cache that can be used to store web pages and controls. The theory behind a cache is that if you store frequently needed items in local memory, you can retrieve those items more quickly than if you had to retrieve those same items from the hard disk or re-create them with a computation. The two types of caches that are supplied are used in different roles in an ASP.NET web application.

By using the `Cache` object, you can place objects in the memory of the server. The `Cache` object is provided in ASP.NET to provide programmable caching through an object that gives us full control of the caching process—including the dependency between cached objects and the life span of the cached object—each ASP.NET web application has one `Cache` object. You store one copy of the item in memory the first time that item is accessed, and after that the item is read from the `Cache` object every time it is requested—this eliminates the duplication of items in the `Cache` object. Using the cached copy of the item also minimizes work duplication for the server and increases performance.

The output cache is more like a traditional cache on a web server—using the output cache we can keep web pages or even portions of web pages in the output cache for faster retrieval of that information.

The Cache Object

The `Cache` object uses references to the items (objects) it stores, and provides the process (business rules) to track the item's policy (expiration and dependency). One of the features of the `Cache` object is that it provides a method for web pages in the ASP.NET web application to pass values between each other.

EXAM TIP   The Cache object can be used to pass values between web pages in the same ASP.NET web application.

The developer configures a web page to request that an item be stored in the Cache object. To save an item in the Cache object, the web page needs to specify a key-value pair. The *key* is what the Cache object uses to reference the item by, and the *value* is the information to be cached. Keys are arbitrary strings that you define.

The following code segment shows how you can store an item in the Cache object:

```
Cache["theKey"] = theValue;
```

To retrieve an item from the Cache object, you use this syntax:

```
theValue = Cache["theKey"];
```

Every time the item is requested, the Cache object checks to see if there is an available cached version of the item—if there is a cached version, it is used, and if there is no cached version available, ASP.NET re-creates the item and stores it in the Cache object for future use.

There is one Cache object per ASP.NET web application, and only web pages in that application can access the Cache object. There is no sharing between applications through the Cache object. Once created, the Cache object's lifetime is the same as the ASP.NET web application.

EXAM TIP   There is only one Cache object per web application.

The Cache object can be used to store information similar to that which would be stored in an application variable, but that would not normally be considered session state information and stored in the Session object. (For a discussion about application and session state, see Chapter 13.)

EXAM TIP   The Cache object has application scope and cannot be used to store session variables.

As you saw earlier in this section, the simple syntax for storing a value in the Cache object is to implicitly assign the value:

```
Cache["theKey"] = theValue;
```

Alternatively, the item can be inserted into the Cache object by using the Insert() method of the Cache object:

```
public void Insert(string key, object value, CacheDependency depend,
DateTime absolute, TimeSpan sliding, CacheItemPriority priority,
CacheItemRemovedCallback callBack);
```

The Insert() method has a number of signatures—the preceding one gives us the most control over how the item is cached. The parameters are listed in Table 17-1.

The following code segment shows the use of the Insert() method:

```
Cache.Insert("theKey", theValue, null, DateTime.Now.AddMinutes(2),
TimeSpan.Zero, CacheItemPriority.High, onRemove);
```

In this example, the key is theKey and the value is theValue. The cached item has no dependency (null) and it will be removed in 2 minutes (DateTime.Now.AddMinutes(2)) with no sliding aging window (TimeSpan.Zero). It has a high priority (CacheItemPriority.High) and will call onRemove() when it is actually removed from the cache.

 EXAM TIP The number and size of the items that are placed in the Cache object must be planned. Storing too many items in the Cache object will actually slow down the server by using too much of the memory for the cache and not leaving enough for the server.

Output Caching

There are times when you'll need to minimize the response time from the web application to the user. By caching pages, or even parts of pages, in memory at the first request, and then using the cached page for all subsequent requests, you will avoid the processing and I/O time that is required to create the page. Output caching is a method that is provided through ASP.NET to give us that caching environment. The difference between

Parameter	Data Type	Description
Key	String	The key for the item that is stored in the Cache object.
Value	Object	The item that is stored in the Cache object.
Depend	CacheDependency	Dependencies for the cached item.
Absolute	DateTime	The absolute date and time when the item will be removed from the Cache object.
Sliding	TimeSpan	A time interval representing the time after the object was last accessed when the cached object expires. If this value is 30 minutes, the object will expire and be removed from the cache 30 minutes after it is last accessed.
Priority	CacheItemPriority	The priority of the cached item. The priority is used to determine the order of removal when the web server is running low on memory.
Callback	CacheItemRemovedCallback	The callback delegate to receive the event notification when the item is removed from the Cache object.

Table 17-1   The Insert() Method's Parameters

output caching and the Cache object is that the output cache stores pages and parts of pages (HTML) while the Cache object can cache any object (item).

Output caching is designed to allow the caching of entire pages, or if it is impractical to cache a complete page because the content of the page is to be customized for each user, you can cache fragments of the page such as a table of data that will be used in many different web pages. To work with cache fragments, you need to identify those parts of the page that should be cached, and turn those fragments into user controls that are then cached. (See Chapter 14 for more information on user controls.) An example of page fragments that would benefit from caching are headers and footers that contain static graphics and menu systems.

 EXAM TIP   To cache page fragments, turn the fragment into a user control first.

The output cache will refresh the page cached when the source for the page changes. Even so, you are not advised to enable output caching for the web forms in an application until the application is debugged, because the caching could return the cached copy of a page rather than the one you are working on, which can lead to confusion in the debugging and testing phase if nothing else.

To direct a page to be loaded into the output cache, you need to add the @ OutputCache page directive to the ASP.NET page. This directive takes two mandatory attributes—Duration and VaryByParam. The Duration attribute specifies how long the page will be cached for in seconds, with 0 (zero) meaning that the page is not cached. VaryByParam is a required attribute, and it specifies one of three methods of caching different versions of a page based on the request from the client. Table 17-2 lists the methods and their attributes.

The following example page directive is for a page that should be cached for 15 minutes and that will not have multiple cached versions:

```
<%@ OutputCache Duration="900" VaryByParam="None"%>
```

Setting the VaryByParam attribute to "None" means that there will only be one version of the page cached. The VaryByParam attribute can be set to any string. For example, setting VaryByParam to "orderID" results in a new version being cached for each orderID. Setting VaryByParam to "*" (the wildcard character) means that a new version will be cached for every different parameter in the GET or POST request.

Attribute	Description
VaryByParam	Allows multiple versions controlled by parameters in the GET or POST request. This attribute is required, so if you do not want multiple cached versions, set VaryByParam to "none".
VaryByHeader	Allows multiple versions controlled by the HTTP header of the request.
VaryByCustom	Allows multiple versions controlled by the client's browser or custom strings.

Table 17-2   Attributes for the @ OutputCache Page Directive

EXAM TIP Both the `Duration` and `VaryByParam` attributes are required. Set `VaryByParam="none"` if it is not needed.

The next step in deploying the application is to configure and optimize the ASP.NET web application using the different configuration files.

Configuring a Web Application

ASP.NET web applications are configured with a combination of configuration files. Each configuration file contains an XML hierarchy that uses tags and attributes to specify the configuration items. There are two types of configuration files: `Machine.config` and `Web.config`. The web server will have only one `Machine.config` file, and it is used to control the entire server. Every web application will have at least one `Web.config` file, and it configures the application. Additional local `Web.config` files can be used to control the behavior of files in individual directories in the application.

The configuration files are well-formed XML documents in which the XML root element is `<configuration>`. The naming convention for the tags and attributes in the configuration files is *camelCasing*, which means that the first character is lowercase and the first letter of any subsequent concatenated word is capitalized. For more information on XML, see Chapter 8.

Machine.config

The system-specific configuration information is stored in the `Machine.config` file located in `C:\WINNT\Microsoft .NET\Framework\`*version*`\Config\Machine.config` on a computer running Windows 2000—the *version* in that path is the version of the installed .NET Framework. The configuration system starts looking for configuration settings in the `<appSettings>` element of the `Machine.config` file, and then in the application's `Web.config` files.

The benefit of using the `Machine.config` file to configure the web server and applications is that all configuration data is in one place. The negative aspect is that the `Machine.config` file is scoped on the server, so it will not be transferred with the application when it is deployed.

Web.config

The central configuration file for a web application is the `Web.config` file located in the root of the web application. You can use this configuration file to share settings and information between web pages in the application. Virtual and local directories can have their own `Web.config` files, as well. If there is a local `Web.config` file in a directory, it will be used when the effective configuration is determined.

The `Web.config` file has elements for each major category of ASP.NET functionality. Table 17-3 lists the elements that correspond to those sections.

Section	Description
`<authentication>`	Contains settings for the security `httpModule`.
`<authorization>`	Contains settings for the security `httpModule`.
`<browserCaps>`	Configures the browser-capabilities component.
`<compilation>`	Includes configuration settings for the compiler options used by ASP.NET.
`<globalization>`	Configures the globalization settings.
`<httpHandlers>`	Configures the mapping of incoming URLs to `IHttpHandler` classes. This section will not be inherited by subdirectories.
`<httpModules>`	Includes settings for the HTTP modules that are used in an application. This is commonly used for security and logging.
`<identity>`	Contains settings for the security `httpModule`.
`<processModel>`	Includes settings for the ASP.NET process model on the IIS (Internet Information Server) web server.
`<sessionState>`	Configures the session state `httpModule`.
`<trace>`	Configures the ASP.NET trace service.

Table 17-3   The Sections in the `Web.config` File

The configuration that is in effect for a page when it is requested by a client browser is the combination of settings in the `Machine.config` file and any `Web.config` files that are in the path for the page. The inheritance of configuration items follows these rules:

- The application `Web.config` file inherits from the `Machine.config` file.
- The application `Web.config` file's settings will override inherited settings.
- Any directory can have a local `Web.config` files that inherit from application `Web.config` files, overriding inherited settings.

The following section will explore the settings in different configuration files and show some examples on the inheritance.

Let's look at some example configuration files. Consider the following `Machine .config` file:

```
<configuration>
   <appSettings>
      <add key = "The answer" value = "42"/>
   <appSettings>
   <authentication mode="Windows">
      <forms name=".ASPXAUTH"
         loginUrl="login.aspx"
         protection="All"
         timeout="30"
```

```
            path="/">
        </forms>
    </authentication>
    <system.web>
        <trace
            enabled="false"
            localOnly="true"
            pageOutput="false"
            requestLimit="10"
            traceMode="SortByTime"
        />
    </system.web>
</configuration>
```

The settings in the preceding Machine.config file sets the authentication to Windows authentication, defines the universal answer to be 42, and turns off tracing (see the highlighted lines).

The following Web.config file is located in the virtual root of the application, (the application Web.config):

```
<configuration>
    <appSettings>
        <add key="marvin"
            value="data source=localhost;
            initial catalog=robotData;
            integrated security=true;" />
    </appSettings>
    <system.web>
        <trace
            enabled="true"
            localOnly="true"
            pageOutput="false"
            requestLimit="30"
            traceMode="SortByCategory"
        />
    </system.web>
</configuration>
```

The effective application-level configuration is the sum of the settings in the Machine.config and the application Web.config files. The authentication is inherited from Machine.config, as is the answer (42). We have changed the trace settings in the Web.config file so trace is now turned on, but we cannot use a remote computer to trace because the localOnly attribute is set to True. In addition, we declared a DSN we called marvin to connect to a database server.

The following Web.config file is from a child directory under the application root:

```
<configuration>
    <appSettings>
        <add key="marvin"
            value="data source=DBServer3;
            initial catalog=robotData;
            integrated security=true;" />
```

```
    </appSettings>
    <authentication mode="Forms">
        <forms name=".ASPXAUTH"
            loginUrl="login.aspx"
            protection="All"
            timeout="30"
            path="/">
        </forms>
    </authentication>
    <system.web>
        <trace
            enabled="true"
            localOnly="true"
            pageOutput="false"
            requestLimit="40"
            traceMode="SortByTime"
        />
    </system.web>
</configuration>
```

The resulting configuration can be seen in Table 17-4. The bold entries are the ones that form the effective configuration.

 EXAM TIP Remember the inheritance chain for configuration—
`Machine.config`, then application `Web.config`, and then local
`Web.config`.

As you saw in the previous example, we stored application data in the `Machine.config` (answer) and `Web.config` file (`marvin`). As you saw, you use the `<appSettings>` section to define key-value pairs that can be used throughout your application.

One very common example is to define database connection strings in the `Web.config` file so you have a common string used everywhere in the application. The element that defines the data item takes this form:

```
<add key="theKey" value="theValue"/>
```

Item	Machine.config	Application Web.config	Child Directory Web.config	Effective Configuration
The answer	42			42
authentication	Windows		**Forms**	Forms
trace	disabled	**enabled**		enabled
localOnly	false	**true**		true
tracemode	SortByTime	SortByCategory	**SortByTime**	SortByTime
requestLimit		30	**40**	40
marvin		localhost	**DBServer3**	DBServer3

Table 17-4 Summary of Configuration Inheritance

The following code segment defines the connection string for connections to the `robotDB` database on the `DBServer3` SQL server:

```
<configuration>
  <appSettings>
    <add key="X3" value="server=DBServer3; initial catalog=robotDB;
         integrated security=true;" />
  </appSettings>
</configuration>
```

Once the key-value pairs are defined in the `Web.config` file, you can access them through the `ConfigurationSettings.AppSettings` static string collection. The following example shows how you can retrieve the value of X3:

```
string strX3 = ConfigurationSettings.AppSettings["X3"];
```

One other issue that we must consider when we build applications is the cost of maintaining them when changes need to be made to the data that the applications use. In the case of Web Forms, we can use the `Web.config` file to store the data for us and bind that data dynamically to properties in our applications. This offers us a central location for defining frequently changing data, which means changes in the data won't require changes in the applications. One excellent candidate for a dynamic property is connection strings that might change frequently. Storing that information in the `Web.config` file will make changes easier to manage.

To configure the connection string as a dynamic property, expand the `DynamicProperties` section in the Properties Explorer for the *xxx*`Connection` object, as shown in Figure 17-1. Note that the `ConnectionString` is listed as an available dynamic property.

Click the ellipsis button to open the Dynamic Property dialog box, shown in the following illustration. You can make the property dynamic by selecting the Map Property to a Key in Configuration File check box. Then click OK.

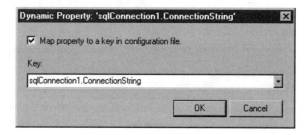

After you click OK, the wizard that configures the project will insert code in the codebehind module to bind the property to the `Web.config` file. The following code segment shows that code:

```
this.sqlConnection1.ConnectionString = ((string)(configurationAppSettings.GetValue
("sqlConnection1.ConnectionString", typeof(string))));
```

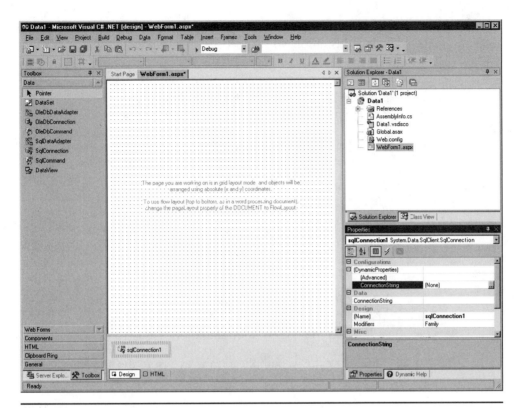

Figure 17-1   The dynamic properties

A key-value pair to hold the connection string has also been added to the Web.config file, as can be seen in this code segment:

```
<configuration>
...
<appSettings>
    <!--  User application and configured property settings go here.-->
    <!--  Example: <add key="settingName" value="settingValue"/> -->
    <add key="sqlConnection1.ConnectionString" value="" />
</appSettings>
...
</configuration>
```

The original `ConnectionString` property is now also marked to indicate that it is dynamic. In the following illustration, you can see the little icon to the right of the property name, which indicates that it is now dynamically set.

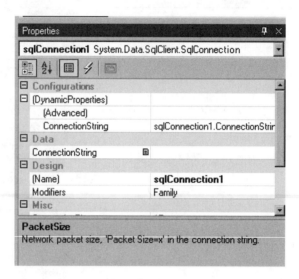

The next step in configuring the web application is to ensure the application is secured according to the design requirements.

Securing a Web Application

The point of a web application is to allow multiple users to access a central resource through a web server. Security is necessary to ensure that users can access the resources they need and are allowed to access, while protecting other resources. In this section, we will look at the issues of authentication and authorization.

Authentication is the process of verifying that the client is truly who he or she claims to be. This is done by collecting credentials (name and password) from the user. The credentials are validated against an authority such as a database; and if the credentials are valid, the client is approved as an authenticated identity.

 EXAM TIP Authentication is the process of ensuring that the client is known and that the credentials submitted are correct for that client.

Authorization is the process of determining whether the authenticated identity has access to the requested resource. The authorization process controls, and limits, access to specific resources, such as web pages, database records, files, and so on.

EXAM TIP Authorization ensures that authenticated clients only have access to the resources they are entitled to.

We have access to three different authentications methods through ASP.NET:

- Windows authentication
- Forms authentication
- .NET Passport authentication

Windows authentication is an extension of the authentication mechanism that is used in the Windows operating systems to authenticate users. ASP.NET uses IIS for this authentication method. When a user requests a secure web page in the web application from IIS, the user supplies the Windows credentials, which are then compared by IIS. If the credentials do not match, IIS will reject the request. All clients using Windows authentication must be using a Windows operating system and must be authenticated to a Windows domain. The Windows authentication method is not appropriate for Internet applications, but it is very functional for intranet applications in networks that already use Windows domain authentication.

The *forms authentication* method presents the user with a form in which the username and password are entered and sent back to the web server. If the credentials are validated, the user will be given a security cookie that is then returned along with any further access requests to the web application. The forms method can be used with clients running on any operating system, but the client must allow cookies.

The *.NET Passport* method is a centralized authentication service supplied by Microsoft. The service allows the user to log in once to a large number of web services using a single Passport account. Web services must have signed up with the .NET Passport service to be able to offer this service. The .NET Passport method is based on cookies, so the client must support cookies. There are possible usage fees involved with registering a web site to use this method. The .NET Passport service is not being tested in the exam, hence we will not discuss it in this chapter.

EXAM TIP Windows authentication requires that the client is running Windows and is authenticated to a Windows domain, so it should be used only for intranet applications. Use forms-based authentication for all other applications.

Secure Sockets Layer (SSL)

The web architecture is based on HTTP, which is used to transfer data between client and server. However, this protocol transmits data in the clear, meaning that the data can be intercepted and read. This is a real problem when you want to send financial data, such as

PART III

credit card numbers, from a client to a server. One option for securing information while it is transferred between the client and server is to use Secure Sockets Layer (SSL) encryptions.

The encryption used in SSL is based on the public-private key scheme—the web server holds a public key that can be used by anyone, while the client generates a session key that the client encrypts with the web server's public key and sends to the server to start the session.

The session key the client generates can come in different lengths (strengths of encryption)—the default is 40 bits, but there is an optional upgrade to support 128-bit session keys. The longer the session key, the longer it will take to crack the encryption using a brute force attack, and the longer the information transmitted is secured.

There is a problem inherent in this scheme—if the server is an impersonator, we could end up sending information to a fraudulent operator rather than to the vendor we thought we were connected to. The solution to this problem is to use certificates. The installation process for SSL requires that the administrator provide a certificate for the server that will act as the server's security credentials. Certificates are issued by certificate authorities (CAs), trusted third-party entities that verify that the server truly is what it purports to be.

In addition to supporting server certificates, SSL supports client certificates that authenticate the browser. To use SSL with a web page once SSL has been installed on IIS, you only need to change the transfer protocol from HTTP to HTTPS (Hypertext Transfer Protocol Secure). For example, if the original URL was http://localhost/page1.aspx, it would change to https://localhost/page1.aspx.

Implementing Windows-Based Authentication

The first step in implementing Windows-based authentication is to configure IIS to use one or more of the following authentication methods: basic, digest, or integrated Windows security. Anonymous access is also permitted as a selection, but it provides no security.

- **Anonymous access** This is the most common authentication method for public Internet sites. The client supplies no authentication credentials, and IIS uses the anonymous IUSR_*servername* account for all access to resources. Browsers will supply the username "Anonymous" and the e-mail address you have configured with the browser when connecting using this method.

- **Basic authentication** When IIS is set to use basic authentication, a client supplies a name and password in clear text to IIS that makes the credentials available to the web application. The basic authentication method is a part of the HTTP specification and is supported by most browsers, but the credentials are sent in clear text, thus exposing a security hole. One possible solution is to implement SSL (Secure Sockets Layer) to encrypt the communication. SSL was described in the preceding section.

- **Digest authentication** This authentication method is similar to basic authentication with the addition that the credentials are encrypted using the MD5 algorithm. The message digest is a hash of the name and password together with additional information (secrets) that is stored on the client's computer. The server compares the submitted information against a copy of the information that is stored with the server to authenticate the user. Digest authentication is only available to clients that have Active Directory domain accounts. Also, this authentication method works only with Internet Explorer 5 or higher, but it works over firewalls and proxies, and over the Internet without any additional configuration.

- **Integrated Windows security**   When using the integrated Windows authentication method, IIS will pass the user's credentials through to the web application when making a request for a resource. The credentials do not include the name and password but are made up of an encrypted token that represents the client. Integrated Windows authentication works with Microsoft Windows NT LAN Manager or Kerberos, and is therefore not suitable for applications that must operate through a firewall.

To configure the IIS authentication methods, start by opening the Computer Management console by right-clicking My Computer and selecting Manage. Once the console is open, expand Services and Applications | Internet Information Services | Web Sites | Default Web Site. Right-click Default Web Site and select Properties. In the Default Web Site Property dialog box, select the Directory Security tab and click Edit in the Anonymous Access and Authentication Control section. The resulting dialog box is shown in the following illustration.

After you select the authentication method, IIS is configured to support the security required. You can also select multiple authentication methods that will be used in order by IIS. If you configure multiple methods and anonymous authentication fails, IIS will attempt to use the other enabled methods.

Once you have selected the authentication method, the next step in implementing Windows-based authentication is to modify the application's `Web.config` file to include the following line in the `<system.web>` section:

```
<system.web>
    <authentication mode="Windows" />
</system.web>
```

Then you need to set the authorization in the `Web.config` file by including an `<authorization>` section:

```
<system.web>
    <authorization>
        <deny users="?" />
        <allow users="Ken" />
    </authorization>
</system.web>
```

In the preceding example, anonymous users are denied access, while the user named Ken is given access.

If you want to specify authorization for specific pages, you need to add `<location>` sections to `Web.config`. The following code segment denies access to the `Statistics.aspx` page to anonymous users, while it is allowed to the user Ken.

```
<location path="Statistics.aspx">
    <system.web>
        <authorization>
            <deny users="?" />
            <allow users="Ken" />
        </authorization>
    </system.web>
</location>
```

Impersonation in ASP.NET allows the server to execute code using the security context of the client, or as an anonymous user. The benefit of impersonation is that the user will have the same access to resources through IIS as if the user connected directly to the same resource using a client application. Impersonation is used when there are existing applications that already have user authorization configured, and we need to build an ASP.NET application that accesses the same resources.

The default impersonation setting is off (disabled), but you can control the impersonation settings using the `<identity>` section in the `<system.web>` section of the `Web.config` file. The following code turns impersonation on and shows the credentials being used.

```
<system.web>
    <identity impersonate="true" username="Ken" password="KungKarl" />
</system.web>
```

After the user is authenticated by IIS, you can read the information using the `User.Identity` object (this is an object of the `WindowsIdentity` class). The following code segment shows how you can read the user information and assign it to variables.

```
...
string strName = User.Identity.Name;
bool bAuthen = User.Identity.IsAuthenticated;
```

 EXAM TIP Windows authentication requires that clients run a Windows operating system.

Implementing Forms-Based Authentication

Forms-based authentication is common because it works with any browser. The process of accessing resources using forms-based authentication is as follows:

1. The client requests a protected page.

2. When IIS receives the request, it will pass it to ASP.NET. The request will be passed on by IIS because the authentication method for IIS is set to anonymous.

3. The ASP.NET process will investigate whether a valid authentication cookie is attached to the request. If there is a valid authentication cookie, it means that the user's credentials already have been validated, so ASP.NET checks for valid authorization by comparing the settings in the Web.config file's authorization section to the client's authorization cookie. If the user is authorized, access to the resource is granted.

4. If there is no valid authentication cookie attached to the request, ASP.NET redirects the request to an authentication (logon) page.

5. The code on the authentication page validates the credentials and, if they are valid, attaches a cookie with the credentials to the request. If authentication fails, an "Access Denied" message is returned.

6. If the user is authenticated, ASP.NET checks for valid authorization by comparing the settings in the Web.config file's authorization section to the client's authorization cookie. If the user is authorized, access to the resource is granted.

The first step in implementing forms-based authentication is to configure IIS to use anonymous authentication. See the section on how to configure IIS security earlier in this section.

After that, you need to configure the <authentication> section in the Web.config file to use mode="Forms" and specify the name of the authentication form the user will be redirected to when authentication is needed. You also need to specify the name attribute that will be added to the cookie as a suffix. The following code segment illustrates this:

```
<system.web>
   <authentication mode="Forms">
      <forms name=".aspxcook" loginUrl="login.aspx" />
```

```
        </authentication>
    </system.web>
```

Next, you need to add the `<authorization>` section to the `Web.config` file to configure security, as shown in this code segment:

```
<location path="Statistics.aspx">
    <system.web>
        <authorization>
            <deny users="?" />
            <allow users="Ken" />
        </authorization>
    </system.web>
</location>
```

You also need to design an authentication login Web Form to validate the user's credentials. The following is an example of a login page:

```
<form id="Form1" method="post" runat="server">
    <asp:TextBox id="txtEmail"
            style="Z-INDEX: 101;
            LEFT: 142px;
            POSITION: absolute;
            TOP: 123px"
            runat="server">
    </asp:TextBox>
    <asp:Button id="Button1"
            style="Z-INDEX: 103;
            LEFT: 146px;
            POSITION: absolute;
            TOP: 191px"
            runat="server"
            Text="Login">
    </asp:Button>
    <asp:TextBox id="txtPassword"
            style="Z-INDEX: 102;
            LEFT: 142px; POSITION:
            absolute; TOP: 152px"
            runat="server"
            TextMode="Password">
    </asp:TextBox>
</form>
```

The code that will perform the validation is in the click event handler for the button, as shown in this code segment:

```
...
using System.Web.Security;
...
private bool login(string a, string b){
    if (a.Length>1 && b.Length>1) {
        return true;
    } else {
        return false;
    }
}
private void Button1_Click(object sender, System.EventArgs e){
    if (login(txtEmail.Text,txtPassword.Text)) {
        FormsAuthentication.RedirectFromLoginPage(txtEmail.Text,false);
    }
}
```

Once the security is configured for the web application, it is essential that it be tested using other systems than the development system to ensure that the security settings are working as designed.

Now we are ready to look at the deployment of the web application on the production server.

Deploying a Web Application

To deploy a web application, you will need to copy the necessary files and folders from the development system to the production server. To deploy the web application on a remote system, you will need to use FTP, whereas local deployment can be done using Windows Explorer. These types of deployment are commonly called *XCOPY deployment* (because it works like the DOS command XCOPY). In addition to the XCOPY deployment method, Visual Studio .NET provides us with a method to Copy Project using the FrontPage Extensions, and there is also the Web Setup Project that can automate the install and uninstall process for the web application.

XCOPY Deployment

The first step in using XCOPY to deploy a web application to a web server is to configure a virtual directory in IIS and mark that directory as the start of an application. Follow these steps to do so:

1. Right-click My Computer and select Manage to open the Computer Management console.

2. Expand Services and Applications | Internet Information Services | Default Web Site.

3. In the left pane of the console, select the directory that is to be the home of your web application.

4. Right-click the directory and select Properties.

5. In the Application Settings section of the Directory tab, click Create.

6. Click OK.

If the directory you need is not in the left pane of the console, right-click on the Default web site and select New | Virtual Directory, and the wizard will help you associate the directory with IIS and mark it as a virtual directory.

Once you have the directory set, the next step is to make sure all the required files are available to be deployed. Start by building the web application and ensure that the application is functioning correctly.

Next, select the files that must be copied. These will include the following:

- The /bin directory—this is where all DLL files for the web application are stored.
- All Web Forms, user controls, and XML web service files (`.aspx`, `.ascx`, `.asmx`).

- Configuration files—`Web.config` and `global.asax`.
- All support files that are needed by the application.

When selecting the files, never include the following types because they are part of the development environment:

- Visual Studio .NET solution files (`.csproj`, `.csproj.webinfo`, and so on).
- Resource files (`.resx`).
- Codebehind pages (`.cs`).

 EXAM TIP Any assembly that is located in the /bin directory does not require registration.

The next step is to copy the files using Windows Explorer or FTP to the production server.

Visual Studio .NET Copy

Visual Studio .NET has a utility that can assist in copying web applications to other servers. The utility is accessed by selecting Project | Copy Project. (The following illustration shows the Copy Project dialog box.) The deployment methods are FrontPage Extensions or XCOPY, and we will look at the FrontPage Extensions later in this chapter.

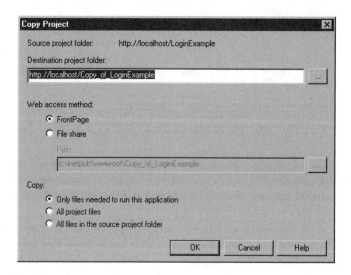

Web Setup Project

There are times when you will need to provide a setup program that an administrator can use to install your web application, rather than providing a collection of files that need to be manually installed. For those circumstances, you can use the Web Setup Projects to produce Windows installer applications that can install and uninstall your applications easily.

 EXAM TIP If you need to easily uninstall a web application, it must be deployed with a setup program.

We will create and deploy a very simple web application here as an example. Follow these steps:

1. Create a web application by selecting File | New | Project from the menu.

2. Select Visual C# Projects in the Project Types pane of the New Projects dialog box. Select ASP.NET Web Application in the Templates pane. In the Location field, name the application `DeployTest` and locate the project on the `localhost` server (http://localhost/DeployTest). Click OK.

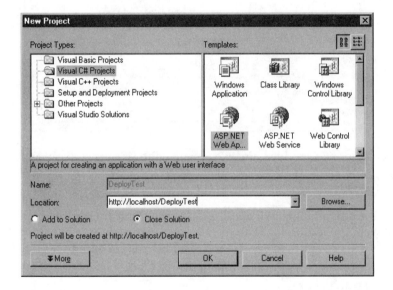

3. Drag a label and a button to the Web Form, and keep all the defaults. In the click handler for the button, set the `Text` property of the label to "Hello World!", like this:

```
Label1.Text = "Hello World!";
```

4. Build the application and test it.

Now you have a very rudimentary web application that will let you display "Hello World!" in the label when the button is clicked. The next step is to create a setup application to deploy the application—the following steps perform that task:

1. With the `DeployTest` project open, select File | Add Project | New Project.

2. In the Add New Project dialog box, select Setup and Deployment Projects in the Project Types pane. Select Web Setup Project in the Templates pane. Name the project `WebDeploy`. Click OK.

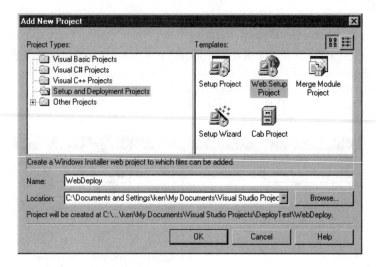

3. After the project is added, the File System editor is opened (see Figure 17-2).

4. Change the `ProductName` property of the Deployment project to `DeployTest`.

5. Add the output of the web application to the Deployment project by selecting the Web Application folder in the left pane of the File System editor. Right-click the Web Application folder and select Add | Project Output.

6. In the Add Project Output Group dialog box, select `DeployTest` from the project combo box.

7. Choose the Primary Output and Content Files groups from the list, and click OK.

8. Select the Web Application folder, and set the `VirtualDirectory` property to Tester.

9. Select the Web Application folder, and set the `DefaultDocument` property to `WebForm1.aspx`.

10. Select Build | Build DeployTest from the menu.

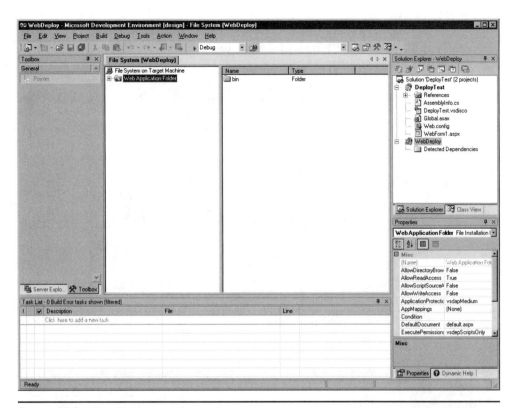

Figure 17-2   The File System editor

These steps will create the installation program, so we can now go ahead with the installation. Start by locating the installation program—if you kept the default locations of files, the installation should be located at this location: `\documents and settings\`*login name*`\My Documents\Visual Studio Projects\DeployTest\DeployTest\Debug\WebDeploy.msi`.

Navigate to the installation file and run it from that location. The web application will be installed—the installation screen is shown in Figure 17-3. Once the application is installed, go ahead and test it: the URL should be http://localhost/Tester.

To uninstall the application, select Start | Settings | Control Panel, and double-click the Add/Remove Programs icon. In the Add/Remove Programs utility, select the application to be removed, and click Remove, as shown in Figure 17-4.

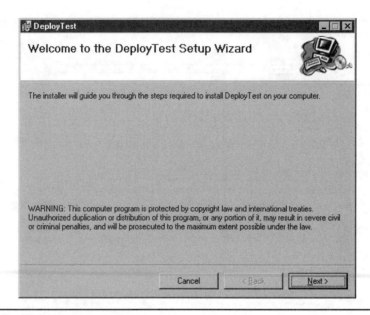

Figure 17-3   The DeployTest installation screen

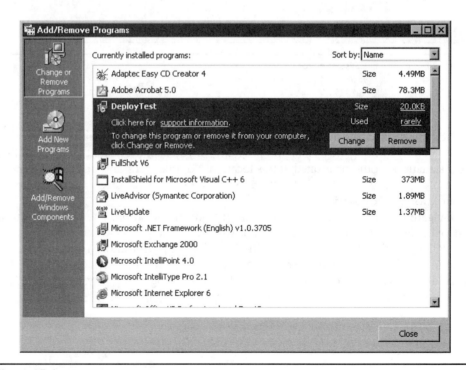

Figure 17-4   Removing the application

Assemblies and the GAC

Up until this point, we have used assemblies that are located in the /bin directory of the web application and thus are private to the application. One of the strengths of the .NET Framework, however, is the option to share assemblies between multiple applications—that is the GAC (Global Assembly Cache). Assemblies are registered in the GAC by using the `gacutil` command-line utility. For more information on assemblies and the use of `gacutil`, see Chapter 6.

One important point about assemblies is that you can keep multiple versions of the same assembly available for applications that need access to a particular version—this is called side-by-side versioning. The search for a suitable version of an assembly always starts in the local /bin directory of the web application and then proceeds to the GAC, where multiple versions can be maintained.

 EXAM TIP   The .NET Framework supports multiple versions of the same assembly in the GAC.

Installing a Web Application

For ASP.NET to work, you need to have the right software installed on your workstation for development, and on your servers for the production environment. Even though Windows 98 and Windows Me are 32-bit operating systems, they are not supported for development of web applications as they do not have a version of IIS (Internet Information Server) available, nor is there a version available for the Windows NT 4 family of operating systems.

The current version of IIS is 5.0, and it is only available for Windows 2000 and Windows XP. Those are the only operating systems that can be used to develop web applications with ASP.NET, and the only ones you can use for production servers. IIS is installed by default on all Windows 2000 servers (Server, Advanced Server, Application Center Server, and Datacenter Server) but not on Windows 2000 Professional. It is also possible that the operating system installer removed IIS from the installation, based on installation standards. Under those circumstances you will need to install IIS.

 EXAM TIP   IIS is not installed by default on Windows 2000 Professional or Windows XP Professional.

To be able to develop XML Web Services, your system also needs to have the FrontPage Server Extensions installed and properly configured.

Installing IIS

To install IIS on a Windows 2000 computer, you must have administrative permissions before you start the installation. If you cannot get administrative rights, you will need to have your computer support group perform the installation.

To install IIS follow these instructions:

1. In the Control Panel (Start | Settings | Control Panel), open the Add/Remove Programs utility.

2. Select Add/Remove Windows Components on the left of the Add/Remove Programs dialog box.

3. Select Internet Information Services.

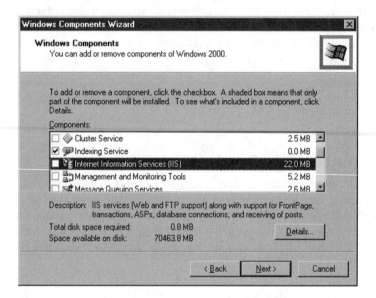

4. Do not add any additional services nor change the defaults for IIS without consulting a security expert.

5. Insert the installation CD if prompted.

6. Repair the .NET Framework installation to use IIS by inserting the Visual Studio .NET Windows Component update CD in your CD drive and running the following command (assuming D:\ is your CD drive):

```
D:\dotNetFramework\dotnetfx.exe /t:c:\temp /c:"msiexec.exe
          /fvecms c:\temp\netfx.msi"
```

7. Immediately connect to the Windows update site at Microsoft to apply any and all security patches and service packs.

 CAUTION IIS is designed to allow other computer users access to web applications on the computer, so it is imperative that you install all available security patches.

Installing FrontPage Server Extensions

The FrontPage Server Extensions are used to allow secure and manageable file transfers between, and administration of, web servers. The FrontPage Server Extensions are installed as part of IIS, but they need to be configured if your IIS installation is on a FAT16 or FAT32 partition. To perform the configuration, follow these steps:

1. Right-click My Computer and select Manage.

2. Expand Services and Applications.

3. Expand Internet Information Service.

4. Right-click Default Web Site, and select Configure Server Extensions.

 NOTE If the Configure Server Extensions option is not available, they are already configured. The Check Server Extensions option is available in the All Tasks menu to check the security of the server extensions.

5. The Server Extensions Configuration Wizard will open. Click Next.

6. Click Yes in the warning dialog box.

7. Select No to configure the mail system, and click Next.

8. Click Finish.

 EXAM TIP The FrontPage Server Extensions are installed with IIS, but they must be configured if the file system is FAT16 or FAT32.

Summary

This chapter dealt with the deployment and configuration of a web application. The most important point is that no configuration of caching is performed until the web application is tested and ready to go into production. All configuration is performed by using the `*.config` files: the `Machine.config` file for the entire web server, and `Web.config` files for the application, and optionally for individual folders. The configuration settings are inherited from `Machine.config` to the application `Web.config` and then to child folder `Web.config` files. Any conflicting settings are applied from the last `Web.config` file read.

Security for the web application was defined as authentication and authorization. Authentication is the client presenting the credentials to a server that validates the login. Authorization matches an authenticated client with the rights (permissions) the client has with respect to a resource. Authentication becomes an important issue if you need to give secure access to multiple users. If they are using both Windows and non-Windows operating systems, the solution is to use forms-based authentication.

You can deploy the web application in three different ways—using XCOPY or project copy, or by creating a setup program. The only way to cleanly uninstall an application is to use a setup program.

You were also introduced to the installation of IIS and to configuring the FrontPage Server Extensions.

Test Questions

1. You are the developer of a web application that is retrieving historical sports information from a database server and displays it to the users of your application. What cache strategy will give you the best performance?

    A. Use the output cache.

    B. Use the `cache` object.

    C. Use the ASP.NET central cache.

    D. Use the client cache.

2. You are the developer of a web application and have decided to use the output cache in ASP.NET. Which of the following statements correctly defines the Web Form if you want to use the output cache, cache all items for 14 minutes, and store different versions of the cached objects for each customer ID?

    A. `<%@ OutputCache Duration="840" VaryByCustom="true" %>`

    B. `<%@ OutputCache Duration="14" VaryByCustom="true" %>`

    C. `<%@ OutputCache Duration="840" VaryByParam="Customer ID" %>`

    D. `<%@ OutputCache Duration="14" VaryByParam="Customer ID" %>`

3. The following `Machine.config` file is installed on the server (http://www.x3.xxx) that will host your web application:

    ```
    <configuration>
       <appsettings>
          <add key = "Home" value = "/bigsite" />
       </appsettings>
    </configuration>
    ```

    You need to ensure that your web application always uses http://www.x3.xxx/smallsite for its `Home` variable. What is the most efficient way of accomplishing that task?

    A. Add an `<appsettings>` section to the application's `Web.config` file, and add the following to the `<appsettings>` section: `<replace key = "Home" value = "/smallsite" />`

    B. Add an `<appsettings>` section to the application's `Web.config` file, and add the following to the `<appsettings>` section: `<add key = "Home" value = "/smallsite" />`

C. Add an `<appsettings>` section to the application's `Web.config` file, and add the following to the `<appsettings>` section: `<key = "Home" value = "/smallsite" />`

D. Add an `<appsettings>` section to the application's `Web.config` file, and add the following to the `<appsettings>` section: `<override key = "Home" value = "/smallsite" />`

4. You are configuring security for a web application that will be used on your company intranet. Your company is using Intel-based as well as Apple computers running Windows and other operating systems. The following is part of the `Web.config` file for the application:

```
<configuration>
   <authentication mode="<<Enter Answer Here>>">
      <forms
         loginUrl="login.aspx"
         protection="All"
         timeout="30"
         path="/"
      </forms>
   </authentication>
</configuration>
```

What will you replace `"<<Enter Answer Here>>"` with to successfully have all users authenticate to the application?

A. Forms

B. Basic

C. Digest

D. Windows

5. What should be added to basic authentication?

A. FTP

B. TCP

C. SSL

D. NHL

6. You are deploying a web application using the `XCOPY` method, and you are now selecting the files that should be included in the deployment. What file extensions must be included in the deployment? Select all that apply.

A. `.resx`

B. `.aspx`

C. `.cs`

D. `.ini`

7. You have just installed IIS on your desktop computer that is running Windows 2000 Professional. Directly after the installation, you try to create a web application and you are given error messages indicating that the Internet server is incompatible with the .NET Framework. You need to create a web application, so what is the fastest way to be able to do so?

   A. Configure the FrontPage Server Extensions.

   B. Repair the .NET Framework installation from the Visual Studio .NET Windows Component update CD.

   C. There is no solution. Windows 2000 does not support .NET Framework web application development.

   D. Re-boot the computer.

8. What is required in order to be able to install and use SSL on a web server?

   A. Export permission.

   B. The SSL add-on CD.

   C. Server certificate.

   D. Encryption key.

9. You have been asked to describe what authentication and authorization are. What statements best describe the two terms? Select two answers.

   A. Authentication is the process of validating permissions for resources.

   B. Authentication is the process of validating security credentials.

   C. Authorization is the process of validating security credentials.

   D. Authorization is the process of validating permissions for resources.

10. True or false. The `Web.config` file can be used to store configuration data for properties of some controls.

    A. True.

    B. False.

11. What tool is used to manage the GAC?

    A. `GacMgr.exe`

    B. `GacSvr32.exe`

    C. `GacUtil.exe`

    D. `RegSvr.exe`

12. What is the effect of the following code snippet from the Web.config file?

```
...
<system.web>
   <authorization>
      <deny users="?" />
   </authorization>
</system.web>
```

    A. Anonymous access is denied.

    B. Only anonymous access is allowed.

    C. Users in the default group are denied access.

    D. There will be a syntax error when the application is executed.

13. You are deploying the web application you have been developing to a production server. Your application uses a number of resource assemblies and also one utility assembly that has been developed for the web application. You deploy the application by using a file-archiving utility to package all the `.aspx` and `Web.config` files into the archive, and the application is installed on the production server by un-packing the archive in the target directory. The deployment did not generate any error messages; but when you are testing the application, you find that it does not work. None of the localized resources display anything, and there are a large number of errors displayed. You need to make the application function normally—what is the most efficient way to achieve that goal?

    A. Enable tracing for the application, trace to an XML file, analyze the output, and correct the source of the problems.

    B. Copy the /bin directory from the development system to the production server.

    C. Install Visual Studio .NET on the production server; enable debugging; and single-step through the application, correcting all problems as they appear.

    D. Abort the deployment, and inform the customer that you will be back as soon as you have found the problem.

14. True or false. The GAC cannot store multiple versions of the same assembly.

    A. True.

    B. False.

15. You are configuring your web application to require digest-based authentication. What must you have in place before you can use digest-based authentication?

    A. A DNS server.

    B. Active Directory.

    C. Strong encryption keys.

    D. A strongly named `Web.config` file.

Test Answers

    1. A. The mostly static nature of the data makes the output cache a best strategy.

    2. C. The `Duration` parameter takes seconds, and the correct attribute is `VaryByParam`.

    3. B. The `Web.config` file will override the `Machine.config` file.

4. **A.** When the clients are not all Windows clients, use forms-based authentication.

5. **C.** Secure Sockets Layer (SSL) will encrypt the clear-text basic authentication method.

6. **B.**

7. **B.** The .NET Framework needs to be repaired.

8. **C.** You need to provide a server certificate.

9. **B and D.**

10. **A.** True.

11. **C.**

12. **A.** `users="?"` is the shorthand for anonymous users.

13. **B.** The assemblies were never deployed, and they are in the /bin directory.

14. **B.** False.

15. **B.** Digest-based authentication requires the use of Active Directory.

PART IV

70-316: Developing and Implementing Windows-Based Applications with Microsoft Visual C# .NET and Microsoft Visual Studio .NET

Introduction
to Windows Forms

In this chapter, you will

- Discover how to create Windows Forms using visual inheritance
- Learn how to set properties on a form
- Become familiar with using controls
- Learn about delegates and event handlers

This chapter is an introduction to creating front-end application code in Visual C# .NET. If you have developed in Visual Studio 6, you are already aware of the capabilities of the integrated development environment (IDE). Although it is possible to develop Windows applications outside of Visual Studio .NET, working within Visual Studio .NET is usually the best option as the IDE is loaded with assistance and shortcuts that help to reduce the amount of time you will spend coding and designing.

The .NET Framework provides many classes for building Windows applications, and we will explore some of them in this chapter. In particular, we will spend time looking at the `System.Windows.Forms` namespace, which is the cornerstone of application development in Windows.

We will also introduce you to the application that we will use in this section of the book to demonstrate Windows development. We will be creating a college registry database application that keeps track of students, instructors, and courses. The application will allow the user to interface with the back-end database. In this chapter, we will introduce form design, place controls on our form, and react to the events that are generated.

Windows Forms

The .NET Framework has provided Windows developers with a new platform on which to create applications—Windows Forms. By using this platform, developers can create Windows applications, front-end interfaces for multiple-tiered applications, and front-end interfaces for client applications. Anything that requires user intervention can be placed inside a Windows Form. If you have just finished Part III of this book, you may be wondering when to use Windows Forms and when to use Web Forms. The key distinction for deciding which one to use is this: If you need an application that can interact with the underlying resources of the system, and you know that you want a lot of the processing to take place on that machine, you need a Windows Form application. ASP .NET Web Forms are used when your application needs to run in a browser.

Windows Forms examples include:

- **A fast response application, like a point-of-sale system**   The "register" needs to be very fast and not dependent on the network connection. The front-end can still connect to a middle-tier or third-tier database, but the calculations and decision-making processing happens on the client.

- **Data-entry programs**   In order to provide the very fast response that is expected of data-entry programs, the work needs to be done on the client. Data can be sent across a network, validated, and returned at the same time as the user is entering new data. The need here is for quick response, and a Windows application provides that.

- **A graphics application**   In order to get the quality, high-performance display, the client needs to quickly interact with the operating system. A Windows Form application can do that.

- **A Windows game**   This type of application needs fast access to the underlying graphics classes that enrich the interface.

ASP .NET Web Form examples include:

- **An application that must be platform independent**   If your application needs to be visible on any machine that has a network connection, you must have a Web Form.

- **E-commerce applications**   For web-based business, a Web Form allows user interaction with the middle and back tiers of your application.

- **Intranet applications**   If your company has internal applications that provide services to employees, a Web Form means that no extra software needs to be installed on the client machines.

However, sometimes the distinction is not as simple as in these examples. If you are interested in learning more about the engineering of front-end applications, we suggest that you find a book on design principles. The Microsoft exams are not going to test you on whether you need to use a Windows Form or a Web Form. Since the two exams are distinct and separate from each other, we have chosen to present the information for the Windows exam in this part of the book (Part IV) and the web exam in Part III.

System.Windows.Forms Namespace and More

Before we get specific and look at the controls within the System.Windows.Forms namespace, let's talk about the categories of classes that relate to Windows application development. These are *controls, user controls, forms, components, common dialog boxes,* and *containers.* Table 18-1 compares and contrasts these important concepts.

It is a good idea to familiarize yourself with the class hierarchy of the categories discussed in Table 18-1. When you want to create a Windows Form, you need to know what classes are available, and you also need to understand the inheritance hierarchy to

PART IV

Class Category	Description
Controls	Simply put, a control has a visual representation. It's something that can be added to a form and displayed visually. The base class is called Control and it provides base functionality for all derived classes. Basic properties can be set, including BackColor, CanFocus, DataBindings, Enabled, and so on. Some of the exposed methods include Show(), Hide(), and GetType(). Events include MouseDown, MouseUp, Paint, and much more.
User Controls	A user control is an empty control from which other controls can be built. To read more about user controls, see Chapter 22.
Forms	A form is a type of control. It inherits from the Control class, so all of the previous applies to forms as well. The Form class represents a window or a graphical interface that can be displayed during an application. Types of windows include dialog boxes, MDI (multiple document interface) windows, and so on.
Components	These classes do not derive from System.Windows.Forms.Control; however, they need to be included here since they provide visual features for your application. For example, System.Windows.Forms.Menu is the base class for classes such as MainMenu, MenuItem, and ContextMenu.
Common Dialog Boxes	In order to achieve consistency between Windows applications, a group of classes have been build that allow interaction with printing, the file system, and so on. These are the common dialog boxes that are displayed in an application when you select File | Open or File | Print from the menus.
Containers	A container can hold zero or more components. The Container class is used when you want to group objects together. It is found in System.ComponentModel.Container. A Form is an example of a container that groups together controls such as buttons, text boxes, and the like.

Table 18-1 Categories of Classes in Windows Forms

be able to work with the functionality of the class. Explore the methods, properties, and events that can be found in the base classes by working your way through the .NET Framework documentation.

Use the following list of derived classes as a basis for understanding the Windows Forms class hierarchy.

- `System.ComponentModel.Component` (parent class)
  - `Control`
    - `ButtonBase`
      - `Button`
    - `ScrollableControl`
      - `ContainerControl`
        - `Form`

This is just a sampling of the hierarchy of classes within Windows Forms. A good exercise would be to build a class relationship diagram in order to see where everything fits.

What Is a Form?

A *form* is the window that is used to present information to or accept information from the end users. The form can be a simple window, an MDI (multiple document interface) window, or a dialog box. We will look at each of these in this chapter.

Having said all that, one point to keep in mind at all times is that a form is actually an object that is instantiated from a class. This means that a form exposes properties, methods, and events. The properties of a form allow you to set the *look* or *appearance* of the form. You can set properties like the size, the background color, and so on. The methods expose the behavior of the form—things like closing and activating. Events define the interaction of the methods—such as loading and deactivating. We will explore the significance of events later in the chapter.

Let's look at the class from which a standard form is created. We will see later in this chapter that you can create a form object using visual inheritance, a technique that allows you to define the base class for your forms. However, for the purposes of this introduction to forms, we will stick to a form that is created from the standard class. Figure 18-1 illustrates the class structure of the `System.Windows.Forms` namespace. Notice that a form is really a type of control.

As this chapter progresses, we will be referring back to Figure 18-1. As you have probably deduced, most of the prebuilt controls come from this namespace—buttons, textboxes, and the like. We will be adding these controls to our form as the chapter unfolds.

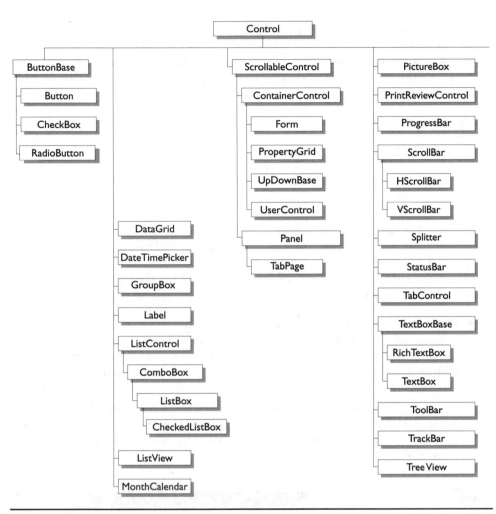

Figure 18-1   Part of the System.Windows.Forms namespace

TIP   C++ programmers will recognize Windows Forms as a replacement for MFC (Microsoft Foundation Classes), which was a wrapper on top of the Win32 API. However, you will see the beauty of the .NET solution when you realize that Windows Forms is a truly OO approach to developing Windows applications.

PART IV

Creating a Windows Form in a Text Editor

Enough theory—let's get to work and build a Windows Form. In this section, we will demonstrate that you can create a form application within a simple text editor. For our purposes, we simply used Notepad as the editor. We will start with a basic application that will create a form and display it to the user:

```
public class MyFirstForm: System.Windows.Forms.Form
{
    public static void Main()
    {
        MyFirstForm m = new MyFirstForm();
        System.Windows.Forms.Application.Run (m);
    }
}
```

The output of this program can be seen in Figure 18-2.

Notice that the default form contains a title bar, a control box to the left of the title bar (to move, size, minimize, maximize, and close the form), and the standard Windows minimize, maximize, and close buttons to the right of the title bar.

Here are the points to notice about our first form:

- Our new form actually derives from the base class `System.Windows.Forms.Form`. To illustrate this, we have provided the fully qualified class path—in reality, you would probably include a `using` statement at the beginning of your code (such as `using System.Windows.Forms`).

- In the `Main()` method, we instantiate our new form and then ask for the assistance of the `Application` class in order to leave the form on the screen. Had we left out the line that invokes the `Run()` method of the `Application` class, our form would not be displayed.

Figure 18-2
Our first
Windows Forms
program

The `Application` class is found in the `System.Windows.Forms` namespace and is used to manage an application. The `Run()` method starts an application message loop and, for our purposes, makes the form visible. The system and your application can generate messages, such as keypresses and mouse clicks, which are interpreted by .NET applications as events. These messages are kept in a queue. (We will examine this in the "Event Handling" section later in this chapter.) By providing the form as an input to the `Run()` method, the `Form` object is displayed on the screen.

 TIP The `Application` class has many other methods that can be used to manage an application. You could invoke `Application.Exit()` in order to terminate a program in an orderly fashion. The remaining messages in the message queue will be executed and then the application will terminate.

We can make our form more interesting by adding a button with the text "Hello World!" on it.

```
using System;
using System.Windows.Forms;
using System.Drawing;
public class HelloWorldForm: Form
{
    private Button buttonHelloWorld;
    public HelloWorldForm()
    {
        buttonHelloWorld = new Button();
        buttonHelloWorld.Text = "Hello World!";
        buttonHelloWorld.Left = 100;
        buttonHelloWorld.Top = 100;
        Controls.Add (buttonHelloWorld);
    }
    public static void Main()
    {
        Application.Run (new HelloWorldForm());
    }
}
```

When we execute this program using `csc HelloWorldForm.cs`, we observe the form as displayed in Figure 18-3.

In order to place a button on our form, we must first declare the existence of a button reference:

```
private Button buttonHelloWorld;
```

Following good OOP guidelines, we then instantiate the button inside the form's constructor. Once the button object is created, we can set the exposed properties of the button—`Text`, `Left`, and `Top`. These are just three of the properties that can be used. If you want to see all of the properties, methods, and events that are available within the `Button` class, be sure to look at the MSDN documentation within Visual Studio .NET.

PART IV

Figure 18-3
Output from
HelloWorldForm

Once the button is created and its properties are set, we then need to tell the constructor to add the button to the list of controls that appear on our form:

```
Controls.Add (buttonHelloWorld);
```

This is accomplished by using the `Controls` collection and the `Add()` method. When the constructor executes, our button object will be added to the form's `Controls` collection and made visible.

One other item of interest is how we have modified the `Main()` method of this application. Instead of spreading the creation of our form object and the presentation of the form over two lines of code, we have simply instantiated the form before passing it as an argument to the `Run()` method. Since we have no need of the form object's reference after the `Run()` method, there is no point in wasting cycles and memory space by creating the object reference.

Creating a Form in Visual Studio .NET

If you are like us and the rest of the world, you probably would prefer not to have to do any more typing than is necessary when you build your application. Enter Visual Studio .NET and its intuitive interface and functional development environment. From this point on, we will be using the IDE to create our Windows Forms applications and to demonstrate the time-saving power of the Visual Studio program.

When you open Visual Studio .NET, you are presented with the Start Page. From the Start Page, select New Project and you will see the New Project dialog box shown in Figure 18-4. You can also get to this screen through the menu system—File | New | Project.

Once you select the Windows Application project type, you will be taken to the graphical interface for forms development (Figure 18-5). Depending on what you have selected from the View menu, you will be able to see the Toolbox (at the left side of the window), from which you will select controls, the Solution Explorer (at the right side of the window), where you can manage the files in the project, and the Properties Explorer, where you set design-time properties for any visible object.

Figure 18-4
The New Project
dialog box

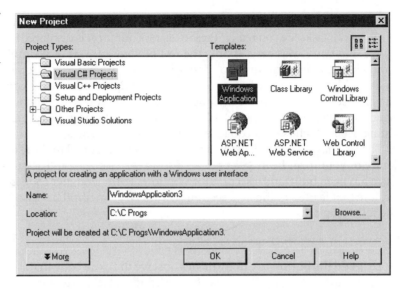

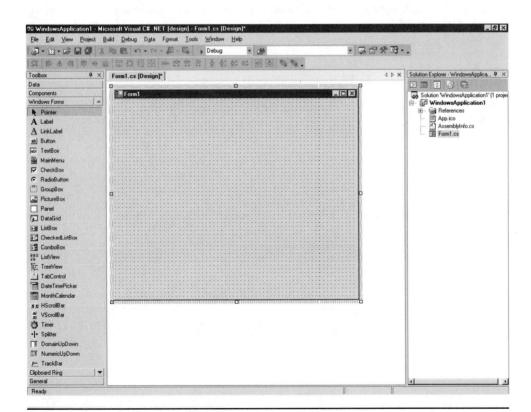

Figure 18-5 A new Forms design window

Let's build the same application as we did in Notepad, and this time, observe the simplicity of our task. Are you ready? Press CTRL-F5. Your form is displayed! (see Figure 18-6).

We told you it was easy. If only the rest of your job was that simple! If it were, you would have no need for this book and we would be unemployed ex-authors. So, let's dig under the hood and see what is going on. If you right-click on the form in the IDE, you can choose View Code from the pop-up list. When you do that, you will see the code window as displayed in Figure 18-7. In order to view the significant elements of the code listing, we have chosen to collapse some of the comments.

The IDE has created a skeleton program for you. Included in the skeleton is the inheritance of your form from `System.Windows.Forms.Form`. The constructor for your form has been built, and a section for Windows Form Designer code is reserved. We will explore that feature in the next section. The `Main()` method has also been created with the following call:

```
Application.Run(new Form1());
```

Let's add the button to our form and observe the extra code that is generated. Return to the Form1.cs (Design) window by selecting its tab in the designer window. Select the Button icon in the Toolbox and double-click it. That will place a button on your form in its default location (top-left corner). You can move the button around by selecting it on the form and dragging it to the position you want. Once the button is

Figure 18-6
Our first
Windows Forms
application

```
1  using System;
2  using System.Drawing;
3  using System.Collections;
4  using System.ComponentModel;
5  using System.Windows.Forms;
6  using System.Data;
7
8  namespace WindowsApplication1
9  {
10     /// <summary>
11     /// Summary description for Form1.
12     /// </summary>
13     public class Form1 : System.Windows.Forms.Form
14     {
15         /// <summary>
16         /// Required designer variable.
17         /// </summary>
18         private System.ComponentModel.Container components = null;
19
20         public Form1()
21         {
22             //
23             // Required for Windows Form Designer support
24             //
25             InitializeComponent();
26
27             //
28             // TODO: Add any constructor code after InitializeComponent call
29             //
30         }
31
32         /// <summary>
33         /// Clean up any resources being used.
34         /// </summary>
```

Figure 18-7   The code window

selected on the form, you can change any of its properties by using the Properties Explorer window (Figure 18-8).

When you press CTRL-F5 to execute the application, you will see a window similar to the one we created through Notepad (refer back to Figure 18-3).

Look at the code window and the extra code that Visual Studio has placed in your application (see Figure 18-9). Not a lot has changed except for the declaration of the Button object. This is because our control has now been created and its properties set by the *design time* of the development environment. In the coming sections, we will look at this concept and compare it to the *runtime* manipulation of controls.

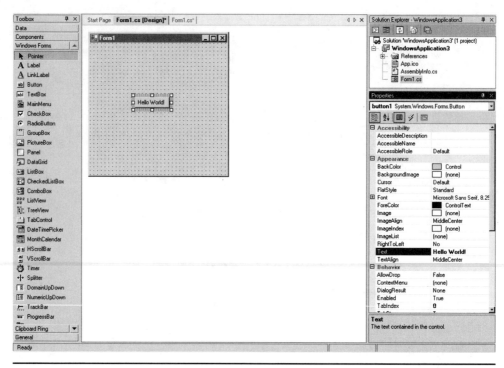

Figure 18-8   Adding a button control to the form

The Windows Forms Designer

What we have just been looking at in Visual Studio .NET is called the Windows Forms Designer. With very little effort, you can create a Windows application with spectacular capabilities. It's nice to have all this built-in assistance, but a good Windows developer has a solid grasp of the code that is written for them. It's the only way you will be able to interact with the help that the Windows Forms Designer supplies for you. In this section, we will examine the code that has been created.

We will start by creating a simple form that will become the basis for our college application. Figure 18-10 illustrates the output from our Windows application. We will then examine the code generated.

```
1  using System;
2  using System.Drawing;
3  using System.Collections;
4  using System.ComponentModel;
5  using System.Windows.Forms;
6  using System.Data;
7
8  namespace WindowsApplication3
9  {
10     /// <summary>
11     /// Summary description for Form1.
12     /// </summary>
13     public class Form1 : System.Windows.Forms.Form
14     {
15         private System.Windows.Forms.Button button1;
16         /// <summary>
17         /// Required designer variable.
18         /// </summary>
19         private System.ComponentModel.Container components = null;
20
21         public Form1()
22         {
23             //
24             // Required for Windows Form Designer support
25             //
26             InitializeComponent();
27
28             //
29             // TODO: Add any constructor code after InitializeComponent
30             //
31         }
32
33         /// <summary>
34         /// Clean up any resources being used.
35         /// </summary>
36         protected override void Dispose( bool disposing )
```

Figure 18-9   Code generated from the Hello World button form

Figure 18-10
Our college
application

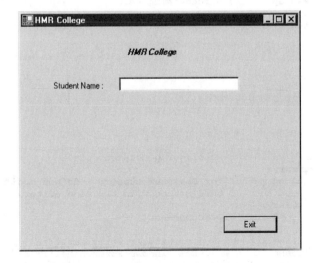

This entire application was created by using the Windows Forms Designer and required no typing of code. However, behind the scenes, the designer has filled in the blanks for us. Let's examine the code:

```csharp
using System;
using System.Drawing;
using System.Collections;
using System.ComponentModel;
using System.Windows.Forms;
using System.Data;
namespace WindowsApplication1
{
    /// <summary>
    /// Summary description for Form1.
    /// </summary>
    public class Form1 : System.Windows.Forms.Form
    {
        private System.Windows.Forms.Label label1;
        private System.Windows.Forms.Label label2;
        private System.Windows.Forms.TextBox textBox1;
        private System.Windows.Forms.Button button1;
        /// <summary>
        /// Required designer variable.
        /// </summary>
        private System.ComponentModel.Container components = null;
        public Form1()
        {
            //
            // Required for Windows Form Designer support
            //
            InitializeComponent();
            //
            // TODO: Add any constructor code after InitializeComponent call
            //
        }
        /// <summary>
        /// Clean up any resources being used.
        /// </summary>
        protected override void Dispose( bool disposing )
        {
            if( disposing )
            {
                if (components != null)
                {
                components.Dispose();
                }
            }
            base.Dispose( disposing );
        }
        #region Windows Form Designer generated code
        /// <summary>
        /// Required method for Designer support - do not modify
        /// the contents of this method with the code editor.
        /// </summary>
        private void InitializeComponent()
        {
            this.label1 = new System.Windows.Forms.Label();
            this.label2 = new System.Windows.Forms.Label();
            this.textBox1 = new System.Windows.Forms.TextBox();
```

```
            this.button1 = new System.Windows.Forms.Button();
            this.SuspendLayout();
            //
            // label1
            //
            this.label1.Font = new System.Drawing.Font("Microsoft Sans Serif", 8.25F,
System.Drawing.FontStyle.Bold, System.Drawing.GraphicsUnit.Point,
((System.Byte)(0)));
            this.label1.Location = new System.Drawing.Point(72, 16);
            this.label1.Name = "label1";
            this.label1.Size = new System.Drawing.Size(328, 24);
            this.label1.TabIndex = 0;
            this.label1.Text = "HMR College";
            this.label1.TextAlign = System.Drawing.ContentAlignment.MiddleCenter;
            //
            // label2
            //
            this.label2.Location = new System.Drawing.Point(56, 88);
            this.label2.Name = "label2";
            this.label2.TabIndex = 1;
            this.label2.Text = "Student Name :";
            this.label2.TextAlign = System.Drawing.ContentAlignment.MiddleRight;
            //
            // textBox1
            //
            this.textBox1.Location = new System.Drawing.Point(176, 88);
            this.textBox1.Name = "textBox1";
            this.textBox1.Size = new System.Drawing.Size(192, 20);
            this.textBox1.TabIndex = 2;
            this.textBox1.Text = "";
            //
            // button1
            //
            this.button1.Location = new System.Drawing.Point(344, 200);
            this.button1.Name = "button1";
            this.button1.TabIndex = 3;
            this.button1.Text = "E&xit";
            //
            // Form1
            //
            this.AutoScaleBaseSize = new System.Drawing.Size(5, 13);
            this.ClientSize = new System.Drawing.Size(488, 421);
            this.Controls.AddRange(new System.Windows.Forms.Control[]
            {
                this.button1, this.textBox1, this.label2, this.label1});
                this.Name = "Form1";
                this.Text = "HMR College";
                this.ResumeLayout(false);
            }
            #endregion
            /// <summary>
            /// The main entry point for the application.
            /// </summary>
            [STAThread]
            static void Main()
            {
                Application.Run(new Form1());
            }
        }
    }
```

Pay particular attention to the following list, which helps explain some of the code that the Designer has added to our project. We have highlighted the code of significance in the code listing.

- VS .NET has added a fair bit of XML documentation comments to our code. Refer back to Chapter 8 to see how these comments will be translated into XML documentation.

- As we mentioned in the previous section, a `Container` object is required if you need to group objects together. The Windows Forms Designer has created an object reference of type `Container` in order to manage the components on the form at run time:

```
private System.ComponentModel.Container components = null;
```

The object reference has been set to null at the start of the code. You may wonder why this is necessary when we talked about a `Controls` collection earlier in this chapter. However, consider that there may be elements in the application that are not controls, and a `Container` object allows us to group everything together. Our controls have been given reference variable names:

```
private System.Windows.Forms.Label label1;
```

TIP   You may want to assign your controls meaningful names at the beginning of the design. Notice how difficult it will be now to go back and change the name of the label to something that represents its function, like `labelStudentName`. The name can be changed in the Properties Explorer window under **Design.**

- The `Dispose()` method is coded in order to perform any operations that are necessary when garbage collection is done. Refer back to Chapter 2 to review the concept of garbage collection. In this case, the `Dispose()` method is called on the `components` object.

- In the `InitializeComponent()` method, the controls are instantiated and are set to their initial behavior. Notice that the `InitializeComponent()` method is called from the constructor. In this method, you will see the code that is created by changing the properties in the Properties Explorer window. Figure 18-11 shows the Properties Explorer for our title label.

- The `Main()` method is assigned as a single threaded apartment. This ensures that drag and drop works properly and also allows the clipboard to function. If you want to learn more about apartments and threading, read about threads in MSDN.

Figure 18-11

Properties of the
`Label` control
viewed in the
Properties
Explorer

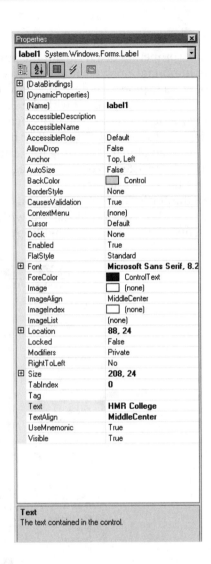

A Closer Look at Forms

Now that we've set the groundwork for developing forms, let's explore some of the finer details. In particular, we'll look at the various properties, methods, and events that come as part of the `Form` class. When we discuss methods and events, we will observe the lifecycle of a form. Visual inheritance is another topic that warrants some discussion here. Not only is visual inheritance covered on the exam, but it is a handy and time-saving method for creating forms.

Form Properties

While there are many properties of a form, for the purposes of this book, we'll focus on some of the more important ones, such as Font, BackColor, and so on. Figure 18-12 illustrates the Properties Explorer window for our form.

Take a minute to familiarize yourself with the Properties Explorer. The drop-down box at the top of the window allows you to move between the visual controls of your application, including the form itself. The toolbar below the drop-down box lets you change your view from an alphabetic listing to a categorized listing. It is often convenient to have the properties listed according to category, especially if your intention is to change properties of the same category.

By clicking the lightning bolt in the toolbar, you can switch the view to the events for the control. Visual Studio .NET provides you with some documentation of these properties and events. At the bottom of the Property Explorer is a short description

Figure 18-12

Form Properties
and Methods

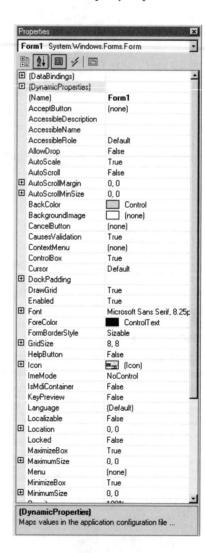

of the selected property or event. In Figure 18-12, you can see the explanation for `DynamicProperties`. It has been cut off because the window was sized too small for the explanation, but you can correct this simply by moving the mouse over the border between the list of properties and the description. You will see a two-headed arrow, and you can click and drag the description window's border higher in order to accommodate the full description.

Some of the more elegant properties of a form are presented in Table 18-2. The best way to familiarize yourself with the extensive list of properties is to actually try them in a test form and see what happens.

 EXAM TIP You will find localization and globalization topics on the Microsoft exam. Please refer to Chapter 7 for an introduction to the concepts and Chapter 24 for the specifics of building localized Windows applications. You will also find an introduction to localization of forms within this chapter.

Property	Description
AcceptButton	When you select this property, you are presented with a drop-down list of buttons on your form. The button you choose will be the one that is "clicked" when the user presses the ENTER key.
AllowDrop	If you are using drag and drop, you may want the form to receive notification of a drag-and-drop activity. The property is set to False by default.
BackColor	This property specifies the color that will be used to display text and graphics on the form.
CancelButton	This is similar to the AcceptButton, except the button will be "clicked" if the ESCAPE key is pressed.
ControlBox	This property determines whether your form will display the standard control box on the left of the title bar, indicating a menu that allows the user to close, maximize, or minimize the window.
Font	When you choose the font, it will be applied to the text on the form as well as on any controls added to the form.
FormBorderStyle	This property sets the appearance of the border of the form. By default, it is set to Sizable. You can change it to FixedSingle, Fixed3D, FixedDialog, FixedToolWindow, or SizeableToolWindow. Your choice depends on your intention for the flexibility of the form.
Icon	By changing the icon, you can set the icon file to be displayed in the top-left corner of your form. It will also be the icon displayed when the form is minimized.
Localizable	This property will set whether localization can happen on your form. When you select True, you can easily have the text of your form displayed in a different language.
StartPosition	When you set this property, you specify the position of the form when it first appears on the screen.
Text	By changing the Text property, you change the text on the title bar.

Table 18-2 Properties of a Form

PART IV

You can use the Object Browser to see the various properties and methods of a class file. When you click View | Other Windows | Object Browser, you will be presented with a window of objects that are included in your project. Drill down through the namespace to find the Form class. On the right side of the window (see Figure 18-13), you can see the methods available within the class.

Some of the key methods of the Form class are listed in Table 18-3.

Form Events

The first thing to happen to your form is the call to the constructor of the Form class by using the keyword New(). Notice in the code generated by the Windows Forms Designer that a call to the method InitializeComponent() is made in the constructor of the form. You can then place any of your initialization code in the InitializeComponent() method.

Certain events are triggered (or *fired*) as a form is opened, closed, moved, and so on. An event is caused by these actions, and these events create the lifecycle of the form. The following are the key events, in order of appearance, that make up this lifecycle:

1. **Load** The Load event is fired just before the form is loaded into memory. The event happens whenever a call is made to the Load() method or the Show() method.

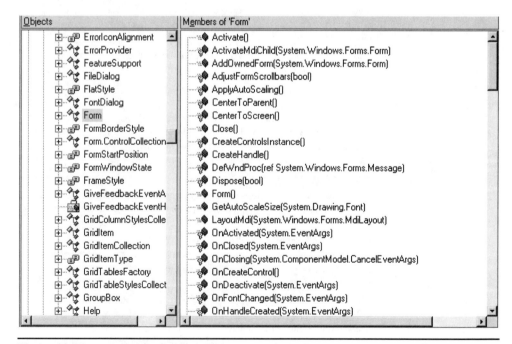

Figure 18-13   Using the Object Browser to explore the Form class

2. **Activated** and **Deactivate**   When a form is activated in code or becomes visible through user movement amongst forms, the Activated event triggers. For example, if a user is working on one form and clicks on a new form, the Activated event fires. You could use this event to code an update routine of information on the original form. Deactivate is caused when the form loses focus.

3. **Closing**   You can use this event to examine the method in which the user closed the form.

4. **Closed**   Just prior to the Dispose event, the Closed event occurs. You could verify the closing intentions of the user at this point.

5. **Dispose**   There is no Terminate event in .NET. In order to provide a place for any final instructions, the .NET Framework includes the Dispose event. You can then code any finalization orders in the Dispose() method.

 TIP   The Dispose method is called automatically on the closing of the main form. If you need to have termination code executed on the closing of any other form, you must explicitly call Dispose().

Using Visual Inheritance

Whenever a form is created by the process of inheriting from an existing base form, it is called *visual inheritance*. This is an extremely powerful technique. Consider its practical uses:

- Your company always has the same "look" to their forms. You can create a base form that exhibits this "look," and all forms can inherit from it.

Method	Description
Show()	This method is actually inherited from the Control class. It displays the form to the user.
Hide()	This method is inherited from Control. As its name suggests, it hides the form. However the form is still in memory.
Close()	This is a method of the Form class that closes the form and releases its resources.
SetDesktopBounds(int, int, int, int)	This method sets the boundaries of the form with respect to the desktop coordinates.
SetDesktopLocation(int, int)	This method provides the location of the form with respect to the desktop coordinates.

Table 18-3   Methods of a Form

PART IV

- You can create a base form as a template for other forms.

- You can reduce development time by having an arsenal of prebuilt templates.

Visual inheritance can only be performed from within Visual Studio .NET. There are two ways to implement it; the first way being the way we have used so far—deriving your new form from an existing form.

```
public class Form1: System.Windows.Forms.Form
```

The second way is by using the Inheritance Picker. From the menus, select File | Add New Item. You will see the Add New Item dialog box displayed in Figure 18-14. Choose Inherited Form from the right-hand pane. You will be presented with the Inheritance Picker window (see Figure 18-15).

In the Inheritance Picker, find the form that you have stored as a base form (click on the Browse button to search for it), and then click OK. This will cause a new form to be created, and the code behind it will include something like this line, depending on which form you picked:

```
public class Form2: VideoCollection.Form1
```

In our case, we chose the first form that we created for our college application, and the code demonstrates that the inheritance will be from Form (the original base class) to Form1 (our template) to Form2 (the new form).

Figure 18-14
The Add New Item dialog box

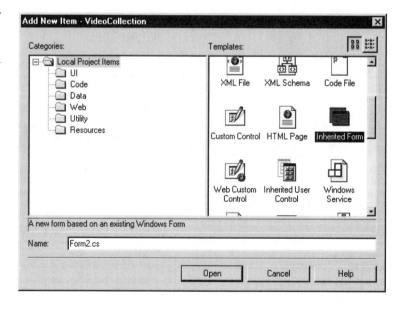

Figure 18-15
The Inheritance
Picker

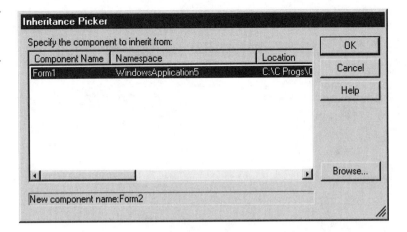

EXAM TIP   Be sure to understand and work with both methods of creating a
form. Visual inheritance is a topic covered on the Windows exam.

Imagine the time you can save by implementing visual inheritance. The whole goal
behind an object-oriented language is to eliminate duplication of effort. By creating a library of template forms and selecting them as base classes for your new applications,
you will reduce the amount of time you spend coding your application and can spend
more time on designing and testing.

Before we leave this subject, though, we must comment on the visual display of the
new form. Examine the form shown in Figure 18-16. This form was created via the Inheritance Picker.

Notice the funny looking characters beside every control. These are called *glyphs*, and
when you select them, you see the border (as in Figure 18-16) that indicates that the control has been inherited. The color of the border will tell you what kind of security has been
applied to the control. Each level of access permissions shows a different shade of gray.

- **Grey border with no sizing handles**   This means that the control is a
  read-only control. You will notice from Figure 18-16 that the properties
  are grayed out. You, as the user of the inherited control, cannot make any
  changes to its properties. You will not be able to move or size it either. This
  occurs when a control is specified with `Private` access modifiers.

- **Standard border with sizing handles**   If a control is specified with either
  `Public` or `Protected` modifiers, you will be able to size and move it.

Localizing Your Form

There will be times when your form will need to be used in a different country or in a different language. In order to accommodate that, you need to build *localization* into your

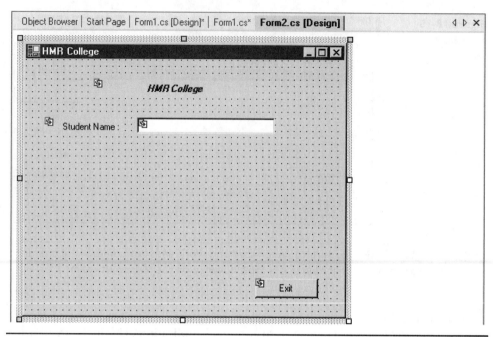

Figure 18-16   The newly inherited form

project. Localization is the process of translating the resources of your application into a different language.

In case you were starting to panic, there's no need. To accomplish localization within Visual Studio .NET, you do the following:

1. Set the form's Localizable property to True.

2. Change the Language property to the new language.

Let's change our Hello World form to provide French and Spanish translations. Here are the steps:

1. Set the form's Localizable property to True.

2. Change the Language property of the form to French (Canada).

3. Change the button's Text property to "Bonjour le Monde".

4. Change the Language property of the form to Spanish (Mexico).

5. Alter the button's Text property to "Hola Mundo".

6. Save and build the solution.

Figure 18-17 illustrates the effect of changing the button's Text property for the Spanish translation. Look under the Solution Explorer, and you will see additional resource files that go with the form. (Be sure to select View All Files first.) The files with the .resx extension are the resource files that are included in the build of the solution.

Once you set the locale of your computer to either French (Canada) or Spanish (Mexico), you will see the button in the language of the locale when you run the project.

 EXAM TIP The Windows exams will include a few questions on localizing the form. Use this chapter as a starting point, and then refer to Chapter 7 for an overall description.

The .NET Framework includes the Windows Forms Resource Editor (Winres.exe), which helps you localize forms when you are using a third party to provide the localization. Figure 18-18 demonstrates the Windows Resource Localization Editor window that opens when you run Winres.exe from the command line.

If you've ever had to create multiple resource files in older versions of Visual Studio, you will appreciate how simple it is in .NET to create applications that can be run on any machine in any culture. For more information, refer to Chapter 7.

We will explore localization further when we discuss deploying our application in Chapter 23. This section has just given you an indication of the power of the resources of the .NET Framework.

Controls

So far we have used a button and a text box on our form. In this section, we will explore the different kinds of controls and their properties, methods, and events. By using the right control in the right place, you can build an extremely effective graphical interface for your users.

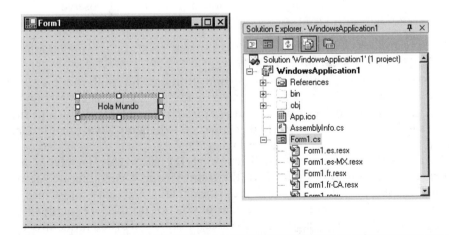

Figure 18-17   Resource files in Visual Studio .NET

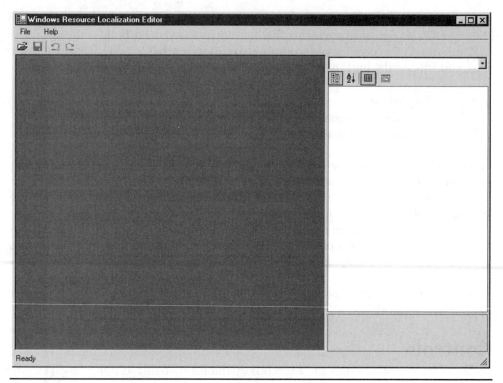

Figure 18-18   Windows Forms Resource Localization Editor

We will also introduce you to the generic elements of working with controls. In the next chapter, we will broaden our discussion of controls and observe how some of the more popular controls interact with the user.

Adding Controls to a Form

There are two ways to add a control to the form—through the Toolbox or programmatically inside your code. The method you use to add the control is entirely up to you. Essentially, you need to decide if the control is one that is available always and therefore can be added in design mode; or whether you need to dynamically create the control at run time depending on specific circumstances.

For instance, you may have a form that prompts the user to enter their name, address, and city. The form also has a field for the country code. Depending on the country selected, you may add another control to the form that asks for state or province or territory or whatever. The point is that the control was not on the form originally and is added based on the input received. In this case, you will need to add the control through the programming code.

Adding Controls Using the Toolbox

The Toolbox contains a list of controls that can be added to your project. Figure 18-19 shows the Toolbox in its entirety. Notice that the window is a floating window. You have a choice of docking the Toolbox (usually to the left of your development window) or sizing it as you prefer and having it float free on the screen.

Figure 18-19

The Toolbox

PART IV

To use the Toolbox to add a control to your form, follow one of these two methods:

- Double-click on the control in the Toolbox. This will create an instance of the control on your form. It will be of its default size and position. You can then click on the control's handles to resize it or move it.

- Click once on the control in the Toolbox. When you move your mouse over to the form, you will see a crosshair and a graphic representing your control. Click on the form at the position of the top-left corner and drag until the control is the desired size. By using this method, you have control over the position and size of the control when you create its instance.

The Toolbox can be customized to accommodate your needs. Notice in Figure 18-19 that there is a tabbed list of the different types of controls. If you right-click anywhere on the Toolbox, you will be presented with a menu from which you can choose Customize Toolbox. The Customize Toolbox dialog box is illustrated in Figure 18-20.

 NOTE The Customize Toolbox dialog box replaces the Components dialog box from Visual Basic, and the Customize dialog box in prior versions of Visual C++.

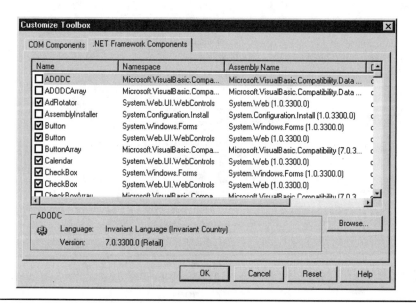

Figure 18-20   The Customize Toolbox dialog box

Once you select the control in the Customize Toolbox dialog box, you can place that control in any of the tabbed lists, or you can create your own tab by right-clicking on the Toolbox and selecting Add Tabs.

Adding Controls Programmatically

As stated earlier, there will be times when you need to create the control in your programming code. Here are the steps that you should follow:

1. Create a reference variable for your control. You would usually make this a private piece of data:

    ```
    private Label myLabel;
    ```

2. Instantiate a new instance of the control.

    ```
    Label myLabel = new myLabel();
    ```

3. Set the properties of the new control.

    ```
    myLabel.Text = "This is my Label control.";
    ```

4. Add the new control to the form's control collection.

    ```
    this.Controls.Add (myLabel);
    ```

5. Implement the event-handling code for the new control. We will explore event handling later in this chapter.

Types of Controls

The following list categorizes controls by their function.

- **Command**   Button, LinkLabel, NotifyIcon, Toolbar
- **Menu**   MainMenu, ContextMenu
- **Selection**   CheckedListBox, ComboBox, DomainUpDown, ListBox, ListView, NumericUpDown, TreeView
- **Text**   TextBox, RichTextBox, Label, LinkLabel, StatusBar
- **Graphics**   PictureBox, ImageList
- **Value**   CheckBox, CheckedListBox, RadioButton, Trackbar
- **Date**   DateTimePicker, MonthCalendar
- **Common Dialog**   ColorDialog, FontDialog, OpenFileDialog, PrintDialog, PrintPreviewDialog, SaveFileDialog
- **Grouping**   Panel, GroupBox, TabControl

Let's investigate the function of each control. Table 18-4 lists the popular controls available in the Toolbox, along with descriptions of their functions. Figure 18-21 illustrates some of the different types of controls and their default sizes on the form. Notice that some controls are not visible on the form—these controls show in the bottom pane of the designer window.

PART IV

Control	Function
Button	Allows a user to click on the control to perform routines.
CheckBox	Sets an option on or off.
CheckedListBox	Presents a list of items preceded by a check box.
ColorDialog	Selects colors from a standard dialog box. When this control is selected, it is added to the bottom of the design window and is not attached directly to the form. This is because it is an invisible control and is used within code. See Figure 18-25 for its positioning in the design window.
ComboBox	Displays data in a drop-down box.
ContextMenu	Presents frequently used menu commands that are associated with a particular object.
DataGrid	Displays data from a dataset. By moving through the DataGrid, the data can be updated at the source.
DateTimePicker	Presents a selection list of dates and times.
DomainUpDown	Allows a user to browse through and select from a list of text strings.
ErrorProvider	Displays error information to the user.
FontDialog	Presents a common dialog box for selecting fonts.
GroupBox	Groups other controls.
HelpProvider	Associates an HTML help file with the application.
HScrollBar	Provides horizontal scroll bars.
ImageList	Collects images that can be displayed on other controls.
Label	Displays text—read only.
LinkLabel	Displays hypertext links—read only.
ListBox	Presents a selection list of text or graphical items.
ListView	Presents a selection list of text, text with icons, text with large icons, or report view.
MainMenu	Displays a menu at runtime.
MonthCalendar	Allows a user to view and set date information.
NotifyIcon	Provides icons for background processes.
NumericUpDown	Allows a user to browse through and select from a list of numbers.
OpenFileDialog	Presents a common dialog box for opening files.
PageSetupDialog	Presents a common dialog box for setting printing options.
Panel	Groups controls in a scrolled list.
PictureBox	Displays graphics.
PrintDialog	Presents a common dialog box for starting printing.
PrintPreviewControl	Allows you to create your own Print Preview dialog box.
PrintPreviewDialog	Presents a common dialog box for viewing a printout.
ProgressBar	Shows the progress of an activity.

Table 18-4   Popular Controls from the Toolbox

Control	Function
RadioButton	Allows the user to select from a set of two or more mutually exclusive options.
RichTextBox	Displays text at run time and allows it to be altered by the user. Text can be formatted as plain text or RTF (Rich Text Format).
SaveFileDialog	Presents a common dialog box for saving files.
Splitter	Allows the user to resize a docked control.
StatusBar	Indicates status information about the application. Status can be set dynamically according to the state of the application.
TabControl	Creates multiple tabs that contain their own controls.
TextBox	Displays text at run time and allows it to be altered by the user.
Timer	Sets intervals for raised events.
ToolBar	Presents buttons on a strip for menu shortcuts.
ToolTip	Provides help text when a user positions the mouse over a control.
TrackBar	Navigates through information or adjusts a numeric setting.
TreeView	Presents a hierarchy of items that can be collapsed or expanded.

Table 18-4   Popular Controls from the Toolbox (continued)

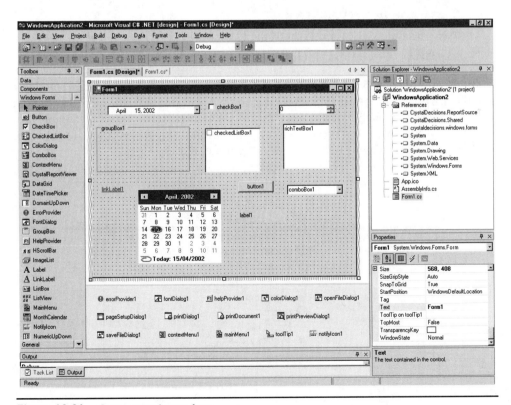

Figure 18-21   Some controls on a form

Setting Properties of Controls

Properties are exposed by the designer of the control and can be set at design time via the Properties window or programmatically at run time. Some properties can only be set at one time or the other. The following are common properties that most controls share:

- **Anchor** Sets the location of the top-left corner of the container to which the control is bound.

- **Backcolor** Sets the background color of the control.

- **BackgroundImage** Adds a background image to the control.

- **Enabled** Specifies whether the control is enabled or disabled (in which case it is grayed-out).

- **Focused** Sets whether the control has focus (in which case it is the control in the foreground).

- **Font** Sets the text properties.

- **Left** Sets the horizontal position of the top-left corner of the control.

- **TabIndex** Specifies the order of the controls. By default, TabIndex is set when you add the control; however, you may want to change that order.

- **Text** Sets the text of the control.

- **Top** Sets the vertical position of the top-left corner of the control.

- **Visible** Determines whether the control is to be displayed or not.

In order to set a property of the control programmatically, use the reference variable and the dot operator. In Visual Studio .NET, the dot operator will automatically present you with a list of available properties—this is called IntelliSense and is a valuable tool for the developer. You don't have to worry about valid properties—they are listed for you by IntelliSense. Figure 18-22 shows an example of this.

Figure 18-22
Using IntelliSense

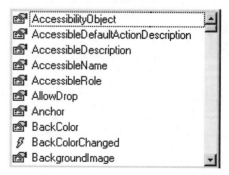

In the design window, you can select multiple controls and, through the Properties window, set the properties for the group. Only common properties will be available to be set. Use the CTRL key while selecting the group of controls.

Event Handling

So far we have avoided too much discussion about events in C# .NET for Windows Forms. It's time now to open this important topic and explore how events are dealt with in the C# language. When you work with controls, you need to understand how to interact with the events that can be triggered by user responses or system requirements.

What Is an Event?

An event is something that happens while the program is executing. It is a message that is sent by a given object in order to inform the program that an action has occurred. It can be generated by a user clicking on a button, pressing a key, moving a mouse, selecting a menu item, and so on. But it's not just the user that can cause an event to happen. The system may trigger an event (for example, when a file transfer is completed) or you can force an event to occur within your program code.

In an event-driven language such as C#, the application is essentially sitting there waiting for events to happen. If a given event is triggered, the program responds with the appropriate code written in the event handler. There is a direct relationship between the sender of the event (whatever raised the event) and the handler of the event (the action taken if the event occurs). However, keep in mind that while many events happen during the course of an application's life, you may only have code written for certain events—this is normal.

Controls have events that are exposed to the developer and can be seen in the Object Browser. They look like methods. However, when you are looking for events in Visual Studio .NET, watch for the lightning bolt icon—this indicates that the item is an event. You can see a list of events in the Properties Window by clicking on the lightning bolt.

The focus of this section of the chapter will be to deal with events, and this is called *event handling*. We will look at the code that is written and talk about *delegates*, which are commonly used classes for building event-handling routines. We will also return to this discussion in the next chapter when we deal with individual controls.

What Happens When an Event Occurs?

Good question. Remember that an event signals to the program that something has happened. The event sender is the object that raises the event. A user clicks on a button, and that button raises the event Click. By some process that we will clarify, a procedure is invoked to perform instructions tied to the raising of that event. The procedure is called the *event receiver*. However, in the middle of the relationship between sender and receiver, there is an object that links the two together. This is called a *delegate*. The .NET Framework will create most of your delegates for you, but there may come a time when you need to create your own delegate. The next section will explore the concept of using delegates as go-betweens for event senders and event receivers.

Delegates

In C#, an event is made transparent by the use of delegates. The concept of a delegate is roughly equivalent to the concept of function pointers in C and C++. The difference between delegates and function pointers lies in the fully object-oriented, type-safe, and secure qualities of a delegate. Not only that, but by using delegates, a developer can create a reference to a method within a delegate object. A delegate object can also call the method that it references. C# does not allow a target method (the method to be run when the event is fired) to be assigned to an event, because the event has to pass parameters to the method.

A delegate is a data structure that is derived from the `Delegate` class. By using delegates, you can tie the actual method to an event at run time. A button is clicked, but the button doesn't know the method that needs to run, so it passes the event to the delegate object, which is tied to the actual method required.

There are two parts to a delegate:

- The definition, which describes the method signature.
- The instance of the delegate, which in turn points to the desired method.

A generic delegate could be coded as follows:

```
public delegate void MyDelegate ();
MyDelegate m = new MyDelegate (<method>);
```

An event delegate includes two parameters that identify the source of the event and the data that belongs to the event:

```
public delegate void MyEventDelegate (object sender, AlarmEventArgs e);
```

These are the generic steps for using a delegate:

- Declare the delegate object. The signature of the delegate must match exactly the signature of the method that is tied to the delegate.
- Create all the methods that match the signature of the delegate.
- Instantiate the delegate object and insert the methods.
- Use the delegate object and call the methods.

Let's look at the code for using a delegate. Start by declaring the delegate object with matching method signature:

```
public delegate void NewDelegate (int i);
```

Next, create the class that contains the methods that match this signature:

```
class DelegateExample
{
    public void MethodA (int i)
    {
        // method code goes here
    }
    public void MethodB (int I)
    {
        // another method with the same signature as the delegate
    }
}
```

Instantiate the delegate object and insert the methods:

```
public static void Main()
{
    DelegateExample d = new DelegateExample();
    NewDelegate n = new NewDelegate (d.MethodA);
    NewDelegate n1 = new NewDelegate (d.MethodB);
}
```

Now for the finale. Call the methods through the delegate object:

```
n();
n1();
```

In the next section, we will relate this technique to a process called event handling. By employing event handling, we can respond to the events that are generated through the user's interaction with a control, through system events, or because of program-raised events.

Creating Event Handlers

Now it's time to tie this all together and investigate how we handle events. An event handler needs to capture the user input and tell the program that something has occurred. The event handler (or event procedure) is written with the program logic required to execute when the event is raised.

Let's start off simply. We have added an Add This Student button to our Video Collection application (see Figure 18-23). By double-clicking on the control, Visual Studio will bind the control to an event handler.

 NOTE A single event handler (procedure) can be tied to multiple events. For example, we could have a menu on this form with a menu item that simulates the clicking of the button. In this case, we could invoke the same event handler.

If you look at the code generated by Visual Studio .NET in the Windows Forms Designer section, you will see code that defines a new event handler:

```
This.button3.Click += new System.EventHandler (this.button3_Click);
```

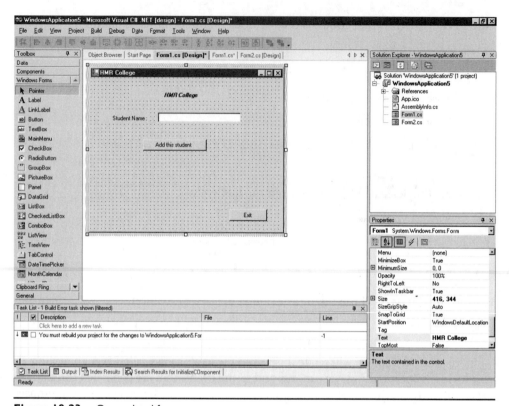

Figure 18-23   Our updated form

Now for the easy part. Follow these steps to build the event-handler stub code:

1. Click on your control in the Designer window.

2. Double-click on the event in the Properties Explorer. Be sure to select the lightning bolt first, in order to list the events.

3. Switch to the code view for your form and—voila!—there is the event-handler stub:

```
private void button3_Click (object sender, System.EventArgs.e)
{
}
```

TIP   The parameter list includes a "sender" object (the originator of the event) and an `EventArgs` object (which contains any information about the event). In Chapter 19, we will look at this further.

The final step is to include the program logic within the stubbed event:

```
private void button3_Click (object sender, System.EventArgs.e)
{
    MessageBox.Show ("This happened because I clicked the button");
}
```

Now, execute your program, click the button, and you will see the message box appear as in Figure 18-24.

Event handlers can be added to your program at run time by adding a new `EventHandler` object:

```
this.buttonx.Click += new System.EventHandler (this.buttonx_Click);
```

You can also remove event handlers at run time:

```
this.buttonx.Click -= new System.EventHandler (this.buttonx_Click);
```

 EXAM TIP Although all the work is done for you by Visual Studio .NET when you double-click on the control (the stubbed event handler is created for you), you will need to understand the process as we described it earlier in this chapter.

You can see how easy this is inside Visual Studio .NET. A lot of coding is done for you. Your role is to simply add the program logic. That's the goal of Rapid Application Development (RAD). It frees the developer to concentrate on the purpose of the application and does a lot of the background grunt work for you.

Figure 18-24
Result of
the button's
`Click` event

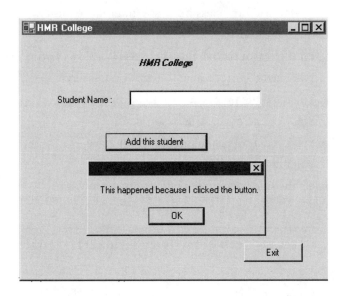

Summary

This chapter has been an introduction to the exciting world of Windows development. In particular, this chapter has made us familiar with working with Windows Forms. However, there is so much more to it than what we've looked at here. In the coming chapters, we will go into the details of using controls. We will also investigate creating our own controls. In the next chapter, you will be introduced to the entire application for our college. We will dissect this application, and by doing so, come to understand how to work with back-end SQL data, learn how to validate input from the user, investigate using services, and finally be able to deploy our final application.

Unless the visual programming world changes drastically (and, if you are a seasoned developer, you know this is possible), you will always find yourself building Windows applications. The web interface is wonderful for many reasons, including platform independence, but eventually you need the rich and consistent look of a Windows application. You may also need to write applications that have access to local resources, and this may not be possible with a Web Form. So get your typing fingers ready and let's delve deeper into the world of Windows applications.

Test Questions

1. Which of the following methods are ways to create a Windows Form?

   A. Visual inheritance.

   B. Building a derived class from `System.Windows.Forms.Form`.

   C. Extending a prebuilt form.

   D. Selecting a form class from the Inheritance Picker.

   E. All of the above.

2. Select the reasons why you would use Windows Forms over Web Forms.

   A. You need the processing to occur on the server.

   B. You need the processing to occur on the client.

   C. You need access to local resources.

   D. You need a consistent graphical interface.

   E. You need platform independence.

3. Select the line of code that will create a new form.

   A. `Form.MyForm m = new MyForm();`

   B. `System.Window.Forms.Form MyForm m =`
      `new System.Window.Forms.Form();`

C. ```
using System.Windows.Forms.Form;
public class MyForm: Form
{
    Form MyForm m = new Form();
}
```

D. ```
using System.Windows.Forms;
public class MyForm: Form
{
    MyForm m = new MyForm();
}
```

E. ```
using System.Windows.Forms;
public class MyForm: Form
{
    MyForm m = new Form();
}
```

4. You want to add a control to your form that allows you to set a particular option on or off. Which control would you choose?

   A. `Button`

   B. `CheckedListBox`

   C. `CheckBox`

   D. `ListBox`

   E. `RadioButton`

5. What is the output from the following code segment?

```
using System;
using System.Windows.Forms;
public class MyForm: Form
{
    private Button MyButton;
    public MyForm()
    {
        IntializeComponent();
    }
    private void InitializeComponent()
    {
        this.MyButton = new Button();
        this.MyButton.Text = "Hello World!";
        this.MyButton.Click += new System.EventHandler(this.MyButton.Click);
    }
    public static void Main()
    {
        MyForm m = new MyForm();
        Application.Run(m);
    }
}
```
```

A. Program compiles and displays "Hello World!" when button is clicked.

B. Program compiles, but clicking the button does nothing.

C. Program compiles but causes a runtime error.

D. Program does not compile.

6. What is the outcome of the following code? Assume that this code has been produced by Visual Studio .NET with a few minor changes by the developer.

```
using System;
using System.Drawing;
using System.Collections;
using System.ComponentModel;
using System.Windows.Forms;
using System.Data;
namespace WindowsApplication4
{
    public class Form1 : System.Windows.Forms.Form
    {
        private System.Windows.Forms.Button button1;
        private System.ComponentModel.Container components = null;
    public Form1()
    {
        InitializeComponent();
    }
    protected override void Dispose( bool disposing )
    {
        if( disposing )
        {
            if (components != null)
            {
                components.Dispose();
            }
        }
        base.Dispose( disposing );
    }
    private void InitializeComponent()
    {
        this.button1 = new System.Windows.Forms.Button();
        this.SuspendLayout();
        this.button1.Location = new System.Drawing.Point(96, 80);
        this.button1.Name = "button1";
        this.button1.Size = new System.Drawing.Size(104, 24);
        this.button1.TabIndex = 0;
        this.button1.Text = "Click Me";
        this.button1.Click += new System.EventHandler(this.button1_Click);
        this.AutoScaleBaseSize = new System.Drawing.Size(5, 13);
        this.ClientSize = new System.Drawing.Size(292, 273);
    this.Controls.AddRange(new System.Windows.Forms.Control[] {  this.button1});
        this.Name = "Form1";
        this.Text = "Form1";
        this.ResumeLayout(false);
    }
    [STAThread]
```

```
static void Main()
{
    Application.Run(new Form1());
}
private void button1_Click(object sender, System.EventArgs e)
{
    MessageBox.Show ("Hello World!");
}
}
```

    A. Program compiles and displays "Hello World!" when button is clicked.

    B. Program compiles, but clicking the button does nothing.

    C. Program compiles but causes a runtime error.

    D. Program does not compile.

  7. When you set the `Localization` property of a form to True, which of the following happens?

    A. You allow the application to accept localization resources.

    B. The form is translated into the language specified in the `Language` property.

    C. The property asks you for the translation language.

    D. The program prompts you to provide a language resource.

  8. By setting the `Text` property on the form, you will cause the value of the `Text` property to display on which part of the form?

    A. Bottom-right corner

    B. Top-right corner

    C. Title bar

    D. Status bar

  9. What causes the following `Load` event to fire? Assume that the form is the only form in the application.

```
private void Form1_Load (object sender, System.EventArgs e)
{
    Form1.Hide();
}
```

    A. The user starts the application.

    B. The `Show()` method is called.

    C. The user ends the application.

    D. A call is made to `Form1_Load` from another method.

10. What would the outcome of an application that contained this code be?

```
private void Form1_Load (object sender, System.EventArgs e)
{
    Form1.Hide();
}
```

A. The application would not compile.

B. The program would run but no form would display.

C. The program would run and display the form.

D. A runtime error would occur.

11. What would the outcome of an application that contained this code be?

```
private void Form1_Load (object sender, System.EventArgs e)
{
    this.Hide();
}
```

A. The application would not compile.

B. The program would run but no form would display.

C. The program would run and display the form.

D. A runtime error would occur.

12. What is the outcome of the following lines of code?

```
button1.Left = 50;
button1.Top = 100;
```

A. The button will display 50 pixels from the top of the form and 100 spaces from the left.

B. The button will display 50 pixels from the left of the form and 100 spaces from the top.

C. The button will display 50 pixels from the top of the window and 100 spaces from the left.

D. The button will display 50 pixels from the left of the window and 100 spaces from the top.

13. Which of the following are not methods of a `System.Windows.Forms.Form` object?

A. `Activate()`

B. `Deactive()`

C. `Form()`

D. `OnCreate()`

14. Which of the following are not events of a
   `System.Windows.Forms.Control`?

   A. `KeyPress`

   B. `KeyDown`

   C. `MousePress`

   D. `MouseMove`

   E. `MouseEnter`

15. In which namespace would you find the class `Application`?

   A. `System.Application`

   B. `System`

   C. `System.Window.Forms`

   D. `System.Windows.Forms`

Test Answers

1. E.

2. B, C, and D.

3. D.

4. C.

5. D. Program does not compile. The error message states that there is a missing event handler.

6. A.

7. A.

8. C.

9. A and B. The user starts the application or a call is made to the `Show()` method.

10. A. The application will not compile because the `Form1_Load` method would need a reference variable to the actual form.

11. C.

12. B.

13. B. `Deactivate()`. It is an event not a method.

14. C.

15. D.

User-Interface Components

In this chapter, you will

- Learn how to work with controls
- Explore the Toolbox controls
- Become familiar with common dialog boxes
- Learn how to create menus
- Be introduced to validation of user input

In this chapter, we will explore the properties and behaviors of the various controls in the Toolbox. If you have been working with previous versions of the Visual C++ or Visual Basic languages, you may want to travel quickly through this chapter. If you're less familiar with the Toolbox controls, you'll probably want to spend a bit more time exploring the material here.

The .NET Framework includes several basic controls that enhance the look of your Windows applications. Knowing how to work with these controls is an important part of creating applications that give the most assistance to the user. You may have worked with several of these controls in previous versions of Microsoft Visual products—they date back to the early days of Windows programming. However, you need to understand and be able to work with the properties, methods, and events that are exposed to the developer. For the exam, you will need to know how to work with groups of controls. We will look at setting the properties of multiple controls, working with collections of controls, and configuring the order through which the controls are tabbed.

Of equal importance is the ability to add functional menus to your application. Towards that goal, we will explore top-level menus, submenus, and context menus. A *context menu* is one that appears when the user right-clicks somewhere within a form. We will also investigate the events that are triggered by using the menus.

Microsoft will also test your understanding of providing user assistance in your applications. We will look at adding validation code that will determine the soundness of the user's input. Two validation techniques will be covered—using the `ErrorProvider` control and the `Validation` event. User assistance can also mean providing meaningful help to the application. With that goal in mind, we'll look at the `HelpProvider` control and talk about ToolTips.

Working with Controls

There are some common features of controls that warrant discussing in this chapter. The problem of programmatically resizing controls when the form resizes has traditionally been a difficulty that GUI developers face. In this section, we will look at how C# resolves this issue. You will also find times that you want to align controls to the position of the form. You may also want to designate the control with focus, making it the "active" control that responds to the ENTER key being pressed, or making it the selected control. Visual C# .NET also now has the capability of docking controls, much like windows can be docked.

Specifying a Control's Location on a Form

When a form is capable of being resized by the user, you need to be aware of how your controls will be positioned after the form is resized. When the user resizes the form, the default behavior is for the controls to maintain their position and size, but this may not be the desired outcome. Consider the first illustration, the start of our college application. We have a tabbed control that should expand when the form resizes, and a row of buttons at the bottom of the form that we would like to anchor to the bottom of the form accordingly. However, when the form is resized, the outcome is as shown in the second illustration.

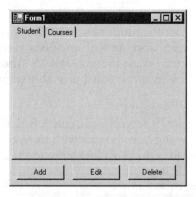

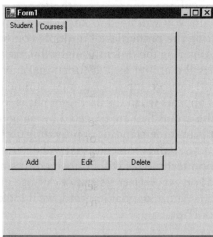

In the resized form, the `TabControl` (with the two tabs—Student and Courses) remains at its original size, and the buttons retain their alignment and size beneath the `TabControl`. In most cases, we would prefer the `TabControl` to size according to the resizing of the form, and we would like the buttons to do the same.

Anchoring a Control

One way to ensure that a control maintains its position when a form is resized is by setting the `Anchor` property. By anchoring a control, you ask Visual C# to maintain the distance between the control and the form. By setting the `Anchor` property to a certain position, you will ensure a more pleasing outcome when resizing.

The following illustration shows our college project and the `TabControl`'s `Anchor` property has been set to Top, Bottom, Left, Right. Notice the `Anchor` property drop-down box—you can set the anchor to position at any combination of Top, Bottom, Left, and Right. By default, the `Anchor` property is set to Top and Left. To clear any part of the anchor, just click on the shaded rectangle.

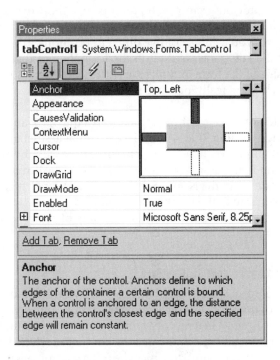

PART IV

Let's observe what happens when we resize the form. Try to resize your form when the `TabControl` is set to anchor to Top, Bottom, Left, and Right. As you will see, things are not quite right yet. The buttons are shifting to bizarre locations—as a matter of fact, we have even lost the Edit button.

Go into the properties of the buttons now (select them as a group) and set the `Anchor` property to Bottom and Left. Now when we run our application, the buttons stay down at the bottom of the form when we resize.

Just a word of warning—this won't solve all of your resizing problems. You may still have to be creative with complicated forms. You may need the help of the `Dock` property (covered in the next section) and some coding.

 EXAM TIP   By using a few panels on your form, you can set controls on the panel and then align the controls using both the `Anchor` and `Dock` properties. (You will see the `Dock` property in the next section.) You will still have to add code for complicated forms, but if you recall resizing in earlier versions of Visual C++ or Visual Basic, you will be pleased by the small amount of coding necessary.

Docking a Control

Another cool technique offered in Visual C# .NET is the docking of controls to ensure their positions upon resizing. If you recall our study of the Visual Studio .NET environment, windows can be docked or undocked. Docking means that the window becomes "attached" to a certain part of the background form and moves and sizes with the form.

We have taken our previous example and reverted the `Anchor` property back to its default of Top and Left, and we have set the `Dock` property of the `TabControl`. The `Dock` property window gives you a choice of five different positions: Top, Left, Bottom, Right, and Middle. Select the Left panel, and rerun the form. Notice that the `TabControl` is "stuck" to the left side of the form and fills the entire side. There is now no space for our buttons and, as such, they really become part of the `TabControl`, which is not our desired result.

Again, you should note that it is the combination of the `Dock` and `Anchor` properties, along with some tricky coding, that will achieve the final aesthetically pleasing result. If you are a Java programmer, you may have spent some time with the different layout managers, and you may find the `Dock` property to be similar to the `BorderLayoutManager` whereby "controls" are set in the North, South, East, West, or Center of the form layout. By experimenting with setting the `Dock` property and using panels to hold your controls, you will find that C# has employed a very similar way of setting control positions and holding them in that position when the form resizes.

Aligning Controls on a Form

If you are coding your form within Visual Studio .NET, you will find that you can use the Format menu to set options for working with your controls. When you work with the Format menu, you set the options in terms of a *primary* control. For example, we will select the three buttons on our form and make sure that the last button selected is the "Add" button. This will become the primary control to which the other controls align. Observe the next illustration—we selected the controls using the CTRL key and choosing the Add button last, and you can see that the primary control has dark resizing handles around it.

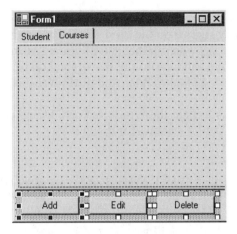

Table 19-1 illustrates the options that are available through the Format menu.

Menu Item	Submenu Item	Description
Align	Lefts Centers Rights Tops Middles Bottoms to Grid	Aligns all controls to the primary control.
Make Same Size	Width Size to Grid Height Both	Allows multiple controls to be resized on the form.
Horizontal Spacing	Make Equal Increase Decrease Remove	Adjusts the horizontal spacing between the controls.
Vertical Spacing	Make Equal Increase Decrease Remove	Adjusts the vertical spacing between the controls.
Center in Form	Horizontally Vertically	Controls the centering of the controls on the form.
Order	Bring to Front Send to Back	Determines whether a control will take a foreground spot, no matter what is placed in front of it.
Lock Controls		Locks all the controls on the form and eliminates any chance of moving or resizing the controls.

Table 19-1   The Format Menu

PART IV

Let's work with the Format menu. Start with a form where the buttons are all different sizes and are not properly aligned on the form. When you select the buttons (being sure to select the Add button last), you can then click Format | Make Same Size | Both. Once this is done, all the buttons will take on the size of the Add button. You can then select Format | Horizontal Spacing | Make Equal, and the buttons will have the same amount of space between them.

For interest's sake, let's look at the Windows Form Designer and examine the code that has been created behind the scenes for us.

```csharp
private void InitializeComponent()
{
    this.tabControl1 = new System.Windows.Forms.TabControl();
    this.tabStudents = new System.Windows.Forms.TabPage();
    this.tabPage2 = new System.Windows.Forms.TabPage();
    this.buttonAdd = new System.Windows.Forms.Button();
    this.buttonEdit = new System.Windows.Forms.Button();
    this.buttonDelete = new System.Windows.Forms.Button();
    this.tabControl1.SuspendLayout();
    this.SuspendLayout();
    // tabControl1
    this.tabControl1.Controls.AddRange(new System.Windows.Forms.Control[] {
        this.tabStudents, this.tabPage2});
    this.tabControl1.Location = new System.Drawing.Point(0, 24);
    this.tabControl1.Name = "tabControl1";
    this.tabControl1.SelectedIndex = 0;
    this.tabControl1.Size = new System.Drawing.Size(544, 416);
    this.tabControl1.TabIndex = 0;
    // tabStudents
    this.tabStudents.Location = new System.Drawing.Point(4, 22);
    this.tabStudents.Name = "tabStudents";
    this.tabStudents.Size = new System.Drawing.Size(536, 390);
    this.tabStudents.TabIndex = 0;
    this.tabStudents.Text = "Students";
    // tabPage2
    this.tabPage2.Location = new System.Drawing.Point(4, 22);
    this.tabPage2.Name = "tabPage2";
    this.tabPage2.Size = new System.Drawing.Size(568, 414);
    this.tabPage2.TabIndex = 1;
    this.tabPage2.Text = "Courses";
    // buttonAdd
    this.buttonAdd.Anchor = (System.Windows.Forms.AnchorStyles.Bottom |
        System.Windows.Forms.AnchorStyles.Left);
    this.buttonAdd.Location = new System.Drawing.Point(8, 456);
    this.buttonAdd.Name = "buttonAdd";
    this.buttonAdd.Size = new System.Drawing.Size(48, 56);
    this.buttonAdd.TabIndex = 1;
    this.buttonAdd.Text = "Add";
    // buttonEdit
    this.buttonEdit.Anchor = (System.Windows.Forms.AnchorStyles.Bottom |
        System.Windows.Forms.AnchorStyles.Left);
    this.buttonEdit.Location = new System.Drawing.Point(152, 456);
    this.buttonEdit.Name = "buttonEdit";
    this.buttonEdit.Size = new System.Drawing.Size(48, 56);
    this.buttonEdit.TabIndex = 2;
```

```
       this.buttonEdit.Text = "Edit";
       // buttonDelete
       this.buttonDelete.Anchor = (System.Windows.Forms.AnchorStyles.Bottom |
          System.Windows.Forms.AnchorStyles.Left);
       this.buttonDelete.Location = new System.Drawing.Point(296, 456);
       this.buttonDelete.Name = "buttonDelete";
       this.buttonDelete.Size = new System.Drawing.Size(48, 56);
       this.buttonDelete.TabIndex = 3;
       this.buttonDelete.Text = "Delete";
       // MainForm
       this.AutoScaleBaseSize = new System.Drawing.Size(5, 13);
       this.ClientSize = new System.Drawing.Size(600, 525);
       this.Controls.AddRange(new System.Windows.Forms.Control[] {
          this.buttonDelete, this.buttonAdd, this.tabControl1, this.buttonEdit});
       this.Name = "MainForm";
       this.Text = "Form1";
       this.Load += new System.EventHandler(this.MainForm_Load);
       this.tabControl1.ResumeLayout(false);
       this.ResumeLayout(false);
}
```

You can tell by looking through the code that the Location and Size properties have been affected by our changes to the Visual Designer. Notice that this code is in the InitializeComponent() method, which, as we discussed in the last chapter, is the method that is called in the form's constructor.

One final option to quickly discuss is the Lock Controls option. When we set the Locked property to True or select the Lock Controls option from the Format menu (shown next), the controls are no longer capable of being moved or resized in the Visual Designer.

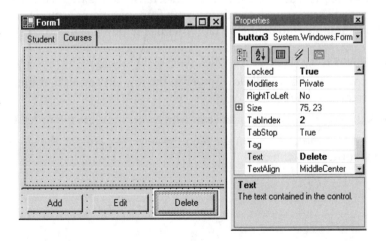

 EXAM TIP Microsoft will expect you to know how to lock controls for the Windows exam. By setting the Lock property to True, you will find that the controls are locked in position.

Managing Control Focus

One final area we need to investigate in this section is managing the *focus* of controls on your form. When a control is in the forefront of the application, it is said to have focus. This is the control that will respond when you press ENTER (although not all controls will have functionality for the ENTER key). The control with focus is usually designated by a darker border or dashes around the control. You can move the focus around the controls on a form by pressing the TAB key.

 EXAM TIP   Microsoft considers configuring the order of tabs to be an objective of the Windows exam. The TabIndex property controls the order of tabs and is 0-based.

When you run the college application, you will notice that you can tab through the controls on the form. If you created the form by adding the controls in order of appearance, meaning the TabControl first, the Add button second, and so on, the order in which you tab is the order in which they were added to the form.

Let's add a new button. We have aligned the Add, Edit, and Delete buttons and made them the same size. The new button is added, visually, before the other three buttons. Yet when you press the TAB key, the first stop is the Add button. It was added to the form first, so it is the first stop.

We can configure the tab order by using the TabIndex property. The first control added to the form has a TabIndex value of 0 (zero). The second control has a value of 1 (one), and so on. You can enter new values to change the tab order.

If you prefer, you can use the View menu to set tab order, as well. This is a very handy technique that will save you a lot of time if your form has many controls that are out of order. Follow these steps to configure tab order using the View menu:

1. Select View | Tab Order.

2. Each control will have a little number in the top-left corner that specifies its current tab order.

3. Click the controls in the sequence in which you want the tab order.

4. Select View | Tab Order from the menu system. You will see the tab order on the form (shown next).

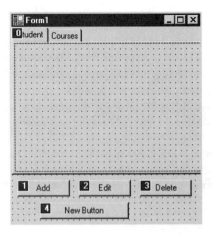

If you want, you can tell C# not to stop at a particular control. Set the TabStop property for that control to False, and you will see that the control is not part of the tab order. A line of code like this will be added to the InitializeComponent() method of the control:

```
this.button1.TabStop = false;
```

As you can see, the .NET Framework has provided us with a number of valuable tools that save hours of programming. Spend some time experimenting with these now, and you will find your development time (from the GUI perspective) greatly reduced.

Windows Forms Controls

In Chapter 18, we introduced the various controls that are included as part of the Toolbox in the Visual Studio .NET IDE. We briefly touched on each control and its use and then went on to discuss the event model that makes up the .NET Framework. In this section, we will work with the controls you might expect to see on the exam and point out the important aspects of each. This is not meant to be a comprehensive study, by any stretch of the imagination. However, it can serve as an introduction to each control. By observing them in our application, you will be able to ascertain each control's effectiveness for the needs of your applications. You will also familiarize yourself with some of the properties, methods, and events that are characteristic of that particular control.

Before we look at these controls specifically, we should take a moment to discuss the events that are common to all controls. In Table 19-2 we present these events and a brief description of how they would be used. Keep these events in mind as we explore the various controls in the Toolbox.

Event	Description
Click	Fires when the control is clicked. This can be the result of a mouse click or the ENTER key being pressed when the control has focus.
DoubleClick	Triggers when the mouse is double-clicked over the control.
Enter	Occurs when the control is entered.
OnFocus	Triggers when the control gets focus either by the user tabbing to the control or clicking on the control. This can also occur programmatically by setting focus on the control.
KeyDown	Fires when a key is pressed when the control has focus.
KeyPress	Fired after KeyDown, which occurs when a control that has focus receives a keypress. You can retrieve the character that was pressed by examining the KeyChar property of the KeyEventArgs parameter. By using the KeyPress event, you can tell whether any of the modifier keys were also pressed (CTRL, SHIFT, ALT).
KeyUp	Occurs when a key is released.
Leave	Occurs when the control is exited (or left).
LostFocus	Occurs when the control loses focus (when the user tabs or clicks on another control).
MouseDown MouseEnter MouseHover MouseLeave MouseUp	A series of events that occurs when mouse actions take place. MouseDown and MouseUp happen when the mouse button is pressed and released. By using the Button property of the MouseEventArgs parameter, you can determine which mouse button was pressed (right, left, or middle).
Move	Occurs when the control is moved.
Validated	Triggers when the control is finished validating. We will look at validation events later in this chapter.

Table 19-2   Common Events for all Controls

Keep in mind that these are just some of the common events that can occur. Each control will have its own list of specific events that have been created just for it. For example, the Timer control has a Tick event that is unique to it.

Buttons, Text Boxes, and Labels, Oh My!

Probably the most common of all controls, buttons, text boxes, and labels are the basic user-interaction controls. By clicking a button, a user can request a certain action; by typing in the text box, a user can present data to the program; and by reading the contents of a label, a user is prompted by its value. New to the .NET Framework is the LinkLabel, which allows you to create a label that contains a hyperlink, and the RichTextBox, which permits formatted text.

Buttons

Including buttons on your form allows the user to select an activity. There are three different kinds of buttons that you can employ—the regular "Click here" type of button, a radio button, and a check box. It may seem strange that we include radio buttons and check boxes in the "button" category, but that is because they all derive from the class `ButtonBase` (a subclass of `Control`). We will return to the discussion of radio buttons and check boxes in a few minutes, but for now, let's concentrate on the standard `Button` class.

To add a new button to your form, either double-click on the Button icon in the Toolbox or click it once and draw the button on your form. Once the button is added to your form, you should immediately change its name property from `Buttonx`, where *x* is the sequentially assigned number of buttons already on the form, to something meaningful like `btnDelete`. The following illustration demonstrates our row of buttons on the main form of our college application. You should then change the `Text` value from `Buttonx` to the visual clue for the user (that is, Delete). Double-click on the new button and you will be taken to the `Click` event. You can then code whatever needs to be done when the user clicks on the button.

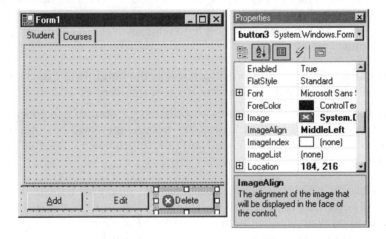

A .NET button can have an image added to it. Notice the graphic to the left of the "Delete" text on the button. This graphic is added by configuring the Image property. We have added one of the common bitmaps that are included with the Visual Studio .NET installation. If you are trying this yourself, you will notice that the graphic appears on top of the text (which we also changed from "Buttonx" to "Delete"). By adjusting the `ImageAlign` property, you can place the graphic to the left of the text (or wherever you want it to be).

TIP Notice the underlined "A" on the Add button. This is created by adding an ampersand (&) in the `Text` property in front of the character you wish underlined. The user can then use the ALT key along with the underlined letter to access the button (instead of clicking on it).

To add the code that should be run when the user clicks on the button, double-click the newly designed button. You will be taken to the code view of the main form. You will see that two things have happened:

1. The `Click` event has been registered (or subscribed to) in the `InitializeComponent()` method:

```
this.btn.Delete.Click +=new System.EventHandler(this.btnDelete_Click);
```

2. The event-handler stub has been created:

```
private void btnDelete_Click (Object sender, System.EventArgs e){ }
```

We can add our own code in the `Click` event that will perform the required `Delete` operation. In Chapter 20, we will code this button to remove a record from the database.

A cool way to determine the valid properties, methods, and events for any control is to type the name of the control in the code view window (for example, `btnDelete`), and then press the period (.), which is also known as the *dot operator*. IntelliSense drops down a list of all the properties, methods, and events for the control. You will be able to determine whether a name is for a property, method, or event by observing the icon beside the name. The hand holding a piece of paper denotes a property, the flying paper signals a method, and the lightning bolt represents an event. A couple properties warrant mentioning:

- **Enabled**   By setting this property to False, the button will display on the form but will not be capable of receiving any user intervention activities.

- **Visible**   This property determines whether the control will appear on the form or not. This is a valuable property, because there will be times that a control should not be visible, and you can control when it is actually displayed programmatically.

Radio Buttons   The look of the radio button is a far cry from the look of the `Button` class; however, they derive from the same base class, `ButtonBase`. A radio button is used when you want to give the user a choice of two or more mutually exclusive options. In our example in the following illustration, the user can choose either Computer Course or C# Course—of course, we *know* they'll choose the C# course!

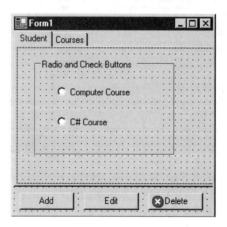

Notice, in this example, that we have placed the buttons in a `GroupBox`. There are many reasons for doing this:

- A `GroupBox` visually keeps all the radio buttons together.
- When you don't use a `GroupBox`, only one radio button can be selected per form. To have multiple areas of selection, you need multiple group boxes.
- When you move the `GroupBox`, the buttons inside move with it, keeping the controls together.

Table 19-3 identifies some of the more common properties and events for a `RadioButton`.

 EXAM TIP A `GroupBox` is very similar to the `Panel` control—both act as containers for other controls. The difference between the two is that a `GroupBox` has a caption on it and a `Panel` can have scroll bars.

Check Boxes A check box allows the user to select an option or answer a question. The following illustration shows a check box that has been added to our college application in the Visual Designer. The difference between a check box and a radio button has to do with the mutually exclusive options of a radio button. With a radio button, you can select only one of the grouped options. By using check boxes, you allow the user to select any number of options, and these options could be very different in nature.

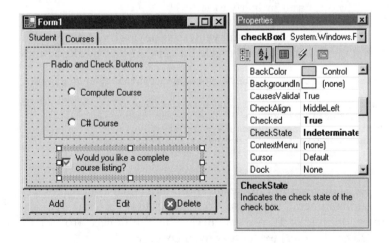

In our example (in the preceding illustration), you can see that the check box is in an indeterminate state (the check mark is grayed out). This is a common practice with Windows applications. The check box can be selected (with a dark check mark), unselected (no check mark), or unchanged (indeterminate). By default, however, you only allow

	Name	Description
Properties	Appearance	A `RadioButton` can be displayed either as seen in the preceding illustration or as a simple click button.
	AutoCheck	The `RadioButton` will automatically change its state (on or off) when it is clicked.
	Checked	You can test whether the button has been selected by determining the True/False value of `Checked`.
Events	AppearanceChanged	This event occurs when the `Appearance` property value changes.
	CheckedChanged	This event is fired when the `Checked` property value changes. When a radio button is clicked, this event happens twice—once to the button that was previously checked and once to the button that is now checked.
	Click	When a radio button is selected, the `Click` event fires once.

Table 19-3 Properties and Events of a `RadioButton`

two options—selected or unselected. In order to add in the indeterminate feature, you must do two things:

- Set the `CheckState` property to Indeterminate.
- Set the `ThreeState` property to True.

To display the check mark as a default value, set the `Checked` property to True.

Let's look at the code that would toggle the `CheckBox` `Checked` property.

```
private void btnToggle_Click (object sender, System.EventArgs e)
{
    if ((cbTest1.CheckState == CheckState.Checked)
        || (cbTest1.CheckState == CheckState.Unchecked))
        cbTest1.CheckState = CheckState.Indeterminate;
    if (cbTest1.CheckState == CheckState.Indeterminate)
        cbTest1.CheckState = CheckState.Checked;
}
```

As you can see in this example, there are enum files (such as `CheckState`) that allow us to use alphanumeric values to compare states (`cbTest1.CheckState == CheckState.Unchecked`). Always check with the Object Browser (View | Other Windows | Object Browser) for these convenient classes.

Text Boxes
When you need the user to enter a value into your application, you can make use of a `TextBox`. The control derives from the `TextBoxBase` class. You will also find a `RichTextBox` control extending from `TextBoxBase`, which allows you to provide

formatted text in a text box. We will also discover later in this chapter that we can use the text boxes to force the user to enter a certain kind of data. For example, you may want to ensure that only numeric values are entered into the text box—in the "Validating User Input" section of this chapter, we will look at this capability in detail.

Let's look at some of the more interesting properties of the `TextBox` class:

- **`CharacterCasing`**   Allows you to set whether the text that is entered is in lowercase, uppercase, or remains the way it was typed. The default value is Normal.

- **`MaxLength`**   Allows you to set the maximum number of characters to be entered into the `TextBox`. By default, the only practical limit is the amount of memory in the host machine.

- **`Multiline`**   Allows the control to display multiple lines of text.

- **`ScrollBars`**   Allows you to specify that the control will show the scroll bars if the control is also set to display multiple lines of text.

- **`PasswordChar`**   Replaces the typed characters with a special password character. For example, most password boxes display asterisks (*) over the typed password for security reasons.

- **`ReadOnly`**   Sets the `TextBox` to be a read-only text box. The user will be unable to change the value in the `TextBox`.

- **`WordWrap`**   Specifies that words will wrap if the text in the control exceeds the width of the control. Used for multiple-line text boxes.

One of the nicer features of a `TextBox` is its ability to provide validation code. We will examine this later in the chapter—just keep in mind that most of the events that you will use for a `TextBox` belong to the validation type.

Rich Text Boxes   The `RichTextBox` class uses a standard for displaying formatted text strings called Rich Text Format (RTF). This allows you to utilize formatting, such as **bold**, *italic*, and <u>underlining</u>. Some properties are supported via the base class and some are new to the `RichTextBox`:

- **`Redo` and `Undo`**   Allows you to specify a True/False value that lets the user undo or redo their keystrokes.

- **`DetectUrls`**   Specifies that a URL will be treated as such and display as an underlined link.

- **`SelectedRtf`**   Allows the user to cut and paste between your application and an application such as Microsoft Word and have the Rich Text Formatting retained between applications.

This is just a sampling of some of the features of a `RichTextBox`. Figure 19-1 illustrates our application with a `RichTextBox` added. We have added a `Button` control

PART IV

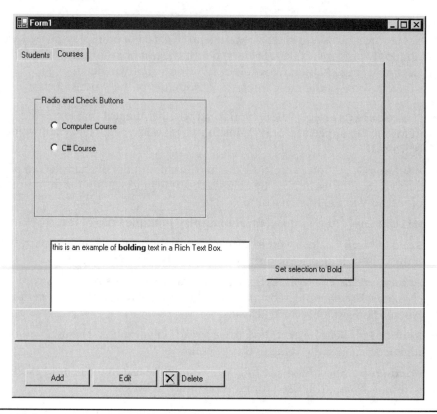

Figure 19-1   Example of a `RichTextBox` control

that will set a selected area of text to bold. The code to implement this in the `Button Click` event is as follows:

```
private void btnSetBold_Click(object sender, System.EventArgs e)
{
    Font oldFont;
    Font myFont;
    oldFont = this.rtfTest1.SelectionFont;
    myFont = new Font (oldFont, FontStyle.Bold);
    this.rtfTest1.SelectionFont = myFont;
    this.rtfTest1.Focus();
}
```

When the button is clicked, whatever text is selected is converted to bold. In our example, we selected the word "bolding" and then clicked the button. As you can see, the text changes to bold font for just the word "bolding". Obviously, this is a trivial example of what you can do to effect formatting changes to the text in a `RichTextBox`. The code demonstrates the `SelectionFont` property, which is just one of the selection properties available for use.

Labels

This is probably one of the most used controls in the Windows application environment. Using a label allows you to provide information to the user. There are two types of label controls that can be added to a Windows form: `Label` is the standard label, and `LinkLabel` allows you to create a hyperlink label.

We have modified our form and added a label (see the next illustration) encouraging students to click on the hyperlink to reach Microsoft's web site.

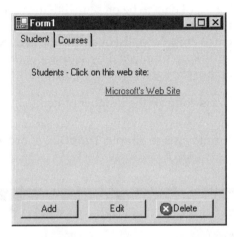

 EXAM TIP Notice that the `Caption` property is not the property to use to set the text of the label. You use the `Text` property in Visual Studio .NET.

We will not spend much time discussing the label controls since they are very basic controls; however, it warrants looking at how you set the properties to support hyperlinks for the `LinkLabel` control. In the `InitializeComponent()` method, the Designer has added the following code:

```
this.linkLabel1.LinkArea = new System.Windows.Forms.LinkArea(0,20);
this.linkLabel1.Location = new System.Drawing.Point (240, 344);
this.linkLabel1.Name = "linkLabel1";
this.linkLabel1.Text = "Microsoft\'s Web Site";
this.linkLabel1.LinkClicked += new
System.Windows.Forms.LinkLabelLinkClickedEventHandler
    (this.linkLabel1_LinkClicked);
```

In the `linkLabel1_LinkClicked` event, we add the following code:

```
private void linkLabel1_LinkClicked (object sender,
    System.Windows.Forms.LinkLabelLinkClickedEventArgs e)
{
    // find out which link was clicked
    linkLabel1.Links[linkLabel1.Links.IndexOf (e.Link)].Visited = true;
    System.Diagnostics.Process.Start ("http://www.microsoft.com");
}
```

Now when you click on the hyperlink in the `LinkLabel` control, you will be taken to a new instance of Microsoft Internet Explorer, and the web site for Microsoft will open.

List Boxes, Combo Boxes, Checked List Boxes, and Such

In order to provide users with a list of options from which to choose, we utilize the `ListBox` and its various adaptations—`ComboBox` and `CheckedListBox`. Look at Figure 19-2 to see the difference between the three of them.

The `ListBox` allows a list of data to be presented to the user with a scrollbar on the right side for scrolling through the list.

The `ComboBox` presents a drop-down list of data to the user. Notice that in our example the data is sorted—this is accomplished by setting the `Sorted` property to True. Other properties that can be set on the `ComboBox` include the following:

- `MaxDropDownItems` controls the number of items shown in the drop-down list.

- `DropDownStyle` can be set to Simple, DropDown, or DropDownList (see Figure 19-3).

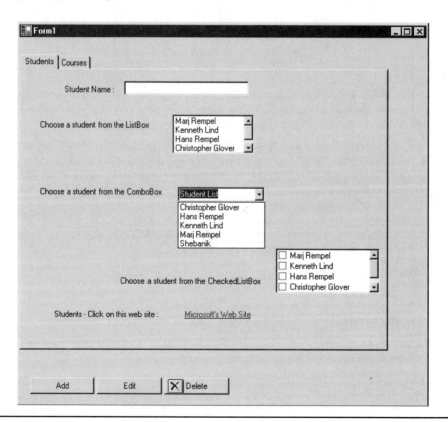

Figure 19-2   Using `ListBox`, `ComboBox`, and `CheckedListBox` controls

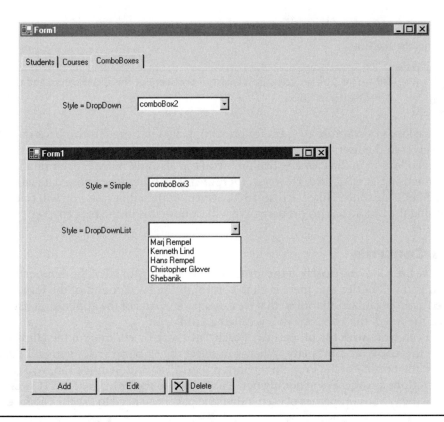

Figure 19-3   Using the `DropDownStyle` settings for a `ComboBox` control

You can see from Figure 19-3 that the `Simple` style presents one item in the box, while both the `DropDownList` and `DropDown` styles allow you to drop down a predefined number of items. The difference between `DropDownList` and `DropDown` has to do with the data itself. `DropDown` style allows the user to type in the top line of the drop-down list and `DropDownList` only lets the user select items that have been displayed.

Here are some important properties of the `ListBox`:

- **MultiColumn**   Permits multiple columns of data to be displayed.

- **SelectionMode**   Allows you to set the maximum number of items that can be selected at a time.

- **SelectedIndex**   Specifies the first selected item by item (or index) number (if no item is selected, this value is 1).

- **Items**   Contains the data that is displayed in the list. `Items` is a collection. The `Count` property will return the number of items in the list. The `Add` property will add items to the list at run time, and the `Remove` property will delete items at run time. `Items.Addrange` allows you to add multiple items to the list box.

 TIP The `Items` collection is also a property of the `ComboBox` and the `CheckedListBox`.

These kinds of controls are great for presenting data retrieved from a back-end database server to the user. In our example, we have simply added to the list by using the `Items` collection in the Property Explorer. You can also add items programmatically at run time using `Items.Add`. However, there are many times when your data will come from an outside source, like Microsoft SQL Server 2000. In that case, you will find yourself using the `DataSource` property. We will explore this in the next chapter.

Tab Controls

If you've been looking closely at the form we've been using for all of the demonstrations so far, you will notice that there is a tab control in the background of the form. It has served as an organization tool so that we can separate parts of the application. Each tab across the top of the `TabControl` is called a `TabPage`.

You can work with the properties of each `TabPage` by clicking on the ellipsis (…) beside the `TabPages` property. When you select the `TabControl`, you will see two links at the bottom of the Properties window—Add Tab and Remove Tab. You can use these buttons as shortcuts to adding new `TabPages` to the `TabControl`. However, to control the various properties of each individual page, you need to use the TabPage Collection Editor, shown next.

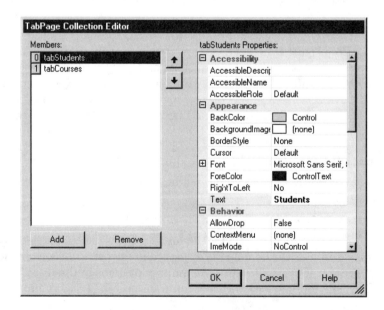

For interest's sake, here are a few tidbits that help when using a `TabControl`.

- **HotTrack**   This property causes the tab page's text to change color as the mouse passes over the tab.
- **SuspendLayout()**   This is really a method of the `Control` class, and it temporarily suspends the layout for the control. You would use this method while you make many adjustments to the layout of a control:

  ```
  tabControl1.SuspendLayout();
  ```

  For example, at some point in your application, you may need to change the `Size` or `Location` properties of a control. Suspend the layout first, make your changes, and when you are finished, you can call this method:

  ```
  tabControl1.ResumeLayout();
  ```

To add a new `TabPage` dynamically to your `TabControl`, follow the example of this code segment:

```
TabPage tpStudentMarks = new TabPage();
tpStudentMarks.Text = "Student Marks";
tpStudentMarks.Size = new System.Drawing.Size (536, 398);
// add code here to insert the controls that will sit on the Tab Page
// For example :
Button b = new Button;
tpStudentMarks.Controls.Add (b);
// Add the new Tab Page to the Tab Control
tcTabControl.Controls.Add (tpStudentMarks);
```

Status Bars

The `StatusBar` control is usually used to display information to the user in an unobtrusive manner. By docking the status bar at the bottom of your application, you can set panels into the bar that will display different information. By default, the `StatusBar` has a single panel (or section for information). By adding panels to the `Panels` collection, you can display more information.

You can access the StatusBarPanel Collection Editor to modify the properties of the panels of the `StatusBar`. You can get to this editor by clicking the ellipsis (…) beside the `Panels` property.

Each panel in a status bar has a zero-based index value, so the first panel has an index value of 0. If we wanted to programmatically change the information in the third panel, we would add the following line of code:

```
this.sbMyStatusBar.Panels[2].Text = "Here is the changed text for the third panel.";
```

 EXAM TIP   If you are adding a status bar to your application, and you are disappointed when you run the program because the panels of the status bar do not show, don't forget to set the `ShowPanels` property to True—its default value is False.

Toolbars

The `ToolBar` control is an area on your window where you can set shortcut buttons for different commands (typically menu options). Figure 19-4 shows a `ToolBar` control on our college application. We have not looked at creating menus yet, so you will see silly buttons on this toolbar. When we work on menus later in this chapter, you will see the true use of a toolbar.

Once the `ToolBar` control is added to your form, you can add buttons to it by clicking on the `Buttons` property and selecting the collection. Use the ToolBarButton Collection Editor in the same fashion as the editors for the `StatusBar` and the `TabPage`. In Figure 19-4, you will notice that there are really four buttons on the toolbar, and each one has a different `Style` property:

- The Canadian flag button is the PushButton style—a typical toolbar button.
- The American flag button is the ToggleButton style, which is either pressed or not pressed.
- The Swedish flag button is the DropDownButton style, which gives extra options when the drop-down arrow is clicked.

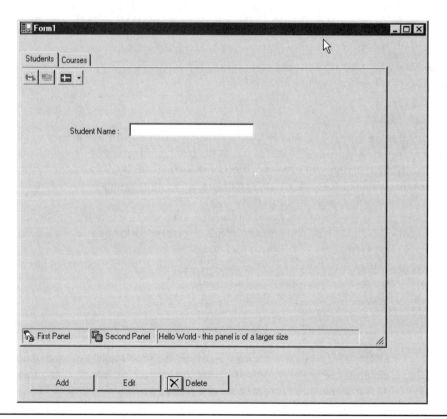

Figure 19-4 Using a `ToolBar` control

- The last button (really the third button) is the one between the American flag and the Swedish flag. It has the style of Separator and acts as a separation point between toolbar buttons.

Notice, as well, that our toolbar has images on each button. This is accomplished by adding the `ImageList` control to your project, and it is simply a holder for images. When you add the control to your application, a little icon appears below the form window (unlike in Visual Studio 6, where the control actually sat on your form, but was invisible at run time). By using the ImageList Collection Editor, you can add any number of images to your application. When you use the images, you reference the ImageList. By using a property named `ImageIndex`, you select from a list of images attached to a particular `ImageList`. The `ImageList` is actually set via the `ImageList` property of the `ToolBar` itself. Once you have set the `ImageList` property, you will have access to all the images associated with the `ImageList`, and you will be able to select them from the ToolBarButton Collection Editor.

We will examine the `ButtonClick` event associated with toolbar buttons later in this chapter when we introduce menus and the handling of menu events.

Dialog Boxes

Using a dialog box is a great way to interact with the user. You may want to simply present some information to the user and wait for a response, but it might also get more complicated than that. In some cases, you will want to ask the user to set common window properties. For example, the user may choose to customize your application by choosing their desired font or colors. This can be accomplished by using the predefined dialog boxes that come with the .NET Framework. In the Visual Studio 6 world, these were called *common dialog boxes* and were part of an ActiveX control. Of course, we are no longer in that world, and the predefined dialog boxes are now class files.

Types of Dialog Boxes

There are many types of dialog boxes available for immediate use, and you can also create your own. In this section, we will explore the prebuilt dialog boxes. Table 19-4 lists the different types and describes their purposes.

The MessageBox   The `MessageBox` control allows the developer to display an informational message and wait for the response. In Figure 19-5, we have adjusted our Courses tab to include a course-selection list box. When the user clicks on any of the items in the list, a message box is displayed as shown in the figure.

The hardest part to creating a message box is determining its look. We used the following code line in the `SelectedIndexChanged` event of the list box, meaning that the box will be displayed as a result of any click within the list box:

```
MessageBox.Show (this, "Sorry, this course if full!", "Course Selection",
        MessageBoxButtons.OKCancel, MessageBoxIcon.Warning);
```

Dialog Box	Purpose
MessageBox	Creates a simple message for the user. Displays a question or message to the user and waits for their response.
ColorDialog	Allows the user to select colors for the application. They can choose from a list of colors or create a custom color.
FontDialog	Allows the user to select a font, the style of the font, and its size, from the fonts that are installed on the computer.
OpenFileDialog	Allows the user to navigate the file system and choose a particular file to open. This is the same dialog box you see when you choose File | Open from a typical Windows menu system.
PageSetupDialog PrintDialog PrintPreviewDialog	Allows the developer to present the standard printer-related dialog boxes. PageSetupDialog presents the dialog box used to specify printer settings. PrintDialog lets the user select a printer and choose the pages to print (exactly as if you chose File | Print from a standard Windows application menu. The PrintPreviewDialog control presents the document on screen as it will look printed.
SaveFileDialog	Allows the user to choose the location for a saved file. This is the dialog box you will see if you select File | Save from a standard Windows application menu.

Table 19-4 .NET Dialog Box Controls

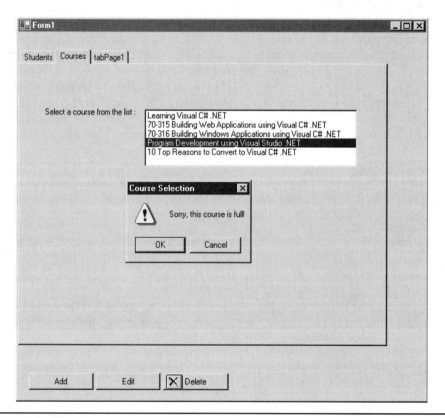

Figure 19-5 Using a MessageBox control

As you can see, there are enumerations that help make the appearance choices for the message box. These include the following:

- **MessageBoxButtons** Select OK, OKCancel, AbortRetryIgnore, RetryCancel, YesNo, or YesNoCancel as the buttons to include on the MessageBox.

- **MessageBoxDefaultButton** Select Button1, Button2, or Button3 as the button to respond to the ENTER key.

- **MessageBoxIcon** In our example, we used the information icon, but you can select from a list of icon choices, including Error, Stop, Warning, and so on.

The Show() method of the MessageBox class is overloaded so that you can display the default message box with only a message and the OK button, or you can create an elaborate box using all of the options.

 NOTE Message boxes are *modal* dialog boxes meaning the user must respond before they will be returned to the rest of the application. Some dialog boxes are modeless, and they will allow the application to continue while the dialog box is running.

You may want to examine the result returned after displaying the message box. The user clicks one of the buttons and your application can deal with the returned value. In order to do this, you make use of the DialogResult class.

```
DialogResult result = MessageBox.Show (this, "Click Yes, No or
    Cancel",,MessageBoxButtons.YesNoCancel);
if (result == DialogResult.Cancel)
{
    // Write your cancellation code here
}
```

The DialogResult enumeration contains named constants (Abort, Cancel, Ignore, OK, Yes, and so on) for comparing against the results of the user clicking one of the option buttons.

Using Dialog Boxes from the CommonDialog Class Aside from the Message Box, all the dialog boxes listed in Table 19-4 are derived from the CommonDialog class, and they all work in approximately the same manner. You use the inherited ShowDialog() method to display the dialog box from your application and the DialogResult class to retrieve the user interaction with the dialog box. As an example, we will use the File | Save dialog box (SaveFileDialog), as shown in Figure 19-6.

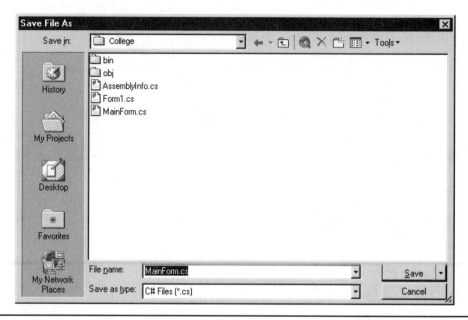

Figure 19-6   The `SaveFileDialog` dialog box

Use the following steps to recreate this section of the application:

1. Add an instance of the `SaveFileDialog` control to your application. The instance will show at the bottom of the white area in the Visual Designer.

2. In the `Click` event of the Save button, add this code:

```
// use the instance of the SaveFileDialog control to set initial properties
saveFileDialog1.InitialDirectory = "c:\\C Progs\\Ch25";
saveFileDialog1.Filter = "C# source files | *.cs";
if (saveFileDialog1.ShowDialog() == DialogResult.OK)
{
    // write your code here
}
```

3. Notice that you can set the initial directory that the Open File dialog box will display. Use the double-slash escape sequence (\ \) to set the directory path. You can also set a filter—in our case, we only want to see C# source files.

4. Run the application and click on the button.

When you click the Save button, the Save File As dialog box is presented. The user can then navigate through the file system and select the file they need saved. The control ensures that the file is saved properly and all error handling is done correctly. For example, if the user tries to save a file in a location where the file already exists, a warning message will appear informing the user that this action will override the existing file.

By making proper use of dialog boxes, you can ensure that your application will retain some consistency between programs. You also save yourself a lot of valuable time by not reinventing the wheel (or, in this case, the dialog box).

Working with Controls at Run Time

Although it is very easy to add controls to your application at design time by making use of the Windows Forms Designer, it is imperative to understand how to add controls at run time. Very often, you will need to create a control on the fly, in response to the circumstances during the running of your application. We will look at the `ControlsCollection` and talk about the `Controls` property, which let you do this.

 EXAM TIP   Microsoft will not likely ask you to add controls at design time using a visual editor—you will need to know the properties and events that we have just covered in this chapter. However, it is a good idea to have a firm grasp on adding controls at run time, since there will be direct questions on adding controls in this fashion.

The Collection Object

All the controls on a Windows Form (or in a container control like the `Panel`) are part of a collection object. The object itself is of type `ControlCollection`. The `ControlCollection` object represents a collection of control objects—buttons, list boxes, and so on. You can access the controls by using the `Controls` property.

The following list demonstrates some of the capabilities of the collection object:

- You can add or remove controls from the collection.
- You can iterate through the collection by using the `GetEnumerator()` method.
- By calling the `Contains()` method, you can check whether a particular control is part of the collection.
- You can use the `Count` property to return the number of controls in the collection.

To test whether a particular control is part of the collection, try the following example code:

```
if (form1.Controls.Contains (btnClickMe))
{
    MessageBox.Show("We found the button");
}
```

You can also clear the full collection by using this line:

```
form1.Controls.Clear();
```

Any control that acts as a container has the `Controls` collection. If we wanted to clear the controls from a `TabPage`, we would code this line:

```
tabPage1.Controls.Clear();
```

Adding a Control at Run Time

We are able to create a customized version of our application by allowing users to add and remove controls at run time. By adding the following code section to our college application, teachers can access a few more controls than students can. In Figure 19-7, we have added a button that, when clicked, displays a text box on the tab page asking for a password. The text box is not part of the form until someone clicks on the If You

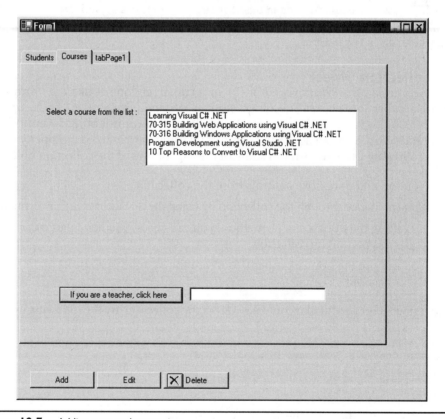

Figure 19-7   Adding a control at run time

Are a Teacher, Click Here button. Once the password is validated, we can then add more functionality via extra controls for a teacher.

The new code looks like this:

```
private void btnTeacher_Click (object sender, System.EventArgs e)
{
    TextBox t = new TextBox();
    t.Text = "Enter your password ";
    t.Width = 200;
    t.Left = 250;
    t.Top = 320;
    tabCourses.Controls.Add (t);
}
```

This code section will add the new control to the `Controls` collection on the tab page—the next step is, of course, to add the extra functionality.

This section has introduced the typical controls with which any Windows programmer will work. Experiment with each one of them—Microsoft expects you to have a full understanding of their functionality.

Working with Menus

Now that we've discussed all the common controls, it's time to move into another big arena for visual presentation of your application. Nearly every Windows Forms program has a menu attached to it—menus give the user a list of options that are available within the application. There are two types of menus in the .NET world—the regular menu that you see attached to the top of any application window, and the menu that appears when you right-click on something. The first type is a `MainMenu`, while the right-click menu is a `ContextMenu`. We will start this section of the chapter by looking at the `MainMenu` object and then conclude the section discussing the `ContextMenu`.

Creating a Main Menu

To our college application, we have added a menu system that contains the standard menus (File, Edit, and Help) as well as an application-specific menu, Students (see Figure 19-8). Creating a menu system from the Visual Designer is very simple.

Building a menu is as easy as adding an instance of the `MainMenu` control to the application. Like the `ImageList` control, it is not added directly to the form, but rather sits at the bottom of the IDE screen.

Once an instance of the control becomes part of your application, you will be presented with the first menu item and a prompt to "Type here." We have added items down to the Exit on the File menu and across to the Help menu, as is shown in Figure 19-8. The menu control leaves open space for us to add to the menu system at any time.

Some special considerations should be taken into account when working with menus:

- To create a menu separator, such as the one between Close and Page Setup in Figure 19-8, type a hyphen (-) in the "Type here" prompt. This will insert the separator, which is really a separate menu item.

- If you want to create submenus, simply type in the "Type here" area that is displayed to the right of the current area. The control will add the appropriate arrows to indicate a submenu.

- The MainMenu is made up of MenuItem children objects. The hierarchy is then created between parent and child objects.

- You can create menu item shortcuts by adding an ampersand (&) to the text of the menu item. Notice in Figure 19-9 that by placing the ampersand in front of a character, that character becomes the shortcut character. The user can then invoke that menu item by pressing a combination of ALT and the shortcut character.

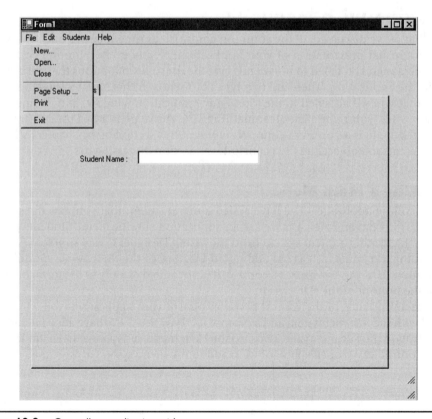

Figure 19-8   Our college application with menus

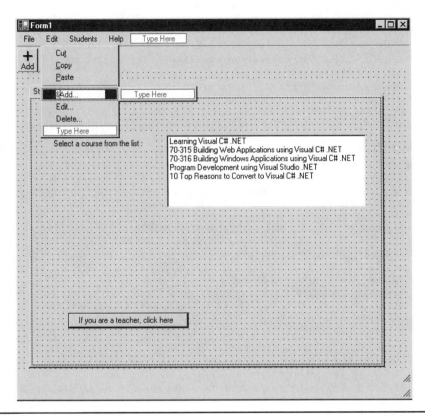

Figure 19-9   Creating a shortcut character

By selecting the MainMenu from your form, you can examine the properties of each MenuItem object. You can set options such as these:

- **Checked**   Displays the menu item with a check mark in front of it.
- **DefaultItem**   Specifies the menu item as the default.
- **Enabled**   Grays out the menu item and makes it inaccessible.
- **RadioCheck**   Does the same as Checked only with a radio button.
- **Shortcut and ShowShortcut**   Deals with the shortcut keys, such as function keys and combinations of function and SHIFT, ALT, CTRL, and so on.
- **Text**   Specifies the actual text of the menu item.

Looking at the Code of a Main Menu

Although the convenience of the Visual Designer abstracts a lot of the coding from us, it is important that we examine the "behind the scenes" coding. We can't just ignore the programming part of this assignment. The following code segments show you just how much work is done for you by the Visual Designer. By acquainting yourself with the coding of menus, you will be able to dynamically add menus to your application.

Each object is declared in the declaration section of the `Form` class:

```
private System.Windows.Forms.MainMenu mainMenu1;
private System.Windows.Forms.MenuItem menuItem1;
// and so on for each menu item
// Please be sure to use more meaningful names in your applications.
```

The next step is to construct each of these objects. This happens in the method: `InitializeComponent()`.

```
this.mainMenu1 = new System.Windows.Forms.MainMenu();
this.menuItem1 = new System.Windows.Forms.MenuItem();
// and so on for each menu item
// did we mention that the names should be changed?
```

The properties are then set for each object:

```
// this is the parent object  mainMenu1
// the code below identifies the top-level menu items that belong to this parent
this.mainMenu1.MenuItems.AddRange (new System.Windows.Forms.MenuItem[] {
    this.menuItem1,
    this.menuItem10,
    this.menuItem18,
    this.menuItem24)};
// menuItem1 becomes the parent for all of the menu items under it
this.menuItem1.Index = 0;
this.menuItem1.MenuItems.AddRange (new System.Windows.Forms.MenuItem[] {
    this.menuItem2,
    this.menuItem3,
    // etc for each menu item that is a child of menuItem1
// and so on until we reach the properties of each individual child menu item
this.menuItem1.Text = "File";
// etc for each one
```

We have just looked at a very standard Windows Forms menu, but you may have need of a menu that spans from the right of the document to the left. In that case, add the following code to the `MainMenu` object:

```
MainMenu1.RightToLeft = RightToLeft.Yes;
```

Handling Menu Events

When you double-click on the menu item that you have added to your form, you will be taken to the code view window and placed inside the `menuItemxx_Click` event. The Visual Designer will add the necessary subscription to the event handler, as follows:

```
this.menuItemxx.Click += new System.EventHandler (this.menuItemxx_Click);
```

You could also change this subscription as follows:

```
this.menuItemxx.Click += new System.EventHandler (<methodname>);
```

In this case, the <methodname> is a method call instead of a reference to a click event. There are many reasons to do it this way, but perhaps the most compelling reason is that there may be different ways of calling that menu item, and they can all make the call to <methodname>. For example, you may have a toolbar on your form that has a button that will produce the same effect as clicking on a particular menu item. Both the menu item and the toolbar button will call the same method.

Context Menus

You know the menus that pop up whenever you right-click on a form? These are called context menus—so called because they respond to the context of the item that is in the foreground. The control that is used to create a context menu is ContextMenu. At design time, you can add a context menu to your form from the toolbox. It is a control that does not reside on the form, similar to a MainMenu. Once the context menu is added to the application, you can set the property of the control to which you wish to associate the context menu. Figure 19-10 illustrates the instance of a context menu added to our project (at the bottom of the screen) and the ContextMenu property of the TextBox set to that instance.

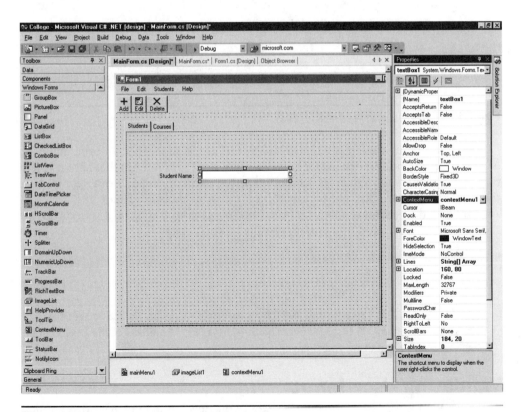

Figure 19-10   A context menu attached to a text box

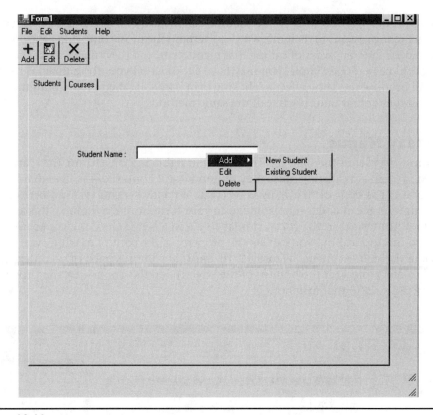

Figure 19-11   Using a context menu

The actual menu items are built much as a `MenuItem` is added to your form. At the top of your form will be a `ContextMenu` instance (invisible at run time) that allows you to type in the menu items. When we run our revised application, the user can right-click on the Student Name text box and see our context menu, as shown in Figure 19-11.

You can add a context menu at run time by adding `MenuItem` objects to the `ContextMenu` collection of menu items called `MenuItems`.

```
MenuItem menuNewItem = new MenuItem();
menuNewItem.Text = "&Window";
contextMenu1.MenuItems.Add (menuNewItem);
```

EXAM TIP   New to the .NET Framework is the ability to add images to menu items. You simply override the `OnPaint()` method of the `MenuItem` object and draw your image.

Validating User Input

Although good form design is very important to the development of Windows applications, it is just as important to pay attention to the data that the user is entering. There are many techniques for validating the information supplied by users of your application. We will discuss two of the methods:

- Using the `Validating` event of a control
- Using the `ErrorProvider` control

Of course, you should also investigate ways of using .NET controls that are designed to restrict user input. But that's another story for another book. We will deal with the two methods that you are likely to encounter on the Microsoft exam.

Validating Events

Certain controls cause a validating event to fire when they are exited. For example, as a user moves from text box to text box on a form, the validating event can be used to ensure that the user has entered correct data.

We have added an extra text box to our Students tab page (see Figure 19-12). A shortcut, when using the Visual Designer, to register a new event with a handler is to click the lightning bolt (for events) in the Properties Explorer.

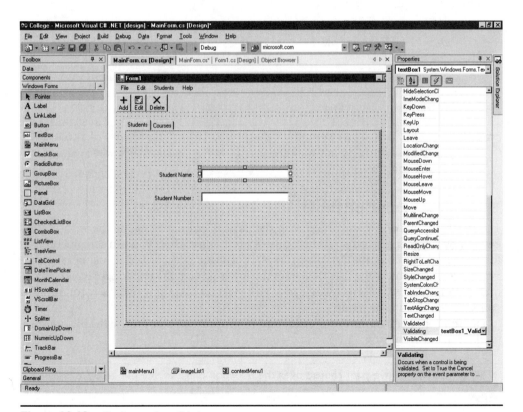

Figure 19-12   Setting up the validating event

A list of that control's events is presented (see Figure 19-12) and by double-clicking on the event, the code is added to your program. We double-clicked on the Validating event, and the Visual Designer added the following code:

```
this.textBox1.Validating += new System.ComponentModel.CancelEventHandler (
    this.textBox1_Validating);
```

A Validating event method is also added to the code:

```
private void textBox1_Validating (object sender,
System.ComponentModel.CancelEventArgs e)
{
    // place your validation code here
}
```

Inside the method, you can add code that will test the value entered by the user and set the Cancel property of the CancelEventArgs object to True if the data is not valid. This has the effect of eliminating the tab or click to the next control and gives you an opportunity to present an error message to the user. The user will then have to correct the data and try to move off the control again. Validation will continue to happen until your method is successfully completed.

Here is an example of validation code:

```
{
    if ( // validation test here)
    {
        e.Cancel = true;
        MessageBox.Show ("Invalid data!");
    }
}
```

 EXAM TIP You can set the CausesValidation property of a control to False if you do not want the Validation event to fire when exiting the control.

ErrorProvider Control

The ErrorProvider control lets you display an error message if the information entered by the user is in error. By using the ErrorProvider, you can set an icon next to the control that contains the data in error. This is more desirable than using a message box, because as soon as the user dismisses the message box, they no longer have a record of the error. A "message" created with the ErrorProvider stays on the form until the correction to the data is made.

Figure 19-13 demonstrates our validation of the first text box. Notice the big question mark beside the text box. The ErrorProvider has placed it there.

 TIP Move your mouse over the question mark to see the error message.

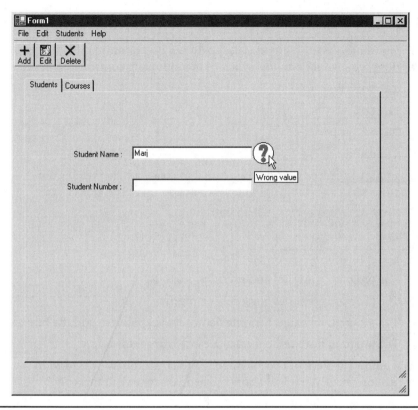

Figure 19-13   Using the `ErrorProvider` control

Summary

We've come a long way in this chapter. By using all the different controls available in the Toolbox, we have been able to create visually pleasing and very functional Windows Forms applications. It warrants mentioning again that you should be very comfortable with all of the concepts in this chapter. Microsoft assumes you are extremely proficient at using the basic controls, creating menus, and working with error validation. On the CD that comes with this book, you can review the entire code for our college project.

In the next chapter, we will work with back-end SQL Server data and continue to build upon our college application. We will access student and course information from the database and demonstrate how to access the data and how to present it. The next chapter is a very significant one for the Microsoft exams. You will find that they like to test you on your data-access knowledge. So once you've tried the following test questions, fasten your seat belts and join us on a data exploration.

Test Questions

1. If you want to ask the user to select between two or more mutually exclusive options, you would employ which of the following controls?

   A. TabControl

   B. Button

   C. RadioButton

   D. CheckBox

2. The following piece of code is intended to create a new TabPage in a TabControl. What will happen when you try to run this code?

```
TabPage tpMyNewTabPage = new TabPage();
tpMyNewTabPage.Caption = "Add Students";
tpMyNewTabPage.Size = new System.Drawing.Size (536, 398);
Button b = new Button();
tpMyNewTabPage.Controls.Add (b);
```

   A. The program compiles and executes properly.

   B. The program compiles and causes a runtime error.

   C. The program does not compile because it is unable to add the button.

   D. The program does not compile because of a syntax error.

3. The following piece of code is intended to create a new TabPage in a TabControl. What will happen when you try to run this code?

```
TabPage tpMyNewTabPage = new TabPage();
tpMyNewTabPage.Text = "Add Students";
tpMyNewTabPage.Size = new System.Drawing.Size (536, 398);
Button b = new Button();
tpMyNewTabPage.Controls.Add (b);
```

   A. The program compiles and executes properly.

   B. The program compiles but the tab page does not show.

   C. The program compiles and causes a runtime error.

   D. The program does not compile because of a syntax error.

4. You want to validate the user input that is retrieved in a text box. Which control will assist you in displaying the error message without moving off the form?

   A. RichTextBox

   B. NotifyIcon

   C. HelpProvider

   D. ErrorProvider

5. You want to validate the user input that is retrieved in a text box. Which event will assist you in the validation of the data?

   A. `UponValidation`

   B. `Validation`

   C. `Validating`

   D. `OnValidation`

6. Which of the following lines of code will produce a message box for the user?

   A. `MessageDialogBox.Show ("This is your message");`

   B. `MessageDialogBox.Show ("Message", "This is your message");`

   C. `MessageBox.Show ("This is your message);`

   D. `MessageBox.Show ("Message", "This is your message");`

7. To dynamically add a context menu to your application, which section of code should be used?

   A. `MenuItem m = new MenuItem();`
      `contextMenu1.MenuItems.Add (m);`

   B. `MenuItem m = new MenuItem();`
      `contextMenu1.MenuItem.Add (m);`

   C. `MainMenu m = new MainMenu();`
      `contextMenu1.MenuItems.Add (m);`

   D. `MainMenu m = new MainMenu();`
      `contextMenu1.MenuItem.Add (m);`

8. To produce a dialog box similar to the Windows Print dialog box, which of the following controls would you use?

   A. `PrintPreviewDialog`

   B. `PrintDialog`

   C. `PrintBox`

   D. `SetupPrintDialog`

9. Which property of the `CheckedListBox` allows you to preset the maximum number of items that can be selected?

   A. `MaxItems`

   B. `MaximumItems`

   C. `SelectionItems`

   D. `SelectionMode`

10. What is wrong with the following piece of code? Assume no other code has been written and you are creating the status bar dynamically.

```
this.sbMyStatusBar.Panels[1].Text = "Panel 1";
this.sbMyStatusBar.Panels[2].Text = "Panel 2";
this.sbMyStatusBar.Panels[3].Text = "Panel 3";
```

A. Nothing is wrong with the code.

B. It will cause a runtime error.

C. There will be a syntax error found.

D. The `Text` property is incorrect for a `StatusBar`.

11. Which line of code must be added in order to show a `StatusBar`?

A. `sbMyStatusBar.Show();`

B. `sbMyStatusBar.Display();`

C. `sbMyStatusBar.Show = true;`

D. `sbMyStatusBar.Display = true;`

12. Which line of code will set the `Link` data for a `LinkLabel`?

A. `this.linkLabel1.Text = "http:\\www.microsoft.com";`

B. `this.linkLabel1.Link = "http://www.microsoft.com";`

C. `this.linkLabel1.HyperLink = "http://www.microsoft.com';`

D. None of the above.

13. Which segment of code will set the selected text in a `RichTextBox` to bold?

A. `myFont = new Font (oldFont, Font.Bold = Bold);`
   `this.rtfTest1.SelectionFont = myFont;`

B. `myFont = new Font (oldFont, FontStyle.Bold);`
   `this.rtfTest1.SelectionFont = myFont;`

C. `myFont = new Font (oldFont, FontStyle.Bold);`
   `this.rtfTest1.SelectedText = myFont;`

D. `myFont = new Font (oldFont, Font.Bold);`
   `this.rtfTest1.SelectedText = myFont;`

14. Which property will allow the user to enter more than one line in a text box?

A. `MaxLines`

B. `MultipleLines`

C. `MultiLines`

D. `MultiLine`

15. Which control would you use to group a lot of controls together?

    A. GroupControl

    B. GroupBox

    C. FrameControl

    D. FrameBox

Test Answers

1. C.

2. D. The syntax error is in the Caption property of the TabPage—it should be the Text property.

3. B. You must add the tab page to the Controls collection of the tab control.

4. D. The ErrorProvider will place the error message next to the text box.

5. C. The Validating event allows you to validate the user input.

6. C.

7. A. The collection is called MenuItems, and you must create MenuItem objects.

8. B.

9. D.

10. B. A runtime error will occur since the Panel collection of the StatusBar is zero-based.

11. C. Show is a property, not a method.

12. D. None of the above. You must use this line of code:

```
System.Diagnostics.Process.Start ("http://www.microsoft.com");
```

13. B. The property is SelectionFont, and the Font constructor takes FontStyle.Bold.

14. D.

15. B.

20

Data in Windows Forms

In this chapter, you will
- Learn to bind data to the user interface
- Get acquainted with displaying and updating data
- Discover how to transform and filter data
- Access and manipulate data from a Microsoft SQL Server database
- Be introduced to handling data errors

This chapter deals with the data-specific portions of the C# Windows exam and assumes a good working knowledge of the information in Chapter 10. If you have not had a chance to review Chapter 10, which presented the concepts of the ADO.NET object model, now would be a good time. You will also find information pertinent to both the Windows and the web exam in Chapter 10. In order to prepare you for the C# Windows exam, we will now take those concepts and apply them to Windows Forms. We will access data from Microsoft SQL Server 2000 using our college application introduced in the last two chapters.

In the past, Microsoft has tended to test heavily on the data side, and you can expect no less on the .NET exams. We will focus on two data-access techniques. The first takes advantage of the Visual Studio .NET support for accessing data—you will find a number of ADO.NET objects in the Toolbox that can be added to your form in order to assist with data access. The second technique involves coding using the ADO.NET object model—using objects such as `Connection`, `Command`, `DataSet`, and so on. These objects were introduced in Chapter 10, and we will use them in our Windows Form in this chapter.

Review of ADO.NET Object Model

There are two main components in data access—data consumers, such as a Windows Form or a Web Form, and data providers, such as a `DataAdapter` or a `DataReader`. A data consumer will request data from a data provider (such as Microsoft SQL Server). Table 20-1 describes the major objects that provide data to a data consumer.

Object	Description
Connection	Represents a physical connection to a specified data source. After providing the necessary properties for the data provider (data source, database, login credentials, and so on), you can then use the open and close connection methods of the Connection object to establish the connection. You can also manage transactions using the Connection object. Review Chapter 10 for information on database transactions.
Command	Creates the command that is executed on the data source. This includes SQL SELECT statements or stored procedures (which are sets of instructions found at the data source).
DataAdapter	Populates a data set and restores updates with the data source. Essentially, this object provides the link between a Connection object and the resulting data set.
DataReader	Reads a forward-only, read-only stream of data from a data source.
DataSet	Represents a "disconnected" set of data. Data can be read from multiple sources (or from a single source) and represented offline as a DataSet. A DataSet is unaware of the source of the data and, in effect, is an in-memory representation of the selected data.

Table 20-1   Common Data Objects

EXAM TIP   Commit the objects in Table 20-1 to memory. You will be tested on your knowledge of each of these objects.

There are a number of classes that assist with data representation, and they are independent of the source of the data (whether it be SQL Server, Oracle, or something else). These classes include DataRow and DataColumn, which as their names imply, represent rows and columns from a table (or spreadsheet), respectively. There is also a DataTable class, which represents the collection of row and column data, and a DataRelation class, which acts as a link between two DataTable objects. You can consider a DataTable to be a collection of DataRow objects, and a DataRelation to be the foreign-key representation between two DataTable objects.

EXAM TIP   Be sure that you understand the source-specific classes for setting up the connection to your data. These include SqlCommand and SqlConnection for specifying the SQL statements or stored procedures and the connection parameters when accessing Microsoft SQL Server 7.0 (and higher) databases. In order to connect to an OLE/DB provider other than Microsoft SQL Server 7.0 (and higher), you would use OleDbCommand and OleDbConnection. The classes specific to these two types of data stores are included in the ADO.NET object model. If you wish to access data providers other than these types, you must download the ODBC classes from Microsoft.

Accessing Data Using Visual Studio .NET

In this chapter we will present data-access concepts and applications using data retrieved from a Microsoft SQL Server, but you should keep in mind that Visual C# and, in particular, the .NET Framework, allows you to access data from any source. Sources include Microsoft SQL Server, Microsoft Access, Oracle databases, flat files, and so on. That data can then, in turn, be bound to objects found in ADO.NET, such as a `DataSet`. The data can be bound to any number of controls that support a data source property. It can also be bound to arrays and collections.

The Visual Studio .NET interface includes many built-in controls that allow you to create a link to a data source and then bind controls to the data retrieved from that source. In this section, we will look at those controls and work with them to present a Windows Form that contains data from our SQL Server database—*College*.

The College Application

Our college application was developed in the last two chapters and will be expanded to include a visual presentation of the data found in our database. Figure 20-1 shows the schematic of the College database, which includes three tables—Student, Program, and Course.

The Student table includes information about the students in our sample college, including the program in which they are enrolled. The program is linked to the Program table for a description and to the Course table for the list of courses that a student must take to complete the program. Using this simple database, we will be able to demonstrate the capabilities of data access, along with some relational aspects.

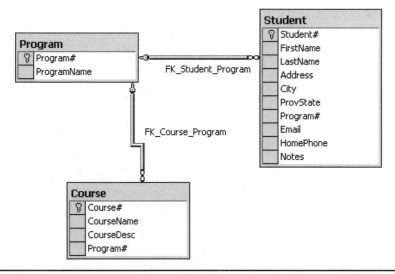

Figure 20-1   The College database

PART IV

At the end of this chapter, you will have a workable model of this application using programmatic access to data. However, for the purposes of this section of the chapter, we will deal with the built-in controls that provide "wizard-like" assistance when connecting to the database and presenting the resulting data. You should keep in mind that, while this technique is quite powerful and certainly reduces the amount of time necessary to build easy applications, a lot of data-driven applications are created by coding the data access directly, without the benefit of prebuilt controls or visual components. In the "Accessing Data Programmatically" section of this chapter, we will work with the classes in ADO.NET programmatically and bind the controls on our Windows Form to data.

ADO.NET Objects in Visual Studio .NET

Let's start by examining the Toolbox in Visual Studio .NET. You will notice in Figure 20-2 that there are many different objects that will provide assistance when retrieving data from a data source. In order to get access to this Toolbox, click on the Data tab.

Figure 20-2
The ADO.NET
Toolbox

Double-click on the `SqlDataAdapter`, which opens the Data Adapter Configuration Wizard. You will be presented with the Welcome screen, which is the first page of the wizard. The wizard allows you to graphically specify the connection information—database server, database name, authentication data, and so on. You start by selecting either a preconfigured or new connection as shown in Figure 20-3. For this example, click the New Connection button.

The next wizard screen asks you to configure the data link properties (see Figure 20-4). Select the appropriate server name from the drop-down list, provide the needed logon credentials, and choose the database from the list. Notice that the database list will not appear if either the server or the credentials are incorrect.

TIP Be sure to test the connection. The wizard provides you with a Test Connection button that will ensure that a connection can be made to the database server.

You also have an opportunity to change the provider using the Provider tab of the Data Link Properties window (see Figure 20-5). Take a moment to investigate the different data providers offered by default within Visual Studio .NET. Should you have need of any other data providers, you will have to download it from either Microsoft's web site or the vendor's web site.

PART IV

Figure 20-3
Choose your
data connection

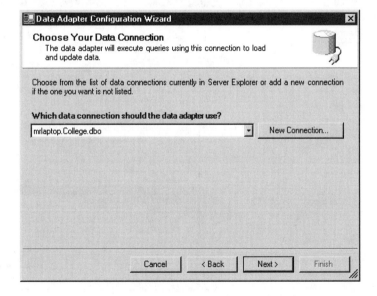

Figure 20-4
Set the data link
properties

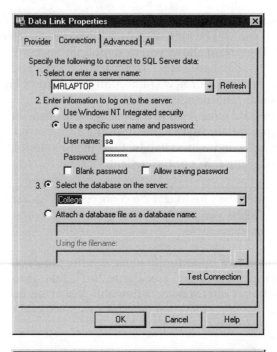

Figure 20-5
Set a data
provider

Once you have finished setting the data link properties, click Next in the Provider tab. The Choose a Query Type wizard window will be displayed (see Figure 20-6). You can choose from the following options:

- **Use SQL statements** These are SQL statements that you code yourself, and they could be `SELECT`, `UPDATE`, `DELETE`, or `INSERT` statements.

- **Create new stored procedures** This lets you create your own stored procedures.

- **Use existing stored procedures** This allows you to use stored procedures that already reside on the database server.

For this example, choose to use your own SQL statements. Click the Next button, and the wizard will ask you to type in the SQL statement (see Figure 20-7). You have three choices when presented with this wizard window:

- Simply type your SQL statement in the box provided.

- Use the Query Builder which is a wizard-like interface for SQL assistance.

- Go to the Advanced Options (see Figure 20-8) to have `UPDATE`, `DELETE`, and `INSERT` statements automatically generated, based on your `SELECT` statement.

EXAM TIP You should be very comfortable with the standard SQL statements. Review Chapter 10 for `SELECT`, `UPDATE`, `DELETE`, and `INSERT` statements.

Figure 20-6

Choose a
query type

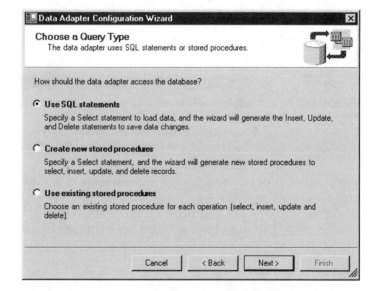

Figure 20-7

Generate your
SQL statements

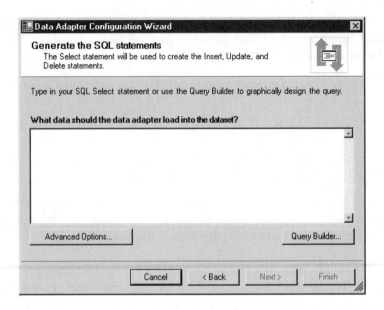

For the purposes of this example, turn off the automatic generation of SQL statements offered in the Advanced options by unchecking the Generate Insert, Update, and
Delete Statements check box.

If you select the Query Builder, the Add Table dialog box opens (see Figure 20-9), displaying a list of the tables contained in the database that was specified in the Data Link
Properties dialog box. Select the tables you wish to add (for this example, choose the
Student table), and the Query Builder will provide you with a graphical interface for
completing your SQL statements, as shown in Figure 20-10. The tables you add can then
be used in any query string that you build through the Query Builder.

Figure 20-8

The advanced
options

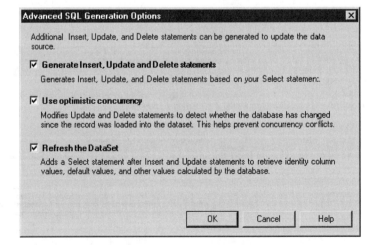

Figure 20-9
The Add Table
dialog box

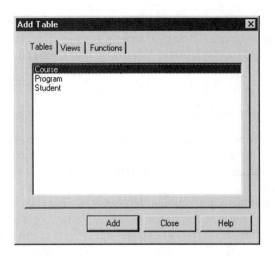

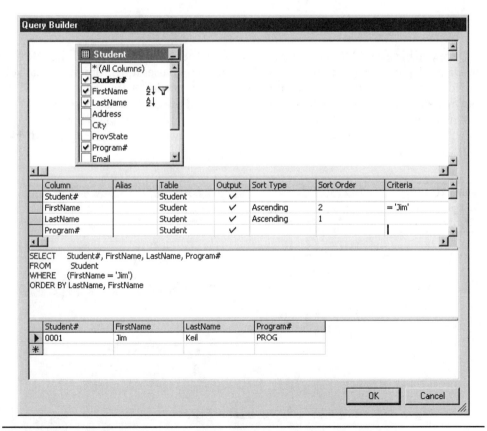

Figure 20-10 The Query Builder

Notice in Figure 20-10 that the Student table columns are listed in the top pane, and you can choose to use all the columns or just specific columns from that pane by checking the appropriate check boxes. When you make your choices (for this example, choose Student#, FirstName, LastName, and Program#), the SQL statement in the third pane down reflects your choice, and in this case displays the following statement:

```
SELECT Student#, FirstName, LastName, Program# FROM Student
```

You can also specify the sort order and selection criteria in the second pane.

To test the command, right-click in the bottom pane and select Run. The command will be run against the connection to the database, and the results will be shown in the bottom pane.

In this example (shown in Figure 20-10), we have asked that LastName be sorted ascending, then FirstName sorted within LastName. We also specified that the FirstName must be equal to 'Jim'. As you can see in the figure, this command returned only one record where the first name is 'Jim'. The corresponding SQL statement has been generated for us:

```
SELECT Student#, FirstName, LastName, Program# FROM Student
    WHERE  (FirstName = 'Jim') ORDER BY LastName, FirstName
```

Once you have tested the command, click OK in the Query Builder, and click Next in the Data Adapter Configuration Wizard. The wizard then uses the information that you provided to generate the desired command and connection statements. You will be shown a window that verifies the success or failure of the exercise (see Figure 20-11).

When you are satisfied with the results, click Finish. You will be returned to your form. Notice in Figure 20-12 that the form now has two objects associated with it—sqlDataAdapter1 and sqlConnection1.

Figure 20-11

Configuration Wizard results

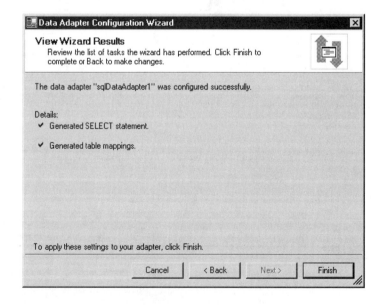

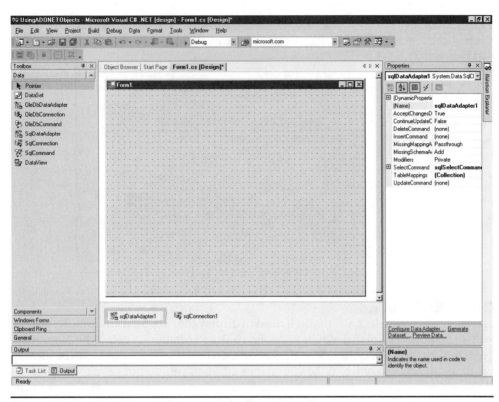

Figure 20-12   The form with the data adapter and connection

You have now created two objects that represent the execution instructions and the physical connection to the data store. The next step is to create an object that will represent the data—a `DataSet`. There are two ways to accomplish this:

- Select Data | Generate Dataset from the menus.
- Right-click on the `sqlDataAdapter1` object and select Generate Dataset.

In either case the Generate Dataset dialog box will be displayed (see Figure 20-13). You can select either an existing dataset or create a new object. For this example, choose a new `DataSet` object and call it `dsStudent` to represent the table from which the data is retrieved. The new `DataSet` object (`dsStudent1`) is created and added to the form along with the `DataAdapter` and `Connection` objects (at the bottom of the screen).

EXAM TIP   To summarize, you use an *xxx*`DataAdapter` (where *xxx* represents SQL or OLE), which encapsulates `Connection`, `Command`, and `DataReader` objects in order to populate a `DataSet`. The `DataSet` is then used to represent the rows and columns (or a table) from the database. Using the `DataAdapter`, you can update the data source through the `DataSet`.

Figure 20-13
Creating a
new DataSet
object

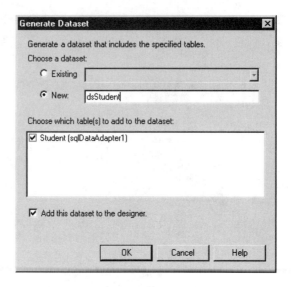

Using the DataGrid
================

Now that you have a DataSet, you'll need to display the data on your form. To do this, we'll start with a control that is built to display rows and columns of data—the DataGrid. From the Toolbox, select the DataGrid and drag it onto the form. Figure 20-14 shows a runtime DataGrid control filled with data. Although you do not need to be aware of the power of the DataGrid control for the Microsoft exams, you should take some time to explore its properties, methods, and events in order to fully appreciate it.

 NOTE Your output may not look exactly like Figure 20-14. As a matter of fact, unless you have read ahead, you will notice that you have no data from the database displayed. You must manually put data into the DataSet using the Fill method of the DataAdapter. We will cover this in the next section.

Figure 20-14
The DataGrid
control

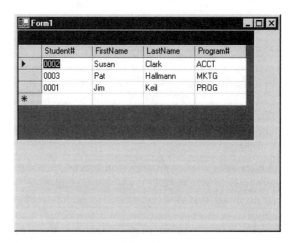

You can set two properties for the DataGrid control in order to have it display data. The first property is the DataSource, which specifies the DataSet object that represents the retrieved data. The second property is the DataMember, which can be used to specify the single table relationship. If a DataSource represents a DataSet created by combining multiple tables, the DataMember must specify the table to which the DataGrid is bound.

 EXAM TIP Be sure to know the difference between the DataSource and DataMember properties.

There are a few important characteristics of a DataGrid control that you should know about. The first is that in order to format the display of data in a manner other than the default display shown in Figure 20-14, you need to work with the properties of the DataGrid, such as GridLineStyle, which can be set to Solid (the default) or None. This can be done programmatically by creating a DataGridTableStyle object and setting its properties to the display you need:

```
DataGridTableStyle myStyle = new DataGridTableStyle();
myStyle.GridLineStyle = DataGridLineStyel.None;
```

You can set the column style by using the DataGrid properties, or programmatically by using a DataGridTextBoxColumn object:

```
DataGridTextBoxColumn myColumns = new DataGridTextBoxColumn();
myColumns.Width = 100;
```

You can also set properties such as Width, Alignment, HeaderText, and so on. Once the desired properties have been set, you can then add the DataGridTextBoxColumn to the GridColumnStyles collection as follows:

```
myStyle.GridColumnStyles.Add (myColumns);
```

Finally, you'll need to add the table style to the data grid:

```
dataGrid1.TableStyles.Add (myStyle);
```

You can also use the AutoFormat tool to select a preset format for your DataGrid. Right-click on the DataGrid on your form, and select AutoFormat. Figure 20-15 shows the Auto Format dialog box that appears.

The DataGrid control can also be used to show the relationship between two related tables. Here's what you would do:

1. Create a DataSet that represents the related tables.

2. Add a DataControl for each related table to your form.

3. Create a DataRelation object that will represent the relationship between the tables. Tie the tables together by setting the relationship properties (table, column, and so on).

PART IV

Figure 20-15

The Auto Format dialog box

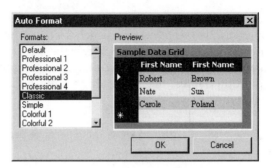

4. Using the `DataSet` object's `Relation` collection, add the `DataRelation`.

5. Bind the grids to the `DataSet` (use the `SetDataBinding()` method of the `DataGrid`).

If you wish to experiment with this process using the `DataGrid`, follow the preceding steps. We will explore table relationships later in this chapter, and we'll look at how to relate them programmatically.

Loading the Data

If you have been following along and creating the sample application in this chapter, you are probably disappointed that your data does not show on the form as it did in Figure 20-14. This is because you still have to manually load the data. This may be new to you (particularly if you have programmed under any earlier ADO object models). ADO.NET does not assume that there is a full-time connection to the data store. In order to retrieve your data, you must manually load the data into the `DataSet`.

 EXAM TIP To manually load data, you use the `Fill()` method of the `DataAdapter`.

To produce the output that you saw in Figure 20-14 you need to load the data into the `DataSet` by using the `DataAdapter`. Where in the application you do this is an important consideration. You don't want to do it too early, because you will be wasting resources before they are actually needed, and you don't want to do it too late, because the process may take some time. Take time to determine the appropriate time to access the actual data.

For the purpose of demonstration only, we will add the following code to the load event of the form:

```
private void Form1_Load(object sender, System.EventArgs e)
{
    sqlDataAdapter1.Fill(dsStudent1);
}
```

Now when you run this application, you will see the actual data retrieved and displayed on your form (as in Figure 20-14).

Using Stored Procedures

The C# Windows exam has as one of its objectives, "Access and manipulate data from a Microsoft SQL Server database by creating and using ad hoc queries and stored procedures." We have covered the ad hoc queries using ADO.NET objects in Visual Studio. Let's take time now to look at using stored procedures, which are bits of executable code that reside on the database server itself. If you need a review of the purpose and intent of using stored procedures, please refer back to Chapter 10.

When you add the xxxDataAdapter to your form (as described earlier in the "ADO.NET Objects in Visual Studio .NET" section), you are taken into the Data Adapter Configuration Wizard. The third screen (shown earlier in Figure 20-6) asks whether you will be creating the SQL code or using stored procedures. For this example, we will take you through the steps of creating a new stored procedure; however, by selecting Use Existing Stored Procedures in that window, you can access code that has been created in advance and stored on the database server.

To create a new stored procedure, select the Create New Stored Procedures option and click Next. You will be taken through the steps of building a query as we saw in the "ADO.NET Objects in Visual Studio .NET" section (Figures 20-9 and 20-10). Once your SQL statements are created, you will be taken to the Create the Stored Procedures screen (Figure 20-16).

Figure 20-16
The Create the Stored Procedures screen of the Data Adapter Configuration Wizard

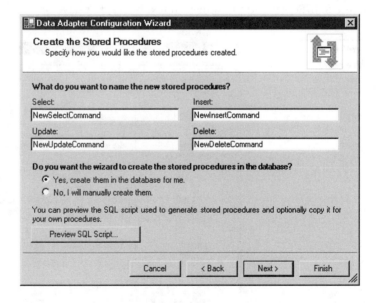

As you can see from the figure, you have several choices. You should give meaningful names to the different SQL statements (SELECT, UPDATE, DELETE, INSERT). You can also ask that the wizard create the stored procedure for you, or you can specify that you will create it yourself. By clicking the Preview SQL Script button, you can see the procedure that has been created (see Figure 20-17).

Once you accept your code, you will see the wizard's Finish window, and your data adapter will have been made a stored procedure instead of it being an on the fly or ad hoc query.

What's Next?

So far we have spent very little time coding. Although this is a very attractive feature of the Visual Studio .NET environment, it may not necessarily provide you with the flexibility that you need when creating data access. However, in this section, we have covered the major topics that deal with ADO.NET objects in Visual Studio.

EXAM TIP   What you have seen so far covers the extent to which Microsoft will test you on Visual Studio ADO.NET objects. As any good programmer knows, though, you should spend more time investigating the power of the development environment and the many classes that have been built to assist with data retrieval and presentation.

The remainder of this chapter will be devoted to programmatically retrieving and displaying data. We will discuss such features as data bindings, formatting, and parsing data. Our goal is to create the form that you see in Figure 20-18, which retrieves data from the SQL Server and presents it in text boxes that have been bound to the data.

Figure 20-17
The Preview window

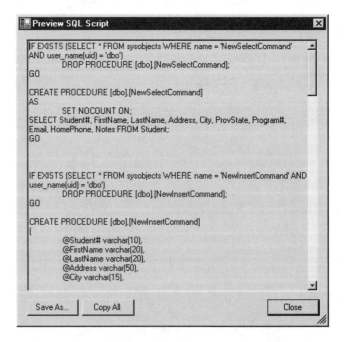

Figure 20-18 The college application form

Data Binding

Just what is data binding? Obviously, as its name implies, it is the process of linking data with something. In prior versions of Microsoft data-object models, you could "bind" data to a control that had data source, data member, and data field properties. For example, a text box could be programmed to contain data from an SQL Server data source, a SELECT statement, and a particular field from the SELECT statement. Although this technique is slightly different in .NET, there are many more possibilities with Windows Forms using the .NET Framework.

The traditional data sources (such as a database) can be used, as well as any object that implements data-binding interfaces—IList, IBindingList, or IEditableObject. Fortunately, you do not need to know any of this for the Microsoft exams, but the possibilities of this new approach are virtually endless. As an example, you can create a collection of values at run time that can then be used to bind to any property of a control.

> **EXAM TIP** For the C# Windows exam, be very aware of the fact that you are not limited to binding to controls that traditionally had "bindable" properties, such as DataSource. A Windows Form control can be bound to virtually any data source. You also do not have to bind the data to a visual property (like the Text property of a TextBox).

The Theory of Data Binding

Data binding involves linking properties of a control to a data source. Data can be bound to both Windows Forms controls as well as Web Forms controls. For a complete look at Web Forms and data binding, refer to Chapter 16.

There are a number of objects that work together to produce data binding. Two important objects are `BindingContext` and `CurrencyManager`:

- `BindingContext`—Every form has a `BindingContext` object associated with it. It acts like the manager of all `CurrencyManager` objects.

- `CurrencyManager` is associated with every data source that you create. The `CurrencyManager` is responsible for managing all the bindings to that data source.

The .NET Framework allows you to use two different techniques for data binding:

- *Simple binding* is used when a control can bind to a single value.

- *Complex binding* is used when the control is capable of holding multiple values.

In this section, we will look at the two different kinds of binding and at setting properties both at design time and run time.

 EXAM TIP   Microsoft will test you on your knowledge of data binding. Pay particular attention in this section to binding programmatically to a data source.

Binding Data at Design Time

Binding data at design time means that you can use the integrated development environment and the Property Explorer to set the binding properties of a control.

Simple Binding at Design Time

Let's take our college application (shown in Figure 20-18) and bind the data source to the text boxes on the form. In the steps that follow, we will work with the Student # text box, but you can set the properties of every text control in a similar fashion.

1. Click on the Student # text box.

2. Right-click to display the Properties Explorer.

3. Expand the `DataBindings` section by clicking the plus (+) sign to the left.

4. Click the ellipsis button (the button with the three dots) beside the Advanced field, and you will see the Advanced Data Binding dialog box shown in Figure 20-19. Notice that the list of properties is large—remember, it's not just the traditional properties that can be bound to data.

5. Select the `Text` property and click the ellipsis button in order to select the data source and the column of data to use (see Figure 20-20). As a shortcut approach for simple binding, you can just set the `DataBindings Text` property in the Property Explorer.

Once you close the Advanced Data Binding dialog box, you can run the application and see that the `Student#` field from the Student table is displayed in the correct text box.

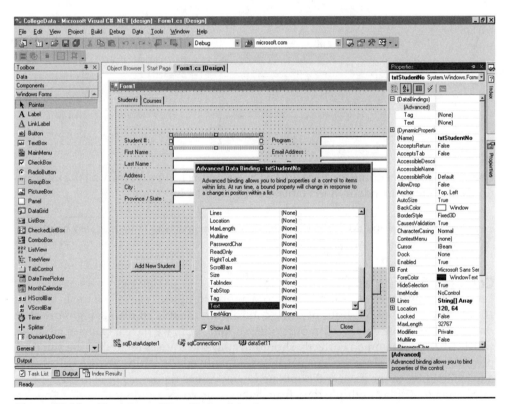

Figure 20-19   The Advanced Data Binding dialog box

Figure 20-20
Setting the
Text property

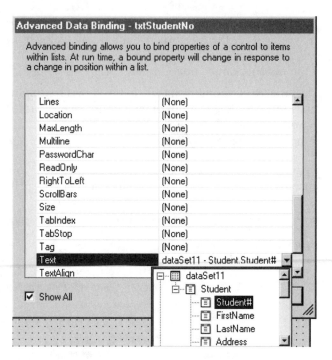

You can do the same thing for all of the text boxes on the form to display all the information about the first student in the table (see Figure 20-21).

TIP If you don't see the data, don't forget that you must manually populate the DataSet.

Complex Binding at Design Time

Let's look now at how to bind data to a more complex type of control, like the ListBox or ComboBox. Both of these controls are capable of displaying more than one record from the database. In our college application, we have a Courses tab page, which when programmed correctly should display the courses related to the student's program. However, since we haven't discussed table relationships yet, we will simply add a ListBox to the page and populate it with course names, as in Figure 20-22.

In order to display multiple rows from a database, you should set the DataSource and DisplayMember properties of the ListBox control as follows:

- DataSource: Choose the DataSet object that represents the table from which the data will be extracted.

- DisplayMember: Select the field (or column) or data that should be displayed.

Form1

Students | Courses |

Student # :	0001	Program :	PROG
First Name :	Jim	Email Address :	jim@CSharp4Us.com
Last Name :	Keill	Home Phone :	555-1212
Address :	123 My Street	Notes :	
City :	MyTown		
Province / State :	ON		

Add New Student   Delete Student   Save Changes

Search   Exit

Figure 20-21   Simple data binding

EXAM TIP   Study the difference between `DataSource` and `DisplayMember` carefully. You may find a question on the exam regarding the difference between the two.

Binding Data at Run Time

Although it is nice and easy to bind data at design time, the reality is that you will usually be binding data at run time. A user of your application may trigger an event or request data based on selection parameters, sort criteria, and the like. You must be prepared to display the data at a requested time rather than at your specific time (i.e. design time). In order to access and display data at run time, you will need to code using the ADO.NET objects.

Simple Binding at Run Time

In our college application, we have removed the `DataBindings` collection's `Text` property and are now ready to bind to the data dynamically. A View Students button

Figure 20-22
The college
application's
Courses page

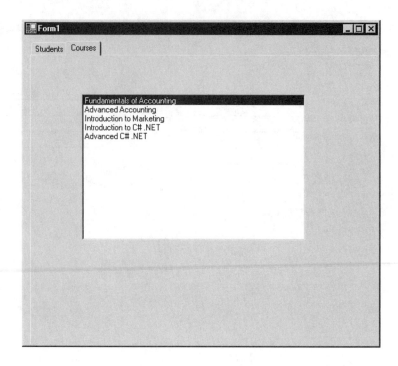

has been added to the form, and the user clicks that button to display the data (see Figure 20-23).

To link our data source and the actual control, you can instantiate a `Binding` object, as shown here:

```
Binding StudentBinding = new Binding ("Text", this.dsStudents1, "Student.Student#");
```

EXAM TIP   The `Binding` constructor takes the control's property as its first parameter and the data source and column as its second and third parameters.

After the `Binding` object has been instantiated, you need to add it to the `DataBindings` collection of the control (in this case, the `TextBox` control):

```
this.txtStudentNo.DataBindings.Add (StudentBinding);
```

You can save yourself programming space and typing by simply sending the `Binding` parameters to the `Add()` method of the `DataBindings` collection. The following code listing demonstrates how to populate each of the text boxes on the form shown in Figure 20-23.

```
this.txtStudentNo.DataBindings.Add ("Text", this.dsStudents1, "Student.Student#");
this.txtFirstName.DataBindings.Add ("Text", this.dsStudents1, "Student.FirstName");
this.txtLastName.DataBindings.Add ("Text", this.dsStudents1, "Student.LastName");
```

```
this.txtAddress.DataBindings.Add ("Text", this.dsStudents1, "Student.Address");
this.txtCity.DataBindings.Add ("Text", this.dsStudents1, "Student.City");
this.txtProvState.DataBindings.Add ("Text", this.dsStudents1, "Student.ProvState");
this.txtProgram.DataBindings.Add ("Text", this.dsStudents1, "Student.Program#");
this.txtEmail.DataBindings.Add ("Text", this.dsStudents1, "Student.Email");
this.txtPhone.DataBindings.Add ("Text", this.dsStudents1, "Student.HomePhone");
this.txtNotes.DataBindings.Add ("Text", this.dsStudents1, "Student.Notes");
```

 EXAM TIP You do not always have to provide the table name as the third parameter of the `Add()` method; however, it is necessary if you have more than one `DataTable` object (such as a `DataSet`).

Complex Binding at Run Time

The preceding section explains how to bind to controls that display a single row of data. We also need to understand how to bind data to controls that are capable of displaying multiple rows of data, like the `DataGrid`. As we saw in the previous "Simple Binding

Form1
Students   Courses

Student # :	0001	Program :	PROG
First Name :	Jim	Email Address :	jim@CSharp4Us.com
Last Name :	Keill	Home Phone :	555-1212
Address :	123 My Street	Notes :	
City :	MyTown		
Province / State :	ON		

View Students

Add New Student   Delete Student   Save Changes

Search   Exit

Figure 20-23 Displaying data dynamically using simple binding at run time

at Run Time" section, the properties of interest are the `DataSource` and the `DataMember`. We can add the following code after the declaration of a list box:

```
dgStudents.DataSource = dsStudent;
dgStudents.DataMember = "FirstName";
```

This code will cause the list box to display all records represented by the data source, but only the `FirstName` column.

 EXAM TIP You can also use the `SetDataBinding` method of the `DataGrid` object to bind both the `DataSource` and `DataMember` properties. A `DataGrid` is also considered a complex control in terms of data binding.

Another thing you can do when displaying data is display a value that is related to but different from the actual bound data. For example, you may wish to provide a user-friendly display of a primary key. The actual primary key value may be an automatically generated number that really means nothing except as a unique key. By using the `ValueMember` property of some controls, you can display the name associated with the primary key and still bind the primary key field for programmatic usage.

BindingContext and CurrencyManager

So far we have discussed ways of displaying data retrieved from a data source. However, we should also explore methods of synchronizing the data with the back-end data source. Remember that a `DataSet` is totally unaware of the data source and therefore has no idea of the actual location of the source records. Earlier in this chapter, we said that every Windows Form has a `CurrencyManager` object with which it is associated. The `CurrencyManager` takes care of knowing the position of the source records in the data source and can inform the control hosting the data when it changes. Some of the important properties of the `CurrencyManager` object are listed in Table 20-2.

In the college application, you can use the `CurrencyManager` and `BindingContext` objects to retrieve information. Recall that a `BindingContext` object exists to manage

Property	Explanation
Current	Contains the value of the current item in the data source.
Position	Returns the position of the current object in the data source.
List	Returns the data source.
Bindings	Returns the collection of bindings that the `CurrencyManager` manages.
Count	Returns the number of rows that are being managed.

Table 20-2   Properties of the `CurrencyManager`

all the `CurrencyManager` objects, and there is one `CurrencyManager` object for every data source. Consider the following code:

```
MessageBox.Show ("We are at position " + this.BindingContext[dsStudents1,
    "Student.FirstName"].Position.ToString());
CurrencyManager cm;
cm = (CurrencyManager)this.BindingContext[dsStudents1, "Student.FirstName"];
MessageBox.Show ("There are " + cm.Count.ToString() + " rows.");
```

The output with the first `MessageBox` is shown in Figure 20-24.

 EXAM TIP   Notice that the `Position` property is zero-based.

The reason this works is that the code `this.txtXXX.DataBindings.Add(…)` creates a new instance of the `Binding` object and adds it to the `Bindings` collection.

Figure 20-24   A `MessageBox` displaying the `BindingContext` object's `Position` property

Exception Handling

Any application that accesses data needs the ability to prevent run-time errors from happening. Consider the following scenario. You design a Windows Form like the college application, and the database server is in a remote location from the user of the Windows Forms (which is a very typical arrangement). For some reason, the connection to the database server fails. What happens to your application?

If you have followed good programming practices, nothing terminal should happen. Obviously, the connection failure is a problem for the user, since the live connection to the data is now disconnected. However, your application should not terminate with some cryptic message generated by the internal exception-handling mechanism. Instead, you want to trap any exceptions and handle them properly. (Refer to Chapter 4 for the basics of exception handling.)

What you need to do is enclose your code in `try ... catch` blocks to make sure that any exceptions that are beyond your control are handled. As a reminder, here is what happens with good exception-handling code:

1. The code instructions that could potentially cause an exception to be thrown (for example, connecting to the database) are enclosed in a `try ... catch ... finally` block.

2. The `try` section says "try this code—if it works without an exception being thrown, move to the `finally` block."

3. If an exception occurs, execution moves to the `catch` blocks and checks whether the exception is listed. If so, the code within that block is executed. Once the exception code has been executed, execution moves to the `finally` block and the code within that block is run.

 EXAM TIP The `finally` block always executes (unless the power plug has been pulled!).

The type of exceptions that can occur when working with data are shown in Table 20-3. All exceptions found in ADO.NET have `System.Data.DataException` as their base class.

Exception	Explanation
ConstraintException	This exception indicates that a constraint has been violated. For example, a primary key record was deleted when foreign key records still exist.
DataException	This is the base class.
DBConcurrencyException	This exception means database write conflicts have occurred. For example, this could happen if one user is updating the database while another is trying to.

Table 20-3 Classes Derived from `System.Data.DataException`

Exception	Explanation
DuplicatedNameException	This exception happens when an object in the database is given a name that already exists.
NoNullAllowedException	This exception occurs when an INSERT into the database contains a NULL value that is not allowed.
ODBCException OleDbException SqlException	These are general exceptions for the three different data providers.
ReadOnlyException	This exception means an attempt to update read-only data has occurred.
SyntaxErrorException	This exception happens when a call to SQL instructions contains syntax errors.

Table 20-4   Classes Derived from System.Data.DataException *(continued)*

Although we have not tried to access data programmatically in our application so far, the code section found in Figure 20-25 demonstrates good practice when connecting to a database. The `try` block attempts to create the connection and "tests" it using a `try` block. If the connection cannot be made, the `catch` block catches the exception.

Without this coding, we would receive the message shown in Figure 20-26, which forces the user to ignore the message or quit the application. If the connection fails, the code within the `catch` block executes (assuming an `SqlException` has been thrown).

```
private void Form1_Load(object sender, System.EventArgs e)
{
    conn = new SqlConnection ("data source=mrlaptop;initial catalog=College");
}


private void btnConnect_Click(object sender, System.EventArgs e)
{
    try
    {
        conn.Open();
    }
    catch (SqlException s)
    {
        MessageBox.Show("A SqlException occurred");
        MessageBox.Show (s.Message);
    }
    finally
    {
        MessageBox.Show("The finally block always executes");
    }
}
```

Figure 20-25   Coding that handles exceptions

Figure 20-26
Unhandled
exception

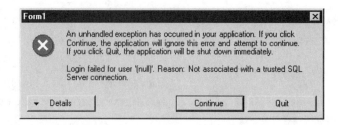

Although we have done nothing exciting within the `catch` block in this example, in a real-life scenario you would provide code that would either prompt the user for additional credentials, or prevent the user from accessing the database, or do whatever is necessary to gracefully exit the error condition. Figures 20-27, 20-28, and 20-29 show the sequence of events when an `SqlException` occurs in the code shown in Figure 20-25. Notice that the `finally` block is executed too.

In Figure 20-29, you can see that we used the exception object that is created (`SqlException s`), and then we displayed its `Message` property to provide a user-friendly message regarding the status of the exception.

EXAM TIP You can create your own data-access exceptions—be sure that they inherit from `System.Data.DataException`.

Some of the properties of the exception object are listed in Table 20-4.

From this point on in our discussions about data, we will be following this convention of catching data exceptions and providing the coding to handle them.

Accessing Data Programmatically

As promised, we will now move our discussion from Visual Studio .NET data controls and wizards to programmatic coding for data access. As mentioned before, accessing data using specialized and prebuilt functions is very valuable, but it may be impractical in some circumstances. For example, you may find that the limitations of a particular control stop you from providing a desired service. In that case, you will need to be able to create your own connections, commands, data adapters, and other objects.

Figure 20-27
The try block—
the first
message box

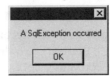

Figure 20-28
The try block—
using the
exception object

Figure 20-29
The finally
block

Property	Description
HelpLink	Provides a link to a help file giving more information about the exception.
InnerException	Contains the exception object that caused the code to enter the catch block. This is used if the exception happened inside a catch block.
Message	Provides a text message to give more information about the exception to the user.
Source	Provides the name of the object that caused the exception.
StackTrace	Provides a means of viewing the call stack (the list of methods in execution order).

Table 20-4   Properties of the Exception Object

PART IV

Creating a Connection Object

The connection object allows us to connect and authenticate against a data source. As you know from Chapter 10, there are two different connection classes associated with ADO.NET—SqlConnection and OleDbConnection. In this chapter, we will deal with the SqlConnection object, since it is the source of many more questions on the Microsoft exams.

 EXAM TIP The SqlConnection class is used for accessing Microsoft SQL Server 7 (and higher). To access an earlier version of SQL Server, you will need to use a different data source provider class.

When you instantiate an SqlConnection object, you must provide the connection parameters to the constructor. The best way to handle this is to create a string object first, and then pass the string object to the SqlConnection constructor, like this:

```
String connString = "data source=mrlaptop;initial catalog=College;user id=sa;password;"
```

The connection string is very similar to those for the ADO or OLE-DB providers in version 6 of Visual C++ or Visual Basic. It consists of three components:

- data source—the server location of the database. If the server was located somewhere other than on the client, the entry would be something like this: "data source=\\SQLServer"
- initial catalog—the name of the database.
- user id and password—the log in credentials.

You could specify integrated security instead of providing the userid and password within the connection string. In that case, you would code "integrated security".

The connection object can be thought of as the bridge between your application and a data provider. Connection strings vary slightly depending on the data provider (OLE-DB, ODBC, and so on). Once the string is created, you then pass it to the connection constructor as follows:

```
SqlConnection myConnection = new SQLConnection (connString);
```

By using this method, you can modify the connection string at any time without touching the actual creation of the connection object.

All that's left to do now is to open the connection, which, essentially, provides us with a link to the data source. No command is being run against the data in the following code, no data is transferred—this simply creates a pipeline to the data.

```
try
{
    MyConnection.Open();
}
catch
```

```
{
... Code your exception handling here

}
```

Be sure to close the connection when you are finished with it. The garbage collector can then destroy the object and free the memory space:

```
try
{
    MyConnection.Close();
}
catch
{   ... Etc...

}
```

Creating a Command Object

The next step is to create the object that encapsulates the code that you want executed on the data source. This could be a stored procedure on the database server or a configured SQL statement located in your code. Either way, you need a Command object to do this for you. The command object will use the connection object to access the database (or it can provide its own connection data). Once the command is executed against the data source, the data is returned to the user in the form of a stream (read by DataReader objects) or a DataSet object. The following code is used to instantiate a command object:

```
SqlCommand MyCommand = new SqlCommand();
```

You can also use the connection object to create the command object. The connection object has a CreateCommand() method that you can use to instantiate your command object.

```
comString = "SELECT * FROM Student";
SqlCommand MyCommand = MyConnection.CreateCommand();
```

Once the command object is created, you can use the execute methods associated with an SqlCommand object:

```
SqlDataReader myReader = myCommand.ExecuteReader();
```

The execute methods include ExecuteScalar() (a command that returns a single value), ExecuteReader() (a command that returns a set of rows), ExecuteNonQuery() (a command that affects the database but only returns the number of rows affected), and ExecuteXmlReader (a command that returns XML data).

 EXAM TIP   ExecuteXmlReader() is used for Microsoft SQL Server 7.0 or later.

Some of the properties of a command object are listed in Table 20-5.

Property	Description
CommandType	The type can be one of StoredProcedure, Text, or TableDirect.
CommandText	This is the name of the stored procedure, the actual SQL statement, or the name of the table.
Connection	This specifies the connection object (or information) required to access the data source.
Name	This is a programmatic name that you can use within your program to refer to the command object.
Parameters	These are the parameters associated with the stored procedure.

Table 20-5   Some Properties of the Command Object

Figure 20-30 shows code that instantiates and uses a command object.

DataAdapter and DataSet

We can now create a DataAdapter and a DataSet in order to get ready to bind our data to the controls on the form. Recall that a DataAdapter is a link between the data source and a DataSet. The DataSet is a representation (or local copy) of the actual data from the data source. These two objects work hand-in-hand to provide a link to the actual data.

Let's start with the DataAdapter. There are two data adapters—SqlDataAdapter and OleDbDataAdapter. Since we are connecting to Microsoft SQL Server 7.0 or higher, we will use the SqlDataAdapter. Create a new DataAdapter using the command object:

```
SqlCommand studentCommand = new SqlCommand();
studentCommand.CommandType = CommandType.Text;
studentCommand.CommandText = "SELECT * FROM Student";
SqlDataAdapter studentAdapter = new SqlDataAdapter(studentCommand);
```

We can then use this data adapter to create the DataSet object that will be a copy of the actual data retrieved through the command object:

```
DataSet studentSet = new DataSet();
studentAdapter.Fill (studentSet, "FirstName");
```

```
private void button1_Click(object sender, System.EventArgs e)
{
    SqlConnection scon = new SqlConnection();
    // another method of passing the connection string information to the connection object
    scon.ConnectionString = "data source=mrlaptop;intial catalog=College;user id=sa;password");
    scon.Open();

    SqlCommand scomm = new SqlCommand();
    scomm.Connection = scon;
    scomm.CommandText = "SELECT * FROM Student";
    scon.ExecuteScalar();
}
```

Figure 20-27   Creating a command object

You can now use all of the binding techniques that you learned earlier in this chapter to bind the data from the data set to any control on your form. The following code listing shows the full code required to fill the form (Figure 20-18) with data retrieved from the Microsoft SQL Server database.

```
using System;
using System.Drawing;
using System.Collections;
using System.ComponentModel;
using System.Windows.Forms;
using System.Data;
using System.Data.SqlClient;
namespace WindowsApplication2
{
    public class Form1 : System.Windows.Forms.Form
    {
        private System.Windows.Forms.Button button1;
        protected SqlConnection studentConnection;
        protected SqlCommand studentCommand;
        protected SqlDataAdapter studentAdapter;
        protected DataSet studentSet;
        private System.Windows.Forms.Button btnGetData;
        private System.Windows.Forms.TextBox txtFirstName;
        private System.ComponentModel.Container components = null;
        public Form1()
        {
            InitializeComponent();
        }
        protected override void Dispose( bool disposing )
        {
            if( disposing )
            {
                if (components != null)
                {
                    components.Dispose();
                }
            }
            base.Dispose( disposing );
        }
        [STAThread]
        static void Main()
        {
            Application.Run(new Form1());
        }
        private void InitializeComponent()
        {
            this.btnGetData = new System.Windows.Forms.Button();
            this.txtFirstName = new System.Windows.Forms.TextBox();
            this.SuspendLayout();
            //
            // btnGetData
            //
            this.btnGetData.Location = new System.Drawing.Point(97, 124);
            this.btnGetData.Name = "btnGetData";
            this.btnGetData.TabIndex = 0;
            this.btnGetData.Text = "GetData";
            this.btnGetData.Click += new System.EventHandler(this.btnGetData_Click_1);
            //
            // txtFirstName
```

```
        //
        this.txtFirstName.Location = new System.Drawing.Point(48, 60);
        this.txtFirstName.Name = "txtFirstName";
        this.txtFirstName.Size = new System.Drawing.Size(169, 20);
        this.txtFirstName.TabIndex = 1;
        this.txtFirstName.Text = "";
        //
        // Form1
        //
        this.AutoScaleBaseSize = new System.Drawing.Size(5, 13);
        this.ClientSize = new System.Drawing.Size(292, 273);
        this.Controls.AddRange(new System.Windows.Forms.Control[] {
            this.txtFirstName, this.btnGetData});
        this.Name = "Form1";
        this.ResumeLayout(false);
    }
    private void btnGetData_Click_1(object sender, System.EventArgs e)
    {
        string strSQL = "user id=sa;initial catalog=College;data source=mrlaptop";
        studentConnection = new SqlConnection (strSQL);
        try
        {
            // open the connection
            studentConnection.Open();
            // create the command object
            studentCommand = studentConnection.CreateCommand();
            studentCommand.CommandType = CommandType.Text;
            studentCommand.CommandText = "SELECT * FROM Student";
            // create the Adapter object
            studentAdapter = new SqlDataAdapter (studentCommand);
            studentSet = new DataSet();
            studentAdapter.Fill (studentSet, "FirstName");
            // bind the data to a text box
            this.txtFirstName.DataBindings.Add ("Text", studentSet, "FirstName");
        }
        catch (SqlException s)
        {
            MessageBox.Show ("Oops, something bad happened");
        }
        finally
        {
            studentConnection.Close();
            studentConnection = null;
        }
    }
  }
}
```

DataReader

If you are looking for an object that will give you a fast and efficient return of rows of data, the DataReader is the object for you. This object provides a stream of rows in a forward-only cursor. There is no opportunity to move forward and backward through the data, and you cannot search for records. However, if you need to quickly scroll through data, the DataReader is what you want. You can create a DataReader from the command object:

```
SqlDataReader studentReader = StudentCommand.ExecuteReader
     CommandBehavior.CloseConnection);
while (studentReader.Read())
{
   // fill a control like a list box with the data using the Items.Add() method
}
studentReader.Close();
```

 EXAM TIP The DataReader provides a read-only, forward-only representation of the data.

Using Format and Parse

Another objective of the Microsoft Windows exam suggests that you need to know how to transform and filter data. To that end, we will explore two techniques—*formatting* and *parsing*. The Binding object exposes two events—Format and Parse. We will discuss these two events in the next two sections.

The Format Event

Whenever data is bound from a data source to a control on a form, the Format event is triggered. It is also triggered when the data returns from the control to the data source (in the example of updating the data). Data is formatted to take it from its native form in the data source to a form that can be displayed to the user. Conversely, displayed data is formatted back to its native form when it is returned to the data source.

Often you will retrieve data from a data source that has a different data type than the type of control to which it is bound. The Binding object is used to bind the data to the control, and it triggers the Format event when doing so. You can create customized formats for your data by using the Format event.

The Format event will fire in these circumstances:

- When the data is bound for the first time to the control
- When the Position property changes (refer back in this chapter for the Position property—it is used to reposition the row indicator)
- When the data is sorted or filtered

Here is some sample code that demonstrates formatting:

```
Binding studentBinding = new Binding ("Text", studentSet, "HomePhone");
studentBinding.Format += new ConvertEventHandler (this.yourFormatName);
```

Of course, you still need to code the yourFormatName method; but the preceding code adds the handler to the Binding object in the text box's DataBindings collection.

The Parse Event

When data is returned to the data source, it triggers the Format event. However, just before the Format event is fired, the Parse event occurs. The Parse event will occur in these circumstances:

- When the Position property changes.
- After a Validation event.
- When the EndCurrentEdit() method is called (a method of BindingManagerBase).

You can use code similar to what we showed for the Format event:

```
StudentBinding.Parse += new ConvertEventHandler (this.yourParseMethod);
```

 EXAM TIP   The Format event is triggered when the data is bound to the control, when the Position changes, or when the data is sorted or filtered. The Parse event is triggered after a Validation event, when the Position changes, or when the EndCurrentEdit() method is called.

Summary

This chapter has covered the exam objectives related to data access in Windows Forms. You should pay particular attention to the sections that deal with binding data to controls (both simple and complex binding) as well as the ADO.NET objects used for retrieving data from a data store (Connection, Command, DataSet, and DataAdapter). Microsoft will also test your understanding of the various data providers (SQL, OLE-DB) and when they are used—remember that the SQL provider is used for versions of Microsoft SQL Server 7.0 and higher.

In order to feel very comfortable with the concepts presented in this chapter, you should find an evaluation copy of Microsoft SQL Server 2000 and set up a simple database (as we have done with the College database). Test yourself by creating connections and commands and displaying the data. That is the one way to make sure that you are ready for Microsoft's exam.

Test Questions

1. Which code segment will populate a DataSet?

   A. sqlDataProvider1.Fill (dsUsers1);

   B. sqlDataProvider.Fill (dataAdapter1);

   C. sqlDataAdapter.Fill (dsUsers1);

   D. sqlDataAdapter.Fill (dataAdapter1);

2. What type of commands can you create?

   A. Text, stored procedures, and tables.

   B. Text, stored procedures, and `TableRows`.

   C. Text, stored procedures, and `TableDirect`.

   D. Text, stored procedures, and `TableColumns`.

3. Data access exceptions all derive from which base class?

   A. `Sql.Data.Exceptions`

   B. `Sql.SqlDataExceptions`

   C. `Exception`

   D. `DataException`

4. You need to get access to a database that is stored on a server running Microsoft Access 2002. Which data adapter would you use?

   A. `SqlDataAdapter`

   B. `OleDbDataAdapter`

   C. `OleDataAdapter`

   D. `ODBCDataAdapter`

5. You need to get access to a database that is stored on a server running Microsoft SQL Server 2000. Which data adapter would you use?

   A. `SqlDataAdapter`

   B. `OleDbDataAdapter`

   C. `OleDataAdapter`

   D. `ODBCDataAdapter`

6. You want to return XML data from a Microsoft SQL Server 7.0 database. Which method would you execute?

   A. `ExecuteXmlReader()`

   B. `ExecuteXmlData()`

   C. `ExecuteOleReader()`

   D. `ExecuteOldData()`

7. The `Parse` event is triggered after which of these occurrences?

   A. Data is sorted.

   B. Data is filtered.

   C. Data is bound to a control.

   D. Data is returned to the data source.

   E. All of the above.

   F. None of the above.

8. The `Format` event is triggered after which occurrences?

   A. Data is sorted.

   B. Data is filtered.

   C. Data is bound to a control.

   D. Data is returned to the data source.

   E. All of the above.

   F. None of the above.

9. What will happen when the following code is executed? Assume the connection is created properly and works fine.

```
try
{
    studentConnection.Open();
    studentCommand = studentConnection.CreateCommand();
    studentCommand.CommandType = CommandType.StoredProcedure;
    studentCommand.CommandText = "SELECT * FROM Student";
    studentAdapter = new SqlDataAdapter (studentCommand);
    studentSet = new DataSet();
    studentAdapter.Fill (studentSet, "FirstName");
    this.txtFirstName.DataBindings.Add ("Text", studentSet, "FirstName");
}
catch (SqlDbException s)
{
    MessageBox.Show ("Oops, something bad happened");
}
finally
{
    studentConnection.Close();
    studentConnection = null;
}
}
```

   A. The program will not compile.

   B. The program will compile but will throw an exception upon execution.

   C. The program will compile but will not display data.

   D. The program will display the data and close the connection properly.

10. What will happen when the following code is executed? Assume the connection is created properly and works fine.

```
try
{
    studentConnection.Open();
    studentCommand = studentConnection.CreateCommand();
    studentCommand.CommandType = CommandType.Text;
    studentCommand.CommandText = "SELECT * FROM Student";
    studentAdapter = new SqlDataAdapter (studentCommand);
    studentSet = new DataSet();
    studentAdapter.Fill (studentSet, "Name");
    this.txtFirstName.DataBindings.Add ("Text", studentSet, "FirstName");
```

```
    }
    catch (SqlDbException s)
    {
        MessageBox.Show ("Oops, something bad happened");
    }
    finally
    {
        studentConnection.Close();
        studentConnection = null;
    }
}
```

A. The program will not compile.

B. The program will compile but throws an exception upon execution.

C. The program will compile but will not display data.

D. The program will display the data and close the connection properly.

11. You are the consultant for HMR Inc. They have a large network that includes a Microsoft SQL Server 2000 database. You have coded a connection and command object to retrieve data from the Student database, but you keep getting an exception. What is wrong with the following code?

```
try
{
    studentConnection.Open();
    studentCommand = studentConnection.CreateCommand();
    studentCommand.CommandType = CommandType.Text;
    studentCommand.CommandText = "SELECT * FROM Student";
    studentAdapter = new OleDbDataAdapter (studentCommand);
    studentSet = new DataSet();
    studentAdapter.Fill (studentSet, "FirstName");
    this.txtFirstName.DataBindings.Add ("Text", studentSet, "FirstName");
}
catch (OleDbException s)
{
    MessageBox.Show ("Oops, something bad happened");
}
finally
{
    studentConnection.Close();
    studentConnection = null;
}
}
```

A. The connection cannot be closed in the `finally` block.

B. You are using the wrong data adapter.

C. You are using the wrong data field.

D. You are using the wrong exception object.

E. Both A and C.

F. Both B and D.

PART IV

12. Which of the following object types allow you to view read-only, forward-only data?

    A. `DataAdapter`

    B. `DataSet`

    C. `DataReader`

    D. `DataCommand`

13. Which of the following statements is correct?

    A. The `DataSource` property refers to the dataset object, and the `DisplayMember` refers to the field.

    B. The `DataMember` property refers to the dataset object, and the `DataSource` refers to the field.

    C. The `DataMember` property refers to the field, and the `DataSource` refers to the dataset object.

    D. The `DisplayMember` property refers to the dataset object, and the `DataSource` refers to the field.

14. Why does the data not display using the following code?

```
studentConnection.Open();
studentCommand = studentConnection.CreateCommand();
studentCommand.CommandType = CommandType.Text;
studentCommand.CommandText = "SELECT * FROM Student";
studentAdapter = new SqlDataAdapter (studentCommand);
studentSet = new DataSet();
this.txtFirstName.DataBindings.Add ("Text", studentSet, "FirstName");
```

    A. The command object is instantiated incorrectly.

    B. The dataset object is instantiated incorrectly.

    C. The data binding is done incorrectly.

    D. The dataset has not been populated.

15. What have you forgotten to do if you see the following dialog box when running your program?

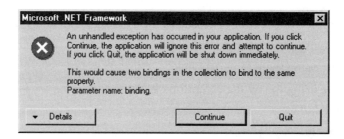

A. Provide the correct database credentials.

B. Handle data exceptions.

C. Populate the dataset.

D. Read Chapter 20.

Test Answers

1. C.

2. C.

3. D.

4. B.

5. A.

6. A.

7. D.

8. E.

9. B. The command type is `Text` not `StoredProcedure`.

10. B. The exception is caused by the column named `Name`.

11. F.

12. C.

13. A.

14. D.

15. B. (Well, it could be D!!)

Web Services and COM

In this chapter, you will
- Learn how to consume (instantiate and invoke) a web service
- Be able to instantiate and invoke a COM or COM+ component
- Understand how to call native functions using platform invoke

Those of you who have done enterprise programming, whereby you create remote objects and invoke their methods from another remote object, will find this chapter exciting. Those of you who have never done any remote-method invocations will also find this chapter exciting. The ability to build objects on a "server" and invoke their methods from a "client" is the true nature of enterprise programming. Remember that a "server" can be an application running on any machine that provides services to a "client," which is simply an application that requests services of the server.

Whether you call it DCOM (Distributed Component Object Model), RMI (Remote Method Invocation), EJB (Enterprise JavaBeans), or CORBA (Common Object Request Broker Architecture), it all has the same objective. You want to instantiate an object that resides elsewhere on a network. Once that object is created, you want to send it messages and ask it to invoke its methods and return the results to you. In the world of Microsoft Visual C# .NET and the .NET Framework, we call this *Web Services*.

In this chapter, we will explore Web Services from the client side (accessing them from our Windows application). The subject of creating Web Services is the topic of Part V of this book and the 70-320 examination, and you will need to understand how to instantiate and invoke a web service. We will also examine connecting to legacy services such as COM and COM+ in this chapter.

Web Services

When we discuss Web Services, we have to think in terms of objects outside our local computer. Think of a program that returns the number of students enrolled in a particular college program. How many of our Windows programs (that make up our college applications) could take advantage of a routine like that? Probably most of the administrative-type programs could use it at one time or another. In that case, it's foolish to think that we would install the service into each and every assembly. Code reusability sometimes implies that the code resides on a server machine somewhere in the world in order to provide accessibility from anywhere. But if the code is located on a server, how do we ask that server to create the object? And once it is created, how do we ask the code to perform its methods? This is the heart of Web Services.

A web service is a component that resides on a server and can be accessed using XML messaging. The front-end application (our Windows Form) can send a request to the server hosting the web service, the server will do some processing as requested, and the server will return the results of the process back to the client application. Traditionally, the concern with component-based architecture (as we have just described) has been the expensive network process. Web Services introduces a lightweight process based on standard protocols such as SOAP (Simple Object Access Protocol), XML (Extensible Markup Language), and HTTP (Hypertext Transfer Protocol). The use of these standard protocols allows Web Services to provide cross-platform and cross-language support. Although our introduction to Web Services in this chapter (and this book) will focus on the Microsoft side of things, keep this fact in mind—Web Services can provide an answer to interoperability concerns.

How Do Web Services Work?

An application can *consume* Web Services, which means that the application can send a request in the form of a message to a web service, which in turn responds with a reply to the message (normally the return data of a method call). A web service has a WSDL (Web Service Description Language) definition file, which defines the type of message the web service will accept and the type of response it will generate.

Web services are hosted by a web server and are located by using a URL. The consuming application (in our case, the front-end Windows Form) will send a request to the web server, and the web server forwards that request to the web service application, which then executes the method call and returns the response to the web server. The web server then forwards the result to the consuming application. There's a little more to it than that, but for the purposes of the Windows exam, you just need to understand the process as described. For more details on how this all works, refer to Part V of this book, which deals with Exam 70-320, "Developing XML Web Services."

Building a Simple Web Service

Although creating a web service is probably not tested on the Windows exam, we'll include it here to give you an idea of how the process works together with your Windows application. Let's build a simple web service that, when called, returns "Hello World" to the caller. Follow these steps to create the web service:

1. Open Visual Studio .NET and start a new project (File | New Project).

2. Select the ASP.NET Web Service template from the Visual C# Projects. Notice in Figure 21-1 that you don't need to name the service. You simply create the URL to the service—**http://localhost/HelloWebService**. Remember that the service is hosted by a web server (in our case, Microsoft IIS).

EXAM TIP The term `localhost` refers to the local computer. If the web service is hosted by a remote server, you would need to insert the server name instead of `localhost`.

3. The web service will be added to the web server (see the following illustration). Any error connecting to the web server will occur at this point.

4. By default, Visual Studio .NET will create a file called `Servicex.asmx` (where *x* is the number of services in the application). You can rename the service by right-clicking on the service and selecting Rename. You may want to rename

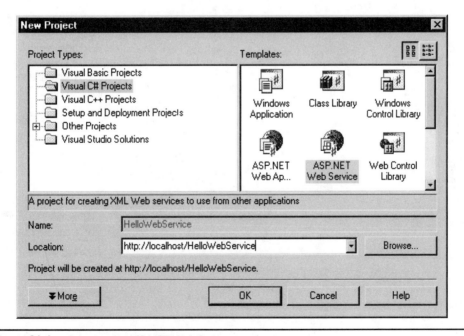

Figure 21-1 Selecting the ASP.NET Web Service template

PART IV

the .vsdisco file as well. In Figure 21-2, you can see that we have renamed both files to HelloWebService.

TIP The .vsdisco file is a discovery file. Discovery services are used to locate a web service, and they will be discussed in Part V of this book. The .vsdisco file is part of that discovery process.

5. Click on the "click here to switch to code view" link (as seen in Figure 21-2). This will take you to the code window for the HelloWebService.asmx.cs class file (see Figure 21-3).

6. As you can see in Figure 21-3, we have made two changes to the default code module. We have changed the name of the class file and the constructor to HelloWebService, and we have also created the simplest of Web Services by removing the comments from the method HelloWorld(). You can make the same changes and see the results.

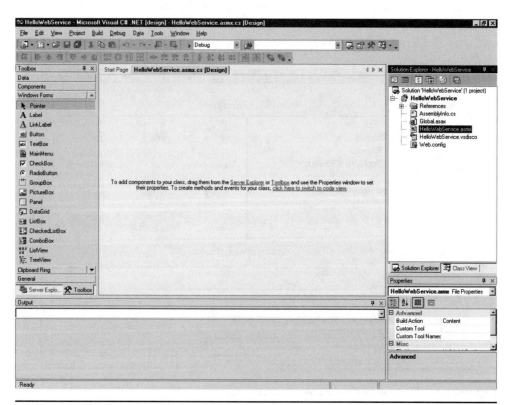

Figure 21-2 The new web service

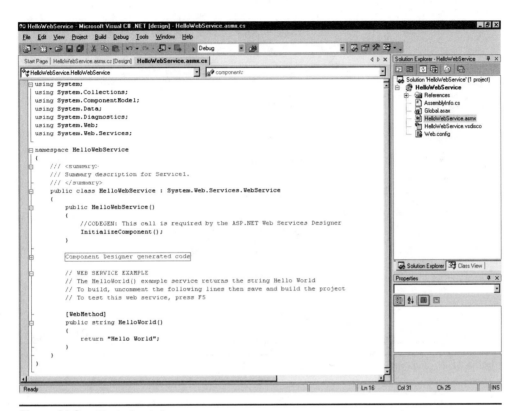

Figure 21-3   The code window

 EXAM TIP   The exposed methods in a web service must be declared as public methods.

7. Build the web service. Select Build from the Build menu.

Several things happen in the background when you build the web service. The first thing that happens is that the virtual root folder in IIS is created (see the selected folder in Figure 21-4). The second thing that happens is that the helper files that you see in Figure 21-4 are created. We will explore the different kinds of files when we reach Part V, which discusses XML web services. For now, notice that `NewHelloService.asmx` is the actual web service file.

You can now test your web service by pressing F5 in Visual Studio .NET. The resulting display is shown in Figure 21-5. The service is presented to you in Internet Explorer, and you can click on the exposed method name, `HelloWorld`.

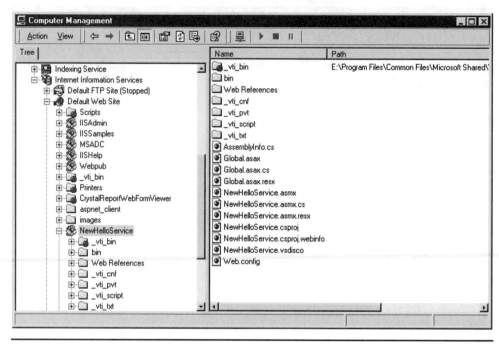

Figure 21-4 The virtual root folder in IIS

When you click on the `HelloWorld` hyperlink, you will see the screen shown at the top of Figure 21-6. To test the method, click Invoke. The resulting output is shown at the bottom of Figure 21-6.

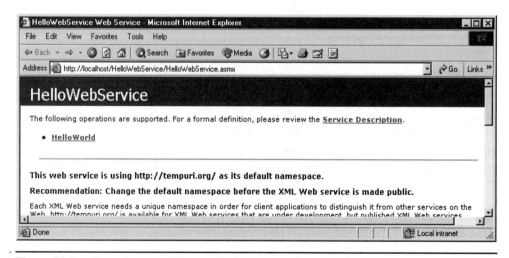

Figure 21-5 The web service in Internet Explorer

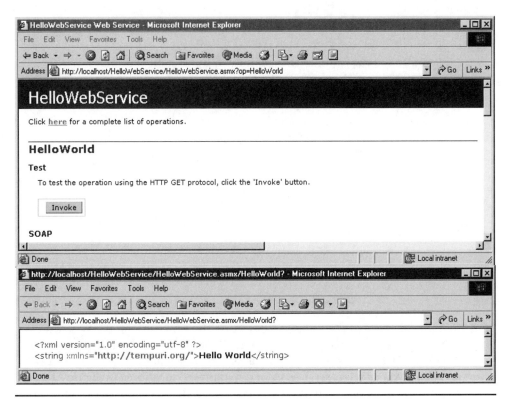

Figure 21-6   The XML output of the web service test

Consuming a Simple Web Service

In the previous section, we looked at how to build a web service; however, the output from our test was less than satisfying. In this section, we will look at the proper way to consume a web service. Consuming a web service means that we will send a request to the service and ask it to perform a method and return the result to our calling application.

The first step is to create the application that will call on the services of the web service. You can do that by building a new project, solution, or assembly. For the purposes of this example, we will simply add a new project (a Windows Form) to our application.

1. Add a new project to the solution. Right-click on the solution name and select Add | New Project.

2. Select a Windows application.

3. Select the new project as the startup project by right-clicking on the Windows project name and choosing Set as Startup Project.

4. Add a button to the form, as shown in the following illustration.

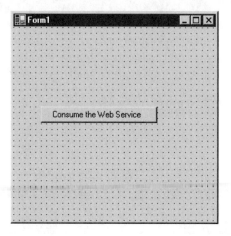

5. Add the reference to the web service. To do this, right-click on the Windows application (in our example, ConsumeHelloWebService) and select Add Web Reference. The Add Web Reference dialog box will open (see Figure 21-7) and allow you to select services from different web locations. In Figure 21-7, you can see that you can request services from a UDDI (Universal Description, Discovery, and Integration) directory or from a Test Microsoft UDDI directory. If you are interested in learning more about UDDI, refer to Chapter 25.

 EXAM TIP The web service doesn't have to be created using Visual C# .NET. That's the wonderful part of this process. You don't have to worry about the language that created the web service—you don't even have to worry about the platform of the web server.

6. In this example, you want to select a service from the local web server. In the Add Web Reference dialog box's Address box, type **http://localhost/ HelloWebService/HelloWebService.asmx?WSDL** and press ENTER.

7. You will see the XML shown in Figure 21-8. You will also have the option of adding the reference to the project. Click on Add Reference.

8. Look at the Solution Explorer (Figure 21-9) and you will see that the web reference has been added to the Windows application. You can now use the proxy object that has been created behind the scenes to make a call to the web service.

9. Add the following code to the click event of the button.

```
private void btnConsume_Click (object sender, System.EventArgs e)
{
    localhost.HelloWebService myService = new localhost.HelloWebService();
    MessageBox.Show (myService.HelloWorld());
}
```

You can now run the project by pressing F5. The output is shown in the following illustration. When the Consume button is clicked, an instance of the web proxy is instantiated and used to run the HelloWorld() method. Except for the fact that we

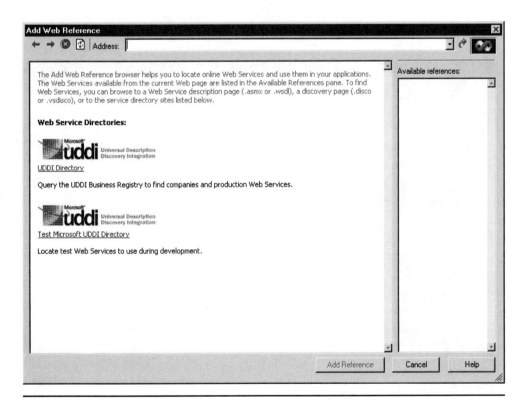

Figure 21-7   Adding a web reference

must instantiate the web service object using the web reference, it seems as if we used a local class.

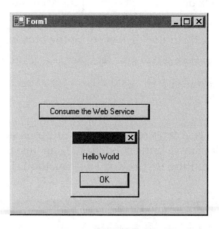

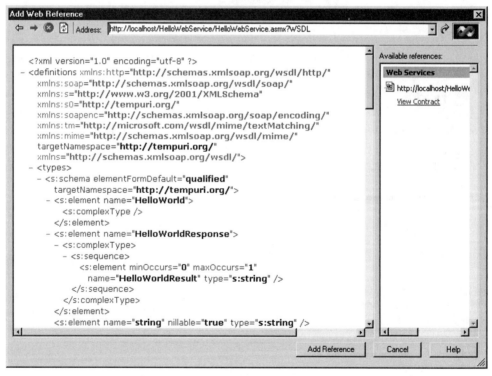

Figure 21-8   XML of the WSDL file

Figure 21-9
The web
reference added
to the project

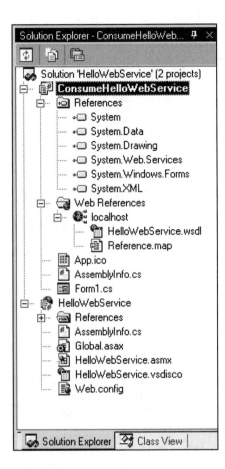

How Web Services Work

When the web reference is added to the application, a proxy object is created from the WSDL file. It is the proxy object that runs on the application's behalf and makes the request of the remote object. In reality, Visual Studio .NET has run WSDL.exe on the WSDL file to create this proxy object. You can do the same thing from a command prompt by using the following line:

```
wsdl /l:cs /o:HelloWebServiceProxy.cs
    http://localhost/HelloWebService/HelloWebService.asmx?WSDL
    /n:HelloService
```

EXAM TIP   The WSDL.exe program creates a proxy class that exposes the methods of the web service.

Let's examine the previous code line:

- wsdl calls `wsdl.exe`, which is the tool that generates the code for web service clients from the WSDL file.

- `/l:cs` specifies the language to be used for the class file. In this case, `cs` is the default language, C#. You could specify VB for Visual Basic or JS for JScript.

- `/o:HelloWebServiceProxy.cs` specifies the output file for the generated proxy class.

- `http://localhost/HelloWebService/HelloWebService.asmx?WSDL` is the path to the WSDL file, which contains the exposed methods of the web service.

- `/n:HelloService` specifies the namespace for the generated proxy class.

The beauty of this system is its simplicity and the convenience for the developer. If you had to code method calls to a remote object, you would have to worry about how the call is *marshaled* to the remote object. Marshalling is the process of sending arguments to the remote object and receiving the results from the method call. The proxy object does all this for you. You simply add the reference or run the WSDL tool, and all this functionality is created for you.

Here's what happens:

1. The proxy object is created from the web service's proxy class:
   ```
   localhost.HelloWebService myService =
   new localhost.HelloWebService();
   ```

 EXAM TIP   The proxy class must be in the search path for the application. Place it in the \bin directory and you will have no problems.

2. The client application makes a call to a method that is exposed by the proxy object. In our example, that call looked like this:
   ```
   myService.HelloWorld()
   ```

3. The proxy object then creates a request packet (using XML) that contains any parameters for the method call.

4. The request packet is sent to the web service.

5. The web service receives the packet, extracts the parameters, and executes the method.

6. The web service then creates a packet with the results of the method call and sends it back to the proxy.

7. The proxy receives the packet and extracts the returned data.

8. The client application then uses the return data.

In order to get a feeling for the proxy class that is generated, we have included the file generated by the `wsdl.exe` tool. Take some time to look through the code listing and realize the amount of work that is done for you behind the scenes. Without this proxy class, there would be no way to request that a remote object do work for you. This class file encapsulates all the functionality to allow that to happen.

```
namespace ConsumeHelloWebService.localhost
{
    using System.Diagnostics;
    using System.Xml.Serialization;
    using System;
    using System.Web.Services.Protocols;
    using System.ComponentModel;
    using System.Web.Services;
    /// <remarks/>
    [System.Diagnostics.DebuggerStepThroughAttribute()]
    [System.ComponentModel.DesignerCategoryAttribute("code")]
    [System.Web.Services.WebServiceBindingAttribute(Name="HelloWebServiceSoap",
            Namespace="http://tempuri.org/")]
    public class HelloWebService :
                    System.Web.Services.Protocols.SoapHttpClientProtocol
    {
        public HelloWebService() {
            this.Url = "http://localhost/HelloWebService/HelloWebService.asmx";
        }
        [System.Web.Services.Protocols.SoapDocumentMethodAttribute
                ("http://tempuri.org/HelloWorld",
                 RequestNamespace="http://tempuri.org/",
                  ResponseNamespace="http://tempuri.org/",
                  Use=System.Web.Services.Description.SoapBindingUse.Literal,
ParameterStyle=System.Web.Services.Protocols.SoapParameterStyle.Wrapped)]
        public string HelloWorld() {
            object[] results = this.Invoke("HelloWorld", new object[0]);
            return ((string)(results[0]));
        }
        public System.IAsyncResult BeginHelloWorld
                (System.AsyncCallback callback, object asyncState) {
            return this.BeginInvoke("HelloWorld", new object[0], callback, asyncState);
        }
        public string EndHelloWorld(System.IAsyncResult asyncResult) {
            object[] results = this.EndInvoke(asyncResult);
            return ((string)(results[0]));
        }
    }
}
```

 EXAM TIP   After the proxy class is created by using the `wsdl.exe` tool, you can compile the proxy using the C# compiler (`csc.exe`). When you compile the proxy class into your assembly, you accomplish everything that Visual Studio .NET does for you (as we saw in the previous section).

Here are some interesting Web Services facts:

- XML is used to encode the data.

- HTTP is the protocol used to pass the data across the network. SOAP is the protocol that transports the messages.

- WSDL is used to describe the contract with the Web Service.

- UDDI is used to publish web services.

- A web service class must extend `System.Web.Services.WebService`.

- To create a method in a web service, add the attribute `[System.Web.Services.WebMethod]`.

- You can use Visual Studio .NET to add a web reference. Once added, all the features of the IDE are available to you. For example, IntelliSense will find the methods for you.

COM and COM+

COM (Component Object Model) was created to enhance software reusability. When a programmer needed the services of an object that had already been developed, they used COM (which is a specification for creating components) to create and store the object. The component was identified in the Windows Registry by means of a globally unique identifier (GUID). When an application needed the services of the component, it used a single copy of the dynamic-link library (DLL). Developers ran into trouble when newer releases were required, however, because the older copy had to be removed (which sometimes was no easy feat) and replaced with the newer copy. However, there sometimes were legacy applications that needed the older component, and sooner or later the developer landed in what is not-so-fondly referred to as "DLL Hell."

In order to assist the developer and provide for remote component storage, Microsoft introduced the Microsoft Transaction Server (MTS) and DCOM (Distributed Component Object Model). Under the Windows 2000 operating system, Microsoft also introduced COM+, the latest in the Component Object Models. One of the services incorporated into this release was Microsoft Message Queue Server (MSMQ), which allowed for asynchronous communication between a client and a server. There's much more to the story than just this, and as a .NET developer, you will have to be able to interoperate with these older component models.

As you have seen, the .NET environment replaces this architecture with assemblies. Assemblies store their own information as metadata in manifests that reside with the component (instead of in the Registry like COM components). This means the component just has to be in the same directory as the application for it to be accessed. As a matter of fact, creating and using components in the .NET environment is much easier than in earlier versions.

In a perfect world, that's all we would have to worry about. Everyone would automatically convert to the newest technology, and our work would be easy. So we issue you a challenge—go to the project manager and tell him that all applications have to convert over to assemblies, and COM and COM+ will disappear. After he stops laughing, come back to this section and find out how you can interoperate with COM and COM+ in a .NET world. For the purposes of this book (and for the purposes of the Microsoft exam), we will treat COM and COM+ as the same thing.

.NET and COM

Let's take a moment to compare the .NET Framework object model and COM. In order to completely understand how they work together, you need to be aware of their differences. Table 21-1 will help with that.

Working with COM

To look at how to add a COM component to a form, let's start a new project called COMProject. When you select Project | Add Reference, you will see the Add Reference dialog box (see Figure 21-10).

For this example, we will add a reference to the `shdocvw.dll` COM component library, which is a library of Internet-style controls. Select the COM tab in the Add Reference dialog box (see Figure 21-11), which gives you the choice of selecting a COM component from the Microsoft libraries or of clicking the Browse button to search for a component using the Select Component dialog box (see Figure 21-12).

For our example, we will choose a Microsoft component library, `msador15.dll`. Scroll down the list of available COM components until you find Microsoft ActiveX Data Objects Recordset 2.7 Library, and double-click on it to add it to the selected components (see Figure 21-13).

COM	.NET
COM is based on a binary standard whereby COM rules dictate the internal layout.	.NET is based on a type standard—the Common Type System (CTS).
COM components are stored in a type library.	.NET components have metadata embedded inside the assembly.
COM uses GUIDs (globally unique identifiers) for identification.	.NET uses strong names.
Object lifetime in COM is managed by reference counting (how many times has the object been used).	A .NET component's lifetime is managed by the CLR through garbage collection.

Table 21-1   Some Differences Between COM and .NET

Figure 21-10
The Add
Reference
dialog box

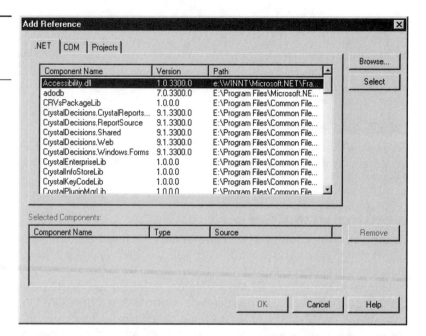

Figure 21-11
Adding COM
references

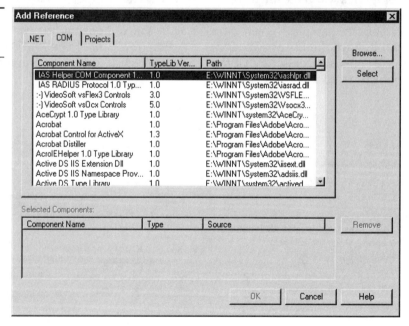

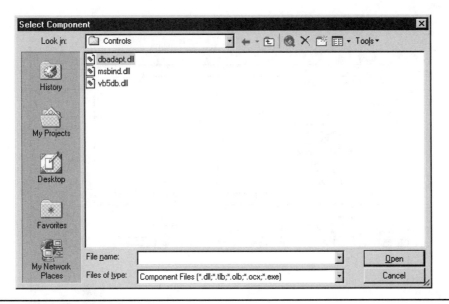

Figure 21-12   Browsing for a COM component

Once the component has been added to the project, you will see it in the References list in the Solution Explorer. Open the Object Browser by selecting View | Other Windows | Object Browser. Figure 21-14 shows the object listing for the ADOR library— `msador15.dll`.

You can now use the COM object by specifying its library and class within:

```
ADOR.RecordsetClass rs = new ADOR.RecordsetClass();
```

Behind the Scenes with COM

Here's what is happening behind the scenes when you add a COM reference to your application:

- A copy of the component is placed in the project directory.
- A proxy is generated for the COM component.
- The proxy is called a Runtime Callable Wrapper (RCW), and it essentially makes the COM component look like a .NET assembly.

PART IV

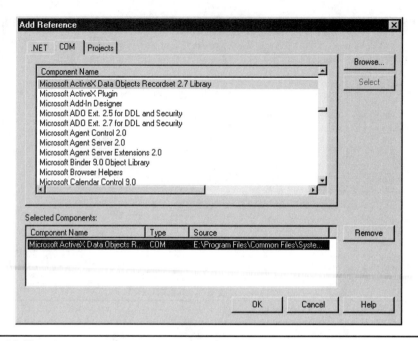

Figure 21-13   The selected components are listed at the bottom of the Add Reference dialog box

Although Visual Studio .NET does the preceding things for you, you may be asked on the Microsoft exam to prove your expertise with the command tool that allows you to manually generate the .NET proxy. The tool is called `TtlbImp.exe`, and it is the Type Library Importer. The importer will convert the definitions in the COM library to equivalent definitions in CLR. The tool will create an assembly that can be looked at by using `Ildasm.exe`, which is the MSIL disassembler utility.

The syntax for using the Type Library Importer tool is as follows:

```
tlbimp <name of file containing the COM type library> [options]
```

Table 21-2 shows some of the syntax options available for the `tlbimp.exe` tool.

EXAM TIP   Use the following list to memorize important COM details.

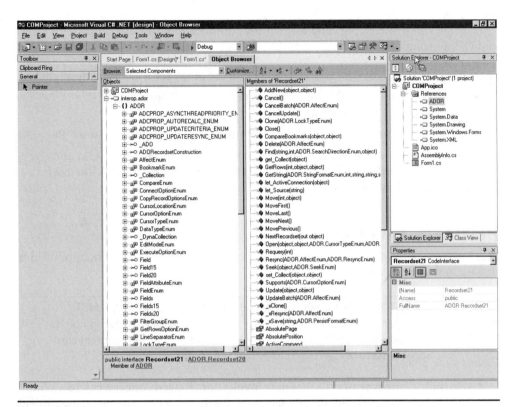

Figure 21-14   Object Browser

Option	Description
/asmversion:versionnumber	Identifies the version number of the assembly.
/help or /?	Returns the command syntax and options.
/out:filename	Identifies the name of the output assembly.
/namespace:namespace	Identifies the namespace in which to produce the assembly.
/primary	Produces a primary interop assembly. There is a description of interop following this table.
/publickey:filename	Identifies the file containing the public key to use in signing the assembly.
/verbose	Displays additional information about the library.
/unsafe	Creates interfaces without runtime security checks.
/reference:filename	Identifies the name of the assembly to use in resolving references.
/silent	Suppresses output display.

Table 21-2   Options for the TlbImp.exe tool

Here are some interesting (and test-worthy) points about interoperating with COM and COM+ components:

- The `TlbImp.exe` tool is used to generate the proxy for a COM component.
- COM components still have to be registered in the Registry. Use `regsvr32.exe` to do this.
- COM components used by .NET applications must be registered in the Registry.
- COM interop is a two-way service that creates a bridge between COM and the .NET framework. This is the way that COM components can "talk" to .NET components and vice versa.

Platform Invoke

Platform invoke allows us to get access to functionality that is in libraries or applications that use unmanaged code.

 EXAM TIP Unmanaged code is code that runs outside of the .NET environment. This means that .NET cannot run garbage collection on it or check the security of the code—it executes in the CLR with minimal services (security, garbage collection, and so on).

An example of the type of calls that may invoke unmanaged code is a call to a Win32 API, which contains many functional pieces of code that you may choose to use instead of creating your own code. Within the Win32 API, you will find `user32.dll`, `gdi32.dll`, and `kernel32.dll`, which will allow you access to some of the Windows platform functionality.

The CLR provides for platform invoke (`pinvoke`), which allows managed code (our .NET code) to call unmanaged native platform code.

 EXAM TIP Make a reference to the `InteropServices` namespace in your C# application in order to communicate with the Win32 API.

Follow these steps to make a call to the Win32 API:

1. Add the namespace like this:

```
using System.Runtime.InteropServices;
```

2. Expose the API method that you want—in our example, we will use the message box from the Win32 API:

```
[DllImport("user32.dll")]
public static extern int MessageBoxW (int Modal, string Message, string Caption,
    int Options);
```

3. Call the method:

```
MessageBoxW (0, "Hello World!", "Hello", 0);
```

If you place the preceding method call inside the click event of a button, you will get the output shown in the following illustration when the user clicks the button.

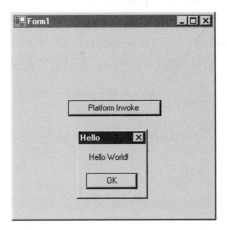

Summary

This chapter has demonstrated the techniques required when working with components. Components can take the shape of a .NET assembly, a COM or COM+ component, or an unmanaged code library, such as the Win32 API. Knowing how to consume these services is the component focus of the Microsoft Windows exam. You may not need to know how to create a component, but rather how to use it.

Keep in mind the various types of components:

- A .NET assembly can contain a .NET component and its metadata.

- A COM or COM+ component can reside in the local Registry or on a remote server.

- A Win32 API DLL exposes methods that allow the developer access to the underlying operating system.

Review the chapter for the utilities that allow these components to be integrated seamlessly into a .NET Framework application. In the next chapter, we will look at deploying the final application for use by the client or end user.

PART IV

Test Questions

1. Where should a web service proxy file be located?

   A. In the \bin directory of My Documents.

   B. In the \lib directory of the application.

   C. In the \bin directory of the application.

   D. In the \lib directory of My Documents.

2. Which code segment would correctly expose the `Convert()` method of a web service?

   A.
   ```
   public int Convert()
   {
       // write the method code here
   }
   ```

   B.
   ```
   private int Convert()
   {
       // write the method code here
   }
   ```

   C.
   ```
   protected int Convert()
   {
       // write the method code here
   }
   ```

   D.
   ```
   public Convert()
   {
       // write the method code here
   }
   ```

3. Which command-line tool will create a web service proxy?

   A. `isdlam.exe`

   B. `ildasm.exe`

   C. `tlbimp.exe`

   D. `wsdl.exe`

4. Which command-line tool will allow you to view an assembly?

   A. `isdlam.exe`

   B. `ildasm.exe`

   C. `tlbimp.exe`

   D. `wsdl.exe`

5. Which command-line tool will generate the proxy for a COM component?

   A. `isdlam.exe`

   B. `ildasm.exe`

    C. `tlbimp.exe`

    D. `wsdl.exe`

6. Which of the following will display the Web Services on a remote IIS server (named www.hmr.com) in an assembly called MyServices?

    A. http://hmr.com/MyServices/ServiceName

    B. http://www.hmr.com/MyServices/ServiceName

    C. url://hmr.com/MyServices/ServiceName

    D. url://www.hmr.com/MyServices/ServiceName

7. Which of the following code segments can be found in a web service proxy class that exposes a method called `CallMe`?

    A.
```
public class CallMeService()
{
    // class code here
}
```

    B.
```
public int CallMeService()
{
    object results = this.Invoke ("CallMeService", new object[0]);
    return ((string)(results[0]));
}
```

    C.
```
public int CallMeService()
{
    object[] results = this.Invoke ("CallMeService", new object[0]);
    return ((string)(results[0]));
}
```

    D.
```
public int CallMeService()
{
    object[] results = this.Invoke ("CallMe", new object[0]);
    return ((string)(results[0]));
}
```

8. What must be done to be ready to consume a web service?

    A. Build a proxy library using `wsdl.exe`.

    B. Build a proxy library using `csc.exe`.

    C. Build a proxy library using `TblImp.exe`.

    D. Build a proxy library using `pl.exe`.

9. You need to call the function, `CallMe()`, located in the `user32.dll` library. The signature of the function is as follows:

```
string CallMe (string Name, string Address, string Phone
```

Which code segment will make the function available to your application?

PART IV

A. `[DllImport("CallMe.dll")]`

`public static extern string CallMe (string Name, string Address, string Phone)];`

B. `[[DllImport("CallMe.dll", EntryPoint="CallMe")]`

`public static extern string CallMe (string Name, string Address, string Phone)];`

C. `[DllImport("user32.dll", EntryPoint="CallMe")]`

`public static extern string CallMe (string Name, string Address, string Phone)];`

D. `[DllImport("user32.dll")]`

`public static extern string CallMe (string Name, string Address, string Phone)];`

10. You have an assembly that includes a web service named `ListCollege`. The `ListAll()` method is a public method that takes an integer value (`studentID`) and returns a Boolean value—True if the student was found, False if no student was found. Which code segment will correctly call this method?

A. `ListCollege.ListAll la = new ListCollege.ListAll();`
`bool response = la.ListAll(studentID);`

B. `ListCollege.ListAll la = new ListCollege.ListAll();`
`la.ListAll();`

C. `ListCollege.ListAll la = new ListCollege.ListAll();`
`bool response = la.ListAll();`

D. `ListCollege.ListAll la = new ListCollege.ListAll();`
`la.ListAll(studentID);`

11. Which namespace is added to a program that calls a web service?

A. `using System.WebServices;`

B. `using System.Web.Services;`

C. `using System.Web.Services.List;`

D. `using System.Web.Services.All;`

12. Which URL will provide access to the web service called `MyWebService`, located in the `WebServices` web on the local machine?

A. http://localhost/MyWebService/WebServices.asmx?WSDL

B. http://localhost/WebServices/WebServices.asmx?WSDL

C. http://localhost/MyWebService/MyWebService.asmx?WSDL

D. http://localhost/WebServices/MyWebService.asmx?WSDL

13. A discovery file used to locate Web Services would have which extension?

    A. .discovery

    B. .discover

    C. .vdisco

    D. .disco

14. When you test a web service, what do you expect to see as output?

    A. The web service running.

    B. The web site.

    C. The XML of the web proxy.

    D. The XML of the web service.

15. Which attribute must be added to create an exposed web service method?

    A. [System.WebServices.WebMethod]

    B. [System.Web.Services]

    C. [System.Web.Services.Web.WebMethod]

    D. [System.Web.Services.WebMethod]

Test Answers

1. C.

2. A. The method must be declared as public.

3. D.

4. B.

5. D.

6. B.

7. D. The method name must be CallMe and the result must be an array.

8. A.

9. C.

10. A.

11. B.

12. D.

13. C.

14. C.

15. D.

PART IV

Build Your Own Windows Control

In this chapter, you will

- Get acquainted with the different types of Windows controls you can create
- Learn to build a composite control
- Understand how to license your control
- Be able to test your control

There will be times during your application development that you will need a control that cannot be found in the Toolbox or in the component libraries. You may also discover that you often create the same combination of controls on your Windows Forms or that you would like a particular control to exhibit extra functionality every time you use it. All of these dilemmas can be solved by creating your own Windows Forms control.

Consider a text box control. It has a number of properties, methods, and events that you can use when you add the control to your form. But what if you wanted that same text box to accept only numeric input every time you used it. Instead of changing its properties every time, you can create a new type of text box control that exhibits the behavior that you desire. Often in a business application, you will find that a combination of controls is used to request a particular response from the user. Each application you build must have the same controls added and their functionality combined. By creating your own control that is built from the combination of these controls, you can reduce your development time greatly. Finally, if you are in the business of creating user controls for development teams, you may find that you regularly take a blank control and draw its interface and provide its functionality from scratch.

In this chapter, we will investigate the ways you can create your own customized controls. You may already be familiar with the term *ActiveX controls*. These were the controls that Visual Basic programmers created and used. Microsoft has moved away from that term, which had mostly Internet connotations, and, in order to simplify and clarify things, now calls any component that has a visible interface a *control*.

At this point in your OOP career, you should not find this kind of coding to be a mystery—after all, isn't this just the same thing as building a class file in order to create reusable objects? The only difference here is that you build a graphical interface into the component, with which the user can interact.

Methods of Building Windows Controls

The Microsoft Visual C# .NET Windows exam will test your knowledge of the three different ways of building custom controls:

- Extending an existing control.
- Combining existing controls into a new composite control.
- Designing and building a control from scratch.

In this section, we will consider the three types of controls and briefly describe their use, and later we will examine the process of creating a composite control from a combination of existing controls in detail.

Microsoft will likely test your knowledge of combining existing controls into a new single control, but we will look at all three methods individually. The combined control is probably the control most commonly built (unless you are a control developer and build your own from scratch).

 EXAM TIP There are three ways to build your own controls: inherit from an existing control, combine existing controls into a new control, or design and build your own control from scratch.

Extending an Existing Control

In order to change or increase the functionality of an existing control, you can simply inherit from the base control, which gives you the base properties, methods, and events, and allows you to add what you need. To illustrate this, we will extend the standard button and add our own fine-tuning to its base functionality. Our new button will have an extra property called `ButtonName` that will allow the user to set and retrieve a name for the button.

Creating the New Extended Control

To begin, start a new project that uses the Windows Control Library by selecting File | New | Project. From the New Project dialog box, choose Windows Control Library as shown in Figure 22-1.

Give the project a name that will reflect the type of control you are building. For this example, name the project `NewButton.cs`. By naming the project, you will also have given a name to the namespace to which your class will belong. Once you are done, click OK.

You will notice that you do not see the standard Windows Form in this type of project. Instead you see a `UserControl` interface (shown in the following illustration). We

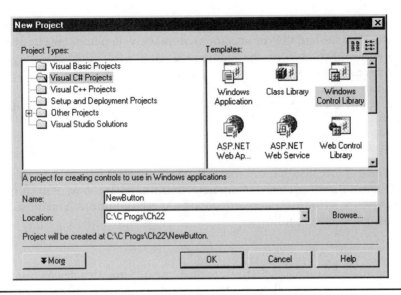

Figure 22-1   Creating a new Windows Control Library project

will explore the UserControl interface in the "Creating Composite Controls" section, when we build controls that are made up of multiple existing controls.

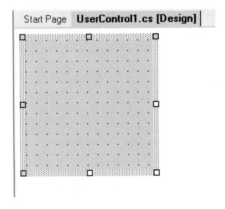

Once the new project has been created, you need to do a little housekeeping in order to name the class file and the constructor appropriately. Rename `UserControl1.cs` in the Solution Explorer to the name you chose (for this example, name it `NewButton.cs`). Then switch to code view and rename the class file to `NewButton` and the constructor to `NewButton`.

Now examine the code carefully. You will see that the class file definition looks like this:

```
public class NewButton: System.Windows.Forms.UserControl
```

This is the inheritance line that you must change if you want to inherit from an existing control. Our specifications state that our new control will have most of the functionality of a regular `Button` control, along with our own special additions. You must, therefore, change this line to read as follows:

```
public class NewButton: System.Windows.Forms.Button
```

By changing this line, you have effectively created a new control that derives from the `Button` class. Your new control will have all the methods, properties, and events of a `Button`, and you can modify or add to that. Save and build your project before continuing.

In order to create a new property that will allow us to set and retrieve the button's name, you now need to add your own property to the code—`ButtonName`. Start by creating a private variable to store the new property:

```
private string varValue;
```

Now create the public property procedure as follows:

```
public string ButtonName
{
    get
    {
        return varValue;
    }
    set
    {
        varValue = value;
    }
}
```

Save and compile the application.

Testing an Extended Control
One method of testing the control is to add a new project to the solution and place your control on the Windows Form of the new project. Follow these steps:

1. Add a new project to your solution (File | Add Project | Windows Application).

2. Set the new form as the startup form. Right-click on the application name in Solution Explorer and select Set as Startup Project.

EXAM TIP A control created in the Windows Control Library will not start up a form on its own—that is why you need the new project and windows form to test your control.

Add a reference to your control to the new project:

1. In Solution Explorer, right-click on the References for the new project and select Add Reference. The Add Reference dialog box will be displayed, as shown in Figure 22-2.

2. Select the Projects tab and choose your new control from the list.

Once you have added the reference to the control, you will see it listed under the References heading in the Solution Explorer (see Figure 22-3).

You need to do one more thing in order to use the control from the Toolbox.

1. Right-click on the Toolbox and select Customize Toolbox.

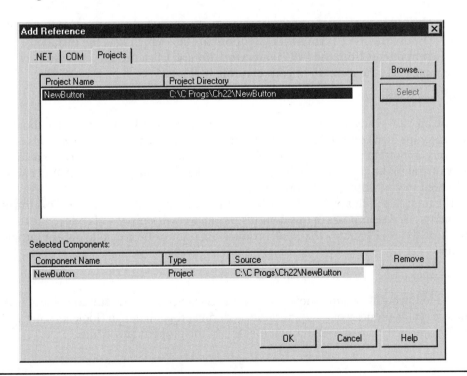

Figure 22-2 Adding a reference to NewButton

Figure 22-3

The `NewButton` reference in the Solution Explorer

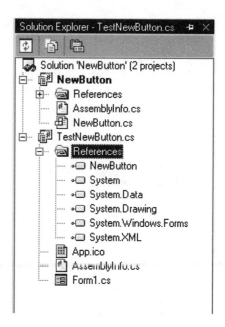

2. You will be presented with the Customize Toolbox dialog box (see Figure 22-4). Choose the .NET Framework Components tab, which lists the installed components from the .NET Framework library. Click the Browse button and select the location of your control.

3. Click OK.

You are now ready to build the new form. When you scroll down in the Toolbox, you will see your own control listed there. Notice that its name is `NewButton`—this is why it is very important to give your control a meaningful name from the start. Your control now operates like any other control. Double-click on it and a default `NewButton` will be added to your form (see Figure 22-5).

The final step in this process is to add the functionality that will set or retrieve the new property. For the purposes of this demonstration, we will simply add code to the `Click` event of the `NewButton` that will produce a `MessageBox` displaying the property value:

```
MessageBox.Show (newButton1.ButtonName);
```

The following illustration shows the result of clicking on the `NewButton` object. Notice that we set the property of the `ButtonName` during program design (look at Figure 22-5), and the property is retrieved through the `Get` in the property procedure.

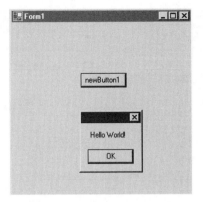

When to Extend an Existing Control

It can get rather confusing to know when to extend an existing control and when to create a new control. The approach just presented of extending an existing control allows

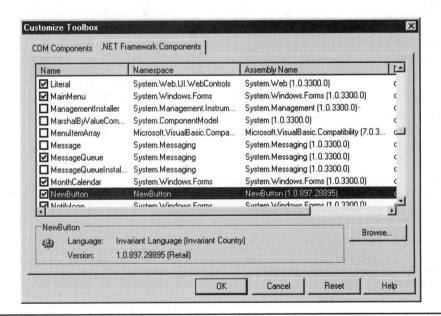

Figure 22-4 Customizing the Toolbox

PART IV

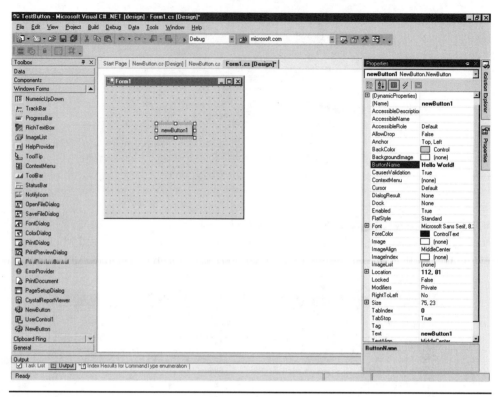

Figure 22-5 The new form with a `NewButton` added

you to derive your control from a base control, maintaining all the properties, methods, and events of the base class. It also allows you to add to the original functionality or to override it.

EXAM TIP Use these next two points to determine whether to extend an existing control or build a new one.

- If you need a control that provides much of the functionality of an existing control, it is wise to derive a new control from the existing one and simply add to it or override the base control's methods.

- If you don't need a combination of existing controls, inherit from a single control. For instance, if you need a button to do the work of a regular button, and also to take on some of your required characteristics.

If you don't need to customize the look of the control, inheriting from an existing control is the way to go. However, if you need your own look on a control, this will require more work than simply overriding the behavior of a base control. In that case, you should create a new control independent of any base controls.

Creating Composite Controls

Very often, you will find that you need a visual interface that is a combination of a number of controls. A control built from several existing controls is called a *composite control*.

For example, you can build a simple control that will display the date and time by combining a `Label` control and the `Timer` control. You can program the label to display the current date and time whenever the `Timer` control's `Tick` event is triggered. This can be set to happen every second or every minute.

Of course, you can add these two controls to your form when you need them, so why would you go to the bother of creating a new control? The answer to that lies in the number of times you will need the combination of these two controls. If every form you create needs to display the date and time in this fashion, then you should create the new control.

The UserControl Class

Before we go into the details of creating a new control based on existing controls, we need to examine the `UserControl` class. Every control inherits from `System.Windows.Forms.UserControl`. You can think of the `UserControl` class as similar to the `System.Windows.Forms.Form` class—the `Form` acts as a container for the visual components of your application, and the `UserControl` acts as a container for the controls that you wish to combine into one.

There is an extensive list of properties, methods, and events associated with the `UserControl` class that provide the basic functionality of your new control:

- Properties such as `Anchor`, `AutoScroll`, `BackColor`, `CanFocus`, `CausesValidation`, `DataBindings`, `Dock`, `Enabled`, `Font`, `ForeColor`, `Location`, `Size`, `TabIndex`, `TabStop`, `Text`, and `Visible`, to name just a few.

- Methods such as `Dispose`, `DoDragDrop`, `Focus`, `Hide`, `Refresh`, `ResetText`, `Select`, `Show`, and `Validate`.

- Events such as `BackColorChanged`, `ControlAdded`, `ControlRemoved`, `DragOver`, `Enter`, `GotFocus`, `KeyDown`, `KeyPress`, `MouseMove`, `Move`, `Resize`, and `TextChanged`.

This is just a short list of the properties, methods, and events that are part of any composite control. You can find the complete listing of control behavior in the help documents attached to Visual Studio .NET. Most of the behavior is inherited from the `Control` class from which `UserControl` is derived.

The UserControl gives the control developer a container that provides basic control support. For example, a design interface is provided, onto which all other controls are placed. These controls keep their own functionality in the control's design phase. However, when the control is completed and is used within another application, only the functions that have been released will be available to the user of the control. This gives the control designer free reign over what properties, methods, and events of the original controls are exposed to the world in the composite control.

 EXAM TIP A control never functions on its own. A control must exist within a hosting application and does not execute independently.

Before we look at how these controls are built, try to keep in mind that a composite control has two different design-time phases. The first phase is when the control itself is designed, and this is when the developer works with the properties of the controls on the UserControl. The second design-time phase is when the developer places the composite control on a new form. At that point, the developer has access to those properties, methods, and events that the control developer has exposed.

 EXAM TIP The controls that make up the composite control are called the *constituent controls*. For example, if you create a control that has a Label and a Timer, the Label and Timer are constituent controls. The new control built from the combination of the two is called the *composite control*.

Creating a Composite Control
Let's examine the overall process of creating a composite control. The following six steps outline the basic procedure, and we will expand upon these as we move through the section:

1. Start a new Windows Control Library project.
2. Add the constituent controls (from the Toolbox) to the UserControl.
3. Adjust the size of the UserControl user interface and the position, size, and properties of the constituent controls.
4. Expose or add any properties to the constituent controls (this involves declaring them as public).
5. Work with methods and events.
6. Test the control.

 EXAM TIP Properties, methods, and events of the constituent controls are, by default, hidden from the user of the composite control.

Starting a New Windows Control Library Project   The first step in building a composite control is to create the project under which it will be developed. From
the menus, select File | New Project. You will be presented with the New Project dialog
box (shown earlier in Figure 22-1). Choose the Windows Control Library and click OK.
You will see the `UserControl` design interface shown in Figure 22-6.

The Windows Control Library template is used to create customized controls that will
be added to Windows Forms. By using the template, you automatically have added all
the references to the solution that are required for a new control. These references include the `System`, `System.Data`, `System.Drawing`, `System.Windows.Forms`,
and `System.Xml` namespaces. You will also notice that the `UserControl1.cs` file
has been added to your solution. This is your `UserControl` interface.

NOTE   The template is unavailable in the Standard Edition of Visual C# .NET.

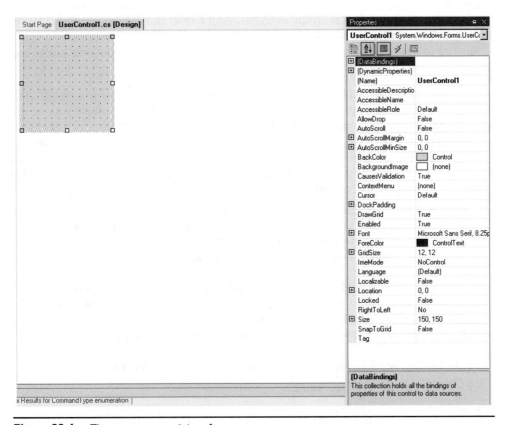

Figure 22-6   The `UserControl` interface

It's a good idea to rename the UserControl to a more meaningful name, as this will be your control's name. Follow these steps:

1. Right-click on the UserControl1.cs file in the Solution Explorer, and select Rename. Enter an appropriate name.

2. In the code module associated with the UserControl interface, find the class name and change it to your new name. You should also ensure that the namespace has a meaningful name as well. (Don't forget to change the constructor name.)

Adding Constituent Controls to the UserControl   The next step is to add the constituent controls to the UserControl. This is done in the same way as placing controls on a Windows Form—double-click on the control from the Toolbox, or select the control and drag it into place.

As an example, create a composite control called StudentValidate that can be used in the college project. This control should contain five constituent controls—two Label controls to display "Student Number:" and "Student Name:", two TextBox controls to contain the student number and student name, and a Button for validating the input. The composite control is shown in Figure 22-7.

Be sure to name all of your controls appropriately and not leave them as Button1, TextBox1, and so forth.

Adjusting the Constituent Controls   You can now go into the constituent controls and adjust their properties. The first properties that should concern you are the size and position of the controls. Place them as you want to see them in your final product. Be aware that the user of your control can adjust the sizes and move the controls if you leave them with that ability—the properties that allow these changes are exposed for the UserControl. If you allow the user to adjust sizes and positions, you must also provide code within the control's interface that adjusts the control accordingly.

TIP   Set the size of the UserControl to be large enough to just hold the constituent controls. Remember that the UserControl will be a control in the Toolbox, and it will be added to another developer's project.

In the StudentValidate example, you could set the ReadOnly property of the student name text box to True, since you don't want to allow the user to initially type into the text box. This text box should act as a display only. You can also add any additional properties to your new control as we did earlier in the chapter for a simple extended control:

1. In the code editor, add the private variables for the properties.

2. Create the property procedures.

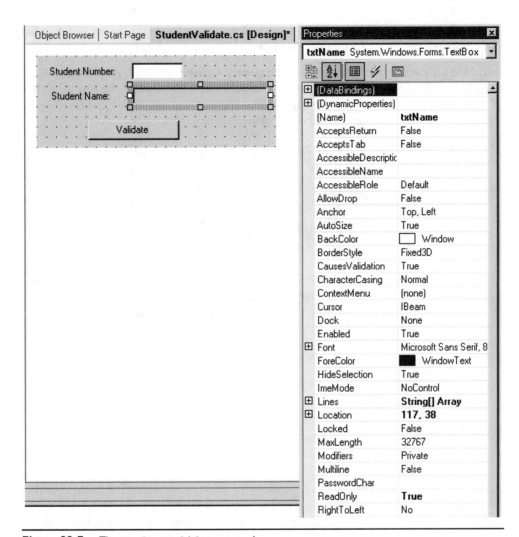

Figure 22-7 The `StudentValidate` control

EXAM TIP Always use properties for your controls (instead of public variables)—the Visual Studio .NET designer program will only display properties, not variables.

In the next section, "Exposing Properties of the Constituent Control," we will examine the code to not only add new properties but also to expose the existing properties of the constituent control—remember, by default, they are hidden from the user of your control.

Once you have set all properties to your initial values, the next step is to decide what you will allow the user of your control to do.

Exposing Properties of the Constituent Control Let's examine how you can allow the user of your composite control to take advantage of the functionality of its constituent controls. For this discussion, add a CheckBox control to the StudentValidate project, as shown in the following illustration.

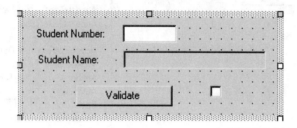

This CheckBox should remain invisible until the student number has been validated since we don't want the user to have access to it until the validation is performed. To accomplish this, you just need to create a public property that exposes the constituent control's Visible property:

```
public bool cbValid_Visible
{
    set
    {
        if (cbValid.Visible == false)
            cbValid.Visible = true;
        else
            cbValid.Visible = false;
    }
}
```

On a request to set the Visible property of the CheckBox called cbValid, this simple code segment will reverse the current value. Obviously, in a sophisticated application, the code would be more extensive. For our purposes, though, we must expose it in this manner so the user of the StudentValidate control (who could be another developer) can set the Visible property. This is what encapsulation is all about—users never need to know how the Visible property is set; they just need to know that they can use it.

EXAM TIP In order to expose the properties of the constituent control, expose them as properties of the composite control.

You can also simply expose a constituent's property without any extra coding:

```
public Color txtName_BackColor
{
```

```
get
{
    return txtName.BackColor;
}
set
{
    txtName.BackColor = value;
}
}
```

This is the easiest way to allow a user of the control access to a constituent property.

You can also add properties as we did for our extended control, NewButton. Add the private variable declaration and then create the public get and set to access the private data:

```
private int var;
public int NewVariable
{
    get
    {
        return var;
    }
    set
    {
        var = value;
    }
}
```

 EXAM TIP   Remember that you can add in all the functionality that is required within the get and set code blocks. This is the value of using properties instead of public variables.

Working with Methods and Events   There is no practical difference between working with methods in any other class file and working with methods in a custom control. Declare your method and provide the body of the method implementation:

```
public void ControlMethod
{
    // implementation of the method goes here
}
```

Events are a little different. An event is the way your control interacts with the rest of the application. There are two different ways of creating events:

- Expose a constituent event (remember, they are private by default)
- Create a custom event

In order to expose a constituent event, the UserControl must raise the event. Start by adding an event handler in the UserControl (for example, add a Click event to a button control).

```
private void btnValidate_Click (object sender, System.EventArgs e)
{
    OnClick(e);
}
```

The "On" before the "Click" in the method is used because all controls have a method that can be called to raise the event. In effect, the OnClick() method raises the Click event from the UserControl.

In order to create a custom event, you can use delegates, which is the .NET standard for using exposing and consuming events in Windows Forms. For example, to create the event that should be triggered upon trying the student number too often in our StudentValidate control, you could use this code:

```
// declare the delegate
public delegate void OutOfLuckEventHandler (object sender, OutOfLuckEventArgs e);
```

Then you could add the event declaration:

```
public event OutOfLuckEventHandler OutOfLuck;
```

And then you would raise the event by creating the "On" method:

```
public void OnOutOfLuck (OutOfLuckEventArgs e)
{
    // invoke the delegate
    OutOfLuck (this, e);
}
```

You are not done yet. You must now allow the hosting application to use this event. You need to add code within the Click event of your Validate button to check the number of times the button has been clicked, and then cause the event to be raised:

```
OnOutOfLuck (new OutOfLuckEventArgs ( <parameters>);
```

Finally, the hosting application would use the control's event to respond to the raising of the event:

```
private void myStudentValidate_OutOfLuck (object sender, OutOfLuckEventArgs e)
{
    // write the code that responds to the 3 click attempts
}
```

If you are still unsure as to how this would work, refer back to Chapter 19 to review the handling of events in Visual C# .NET.

Testing the Composite Control   Remember that controls are not stand-alone applications—they must be added to a hosting application first and then tested from there. Follow these steps to test your control:

1. Build your control. Select Build | Build from the menus.

2. Create a test project. Select File | Add Project | New Project.

3. Select Windows Application, and give the new project a name.

4. Add a reference to your control. Right-click the References for your new project in the Solution Explorer and select Add Reference. This will display the Add Reference dialog box (see Figure 22-8).

5. Add your control to the Toolbox. Right-click the Toolbox and select Customize Toolbox. Then, from the .NET Framework Components tab, click Browse and find the directory containing your custom control. Drill down into the Bin\ Debug directory and add the control (see Figure 22-9).

6. Set the test project as the startup project. Right-click on the test project and choose Select as Startup.

7. Run the test project.

You should notice that these steps are very similar to the steps taken to test a control that is created by extending an existing control. There is very little difference between the two methods.

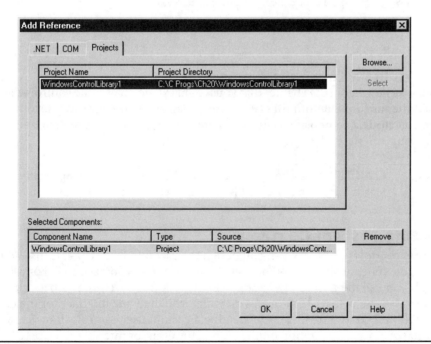

Figure 22-8   The Add Reference dialog box

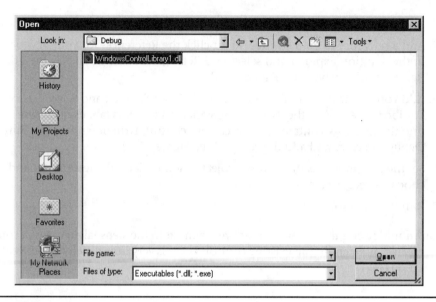

Figure 22-9 Selecting the control from the Debug directory

When to Use a Composite Control

We suggested earlier in the chapter that you would extend an existing control when you wanted the functionality of a single control enhanced with your own customization. When you create a composite control, you are pulling together more than one control into a visual interface (the `UserControl`).

 EXAM TIP Use a composite control when you want to bring together the functionality of many controls into one, reusable control.

Building Custom Controls

A custom control is one for which you design the user interface elements instead of extending the functionality of one or many controls already in existence. For a custom control, you use the `System.Windows.Forms.Control` class as a base class, and this provides you with a blank canvas on which you draw the interface for the user.

We will not go into the details of creating a custom user control, since you are not likely to see its implementation on the exam. However, for interest's sake, here is some sample code that would start the process:

```
using System;
using System.Drawing;
using System.ComponentModel;
using System.Windows.Forms;
public class MyCustomControl: System.Windows.Forms.Control
{
// override the OnPaint event of the Control class
// draw your own user interface using GDI+
    protected override void OnPaint (System.Windows.Forms.PaintEventArgs e)
    {
        // using the PaintEventArgs object, call the methods of GDI+
        e.Graphics.Draw<Method> (<arguments>);
    }
}
```

We have not examined the drawing capabilities of GDI+ (Graphics Device Interface) yet—that will be covered in Chapter 24; however, the preceding code demonstrates the way in which you would start to code your custom control.

The base class contains a default event handler, `OnPaint`, which really does nothing. You must override it and insert the code that will make your control look the way you want it to. Notice that the event handler is sent an argument of type `System.Windows.Forms.PaintEventArgs`. Using that object, you can work with its most significant property—an object of type `System.Drawing.Graphics`. The methods of the `Graphics` object allow you to work with the GDI+ code of the .NET Framework. The draw methods, such as `DrawString`, allow you to paint a graphics object (in this case a `String`) onto the drawing surface. Refer to Chapter 24 for more information on GDI+.

EXAM TIP   To build a composite control, extend the `UserControl` base class. To build a custom control, extend the `Control` base class.

Visual Studio .NET Support

In this section, we will look at a few of the shortcut techniques you can use to build your controls. The goal behind any good integrated development environment is to save the developer time, and the Visual Studio program is no exception.

Using Visual Inheritance

One of Microsoft's stated exam objectives for building your own control is "Create a Windows control by using visual inheritance." As we have noted already, you can create a control whose base control is just another control. For example, our `NewButton` is inherited from the base class `Button`. We accomplished this through code. You can use Visual Inheritance to accomplish the same thing.

Follow these steps to access the Inheritance Picker dialog box, from which you can choose an existing control:

1. Start a new Windows Application project and name it UsingVIDemo (see Figure 22-10).

2. If you wish, you can add references to existing components. For example, add a reference to the NewButton control by right-clicking on the project References in the Solution Explorer and choosing Add Reference. This opens the Add Reference dialog box (shown in Figure 22-11). From the Projects tab, browse to find your component, and add it to the reference list by clicking Select and then OK.

3. You can also add an inherited control. Select Project | Add New Item to open the Add New Item dialog box (see Figure 22-12). Select Inherited User Control from the Templates list on the right side of the dialog box.

4. If you are just starting your project, and you have not performed the Build operation on it, you will receive a warning message from the Inheritance Picker, as shown in the following illustration. If the control from which you intend to inherit is not found in the current assembly, you will receive this message as well. If you do not receive this message, skip to step 6.

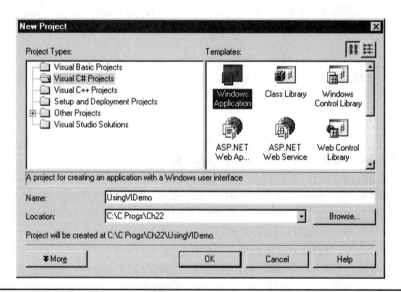

Figure 22-10 Creating a new Windows Application project

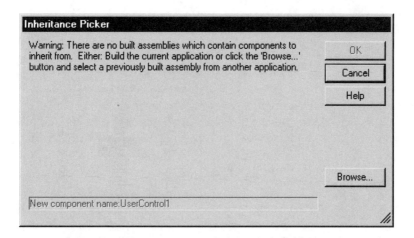

5. Click the Browse button in the Inheritance Picker warning dialog box, and find the directory with the assembly that contains your base control.

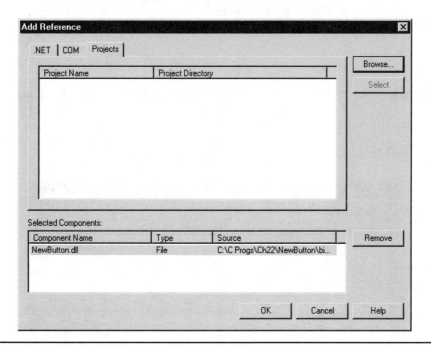

Figure 22-11   Adding a reference to an existing component

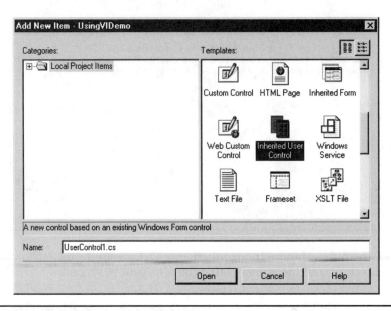

Figure 22-12   Adding an inherited control

6. You will now see the Inheritance Picker, as shown in the following illustration. You can either select the component from the list or click the Browse button to point the directory system to the component you wish to use. For this example, find and select the StudentValidate control created earlier in this chapter. Click OK, and the control will be added to your project.

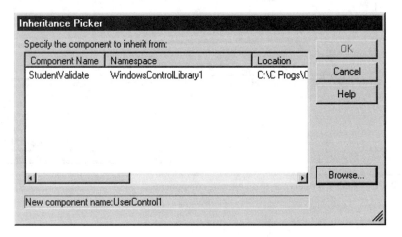

7. If you wish to alter any of the `StudentValidate` control's properties, right-click on the reference to the control in the Solution Explorer and select View Designer. This will take you to the design-time instance of the control (see the following illustration).

Notice that the Property Explorer window allows you to see the properties of the `StudentValidate` control. However, they are grayed out and are inaccessible to the developer. This is because all properties are deemed to be private unless the control designer chooses to expose them. In developing the `StudentValidate` control, you could create public properties for those constituent properties that you want to let users of the control work with.

EXAM TIP   You can only modify properties for which there is a public property in the `UserControl`.

Adding Design-Time Support to Your Control

So far, we have not been very friendly to the user of our controls. In this section, we will look at how to add a Toolbox bitmap for the `StudentValidate` control. We will also add attributes to the control, which can then be applied to properties, methods, or events. Finally, we will look at some of the features included in the .NET Framework to assist in developing controls.

Adding a Toolbox Bitmap

A Toolbox bitmap provides a related graphic appearance for your control in the Toolbox. For example, the `Label` control has an "A" as its graphic, and a `Button` has a small button as its graphic. The `NewButton` and `StudentValidate` controls show default graphics when you add it to the Toolbox (see Figure 22-13). Notice that `NewButton` has one graphic and `StudentValidate` has another. It depends on how the control is created and what kind of control it is (simple, composite, custom) as to which bitmap is used.

EXAM TIP   A very important concept that we will introduce here is that you have your own copy of the control when it is added to your project. This is good news to developers who have, in the past, struggled with versioning of controls. Version 1 might have belonged to a certain number of applications, while version 2 belonged to different applications. By making the control part of the new application, the version is implicitly bound to the application.

Here are the steps for adding a Toolbox bitmap to your control:

1. Open your control project.

2. Select Project | Add Existing Item from the menus. You will see the Add Existing Item dialog box, as shown in Figure 22-14. Change the Files of Type filter to "All files (*.*)."

3. Find an appropriate icon in the file system. In this example, we have chosen the MSN icon to represent the `StudentValidate` control (for no reason, other than we like MSN).

Figure 22-13
The default
Toolbox bitmaps

4. Once the icon file (MSN.ico) has been added to the project, you need to treat it as an embedded resource. Click on the icon file in Solution Explorer, and

then move to the Properties Explorer (see the following illustration). You can see that there is a Build Action property that you need to set to Embedded Resource.

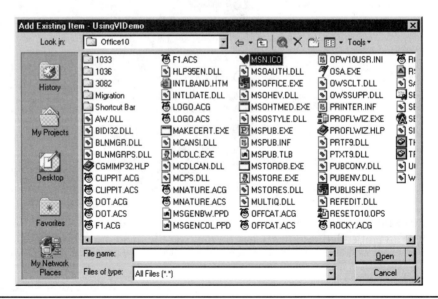

Figure 22-14 The Add Existing Item dialog box

5. Finally, you need to add the code that will associate the icon with the control. In the line preceding the class definition, add the following code:

```
[ToolboxBitmap(typeof(StudentValidate), @"MSN.ico")]
```

The MSN.ico string specifies the file (you can also add the path to the file in the string) and the typeof parameter specifies that the icon is to be associated with the StudentValidate type.

There are two other forms of this statement. Use whichever you need to access your icon for the Toolbox bitmap:

```
// insert the icon associated with the control type only
[ToolboxBitmap(typeof(StudentValidate)]

// insert the icon associated with the path
[ToolboxBitmap(@"MSN.ico")]
```

 EXAM TIP   Remember that this line of code appears before the class definition in your code module.

Adding Attributes to Properties

By adding attributes to properties and events (or to the control itself), you can add design-time functionality to the control. The attributes become part of the metadata of the control and allow you to specify how your custom properties will be grouped together within the Properties Explorer, what types of default values exist for your properties, and whether there are any custom editors for your custom properties.

Table 22-1 identifies the types of attributes that you can add to your control.

Property Attribute	Description
Browsable	Indicates whether a property or event can be displayed in the Property Browser/Explorer.
Category	Indicates the name of the category that will be used to group the property in the Properties Explorer.
Description	Specifies the description the user will see when the property or event is selected from the Property Browser.
DefaultProperty	Indicates the default property for the control.
DefaultValue	Indicates the default value of the property.
TypeConverter	Indicates the type converter to use when converting the property to another type.
Editor	Specifies the editor to be used when changing the property.
RefreshProperties	Specifies how the forms designer will refresh when changes are made to the property values.

Table 22-1   Property Attributes That Can Be Added to a Custom Control

These attributes can be inserted into the code module for your control. Place them in front of the property or event to which you are adding this functionality. Here is an example:

```
[Category("StudentValidate"), Description ("The Validate button will check
for the existence of the Student Number in the database")]
public override Button Validate
```

Providing Other Design-Time Support

In order to give the user of your control extra design-time support, the features listed in Table 22-2 are available to your control.

To go into any more detail on these features is beyond the scope of the Microsoft C# Windows exam. You may just need to be aware that these features exist.

Hosting Your Control in Internet Explorer

There will be times when your control will be added to a browser page and displayed in Internet Explorer. Be aware that support for this exists only in versions of Internet Explorer 5.5 and higher.

The control is loaded from the web server by adding an OBJECT tag into the HTML page as follows:

```
<OBJECT id="StudentValidate" classid="StudentValidate.dll#StudentValidate"
width="100" height="100">
<PARAM name="//your parameter goes here" value="//set the value"
</OBJECT>
```

.NET Feature	Description
Property Browser	You will see all exposed properties in the Property Browser. The browser provides built-in capabilities for testing the type of data that the user enters for a property at design time.
Type Converter	Most type conversions are from a string to a given type (such as an integer). The primitive types have their own type converters (Int32), but you can create your own type converter by extending the System.ComponentModel.TypeConverter class and then applying the new converter to a property.
Custom editors	Define and create a class that is derived from System.Drawing.Design.UITypeEditor. This class can then be applied to a certain property for your control.
Customer Designers	You can create a class that implements the IDesigner interface in order to create your own visual clues for design-time use of your control.

Table 22-2   Built-in Design Support for Controls

Here are a few points about running your controls in Internet Explorer:

- The client must have the .NET Framework Redistributables installed.

- Your control will run in a browser page.

- You can only host controls that you have built (or custom or user controls) in Internet Explorer—you cannot host controls from the standard Toolbox.

- This is supported in Internet Explorer 5.5 or higher only.

Licensing a Control

Now that you have created a fabulous control that you will sell to millions of developers, you need to ensure that your control is being used in a controlled fashion. This involves licensing your control and then checking whether the user is authorized to use the control. Remember that a developer, who is your user, will be incorporating your control into an application at design time. This is when you will want to issue a runtime license so that users of the application will be able to use your control.

There are two modes of licensing:

- **Design-time licensing**   This allows a developer to use your control in their new application.

- **Runtime licensing**   This allows the user of the new application to run your control.

When you add a licensed component to your application, the following things will happen:

- The `LicenseManager` will look for a valid `.LIC` file. Remember that by default it will look for the file in the same folder as the assembly.

- Upon finding a valid `.LIC` file, the `LicenseManager` creates and populates the `License` object.

- The `.LICX` file is created automatically by Visual Studio .NET and is added to the assembly.

- After the application has been built, the `LC.exe` utility gets to work. It does the following things:

  - Looks for the list of licensed controls in the `.LICX` file.

  - Creates objects for all the controls found.

  - Extracts the runtime license key.

  - Creates the binary `.Licenses` file with the collection of runtime keys.

EXAM TIP All of the licensing support resides in the `System.ComponentModel` namespace.

Here are the steps to enable licensing for your control:

1. Add a `LicenseProvider` to your class. The license provider derives from `System.ComponentModel.LicenseProvider`—you specify the actual type and .NET will supply the default `LicFileLicenseProvider` for you. The default is easy to use, but not very secure. You will want to extend this class to provide for more security and functionality.

   `[LicenseProvider(typeof(LicFileLicenseProvider))]`

2. Create a license object that will represent the valid license:

   `private License myLicense = null;`

3. The license object is instantiated and filled with the valid license through the use of a `LicenseManager` object. Use either the `Validate()` or `IsValid()` methods. (Use the `IsValid()` method to test the validity and limit usage of the control based on the result.) The `Validate()` method will throw an exception (`LicenseException`) when there is no valid license present. The `LicenseManager` has properties and methods to add a license to a component.

   `MyLicense = LicenseManager.Validate (typeof(StudentValidate), this);`

You will also need the files listed in Table 22-3 to complete the licensing scenario.

EXAM TIP Add the `xxxx.LIC` file to the assembly folder in the obj\Debug folder.

File	Purpose
`xxxx.LIC`	This is the design-time license file. It is a text file that should be in the same directory as the assembly. The file must contain this statement: "<namespace.classname> is a licensed component," where you provide the namespace and classname.
`xxxx.LICX`	This is the design-time license file. This file consumes a licensed component. It is a text file, and it lists all of the licensed components in an application. This file is created automatically when you add a licensed component to an application.
`xxxx.Licenses`	This is a binary runtime license file. It is generated by the `LC.exe` utility.

Table 22-3 License Files

Dispose of a `License` object when you are done with it. In the `Dispose` method, add the following code:

```
if (myLicense != null)
{
    myLicense.Dispose();
    myLicense = null;
}
```

Summary

In this chapter, we explored three ways of creating your own custom controls. We created a control by inheriting from an existing control, by using a `UserControl` object to host a number of existing controls, and by using a `Control` object to create our own design. Depending on your position within the development team, you may or may not have to ever create your own controls. Often a company has a team of "control developers" or uses controls developed by third parties.

The Microsoft exam will focus on your ability to derive a new control from a single existing control, or to build a new control that is based on a combination of many existing controls. Spend some time creating your own controls until you are comfortable with the concepts presented in this chapter. In the next chapter, we will create the foundations for deploying an application and look at the various techniques for packaging and shipping an application.

Test Questions

1. Which file must be included in the assembly in order to provide a list of licensed controls within the application?

   A. xxxx.LIC

   B. xxxx.LCX

   C. xxxx.LICX

   D. xxxx.Licenses

2. You are planning to create a new control that will be used in place of the `Button` control. The new control will blink and change color whenever the user moves the mouse over the control. Which control type would you use?

   A. Derived control from the `Button` class.

   B. Derived control from the `Control` class.

   C. Derived control from the `UserControl` class.

   D. Customized control using GDI+.

PART IV

3. Which of the following techniques will expose a new procedure for a newly created control?

A. `public string newProperty;`

B. `private string newProperty;`

C.
```
public string newValue;
public string newProperty
{
    get
    {
        return newProperty;
    }
    set
    {
        newValue = newProperty;
    }
```

D.
```
public string newValue;
public string newProperty
{
get
{
    return newValue;
}
set
{
    newValue = Value;
}
}
```

E.
```
private string newValue;
public string newProperty
{
    get
    {
        return newValue;
    }
    set
    {
        newValue = Value;
    }
}
```

4. Which set of steps will enable you to test your new control? Assume that a Windows Control Library application has been created, and a single control has been built by extending an existing control.

A. Version A

   i. Build the project.

   ii. Run the project, which will open Internet Explorer to host your control.

B. Version B

   i. Build the project.

   ii. Add a new Windows Forms project.

   iii. Set the new project as the startup project.

   iv. Run the project.

C. Version C

   i. Build the project.

   ii. Add a new Windows Control Library project.

   iii. Set the new project as the startup project.

   iv. Run the project.

D. Version D

   i. Build the project.

   ii. Add a new Web Forms project.

   iii. Set the new project as the startup project.

   iv. Run the project.

5. You are planning to create a control that will display two text boxes, ask the user to enter a value in each box, and compare the contents for equality. Which type of control would you build?

   A. Derived control from the `Button` class.

   B. Derived control from the `Control` class.

   C. Derived control from the `UserControl` class.

   D. Customized control using GDI+.

6. Which name is given to the controls that make up part of a composite control?

   A. Extenders

   B. Constituents

   C. Hosts

   D. Children

PART IV

7. Why would you use properties instead of variables to expose attributes for your new control?

   A. Properties can be displayed in the Property Explorer.

   B. Properties can be made public, and variables must be private.

   C. Variables expose a security risk.

   D. Variables are, by default, hidden from view.

8. Which of the following code segments would properly extend a `TextBox` control?

   A. `public class myTextBox:`
      `System.Windows.Forms.Controls.TextBox`

   B. `public class myTextBox: System.Windows.Forms.TextBox`

   C. `public class myTextBox: System.Forms.TextBox`

   D. `public class myTextBox extends`
      `System.Windows.Forms.TextBox`

9. Which segment of code will instantiate and populate a new `License` object?

   A. `MyLicense = new License (typeof (StudentValidate, this));`

   B. `MyLicense = License.Create(typeof(StudentValidate, this));`

   C. `MyLicense =`
      `LicenseManager.Create(typeof(StudentValidate, this));`

   D. `MyLicense =`
      `LicenseManager.Validate(typeof(StudentValidate, this));`

10. Which of the following advantages of .NET controls is most significant when compared to prior releases of ActiveX components?

    A. .NET controls extend the `Control` class.

    B. .NET controls manage versioning better.

    C. .NET controls can be created one of three different ways.

    D. .NET controls replace ActiveX controls.

11. Which of the following can you use to add a Toolbox bitmap to your control?

    A. `[ToolboxBitmap(typeof(NewControl),`
       `@"C:\MyIcons\NewControlIcon.ico")]`

    B. `[ToolboxBitmap(typeof(NewControl)]`

    C. `[ToolboxBitmap(@"C:\MyIcons\NewControlIcon.ico")]`

    D. All of the above.

    E. None of the above.

12. Which set of steps will enable you to test your new control? Assume that a Windows Control Library application has been created, and a composite control has been built by creating a `UserControl` and adding the constituent controls.

   A. Version A

      i. Build the project.

      ii. Run the project, which will open Internet Explorer to host your control.

   B. Version B

      i. Build the project.

      ii. Add a new Windows Forms project.

      iii. Set the new project as the startup project.

      iv. Run the project.

   C. Version C

      i. Build the project.

      ii. Add a new Windows Control Library project.

      iii. Set the new project as the startup project.

      iv. Run the project.

   D. Version D

      i. Build the project.

      ii. Add a new Web Forms project.

      iii. Set the new project as the startup project.

      iv. Run the project.

13. Which object can you use from the `PaintEventArgs` object in order to draw on your new control?

   A. `Graphics` object.

   B. `Drawing` object.

   C. GDI+ object.

   D. `Control` object.

14. What is wrong with the following code?

```
using System;
using System.Drawing;
using System.Windows.Forms;
public class MyCustomControl: System.Windows.Forms.Control
// override the OnPaint event of the Control class
// draw your own user interface using GDI+
protected override void OnPaint (System.Windows.Forms.PaintEventArgs e)
```

```
{
    // using the PaintEventArgs object, call the methods of GDI+
}
```

A. The `OnPaint` declaration is wrong.

B. The `OnPaint` arguments are wrong.

C. There is invalid inheritance.

D. There is a missing declaration.

15. Which of the following class definitions will correctly define a new control from an existing control?

A. `public class NewLabel : System.Windows.Forms.Label`
```
    {
        private System.ComponentModel.Container components = null;
        private string varValue;
        public NewLabel()
        {
            InitializeComponent();
        }
        protected override void Dispose (bool disposing)
        {
            if (disposing)
            {
                if (components != null)
                    components.Dispose();
            }
            base.Dispose(disposing);
        }
        private string LabelColor
        {
            get
            {
                return varValue;
            }
            set
            {
                varValue = value;
            }
        }
    }
```

B. `public class NewLabel : System.Windows.Forms.Label`
```
    {
        private System.ComponentModel.Container components = null;
```

```
        private string varValue;
        public NewLabel ()
        {
            InitializeComponent ();
        }
        protected override void Dispose (bool disposing)
        {
            if (disposing)
            {
                if (components != null)
                    components.Dispose ();
             }
            base.Dispose (disposing);
        }
        public string LabelColor
        {
            get
            {
                return varValue;
            }
            set
            {
                varValue = value;
            }
        }
    }
```

C. `public class NewLabel : System.Windows.Forms.Label`

```
    {
         private System.ComponentModel.Container components = null;
        private int varValue;
        public NewLabel ()
        {
            InitializeComponent ();
        }
        protected override void Dispose (bool disposing)
        {
            if (disposing)
            {
                if (components != null)
                    components.Dispose ();
             }
            base.Dispose (disposing);
```

```
        }
        private string LabelColor
        {
           get
           {
              return varValue;
           }
           set
           {
              varValue = value;
           }
        }
     }
```

D. ```
public class NewLabel: System.Windows.Forms.Control
   {
        private System.ComponentModel.Container components = null;
     private int varValue;
     public NewLabel()
     {
        InitializeComponent();
     }
     protected override void Dispose (bool disposing)
     {
        if (disposing)
        {
           if (components != null)
              components.Dispose();
        }
        base.Dispose(disposing);
     }
     private string LabelColor
     {
        get
        {
           return varValue;
        }
        set
        {
           varValue = value;
        }
     }
   }
```
```

Test Answers

1. C.
2. A.
3. E.
4. B.
5. C.
6. B.
7. A.
8. B.
9. D.
10. B.
11. D.
12. B.
13. A.
14. D.
15. B.

Deploying a Windows-Based Application

In this chapter, you will

- Plan and set up a web-based deployment
- Plan and set up a network deployment
- Learn the Windows Installer files and requirements
- Be able to register components and assemblies
- Recognize security policies

In this chapter, we will explore how you package and deploy an application, as it pertains to the Microsoft exam. You will need to know how to plan the deployment of a Windows-based application from removable media, from the Web, and from a network. You will also need to understand the Windows Installer requirements. One topic of great concern to developers is how you install an application that allows components and assemblies to be registered properly. Over the past few years, it has been difficult to ensure that an uninstalled application actually removed all of its components. Users often have to "clean out" the Registry of entries left behind when an application is dropped from the system. We will see, in this chapter, how that concern is addressed by .NET.

If you haven't had a chance to look at Chapter 6 in any detail, you should take the time now. We will briefly review assemblies and the Global Assembly Cache (GAC) in this chapter, but it has been covered in detail in Chapter 6. Security plays a big part in a properly deployed application, and we will discuss security policies and look at configuration files.

Review of Assemblies

An *assembly* is a group of files and resources that make up a single, executable unit. The unit can be deployed, it has a version number, and it can be secured. An *application* is made up of one or more assemblies.

Each assembly is self-describing. This means that there is metadata (data about data) for each assembly. The metadata identifies the version of the assembly, the security restrictions, the types that are implemented by the assembly, the list of files included in the assembly, and so forth.

For years, developers have been plagued by versioning and security issues, which arise from component information being stored in the Windows Registry. By using assemblies, the .NET Framework includes the metadata information with the assembly files and, as a result, has removed it from the Registry and has eliminated the problems associated with it. The previous problems included having a newer component replace an older one when some applications needed the old component and some needed the new one. .NET has solved this problem by having every application keep track of its own components. Now we can have several applications using different versions of the same type of component (this is called side-by-side versioning). This is a huge improvement over earlier component versioning, and developers are very excited by the possibilities.

An assembly contains the following:

- **Assembly name**   This can be private or strong.
- **Cryptographic hash**   This provides a check for version and security.
- **Locale**   This identifies the .culture.
- **Manifest**   This is the metadata describing all the rest.
- **Security**   This specifies the permissions.
- **Types**   This identifies the scope of all types.
- **Version**   This is the version number.

Strong Named Assemblies

By default, assemblies are private. This means that they run within the context of the application domain and will never cross the boundary into another application's namespace.

However, assemblies can be shared. Shared assemblies are installed into the Global Assembly Cache (GAC) and can be made available to other applications. In that case, a shared assembly must have a unique name that is referred to as the *strong name*. A shared assembly is created in order to provide code reusability between applications or to control versions.

You can create a strongly named assembly by using the Strong Name utility included in the SDK:

```
Sn -k myAKeys.snk
```

This will create a file with public and private keys that will be used to give the assembly a guaranteed unique name. Refer to Chapter 6 for more information on creating the strong-name key file.

The next step is to tell your application to use the key. You do this by *signing* the assembly (adding the key to the assembly). Locate the file in the Solution Explorer called `AssemblyInfo.cs`. Open the file and change this line:

```
[assembly: AssemblyKeyFile("")]
```

to this:

```
[assembly: AssemblyKeyFile("myAKeys.snk")]
```

The compiler will now know to digitally sign the assembly using the keys found in the `.snk` (strong-name key) file.

 EXAM TIP   You must recompile your program in order to apply the changes made to the `AssemblyInfo.cs` file.

Installing an Assembly into GAC

The Global Assembly Cache is a local machine storage area that holds shared assemblies. It is used to store assemblies that can be shared among several applications.

 EXAM TIP   The cache can contain one or more versions of the same assembly. This is called side-by-side versioning.

You can find the GAC in one of two locations, depending on the version of Windows:

- c:\Winnt\Assembly for Windows NT or Windows 2000 versions
- c:\windows\assembly for Windows 98/XP versions

The cache can be accessed using the GAC tool—`gacutil.exe`. This tool allows you to view and change the contents of the GAC. In particular, it allows you to install assemblies into the cache or remove them from the cache. The syntax is as follows:

```
gacutil [options] [assembly]
```

Table 23-1 displays the options available for the GAC tool.

 EXAM TIP   You need administrative privileges to access the GAC.

Table 23-1 The gacutil.exe Options	Option	Description
	/h	Displays help topics for the `gacutil.exe` tool.
	/I	Installs an assembly into the GAC.
	/u	Uninstalls an assembly from the GAC.
	/l	Lists the contents of the GAC.

EXAM TIP Here is an example of installing `myFile.dll` into the GAC— `gacutil /i myFile.dll`.

Before we leave the discussion of assemblies, keep the following in mind. Shared assemblies allow you to

- Reuse code modules.
- Maintain a unique namespace for the assembly (using strong names).
- Maintain versions of assemblies (side-by-side versioning).

Precompiling Assemblies

Instead of having your assemblies generated on the fly, you can run the `Ngen.exe` utility and create a native image. This should cause the application to load faster, since the work of compiling the code has been done in advance.

When an assembly is executed, the runtime searches for the native image (a file containing compiled processor-specific code). If it is unable to find it, the runtime will look for the JIT (just-in-time) compilation of the assembly.

 EXAM TIP The syntax of the `Ngen.exe` utility is as follows: `ngen [options] [AssemblyName]`.

Some of the `Ngen.exe` options are shown in Table 23-2.

 EXAM TIP Remember that the reason to use `Ngen.exe` is to allow the assembly to load and execute faster.

Not every application will benefit from using a precompiled assembly. You must do a comparison between the JIT compiler and a precompiled assembly. The most benefit will be seen in startup times and, in that case, a CPU-intensive startup would benefit greatly from precompiling assemblies with `Ngen.exe`.

Table 23-2	Option	Description
Options for	/debug	Generates the image used by a debugger.
Ngen.exe	/delete	Deletes the native image files in the native image cache.
	/help	Provides assistance.
	/show	Lists the existing files in the native image cache.

EXAM TIP   Using Ngen.exe eliminates the possibility of creating runtime optimizations on the code. It also doesn't allow for deploying your application with the .NET redistributables (CLR for applications).

Deploying a Windows Application

This section will cover the deployment of a Windows-based application. When you finish an application, you work through the deployment process in order to create something that can be run on a client's machine. The "something" is made up of different solutions—an executable file, an installer package, a web download, and so forth. When you deploy a solution, you must answer a number of questions—What files are needed? Where will the solution be hosted? and so on. Depending on your deployment scenario, the answers may be simple or as complicated as you wish.

The good news is that you could very easily deploy a Windows-based application by simply copying the assembly into a new machine. Sound simple? It is. You don't need to worry about the Registry as you did in days gone by. Just copy the executable created from your project into the new machine and Presto! It works!

Having said that, we all know that large applications will be more difficult to approach in this manner. What about shared assemblies? What about security? What about location and icons? All these questions can be answered by deploying your application in one of the following ways:

- **Setup project**   You can create a Windows Installer package that includes setup files that will handle the actual installation. The setup files manage your application files and resources and create an uninstall procedure to remove the application.

- **Web Setup project**   This is the same process as the Setup project, but you can deploy your application from a web server.

- **CAB project**   Remember the days of cabinet files? Well, they're still around. This is similar to having a ZIP file that contains all the necessary files and resources. You can deploy it from an HTML page using a CAB project.

- **Merge Module project**   This is the first step in creating a deployment project that includes many different modules that must be brought together into one.

Let's look at each one of these in more detail.

Creating a Setup Project

A Setup project allows you to create an installer for a Windows application. Visual Studio .NET provides you with many tools to customize your installer package. In this section, we will create an installation package for the college application.

To create the Setup project, start with these steps:

1. Open Visual Studio .NET.
2. Open the college application.
3. Add a new project by selecting File | Add Project | New Project.
4. Select Setup and Deployment Projects from the Project Types list.

 EXAM TIP   Notice that the templates available from Setup and Deployment Projects include Setup Project (which creates a Windows installer), Web Setup Project (for deploying from a web server), Merge Module Project (which accumulates modules), Setup Wizard, and Cab Project.

At this point you have two choices for a Setup project. You can either let the Setup Wizard assist you through the process, or you can choose Setup Project and customize the setup on your own (see Figure 23-1). We will start with the Setup Wizard here, and then examine the more hands-on approach using Setup Project in the next section.

Using the Setup Wizard
When you use the Setup Wizard, it will take you through five different windows, each one designed to let you customize the Setup project. Although the wizard will do most of the work for you, you will still be able to customize the project after it is completed. Refer to the next section for customization options.

To use the Setup Wizard, follow these steps:

1. Choose Setup Wizard from the Templates in the Add New Project dialog box (see Figure 23-1).

Figure 23-1
New project templates

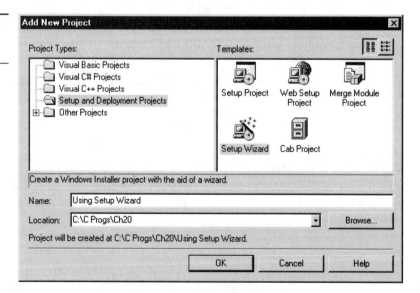

2. The Setup Wizard will first display the Welcome screen. Click Next.

3. The second wizard screen of the Setup Wizard (see the following illustration) asks you to choose a project type—whether you are creating a Setup project for a Windows or a web application. For this example, choose the Windows application. This screen also asks whether you want to create a redistributable package—a merge module or downloadable CAB file.

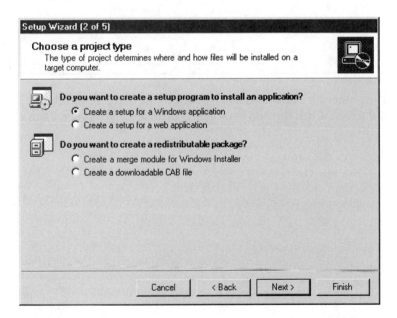

EXAM TIP A redistributable package is required for applications that will be installed on machines that don't have the .NET Framework installed. The package will contain the CLR, which needs to be installed for applications to run, and it is supported for Windows 98, ME, NT 4.0, 2000, XP, and .NET Server. Internet Explorer 5.01 or later must be on the machine, as well. If the redistributable package is to be installed on a server, the server must have MDAC 2.6 (MDAC 2.7 recommended for data applications) installed.

4. The third wizard screen asks which output groups you want to include in the Setup project. Notice that you can select from documentation files, localized resources, source files, and so forth.

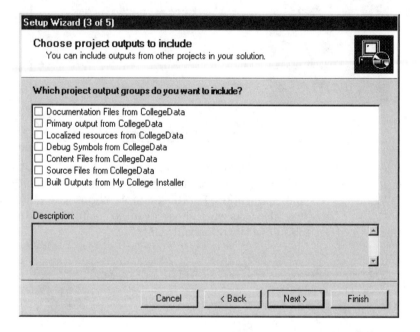

5. Add any other files that need to be added to the Setup project in the fourth wizard screen. Click the Add button and browse for your files. Then click Next.

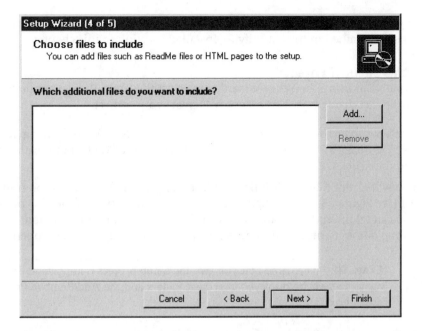

6. The last wizard screen is the summary window. It's a good idea to read the summary and make sure that you have included everything you need in the project. The summary window will tell you if there were any errors and specifies the output directory for the Setup project. If everything is okay, click Finish.

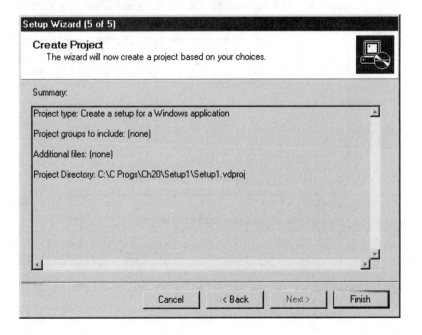

Once your project has been created with the Setup Wizard, you can make modifications. This is explained in the "Modifying Installers" section in this chapter.

Using the Setup Project

The alternative to using the Setup Wizard is to select the Setup Project template in the Add New Project dialog box. These steps will create your project:

1. Select Setup Project from the Templates in the Add New Project dialog box (see Figure 23-2). For this example, name the project "My College Installer" and then click OK.

2. You will notice that the Solution Explorer has added your Setup project to the list (see Figure 23-3). This figure also shows the properties of the new project. You can set the author's name, a description, manufacturer information, support phone numbers, and version numbers, to name just a few of the properties.

 EXAM TIP The name that you give the Setup project is important. This is the name that will be displayed in project folders and the Add/Remove Programs dialog box.

3. In Figure 23-4, you will see the format of the installer, and you can work with the properties of the destination machine. In the File System on Target Machine section, you can adjust the application folder, the user's desktop, and the user's program menu as it pertains to your application.

Figure 23-2
Choose the Setup Project template

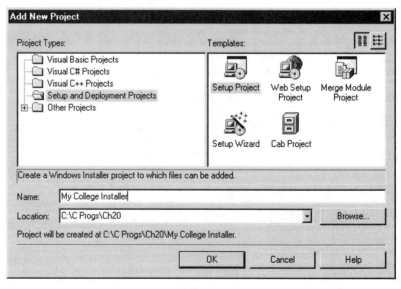

Figure 23-3
The Setup project
is shown in the
Solution Explorer

4. The next step is to add your application to the installer. Select your Setup project in the Solution Explorer, right-click on it, and choose Add | Project Output. You will see the Add Project Output Group dialog box shown in the following illustration. Here you can specify the parts of the project that will be added to the installer. For example, you can add documentation files,

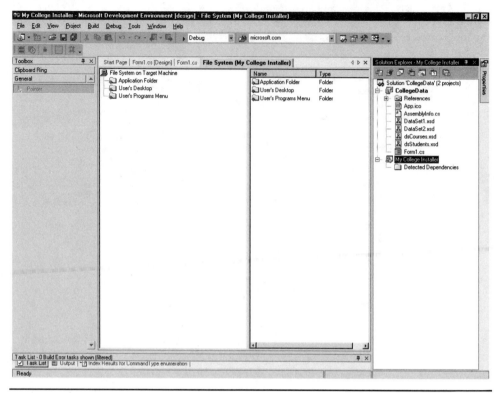

Figure 23-4　Set the file system for the application

localized resources, or, as shown in the illustration, the primary output, which
is the actual `.DLL` or `.EXE` built by the project.

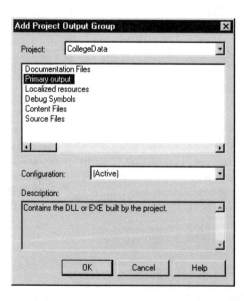

5. The final step in this process is to build the installer. Select Build | Build <Setup Project Name> from the menus to create the installer.

Once the basic installer program is created, you can check the local file system for your project directory, and you will see the files that have been created (see Figure 23-5). The Windows Installer package has been created (`My College Installer.msi`), along with the Setup application.

EXAM TIP   Notice that our files are listed in a subdirectory called "Debug". You must ensure that you use a Release Build to create Setup projects. Use the properties of the solution to set the Configuration to Release (see Figure 23-6).

Modifying Installers

There are a number of modifications you can make to your installer package after it's been created. You may want to create a shortcut on the user's desktop or insert additional files in the package. This can all be done from Visual Studio .NET. The following list explains three of the modifications you can make to the package:

- **Add a shortcut to the user's desktop**   Select the Primary output from <application> from the Solution Explorer. Find the "Primary output from <application>" in the File System Editor, right-click on it, and choose Create Shortcut To. This will create a shortcut (which you can rename). Drag the new shortcut to the User's Desktop folder.

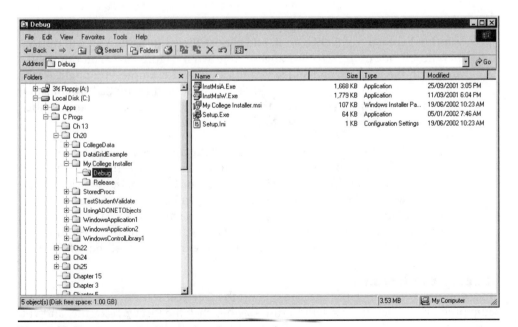

Figure 23-5   The installer files that have been created

PART IV

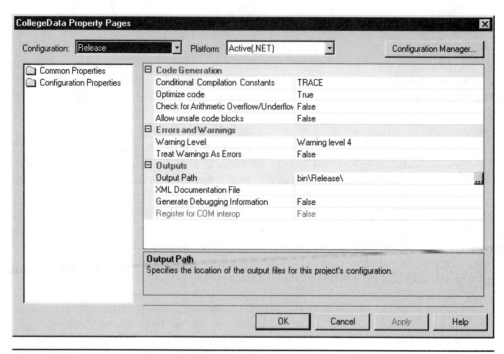

Figure 23-6   Setting the project to create a release build

- **Add Registry entries for the application**   Select the installer project from the Solution Explorer, right-click on it, and choose View | Registry. You will notice that the left side of the screen changes, as shown in Figure 23-7. You can then work with the Registry, and add keys and values. For example, you might want to set an application property in the Registry called "Start-up mode." By adjusting the entry at this point, you can set the default value for the Registry and, in the actual application, allow the user to change it.

- **Set up custom installation windows**   Select the installer project from the Solution Explorer, right-click on it, and choose View | User Interface. In the User Interface tab (see Figure 23-8), choose the Start tab, right-click on it, and make your choice. In the example shown in Figure 23-8, we asked for Checkboxes from the Add Dialog dialog box. This will insert an additional, customized dialog box into the installation procedure. Using this customized dialog box, the user can make choices during the installation of the software.

Running the Installer
Once you have the installation package set up the way you want it, you can run your setup program and let the installation run. Double-click the Setup.exe file, and you

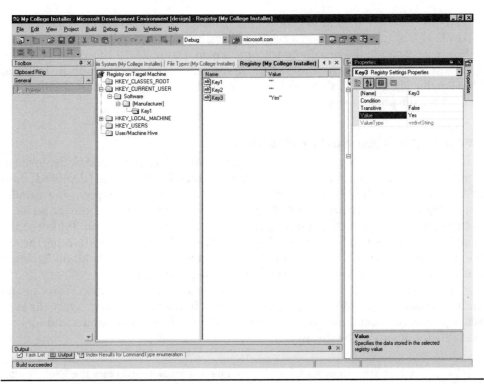

Figure 23-7   Adding Registry entries

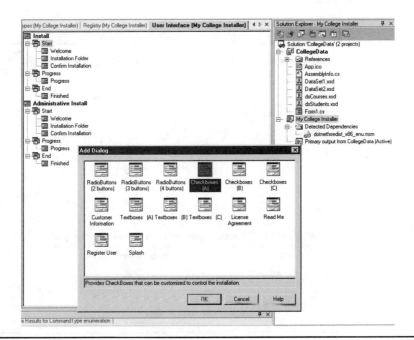

Figure 23-8   Adding custom installation procedures

will see the installation windows shown in Figures 23-9 through 23-11. (Figure 23-11 will only be displayed if you add a custom dialog box to the installation.)

Figure 23-9 shows the installer's welcome screen. Figure 23-10 shows the Select Installation Folder screen, which allows the user to choose the location of the installed files. Finally, Figure 23-11 shows our customized dialog box (it's not too exciting, but you can see the possibilities).

Creating a Web Setup Project

In the previous section, we discussed creating a Setup project that would be deployed in a traditional manner. The output from the Setup project can be copied (deployed) onto a CD or onto a hard disk. However, you can also deploy from a web server—the installer can be deployed to a web server so that a user can download and run it from the server.

In order to create a Web Setup project, you need to select Web Setup Project in the Templates list in the Add New Project dialog box (Figure 23-1). Instead of seeing the Application Folder, User's Desktop, and User's Programs Menu in the Solution Explorer, you will simply see the Web Application Folder (see Figure 23-12).

At this point, little is different from creating a standard Setup project. You can add project output groups, add resources, and so forth, in the same fashion. Once the Web Setup project has been built, you can copy it to the web server computer and make it available for download by the users.

EXAM TIP In order to deploy to a network solution, create the Web Setup project and copy the installer to a server computer. The installer can then be downloaded over a network.

Figure 23-9
Windows
Installer

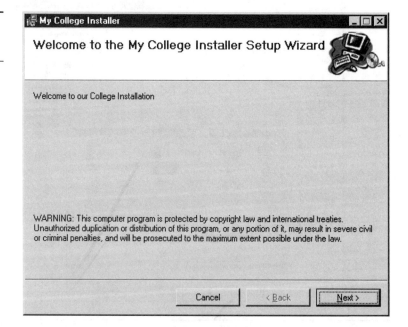

Figure 23-10
Setup Installation
Folder

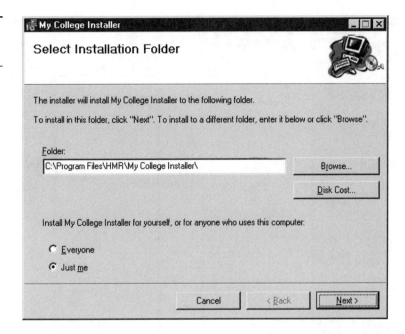

Creating a CAB Project

Creating a CAB project is perhaps the easiest of all solutions. A CAB project (a project containing cabinet files) consists of a single, compressed file that contains all of the

Figure 23-11
Customized
dialog box

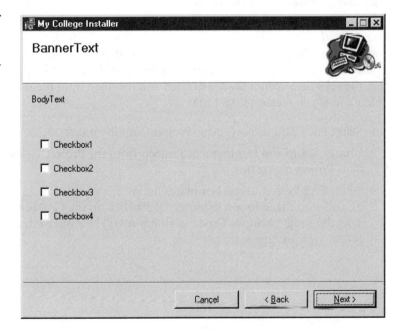

PART IV

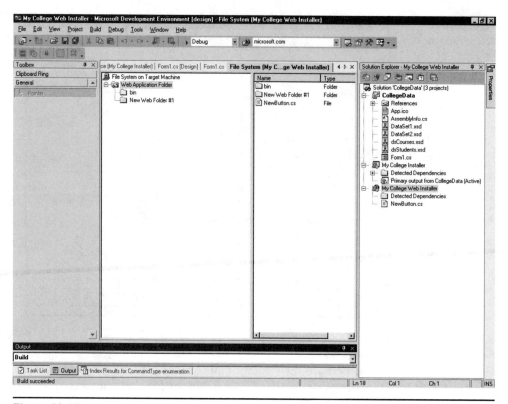

Figure 23-12   Creating a Web Setup project

setup files. The project can be placed into an HTML page on an intranet or Internet site and downloaded to the client computer from there. Once the user runs the setup program, the CAB file's contents are extracted and installed onto the user's computer.

Here's how you create a CAB project:

1. Select File | Add project | New Project from the menus.

2. Choose Setup and Deployment Projects from the Project Types list in the Add New Project dialog box.

3. Select CAB Project in the Templates list. When you choose it, a CAB file will be added to the Solution Explorer. Right-click on the CAB file and select Add. The Add Project Output Group dialog box will be displayed, as shown in the following illustration.

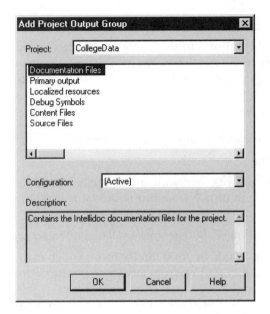

EXAM TIP   Creating a CAB project packages the files into a single, compressed file with a `.cab` extension.

Creating a Merge Module Project

You create a Merge Module project to package files and components that will be shared amongst multiple applications. All of the files, resources, and Registry entries will be found in the merge module file. The file has an extension of `.msm`. A component that will be shared amongst applications should be placed into its own merge module.

EXAM TIP   A merge module (`.msm`) is added into other deployment projects and is used by developers. A Windows installer (`.msi`) is created for an end user of the application.

To create a Merge Module project, select Merge Module Project from the Setup and Deployment Projects dialog box. To add a Merge Module project to an existing solution, select File | Add | Existing Project from the menus.

EXAM TIP   A merge module can also be used to deploy patches or new versions of a component.

Conforming to Windows Standards

An application should conform to the Windows Installer requirements, and you may also want to conform to the Windows logo program requirements. The Microsoft exam objectives suggest that you need to understand that the application must conform to both of them. In order to comply with Windows Installer requirements, your application must do the following:

- Manage version-checking of shared components.
- Be self-repairing.
- Have a reliable uninstall program and correctly handle shared components. For example, the uninstall procedure should not arbitrarily uninstall shared components.
- Be able to install on client machines for which the user is not an administrator.
- Make full use of Windows 2000 IntelliMirror, which essentially allows the user access to their policy settings from anywhere on the network.

In order to ensure that your application meets with the requirements for the Windows logo program, which allows you to distribute your application with "Designed for Windows" attached to it, you must follow the requirements set forth in this web site: http://www.microsoft.com/winlogo/software/.

Security Policies

In the next chapter, we will deal with security issues you should be aware of when preparing your application for user delivery. In short, policies are the set of rules that the runtime uses when it loads your code. These policies can be configured in one of two ways:

- By editing the XML configuration file (see Chapter 24).
- By using the .NET Framework Configuration tool—`Mscorcfg.msc`.

The configuration tool can be run by selecting Start | Programs | Administrative Tools | Microsoft .NET Framework Configuration. Figure 23-13 shows the .NET Framework Configuration tool.

We will explore this tool in greater detail in the next chapter. Notice in Figure 23-13 that you can configure the assembly cache, manage assemblies, adjust remoting services, manage applications, and configure security policies. If you select the latter, you will see the Code Access Security Policy window shown in Figure 23-14. Stay tuned to Chapter 24 for more information on security and security policies.

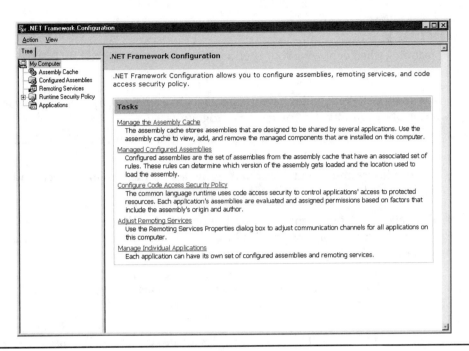

Figure 23-13   The .NET Framework Configuration tool

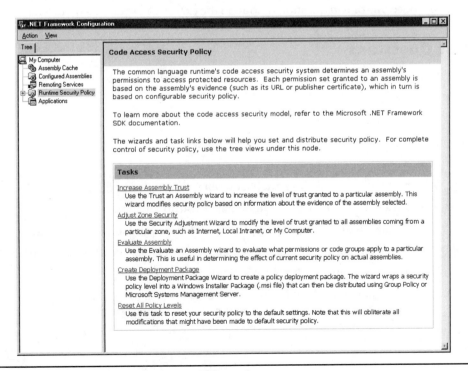

Figure 23-14   The Code Access Security Policy window

Summary

Proper planning when deploying your application is crucial to its success. In this chapter, we discussed the various methods of packaging your application:

- Windows Installer 2.0 files have the packages in a single `.msi` file, and they are installed by running the `Setup.exe` program.
- CAB files have the packages in a single `.cab` file, and they can be downloaded from a network server or an HTML page.
- The assemblies and executables can be provided in their original folders and can be copied to the client machine using XCOPY or FTP.

We also looked at deployment of an application, which takes the packaged files and sends them to a location for download or installation. Keep the advantages and disadvantages of each technique in mind when studying for the exam.

 EXAM TIP Windows Installer is the preferred method of packaging and deploying.

In the next chapter, we will look at security issues and expand on the discussion we started in this chapter. We will also look at how you can optimize your final product. Finally, we will wrap up all the loose ends that have not been covered yet, but that you are liable to see one or two questions about on the exam. You're almost there—hang in.

Test Questions

1. Which tool allows you to install an assembly into the GAC?

    A. `Ngen.exe`

    B. `Mscorcfg.msc`

    C. `Setup.exe`

    D. `sn.exe`

2. Which of the following accurately describes a strong named assembly?

    A. A private assembly with a unique name within an application domain.

    B. A private assembly with a unique name within a global domain.

    C. A shared assembly with a unique name within an application domain.

    D. A shared assembly with a unique name within a global domain.

3. Which template must be chosen from the Add New Project dialog box's Templates list in order to have an application downloaded from an IIS (Internet Information Server) server?

A. Windows Setup Project.

B. CAB Project.

C. IIS Project.

D. Web Setup Project.

4. You have followed the steps in creating a Windows Installer Setup project, and after deployment you notice that it does not install properly on the client. Which of the following could be the problem?

A. You forgot to run the `sn.exe` utility.

B. The shortcut was not configured properly.

C. The release type is set to Debug.

D. The Registry entry is incorrect.

5. Why did Microsoft invent assemblies?

A. To allow applications to take care of their own components.

B. To speed up processing.

C. To confuse developers studying for the .NET development exams.

D. To ensure that all components register properly in the Registry.

6. Select two techniques for viewing the GAC.

A. .NET Configuration Viewer.

B. .NET Configuration tool.

C. `gacutil.exe`

D. `gacview.exe`

7. What can be configured using the .NET Configuration tool?

A. GAC cache.

B. Assemblies.

C. Security.

D. Policy levels.

E. All of the above.

F. None of the above.

8. Which of the following command-line entries would allow you to install an assembly into the GAC?

A. `gacutil /l myAssembly.exe`

B. `gacutil /i myAssembly.exe`

C. `gacutil /s myAssembly.exe`

D. `gacutil /h myAssembly.exe`

9. Which command would you use to list the existing files in the native image cache?

   A. Ngen.exe /list

   B. Ngen.exe /cache

   C. Ngen.exe /debug

   D. Ngen.exe /show

10. What kind of project can you create from the Setup and Deployment Projects list?

    A. Web Setup project.

    B. GAC project.

    C. Setup project.

    D. CAB project.

    E. B, C, and D.

    F. A, C, and D.

11. If the redistributable package is to be installed on a server, what must be in place?

    A. .NET Framework

    B. SQL Server

    C. MDAC 2.6

    D. CLR

12. Why is the Setup project name important?

    A. Setup looks for files under that name.

    B. It is the name in the Add/Remove Programs dialog box.

    C. There cannot be any spaces in the name.

    D. The name goes in the Registry.

13. What can you expect to find in an assembly? Choose all that apply.

    A. Security hash.

    B. Locale specifications.

    C. Registry GUID.

    D. Version numbers.

    E. Program ID.

14. Which line must exist in the AssemblyInfo.cs file in order to "sign" the assembly?

    A. [assembly: AssemblyKeyFile("")]

    B. [key: AssemblyKeyFile("")]

    C. `[assembly: AssemblyKeyFile("myKeys.snk")]`

    D. `[key: AssemblyKeyFile("myKeys.snk")]`

15. Where is the GAC located by default?

    A. Windows directory.

    B. Programs directory.

    C. Documents and Settings directory.

    D. Application directory.

Test Answers

1. A.

2. B.

3. D.

4. C.

5. A.

6. B, C.

7. E.

8. B.

9. D.

10. F.

11. C.

12. B.

13. A, B, D.

14. C.

15. A.

Configuring a Windows Application

In this chapter, you will

- Become familiar with configuring a Windows application
- Optimize the performance of a Windows application
- Configure security
- Implement online user assistance
- Set globalization properties
- Build GUI elements using `System.Drawing`

This is the chapter that will bring together the remaining objectives of the C# Windows exam. In the last chapter, we looked at deploying an application. In this chapter, we will examine the ways of configuring your application. This will include setting application properties that optimize and secure your application. In prior chapters, we have discussed localization and globalization issues in general terms. Here we will look at applying localization to a Windows application.

The C# Windows exam also expects you to be conversant in providing online assistance for the user of your application. Towards that goal, we will look at creating ToolTips, adding a help menu, and providing context-sensitive help. The final objective to be covered for the Windows exam involves working with `System.Drawing`. We will discuss the issues related to building your own graphical elements as they pertain to the exam.

Configuring a Windows Application

You can configure a .NET application by using a number of XML configuration files that specify the configuration elements. The advantage to keeping the configuration data in XML files is that it can be changed as needed. Many hands can take part in the configuration duties—the network administrator may need to set security policies, the application developer may use the files to change settings without recompiling the application, and so forth.

In this section, we will look at the .NET Framework Configuration tool, along with the three types of configuration files:

- **Machine configuration file** Contains the settings that apply to the entire computer.

- **Application configuration file** Contains the settings that apply specifically to the application.

- **Security configuration file** Contains the permission settings associated with a security policy.

We will examine these three types of files individually and then look at the configuration tool, which will help you ensure that the files are maintained properly.

Machine Configuration File

The machine configuration file is used to set system wide configuration options. On a Windows 2000 machine, this file is found at this location: <system drive>:\winnt\Microsoft.NET\Framework\<version>\CONFIG\Machine.config

Figure 24-1 shows an example `machine.config` file. If you need a refresher on reading XML, refer back to Chapter 8. The configuration files contain elements (logical data structures) that define the configuration information and set its values. Notice in Figure 24-1 that the first element is called `<configuration>` followed by `<configSections>` and then the more specific `<section name>`. These elements define the configuration data to the application.

Every .NET-aware machine has the `machine.config` file in its Windows directory. If you find the file and scroll through its contents, you will find a section starting with the following tag:

```
<appSettings>
```

The configuration system starts looking for the application configuration settings in this section.

EXAM TIP Using an XCOPY deployment will not copy the `machine.config` file. Remember that the `machine.config` file is specific to the host machine, and it would make no sense on another machine.

By setting configuration properties within the `machine.config` file, you will be able to place the configuration data in a single location. However, keep in mind that this file is specific to the computer system or server. The file is not transferred when the application is deployed.

```
machine.config - Notepad
File  Edit  Format  Help
<?xml version="1.0" encoding="UTF-8"?>
<configuration>

    <configSections>
        <!-- tell .NET Framework to ignore CLR sections -->
        <section name="runtime" type="System.Configuration.IgnoreSectionHandler, System,
Version=1.0.3300.0, Culture=neutral, PublicKeyToken=b77a5c561934e089"
allowLocation="false"/>
        <section name="mscorlib" type="System.Configuration.IgnoreSectionHandler, System,
Version=1.0.3300.0, Culture=neutral, PublicKeyToken=b77a5c561934e089"
allowLocation="false"/>
        <section name="startup" type="System.Configuration.IgnoreSectionHandler, System,
Version=1.0.3300.0, Culture=neutral, PublicKeyToken=b77a5c561934e089"
allowLocation="false"/>
        <section name="system.runtime.remoting"
type="System.Configuration.IgnoreSectionHandler, System, Version=1.0.3300.0,
Culture=neutral, PublicKeyToken=b77a5c561934e089" allowLocation="false"/>

        <section name="system.diagnostics"
type="System.Diagnostics.DiagnosticsConfigurationHandler, System, Version=1.0.3300.0,
Culture=neutral, PublicKeyToken=b77a5c561934e089"/>
        <section name="appSettings" type="System.Configuration.NameValueFileSectionHandler,
System, Version=1.0.3300.0, Culture=neutral, PublicKeyToken=b77a5c561934e089"/>

        <sectionGroup name="system.net">
            <section name="authenticationModules"
type="System.Net.Configuration.NetAuthenticationModuleHandler, System, Version=1.0.3300.0,
Culture=neutral, PublicKeyToken=b77a5c561934e089"/>
            <section name="defaultProxy" type="System.Net.Configuration.DefaultProxyHandler,
System, Version=1.0.3300.0, Culture=neutral, PublicKeyToken=b77a5c561934e089"/>
            <section name="connectionManagement"
type="System.Net.Configuration.ConnectionManagementHandler, System, Version=1.0.3300.0,
Culture=neutral, PublicKeyToken=b77a5c561934e089"/>
            <section name="webRequestModules"
type="System.Net.Configuration.WebRequestModuleHandler, System, Version=1.0.3300.0,
Culture=neutral, PublicKeyToken=b77a5c561934e089"/>
        </sectionGroup>
```

Figure 24-1   A sample `machine.config` file

The machine configuration file can specify remoting configurations as well as assembly-binding specifications.

 EXAM TIP   The `machine.config` file is consulted prior to the application configuration file. This means that the application file will override any settings in the `machine.config` file.

Application Configuration File

More significant to the Windows application is the application configuration file. This file contains the settings that are particular to the specific application. The CLR will read these settings and apply them to the runtime environment.

 EXAM TIP   The application configuration file must be in the same directory as the application files and is named `<application_name>.exe.config` (where `<application_ name>` is the name of the application).

The application configuration file is read after the machine configuration file. This means that any settings in the application file will override the machine file. However, you may wish to keep common configuration information in a single location. For example, a component that is used by different applications may have its settings in the machine configuration file for easier manageability.

 EXAM TIP This file is called `web.config` for an ASP.NET application.

Here's an example of the kind of data you might want to keep in an application configuration file. Suppose you have a client application that uses a particular shared component. There may be different versions of the component, and you would like your application to use the most current version. By creating an application configuration file, you can easily enter the version number into the file. The following code could be added to the file:

```
<runtime>
    <assemblyBinding ....>
        <dependentAssembly>
            <assemblyIdentity name="MySharedComponent" ... />
            <bindingRedirect oldVersion="1.0.0.1"
                newVersion="1.0.0.2" />
        </dependentAssembly>
    </assemblyBinding>
</runtime>
```

This is a simplistic overview of how you might set the version number of a referenced component. In this XML example, we use the `<runtime>` tag to set runtime configuration elements. Drilling down through the sub-elements (`<assemblyBinding>`, `<dependentAssembly>`), we reach the `<bindingRedirect>` sub-element that allows us to set the version redirection to version 1.0.0.2. When the application is started, it will be redirected to the new component version.

If you are concerned right now about all the XML coding that you will have to do to set these kinds of configuration elements, don't worry. The .NET Framework includes a tool that will create the files for you. It's called the .NET Framework Configuration tool and will be covered shortly.

Security Configuration File

In the security configuration file, you can specify data about the permissions that are associated with policy levels for your application. We will be covering this in more detail in the "Securing a Windows Application" section of this chapter.

EXAM TIP Microsoft strongly recommends that you use the .NET Framework Configuration tool (`Mscorcfg.msc`) or the Code Access Security Policy tool (`Caspol.exe`) to set security data. You know that if Microsoft "strongly" recommends something, you should be very aware of it for an examination.

The security configuration files can be found in the following locations:

- **Enterprise policy configuration file** `<runtime install path>\Config\Enterprisesec.config`

- **Machine policy configuration file** `<runtime install path>\Config\Security.config`

- **User policy configuration file** `<userprofile path>\Application data\Microsoft\CLR security config\Security.config`

.NET Framework Configuration Tool

The .NET Framework Configuration tool is installed as part of the .NET Framework. It is a graphical interface that allows you to manage and configure assemblies, security policies, and remoting services. It can be used to configure machine and application configuration files. The following configuration tasks can be accomplished by using the .NET Framework Configuration Tool:

- Adjust remoting services

- Manage and configure assemblies in the Global Assembly Cache

- View the current security settings

- Increase the assembly trust

- Adjust the zone security

- Create a deployment package

- Reset all policy levels

- View and add applications to be configured with the tool

- Configure an assembly for an application

- View the properties and assembly dependencies for an application

Running the Configuration Tool

To run the .NET Framework Configuration tool (shown in Figure 24-2), select Start | Programs | Administrative Tools. Under administrative tools, click Microsoft .NET Framework Configuration.

PART IV

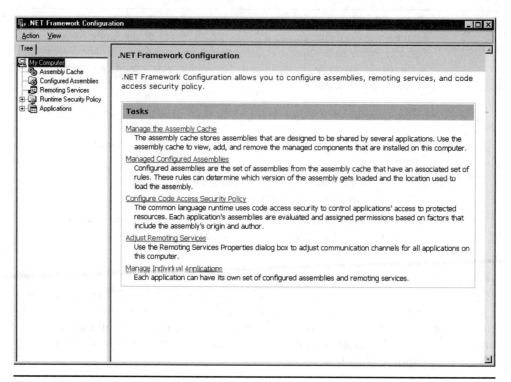

Figure 24-2   The .NET Framework Configuration tool

The tool can also be installed in a Microsoft Management Console as follows:

1. Select Start | Run.

2. Type in the command **mmc**. This will open a new management console (see Figure 24-3) that you can customize for your purposes. (Note that you can also add the tool to an existing management console.)

3. Select Console | Add/Remove Snap-In from the menus.

4. Click the Add button, and the Add Standalone Snap-In dialog box will be displayed (see the following illustration).

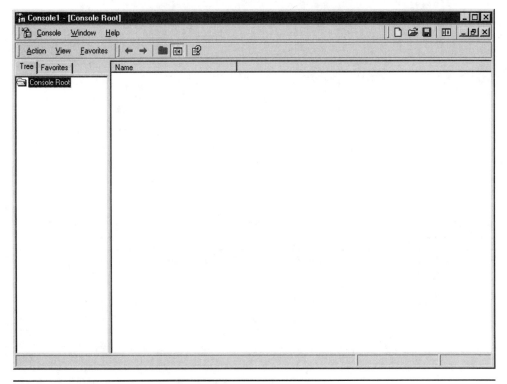

Figure 24-3 A new Microsoft Management Console

5. Select the .NET Framework Configuration snap-in, and click Add. Click Close to close the Add Standalone Snap-In dialog box.

6. Click OK, and you will see that the .NET Configuration tool has been added to your management console (see Figure 24-4).

7. Save the management console—select Console | Save As, and choose the location and name of your management console as shown in the following illustration. For this example, place the console on the desktop and name it ".NET tools". Close the console, and you will see the icon on the desktop

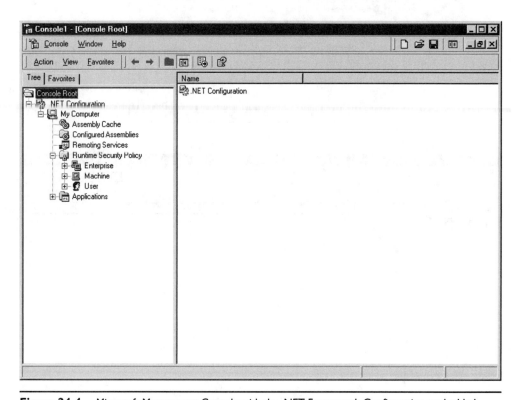

Figure 24-4   Microsoft Management Console with the .NET Framework Configuration tool added

labeled ".NET Tools.msc". You can now access the console by double-clicking on the icon.

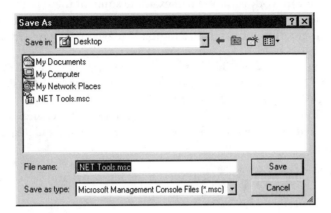

 EXAM TIP If you are asked the specific location of the .NET Framework Configuration tool, it is found in `<winnt>\Microsoft .NET\Framework\ <version number>\mscorcfg.msc` (see the following illustration).

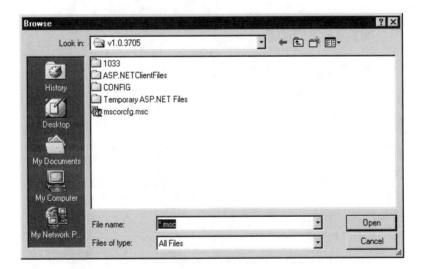

Using the Configuration Tool

Now that you know how to run the configuration tool, let's examine the configuration elements that you can work with. We will examine some of these in more detail as the chapter progresses, but for now, just get comfortable with the tool itself. Open the .NET Framework Configuration tool and click on the Manage the Assembly Cache link. You will see a list of assemblies, as shown in Figure 24-5.

All of the assemblies in the Global Assembly Cache are listed on the right side of the display in Figure 24-8 (refer to Chapter 6 for more about the Global Assembly Cache). You can delete assemblies or add assemblies.

Let's look at how to add an assembly to the Global Assembly Cache. We will be using the assembly created in Chapter 6, which includes the `Hello.cs` and `Heja.cs` modules. Follow these steps:

1. Right-click on Configured Assemblies in the left panel and select Add. This will start the Configure an Assembly Wizard.

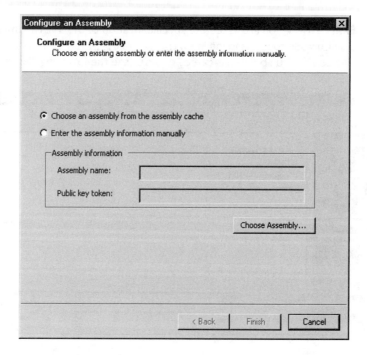

2. At this point, you can either choose to add an assembly that is in the assembly cache or enter the information manually. We have selected the `Hello.dll` component from Chapter 6. Once you provide the assembly information, you will see the dialog box.

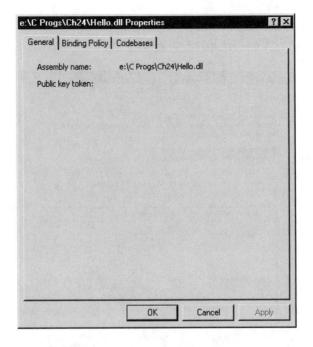

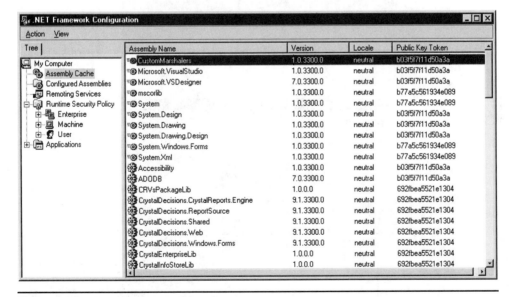

Figure 24-5 Managing the assembly cache

3. In the Binding Policy tab, you can specify the binding redirections, which redirect to a different version of the component.

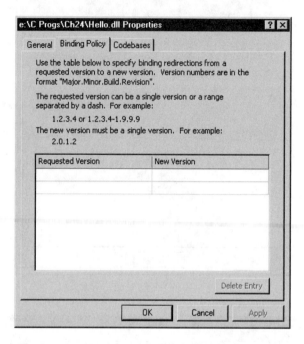

4. In the Codebases tab, you can specify the codebases for specific versions of the assembly.

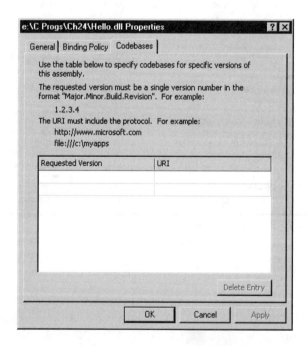

The preceding procedure allows you to work with the assembly configuration. In the coming sections, we will work with the .NET Framework Configuration tool to configure remoting and security.

 EXAM TIP Working with versioning in .NET is much improved over previous versions. By using these XML configuration files, a developer can use a new version of a component simply by changing the versioning information. The client application never needs to be rebuilt.

XML Configuration Tags

We will now look at some of the important XML tags that can be found in a configuration file. Table 24-1 lists these tags and their purposes. These tags are significant for the Microsoft C# .NET Windows exam. Remember that the configuration files can be created or modified by using the .NET Framework Configuration tool.

Optimizing a Windows Application

In this section, we will examine the various techniques for optimizing your Windows application. There are many different ways to create the final, "shippable" product, keeping in mind that your final goal is to create an executable application that is as small as possible and runs as efficiently as possible. That is the goal of this section.

Debug vs. Release Versions

The first thing to worry about is whether you are creating a Debug version of your application or a Release version. The Debug version allows a lot of debugging techniques to be built into the application, but when you give your application to the user, it is not necessary to include the debugging code. In order to create a smaller executable without the debugging options, you must change the build type to the Release version.

Tag	Purpose
`<configuration>`	This is the root element.
`<runtime>`	Contains information about the runtime assembly binding. It is a sub-element of `<configuration>`.
`<assemblyBinding>`	Contains information about the location of assemblies and any version redirection. It is a sub-element of `<runtime>`.
`<dependentAssembly>`	Contains information about each assembly. It is a sub-element of `<assemblyBinding>`.
`<assemblyIdentity>`	Contains assembly identification information. It is a sub-element of `<dependentAssembly>`.
`<bindingRedirect>`	Contains information that redirects the runtime from one version to another version. It is a sub-element of `<dependentAssembly>`.
`<codeBase>`	Contains the position of a strong named assembly.

Table 24-1   XML Tags for Configuration Files

PART IV

To change the build type of your solution, right-click on the solution name in Solution Explorer, and you can select the property page for your solution (see the following illustration). You can configure the common properties of the application or the configuration properties.

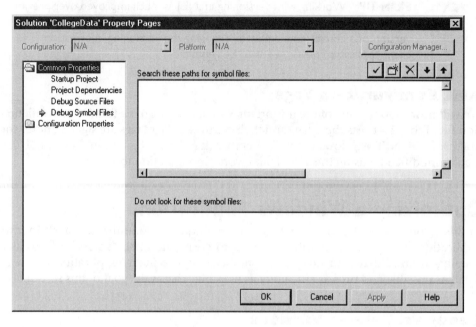

Under the Common Properties heading, you can set the following:

- **The startup project**   Specifies whether this is a single startup project or there are multiple startup projects.

- **Project dependencies**   Specifies which projects must be built in which order.

- **Debug source files**   Sets the location where the debugger will look for source files when debugging the solution.

- **Debug symbol files**   Sets the location where the debugger will look for symbols when debugging the solution.

In order to access the configuration properties, click on Configuration Properties in the left panel (see the following illustration). These options will allow you to set how the different versions of the solution will be built. Notice in the illustration that you can set the configuration type for each project. The type can be either Debug or Release. Set this to Release when the application is ready for shipping. This will reduce the size of the released code.

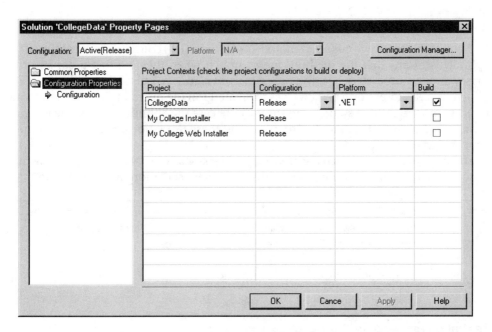

You can also click the Configuration Manager button to further configure your solution. When you click this button, you will see the window shown in the following illustration. You can use this window to create or edit solution build configurations and project configurations. Any changes that you make here will also be reflected in the Solution Explorer.

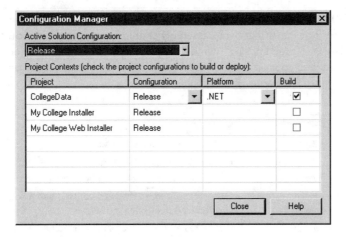

Precompiling

In Part I of this book, we talked about the just-in-time (JIT) compile nature of Visual C# .NET. This means that the methods are compiled when they are first used, and this causes a small time lag when the program is first run. A Windows application uses shared libraries to perform certain tasks that call upon the operating system (rendering visual components, and so on), and this can increase the application's overhead when the application is first started. In order to avoid these limitations, you can precompile your application.

The tool that you use to create precompiled versions is the Native Image Generator (ngen.exe). The precompiling can be done during installation or at build time.

 EXAM TIP In most cases, it makes more sense to run ngen.exe on the destination machine (at installation time) since it will create a precompiled version of the application specific to the local host.

This is the syntax of the ngen.exe command:

```
ngen [options] <assembly path or display name>
```

The options are listed in Table 24-2.

The ngen.exe command creates a native (machine-specific) image from your application and installs it into the native image cache on the host computer. The runtime will automatically try to locate and run the native image each time it runs the assembly. The performance of the application may improve, because a lot of the work that is required to compile methods in a just-in-time implementation will be avoided.

 NOTE Just because there is a perceived performance boost from precompiling does not mean that every assembly should be precompiled. You can see a big benefit in precompiling Windows applications; however, it may not make sense for a web application. Good developers will do bench-testing on precompiled versus JIT versions of their applications.

Table 24-2	Option	Description
Options for the ngen.exe Command	/show	Shows existing native images
	/delete	Deletes existing native images
	/debug	Generates an image that can be used under a debugger
	/debugopt	Generates an image that can be used under a debugger in optimized debugging mode
	/prof	Generates an image that can be used under a profiler
	/? or /help	Returns the help message
	/nologo	Prevents the display of the logo
	/silent	Prevents the display of success messages

Other Performance Enhancements

There are a number of other things to consider when it comes to determining how to improve the performance of a Windows application. In this section, we will quickly visit a lot of these methods. However, keep in mind that you must, as a good developer, determine which of these methods will work for your application. Not all optimization techniques will improve the performance of every application—if they did, then all applications would be optimized in the same way, and you wouldn't need this section of the book.

The following are some of the techniques that can be used to optimize a Windows application:

- **Exception throwing**   Watch the number of exceptions you throw in your application. Throwing exceptions is very expensive in terms of system resources. Remember that the runtime environment will throw its own exceptions as well—you may not explicitly call for an exception to be thrown, it can happen as a result of the runtime. This does not include exception handling, where you try code blocks with a `try ... catch` block. However, it does include using exception throwing to control program flow. In the following piece of code, the programmer has caused a number of exceptions to be thrown that could easily be handled through the use of flow-control statements (such as `break`, `continue`, and the like).

```
for (int i = 0; i < 100; i++)
{
    try
    {
        if (j = i)
        {
            throw new System.Exception.WrongValue();
        }
    } catch { }
}
```

- **Chunky calls**   Your method calls can be expensive. By making a method perform several related tasks (such as initializing all variables) rather than having many calls to the method, you can improve the overall performance of your application. Keep in mind that your methods may have to be called through remote calls, and several calls to the same method will invoke many transitional calls to the remoting technique (such as marshalling the parameter data to the method). Instead of having five calls to the five different methods, incorporate the common operations into a single method that will involve a single call.

- **Use value types instead of objects**   Alright—not all the time, of course! However, there are times when an object is not required, and a value type can handle the problem more efficiently. Keep in mind the overhead required when you create an object. If you must do a lot of boxing and unboxing, though, don't consider the value type as an option—use an object instead.

- **AddRange** Rather than adding one item at a time to a collection, use the `AddRange()` method to add a whole collection of items. Windows Forms controls (or at least most of them) have an `AddRange()` method that will improve performance when adding multiple items to a collection.

- **foreach** Replacing `for` loops with `foreach` loops will significantly improve performance. Instead of having the overhead of a `for` loop, the `foreach` acts as an enumerator over many different types.

- **StringBuilder** String manipulation can often be very expensive. Each time a string is modified, a new string is created and the old string must be garbage collected. If you plan to manipulate the string many times, this can become very costly for the performance of your application. Instead use a `StringBuilder` object to modify the string. Consider the following code:

```
string myString = "Counting from 1 to 100: ";
for (int i=0; i < 100; i++)
{
    myString = myString + i;
    System.Console.WriteLine (myString);
}
```

This code section causes 100 instances of the string to be created. Instead, use the `StringBuilder` as follows:

```
System.Text.StringBuilder s = new System.Test.StringBuilder ("Counting from 1 to 100: ";
for (int i=0; i < 100; i++)
{
    System.Console.WriteLine (s.append(i));
}
```

In this case, there is only 1 object instead of the 100 objects in the first example.

- **Jagged arrays** A jagged array (or an array of arrays) is more efficient than rectangular arrays. The JIT compiler optimizes a jagged array better.

- **DataReader** Use a `DataReader` instead of a `DataSet` whenever possible. A `DataReader` gives you a fast read of the data and doesn't leave the object's contents around. The reader is a stream of data instead of an object that holds the state.

- **Stored procedures** Whenever possible, use stored procedures for data manipulation. The request is made from the client, and the processing is done on the server. There is no additional network traffic, and the code does not have to be interpreted or compiled on the client.

The preceding list encompasses some of the techniques for optimizing Windows applications. As an exam caution, the most significant startup time-performance improvement can be had by precompiling the application.

Securing a Windows Application

Working with the .NET security model allows the developer to protect the application code as well as the data that moves through the application. The security model deals with type safety, code signing, data encryption, access permissions, and role-based security. For the .NET Windows exam, you should become very familiar with code-access security and role-based security. We will cover both of these topics in detail in this section.

Code-Access Security

The code-access security model sets permissions for access to protected resources. The permissions restrict or grant access. The set of permissions are granted through the use of *evidence*, which is information about an assembly. When an attempt to access protected resources is made, the .NET Framework security system checks to see if the code caller has the necessary permissions.

Evidence

In order to decide which permissions can be granted to an assembly, the security system uses *evidence*, which is a set of information about the identity and origin of the assembly. Evidence data includes the following:

- **Assembly's directory**   This is the directory into which the application has been installed.
- **Assembly's publisher**   This is the signature of the software publisher or the Microsoft Authenticode signer of the code.
- **Site**   This is the originator's site, such as http://www.yoursite.com. It can also be expressed as a UNC (Universal Naming Convention) path, or the folder on a local computer.
- **Strong name**   This is the assembly's strong name, which includes a public key, a name, and a version.

The evidence is passed along to the runtime through the trusted application domain or directly from the loader. For example, the digital signature is validated when the code is loaded. Custom evidence can also be included by the creator of the assembly.

Permissions

Certain activities can be performed only if the proper permissions are attached to the call. For example, you might restrict access to reading and writing files on the local file system, or control access to environmental variables based on permissions. Code-access permissions are used to represent the access rights to the resources. Table 24-3 lists some of the built-in code-access classes. You can also create your own custom permission classes.

Class	Description
DirectoryServicesPermission	Directory services
DnsPermission	Domain Name System
EnvironmentPermission	Environmental variables
EventLogPermission	Event logs
FileIOPermission	Local files and folders
OleDbPermission	OLE DB databases
PrintingPermission	Printers
RegistryPermission	Registry
SocketPermission	Connections to other computers (using sockets)
UIPermission	Windows and other user-interface elements
WebPermissions	Access using HTTP

Table 24-3   Code-Access Permission Classes

Putting It Together

Every assembly that is loaded is granted a permission set (a group of permissions) based on the policy. The policy is created from evidence, permissions, code groups, and security policies. The evidence is used to put the assembly into a code group. The code group has been assigned permissions that become permissions for the assembly. A union (all permissions from the code group) is assigned to the assembly. An intersection is the combination of union and security policies.

Let's look at the steps involved in granting permissions:

1. Evidence is gathered for the assembly.

2. The assembly is assigned a code group, and it is tested against certain conditions by the runtime. If the assembly meets the conditions, the permission set associated with the code group is granted. The assembly is then considered to be a member of the code group.

3. All code groups are put together to create a *union of permissions* for the assembly.

4. Steps 1 through 3 are repeating for all security policy levels. These include enterprise, machine, user, and optionally any belonging to the application domain. Enterprise policies are created by the network administrator. Machine policies are specified by the local administrator, and user policies are managed by individual users.

5. The assembly is granted an *intersection of permissions* that represents all policy levels.

 EXAM TIP   Table 24-4 shows evidence types, permissions, code groups, and security policy levels.

Security Piece	Type	Description
Evidence	Application Directory	Installation directory
	Hash	Cryptographic hash
	Publisher	Software publisher's signature
	Site	URL, directory, or other location of the software
	Strong Name	Assembly's strong name
	URL	URL of the software
	Zone	Originating zone of the software
Permissions	FullTrust	No limitations
	Everything	All but security verification
	LocalIntranet	Enterprise permissions
	Internet	Origin is unknown
	Execution	No access to system resources
	Nothing	No permissions
Code group	Root	Represents all code
	Child groups	Made up of group name, membership condition, and permission; examples are Site, Internet, Publisher, etc.
Security policy levels	Enterprise	Code belonging to the enterprise
	Machine	Code on the computer
	User	Code belonging to the user
	Application Domain	Code in the application domain

Table 24-4   Evidence, Permissions, Code Groups, and Security Policy Levels

Here's a series of steps that provides an example of security at work:

1. An assembly is located locally in the application directory on the computer and has a publisher certificate.

2. The assembly belongs to the Root Code group by default, since its membership criteria is all code.

3. The assembly belongs to a publisher group.

4. The assembly belongs to the application directory, as well.

5. Permissions thus are the combination of the Root, the publisher, and the application directory.

Working with Security Policies
The .NET Framework comes with a Code Access Policy command-line utility you can use to view and configure security policies: `caspol.exe`.

Using this tool, you can modify the security policy for the machine, the user, or the enterprise policy level. We don't need to go into great detail for this tool, since you just need to know that it exists for the Microsoft exam; however, it warrants spending a bit of time on its use.

To view the security policies for the various levels, you can use the following statement at a command prompt, choosing the appropriate level:

```
caspol [-enterprise | -machine | -user | -all] -list
```

Figure 24-6 shows an excerpt from the command output from `caspol -machine -list`.

From the output in Figure 24-6, you can see the different code groups and the reference number or name that you can use to specify them. You will also see the membership condition name and the condition value, along with the name of the permission set associated with it.

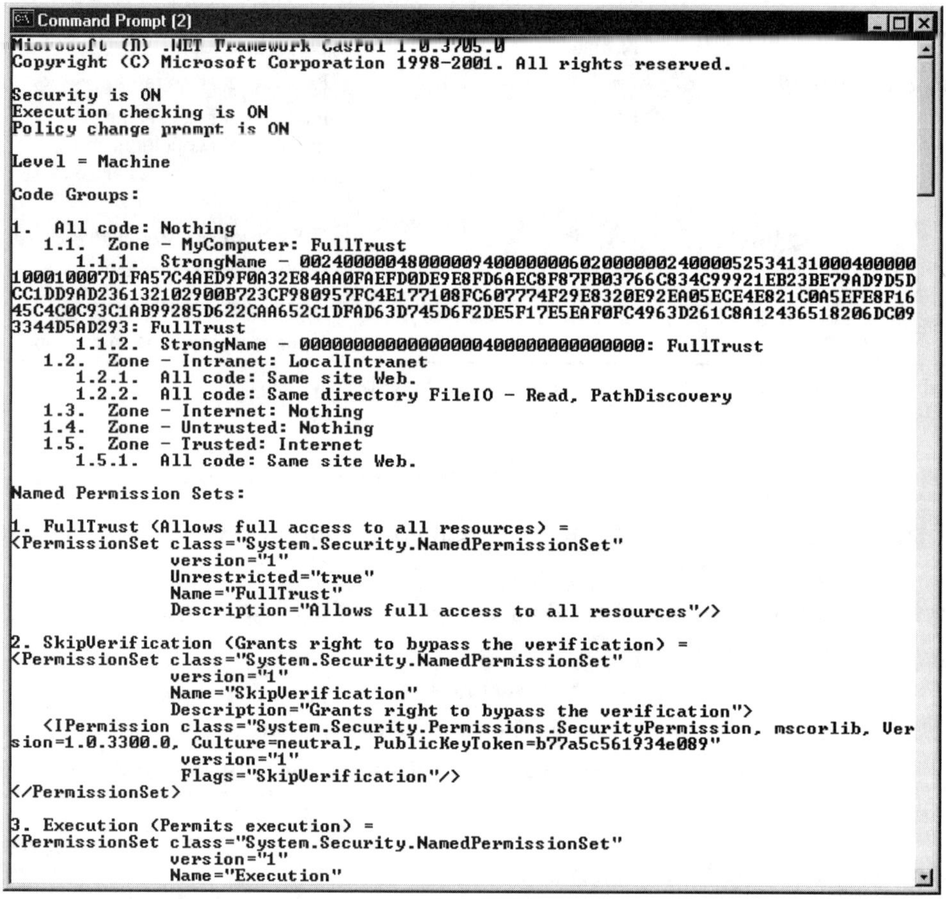

```
Microsoft (R) .NET Framework CasPol 1.0.3705.0
Copyright (C) Microsoft Corporation 1998-2001. All rights reserved.

Security is ON
Execution checking is ON
Policy change prompt is ON

Level = Machine

Code Groups:

1.  All code: Nothing
   1.1.  Zone - MyComputer: FullTrust
      1.1.1.  StrongName - 002400000480000094000000060200000024000052534131000400000
100010007D1FA57C4AED9F0A32E84AA0FAEFD0DE9E8FD6AEC8F87FB03766C834C99921EB23BE79AD9D5D
CC1DD9AD236132102900B723CF980957FC4E177108FC607774F29E8320E92EA05ECE4E821C0A5EFE8F16
45C4C0C93C1AB99285D622CAA652C1DFAD63D745D6F2DE5F17E5EAF0FC4963D261C8A12436518206DC09
3344D5AD293: FullTrust
      1.1.2.  StrongName - 00000000000000000400000000000000: FullTrust
   1.2.  Zone - Intranet: LocalIntranet
      1.2.1.  All code: Same site Web.
      1.2.2.  All code: Same directory FileIO - Read, PathDiscovery
   1.3.  Zone - Internet: Nothing
   1.4.  Zone - Untrusted: Nothing
   1.5.  Zone - Trusted: Internet
      1.5.1.  All code: Same site Web.

Named Permission Sets:

1. FullTrust (Allows full access to all resources) =
<PermissionSet class="System.Security.NamedPermissionSet"
               version="1"
               Unrestricted="true"
               Name="FullTrust"
               Description="Allows full access to all resources"/>

2. SkipVerification (Grants right to bypass the verification) =
<PermissionSet class="System.Security.NamedPermissionSet"
               version="1"
               Name="SkipVerification"
               Description="Grants right to bypass the verification">
   <IPermission class="System.Security.Permissions.SecurityPermission, mscorlib, Ver
sion=1.0.3300.0, Culture=neutral, PublicKeyToken=b77a5c561934e089"
                version="1"
                Flags="SkipVerification"/>
</PermissionSet>

3. Execution (Permits execution) =
<PermissionSet class="System.Security.NamedPermissionSet"
               version="1"
               Name="Execution"
```

Figure 24-6 Output from the `caspol` command

You can use the Code Access Policy tool to add code groups (among other things). To add a new code group, type the following:

```
caspol -machine -addgroup <parentName> <pset_name> <mship>
```

For example, suppose you wanted to add a code group that targets code from Internet Explorer trusted sites. You could use the following command:

```
caspol -addgroup All_Code -zone Trusted LocalIntranet
```

Before we get too carried away with information not required for the Windows exam, remember that you can configure a lot of the security by using the .NET Framework Configuration tool. Figure 24-7 illustrates the configuration possibilities available using this tool.

 EXAM TIP For the exam, remember that *evidence* is the set of information about the identity and origin of an assembly; *permissions* are the rights to protected resources, and *security policies* are used to map evidence with the permissions. Security policies include Enterprise, Machine, User, and Application Domain. Also remember that the most restrictive rules are applied.

PART IV

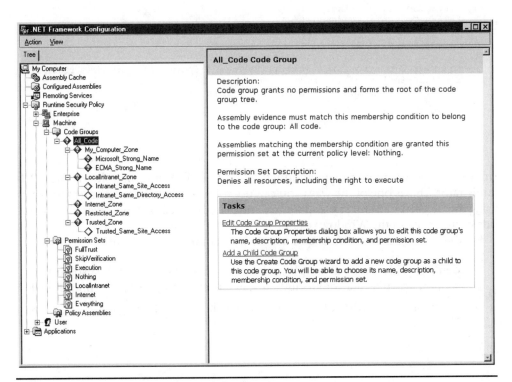

Figure 24-7 Using the .NET Framework Configuration tool for configuring security

Role-Based Security

The second type of security that can be set on an application is role-based security. This involves determining the type of user (or the role that the user plays) and granting permission or denying permission based on that role. For example, you may have an application that requires managers to perform a certain duty. However, clerks may be using the same application but are not permitted to perform the same duty. These restrictions may be as simple as letting a manager change customer details, and letting only a clerk view those details. By implementing role-based security, you can control this.

Role-based security is controlled by passing information about the principal (the identity) of the caller on the current thread. This can take the form of a Windows account, or some other form. The application then makes decisions based on the principal and the role to which the user has been assigned. The role is a collection of principals that have the same permissions—for example, all clerks would be one role, all managers would be another role. Note that a principal can be a member of several roles. The manager may also be a member of the clerk role, thereby permitting the manager to view customer details as well as change them.

The following program demonstrates the use of principals and role-based security.

```
using System;
using System.Threading;
using System.Security.Principal;
public class TestRoleBasedSecurity
{
    public static void Main()
    {
        AppDomain.CurrentDomain.SetPrincipalPolicy ( PrincipalPolicy.WindowsPrincipal);
        WindowsPrincipal w = (WindowsPrincipal) Thread.CurrentPrincipal;
        if (w.IsInRole(WindowsBuiltInRole.Administrator))
        {
            // execute code for Administrators
        }
    }
}
```

Notice that the IsInRole() method tests for a built-in Windows role—namely Administrator. This is one of the ways you can use roles. You can also create generic roles using the GenericIdentity and GenericPrincipal classes; however, that is outside of the scope of the Windows exam.

For the exam, just be aware of two key elements of role-based security:

- **Identity** This can be as simple as the user's login name. It could also be a Passport account or a cookie-authenticated user (for an ASP.NET application).
- **Principal** This is the role (or roles) to which the user belongs.

EXAM TIP Role-based security can be useful for Windows 2000 accounts, Microsoft Passport, or user directories, to manage access to resources.

You may also be tested on your knowledge of the difference between authentication and authorization. These are the basics, in a nutshell:

- **Authentication** is the process of verifying a user's identity. Examples of processes that will find the user's identity and then validate them are operating system user names and Microsoft Passport. These are then validated against such mechanisms as Kerberos (Windows 2000 authentication protocol) or NTLM (Windows NT authentication protocol).

- **Authorization** is the process of finding out whether the authenticated user can proceed with an activity. This happens after the authentication process and uses the role to which the user is assigned to determine which resources the user may access.

Providing User Assistance

There are a few things that can be done to enhance the appearance and the user friendliness of your application. For example, you may give assistance to the user of your application through ToolTips, context-sensitive help, or Help menus. You may also wish to add accessibility features to your application—assistance for vision-, hearing-, or mobility-impaired people. In this section, we will explore these tools.

Providing User Help

Adding help to a Windows application is a necessity. Although you might be very familiar with moving around your forms, the user is not. As a rule, you should try to make your forms as consistent in nature as possible. If you usually put a button in a certain location, try to be sure that it is located there for all related applications. Just as Microsoft does, ensure that your menus are positioned and labeled following Windows standards—File, Edit, View, and so forth. In addition to these techniques, provide assistance to the user with ToolTips, Help menus, and context-sensitive help.

ToolTips

In order to provide assistance through the use of ToolTips, you must add the `ToolTip` control to each form. Figure 24-8 demonstrates the college application form with an instance of the `ToolTip` control added to the form.

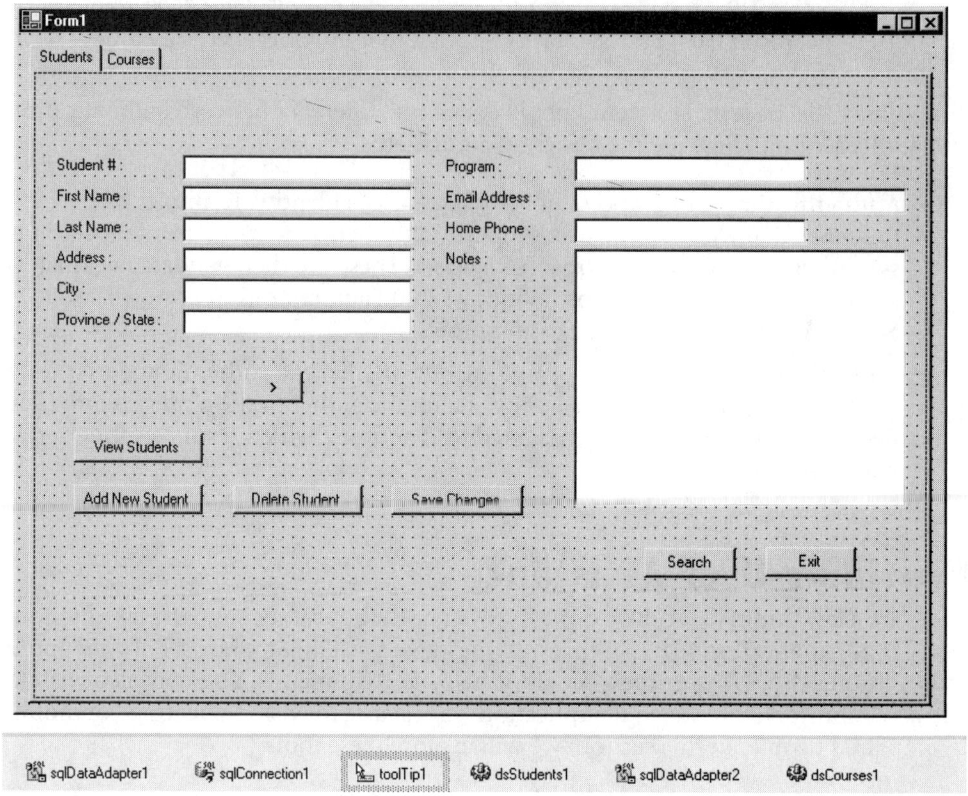

Figure 24-8   Adding a `ToolTip` control to the college application form

Once the instance of the control has been added to the form, you can set the `ToolTip` property of any control on the form. In our example, we have set the property of the Add New Student button to read "This button allows you to add a new student." (see Figure 24-9).

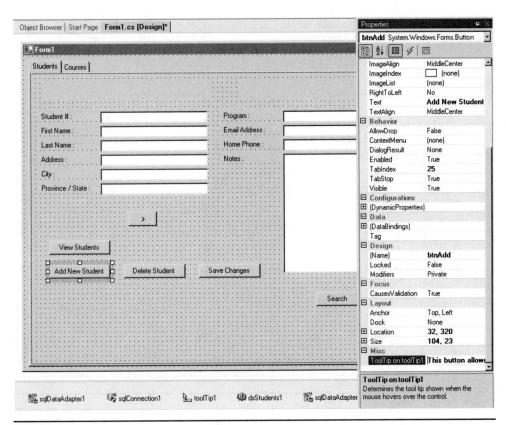

Figure 24-9   Setting the `ToolTip` property

When we execute the application, the user can run the mouse pointer over the button and view the ToolTip (see Figure 24-10).

Context-Sensitive Help

Context-sensitive help occurs when the user presses F1 or clicks the Help button on a form. We will again use our college application as an example and add context-sensitive help to the main form.

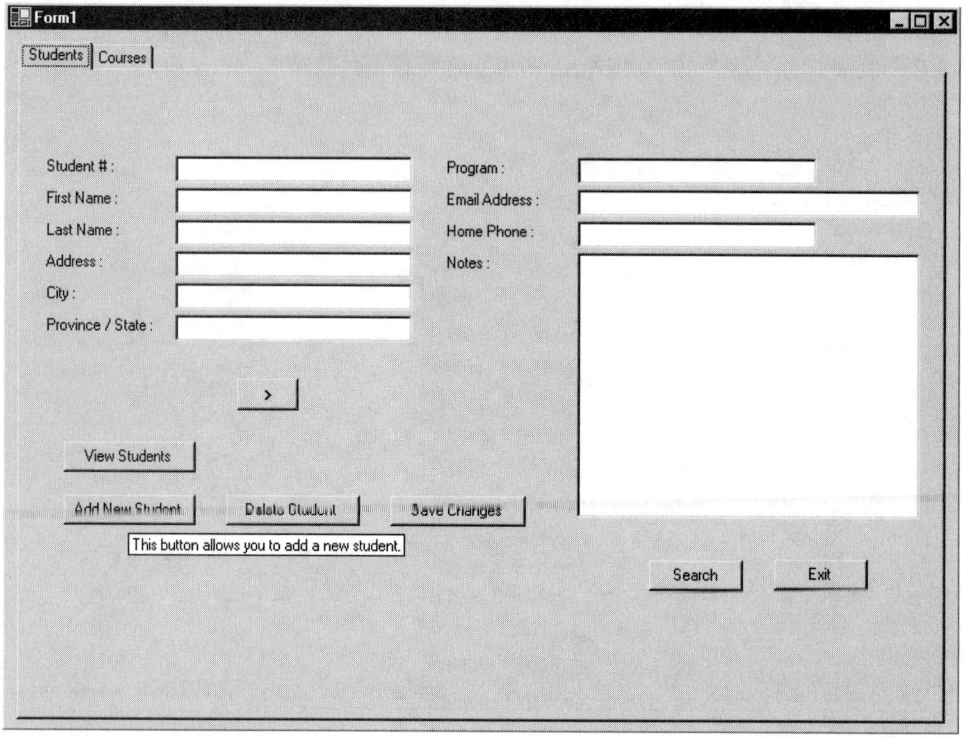

Figure 24-10   Using the `ToolTip` property

The first step is to add an instance of the `HelpProvider` control to the form as shown in Figure 24-11.

Once the `HelpProvider` control is added to the form, you can set the `HelpNamespace` property of the `HelpProvider` control.

- If you set the `HelpNamespace` property, the help will come from the location specified in the property setting when the user presses F1. For example, you could point to a URL or file, and the help will be extracted from there.

- If you do not set the `HelpNamespace` property, the help will be displayed in a small pop-up window beside the control when the user presses F1.

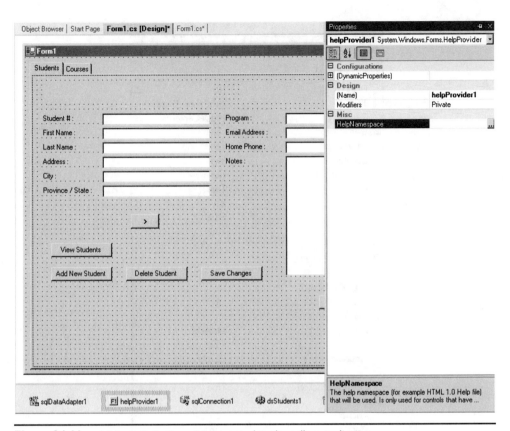

Figure 24-11   Adding a `HelpProvider` control to the college application

For this example, leave the `HelpNamespace` property blank. Now when you click on the button to which you wish to add help, you will see help properties in the Property Explorer (see Figure 24-12). Set the `HelpString` property to provide the needed assistance.

The final step is to set the help properties of the form:

1. Select the form and open the Property Explorer.

2. Find the `HelpButton` property and set it to True.

3. Set the `MaximizeBox` and the `MinimizeBox` properties to False.

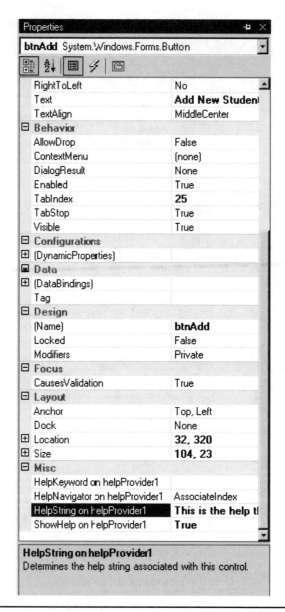

Figure 24-12   Setting the help properties

When you run the application now, you will see the Help button (?) in the top right corner (see Figure 24-13). When you click the Help button, it displays a large question-mark symbol. The user can then move the question mark over the desired control (in

Figure 24-13   The Help button

this example, the Add New Student button) and click the button. The `HelpString` text
will be displayed.

EXAM TIP   Do not forget to set the `MaximizeBox` and `MinimizeBox` to
False; otherwise the Help button will not appear.

Linking Help Topics to a Help Menu

The `MainMenu` control can be used to add menus to your application. Double-click on
the `MainMenu` control in the Toolbox, and the menu will be added to your form. Type
in the spaces provided to show the menu items. In the example shown in Figure 24-14,
we have added a File and a Help menu to the form.

You will then need to add the following code to the form:

```
private void menuItemx_Click (object sender, System.EventArgs e)
{
    Help.ShowHelp (this, HelpProvider.HelpNamespace);
}
```

Figure 24-14 Adding menus to a form

The `HelpNamespace` object identifies the location of the help file. This could be in the form of a URL or a local file.

Adding Accessibility Features

Another way of adding user assistance to your application is to provide accommodation for the accessibility needs of your users. This can include assistance for poor vision, voice input utilities for hand-impaired users, narrators, and many other options. In this section, we will look at adding some of these features to your Windows application.

 TIP For guidelines on the standards associated with accessibility features, visit Microsoft's web site: http://www.microsoft.com/enable/.

In order be "Certified for Windows", an accessible application will:

- Support Control Panel size, color, font, and input settings.

- Support High Contrast mode.

- Provide documented keyboard access to all features.

- Expose location of the keyboard focus visually and programmatically.

- Avoid conveying important information by sound alone.

These five requirements are verbatim from MSDN and, if followed, mean that your application can add the "Certified for Windows" logo to its packaging.

Every control in the Toolbox supports many of the accessibility guidelines, and Table 24-5 illustrates some of these properties.

 EXAM TIP Use the `SystemInformation.HighContrast` (which takes a Boolean value) to determine whether the High Contrast mode has been set. If it is True, use the system color scheme for the application. When the `HighContrast` changes, the `UserPreferenceChanged` event is raised.

Here are some extra tips for making your application more accessible:

- The user can resize menu bars, title bars, and the like through the Control Panel. You do not need to code to accommodate for this.

- Use the Windows API function `FlashWindow` to make the title bar flash. This can provide a means of alerting the user to some condition that otherwise would have relied on sound.

- Make use of status indicators in the status notification area of the task bar.

Property	Description
AccessibleDescription	Screen readers (specialized programs or devices) will be able to report this property to the disabled user.
AccessibleName	Screen readers will use this name.
AccessibleRole	Screen readers will understand the use of this element.
TabIndex	This is the order in which the controls are tabbed.
Text	This will make use of the & to provide alternate methods for accessing the control.
FontSize	The font size should be set to an acceptable level for the form.
Forecolor	The property should be set to a default and the user's preferences will apply.
Backcolor	This should be treated in the same way as Forecolor.
BackgroundImage	Using this property can muddle the screen—leave it blank.

Table 24-5 Accessibility Properties for Controls

PART IV

Localizing a Windows Form

In Chapter 7, we spoke generically about localizing an application. In this section we will apply those concepts to a Windows Form. Two key terms are used here:

- **Globalization**   This is building the functionality of the application without localization.
- **Localization**   This involves translating the resources.

 EXAM TIP   The `CultureInfo` class contains culture-specific information.

The .NET Framework includes the `CultureInfo` class, which contains specific information for a particular culture. For instance, it would contain information about language, calendars, country or region, date formatting, and currency formatting, to name but a few elements. A unique name exists for each culture—these names can be found in the SDK documentation that comes with the .NET Framework.

In our college application, we will localize the text on the Add New Student button and then change the display by changing the locale settings in the Control Panel. Follow these steps to accomplish this:

1. Set the `Localizable` property of the form to True.

2. Set the needed languages for the form using the `Language` property. Each language will have its own resource file.

3. With the `Language` property of the form set to the new language, change the text of the controls.

4. Add any localized text strings by selecting Project | Add New Item | Assembly Resource File from the menus. Add entries into the resource file.

5. Add the necessary `using` directives:

```
using System.Globalization;
using System.Resources;
using System.Threading;
```

6. Retrieve the locale from the Control Panel settings:

```
Thread.CurrentThread.CurrentUICulture = Thread.CurrentThread.CurrentCulture;
```

 EXAM TIP   To set the locale for the application, use the preceding code.

---

7. Create a resource manage object:

```
ResourceManager rm = new ResourceManager ("<resource file>",
Assembly.GetExecutingAssembly());
```

8. Set the Regional Options of your computer to the new language.

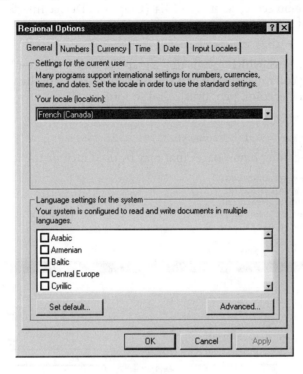

9. Run your application under the new regional settings. Notice in Figure 24-15 that the Add New Student button has changed to the French version.

EXAM TIP The `Localizable` property, when set to True, creates a new resource file for each new language that the user adds.

Using System.Drawing

If you want to build your own controls, or draw your own elements on a form, you will need to use the `System.Drawing` namespace. The namespace contains many classes that will help you draw on a form, such as `Color`, `Point`, `Rectangle`, `Icon`, `Image`, `Graphics`, `Pen`, `StringFormat`, and many, many more.

We will only deal with the issues that may be pertinent to the Windows exam, since this is a very specific area of study. Keep the following points in mind for the exam:

- The `Graphics` class contains many of the methods that you will use to draw. Some of these methods include: `DrawArc`, `DrawCurve`, `DrawLine`, `DrawRectangle`, `FillRectangle`, and `RotateTransform`, along with many others.

- Create a `Graphics` object in order to draw lines and shapes or manipulate images. The object represents a GDI+ (Graphical Device Interface) drawing surface and is used to create graphical images.

```
Graphics g = this.CreateGraphics();
```

- GDI+ is stateless, which means that a graphics object will not hold its properties. You must always pass the properties to any of the methods (properties like color, pen, brush, and so forth).

- Create a new `Color` object as follows:

```
Color myColor = Color.FromArgb (127, 182, 145);
```

- Some of the other namespaces that may be used include the following:

```
System.Drawing.Drawing2D
System.Drawing.Imaging
System.Drawing.Printing
System.Drawing.Design
System.Drawing.Text
```

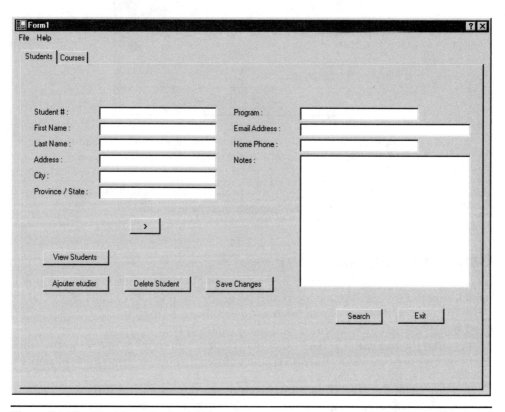

Figure 24-15   The form with a localized button

The following code segment will produce a small graphic and show you how to manipulate the Graphics object.

```
// create a new Graphics object
Graphics g = this.CreateGraphics();
// display the window
this.Show();
// create a pen object with which to draw our rectangle
Pen redPen = new Pen (Color.Red, 3);
// draw a rectangle
g.DrawRectangle (redPen, 100, 100, 100, 100);
```

The result of the preceding code is shown in the following illustration.

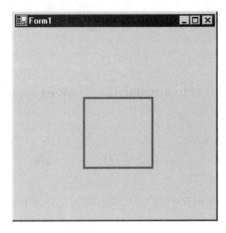

Summary

In this chapter, we have dealt with a number of exam topics. Make sure that you feel comfortable with configuring a Windows application and setting security—both role-based and code-access security. You should also know the techniques for optimizing the performance of a Windows application, paying close attention to precompiling as a valuable technique for saving system resources. You may find a little on the exam regarding user assistance in the form of ToolTips, help menu items, and context-sensitive help. Also spend some time on localizing a Windows Form, as you will need to know the classes that retrieve system information from the local computer and determine the locale of the application's runtime.

This completes the fourth part of this book—the Windows exam. By now you should be experienced at creating Windows applications and working with the code that accompanies the graphical interface. Prepare yourself for the exam by going through the questions at the end of each chapter, and then take the practice test on the accompanying CD. That should prepare you for the exam. Of course, there's nothing like experience—so work with C# as much as you can.

Test Questions

1. You are responsible for adding localization to an existing Windows Form. What class will determine the locale of the runtime environment?

   A. `ResourceManager`

   B. `Localization`

   C. `Globalization`

   D. `CurrentUICulture`

2. Which tool can you use to configure the security settings for an application?

   A. `mscorcfg.msc`

   B. `ngen.exe`

   C. `caspol.exe`

   D. `caspol.msc`

3. Which tool can you use to precompile a Windows application?

   A. `mscorcfg.msc`

   B. `ngen.exe`

   C. `caspol.exe`

   D. `caspol.msc`

4. Which security file will override the machine configuration file?

   A. Enterprise configuration

   B. Application configuration

   C. Security configuration

   D. User configuration

5. Which of the following code segments will produce an ellipse on the form?

   A. `Graphics g = new Graphics();`
      `g.DrawEllipse(myPen, 10, 10, 10, 10);`

   B. `Graphics g = new Graphics();`
      `g.DrawEllipse (10, 10, 10, 10);`

   C. `Graphics g = this.CreateGraphics();`
      `g.DrawEllipse (myPen, 10, 10, 10, 10);`

   D. `Graphics g = this.CreateGraphics();`
      `g.DrawEllipse (10, 10, 10, 10);`

6. Where would you find the `machine.config` file on a Windows 2000 machine?

   A. `<system drive>\Program Files\Microsoft .NET\Framework\`
      `CONFIG\`

   B. `<system drive>\Winnt\Microsoft.NET\Framework\<version>\`
      `CONFIG\`

C. `<system drive>\Winnt\CONFIG`

D. `<system drive>\Documents and Settings\Framework\CONFIG`

7. Which of the following XML segments will redirect the bindings of a component?

A.
```
<runtime>
    <assemblyBinding  >
        <redirectBinding name="MyComponent"
            oldVersion="1.0.0.01" newVersion="1.0.0.02" />
    </assemblyBinding>
</runtime>
```

B.
```
<runtime>
    <assemblyBinding  >
        <oldVersion="1.0.0.01" newVersion="1.0.0.02" />
    </assemblyBinding>
</runtime>
```

C.
```
<runtime>
    <assemblyBinding  >
        <dependentAssembly>
            <assemblyIdentity name="MyComponent" />
                <redirectBinding oldVersion="1.0.0.01" newVersion="1.0.0.02" />
        </dependentAssembly>
    </assemblyBinding>
</runtime>
```

D.
```
<runtime>
    <assemblyBinding  >
        <dependentAssembly>
            <assemblyIdentity name="MyComponent" />
                <bindingRedirect oldVersion="1.0.0.01" newVersion="1.0.0.02" />
        </dependentAssembly>
    </assemblyBinding>
</runtime>
```

8. What is the name and path of an application configuration file if the application name is `MyApplication.exe` and is found in `c:\MyProgs`?

A. `c:\Winnt\Microsoft.NET\Framework\<version>\CONFIG\MyApplication.exe.config`

B. `c:\MyProgs\MyApplication.config`

C. `c:\MyProgs\MyApplication.exe.config`

D. `c:\Winnt\Microsoft.NET\Framework\<version>\CONFIG\MyApplication.config`

9. What are the three different policy-configuration files?

   A. Enterprise, Machine, User.

   B. Enterprise, Machine, Local.

   C. Enterprise, Security, Local.

   D. Enterprise, Security, User.

10. Which code segment represents the most efficient way to manipulate a string?

    A.
    ```
    string s = new string("Hello");
    for (int j = 0; j <10; j++)
    {
       s = s + NameCollection(j);
     }
    ```

    B.
    ```
    String s = new String ("Hello");
    for (int j = 0; j < 10; j++)
    {
       s = s + NameCollection(j);
    }
    ```

    C.
    ```
    StringBuilder s = new StringBuilder ("Hello");
    for (int j = 0; j < 10; j++)
    {
       s.append(NameCollection(j));
    }
    ```

    D.
    ```
    StringBuffer s = new StringBuffer ("Hello");
    for (int j = 0; j < 10; j++)
    {
       s.append(NameCollection(j));
    }
    ```

11. What type of array is the most efficient to work with?

    A. Rectangular array

    B. One-dimensional array

    C. Two-dimensional array

    D. Jagged array

12. Which code-access class can be used to represent permissions related to network access?

    A. NetworkPermission

    B. RemotePermission

    C. URLPermission

    D. SocketPermission

13. Which of the following represents a union of permissions?

    A. A collection of code groups.

    B. A collection of permissions.

    C. A collection of intersections.

    D. A collection of evidence.

14. Which code segment would test the validity of a role-based user?

    A.
```
AppDomain.CurrentDomain.SetPrincipalPolicy (PrincipalPolicy.WindowsPrincipal);
if (WindowsBuiltInRole == Administrator)
{
    // do something here
}
```

    B.
```
AppDomain.CurrentDomain.SetPrincipalPolicy (PrincipalPolicy.WindowsPrincipal);
WindowsPrincipal w = (WindowsPrincipal) Thread.CurrentPrincipal;
if (w.WindowsBuiltInRole == Administrator)
{
    // do something here
}
```

    C.
```
AppDomain.CurrentDomain.SetPrincipalPolicy (PrincipalPolicy.WindowsPrincipal);
WindowsPrincipal w = (WindowsPrincipal) Thread.CurrentPrincipal;
if (w.IsInRole(WindowsBuiltInRole == Administrator))
{
    // do something here
}
```

    D.
```
AppDomain.CurrentDomain.SetPrincipalPolicy (PrincipalPolicy.WindowsPrincipal);
WindowsPrincipal w = (WindowsPrincipal) Thread.CurrentPrincipal;
if (w.IsInRole(WindowsBuiltInRole.Administrator))
{
    // do something here
}
```

15. What must be done to create a ToolTip on a new Windows control?

    A. Add a `ToolTip` control and set the `ToolTip` property of the new control.

    B. Set the `ToolTip` property of the new control.

    C. Set the `Help` property of the new control.

    D. Create a `MessageBox` that displays when the user clicks the new control.

Test Answers

1. D.
2. A.
3. B.
4. B.
5. D.
6. B.
7. D.
8. C.
9. A.
10. C.
11. D.
12. D.
13. A.
14. D.
15. A.

Exam 70-320: Developing XML Web Services

Introduction to XML Web Services and Server Components

25

In this chapter, you will
- Be introduced to SOAP, UDDI, XML, WSDL, XSLT, XPath, and XSD
- Configure debugging in an XML web service
- Implement logging in an XML web service
- Implement tracing in an XML web service

This chapter introduces you to the concepts that we will be exploring in detail in this part of the book. In order to fully understand the questions you will see on Exam 70-320, "Developing XML Web Services and Server Components," you must take the time to understand the protocols and alphabet soup that you see in this chapter's objectives. Most of the questions are very detailed and explore complicated scenarios that will call upon your understanding of the technologies.

As a result, you will see very little in this chapter that is directly on the exam; however, you will need to know this chapter inside and out to be successful on the exam. If you are fairly new to XML (Extensible Markup Language), be sure to review the information in Chapter 8. We will quickly review the concepts here, but we will also be going into the detail that is required for the 70-320 exam. A fair bit of this chapter will be spent on SOAP (Simple Object Access Protocol), and then we will briefly explore technologies such as UDDI, XSLT, XPath, and XSD.

We will also take some time to review the testing methods for XML web services and server components. In Chapter 9, we looked at the generic concepts related to testing—creating a unit test plan, tracing, and so forth. In this chapter, we will specifically consider the testing of an XML web service. We will also look at the log test results. The focus of our work on testing in this chapter will be on debugging control within the `web.config` file and using SOAP extensions for debugging.

The Standards

Many of the questions on the 70-320 exam describe complicated scenarios that require your understanding of the standards involved in server-based services. In this section, we will examine some of these standards and protocols. Here is a quick summary:

- **XML (Extensible Markup Language)** A language that allows data and data definitions to be included in a structured document.

- **SOAP (Simple Object Access Protocol)** A lightweight protocol for exchanging information in a decentralized, distributed environment.

- **XML Web Services** Application logic (components) that provide data and services to other applications. XML web services are accessed using web protocols such as HTTP, XML, and SOAP.

- **WSDL (Web Services Description Language)** A language that describes a web service in terms of the messages that it accepts and creates.

- **UDDI (Universal Description, Discovery, and Integration)** A method of publishing and discovering information about web services. UDDI provides a directory of web services.

- **XSL (Extensible Stylesheet Language)** A style-sheet language that renders the presentation of data from the data content. It is a transformation language that is usually used to translate XML data content to HTML for displaying in a browser.

- **XSLT (Extensible Stylesheet Language Transformations)** A component of XSL that transforms data content from one XML format to another XML format.

- **XPath** A technology that addresses part of an XML document. It is used by XSLT.

- **XSD (XML Schema Reference)** Files that allow you to define the structure and data types for XML documents.

In this section, we will start with XML and work our way through the preceding list. Remember that most of the information in this section is provided as a reference for the material that comes after it. You will see very little on the exam that is directly related to this section.

XML (Extensible Markup Language)

Hang onto your hats—we are going to cover in this section what took us all of Chapter 8 earlier. However, we understand that you might only be interested in this part, since you want to write the 70-320 exam, so we'll give you the Reader's Digest version of XML here.

What Is XML?

XML stands for Extensible Markup Language and was designed to describe data. Since it is a markup language, it looks a little like HTML (Hypertext Markup Language), but it is not the same thing. HTML is used to display data and XML is used to describe data. XML uses tags that you define (or that a schema document defines) to define pieces of data within the XML document. The following is an example of an XML document:

```
<recipe>
    <name>Chicken Soup</name>
    <ingredient>Chicken</ingredient>
    <ingredient>Soup</ingredient>
</recipe>
```

This XML document does nothing except describe some data. Although it looks like HTML with its tags, it really does nothing. If you try to "open" this file in a browser, such as Internet Explorer, you will see the result shown in Figure 25-1.

In order to display the data described in our XML document, we need a program that will do something with it. In reality, for the purposes of this part of the book, XML is a tool for transmitting data. We will find a way to send the data (SOAP). The data can be sent to any platform, any software or hardware, and be received there and processed. When data is described using XML, it can be easily transmitted through Internet protocols and received by any type of application at the server end. XML allows developers to spend less time worrying about how to move data and more time developing their applications.

Businesses can use XML to exchange and share data (well, that's been done for ages, but now the data is self-describing and is easily transmitted over the Internet). As an analogy, think of a word processing document. In the past, if you wanted to send the document to someone else, they had to have the same word processing program to read the document because the encoding must be read by that one application. With a standard way of describing data through XML, anyone can read the document.

PART V

Figure 25-1
The XML
document in
Internet Explorer

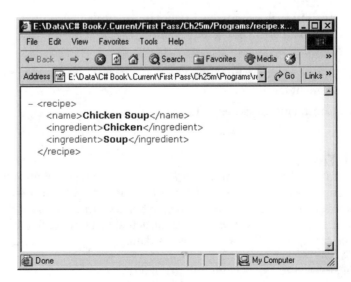

XML Rules

As a standard, XML boasts very simple and very tight syntax rules. Following these rules means that your XML document can be easily read and used. These rules are as follows:

- The first line in the document is an XML declaration describing the version and encoding:

  ```
  <?xml version="1.0" encoding="utf-8"?>
  ```

- There can only be one root element. An *element* is a tag that describes the data, and in a well-formed XML document, there is only one *root element*. The root element in our example is `<recipe>`.

- All other elements are considered *children* of the root element. Therefore, `<name>` is a child element.

- XML elements must have closing tags:

  ```
  <name>Chicken Soup</name>
  ```

  The `<name>` element is closed using `</name>`.

- XML tags are case sensitive. This means that the tag `<name>` is different from the tag `<Name>`.

- XML elements must be properly nested. For example, the following XML is invalid because the `<ingredient>` is not closed within the `<ingredients>` tag.

  ```
  <recipe>
      <name>Chicken Soup</name>
      <ingredients>
          <ingredient>Chicken
      </ingredients>
      </ingredient>
  </recipe>
  ```

- Attribute values must be in quotes. An *attribute* describes name-value pairs within an element tag. For example,

  ```
  <name serves="4">Chicken Soup</name>
  ```

  In the preceding line, `serves` is an attribute that doesn't need it's own element tag.

- Comments are coded as follows:

  ```
  <!--This is a comment-- >
  ```

XML Elements

Elements are the most common type of markup that you will see in an XML document. Elements describe the data and formulate the hierarchy of the data in the document. Tags are used to define data elements. In between the start tag, `<element_name>`, and the end tag, `</element_name>`, is the actual text or data that belongs to the element. In this example, `Chicken Soup` is the data:

```
<name>Chicken Soup</name>
```

Elements can be hierarchical. This means that you can have child elements of an element. In our earlier example, `<ingredient>` was a child of `<recipe>`, and `<name>` was a child of `<recipe>`. To be more correct, you may want to formulate the XML document like this:

```
<recipe>
   <name>Chicken Soup
      <ingredient>Chicken</ingredient>
      <ingredient>Soup</ingredient>
   </name>
</recipe>
```

In this case, `<ingredient>` is a child of `<name>`, which is a child of `<recipe>`. Notice that this document follows the rules of the previous section, in that there is one and only one root element—`<recipe>`.

Element names must conform to the following rules:

- They must contain letters, numbers, or other characters.
- They must not start with a number or punctuation character.
- They must not start with the letters "xml" (in any case combination).
- They cannot contain spaces.

XML Attributes

An XML attribute can be used to give more information about the data. However, an attribute is not an element. Rather, it is a part of the element and gives more information about the element. In the earlier example, we used this line to describe the data regarding the name of the recipe:

```
<name>Chicken Soup
```

We could add an attribute (which is simply a named pair of values) to give more information about the name of the recipe:

```
<name Category="soup" Chicken Soup
```

`Category` is the attribute, and it is followed with an equal sign (=) and double quotes surrounding the value. You can use either double or single quotes to surround the attribute value, but they must match.

For more information on XML, refer back to Chapter 8. However, keep in mind that this book's intention is not to teach you XML. You simply have to know how it is formed and how it is used in web services or server components.

SOAP (Simple Object Access Protocol)

At the time of writing, the SOAP protocol is at version 1.1 and the specifications for the protocol can be found at http://www.w3.org/TR/SOAP. The official definition of SOAP is "a lightweight protocol for exchange of information in a decentralized, distributed environment." In this section, we will examine the protocol in detail.

PART V

What Is SOAP?

Many developers were keen to anticipate the release of SOAP because they were looking for a method of using RPCs (remote procedure calls) over HTTP (Hypertext Transfer Protocol). Remote procedure calls are used by many different distributed solutions to define the way requests and data are transmitted from one application to another. This means that one program can request the services of another program that is located on a remote system. The calling program (client) does not need to understand the network details. How the request gets there is unimportant to the client.

Using RPCs entails the use of *stubs*, which are compiled into the client code and act as the local representative of the called code (which is on the server). The stub actually receives the client request and marshals it to the server. The server then intercepts the request, processes the call, wraps the results up (using a proxy—a representative of the server), and marshals them back to the stub.

One of the problems with using RPCs is that HTTP does not support them. This means that typically firewalls will block RPC calls. Using HTTP means that port 80, which is usually open on a firewall, can be used for remote calls.

So is this SOAP?—a method of using RPCs over HTTP? Not really, although that is certainly part of the specification. SOAP is "a lightweight protocol that passes structured data between applications using XML." It doesn't matter what transports the data. HTTP can be used, SMTP (Simple Mail Transfer Protocol) can be used—SOAP simply defines the way in which the message is constructed. How it is transported is immaterial.

The Three Faces of SOAP

SOAP is an XML-based protocol that is made up of three parts:

- **The envelope**   The envelope describes what is in the SOAP message and explains how the message can be processed.

- **The encoding rules**   The encoding rules define the serialization mechanism (encoding, sending, and decoding) that can be used to exchange the data.

- **The RPC representation**   This is the convention that can be used to represent remote procedure calls and the responses from the server.

Let's look at how a SOAP message is created, and how the mechanism works.

The Envelope   Every SOAP message is an XML document. The document includes an XML envelope element, which is the root element (see Chapter 8 for the definition of root elements). The envelope element optionally may contain a header element, but must contain a body element. If a header is not used, the body element must be the immediate child of the envelope element.

 EXAM TIP   A SOAP message is made up of (1) the envelope, the top element in the XML document that represents the message; (2) the header, an optional element that includes definitions of extra features; and (3) the body, a mandatory element that contains the message.

The SOAP header is used to describe extra information regarding the message but will not directly affect the message. Some of the information that you might find in a SOAP header includes the following:

- Transaction information
- Authentication information
- Language, country, currency, and so on
- Next recipient of the message
- State information to be carried between requests

The SOAP body is the actual message that is intended for the recipient of the message. The body element will contain multiple child elements, which are called body entries.

SOAP Encoding   Serialization (the rules for representing types such as integers, strings, and so forth) of data inside a SOAP message is called *encoding*. You can use an attribute called `encodingStyle` within the `Envelope` element to identify the encoding rules. Encoding style can be defined right down to a specific element, if you want. However, we won't spend too much time on this concept because you'll begin to think that the "Simple" in SOAP is a misnomer.

There is no default encoding style, but you can use the SOAP specification's set of encoding rules. These will work well in most cases because they map nicely to most programming types. The SOAP encoding rules are found at http://schemas.xmlsoap.org/soap/encoding/.

To read more on SOAP encoding, refer to the SOAP specifications at http://www.w3.org/TR/SOAP. Section 5 covers the rules for encoding types in XML, simple types, strings, enumerations, compound types, arrays, structs, and references.

RPC Representation   The final piece that brings the picture together is the representation that defines the convention that can be used to represent method calls and responses. For the purposes of this part of the book, we will cover SOAP in HTTP. Keep in mind, however, that SOAP can be used for remote procedure calls (RPCs). The SOAP specification (http://www.w3.org/TR/SOAP) covers both of these.

The SOAP Message
Figure 25-2 shows how a SOAP message is constructed. Notice that HTTP (the transportation protocol) wraps the entire message. Within the package is the SOAP document, and it contains an optional header with delivery information and a mandatory body with the actual method parameters.

A very simple SOAP message would look like this:

```
<SOAP:Envelope xmlns=http://schemas.xmlsoap.org/soap/envelope/>
    <SOAP:Body>
        <m:helloWorld xmlns:m="http://www.osborne.com/"/>
    </SOAP:Body>
</SOAP:Envelope>
```

PART V

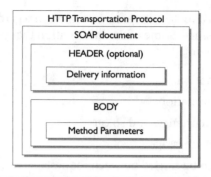

Figure 25-2   SOAP message structure

If we take this message apart, we have the following:

- An envelope element starting with `<SOAP:Envelope` and ending with `</SOAP:Envelope>`

- The namespace URL, which is determined by `xmls=http://schemas.xmlsoap.org/soap/envelope`. The elements and attributes are defined at that location.

- The next element (defined by the schema) is `<SOAP:Body>`.

- Following the declaration of the body element is the actual remote method call—`m:helloWorld`. The `m` represents the namespace of the method call and is defined in the namespace declaration `xmlns:m="http://www.osborne.com/"`.

Note that if you go to the namespace URL (`http://schemas.xmlsoap.org/soap/envelope`) mentioned in the second point in the preceding list, you will find something that looks like this:

```
<xs:schema xmlns:xs=http://www.w3.org/2001/XMLSchema
        xmlns:tns=http://schemas.xmlsoap.org/soap/envelope/
        targetNamespace="http://schemas.xmlsoap.org/soap/envelope/">
- <!--
 Envelope, header and body
  -->
<xs:element name="Envelope" type="tns:Envelope" />
<xs:complexType name="Envelope">
<xs:sequence>
     <xs:element ref="tns:Header" minOccurs="0" />
   <xs:element ref="tns:Body" minOccurs="1" />
   <xs:any namespace="##other" minOccurs="0" maxOccurs="unbounded" processContents="lax" />
</xs:sequence>
   <xs:anyAttribute namespace="##other" processContents="lax" />
   </xs:complexType>
   <xs:element name="Header" type="tns:Header" />
- <xs:complexType name="Header">
- <xs:sequence>
   <xs:any namespace="##other" minOccurs="0" maxOccurs="unbounded" processContents="lax" />
</xs:complexType>
```

```
    <xs:element name="Body" type="tns:Body" />
-   <xs:complexType name="Body">
-   <xs:sequence>
    <xs:any namespace="##any" minOccurs="0" maxOccurs="unbounded" processContents="lax" />
</xs:sequence>
-   <xs:anyAttribute namespace="##any" processContents="lax">
-   <xs:annotation>
    <xs:documentation>Prose in the spec does not specify that attributes are allowed on
the Body element</xs:documentation>
    </xs:annotation>
    </xs:anyAttribute>
    </xs:complexType>
```

In this code, you can see the schema that describes some of the elements and attributes that will be included in your SOAP document. For the complete schema, go to http://schemas.xmlsoap.org/soap/envelope.

Here is a template for a SOAP message:

```
<SOAP:Envelope xmlns:"http://schemas.xmlsoap.org/soap/envelope/"
               soap:encodingStyle="http://schemas.xmlsoap.org/soap/encoding/">
    <SOAP:Header>
    <!--
     Header information goes here
     e.g.
        <t:Transaction xmlns:t="URL" /t:Transaction>
    -->
    </SOAP:Header>
      <SOAP:Body>
      <!--
     Body goes here
     e.g.
        <m:runMethod xmlns:m="URL" />
    -->
        <SOAP:Fault>
        <!--
     Fault information goes here
     Carries error and/or status information within a SOAP message
     e.g.
         <faultcode>SOAP:Server</faultcode>
         <faultstring>Server Error</faultstring>
    -->
        </SOAP:Fault>
      </SOAP:Body>
  </SOAP:Envelope>
```

SOAP in HTTP

Developers can use SOAP within HTTP. SOAP and HTTP are a natural fit, since they both use a request/response messaging model. In this section, we will examine how you can bind SOAP to the network protocol, HTTP. Keep in mind that a lot of this is beneath the surface of what you see when you code using Visual Studio .NET and create web services.

SOAP allows you to embed method calls within an XML document and have those calls transmitted over HTTP. Here are the steps:

1. The client identifies the server by its URL.

2. The TCP/IP network protocol, HTTP, is used to connect to the server.

PART V

3. The HTTP request message has a SOAP request embedded within it.

4. The SOAP request is then "bound" to HTTP.

Here is a simple SOAP HTTP header:

```
POST /objectURI HTTP/1.1
HOST: www.osborne.com
SOAPMethodName: namespace:IRecipe#getRecipe
Content-Type: text/xml
Content-Length: xxxx
```

The header indicates that the `getRecipe` method (found in `namespace:IRecipe`) should be called from server www.osborne.com.

The corresponding SOAP document would include the following:

```
<?xml version="1.0"?>
<SOAP:Envelope xmlns:"http://schemas.xmlsoap.org/soap/envelope/">
   <SOAP:Body>
      <m:getRecipe xmlns:m="namespace:IRecipe">
         <recipeName>Chicken Soup</recipeName>
      </m:getRecipe>
   </SOAP:Body>
</SOAP:Envelope>
```

Notice that within the `<SOAP:Body>` element, the element `<m:getRecipe>` matches the `SOAPMethodName` in the HTTP header. (Remember that `<m:getRecipe>` translates into `<namespace:IRecipe:getRecipe>`.) Because of this, the code within HTTP can be used to process the call on the server side without having to parse the XML first.

We have added one more element to the SOAP message—`<recipeName>`. This is the parameter information that the method `getRecipe` is expecting. So, what happens at the server side? The SOAP protocol doesn't really care. The request may be to an ASP page or any other server component, such as Java Server Pages, CGI programs, Apache modules, and so on. The point here is that it doesn't matter what is on the server side. That's the beauty of SOAP—it's transparent to the server. Issues like interoperability, firewalls, and the like all disappear by using SOAP.

This is a very simplified explanation of SOAP, mainly because you don't need to know all of the mechanics behind it.

 EXAM TIP Microsoft will ask you questions regarding the protocol to use when requesting services outside of the local application. Your answer very often should be SOAP. Read the question carefully and ensure that SOAP will answer the problem.

Things to Remember About SOAP

SOAP messages are made up of the following parts:

- **Envelope** This is the mandatory root element of a SOAP document.

- **Header** This is an optional element that provides extra information to the server.

- **Body** This is a mandatory element that contains the actual data of the message.

SOAP messages are embedded in an HTTP request. The message is sent to the server identified by its URL in the message. Figure 24-3 illustrates the process.

SOAP in HTTP is used to provide an interoperable, standards-driven, and flexible transmission of message calls between a client and a server. XML web services use SOAP as the protocol for network messages. These messages can pass data and use complex data, such as objects and structures.

XML Web Services

XML Web Services is Microsoft's latest entry into the remote execution of application code in a *multi-tiered application*. In a multi-tiered application, the client request is generated by one application and sent to a server for processing through a transmission protocol. There can be many different machines involved in the process or, in the simplest sense of the term, everything could happen on a single machine. Figure 25-4 illustrates the relationship between the different pieces of the multi-tier puzzle.

The web service architecture begins with the XML web service consumer, as shown in Figure 25-4. The client can be a browser program (such as Internet Explorer), a Windows application, or a console application. The client makes a request of a web service broker, which acts like a directory service and looks up the location of the web service. (This step can be avoided if the location is hard-coded for the client.) The location is the URL address

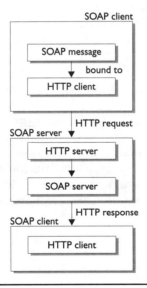

Figure 25-3   The steps in the SOAP message process

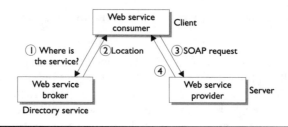

Figure 25-4   Web services at work

of the web service provider. The location is returned to the consumer, who then makes the remote call to the web service provider. The provider services the request and returns the response to the consumer.

XML web services use HTTP, XML, and SOAP. Since the protocols are easily transferred throughout the World Wide Web, XML web services are gaining in popularity and will ultimately replace many of the older standards, such as DCOM, CORBA, and so forth. XML web services can be used by virtually any application, since the technologies are platform independent.

It is not always necessary to use XML web services—XML web services operate at a higher level of networking, which requires extra overhead. However, if you have little or no control over the location of the client or the server, you will find that the answer to platform limitations is to use XML web services.

The web service consumer must be able to create the messages that are destined for the web service and understand the messages that are returned from the web service. Although it is possible to do the coding yourself, it is much easier to allow the .NET Framework to build the *proxy* class that will encapsulate the message-parsing and creation code. The idea behind a proxy is that it works on behalf of the application and acts as a go-between between the technology and the application.

WSDL (Web Services Description Language)

The Web Services Description Language is used to describe a web service in terms of the messages that it creates and accepts. The WSDL document is an XML file that contains the interface schema for the web service; it identifies the methods that are used in the exchange between a web service consumer and a web service provider. Essentially, it is a file that contains a whole lot of definitions. These are the elements in the WSDL document:

- **Types** These XML elements describe the various data types that are used to exchange messages between the consumer and the provider.

- **Message** This XML element describes the actual message or method call.

- **portType** This element describes the set of operations and each related message.

- **binding** The binding elements describe the protocol details.

- **service** This element groups a set of related ports together.

Unless you like to type, you can get the .NET Framework to generate this file for you. Let's look at creating a simple web service.

Creating a Web Service

We will use Visual Studio .NET to create an XML web service, since it contains all of the tools to generate the surrounding documents. For the full details on creating and consuming XML web services, refer to Chapter 28. We will use the web service that is created in that chapter for our example.

Follow these steps to create a simple web service provider:

1. Open a new ASP.NET Web Service project in Visual Studio .NET, and name it `CImperial`. Be sure to locate the project on the `localhost` server (or your web server of choice).

2. Rename the file to `Imperial.asmx` in the Solution Explorer.

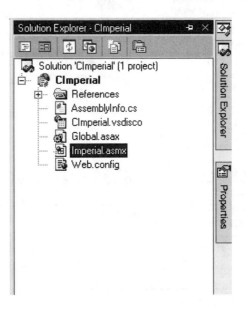

3. Remove the comments from the `HelloWorld()` method.

4. Test the web service (press F5). You will see the information page displayed in Internet Explorer, as shown in Figure 25-5. Notice the SOAP request and response code.

5. Click the Invoke button, and you will see the XML document that represents the return value from the HelloWorld() method (see Figure 25-6).

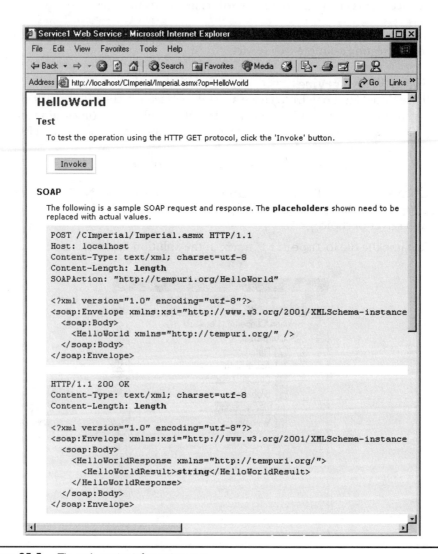

Figure 25-5 The web service information page

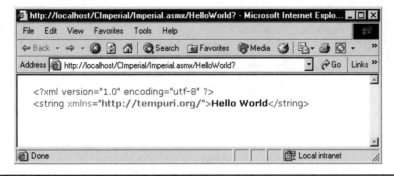

Figure 25-6   The XML document with the return value

6. Add the code to tell the service its namespace (see Figure 25-7). This step is required to locate the service correctly.

7. Build and run the solution (F5) and click on the Service Description link that appears in the web browser. You will see the WSDL file that has been created for you. You can see in Figure 25-8 that the methods have been described in this file. This document is the contract between the provider and the consumer of the web service.

```csharp
using System;
using System.Collections;
using System.ComponentModel;
using System.Data;
using System.Diagnostics;
using System.Web;
using System.Web.Services;

namespace CImperial
{
    /// <summary>
    /// Summary description for Service1.
    /// </summary>
    [WebService(Namespace="http://localhost/")]
    public class Service1 : System.Web.Services.WebService
    {
        public Service1()
        {
            //CODEGEN: This call is required by the ASP.NET Web Services Designer
            InitializeComponent();
        }
```

Figure 25-7   Adding the web service namespace

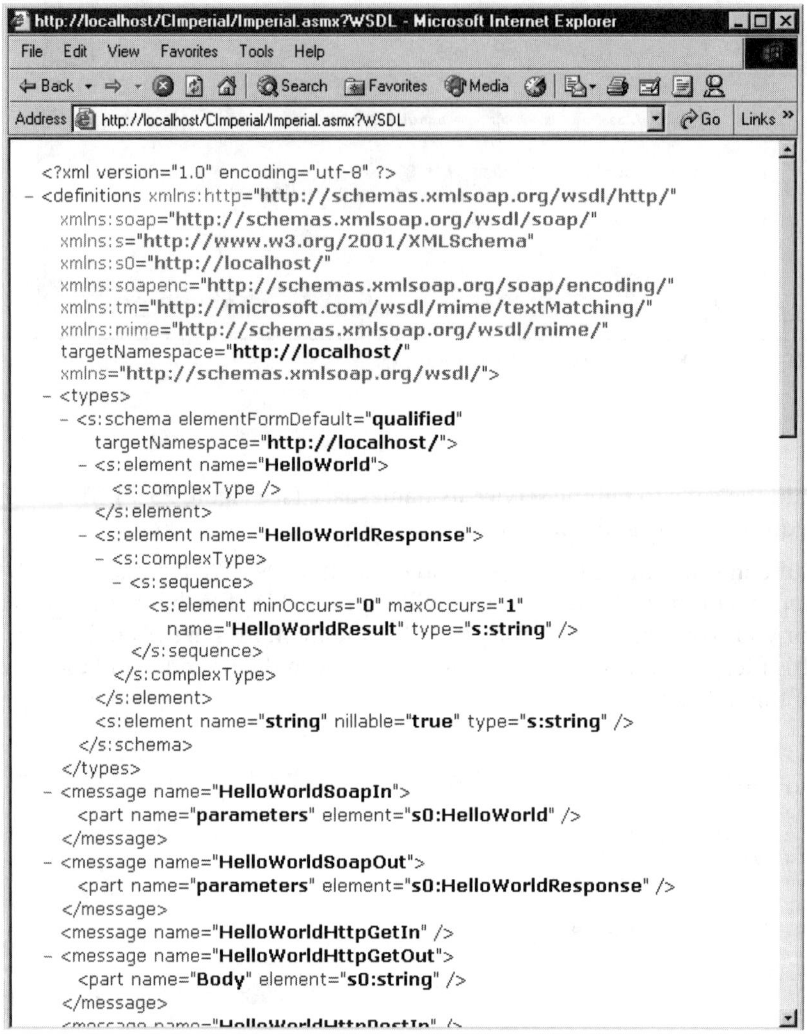
http://localhost/CImperial/Imperial.asmx?WSDL - Microsoft Internet Explorer
File Edit View Favorites Tools Help
Back Search Favorites Media
Address http://localhost/CImperial/Imperial.asmx?WSDL
Go Links
<?xml version="1.0" encoding="utf-8" ?>
- <definitions xmlns:http="http://schemas.xmlsoap.org/wsdl/http/"
xmlns:soap="http://schemas.xmlsoap.org/wsdl/soap/"
xmlns:s="http://www.w3.org/2001/XMLSchema"
xmlns:s0="http://localhost/"
xmlns:soapenc="http://schemas.xmlsoap.org/soap/encoding/"
xmlns:tm="http://microsoft.com/wsdl/mime/textMatching/"
xmlns:mime="http://schemas.xmlsoap.org/wsdl/mime/"
targetNamespace="http://localhost/"
xmlns="http://schemas.xmlsoap.org/wsdl/">
- <types>
- <s:schema elementFormDefault="qualified"
targetNamespace="http://localhost/">
- <s:element name="HelloWorld">
<s:complexType />
</s:element>
- <s:element name="HelloWorldResponse">
- <s:complexType>
- <s:sequence>
<s:element minOccurs="0" maxOccurs="1"
name="HelloWorldResult" type="s:string" />
</s:sequence>
</s:complexType>
</s:element>
<s:element name="string" nillable="true" type="s:string" />
</s:schema>
</types>
- <message name="HelloWorldSoapIn">
<part name="parameters" element="s0:HelloWorld" />
</message>
- <message name="HelloWorldSoapOut">
<part name="parameters" element="s0:HelloWorldResponse" />
</message>
<message name="HelloWorldHttpGetIn" />
- <message name="HelloWorldHttpGetOut">
<part name="Body" element="s0:string" />
</message>

Figure 25-8 The WSDL document

Now that you have created the web service provider, you need to build the client. The following steps describe how to build the client (the web service consumer).

1. Open a new Visual Studio Windows Application project, call it `Practice`, and locate it on the `localhost`.

2. Add a new button to the form, and change its `Text` property to read **Call on a Web Service**.

3. In Solution Explorer, right-click on the project name and select Add Web Reference from the menu. The Add Web Reference dialog box will open. Type **http://localhost/CImperial/Imperial.asmx** in the Address field.

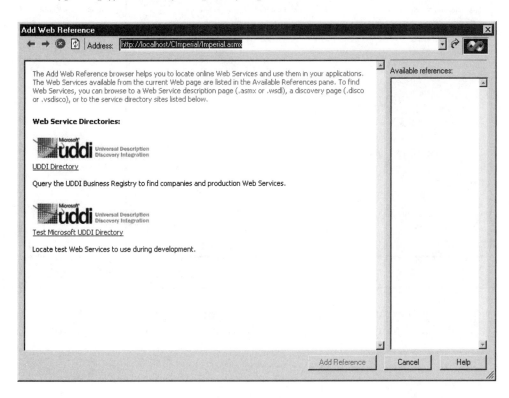

4. Press ENTER, and you will see the window shown in the following illustration. This window allows you to select from the web services found at the location in

the Address box. In this case, there is only one web service, called HelloWorld. Click the Add Reference button to add the web reference to your project.

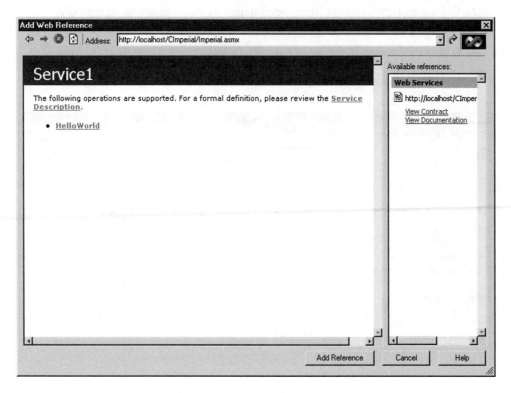

5. When you expand the Web References and localhost sections in the Solution Explorer, you will see the WSDL file that has been created for you.

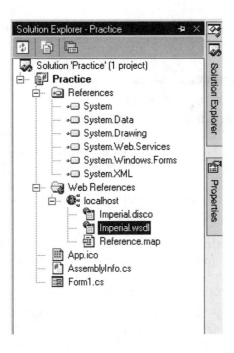

6. Add the following code to the button:

```
localhost.Service1 s = new localhost.Service1();
MessageBox.Show (s.HelloWorld());
```

7. Finally, press F5 to build and run the project. Click on the button to instantiate a new instance of the web service, and then call on its HelloWorld() method. The result is shown in the following illustration.

PART V

This section has demonstrated the simple creation and consumption of a web service. For more details and exam-specific information, read Chapter 28.

UDDI (Universal Description, Discovery, and Integration)

In our previous example of creating and consuming a web service, we kept the actual service component on the local machine (http://localhost/CImperial/Imperial.asmx). In reality, the service will likely be hosted on a remote server. The process of locating (or discovering) documents that describe XML web services using WSDL is called *web service discovery*.

Chapter 28 goes into the details of static and dynamic discovery—but for the purposes of an introduction, here is the difference:

- **Static discovery**   This means that a discovery document (with an extension of .disco) can be found and interpreted. The discovery document contains the information necessary to describe the services that are located at the server endpoint (in our example, localhost).

- **Dynamic discovery**   In this case, the consumer application does not know any location information. Instead, all that is known is the endpoint (the web service provider). Dynamic discovery is not enabled by default and must be turned on within the configuration files (either in machine.config or web.config). Refer to Chapter 28 for more information.

 EXAM TIP   A static discovery document can usually be identified by its .disco extension. A dynamic discovery document usually has an extension of .vsdisco.

Consider the World Wide Web and all of the services located there. How is an application developer to find out about the web services that are available? In order to help in the search for XML web services, XML web service directories are used. Web services are published to the directories, and the information is then available to any queries.

The UDDI (Universal Description, Discovery, and Integration) specifications define the standards for publishing and discovering information about XML web services. These standards have been built in cooperation with companies such as Microsoft, Ariba, Novell, and IBM (to name but a few). For more information on the UDDI specifications, visit http://uddi.org/.

Two services are provided by UDDI:

- XML Schema for business descriptions including information about the service publisher (contact name, address, and so on) and specifications on the web service
- Web Registry of Web Services including business, service, and binding information for the web service

Think of UDDI as a yellow-pages service. Businesses register their web services with UDDI, which, in turn, publishes them for use by consumer applications. The consumer applications can then search for the available web services and receive information about them.

Let's look at the process of discovering information about web services. The following steps describe what happens when a consumer application searches for and finds a web service directory:

1. The web service consumer application searches for a service by sending a request to a UDDI to locate the service. (UDDI is actually a web service that allows a request to drill down into the directory.)

2. UDDI returns a link to the service description.

3. The consumer then connects to the returned link and requests the service description.

4. The web service returns the WSDL file, which is a contract between the consumer and the provider and contains the description of the actual web service (as explained earlier in the chapter).

5. The consumer then requests that a method be executed by sending a SOAP message that encompasses the SOAP request for the method.

6. The provider then returns a SOAP response with the results of the method invocation.

In the HelloWorld consumer example created in the "Creating a Web Service" section earlier in the chapter, you right-clicked on the project and selected Add Web Reference from the menu, and you saw the screen shown in the following illustration. Notice that there are currently two UDDI directories listed there—the UDDI Business Registry and the Microsoft development directory. When you select the UDDI Business Registry, you will

PART V

be redirected to http://uddi.microsoft.com/visualstudio/, and from there you can type in the business name and press ENTER.

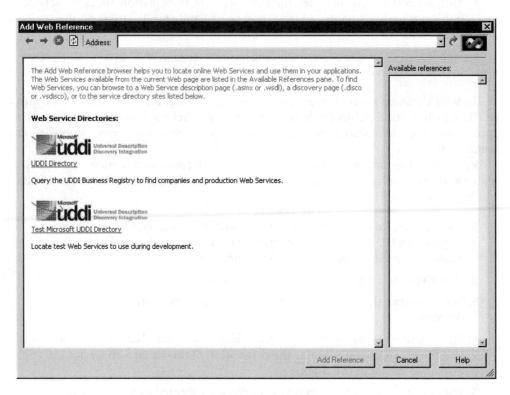

In the following illustration, we typed in **Microsoft** as the business name and then expanded the root UDDI Web Services to receive the namespaces you see in the list.

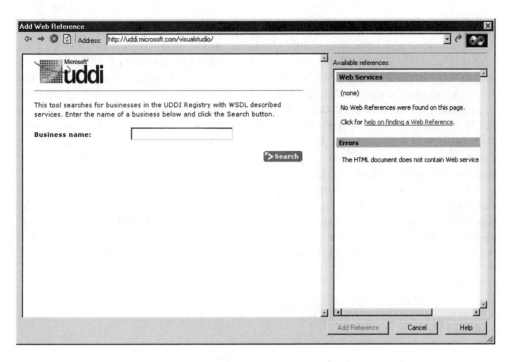

This is simply an example of how the process works when you statically select a UDDI directory. Remember that dynamic discovery will return information about web services that might not be statically known.

 EXAM TIP To add discovery capabilities to your .NET application, add the `System.Web.Services.Discovery` namespace to the application.

XSD, XSLT, and XPath

In this section, we will quickly introduce the renaming acronyms that may be subject to testing on the Microsoft exam. Remember that you will not be tested directly on these technologies. Rather, you can expect to see the acronym in a question, and you must understand the context under which it is used.

PART V

XSD (XML Schema Definition Language)

The World Wide Web consortium published a recommended standard in 2001 for XML Schema Definition (XSD). (Refer to Chapter 8 for more information on XSD.) This standard should bring a level of consistency to software development, and Microsoft has chosen to accept the standard in its XML parser, which supports XSD. An XML parser is an application that can read XML and render it to the reader. For example, a parser would be needed to display the XML data in a web browser—remember that, by default, the browser will only show the XML code because XML by itself does not display data, it simply describes data. An XML parser can be used to display the data, and until now, those parsers have understood DTDs (Document Type Definitions).

XSD schemas will eventually replace DTDs and XDRs (Microsoft XML-Data Reduced schemas). You may find that you will still have to support both of these methods of defining the XML grammar; however, the push is to move toward XSD. The .NET Framework provides a great deal of support for XSD.

Let's return to the simple XML file we looked at earlier in the chapter:

```
<recipe>
   <name>Chicken Soup
      <ingredient>Chicken</ingredient>
      <ingredient>Soup</ingredient>
   </name>
</recipe>
```

We can take this file and add the XSD to it, as follows:

```
<?xml version="1.0"?>
<xsd:schema xmlns:xsd="http://www.w3.org/2001/XMLSchema">
   <xsd:element name="Recipe" type="RecipeType"/>
   <xsd:simpleType name="RecipeType">
      <xsd:sequence>
         <xsd:element name="RecipeName" type="xsd:string"/>
      </xsd:sequence>
   <xsd:simpleType name="Ingredient">
```

We could start to make a lot of mistakes by doing it this way. Let's look at how Visual Studio .NET assists us in the process:

1. Open a new file in Visual Studio (File | New File). This file can be added to an existing project or be created on its own. You will see the New File dialog box.

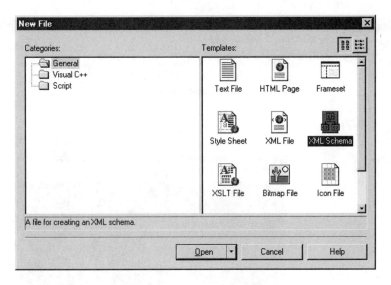

2. Select XML Schema from the list of templates and click Open.

3. The new file is shown in Figure 25-9. Notice that the Toolbox has a new tab—XML Schema. From the Toolbox, you can select and drag any of the following XML Schema descriptors to the Design window: `element`, `attribute`, `attributeGroup`, `complexType`, and so forth.

4. Experiment by adding a `complexType` called `Recipes`, and insert the element's name and ingredient. When you switch over to the code window, you will see the code shown in Figure 25-10.

In order to link your XML file to the XSD file, add the following to the `recipe.xml` file:

```
<?xml version="1.0"?>
<RecipeSummary RecipeSummary="MyRecipes"
        xmlns:xsi="http://www.w3.org/2001/XMLSchema-instance"
        xsi:noNamespaceSchemaLocation="file://MyFirstXSD.xsd">
   <recipe>
     <name>Chicken Soup
        <ingredient>Chicken</ingredient>
        <ingredient>Soup</ingredient>
     </name>
   </recipe>
 </RecipeSummary>
```

PART V

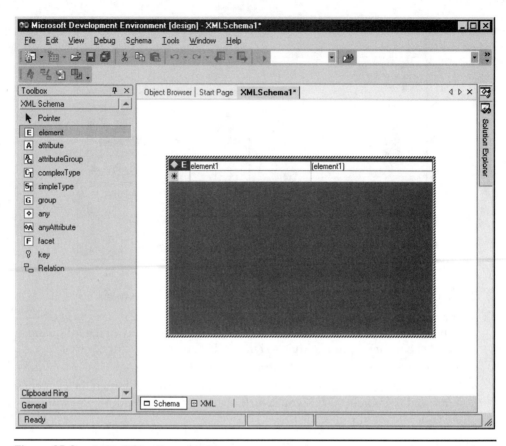

Figure 25-9 Adding XML schema descriptors

Notice that in this example, we have no namespace for the XML. We are simply pointing to the local filesystem for the .xsd file. Properly formed XML and XSD would include namespaces to identify locations.

XSLT (Extensible Stylesheet Language Transformations)

Simply put, XSLT is a technology that transforms the content in one XML document into a new XML document. By using XSLT, you can parse an XML document and create a new document that uses the data differently. For example, the new document may contain values calculated from the old XML document. XSLT can also be used to create HTML, which can then render the XML source document in a web browser.

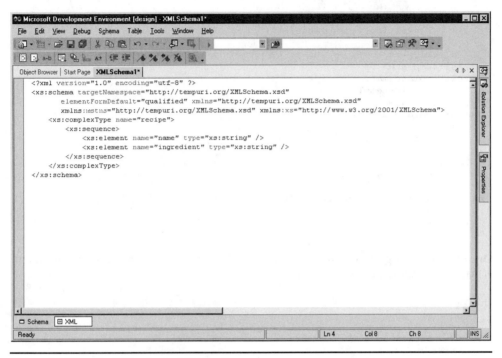

Figure 25-10   The XML schema definition file

XSLT documents are stored in style sheets that are used to transform the XML data. Let's look at our recipe XML file and combine it with an XSL style sheet.

```
<?xml version="1.0"?>
<?xml-stylesheet type="text/xsl" href="Recipe.xsl"?>
 <recipe>
     <name>Chicken Soup
         <ingredient>Chicken</ingredient>
         <ingredient>Soup</ingredient>
     </name>
   </recipe>
 </RecipeSummary>
```

The next step is to build the simple XSLT style sheet:

```
<?xml version="1.0"?>
<xsl:stylesheet xmlns:xsl="http://www.w3.org/1999/XSL/Transform">
   <xsl:template match="/">
       <html>
```

```
            <body>
                <xsl:apply-templates/>
            </body>
        </html>
    </xsl:template>
    <xsl:template match="recipe">
        <xsl:apply-templates/>
    </xsl:template>
    <xsl:template match="name">
        <H1>
            <xsl:value-of select="."/>
        </H1>
    </xsl:template>
    <xsl:template match="ingredient">
        <li>
            <xsl:value-of select="."/>
        </li>
    </xsl:template>
</xsl:stylesheet>
```

Once a parser program (such as MSXML) works through the XML file, it outputs an HTML file, as shown here:

```
<html>
    <body>
        <H1>
            Chicken Soup
        </H1>
        <li>Chicken</li>
        <li>Soup</li>
    </body>
</html>
```

The style sheet contains the templates that tell the parser how to process the XML. These templates could tell the parser to work with the data or, as in our example, create the HTML to display the data.

XPath (XML Path Language)

XML Path Language (XPath) allows you to create expressions that can address sections of an XML document. Using XPath, you can manipulate strings, numbers, and so forth. XPath is used by XSL Transformations (XSLT), covered in the preceding section.

When XSLT is working through parts of an XML document, it uses XPath to select a portion of the XML document by using expressions to query for particular elements in the document. For example, in our demonstration in the previous section, `<xsl:template match="/">` is an XPath expression that says "find the beginning of the XML document" (or the first line following the XML declarations).

System.XML Namespace

In order to use these technologies programmatically, you need to know the classes that represent them. The `System.XML.XSL` namespace is where you will find the classes that are used to perform XSLT transformations. These include

- `XslTransform`   Used to perform transformations.
- `XsltArgumentList`   Used to pass arguments to the transformation.

The `System.Xml.XPath` namespace contains the classes that allow XPath expression parsing and evaluating. Look for

- `XPathDocument`   Used to perform XSLT transformations
- `XPathExpression`   Used to represent XPath expressions
- `XPathNavigator`   Used to access XML documents with XPath expressions

This whole section has been a quick introduction to the technologies that you will use with XML. Keep the various acronyms in mind as you go through the rest of the chapters in this part of the book. You will be able to see where they are used and how they are used as we cover the requirements for exam 70-320.

Logging Test Results and Debugging

We have included a section in this chapter on testing and debugging, since the Microsoft exam requires that you understand how to test your services. This can include testing of web services, Windows services, .NET remoting objecting, and so forth. Each will be covered in their respective chapter and, of course, Chapter 9 introduces the concepts of testing and debugging. However, in this chapter, we will deal with XML Web Services and configuring debugging and testing for your web services.

We will look at logging test results, since that is the focus of the Microsoft 70-320 exam. However, remember that you should become comfortable with debugging the services that you create, and you will find that information in the chapters that focus on each service. The next chapter, for instance, is on Windows Services, and you will find a section on testing in that chapter.

Control Debugging in web.config

In order to test your web service within Visual Studio .NET, you need to make sure that the `web.config` file is set up properly. The `web.config` file is a configuration file that contains XML code specific to the settings of your application. In the Solution Explorer, double-click the `web.config` file to look at the configuration file (see Figure 25-11).

Make sure that the `debug` attribute of the `compilation` element is set to True, as follows:

```
<compilation
   defaultLanguage="c#"
   debug="true"
/>
```

EXAM TIP   By setting the debug attribute to True, the debug information will be compiled into your solution. Be sure to change this attribute before you deploy your application.

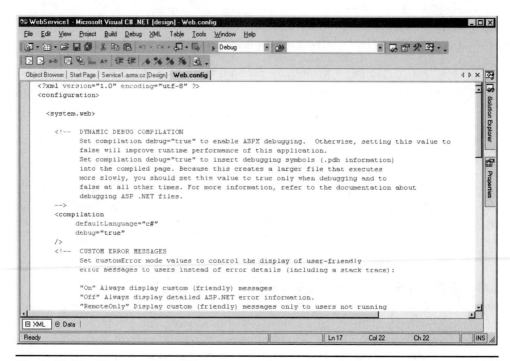

Figure 25-11   The web.config file

You should also ensure that the project configuration shows ASP.NET Debugging as enabled. Right-click on the project in Solution Explorer and select Properties from the menu. You will see the Property Pages dialog box shown in the following illustration. Select the Configuration Properties on the left side, and set the Enable ASP.NET Debugging option to True.

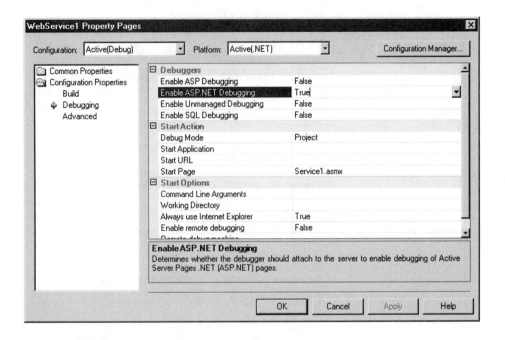

Logging Test Results in an XML Web Service

Log entries can be written into the Application Log (viewed by using the Event Viewer—see Figure 25-12). A network administrator can then track the errors that might need to be resolved by looking at the Application Log. As the developer, you must write pertinent information to the log file without recording too many events that would cause the file to explode.

In order to write to the Application Log, add the following namespace declaration:

```
using System.Diagnostics
```

PART V

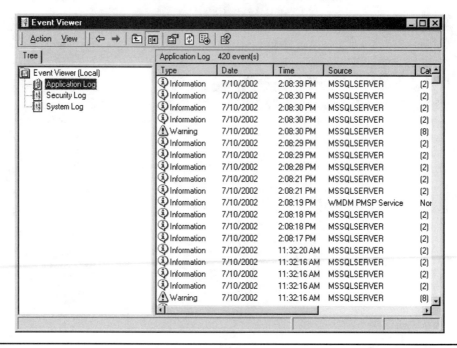

Figure 25-12   Viewing the Application Log in the Event Viewer

The `System.Diagnostics` namespace contains classes that allow you to write to the Application Log. In the code section of your web service, locate the method that contains the error (or write an error-handling routine) and add the following:

```
// Create a string that contains the error message and code
string strMessage = "Error message from my web service";
string strLogName = "Application";
// test if the event log exists
// if it doesn't exist, create it
if (!EventLog.SourceExists (strLogName))
{
    EventLog.CreateEventSource (strLogName, strLogName);
}
// Instantiate an EventLog object and insert the message
EventLog l = new EventLog();
l.Source = strLogName;
l.WriteEntry (strMessage, EventLogEntryType.Error);
```

This method will now write a message out to the Application Log after checking that the log file actually exists first. If the log file does not exist, this method will create it with this line:

```
EventLog.CreateEventSource (strLogName, strLogName);
```

The `EventLog` class also contains a method that will write the message out to the Application Log file:

```
l.WriteEntry (strMessage, EventLogEntryType.Error);
```

Implementing Tracing in an XML Web Service

While implementing debugging during production is an excellent way of proving the validity of your application, it is a terrible way to ensure application success during production. During production, your application must stay up and running. However, in order to provide more information than what is written out to the application log, you can implement tracing. Tracing allows a production environment to benefit from reporting on errors and exceptions while not compromising the success of the application. Refer to Chapter 9 for a full description of implementing tracing within Microsoft .NET applications.

To implement tracing within your XML web service, you need to write the tracing code within the application and then set the production environment to either implement it or not. That way, the code stays with the application, but it will not execute unless the environment tells it to. For example, you can code the following anywhere within your XML web service:

```
if (HttpContext.Current.Trace.IsEnabled == True)
{
    HttpContext.Current.Trace.Write ("MyWebService", "We are here!");
}
```

This code will check the context under which the service is running (the configuration file sets the context) and determine whether it should write the tracing information out or not.

To set the runtime environment, code the following in the `web.config` file:

```
<trace enabled="true" requestLimit="10" pageOutput="false"
    traceMode="SortByTime" localOnly="true" >
```

Turn off the `pageOutput` property, since normally this tracing is found at the bottom of an HTML page. An XML web service is not typically outputting any HTML, so the information will not be seen.

Summary

In this chapter, we have provided you with an introduction to the technologies that will be explored throughout this part of the book. We have looked at XML again and reviewed the technologies associated with it. We have also explored the concepts and implementation of Simple Object Access Protocol (SOAP).

 EXAM TIP Remember that these technologies, SOAP, HTTP, and XML, work together to provide XML web services.

In Chapter 28, you will look in depth at XML Web Services, which is a large focus of the 70-320 exam. In this chapter, we explored the overall process and talked about the three components—web service provider, web service consumer, and web service broker. Be very sure that you are comfortable with all of these technologies before moving on in this part of the book.

In the next chapter, we will introduce Windows Services, the first service in three services covered by the 70-320 exam—Windows Services, .NET Remoting Services, and XML Web Services. Later in this part of the book, we will revisit data access as it applies to server components. Finally, we will end Part V with security and deployment.

Test Questions

1. What is the result of opening the following XML file in Internet Explorer?

```
<Books>
    <Book>
        <Title>
            All-in-One Certification Guide
        </Title>
    </Book>
</Books>
```

A. The file will not open because it is not well-formed XML.

B. Figure 25-13.

C. Figure 25-14.

D. An XML file cannot be opened by Internet Explorer.

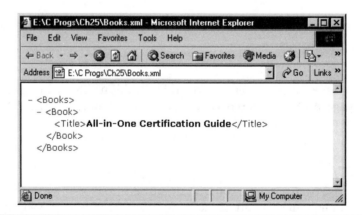

Figure 25-13   Answer B

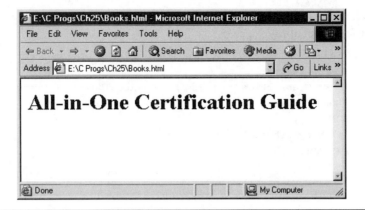

Figure 25-14 Answer C

2. Which line of code will write an event out to an Event Log file?

   A. `EventLog.CreateEventSource (strLogName, strMessage);`

   B. `EventLog.WriteEntry (strMessage,`
      `EventLogEntryType.Error);`

   C. `eventLogInstance.WriteEntry (strMessage,`
      `EventLogEntryType.Error);`

   D. `EventLog.Source = eventLogInstance.WriteEntry`
      `(strMessage, EventLogEntryType.Error);`

3. Which namespace must be added to the XML web service in order to write to an event log?

   A. `System.EventLog`

   B. `System.Events`

   C. `System.Diagnostics`

   D. `System.Diagnostics.Event`

4. Which technology allows you to publish XML web services?

   A. XMLPub

   B. XSLT

   C. XPath

   D. UDDI

PART V

5. Which of the following SOAP messages will result in a valid message transfer? Choose all that apply.

A.
```
<SOAP:Envelope xmlns="http://schemas.xmlsoap.org/soap/envelope/">
    <SOAP:Header>
        <t:Transaction xmlsn:t="http://localhost" /t:Transaction>
    </SOAP:Header>
    <SOAP:Body>
        <m:MyMethodCall xmlns:m="http://localhost" />
    </SOAP:Body>
    <SOAP:Body>
        <m:MyMethodCall2 xmlns:m="http://localhost" />
    </SOAP:Body>
</SOAP:Envelope>
```

B.
```
<SOAP:Envelope xmlns="http://schemas.xmlsoap.org/soap/envelope/">
    <SOAP:Header>
        <t:Transaction xmlsn:t="http://localhost" /t:Transaction>
    </SOAP:Header>
    <SOAP:Body>
        <m:MyMethodCall xmlns:m="http://localhost" />
    </SOAP:Body>
</SOAP:Envelope>
```

C.
```
<SOAP:Envelope xmlns="http://schemas.xmlsoap.org/soap/envelope/">
    <SOAP:Header>
        <t:Transaction xmlsn:t="http://localhost" /t:Transaction>
    </SOAP:Header>
</SOAP:Envelope>
```

D.
```
<SOAP:Envelope xmlns="http://schemas.xmlsoap.org/soap/envelope/">
    <SOAP:Body>
        <m:MyMethodCall xmlns:m="http://localhost" />
    </SOAP:Body>
    <SOAP:Body>
        <m:MyMethodCall2 xmlns:m="http://localhost" />
    </SOAP:Body>
</SOAP:Envelope>
```

E. A and C.

F. A and D.

G. A, B, and D.

6. Which of the following describes the elements that make up a SOAP message?

A. Envelope, Header, Body, Fault.

B. Envelope, Header, Body, Error.

    C. Envelope, Body, Fault.

    D. Envelope, Header, Fault.

7. Which of the following technologies are used to describe a web service in terms of the messages that it creates and the messages that it accepts?

    A. XMLS

    B. XSLT

    C. CORBA

    D. WSDL

8. What is the default namespace for a new web service?

    A. http://localhost

    B. http://www.w3.org

    C. http://tempuri.org/

    D. http://www.microsoft.com

9. Which segment of code will cause the web service method to be invoked?

    A. `localhost.Service1 MyWebService = new localhost.Service1();`
       `MyWebService.Method();`

    B. `proxy.Service1 MyWebService = new proxy.Service1();`
       `MyWebService.Method();`

    C. `Service1 MyWebService = new Service1();`
       `MyWebService.Method();`

    D. `WebService MyWebService = new WebService();`
       `MyWebService.Method();`

10. How would you add a web service component to your Visual Studio .NET application?

    A. Project | Add Web Component

    B. Project | Add Component

    C. Project | Add Web Service

    D. Project | Add Service

11. A static discovery file will usually have a file extension of which of the following?

    A. `.vsdisco`

    B. `.vdisco`

    C. `.sdisco`

    D. `.disco`

PART V

12. Which of the following technologies is a lightweight protocol for exchange of information in a decentralized, distributed environment?

    A. XML

    B. WSDL

    C. XSD

    D. SOAP

13. Which of the following technologies is a file that defines the structure and data types for XML documents?

    A. XSD

    B. XMLD

    C. XSLT

    D. XSL

14. You are creating an application that will employ the services of an application that resides on a remote server. Which of the following protocols should be used to encode the message to the remote server?

    A. SOAP

    B. XML

    C. RPC

    D. DCOM

15. A WSDL document is a file that contains definitions for which of the following?

    A. Types, Messages, Bindings.

    B. Types, Messages, portTypes, bindings, services.

    C. Types, portTypes, bindings, services.

    D. Messages, portTypes, bindings, services.

Test Answers

1. B. Only the XML code will be displayed.

2. C. You need an instance of the class `EventLog` in order to write to the log file.

3. C.

4. D.

5. G. A SOAP message must have a `<BODY>` element and may have a `<HEADER>` element.

6. A.

7. D.

8. C.

9. A.

10. C.

11. D.

12. D.

13. D.

14. A.

15. B.

Windows Services

In this chapter, you will

- Learn how to create a Windows service
- Write code that is executed when a Windows service is started and stopped
- Implement a serviced component
- Create interfaces that are visible to COM
- Create a strongly named assembly
- Register the component in the Global Assembly Cache
- Manage the component by using the Component Services tool

In this chapter, we will cover two of the major objectives of Exam 70-320. The first objective deals with Windows Services—we will look at how to create and manage a Windows service, which is a component that runs in the background of the Windows operating system. The second objective is to create and consume a serviced component. Towards this objective, we will investigate serviced components and create interfaces that are visible to COM and work with strongly named assemblies.

The goal of this chapter is to provide you with the framework for developing middle-tier components (serviced components) and background services. Services that you may already be familiar with include file-transfer services (like FTP Server), web server services, and so forth. You can also build your own types of services that users can access locally or over the network.

Introducing Windows Services

A Windows service is a program that loads automatically when the operating system starts up. The idea behind a Windows service is that it runs in the background without any user interaction or intervention. In order to see the services that are part of your Windows computer, you can do one of the following:

- If you are running Windows 2000 Professional, select Start | Programs | Administrative Tools | Services, and you will see a screen similar to the one displayed in Figure 26-1.

- If you are running an operating system other than Windows 2000 Professional, be aware that Windows services only run under the Windows NT kernel, meaning that Windows 95, 98, and ME do not have Windows services. However, Windows NT, Windows 2000, and Windows XP all have Windows services.

In Figure 26-1, you can see that some of the background services include Simple Mail Transport Protocol, Task Scheduler, Telephony, Telnet, Workstation, and more. Each system will display a different list of services depending on the services installed on the machine. These services can be active (providing a service) or waiting to be activated (listening for activity that requests their service). For example, SMTP is started but not active until an e-mail message needs to be moved. (The SMTP service is the service that allows e-mail to leave your computer.) The Workstation service is started and waiting for requests to be made of remote hosts.

Let's take a closer look at the SMTP service. If you were to right-click on the service name and select Properties from the submenu, you would see a Properties dialog box, as shown in Figure 26-2. Notice the different properties on the General tab:

1. The display name can be modified.

2. A description can be provided for the service.

3. You can see the actual path or file location of the executable file (E:\WINNT\System32\inetsrv\inetinfo.exe)

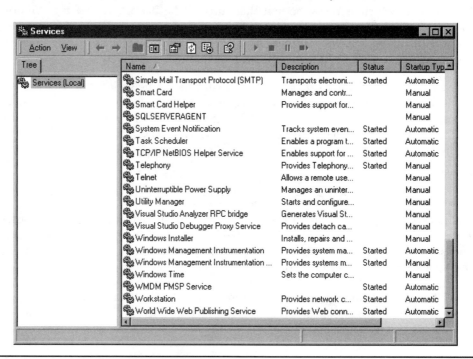

Figure 26-1   Windows 2000 services

4. A startup type can be set. If you were to click on the down arrow, you would see three different startup types—Automatic (starts when the operating system starts), Manual (starts when an administrator selects Start from the Service Status section of the dialog box), and Disabled (will only be capable of starting after an administrator changes the startup type to Enabled).

5. The Service Status section shows whether the service is started, paused, stopped, or disabled.

6. Start parameters can be added (if the service is capable of receiving start parameters).

For our purposes, we should also investigate the Log On tab of the Properties dialog box (see Figure 26-3). This is where you can set the account that is used when the service starts. Since a service really doesn't operate through user intervention or user logon, the service needs a user account under which it "logs on."

The logon account can be a local system account or a user account that has been added specifically for it (actually, it can use any account, like the Administrator account, but it is advisable for it to have its own account. That way, if an account is deleted, the service can still run under its own account). Notice in Figure 26-3 that you can also set the service to be able to interact with the desktop. You may have need of a service that provides a user interface to the logged on user account. For example, an Event Log service needs a user interface in which to display the logged entries. In this case, the Allow Service to Interact with Desktop check box should be selected.

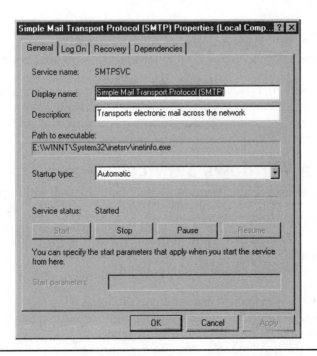

Figure 26-2   General properties of the SMTP service

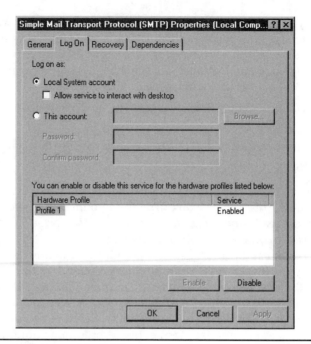

Figure 26-3   Logon properties of the SMTP service

 EXAM TIP   Make sure that you have a separate "log on" account configured for your Windows service. It is not a good idea to use a normal user account.

Using Microsoft Visual C#, we can build our own Windows services that will operate similarly. In the next section, we will look at how you can build a Windows service using Visual Studio .NET, and then we'll explore how you can use and configure the service.

Building a Windows Service

Let's start by building a simple Windows service, and then we will look into the complexities of working with the service. We will create a very simple service that can be started and stopped with the Services manager program shown in Figure 26-1. We will call our service `ClockService`, and its purpose will be to provide the time of day to a consumer of the service.

Follow these steps to build and deploy your first Windows service:

1. Start a new project from Visual Studio .NET. Select File | New | Project and select Visual C# Projects in the left pane. Select Windows Service in the Templates pane (shown here). Name the service `ClockService` and locate it in the `E:\C Progs\Ch26` folder. Click OK.

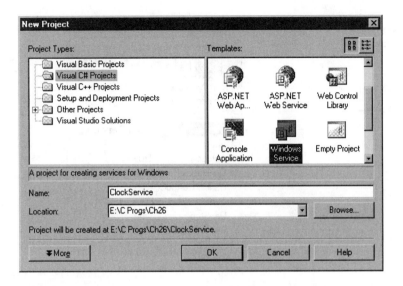

 EXAM TIP   Make sure that you select Windows Service from the template list in the New Project dialog box. You cannot choose Web Service.

2. Click on the tab for the Design view:

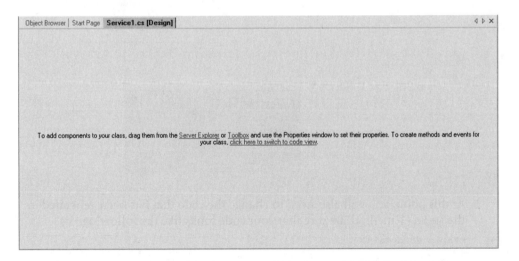

3. In the Properties Explorer, you can set the name of the service (see Figure 26-4). This should be done immediately, as the IDE calls the service `Service1`, and code will be automatically built for you using that name. You need to change that name to `ClockService`.

4. Switch to the Code Editor and change the class name to `ClockService` (don't forget to change the constructor as well).

Figure 26-4

The Properties Explorer showing the ClockService project

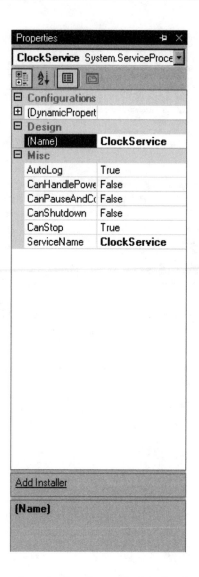

5. At this point, you will also need to change the code that has been generated in the Main() method. Be sure that your code looks like the following:

```
static void Main()
{
    System.ServiceProcess.ServiceBase[] ServicesToRun;
    ServicesToRun = new System.ServiceProcess.ServiceBase[]
                        {
                            new ClockService();
                        }
    System.ServiceProcess.ServiceBase.Run (ServicesToRun);
}
```

The preceding steps are the first in creating your new Windows service. The next thing to do is associate the new service with an Event Log. By doing this, you will be able to watch your service start up, stop, and pause in the Event Viewer—essentially, anything that you want recorded can be watched in the Event Viewer.

Let's look at the steps:

1. Add an `EventLog` component to your design. Return to the Design view and add the `EventLog` component from the Toolbox. Be sure to select the Components tab on the Toolbox:

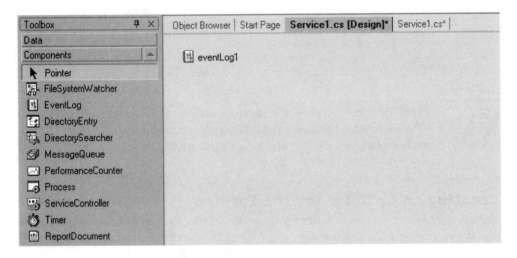

2. When you add the EventLog component to the Design view, you get a new instance of the component—eventLog1.

3. Return to the code window and add the following code to the service constructor. This code can be added anywhere—if you add it to the constructor, the event log will be ready when you need it.

```
public ClockService()
{
    //This call is required by the Windows.Forms Component Designer
    InitializeComponent();

    // Check if the event log exists—if not, create the event log
    if (!System.Diagnostics.EventLog.SourceExists ("MySource"))
    {
        System.Diagnostics.EventLog.CreateEventSource ("MySource", "MyNewLog");
    }

    // Set the Source and Log properties for the EventLog component
    eventLog1.Source = "MySource";
    eventLog1.Log = "MyNewLog";
}
```

PART V

Now that you have told the service to log to the Event Log, you need to tell the service what to do when the service is started or stopped. You can also code what will happen when the service is paused, continued, or shut down by using the OnPause(), OnContinue(), and OnShutdown() methods respectively. For the purpose of our demonstration, we will set the OnStart() and OnStop() methods:

1. In the code editor, find the OnStart() method and code the following:

```
protected override void OnStart (string[] args)
{
    eventLog1.WriteEntry ("We are in the Start method");
}
```

2. Find the OnStop() method and code the following:

```
protected override void OnStop()
{
    eventLog1.WriteEntry ("We are in the Stop method");
}
```

EXAM TIP When a service is started, the OnStart() method is called. When a service is stopped, the OnStop() method is called. Other methods include—OnPause(), OnContinue(), OnShutdown(), and OnCustomCommand().

Creating an Installer for the Service

The next step is to create an installer for the service. You can then use the installer to install the service onto the destination computer and make sure that it is recording to the Event Log properly. Follow these steps to create the installer:

1. Change back to the Design view and click on the background. Do not select anything.

2. Make sure that the Properties Explorer is displayed, and click the Add Installer link from the bottom of the Properties Explorer window. (The mouse pointer in Figure 26-5 points out the link).

EXAM TIP The Add Installer link is found in the Properties Explorer window.

3. Change to the Design view for ProjectInstaller.cs (the class that is created by adding the installer). You will notice two instances of the installer—serviceProcessInstaller1 and serviceInstaller1 (shown here).

One is the installer for your service (the latter), and the other is the installer for the service's associated process, which we will discuss in the "Windows Service Architecture" section later in this chapter.

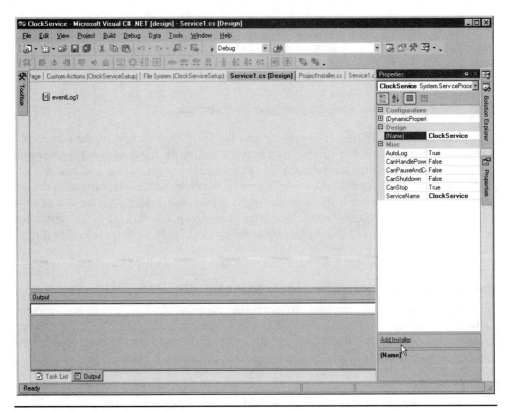

Figure 26-5   Add an installer link

4. Select `serviceInstaller1` and set the `Name` and `ServiceName` properties in the Properties Explorer:

5. Make sure that the `StartType` is set to Automatic.

You are now ready to build the project. As a final step, you should set the startup object to `ClockService`. Do this by selecting the project in the Solution Explorer and right-clicking to access the submenu. Select Properties from the menu, and you will see the Property Pages dialog box shown in Figure 26-6. Select the General option in the left pane, the Startup Object option in the right pane, and select your new service—`ClockService.ClockService` from the drop-down list. Click OK to accept the properties, and then build the project by pressing CTRL-SHIFT-B (or by selecting Build | Build from the menus).

Creating the Setup Project for the Windows Service

In order to be able to add the new service to any computer, you need to create a mechanism to deploy the service. We will create a deployment scenario by building a Setup project. The executable for our service, `ClockService.exe`, will be added to the Setup project, and then we can see what happens as the service is loaded into a computer.

Follow these steps to create the Setup project:

1. Add a Setup project to the solution. Select File | Add Project, and choose New Project. Select Setup and Deployment Projects in the left pane of the Add New Project dialog box, and select Setup Project from the list of templates.

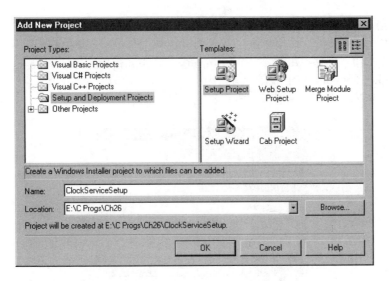

2. Name the Setup project `MyClockServiceSetup` in the Solution Explorer.

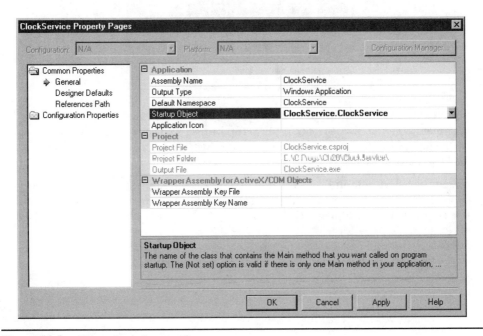

Figure 26-6   The project's Property Pages

3. Add the executable to the Setup project by right-clicking on
   `MyClockServiceSetup` and selecting Add | Project Output.

4. You will see the Add Project Output Group dialog box shown next.
   Make sure your project (`ClockService`) is in the Project field. Choose
   Primary Output and click OK to add the executable to the project.

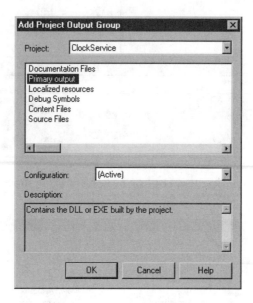

5. Now you need to add a custom action to the Setup project to install the
   executable file. Right-click on the Setup project and select View | Custom
   Actions from the menu. You will see the Customer Actions editor. Choose
   Add Custom Action.

6. In the Select Item in Project dialog box, select the Application Folder from
   the Look In drop-down box. Then select Primary Output from ClockService
   (Active), as shown next.

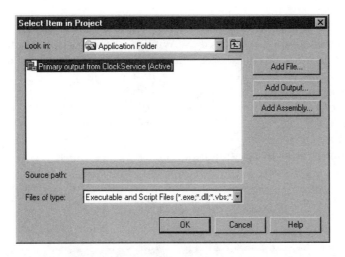

7. You will notice that the primary output has been added to all four nodes—
Install, Commit, Rollback, and Uninstall:

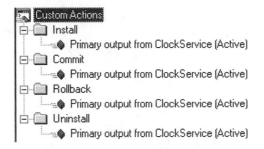

8. Build the Setup project and exit Visual Studio .NET.

You have now successfully created a Setup project for your Windows service. If you
are unsure of the purpose of any of the preceding steps, be sure to spend some time in
Chapter 30. The setup and deployment of Windows services, .NET Remoting, and XML
Web Services will be covered in that chapter.

PART V

Installing the Windows Service

You're almost there! You have created the Windows service, attached an installer, and created the Setup project for the service. The last phase of this process involves installing the service on any machine and watching it run.

If you had set the configuration properties of the ClockService to Release mode (see Figure 26-7), you could now navigate to the folder containing the service, find the Release folder, and select the ClockServiceSetup.msi file, which would run the installer program for your service.

Let's step through the installation process:

1. Double-click the ClockServiceSetup.msi file, and you will see the Welcome screen of the ClockServiceSetup Setup Wizard. There is nothing to do here except click Next.

2. You will be requested enter the username and password that will be used to log into the service in the Set Service Login dialog box (shown next). As we mentioned previously, you should have an account prepared for the service. We have created an account called ClockServiceUser. If you know how to

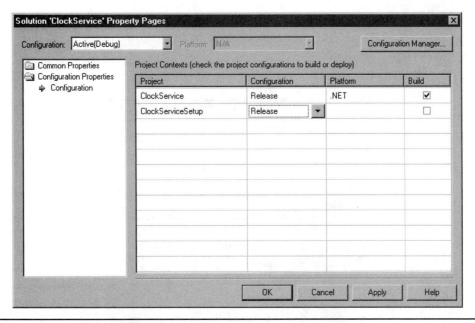

Figure 26-7 Setting configuration properties in the Property Pages dialog box

set up a user in Windows 2000 (our platform for development) and have already done so, skip to step 7.

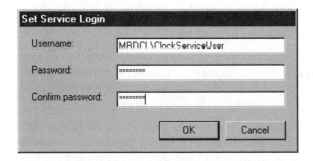

3. In order to set up a new user in Windows 2000 that can be used for the service, select Start | Settings | Control Panel | Administrative Tools | Computer Management. This will open the Computer Management console. Locate

the Users folder under Local Users and Groups, and right-click on Users. Select New User to open the New User dialog box (shown next). Fill in the username (**ClockServiceUser**—remember this is not a person, just an account for the service).

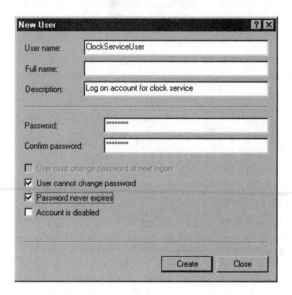

4. Check the User Cannot Change Password check box and the Password Never Expires check box, which do exactly what they say. This is important, since you don't want a service's password to expire—the next time the service was started, it would not be able to start under the old password. Click Create to add the new user to the accounts database.

5. Select the account from the right pane of the Computer Management console and right-click on it to access the account properties. You will see a window similar to that displayed in Figure 26-20.

6. Make sure that the account belongs to the Administrators local group. You may want to read Chapter 30 and look at security issues here, but in order to have the service start up while the operating system starts, you will need an account with more power than just a local user. Click on the Member Of tab, select the Administrators group, and click the Add button. Click Close to exit the properties of the new user.

7. You have now added the new user and set the group membership. Specify the user account for service log in, and the installation process continues to completion.

8. To test the newly installed service, open the Computer Management console and look at the services (in Windows 2000, select Start | Settings | Control Panel | Administrative Tools | Computer Management). You should see your new service listed in the group of services:

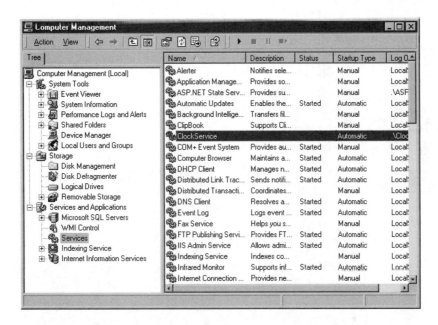

PART V

9. Start the service—right-click on ClockService and choose Start from the menu. Windows will attempt to start the service (as shown here), and if successful will show the status of the new service as started.

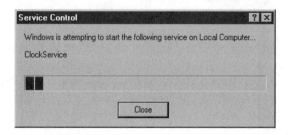

Verifying the Service Logging

You need to make sure that your new service is logging to the Event Log as you programmed it to do.

1. In the Computer Management console, expand System Tools and the Event Viewer in the left panel (as shown next).

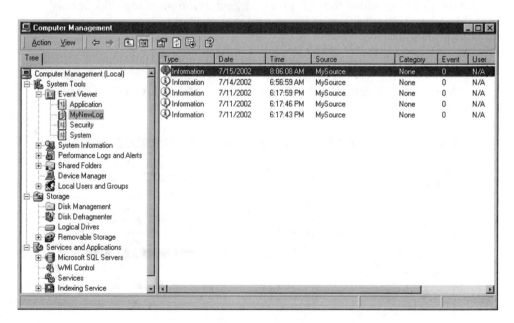

2. You will notice that there is a new log file in this list. Typically, Windows 2000 will display three different logs—Application, Security, and System logs. The Application log is typically the log file to which application messages are sent. The Security log tracks event messages regarding file access, logon attempts, and so forth. The System log maintains event messages regarding system activities, such as starting services and the like. However, you have added a new log in our service program—MyNewLog. Select this log, as shown in Figure 26-24, and you will see the log entries on the right side of the console.

3. Select one of the log entries and double-click on it. This will open the entry and allow you to see the details (shown next). In our example, we are looking at the log entry that was written to MyNewLog when ClockService was started.

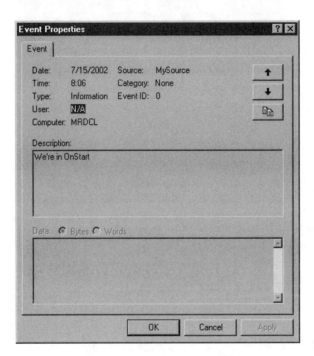

4. To test whether you are getting a log entry when the service is stopped, return to the Services node on the left side of the console. Right-click on ClockService and select Stop from the menu. The service will then be stopped.

5. Click on the Event Viewer and then on MyNewLog. You should see a new log entry. Double-click the new entry, and you should see the log entry for stopping the service:

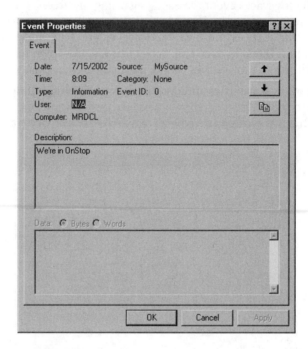

You have now verified that your Windows service is running and is responding to the start and stop commands.

Windows Service Architecture

In order to be sure that you are properly prepared for the 70-320 exam, let's take a few moments to cover the architecture of Windows Services. There are three components (or programs) that are necessary to make sure that a Windows service operates successfully:

- **Service program** This is the actual program code that you created at the beginning of the chapter. This program tells the service what to do if stopped, started, or sent any other type of command.

- **Service control program** In our example, the service control program was found in the Computer Management console under Services. Through this program, you are able to send the service commands, such as Start, Stop, and so on.

- **Service configuration program** Services must be registered in the Windows Registry, meaning that you must deploy a service as you did the one demonstrated in the last section. A simple xcopy will not work. Using the installation program, you can set configuration parameters and properties. For example, you can set the startup mode—started, stopped, or disabled.

EXAM TIP Don't forget that a Windows service cannot be installed by using xcopy. The xcopy utility does not affect the Windows Registry, and a Windows service must access the Windows Registry in order to set the configuration properties.

All Windows services inherit from System.ServiceProcess.ServiceBase. You will see this if you look at the code designer for your ClockService. The class definition looks like this:

```
public class ClockService: System.ServiceProcess.ServiceBase
```

This base class is necessary in order to communicate with the service control program, which makes the necessary calls to the service's Main() method, and through the ServiceBase class calls the native methods that will ensure the successful start of the service.

EXAM TIP Although this is a simplistic explanation of the process, it is not necessary for you to know the details for the exam. You just need to know that your service program must inherit from the base class, ServiceBase.

Quick Facts on Windows Services

In this section, we will briefly highlight some of the "quick facts" about Windows Services that you should be aware of in order to write the 70-320 exam. If Windows Services is a topic of interest to you, spend some time working through the examples in MSDN and experiment creating services of your own. For the exam, you'll need to know the following.

The System.ServiceProcess namespace includes the following classes that are required for a Windows service to operate:

- **ServiceBase** This is the parent class of your Windows service. This is the class that handles the start and stop requests.

- **ServiceProcessInstaller** Along with ServiceInstaller, this class is used to install and configure the service programs.

- **ServiceController** This class implements the service control program and is used to send requests to services. See the next section for more information on the ServiceController class. The configuration of your Windows service can be done in the local Registry. Access the Registry by typing **regedt32.exe** at the Run prompt (select Start | Run). This will open the Windows Registry (we are using Windows 2000 Professional—check the operating system documentation for other versions of the Windows NT kernel). Locate the service in HKEY_LOCAL_MACHINE\System\CurrentControlSet\ Services, and make any necessary changes (see the following illustration). You can modify such properties as the type of service, the display name, startup configuration (Automatic, Disabled, or Manual), the path to the .exe file, and so forth.

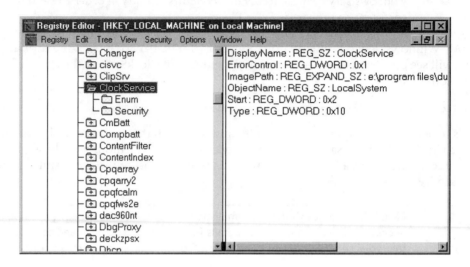

EXAM TIP A service must be configured in the Registry. All services can be found in `HKEY_LOCAL_MACHINE\System\CurrentControlSet\Services`. Using the `regedt32` program, you can make modifications to the service configuration.

Monitoring the Windows Service

As you have seen, we can monitor the service in the Computer Management console or through the Event Viewer. You can also work with the service through a command prompt by using the `net.exe` commands. The following illustration shows starting and stopping the service by using the command prompt in Windows 2000 Professional.

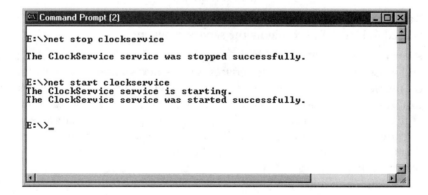

You can also work with Windows services by using a command-line tool called `sc.exe`. This tool can be found in the `\Microsoft Platform SDK\Bin\WinNT` folder (if installed) for Windows NT or 2000 or in the `Windows\system32` folder on Windows XP. The `sc.exe` command is installed automatically for Windows XP, but it must be installed manually for earlier versions. Using this command, you can check the status of a service, work with the configuration, or install or remove the service. Figure 26-8 shows the syntax of the command.

Finally, an instance of the `ServiceController` class can be added to your service project in Visual Studio .NET, and it can be used to control the service. Figure 26-9 shows the class added to the project.

```
Command Prompt (2) - sc                                        _ □ X

F:\WINDOWS\system32>sc
DESCRIPTION:
        SC is a command line program used for communicating with the
        NT Service Controller and services.
USAGE:
        sc <server> [command] [service name] <option1> <option2>...

        The option <server> has the form "\\ServerName"
        Further help on commands can be obtained by typing: "sc [command]"
        Commands:
          query-----------Queries the status for a service, or
                          enumerates the status for types of services.
          queryex---------Queries the extended status for a service, or
                          enumerates the status for types of services.
          start-----------Starts a service.
          pause-----------Sends a PAUSE control request to a service.
          interrogate-----Sends an INTERROGATE control request to a service.
          continue--------Sends a CONTINUE control request to a service.
          stop------------Sends a STOP request to a service.
          config----------Changes the configuration of a service (persistant).
          description-----Changes the description of a service.
          failure---------Changes the actions taken by a service upon failure.
          qc--------------Queries the configuration information for a service.
          qdescription----Queries the description for a service.
          qfailure--------Queries the actions taken by a service upon failure.
          delete----------Deletes a service (from the registry).
          create----------Creates a service. (adds it to the registry).
          control---------Sends a control to a service.
          sdshow----------Displays a service's security descriptor.
          sdset-----------Sets a service's security descriptor.
          GetDisplayName--Gets the DisplayName for a service.
          GetKeyName------Gets the ServiceKeyName for a service.
          EnumDepend------Enumerates Service Dependencies.

        The following commands don't require a service name:
        sc <server> <command> <option>
          boot------------(ok | bad) Indicates whether the last boot should
                          be saved as the last-known-good boot configuration
          Lock------------Locks the Service Database
          QueryLock-------Queries the LockStatus for the SCManager Database
EXAMPLE:
        sc start MyService

Would you like to see help for the QUERY and QUERYEX commands? [ y | n ]:
```

Figure 26-8   The `sc.exe` command

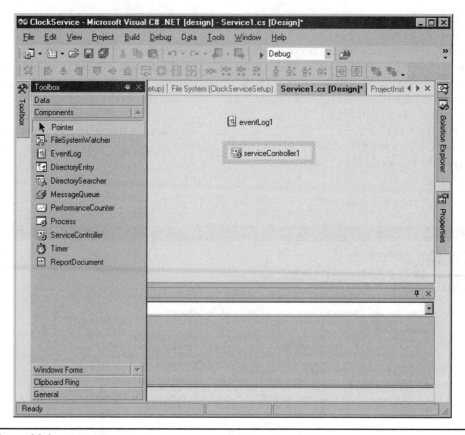

Figure 26-9   Adding the ServiceController class to the project

Some of the properties of the ServiceController class that you may find useful are listed in Table 26-1. Figure 26-10 illustrates the members of the ServiceControllerStatus enumeration, which is described in the table.

Property	Description
ServiceName	Identifies the name of the service.
MachineName	Identifies the name of the machine running the service.
DisplayName	Specifies the name that will be displayed for the service.
ServiceType	Identifies the service type. If the service interacts with the desktop, this will be InteractiveProcess. If the service runs along with other services inside a shared process, ServiceType will be Win32ShareProcess. Otherwise, a service running by itself in its own process space will have a ServiceType of Win32OwnProcess.

Table 26-1   Properties of the ServiceController Class

Property	Description
DependentServices	Sets the dependencies of your service. Some services can only run if another service or services are running. For example, the Browser service in a Windows 2000 Professional computer cannot run without the Workstation and Server services running.
Status	Indicates the status of the service—running, stopped, paused, and so on. The ServiceControllerStatus enumeration lists the different statuses.

Table 26-1   Properties of the ServiceController Class *(continued)*

 EXAM TIP   The ServiceController class allows you to set configuration information and to get information about the service programmatically.

The service can also be controlled programmatically by using the methods of the ServiceController class listed in Table 26-2.

Object Browser | **ServiceControllerStatus Enumeration** | Custom Actions (ClockServiceSetup) | File System (C ◄ ►

[✗] [✓] [▼] *.NET Framework Class Library*

ServiceControllerStatus Enumeration

Remarks

The **ServiceControllerStatus** class is used by an instance of the ServiceController class to indicate whether an existing service is running, stopped, paused, or whether a Start, Stop, Pause, or Continue command is pending.

Members

Member name	Description
ContinuePending	The service continue is pending.
Paused	The service is paused.
PausePending	The service pause is pending.
Running	The service is running.
StartPending	The service is starting.
Stopped	The service is stopping.
StopPending	The service is not running.

Requirements

Namespace: System.ServiceProcess

Platforms: Windows NT Server 4.0, Windows NT Workstation 4.0, Windows 2000, Windows XP Home Edition, Windows XP Professional, Windows .NET Server family

Assembly: System.Serviceprocess (in System.Serviceprocess.dll)

Figure 26-10   ServiceControllerStatus enumeration

Method	Description
Start()	Informs the service control program to start the service. The Start() method actually calls the OnStart() method of the service.
Stop()	Informs the service control program to stop the service—calls OnStop().
Pause(), Continue()	Informs the service control program to pause or continue the service—calls OnPause() or OnContinue(), respectively.
ExecuteCommand()	Sends a custom command to the service.

Table 26-2   Methods of the ServiceController Class

As a final note on Windows Services, let's create an application that will use our service and control the service through a service controller. Follow these steps:

1. Start a new Windows Application project.

2. Add a reference to System.ServiceProcess.dll. Right-click the project name in Solution Explorer and choose Add Reference from the menu. You will see the Add Reference dialog box shown next. Scroll through the list until you find System.ServiceProcess.dll, select it, and click Add.

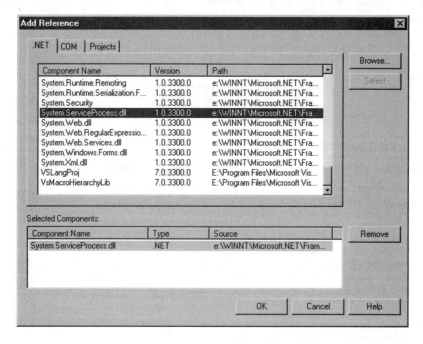

3. Add a button to your form with the text "Start Service" (see Figure 26-33). Add the following code to the Click event of the button.

```
void btnServiceStart_Click (object sender, System.EventArgs e)
{
    // instantiate a new ServiceController object connected to the ClockService
    ServiceController sc = new ServiceController("ClockService");
    // make a call to the Start() method of the service controller
    // this will call the OnStart() method of the service
    sc.Start();
    // wait for the service to start
    sc.WaitForStatus (ServiceControllerStatus.Running);
    // verify that the service is running
    ServiceControllerStatus status = sc.Status;
    if (status == ServiceControllerStatus.Running)
        MessageBox.Show("It's running!");
}
```

The result of running this Windows service is shown here:

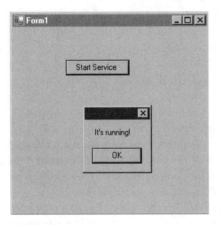

Server Components

In this section of the chapter, we will look at working with components that are handled by a middle-tier server. In order to set the stage for this kind of .NET development, let's take a few moments to review the architecture of a multi-tiered solution. Chapter 10 covered this when dealing with data—most of the time, middle-tier components provide data services to a client component, but that doesn't have to be the case.

Multi-Tiered Architecture

An application can be broken down into three distinct services that can be provided by the same program or split between two or more programs that work together to provide the overall solution. These are the services:

- **Presentation**   This service is responsible for the rendering of the user interface. Typically, you can think of this service as the Windows or Web Form. The program displays the interface on a client computer. Examples of this include programs that allow data entry (a bank entering customer information), and that display data (web or Windows pages that display customer details).

- **Business** This service is responsible for ensuring that the business rules are followed. In our example of a bank entering customer information, every customer must have a valid piece of identification. That identification has to follow specific rules, and the business service will validate the data. In a multi-tiered application, the business rules are found in components that are serviced by a server computer.

- **Data** This service is where the data source sits. This can be a database (or any data source). Typically, a multi-tiered application allows the business service to access the data.

 EXAM TIP It is a good idea to commit this model to memory. Microsoft exams assume your understanding of the three distinct service layers.

As mentioned, these services can be separated by machines or could run on a single machine. The services could also be provided by a single program or by multiple programs. This creates the distinction between single-tier, two-tier, three-tier, or n-tier (multi-tier) applications. Let's look at each one separately.

Single-Tier Model

A single-tier (1-tier) model is typical of a mainframe application. Dumb terminals gain access to the mainframe computer, which is running the application. The application combines all three services into a single location or a single program. All users of the application must connect to the mainframe computer and access the application remotely. Every process runs on the mainframe computer.

Since all of the services are located physically in one spot, there are limitations to this model. The first and foremost is that there is a single point of failure—a network breakdown or application bug causes the whole application to fail, and every user is affected directly. Equally as important is the concern that a small change can cause. One simple business-logic change can affect the application so greatly that the whole thing needs to be redeveloped.

On the flip side of that, an application of this sort is comparatively easier to develop because all the services are in one location and become easier to manage.

Two-Tier Model

Many years ago, developers introduced a new architecture designed to replace (or augment) the mainframe single-tier model. This is called *client/server* architecture, whereby a client application connects to a server application. The server application handles the back-end functionality, which in a two-tier model would include database connectivity and perhaps business logic.

Since the presentation service is now separated from the business and data services, small logic changes are easier to manage and less intrusive to the client application. However, in reality, true abstraction was not achieved. Some of the business logic remained on the client, and some was removed to the server. This causes problems when controlling the application because the developer must be aware of the location of the services. Scalability is also a big issue for 2-tier modeled applications. The larger the application and user base becomes, the harder it is to manage.

Three-Tier Model

Arising from the concerns of the two-tier model came the establishment of the three-tier model. In this case, all three services are handled by different applications and, in most cases, by three different machines. The *client* or *front-end* application provides the visual interface for the user. Business logic is retrieved from components running on remote servers (although this is not absolutely necessary—it can be found on the same machine). Business services attach to the back-end data store and retrieve the data for the presentation service.

The advantages of this model are many. Different platforms can provide separate service functionality. The client can be a browser-based application connecting to a middle-tier provided by an entirely different operating system. The middle tier can be ignorant of the type of service on either side of it, meaning that the database engine is not important to it, and the vehicle producing the user interface is immaterial to it. It is a separate and distinct component that can be used by multiple applications.

n-Tier Model

We now get to the crux of the matter—by taking the services and separating them (making them completely distinct and non-cohesive), we now can take advantage of the scalability that this model provides. The business service can be split among many different applications or servers. Data services can be provided by multiple platforms and data vendors. The interaction of these services brings us to the topic of the rest of this chapter.

Components provide the functionality and separation that we have been talking about in an n-tier model. Life would be wonderful if everyone in the development world chose the same platform and techniques to produce these components, but that is just not the case. We have spoken in earlier chapters about working with COM components in Windows and web applications. In this chapter, we will look at implementing a COM+ component, creating interfaces that are visible to COM, and working with strongly named assemblies. The goal is to make sure that the middle-tier (the business services) are dealt with in an n-tiered environment.

COM and COM+

As you may have been able to determine, one of the goals of multi-tiered applications (or applications that make use of middle-tier services) is to provide for code reuse. You may have created a module that connects to a database and retrieves the information about a single customer. Many different applications can make use of that generic type of code. As you will see in Chapter 28, the .NET Framework allows you to create XML web services that may eventually replace the COM (Component Object Model) architecture. However, because the world will not change overnight, you need to understand and work with component architecture, such as COM and COM+.

PART V

COM is an object-oriented approach to components and code reuse. In order for client code (any code making use of the component) to "talk" to components, COM provides standard interfaces to which developers must adhere. Language-specific details are unimportant, since the client must communicate through these standard interfaces. As a result, the component can be written in C++ and the client can get access to it through Visual Basic.

All COM objects implement the IUnknown interface. This interface keeps track of the number of clients accessing the component and is responsible for determining when the component (object) can be removed. COM components are installed and registered in the local machine's Registry. When registered, the component is uniquely identified by a globally unique identifier (GUID). The GUID information is written to the Registry and provides the client with information as to the location of the component and some of the configuration information. When a COM component is requested, the COM provider (which may be a middle-tier server) determines if the component needs to be instantiated or can be retrieved from the component pool (where there are previously instantiated objects ready for use). Once the services have been used, the component is either returned to the pool or destroyed. The component can be involved in complicated transactions, can have extensive security applied to it, and can be pooled (as noted previously).

The biggest benefit to the development world of the release of COM was the standard, cross-language object model that it provides. With a single definition of what a remote object looks like and acts like, the developer's life is made much easier.

COM+ was introduced in 1997 and furthered the ease of development. COM+ hides many of the details from the coder, thereby making developers' lives easier. Vendors creating tools that work with COM+ have to use the common library. Metadata (information about the component) is now stored with every COM+ object. A common set of types is implemented for COM+, so the problems of different language types are alleviated. Another huge benefit to COM+ is the abstraction (for the developer) of the Interface Definition Language (IDL).

Remember that XML web services are designed to replace the COM architecture and provide a method of accessing remote objects over common protocols such as SOAP and HTML. However, until the time comes, if ever, that they totally replace COM and COM+, you need to understand how to integrate the older technology into your .NET applications.

Serviced Components

A *serviced component*, according to Microsoft's definition, is "a class that is authored in a CLS-compliant language and that derives directly or indirectly from the class System .EnterpriseServices.ServicedComponent." This means that the class can be hosted by a COM+ application and can use COM+ services. A serviced component can take advantage of context sharing between COM+ and .NET Framework classes.

COM+ services used to be hosted by Microsoft Transaction Server (MTS) and provided robust enterprise services to applications. In other words, using COM+ services made your application a multi-tiered application in which the following parts worked together:

- Front-end application programs (user-interface applications) made calls to a component hosted by MTS on a server.

- COM+ services responded to the call and provided middle-tier functionality.

- Calls were made from the middle-tier service to the back-end database. The database returned the information to the service, which, in turn, returned the result to the front-end application.

COM+ services added the following robust features to middle-tier functionality:

- Database transaction handling, which wraps database commands in a transaction that cause an "all or nothing" transaction. See Chapter 10 on data handling for transaction properties (ACID).

- Security, meaning that restrictions on who has access to the component can be enforced.

- Object pooling, which allows multiple users of the component to access a single instance of the component. Components are pooled (instantiated and left to wait for calls), and that saves time on the server side of the call.

In order to create an environment whereby the developer can take advantage of .NET Framework objects and COM+ services working together, you need to understand the architecture of a COM+ application hosting serviced components. Figure 26-11 shows the two environments and the boundaries created between them.

Services can flow between .NET objects and COM+ services. Each environment is responsible for the implementation and the execution of the object, but COM+ provides the context for the object: transaction control, pooling, and so on.

 EXAM TIP COM+ services include automatic transaction handling, JIT object activation, security, object pooling, message queuing, and load balancing.

There are three remaining services:

- **JIT object activation** COM+ services will deallocate memory occupied by objects when they are not being used and will bring them back to life when needed.

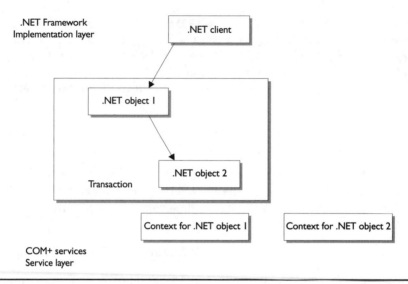

Figure 26-11   .NET Framework and COM+ services

- **Message queuing**   COM+ services will deal with queuing messages that may not be received by resources (for example, if a database server crashes and doesn't respond for a while). The queuing service records the method calls so that they can be played back when the target server responds.

- **Load balancing**   COM+ services will distribute object calls across a "farm" of servers, thereby keeping one or more servers from becoming congested.

Building a Serviced Component

The .NET Framework, as we have seen, uses COM+ to provide runtime services to .NET components. Services include transaction handling, object pooling, JIT activation, and so forth. Three pieces work together to provide this functionality:

- **Enterprise service**   A COM+ service that is exposed through the `System.EnterpriseServices` namespace.

- **Serviced component**   A .NET class that will use the enterprise service.

- **Serviced assembly**   A .NET assembly that contains at least one serviced component.

Let's build a class as a serviced component:

1. Start a new project using the Console Application template and add a reference to `System.EnterpriseServices.dll`. Right-click on the project and select Add Reference from the menu. The Add Reference dialog box will open, as

shown next. Double-click the `System.EnterpriseServices` component and click OK.

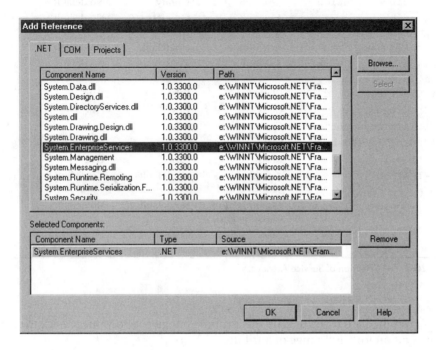

2. Set your class to inherit from `System.EnterpriseServices.ServicedComponent`:

```
public class MyServicedComponent:
    System.EnterpriseServices.ServicedComponent
```

3. Add a constructor to your class, like this:

```
public MyServicedComponent()
{
}
```

4. Specify the attributes that will work with the COM+ services. In order to do this, you need to add attributes to the `AssemblyInfo.cs` file. (Review Chapter 6 if you are unsure of how to do this). The following code listing gives you an example:

```
[assembly: ApplicationName("MyServicedApplication")]
[assembly: Description("My First Serviced Application")]
```

The attributes that are available within the `System.EnterpriseServices` namespace are listed in Table 26-3. In the table, you will see the scope value that specifies whether the attribute belongs to the method, the class, or the assembly. You will also see the unconfigured default value, which represents the value that COM+ assigns to the field if the attribute is omitted from your code. The configured default value is the value

Attribute	Scope	Unconfigured Default Value	Configured Default Value
ApplicationActivation	Assembly	Library	No default
ApplicationID	Assembly	Generated GUID	No default
ApplicationName	Assembly	No default	No default
Description	Assembly/ Class	No default	No default
EventTrackingEnabled	Class	False	True
JustInTimeActivation	Class	False	True
LoadBalancingSupported	Class	False	True
MustRunInClientContext	Class	False	True
ObjectPooling	Class	False	True
SecureMethod	Assembly/ Class/Method	No default	No default
SecurityRole	Assembly/ Class/Method	No default	No default
Transaction	Class	False	TransactionOption. Required

Table 26-3   A Selection of Service Attributes

COM+ gives the field if you specify the attribute but give it no value. Check the MSDN documentation for a full range of attributes.

EXAM TIP   The `ActivationOption.Library` option is used for component classes that are created within the process of the calling client. The `ActivationOption.Server` option is used for component classes that run in a dedicated process space.

The following code segment shows an example of coding to get the configured default value for `LoadBalancingSupported`:

```
using System.EnterpriseServices;
[LoadBalancingSupported]
public class MySC: ServicedComponent
{
    static void Main()
    {
    }
}
```

Example of a Serviced Component
In this section, we will create the client and server part of a serviced component. Our class will be called `CustomerComponent` and, when completely coded, will make a

call to the Customer table and update the table based on a client's request. We will not code the method, but will simply provide the skeleton of the serviced component.

Here is the server code:

```
using System.EnterpriseServices;
using System.Reflection;

[assembly: ApplicationName("CustomerComponent")]
[assembly: AssemblyKeyFileAttribute("CustomerComponentKeys.snk")]

namespace CustomerComponent
{
    [Transaction(TransactionOption.Required)]
    public class Customer: ServicedComponent
    {
        public Customer()
        {
        }
        public void Update(string custCode)
        {
            // perform the database operations here
        }
    }
}
```

 EXAM TIP A serviced component must be strongly named.
Notice in the preceding code that we add the attribute [assembly:
AssemblyKeyFileAttribute("CustomerComponentKeys
.snk")]. To learn more about strongly named assemblies, review
Chapter 6.

The client code looks like the following:

```
using CustomerComponent;
namespace CustomerComponentConsoleClient
{
    public class CustomerClient
    {
        public CustomerClient
        {
        }
        public static int Main()
        {
            Customer c = new Customer();
            c.Update("Matthew");
        }
    }
}
```

Compile the two classes as follows (refer to the "Review of Strongly Named Assemblies" section for more information on the sn.exe utility):

```
sn -k CustomerComponentKeys.snk
csc /t:library /r:System.EnterpriseServices.dll Customer.cs
csc /r:Customer.dll CustomerClient.cs
```

Registering the Component

The easiest way to deploy a serviced component is with dynamic registration. This means that you copy the assembly containing the component(s) to the COM+ application's directory. By using dynamic registration, clients such as web clients (ASP.NET and Web Forms) can call serviced components that are unregistered. When the client creates an instance of the serviced component for the first time, the CLR will register the assembly and configure the COM catalog.

 EXAM TIP Using dynamic registration means that the assemblies are not placed in the Global Assembly Cache (GAC). You must use manual registration to place them in the GAC.

However, if you want to have a server application that is called by COM clients, you must register the assembly manually. In order to do this, you use the .NET Framework Services Installation tool—regsvcs.exe. The regsvcs.exe tool will manually register an assembly that contains serviced components.

 EXAM TIP Before you register the assembly, be sure to add the assembly to the GAC using gacutil.exe. Review Chapter 6 for more information.

Let's step through the process:

1. Add the assembly to the GAC:

   ```
   gacutil -i CustomerComponent.dll
   ```

2. Register the assembly with COM+ services:

   ```
   regsvcs CustomerComponent.dll
   ```

 EXAM TIP By using regsvcs.exe, the differences between .NET assemblies and COM components are resolved. COM+ services will now recognize the interfaces.

The regsvcs.exe tool does the following:

- Loads and registers the .NET assembly
- Creates a type library for the .NET assembly
- Imports the type library into a COM+ services application
- Configures the type library using the metadata from the DLL

Review of Strongly Named Assemblies

By default, assemblies are private. This means that they run within the context of the application domain and will never cross the boundary into another application's namespace. Since we are creating shared assemblies for our serviced components, we need to install them into the Global Assembly Cache. A shared assembly must have a unique name that is referred to as the *strong name*. You create a strongly named assembly by using the Strong Name utility (`sn.exe`) included in the SDK:

```
sn -k CustomerComponentKeys.snk
```

This will create a file with public and private keys that will be used to give the assembly a guaranteed unique name. Refer to Chapter 6 for more information on creating the strong-name key file.

The next step is to tell your application to use the key. You do this by *signing* the assembly (adding the key to the assembly). Locate the file in the Solution Explorer called `AssemblyInfo.cs` and add the following line:

```
[assembly: AssemblyKeyFile("CustomerComponentKeys.snk")]
```

The compiler will now know to digitally sign the assembly using the keys found in the `.snk` (strong-name key) file.

Installing an Assembly into GAC

The Global Assembly Cache is a local machine storage area that holds shared assemblies. It is used to store assemblies that can be shared among several applications. The cache can be accessed using the GAC tool, `gacutil.exe`. This tool allows you to view and change the contents of the GAC. In particular, it allows you to install assemblies into the cache or remove them from the cache. The syntax is as follows:

```
gacutil [options] [assembly]
```

 EXAM TIP   You need administrative privileges to access the GAC.

Table 26-4 displays the options available with the GAC tool.

 EXAM TIP   Example of installing our serviced component into the GAC—
`gacutil /i CustomerComponent.dll`

Table 26-4	Option	Description
gacutil.exe Options	/h	Displays help topics for the `gacutil.exe` tool
	/I	Installs an assembly into the GAC
	/u	Uninstalls an assembly from the GAC
	/l	Lists the contents of the GAC

Using the Component Services Tool

In the Windows 2000 operating system, COM+ services are easier to manage. In Windows NT, you may remember that you had to add the MTS (Microsoft Transaction Server) from the Windows Option Pack. Fortunately, with Windows 2000, it is an integral part of the operating system. Access the Component Services Tool from Start | Settings | Administrative Tools (in Windows 2000 Professional). This will open a Component Services console, as shown in Figure 26-12.

Expand Component Services in the left panel, as shown in Figure 26-13. You will see the hierarchical display on the left side and the details on the right side of the console. By expanding COM+ Utilities, you can drill into the actual components and manage them.

Each component is represented by the round circle with a plus (+) sign in the middle (see Figure 26-13). When a component is being accessed, the circle will spin. You can

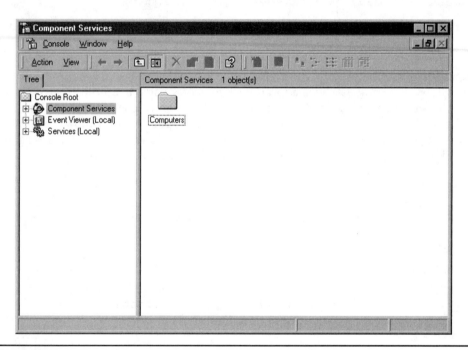

Figure 26-12   The Component Services tool

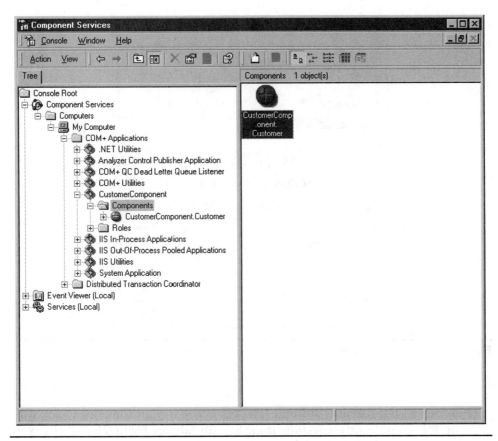

Figure 26-13   Looking at the components

see the properties of the component by right-clicking on the component (in the right pane) and selecting Properties (see Figure 26-14).

Figure 26-14 shows the General properties—name, description (this can be modified), the DLL, class ID (CLSID), and the application identifier. You can manage the component using the following tabs on the Properties dialog box:

- **Transactions**   In the Transactions tab (see Figure 26-15), you can specify the transaction support—Disabled, Not Supported, Supported, Required, and Requires New. You can also specify the transaction timeout if supported.

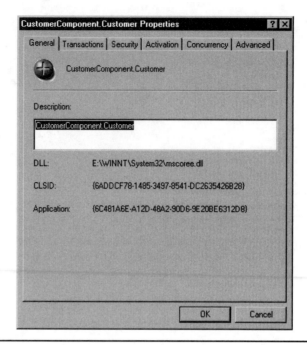

Figure 26-14   Properties of the component

- **Security**   If the security attribute has been added to your component, you will be able to configure the security using Security tab (see Figure 26-16). Here you can set the authorization and the security roles.

- **Activation**   Using the Activation tab (see Figure 26-17), you can set object pooling properties, as well as JIT (just-in-time) activation. Remember that these properties are all COM+ services.

- **Concurrency**   In Figure 26-18, you can see that threading and synchronization support can be configured through the Concurrency tab. Notice that our threading model is set, by default, to Any Apartment. An apartment is a logical container for processes.

Take a moment to look at the interfaces that have been created to make your component visible to COM. Figure 26-19 shows the Component Services console tree expanded to dig deeper into the `CustomerComponent.Customer` component.

By opening the Interfaces folder (see Figure 26-19), you can see that behind the scenes a number of interfaces have been created to work with COM. By right-clicking on the Interface name and selecting Properties from the menu, you can see the properties

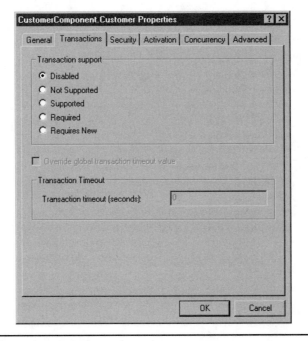

Figure 26-15   Transaction properties

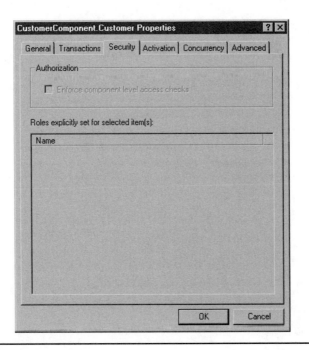

Figure 26-16   Security properties

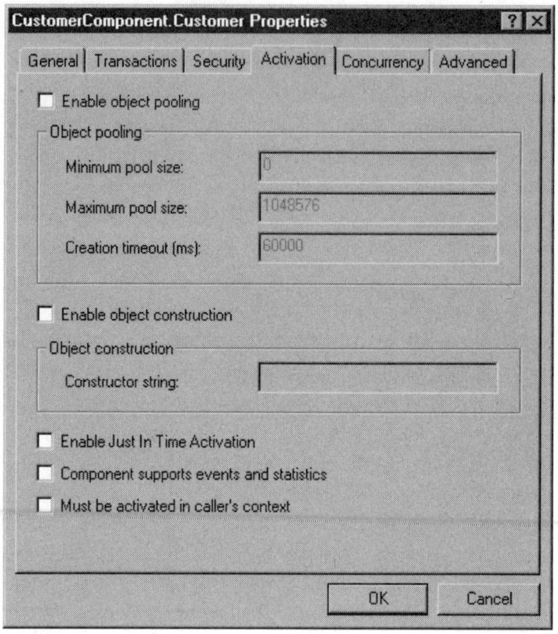

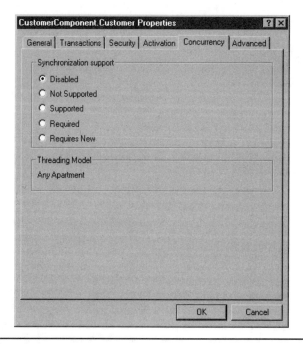

Figure 26-17 Activation properties

Figure 26-18 Concurrency properties

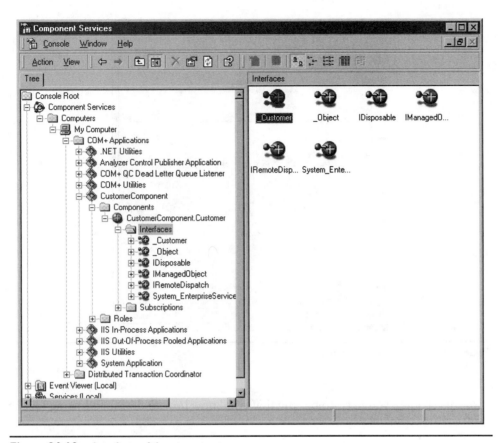

Figure 26-19   Interfaces of the component

that can be set for each particular interface (see Figure 26-20). Each interface exposes the methods specific to the COM requirements. We have opened the Object interface (which is not really too exciting, but useful for our demonstration).

In Figure 26-21 you can see the methods of the Object class exposed to COM. This is the crux of the whole process—our .NET Framework component has been resolved in order to expose interfaces that are visible to COM.

Summary

When building enterprise applications, you can take advantage of the support that COM+ services gives to your components. In this chapter, we have reviewed creating and working with Windows services (components that run in the background of the current Windows session) and serviced components (components that are run on a server and accessed using COM+ services).

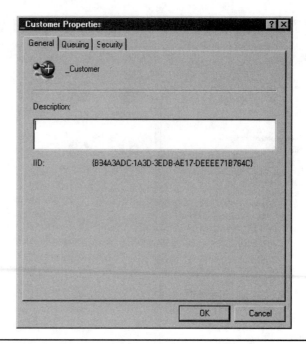

Figure 26-20   Interface properties

In this chapter, you need to be sure that you know how to do the following for the exam:

- Create and work with a Windows service.
- Create and work with a serviced component.
- Expose interfaces that are visible to COM. This involves making sure that you use the `regsvcs.exe` tool.
- Register components using `gacutil.exe`
- Work with the Component Services management console.

Test Questions

1. You have created a serviced component that will interface with COM+ services. You want to install the component in the Global Assembly Cache. Which utility will allow you to do this?

   A. `gacutil.exe`

   B. `regsvcs.exe`

   C. `install.exe`

   D. `sc.exe`

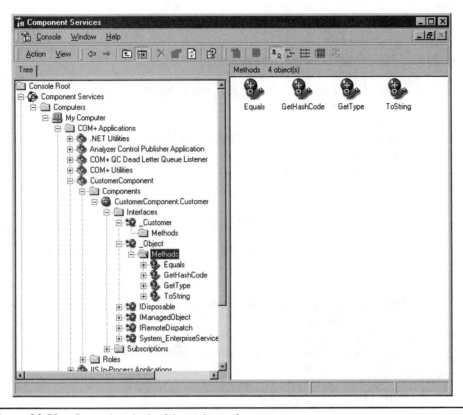

Figure 26-21   Exposed methods of the **Object class**

PART V

2. You are creating a Windows service for Windows ME. You want to install the service in the Registry. What utility will do this for you?

   A. gacutil.exe

   B. regsvcs.exe

   C. sc.exe

   D. installer.exe

   E. None of the above

3. Which project template will allow you to create a background service in Visual Studio .NET?

   A. Windows service

   B. Web service

   C. Windows application

   D. Service

4. Which of the following code modules will create a serviced component that will work with COM+ services?

A.
```
using System.EnterpriseServices;
using System.Reflection;
[assembly: ApplicationName("Price")]
namespace Price
{
    public class Price: ServicedComponent
    {
        public Price()
        {
        }
        public void SomeMethod()
        {
            // perform the database operations here
        }
    }
}
```

B.
```
using System.EnterpriseServices;
using System.Reflection;
[assembly: ApplicationName("Price")]
[assembly: AssemblyKeyFileAttribute("PriceKeys.snk")]
namespace Price
{
    public class Price
    {
        public Price()
        {
        }
        public void SomeMethod()
        {
            // perform the database operations here
        }
    }
}
```

C.
```
using System.EnterpriseServices;
using System.Reflection;
[assembly: ApplicationName("Price")]
[assembly: AssemblyKeyFileAttribute("PriceKeys.snk")]
namespace Price
{
    public class Price: ServicedComponent
```

```
        {
            public Price()
            {
            }
            public void SomeMethod()
            {
                // perform the database operations here
            }
        }
    }
```

D.
```
    using System.Reflection;
    [assembly: ApplicationName("Price")]
    [assembly: AssemblyKeyFileAttribute("PriceKeys.snk")]
    namespace Price
    {
        public class Price
        {
            public Price()
            {
            }
            public void SomeMethod()
            {
                // perform the database operations here
            }
        }
    }
```

5. You have created a serviced component that will interface with COM+ services. You want to register the component manually. Which utility will allow you to do this?

   A. gacutil.exe

   B. regsvcs.exe

   C. install.exe

   D. sc.exe

6. You have created a serviced component that will interface with COM+ services. You want to register the component automatically. Which utility will allow you to do this?

   A. gacutil.exe

   B. regsvcs.exe

   C. xcopy.exe

   D. sc.exe

7. Which of the following code segments will send an event message to the
   Application log when the Windows service is stopped?

A.
```
public MyService()
{
    InitializeComponent();
    if (!System.Diagnostics.EventLog.SourceExists("Application")
    {
        System.Diagnostics.EventLog.CreateEventSource ("Application", "Application");
    }
    eventLog1.Source="Application";
    eventLog1.Log = "Application";
}
protected override void OnStart (string[] args)
{
    eventLog1.WriteEntry ("Here we are!");
}
```

B.
```
public MyService()
{
    InitializeComponent();
    if (!System.Diagnostics.EventLog.SourceExists("Application")
    {
        System.Diagnostics.EventLog.CreateEventSource ("Application", "Application");
    }
    eventLog1.Source="Application";
    eventLog1.Log = "Application";
}
protected override void OnStop (string[] args)
{
    eventLog1.WriteEntry ("Here we are!");
}
```

C.
```
public MyService()
{
    InitializeComponent();
    if (!System.Diagnostics.EventLog.SourceExists("System")
    {
        System.Diagnostics.EventLog.CreateEventSource ("System", "System");
    }
    eventLog1.Source="Application";
    eventLog1.Log = "Application";
}
protected override void OnStart (string[] args)
{
    eventLog1.WriteEntry ("Here we are!");
}
```

D.
```
public MyService()
{
    InitializeComponent();
    if (!System.Diagnostics.EventLog.SourceExists("Application")
    {
        System.Diagnostics.EventLog.CreateEventSource ("Application", "Application");
    }
    eventLog1.Source="System";
    eventLog1.Log = "Application";
}
protected override void OnStop (string[] args)
{
    eventLog1.WriteEntry ("Here we are!");
}
```

8. Where would you find the Add Installer link within Visual Studio .NET?

   A. Under the Project menu

   B. Under the Build menu

   C. In the Toolbox

   D. In the Properties Explorer window

9. Which of the following methods will install a Windows service? Choose all that apply.

   A. `xcopy.exe`

   B. `regedit.exe`

   C. `setup.exe`

   D. `service.exe`

10. A Windows service must inherit from which class?

    A. `System.Service.ServiceBase`

    B. `System.ServiceProcess.Service`

    C. `System.ServiceProcess.ServiceBase`

    D. `System.Service.Service`

11. Which Registry key would lead you to find the installed Windows service?

    A. `HKEY_LOCAL_MACHINE\Services`

    B. `HKEY_LOCAL_MACHINE\System\CurrentControlSet\Services`

    C. `HKEY_LOCAL_MACHINE\System\Services`

    D. `HKEY_LOCAL_MACHINE\CurrentControlSet\Services`

12. You want to configure your new Windows service. Which of the following tools will allow you to set configuration properties for the service? Choose all that apply.

   A. `regedt32.exe`

   B. `sc.exe`

   C. `regsrvs.exe`

   D. `net.exe`

13. Which class will allow you to programmatically work with your Windows service?

   A. `ServiceController`

   B. `ServiceConfiguration`

   C. `ServiceStatus`

   D. `ServiceControl`

14. Which method of the `ServiceController` class will allow you to send a command to the service?

   A. `Stop()`

   B. `Start()`

   C. `Pause()`

   D. `ExecuteCommand()`

15. Which of the following services represent the services that together provide an enterprise application?

   A. Business, Logic, Application

   B. Application, Business, Data

   C. Presentation, Business, Data

   D. Presentation, Logic, Data

Test Answers

1. A.

2. E. Windows services do not run under Windows ME.

3. A.

4. C. Answer A is missing the key file that will establish a strongly named assembly. Answer B does not derive from `ServicedComponent`, and D is missing the namespace.

5. B.

6. C.

7. B.

8. D.

9. C.

10. C.

11. B.

12. A and B.

13. A.

14. D.

15. C.

.NET Remoting

In this chapter, you will

- Implement server-activated components
- Implement client-activated components
- Select a channel protocol and a formatter
- Create client and server configuration files
- Instantiate and invoke a .NET Remoting object

The .NET Framework has included developer-friendly mechanisms for calling on objects that are running in a different *application domain*. An application domain is a secure processing unit that the CLR (Common Language Runtime) uses to isolate applications. Since applications are separated by application domains, you cannot pass a reference variable from one process to another. This means that you cannot ask an object running in one application domain to perform operations or provide data for an object running in another application domain. In order to send messages to a remote object, you must take advantage of remote-access mechanisms within the .NET Framework. These include .NET Remoting, which is the subject of this chapter, and XML Web Services, the subject of the next chapter.

The Microsoft exam will test your knowledge of both of these remote-object frameworks. You will also be expected to know when to use XML Web Services instead of .NET Remoting, and vice versa. In this chapter and in Chapter 28, we will look at the advantages and disadvantages of one technique over the other.

We will start this chapter by providing the background and details of the architecture of .NET Remoting. The second half of the chapter will concentrate on creating examples and using the technology.

What Is .NET Remoting?

Traditionally, programmers wanting to take advantage of objects running on a remote server had to be concerned with issues such as

- *Coding the network calls.* The programmer had to deal with creating sockets, passing the data over the network socket, and allowing the component on the server side to accept the data, process the request, and pass the data back to the client component.

- *Listening to a specific port.* The developer had to worry about maintaining an open port connection. Typically, the application on the server side would register on a port and wait for incoming messages. A port is a logical communication channel to which an application binds. When a client request is received, it specifies the application by the port number.

In order to abstract all the background network tasks from the developer, Microsoft introduced DCOM (Distributed Component Object Model), which is a programming model for calling methods on objects running on a server. The trouble with DCOM is that the model is intended for communication between COM objects. As we have seen in this book, COM is not the technology on which the .NET Framework is built. Table 27-1 outlines some of the differences between DCOM and .NET Remoting.

Other advantages of using .NET Remoting over DCOM include:

- The overhead of COM InterOp is not involved with .NET Remoting.
- More deployment options exist with .NET Remoting.
- .NET Remoting calls can easily be transmitted through a firewall (when using HTTP).

Distributed computing under the .NET Framework is handled by .NET Remoting. A managed object can be accessed by a remote client using .NET Remoting. When a client makes a call to an object in another application domain (sometimes called an *app domain*), a proxy object grabs the call first. The proxy object behaves like the remote object, except that the proxy object is running locally. We will look at the architecture in detail in the coming sections.

Terms and Terminology

Before we start into this vast subject of distributed computing, let's take a few moments to examine the terms that you will encounter. In this section, you will get a bird's-eye

DCOM	.NET Remoting
A server process is launched automatically upon the first call from a client.	A server process can be launched when the server is hosted by an IIS (Internet Information Server) application; however, .NET Remoting supports multiple processes accessing the same server component.
The lifetime of a server component is managed by the server "asking" the client if it still needs it.	The lifetime of a server component can be managed using "leases," whereby the client establishes the lifetime of the remote object.
DCOM is a closed system and does not allow for much in the way of creating custom mechanisms.	.NET Remoting is an open architecture, and it allows the developer to create custom channels (communication mechanisms) and custom serialization.
DCOM is very secure.	.NET Remoting has no built-in security mechanisms (except when hosted by IIS).

Table 27-1   Differences Between DCOM and .NET Remoting

view of the terminology that we will be using in the coming sections of this chapter. If you are very familiar with remote method invocation (the calling of methods on a remote object), you may want to briefly skim these definitions and then move to the meat of this chapter—the architecture and examples. If this is your first experience with distributed object handling, spend some time here to familiarize yourself with these terms—we will be going into the details in coming sections:

 EXAM TIP   Be very familiar with all of the following terms.

- **Remote method invocation**   When a method in one object that exists in one application domain needs to call on a method that exists within an object in another application domain, this is called a *remote method invocation*. The objects are not situated so that the call can be made locally. The call must be handled and marshaled to the remote object. Keep in mind that the objects can actually be running on the same machine, but in separate application domains, and still be remote to each other.

- **.NET Remoting**   The *.NET Remoting* framework offers developers a distributed object model. The model means that remote method invocations can be made between different CLRs (Common Language Runtimes) or different application domains. One runtime environment can support multiple application domains.

- **Client**   A *client* is any component that is making a call to a remote component's method. The client can be on the same machine as the server or be on a machine on the other side of the world.

- **Server**   A *server* is any component that responds to the requests of a client component.

- **Marshal by reference**   When an object is created remotely, a reference to that object can be passed as a parameter to a method call. That object can be passed *by reference* or *by value*. In order to pass the object by reference, the server must implement the `MarshalByRefObject` interface.

- **Marshal by value**   If the remote object does not implement the `MarshalByRefObject` interface, objects must be passed by value to the server. In this case, the server must implement the `ISerializable` interface.

- **Proxy objects**   As soon as a client creates an instance of the remote object on the server, a *proxy object* is created that resides on the client side. The proxy object is a local representation of the remote object and is responsible for forwarding method calls to the server.

- **Client-activated components**   A *client-activated component* is created when the client passes parameters to the constructor of the remote object. In this case, the server maintains an instance of the object that belongs to that client only.

PART V

- **Server-activated components** A *server-activated component* is created by the server. Two possible modes exist here—`Singleton` and `SingleCall`. See the description of *activation* in this list for more information.

- **Channels** A *channel* is a conduit for the actual transmission of the remote calls over the wire.

- **HTTPChannel** Remote calls are transmitted over the HTTP protocol. `HTTPChannel` is part of the .NET Framework.

- **TCPChannel** Remote calls are transmitted over the TCP protocol. `TCPChannel` is part of the .NET Framework.

- **Formatters** A *formatter* is responsible for transforming the data intended for the remote object into the transmission format, and vice versa—a formatter is required to transform the response from the server into the transmission format.

- **SOAP formatter** A *SOAP formatter* transforms the remote data using SOAP (Simple Object Access Protocol). The SOAP formatter is included as part of the .NET Framework.

- **Binary formatter** A *binary formatter* transforms the remote data via a binary data stream. The binary formatter is part of the .NET Framework.

- **Sink chains** The combination of a channel and a formatter is a *sink chain*. Messages pass from one sink chain to another in the remoting architecture.

- **Remoting host** A *remoting host* provides a runtime environment on the remoting server for the remote object. Examples include IIS (Internet Information Server) and Windows Forms. Almost any .NET executable can serve as a remoting host.

- **Stateful vs. stateless** *State* is the data that an object contains. If a remote object maintains state between method calls, it is called a *stateful* object. This means that if multiple clients are accessing the same object, they will be able to see the changes that another client object has made to the server object's state. If a remote object does not keep state between method calls (if there is no data held), the object is called *stateless*. Stateless objects can be used easily between multiple clients because there is no fear that data created by one client will be destroyed by another client (since there is no data stored).

- **Activation** When a server object's methods are requested, this is called *activation,* and it can be done through server-object instantiation. There are two ways in which a remoting object can be activated. The first is by using `SingleCall` mode, which means that a new instance of the server object is created with every client call. The second is by using `Singleton` mode, which means that a single instance of the server object can serve several clients. The third method of activation is called client-activated object (CAO). In this case, the client application creates an exclusive instance of the object. The object can then maintain state without any other client object making changes to it.

If your head is spinning right now, don't worry. We will cover each of these concepts in detail in this chapter. The preceding list is a quick reference for you when you go to take the exam. These terms and their meanings must be at the tip of your tongue if you are to be successful on the exam.

.NET Remoting Architecture

Understanding the architecture of .NET Remoting will help you when working with this technology. Remember that a lot of what happens is abstracted from the developer in an effort to reduce the amount of coding work and make better use of development time. This is true of any remote object architecture, whether it is .NET Remoting, Web Services, Enterprise JavaBeans, or any other development environment. The goal of these architectures is to reduce the amount of time that you, the developer, have to spend working on the remote and networking issues. Your development time should be spent on making the objects as flexible as possible. These objects should encapsulate the business logic, rather than the networking logic.

Having said all that, you should be aware of the background work that is done for you in order to fully appreciate the significance of this technology. We will start off with a simplistic overview of .NET Remoting. Figure 27-1 illustrates the overall process.

Let's examine all the parts of Figure 27-1. (In the coming sections, we will look at each in detail.) Two separate application domains are shown in Figure 27-1: the server environment, where the remote object will be created, and the client environment, which will make the call to the remote object. Under normal circumstances (without remoting), these objects are unable to send messages to each other.

Here are the steps involved in remote calls:

1. The client object creates an instance of the server object.

2. The remoting system creates a proxy object that represents the server object, and returns a reference to the proxy to the client.

3. The client makes a method call to the server object.

4. The remoting system that envelops the client will intercept the call, check the request for type safety, and send the request over a channel to the server.

5. A channel on the server side listens for such calls and picks up the request.

Figure 27-1
.NET Remoting
overview

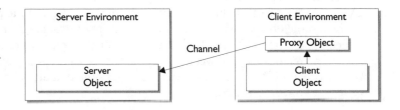

6. The remoting system that envelops the server will then either create the object or use a previously instantiated object and make the call to the object.

7. The server remoting system will put the response in a message to be returned via a reverse process. The proxy object then returns the result of the call to the client object.

That is the simplified process in a nutshell. Not much code is needed on either side to make this work. We will examine the code required later on in this chapter. However, in order for the entire system to work, many elements must cooperate. You must be sure that the URI (Uniform Resource Identifier) is correct in order to be able to find the server object. The configuration files on the client and the server side must also be absolutely correct for the remote call to succeed. In order to be confident that you can accomplish this, let's break down the architecture even further.

The Remote Object

The remote object is the object that is considered to be the *server*. Typically, this object will run on a server machine either hosted by Internet Information Server (IIS) or another remoting host. The client does not call the actual methods of the remote object. Instead the client calls the methods of a proxy object, which is a representative of the server object.

A server object is one that inherits from `MarshalByRefObject`. This is the class definition of a remote object:

```
public class MyRemoteServerObject: MarshalByRefObject
```

 EXAM TIP   Any remote object that can be passed by reference must inherit from `MarshalByRefObject`.

Client Object and Proxies

The client object is the object that is considered to be the *client*. The client object will request a method invocation of a remote object. However, since the remote object can never leave its application domain, the client must make the request of a proxy object. To complicate things further, there are actually two proxy objects that are created:

- **Transparent proxy**   The transparent proxy actually looks like the real remote object, which means that it provides the implementation of the public methods of the remote object. Using reflection, it reads the metadata of the assembly, which makes the public methods known to the transparent proxy. Figure 27-2 shows the relationship between the client, the transparent proxy, and the real proxy. The .NET Remoting framework provides the default proxy, which is called `TransparentProxy`.

Figure 27-2
The client and
the proxies

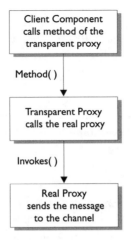

• **Real proxy**   The real proxy (`RealProxy`) is the object that knows how to send
the message on to the channel. Remember that the channel is responsible for the
wire transmission of the message. The real proxy is automatically generated by
.NET tools; however, you can customize this object to make it do what you want.
Suppose you want to log events as they happen through the process—you could
code the real proxy to do that for you. By default, the real proxy will locate the
sink (formatter), which can transform the message for channel transmission.

Formatters

The formatter is responsible for transforming the message so that it can be sent over the
network. To do this, it must serialize the parameters (the data of the method call) into a
format that the wire understands. There are two formatters that ship with the .NET
Framework:

• SOAP formatter:

    System.Runtime.Serialization.Formatters.Soap.SoapFormatter

• Binary formatter:

    System.Runtime.Serialization.Formatters.Binary.BinaryFormatter

By default, an HTTP channel uses a SOAP formatter to transport XML messages, and a
TCP channel uses sockets to transport binary messages using the binary formatter. You
can also create custom formatters or use third-party formatters.

EXAM TIP   A formatter encodes and decodes the messages between a
server and a client over a channel. HTTP channels use SOAP formatters.

Channels

Channels are the objects that transport the messages over the wire (or, to be more correct, across boundaries, whether they are application domains, processes, or computers). Two types of channels are shipped with the .NET Framework:

- **HTTPChannel** Messages are transported to and from the remote object using the SOAP protocol. The message is transformed into XML and serialized, and SOAP headers are added to the stream. HTTP is the transport protocol and SOAP and XML are the encoding protocols. The channel is found in the following namespace:

```
System.Runtime.Remoting.Channels.Http
```

- **TCPChannel** Messages are transported to and from the remote object using binary formatters. Messages are serialized into a binary stream and then transported using the TCP protocol. The binary stream provides a faster and more efficient process; however, you may need an `HTTPChannel` to bypass firewall restrictions, and so forth. The channel is found in the following namespace:

```
System.Runtime.Remoting.Channels.Tcp
```

A channel listens for messages and is registered with the remoting infrastructure by coding the following:

```
ChannelServices.RegisterChannel()
```

The client can select any channel that is available to communicate with the server object.

 EXAM TIP At least one channel must be registered with the remoting system in order for a client to call on a remote object. Channels are registered in the application domain.

Channel names must be unique within the application domain. In order to register two HTTPchannels, you must create unique names for each one. We will look at registering channels in the coming sections.

 EXAM TIP A channel cannot be registered more than once if it listens on the same port. This means that different application domains on the same machine cannot register the same channel on the same port.

Putting It All Together

Let's look at the complete architecture picture, now that we have described the individual components of the structure in more detail. Figure 27-3 illustrates the complete process from client method invocation to server method response.

Figure 27-3
The complete
remoting process

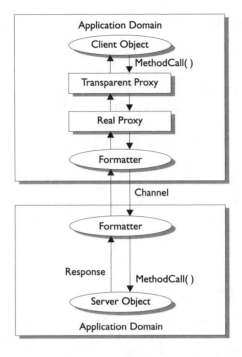

Steps for Invoking a Server Object's Methods

Before we take a look at the code required to create client and server objects, let's step through the process. Keep the architecture in mind as we do this.

1. The client object registers a channel. This channel will provide the communication link between the client and the remote object.

 EXAM TIP   The server object has to be listening on a similar channel.

2. The client activates the remote object. This can be done in one of three ways:

- Create a new instance using the new keyword:
  `ServerObject s = new ServerObject();`

- Retrieve an existing remote object:
  `ServerObject s = (ServerObject) Activator.GetObject`
  `(typeof(ServerObject), "<location>");`
  We will examine the <location> parameter in the next section.

- Create a new (client-activated) instance of the remote object:
  `ServerObject s = (ServerObject) Activator.CreateInstance(...);`

We will fill in the parameters in the next section.

3. The framework creates the proxy object based on the information provided by the activation request. At this point, we are working with local objects, since no call has yet been made to the remote object. This is why proxies work—they are local to the client object. The server object is remote from the client.

4. The client calls a method on the remote object. The proxy intercepts the method call and sends it to the formatter.

5. The formatter converts the request to a transmission protocol and sends the request (via a `Message` object) through the channel object.

6. At the server side, the framework works backwards through the process. The formatter transforms the message to a call that can be understood by the object.

7. The object performs the action requested of it and sends the results through the same process.

In the next section, we will look at the code that will accomplish this process.

Using .NET Remoting

Now that we have discussed the architecture of .NET Remoting, let's put together a few examples to see how this works. In this section, we will look at creating the component, building a server, and coding a client to call the server's methods. The code will be built using Notepad and the command line in order to see the actual internal workings. We will also discuss the difference between client-activated objects and server-activated objects. For the Microsoft exam, you will need to know how to code both of these activation techniques. We will finish this section off by looking at how the coding can be done through Visual Studio .NET.

Building the Remote Object

Any object that will be called upon from a different application domain or machine must be built as a remote object. This means that it must derive from `System .MarshalByRefObject`. Any object that derives from `MarshalByRefObject` is not allowed to transverse application domains. A proxy is needed to communicate with objects such as these.

 EXAM TIP The `MarshalByRefObject` class allows access to objects across application boundaries. The application must support remoting. Some of the methods of the `MarshalByRefObject` class include `CreateObjRef()`, which creates an object that contains all of the information to create the proxy; `GetLifetimeService()`, which retrieves the object that controls the lifetime policy of the remote object; and `InitializeLifetimeService()`, which gets a lifetime service object to control the lifetime.

To build the remote object, create a new class in Notepad as follows:

```
using System;
namespace HelloWorld
{
    public class Hello: MarshalByRefObject
    {
        // constructor for remote object
        public Hello()
        {
            // output to the console a message that indicates
            // that we are in the constructor of the object.
            System.Console.WriteLine ("We are in the constructor.");
        }
        // public method that the client will call
        public string HelloWorld()
        {
            // output to the console a message that indicates
            // that we are in the HelloWorld() method
            System.Console.WriteLine ("We are in the HelloWorld() method.");
            // return the Hello World string to the caller of the method
            return "Hello World!";
        }
    }
}
```

Save the file as `Hello.cs` and compile the remote object as follows:

```
csc /t:library Hello.cs
```

You should find that you have `Hello.dll` in the same folder as `Hello.cs` after a successful compilation.

In this example, we have created a library class with a single method, `HelloWorld()`. The class inherits from `System.MarshalByRefObject`, which supports the class becoming a remote, callable component. We have included a few console write lines that will let us see the component moving from constructor to method call—these are for demonstration only. Notice that the `HelloWorld()` method does not write out to the console; rather, it returns the string to the caller of the method. It is a common mistake of first-time remote-component coders to write to the console instead of returning the string. Remember that your calling program will probably not be on the same machine as the remote component, so writing to the console is only useful to the server computer—not to the client computer.

Building the Remote Server

Our next step is to create the remote server. For this example, we will create a simple console application that will instantiate a `TCPChannel` and register our remote component.

In Notepad, create the following console application:

```
using System;
// the following assembly includes the TcpServerChannel
using System.Runtime.Remoting;
```

```
using System.Runtime.Remoting.Channels;
using System.Runtime.Remoting.Channels.Tcp;
namespace HelloWorld
{
    public class HelloWorldServer
    {
        [STAThread]
        public static void Main ()
        {
            // instantiate the channel object
            TcpServerChannel tc = new TcpServerChannel (4242);
            // register the channel to make it available to
            // the remote object
            ChannelServices.RegisterChannel (tc);
            // register the remote object
            RemotingConfiguration.RegisterWellKnownServiceType (
                    typeof(Hello), "HelloWorld",
                    WellKnownObjectMode.SingleCall);
            // the server will remain running until the user presses
            // any key on the console
            System.Console.WriteLine ("To stop the application, press Enter.");
            System.Console.ReadLine();
        }
    }
}
```

Let's dissect the important lines of code:

```
TcpServerChannel tc = new TcpServerChannel (4242);
```

This line creates a new channel object, using a TCP channel, and creates it on port 4242. Use port numbers greater than 1026 in order to avoid using a port number that a well-known application may be using. For example, a web server uses port 80, an SMTP mail server uses port 25, and so on.

 EXAM TIP There are two channel types that ship with the .NET Framework— `TcpServerChannel` and `HttpServerChannel`.

The next line of code looks like this:

```
ChannelServices.RegisterChannel (tc);
```

This line registers the channel so that the remote object will have a channel that it can use for transmitting the response from the method call.

The following line registers the remote object in such a way that the client can find the object:

```
RemotingConfiguration.RegisterWellKnownServiceType (
                typeof(Hello), "HelloWorld",
                WellKnownObjectMode.SingleCall);
```

The parameters of the RegisterWellKnownServiceType() method include the following:

- The type of class in the remote object—typeof(Hello) in the preceding example.

- The name by which the client can call the remote object—"HelloWorld" in this case. This is called the URI (Uniform Resource Identifier). For a TCP channel, it is a simple string as seen here. For an HTTP channel, it is the actual server location—"http://localhost/ServerApp" for example.

- The SingleCall mode means that a new instance is created for every method call.

 EXAM TIP There are two different well-known object modes for server-activated objects: SingleCall, where there is a new instance for every method call and no state is maintained between method calls, and Singleton, where every method call uses the same instance of the remote object.

The last lines of the remote server code consists of console output lines that will allow the server to continue running until the user presses ENTER on the console application. The code demonstrates a hosting application—in our case a console application.

An alternative approach would be to create the remote object and register it in Internet Information Server (IIS) as a web service object. In that case, you would have created an HTTPServerChannel within the remote object itself. We will look at code that does this later.

Save the file as HelloWorldServer.cs and compile it as follows:

```
csc /r:Hello.dll HelloWorldServer.cs
```

Building the Client

The client application is the last step for this demonstration. We will create a simple console application that will create a TcpClientChannel object which will be used to transmit the client's request. We will then use the Activator class to find the remote object and invoke its method. Here is the code:

```
using System;
using System.Runtime.Remoting.Channels;
using System.Runtime.Remoting.Channels.Tcp;
namespace HelloWorld
{
    public class HelloWorldClient
    {
        [STAThread]
        public static void Main()
        {
            ChannelServices.RegisterChannel (new TcpClientChannel());
            Hello h = (Hello) Activator.GetObject (typeof(Hello),
                                    "tcp://localhost:4242/Hello");
```

```
            System.Console.WriteLine (h.HelloWorld());
        }
    }
}
```

Let's look at the key lines of code:

```
ChannelServices.RegisterChannel (new TcpClientChannel());
```

Notice that we do not select a port number here—any free port will do. The client is simply using the port as an exit mechanism for the remote call. On the server side, we will connect to port 4242, which is where the server is running.

In the next line of code, the client instantiates the `Hello` object by using the `GetObject()` method of the `Activator` class:

```
Hello h = (Hello) Activator.GetObject (typeof(Hello),
                              "tcp://localhost:4242/Hello");
```

Notice the parameters that are sent to the `GetObject()` method:

- `typeof(Hello)` tells the method the class type of the remote object.
- `"tcp://localhost:4242/Hello"` tells the method where to find the remote object. We have selected the `localhost` (the local computer), port 4242 (where the component is registered and waiting for calls), and the URI (`Hello`), a named identity.

 EXAM TIP Now for the $64,000.00 question! The reference `Hello` `h` is what type of variable? Remember that the client never talks to the remote object directly. The variable *h* refers to the proxy object. Actually, it refers to the transparent proxy object, which then communicates with the real proxy object.

Running the Remote Application

All the pieces are now in place, and we are ready to test our remote application. The first step is to start the hosting server application, `HelloWorldServer.exe` (see Figure 27-4). In Figure 27-5, you can see that we have compiled all of our programs and have started the client application.

Notice in Figure 27-5 that the server has responded with "Hello World!" indicating that the client application has successfully sent a message to the remote server. You can also examine the hosting application's response to the method calls—recall that we inserted console output to indicate method calls. Figure 27-6 shows the console output from the hosting server.

While you are in the process of developing remote components and testing them as we have done in this example, it is a good idea to place `System.Console.WriteLine` statements in your methods. By doing this, you can see what is happening as the remote calls come through to the server object. Notice in our example that the constructor is called and then the `HelloWorld()` method is called. By looking at the output, you can see that we were successful in creating a remote component and building a remote server for it to execute through.

Figure 27-4   Starting the hosting server

Figure 27-5   Starting the client

Figure 27-6   Console output

Configuring .NET Remoting

In this section, we will look at another method of hosting the remote component. As we have mentioned, the remote component can be hosted by any type of application. In our previous example, we created a server console class to host our component. In this section, we will use IIS and take advantage of an HTTP channel for transmission.

In addition to exploring the technique for using a remote component in IIS, we will look at the configuration file that can be created to provide information to the runtime environment. We will also create our application within Visual Studio .NET in order to take advantage of some of the shortcuts available to developers.

Creating the Remote Object

Create the remote server object within Visual Studio .NET by following these steps:

1. Start a new class library application in Visual Studio. Name it HelloWorldIIS.

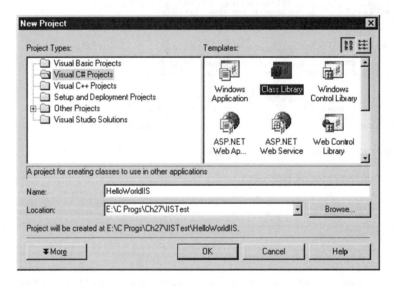

2. Rename the Class1.cs module to Hello.cs, and adjust the code for the class definition and the constructor. Be sure to make your new class inherit from System.MarshalByRefObject:

```
public class Hello: System.MarshalByRefObject
{
    public Hello()
```

3. Add the HelloWorld() method to the class file:

```
public string HelloWorld()
{
    return "Hello World!";
}
```

4. Build the remote object by selecting Build | Build HelloWorldIIS from
   the menus.

Creating the Remote Object Configuration File

In order to specify the necessary operating parameters to the runtime environment, you
need to provide a configuration file for the remote object. This configuration file is
called web.config, and it looks like this:

```
<configuration>
   <system.runtime.remoting>
      <application>
         <service>
            <Wellknown mode="SingleCall"
                       type="HelloWorldIIS.Hello, Hello"
                       objectUri="Hello.soap" />
         </service>
      </application>
   </system.runtime.remoting>
</configuration>
```

Place the web.config file in the same directory as the Hello.dll file. The configuration file has a section for configuring the remoting instructions. Under the <service>
tag, you can see the information pertaining to the server mode, SingleCall, as well as
to the type and location (URI) of the remote object. The type includes the fully qualified
name of the remote object as its first parameter, and the executable filename as the second
parameter.

EXAM TIP   The web.config file must be placed in the same directory as
the component.

Choosing the Mode

At this point, it is probably a good idea to discuss the differences between SingleCall
and Singleton mode. Either of these modes can be used when the object is server activated (that is, when the server is responsible for instantiating the object).

SingleCall mode objects are activated when the method call is received, and they
live until the method is complete. In other words, the object is only around as long as
the method is alive. As soon as the method is finished, the remote component is no longer available. There is no state maintained between calls (there can't be—the object is
destroyed after the method call). Each client will receive a reference to its own server object
for the life of the method. This is a more scalable option, since any number of clients can
be added and, as long as the hardware and memory requirements do not explode, the
remoting environment will keep on making server objects for each client call. On the down-
side, there is no state maintained between method calls, so that data that is created or received during the method is destroyed when the method is finished.

`Singleton` mode objects are created after the first remote method call, and they stick around for the duration of the hosting application. In other words, every client will receive a reference to the same object as every other client receives. There is only ever a single instance of any particular remote component alive. This is an excellent solution for sharing data between clients. One client can make a change that another client will see, since they are looking at the same object. This is not a very scalable approach, but it is good to use if you want to share objects between clients.

 EXAM TIP   You cannot mix modes for a single class. A class can only have one mode—either `SingleCall` or `Singleton`.

Creating the Client

When we write the client code, we treat the remote object as if it were a local object (remember that we get a reference to a local proxy object). However, we must write code to find out the type and the location of the remote object.

In this example, we will create a Windows application that has a button on the screen. The button click event will cause a remote method call to the server object, which will be deployed into IIS. Follow these steps to create the client application:

1. Start a new project and select Windows application. Name the application `HelloWinClient.cs`.

2. Add a button to the form, and name the button `btnCallRemote`.

3. Add the following code to the click event of the button:

```
private void btnCallRemote_Click (object sender, System.EventArgs e)
{
    Hello h = (Hello) Activator.GetObject (typeof (Hello),
                "http://localhost:8080/HelloWorldIIS",
                WellKnownObjectMode.Singleton);
    MessageBox.Show(h.HelloWorld());
}
```

4. Add a reference to the server DLL. Right-click on the Windows application in Solution Explorer and select Add Reference to `Hello.dll`. This will open the Add Reference dialog box.

5. Add a reference to `System.Runtime.Remoting`.

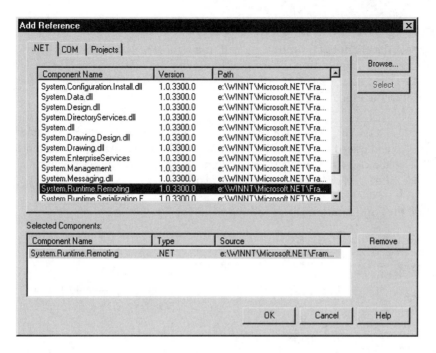

6. Add the following `using` statements to the Windows application:

```
using System.Runtime.Remote;
using System.Runtime.Remoting.Channels;
using System.Runtime.Remoting.Channels.Http;
using HelloWorldIIS;
```

7. Add the following code to the form constructor to create a channel:

```
public Form1()
{
    InitializeComponent();
    HttpChannel c = new HttpChannel();
    ChannelServices.RegisterChannel (c);
}
```

8. Set the Windows project as the startup project—right-click on `HelloWinClient` and select Set as Startup Project.

9. Build the project.

At this point, everything is ready. You just need to create the configuration file for the client and deploy the component to the Internet Information Server (IIS).

Creating the Client Configuration File

In order for the client to communicate with the remoting system (in this case IIS), you need to create a configuration file for the client with the information that it needs. This file will be called `HelloWinClient.exe.config`, and it will provide the channel information to the executable file.

 EXAM TIP   The client configuration file is named after the executable file and placed in the bin directory with the client executable. For example, if the client executable is `HelloWinClient.exe`, the configuration file is `HelloWinClient.exe.config`.

Create the configuration file as follows:

```
<configuration>
    <system.runtime.remoting>
        <application name="HelloWinClient">
            <channels>
                <channel type="System.Runtime.Remoting.Channels.Http.HttpChannel,
                              System.Runtime.Remoting" />
            </channels>
        </application>
    </system.runtime.remoting>
</configuration>
```

The configuration file uses an `<application>` tag to identify the name of the client class. The channel information is provided by the `<channel>` tag. The first attribute tells the client what type of channel to use, and the second parameter associates the namespace with the channel.

Setting Up IIS to Host the Server

The last step is to set up IIS to host the remote server component. Start by mapping out the directory structure for the actual component. The following files must be placed in the structure:

```
<path>IISTest\Server\HelloWorldIIS.cs
<path>IISTest\Server\Web.config
<path>IISTest\Server\bin\HelloWorldIIS.dll
<path>IISTest\Client\HelloWinClient.exe
<path>IISTest\Client\HelloWinClient.exe.config
```

Set up the IIS server by following these steps:

1. Open Internet Services Manager. In Windows 2000, you can select Start | Settings | Control Panel | Administrative Tools | Internet Services Manager. You will see the Internet Information Services window shown in Figure 27-7.

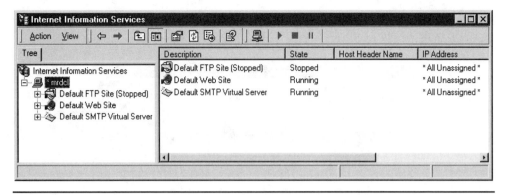

Figure 27-7   The Internet Services Manager

2. Double-click on Default Web Site in the left pane. Right-click on the Default Web Site and select New | Virtual Directory. You will see the Welcome screen of the Virtual Directory Creation Wizard. Click Next.

3. Create the alias for the virtual directory. This can be given any name you choose. For this example, call it `IISTest`. Click Next.

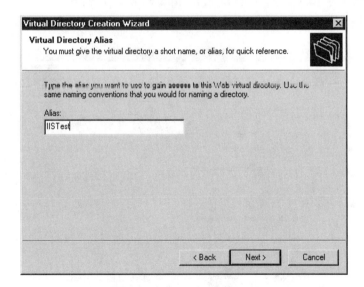

4. Enter the physical path to the remote object directory—`<path>\IISTest\`
   `Server` in our example. Click Next.

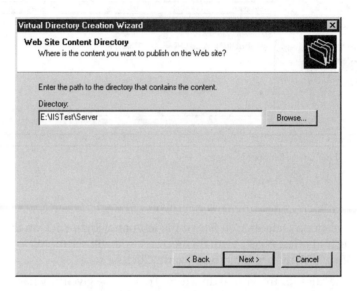

5. Set any security settings in the next window. The default settings allow a user
   to read and run scripts, but you can modify those permissions through this
   window. Click Next when you are done.

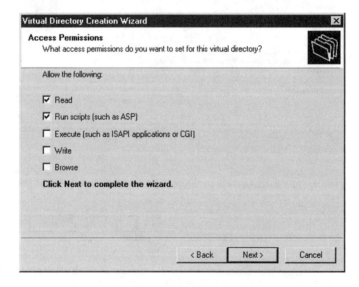

6. Click Next to finish the Wizard program. You will now see your virtual
   directory listed under the Default Web Site (see Figure 27-8).

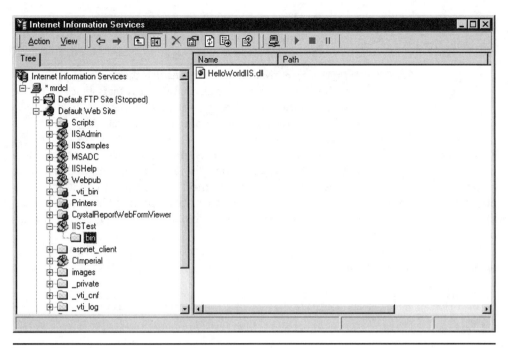

Figure 27-8   The new virtual directory

The final step is to test the client application. Click the Call Remote Method button on the form, and you will see a message box that displays the output from the server object's `HelloWorld()` method.

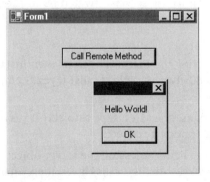

Client-Activated Objects

So far we have discussed server-activated objects and reviewed the difference between `Singleton` and `SingleCall` activation modes. The third type of remoting object is the client-activated object (CAO). In this case, the client application creates the remote object for exclusive use (this is very similar to the COM world).

 EXAM TIP   Singleton activation mode means that there is only a single instance of the object running and all clients access that object. The SingleCall activation mode means that every client gets their own object, which is destroyed at the end of the method call.

Although this may seem to be the same as using SingleCall for server-activated objects (SAOs), it is not. With SAO objects, there is no state maintained between method calls. The object is destroyed when the method is finished. A client-activated object maintains state between method calls, and the state maintained is exclusively for the calling client—no other clients will have access to the state data, since there is a unique object for every client.

To make the client-activated object ready for client activation, modify the configuration file on the server as follows:

```
<service>
  <activated type="HelloWorldIIS.Hello, Hello" objectUri="Hello.soap" >
  </activated>
</service>
```

You will also need to modify the client configuration file:

```
<client url="http://localhost:8080">
  <activated type="HelloWorldIIS.Hello, Hello" />
</client>
```

The final step is to make sure that the client uses the new keyword to instantiate the remote object.

How do you know when to use server-activated (SingleCall or Singleton) or client-activated objects? Consider the following questions when making the design decision:

1. Does every client calling the method need its own instance of the object and its own data maintained between method calls? If yes, then you need a client-activated remote object.

2. Can multiple clients use the same server object? If yes, then you need a server-activated Singleton remote object.

3. Do you have a lot of clients accessing the server object, and there is no need for maintaining state between method calls? If yes, then you can use a server-activated SingleCall remote object.

Managing the Lifetime of a Server Object

By default, a remote server object lives a certain amount of time and then is set to null and made available for garbage collection. The "certain amount of time" depends on the activation type of the server component. In order to give the developer control over the lifetime of a server component, the remoting framework has included a lifetime-management mechanism called *remote leasing*.

A client application can register with the lease manager in order to be notified when a server object is about to be destroyed. The lease manager will notify the client and then wait a designated amount of time for the client to respond. The client will return the amount of time that it wants the server to be kept alive (if necessary), and the lease manager will adjust the time to live for the server object.

A client class must implement the `ISponsor` interface before it can take advantage of the lifetime-management lease manager:

```
public class RemoteClient: ISponsor
```

There is a single method defined in the `ISponsor` interface—`Renewal()`. The lease manager will call this method when the lifetime of the server component needs to be updated.

The client instantiates a new leasing manager:

```
ILease lease = (ILease) servercomponent.InitializeLifetimeService();
```

In the preceding line, `servercomponent` is the remote server object reference.

The client then registers with the lease manager to receive lifetime updates:

```
// A TimeSpan object is used to control the hours, minutes and seconds
//   for the lease notification
lease.Register (this, new TimeSpan(0, 0, 5);
```

The last step is to implement the `Renewal()` method and provide the details of the renewal to the lease manager:

```
public TimeSpan Renewal (ILease ls)
{
   TimeSpan ts = new TimeSpan (0, 0, 5);
   return ts;
}
```

That's all there is to it! The lease manager will notify the client of an object's impending destruction, and the client will send back a `TimeSpan` object that tells the leasing manager to inform the runtime environment that the server will live for the amount of time specified.

Final Considerations

Since there is so much to consider with this type of remote-method invocation, we will summarize the concepts and design considerations presented throughout this chapter.

 EXAM TIP   Use this section as a final study guide for the topic of .NET Remoting.

Performance Considerations

You should consider the type of channel to use when configuring .NET Remoting. There are two types shipped with the .NET Framework—TCP and HTTP. Performance is affected as follows:

- The HTTP protocol must negotiate connection information (host to host) in order to function. This makes it a slower solution than using TCP.
- The TCP channel provides the fastest throughput; however, it may not be the solution for network communication through firewalls.

Two types of formatters are provided with the .NET Framework: the SOAP formatter and the binary formatter:

- The binary formatter is faster and more efficient because it uses a binary stream of data.
- The SOAP formatter is slower since it has to handle the SOAP protocol.

Both formatters can be used over an HTTP channel, but for the best performance, use a binary formatter over a TCP channel. Remember, though, there may be circumstances that make it impossible to use a TCP channel.

.NET Remoting vs. Web Services

In the next chapter, you will be looking at creating XML Web Services that allow remote objects to be hosted as web applications and allow communication using HTTP and SOAP protocols. When considering whether to use .NET Remoting over Web Services, consider the following:

- A .NET Remoting server object can be hosted by any type of application—Web Services need a web server, such as Internet Information Server.
- XML Web Services are tied directly to HTTP and SOAP formatting. This may not always be the best solution. You must analyze the requirements fully before making the decision between .NET Remoting and Web Services.
- A .NET Remoting server object can maintain state between method calls.

Having said all that, you might be wondering why you would ever use XML Web Services. Well, hold on to your hats. In the next chapter, you will see a lot of the complexity of remote objects eliminated through the use of Web Services. You will also see that many solutions can take advantage of the HTTP and SOAP capabilities of Web Services.

The bottom line is that you must look at the user requirements thoroughly before making the decision. If you need a flexible, fully controllable solution (one for which you can create your own plug-ins), then maybe .NET Remoting is for you. However, if your needs are for fast development over common platforms, then XML Web Services will be the right solution.

If you are asked on a Microsoft exam which technique to use, remember to examine the surrounding elements:

- What is the physical connection?
- What protocols can be used?
- How fine-tuned do the networking components have to be?

These are all questions that will help you in the final design decision.

Points to Remember

The following list will help when considering .NET Remoting:

- A remoting host is needed on the remoting server in order to provide a runtime environment for your remote object. This can be any application, such as a console application, web server, and so forth.
- IIS can be the remoting host. However, only objects using the HTTP channel can be used for IIS. Either formatting option will work with IIS.
- Configuration files can be changed without recompiling the components. However, configuration can also be done programmatically. This might create a more secure solution in some cases. If configuration is done programmatically, then the component needs to be recompiled when the information changes.
- Activation is the process that determines how and when remote objects are created.
- Server-activated objects have their lifetime controlled by the server. When the client makes the first call, the object is activated. `SingleCall` mode means that a new instance is given to each client requesting the object. `Singleton` mode means that a single instance of the object is created, and every client communicates with that instance.
- Client-activated objects have their lifetime controlled by the client. The server object is created when the client creates the proxy.
- Remotable objects must inherit from `System.MarshalByRefObject`.

Summary

In this chapter, we have investigated .NET Remoting, a mechanism for gaining access to objects running in separate and distinct application domains. There are many techniques for doing this. We looked at Windows Services in the last chapter, which is a way to create applications that run in the background, waiting for client requests for their services. In the next chapter, you will find out how to create XML Web Services, another method for requesting services of a remote application.

Using .NET Remoting, you can create client applications that work with a configuration file to retrieve information about the server object. You can also bypass configuration files by registering the remote object and providing the location of the server object programmatically. You can have the client activate the object or you can create an object that is self-activating.

The architecture of .NET Remoting allows for different protocols for transmission—we have looked at HTTP and TCP, but anything can be plugged into these applications. The framework for .NET Remoting is so flexible that most remote method invocations, no matter which protocol is used or type of objects are required, can be accommodated. You have seen that it is also possible to create your own channels, proxies, and formatters, and plug them into the architecture. You will not be asked to do that for the Microsoft exam, but you should be aware of the flexibility of this architecture.

Test Questions

1. You have developed a remote object library class for deployment into a console application. The console application will remain running on the server computer and respond to client requests for the remote object. However, when you try to run the remote hosting application, you receive an application exception. The following is the code for the hosting application:

```csharp
using System;
using System.Runtime.Remoting;
using System.Runtime.Remoting.Channels;
using System.Runtime.Remoting.Channels.Tcp;
namespace ChatServer
{
    public class ChatServerHost: MarshalByRefObject
    {
        [STAThread]
        public static void Main ()
        {
            TcpServerChannel tc = new TcpServerChannel (4242);
            ChannelServices.RegisterChannel (tc);
            RemotingConfiguration.RegisterWellKnownServiceType (
                        typeof(Chat), "ChatServer",
WellKnownObjectMode.SingleCall);
            System.Console.WriteLine ("To stop the application, press Enter.");
System.Console.ReadLine();
        }
    }
}
```

Here is the code for the remote object:

```csharp
using System;
using ChatServerHost;
namespace ChatServer
{
    public class Chat
    {
        public Chat()
```

```
        {
        }
        public string Talk(string message)
        {
            return message;
        }
    }
}
```

What is the most likely cause of the exception error?

A. The remote object class is missing a using declaration.

B. The format of the Talk() method is incorrect.

C. The Talk() method is not called from the hosting application.

D. The remote object class is not capable of receiving remote method calls.

E. The remote hosting class is not capable of receiving remote method calls.

2. In order to have your server component accept method calls that pass the object by value, your remote server object must implement which interface?

A. IUnknown

B. IMarshalByValue

C. IMarshalByRef

D. ISingleCall

E. ISerializable

3. You are in charge of creating a remote object that will return database records to the caller of the method. You want to ensure that the object keeps track of the number of requests, and writes the number out to the database. Which activation mode would you use?

A. SingleCall

B. Singleton

C. Client-activated

D. Server-activated

4. You have created a remote object, ChatServer.dll, that is to be deployed to an IIS server. You need to create a configuration file that will provide location and type information. Which file would you create?

A. web.config

B. machine.config

C. application.config

D. ChatServer.exe.config

5. You need to create a configuration file for the client component that will gain access to your `ChatServer.dll` server component running on the IIS server. Which of the following configuration file entries is correct?

A.

```
<configuration>
    <system.runtime.remoting>
        <application name="ChatServerClient">
            <channels>
                <channel
                    type="System.Runtime.Remoting.Channels.Tcp.TcpChannel,
                                    System.Runtime.Remoting"
                    />
                </channels>
        </application>
    </system.runtime.remoting>
</configuration>
```

B.

```
<configuration>
    <system.runtime.remoting>
        <application name="ChatServerClient">
            <channels>
                <channel
                    type="System.Runtime.Remoting.Channels.Http.HttpChannel,
                                    System.Runtime.Remoting" />
                </channels>
        </application>
    </system.runtime.remoting>
</configuration>
```

C.

```
<configuration>
    <system.runtime.remoting>
        <application>
            <service>
                <Wellknown mode="Singleton"
                    type="ChatServer.ChatServer, Chat"

                    objectUri="Chat.soap" />
            </service>
        </application>
    </system.runtime.remoting>
</configuration>
```

D.

```
<configuration>
    <system.runtime.remoting>
        <application>
            <service>
                <Wellknown mode="SingleCall"
                    type="ChatServer.ChatServer, Chat"

                    objectUri="Chat.soap" />
            </service>
        </application>
    </system.runtime.remoting>
</configuration>
```

6. Which of the following formatters can be used over an HTTP channel. Choose all that apply.

A. SOAP formatter.

B. RPC formatter.

C. Binary formatter.

D. DCOM formatter.

7. You are developing a remote component that will make a call to a Customer database and return a customer's account number to the caller of the method. You have built the server object and will deploy it as an XML Web Service. The method `public int GetCustomerAccount()` uses a stored procedure to retrieve a given customer's account number and returns the number to the calling component. You must decide what type of activation to use. Which of the following is the best choice?

A. `SingleCall`

B. `Singleton`

C. Client-activated

D. Server-activated

8. You need to create a configuration file for the client component that will gain access to your `ChatServer.dll` server component running via a console application. Which of the following configuration file entries is correct?

A.

```
<configuration>
    <system.runtime.remoting>
        <application name="ChatServerClient">
            <channels>
                <channel
                    type="System.Runtime.Remoting.Channels.Tcp.TcpChannel,
                                    System.Runtime.Remoting" />
            </channels>
        </application>
    </system.runtime.remoting>
</configuration>
```

B.

```
<configuration>
    <system.runtime.remoting>
        <application name="ChatServer">
            <channels>
                <channel
                    type="System.Runtime.Remoting.Channels.Http.HttpChannel,
                                        System.Runtime.Remoting" />
            </channels>
        </application>
    </system.runtime.remoting>
</configuration>
```

C.

```
<configuration>
   <system.runtime.remoting>
      <application>
         <service>
            <Wellknown mode="Singleton" type="ChatServer.ChatServer, Chat"
                                         objectUri="Chat.soap" />
         </service>
      </application>
   </system.runtime.remoting>
</configuration>
```

D.

```
<configuration>
   <system.runtime.remoting>
      <application>
         <service>
            <Wellknown mode="SingleCall" type="ChatServer.ChatServer, Chat"
                                          objectUri="Chat.soap" />
         </service>
      </application>
   </system.runtime.remoting>
</configuration>
```

9. You have developed a remote object library class for deployment to a web server. You have established that your configuration files are correct, and now you feel that your component classes may have an error. The following is the code for the remote object:

```
using System;
using System.Runtime.Remoting;
using System.Runtime.Remoting.Channels;
using System.Runtime.Remoting.Channels.Http;
namespace HelloServer
{
   public class Hello: MarshalByRefObject
   {
      public Hello()
      {
      }
      public string HelloWorld(string message)
      {
         return message;
      }
   public static void Main()
   {
      HttpChannel c = new HttpChannel (4242);
      RemotingConfiguration.RegisterWellKnownServiceType {
              Type.GetType("HelloServer"), "Hello",
              WellKnownObjectMode.SingleCall);
   }
}
}
```

What is the most likely cause of the exception error?

A. You are missing a `using` declaration.

B. You have used the wrong channel type.

C. You have used the wrong activation mode.

D. You have not registered the channel.

E. There is no error.

10. Which of the following activation requests would you use in client code to have a client-activated remote object?

A. `ServerObject s = new ServerObject();`

B. `ServerObject s = (ServerObject) Activator.GetObject ( …);`

C. `ServerObject s = (ServerObject) new ServerObject();`

D. `ServerObject s = (ServerObject)`
   `Activator.CreateInstance(…);`

11. To which namespace does the `Activator` class belong?

A. `System`

B. `System.Remoting`

C. `System.Remote`

D. `System.Remoting.Activation`

12. You have developed a remote object library class for deployment to a web server. You have established that your configuration files are correct, and now you feel that your component classes may have an error. When you try to run the remote hosting application, you receive an application exception. The following is the code for the remote object:

```
using System;
using System.Runtime.Remoting;
using System.Runtime.Remoting.Channels;
using System.Runtime.Remoting.Channels.Http;
namespace HelloServer
{
    public class Hello: MarshalByRefObject
    {
        public Hello()
        {
        }
        public string HelloWorld(string message)
        {
            return message;
        }
    public static void Main()
    {
        HttpChannel c = new HttpChannel (4242);
        ChannelServices.RegisterChannel (c);
        RemotingConfiguration.RegisterWellKnownServiceType {
                Type.GetType("HelloServer"), "Hello",
                WellKnownObjectMode.SingleCall);
        HttpChannel d = new HttpChannel (4242);
        ChannelServices.RegisterChannel (d);
        RemotingConfiguration.RegisterWellKnownServiceType {
                Type.GetType("GoodbyeServer"), "Goodbye",
                WellKnownObjectMode.SingleCall);
    }
}
```

What is the most likely cause of the exception error?

A. You are missing a `using` declaration.

B. You have used the wrong channel type.

C. You have registered the channels incorrectly.

D. You have not registered the channel.

E. There is no error.

13. To which namespace does the `HttpChannel` class belong?

A. `System.Remoting`

B. `System.Runtime.Remoting.Channels.Http`

C. `System.Runtime.Remoting`

D. `System.Runtime.Remoting.Channels`

14. Which line of code will register a channel?

A. `ChannelServices.Register (channel);`

B. `ChannelServices.RegisterChannel(4242);`

C. `ChannelServices.Register (4242);`

D. `ChannelServices.RegisterChannel(channel);`

15. In which directory does the `<application_name>.exe.config` file belong?

A. In the bin directory of the application.

B. In the root directory of the application.

C. In the `\Winnt\System32` directory.

D. In the `\Program Files\Microsoft.NET` directory.

Test Answers

1. D. The remote object class must extend `MarshalByRefObject`.

2. E.

3. B. `Singleton` mode means that there is a single instance of the component and state is maintained between method calls.

4. A.

5. B. The client uses an HTTP channel to access an IIS server.

6. A, C.

7. A. There is no need to maintain state between calls. This is the most scalable option.

8. A.

9. D.

10. D.

11. A.

12. C. Only one channel registration is allowed.

13. B.

14. D.

15. B.

XML Web Services

In this chapter, you will
- Control characteristics of web methods by using attributes
- Create and use SOAP extensions
- Create asynchronous web methods
- Control XML wire format for XML Web Services
- Instantiate and invoke an XML web service

XML Web Services is Microsoft's name for the distributed software environment that Microsoft hopes will be the answer to metered software—software that can be billed for on a per-use basis. XML Web Services is also the environment that will enable loosely coupled software components to be dynamically located by the client software at run time.

In this chapter, you will learn how to design, create, and use XML Web Services, and most importantly from the exam point of view, you will learn how to control the environment of particular XML Web Services. You will work with both static and dynamic discovery of XML Web Services using the UDDI protocol. The exam draws heavily from material in this chapter, so be certain that you are familiar with the terms and concepts we discuss.

Introducing XML Web Services

We will start by looking at distributed applications and where XML Web Services fit. This section focuses on distributed applications and the protocols that are used to communicate between components. Some of those protocols are RPC, message-based systems, and the web standards like XML.

Distributed Applications

Distributed applications are made up of many software components that are distributed between multiple computers connected by a network. This decentralization of the software components offers a number of benefits when the sum of the processing power of the different physical computers is available to the application, and the data can be physically distributed across many different systems.

Some of the forces that moved the application architecture from the monolithic single-tier model to the distributed model are

- **Cost**   The cost of centralized systems is higher than the cost of individual computers that, as a group, have more processing and storage capacity.

- **Data**   The change in usage and ownership of the data that an organization uses is more easily managed if the individual departments have full control of their own data.

- **Security**   Varying levels of security are needed for an organization that offers publicly available data and also keeps highly secured marketing and financial data, and this is easier to manage on physically different computers than it is on a centralized system.

The Web is one of the architectures that has grown almost overnight, and it is one natural environment where distributed applications can reside. The standardized protocols that components can use to communicate over the Web are the foundation for distributed applications on the Web.

The protocols that are used on the Web include the latest interoperability protocols to be released (XML, SOAP for example), along with remote procedure call (RPC) and message-based protocols.

Remote Procedure Calls

One of the first protocols introduced for use with distributed applications was the remote procedure call (RPC). An RPC is a call to a function that resides on another (remote) computer. To the developer, RPCs look like regular function calls, and they provide location transparency, in that the location of the provider of the service is not known when the client software is designed. RPCs also provide a very familiar call sequence that makes them easy to use.

RPCs make use of a stub that packages the function call and any parameters (the packaging of call and parameters is called *marshalling*) in a buffer that is then transmitted across the network to the RPC server. Another stub in the RPC server unpacks the function call and the parameters and calls the function on the client's behalf. Any return data is sent to the client using the same procedure.

The RPC function call looks almost the same as a local call and behaves in the same way as a local call. This means that the RPC is a synchronous call and, as such, a blocking call—the call to the remote function will not return until it is finished. This model is very common and familiar to most developers, but there are potential problems with the synchronous model when used with a distributed architecture.

Other issues that have plagued the RPC-based model include the hard-coding of endpoints (the locations of the distributed components), which results in problems with load balancing and failovers. It is also almost impossible to set priorities for the RPC calls—they are always served on a first come, first served, basis.

Message-Based Architecture

The message-based architecture uses message queues, such as Microsoft Message Queue Server (MSMQ). Message queues are asynchronous in nature and can be routed based on load and priority. The application developer must provide for the higher-level protocols that are used to pack and unpack the messages, and because the message queue architecture is asynchronous, the developer might also need to use synchronous messages to support workflow scenarios when the order of messages is important.

Web Standards and XML

RPC-based environments have been successfully implemented by many different organizations in the form of Distributed Component Object Model (DCOM) from Microsoft, Common Object Request Broker Architecture (CORBA) from HP et al, and Remote Method Invocation (RMI) from Sun. These implementations are designed around binary protocols that have inherent problems:

- **Interoperability**   The protocols are not interoperable because they were developed to be monolithic standards within the context of the specific distributed environment. Translation services can and have been developed, but these services are not only unwieldy, but they also tend to lose some information as is normal in any translation process. The problems arise when different partners have selected a different binary protocol resulting in translation problems.

- **Firewalls**   Firewalls are network components that control what network traffic is allowed to pass between the internal and external networks. RPC communication is point-to-point and uses ranges of TCP ports that must be opened (made available) in the firewall for communication to function. Opening ports in the firewall is considered to be a security risk by most organizations.

- **Data types**   The different binary protocols encode data in different ways, which creates a huge problem when the call must be translated. If there is no direct relationship between the data types in the systems, the result is inevitable data loss.

The solution to the binary protocol quandary is to use standard protocols that can be used and understood by all parties who want to participate in the distributed application. The following list is a refresher of the different web protocols:

- **HTTP**   Hypertext Transfer Protocol is the protocol that transfers any kind of document across the Web from client to web server and back again. HTTP traffic uses only one TCP port, making the firewall configuration more secure.

- **HTML**   Hypertext Markup Language is the language that is used to describe the web pages you see and use on the Web. They are delivered to the browser from the web server using HTTP.

- **XML** Extensible Markup Language is the standard that gives you the ability to package data and the structural definition (metadata) of that data in one document. XML documents offer the following benefits:

  - Easy to use across the Internet.
  - Easy to process.
  - Easy to create.
  - Extensible.
  - Platform independent.
  - Easy to localize.
  - Clear data model.

For a full discussion of protocols, refer to Chapter 25.

The adoption of XML by web server and web solution vendors has brought XML into the forefront as the most important web technology of this decade. XML is also the solution to transmitting documents between partners in most e-commerce scenarios. Some developers think that XML has yet to prove itself, but the web world seems to have adopted XML, and we are not likely to go back to the monolithic environments of the past, with their vendor-specific protocols.

That being said, there are some problems involved in transmitting information on the Internet that must be solved:

- **Performance** The client still connects to the Internet mostly through dial-up connections, resulting in the need to send small amounts of data back and forth between the client and web server. This is not a major concern when you develop for intranets.

- **Security** The Internet is a public place, presenting opportunities for shadowy individuals to intercept, modify, spoof, or steal data using any one of many hacking techniques. We will deal with the defenses against these attacks in Chapter 30.

XML is an excellent choice when it comes to solving these two problems. XML transmits data and the structure of that data in a compact text format. This data can be encrypted for security.

XML Web Services in a Nutshell

XML Web Services is the end result of research into the problems with distributed applications based on binary protocols. The fast adoption of web protocols was one of the factors that made XML Web Services possible. XML Web Services is based on the XML standard, as the name implies, but there are a number of other standard protocols, including HTTP and Simple Object Access Protocol (SOAP) that are instrumental in making XML Web Services functional. The standard protocols are detailed in Chapter 25.

An *XML web service* is a URL-addressable set of functionality that is exposed over a network to serve as a part of a distributed application. All communication between a client and the XML web service server uses the HTTP protocol.

The XML web service acts as a building block of a distributed application and, as such, acts as a component, a black box. The design for the XML web service uses common object-oriented (OO) techniques that encapsulate the implementation and the data of the XML web service, thus making the XML web service suitable for building distributed applications.

An XML web service can be a very simple static service that provides information to the user, or a fully aggregated system of XML Web Services that provide a dynamic, complex software system. Aggregated XML Web Services are also known as federated XML Web Services.

The following features of XML Web Services will contribute to its success:

- **Standards** The standards that support XML virtually guarantee that XML Web Services will be one of the major environments. The adoption of the XML standard and the technologies that support XML has not been seen in the Information Systems sector before. For example, an XML web service written in C# .NET and exported in IIS can be used by a Common Gateway Interface (CGI) application written in C++, and the use is seamless.

- **Reuse** Microsoft has made tools and technologies available that enable developers to take software components and expose them (make them available) as XML Web Services without rewriting them.

- **Interoperability** The use of SOAP guarantees that XML Web Services are interoperable with CORBA, DCOM, and any other binary protocols. XML Web Services can be hosted and accessed by any computer that supports HTTP and XML. HTTP is the only communication protocol that is needed. XML is a markup language.

- **Languages** XML Web Services can be written in any .NET language (C# .NET, VB .NET, COBOL .NET, and so on), enabling the developer to be productive in a familiar language, rather than having to learn yet another new language.

Wire Formats

The term *wire protocol* is used to describe the protocol that is used for components to communicate with each other. XML Web Services can use the legacy binary wire protocols (RPC) that were used to let components communicate via DCOM, or a number of different internet protocols.

The following wire protocols are available to developers when creating XML Web Services:

- **HTTP-GET and HTTP-POST** These are standard protocols that have been evolving since the Web was invented. They use HTTP encoding to pass name-value pairs as part of the request. All non-text characters must be quoted and encoded. Both of these protocols are very low weight (low use of processing and transmission resources), but can be cumbersome to work with due to the URL encoding that must take place to put data in the request.

- **SOAP** The Simple Object Access Protocol is XML-based. Messages sent using SOAP can be passed between nodes using HTTP packets without requiring any special encoding. Because SOAP uses XML, the data and the structure is very clear, so SOAP is the choice protocol. For a refresher on SOAP, see Chapter 25.

 EXAM TIP When faced with a choice about the protocol to use, SOAP is the best choice because it is the most portable and can be encrypted at will.

XML Web Services Architecture

The architecture used for XML Web Services is one in which the XML web service is loosely coupled to the clients that will use it—the resources of the service and the client are separate and distinct. The communication to and from the service must meet the Internet standards, and the methods that will be called from a client of the XML web service must be published for public use and be publicly accessible.

There are three services in the XML Web Services architecture, as can be seen in Figure 28-1.

The service provider hosts the XML web service and is responsible for providing access to the public interface of the software service. The service consumer is the client and will bind to the interface of the service provider. Note that in this architecture, the service consumer is not the end user—it is a software node in an application. The service broker is a node that is used to locate the service provider of a specific XML web service.

The interactions in Figure 28-1 are as follows:

- **Publish service** The service provider publishes the XML web service to a service broker.
- **Find service** The service consumer uses the service broker to find the service.
- **Bind to service** The service consumer binds to the service from the service provider.

The find and bind actions can be dynamic, giving applications the ability to be configured dynamically at run time.

Figure 28-2 shows the protocols that are used between the three services in the XML Web Services architecture.

The service broker is a node in the network that implements a Universal Description, Discovery, and Integration (UDDI) registry (see Chapter 25 for a description of UDDI). The service provider exposes (provides) XML services through an ASP.NET file that has the file extension .asmx. The service consumer can be any node in the network that can communicate using SOAP or HTTP, can supply the required authentication, and understands the service interface.

Figure 28-1
The objects
in the XML
Web Services
architecture

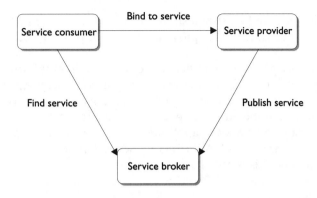

EXAM TIP   The service consumer does not have to be a client application—
it can be another XML web service.

In the following sections, we will look more closely at the nodes in the XML Web Services architecture.

XML Web Service Provider

The central role of the XML Web Services architecture is that of an XML web service provider (we will use the term service provider for short). The service provider must supply HTTP protocol handling and authentication services. If the service provider can't supply these infrastructure services, the XML web service must implement them on behalf of the provider.

The minimum requirement for the service provider is that it must supply a protocol listener for the HTTP protocol. A protocol listener is a software component that waits (listens) for connections using a specific protocol, in this case HTTP. The service provider

Figure 28-2
The protocols
in the XML
Web Services
architecture

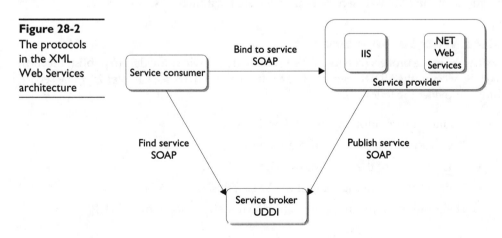

must also be able to distinguish between calls to different XML Web Services that are hosted on the same service provider, as well as provide basic security at the protocol level.

The service provider that Microsoft offers is Internet Information Server (IIS). IIS is a web server that provides all the services required of a service provider. IIS has the ability to redirect client calls to invoke service components on the server based on the configuration of IIS and the extension of the file being requested on the web server. For example, IIS can invoke CGI applications, Active Server Pages (ASP) and ASP.NET applications, as well as ISAPI (Internet Server Application Programming Interface) applications, and this is not an exhaustive list.

XML Web Service Consumer

The XML web service consumer (service consumer) is the node in the network that uses XML Web Services to provide its functionality. The service consumer is usually not the client application—rather it is one node in the network that aggregates other services to provide some specific part of the distributed application. The minimum requirement of a service consumer is that it can call the XML web service using the wire protocol that the service supports—this can be any of the standard protocols. The .NET Framework provides classes that encapsulate the details of building custom communications packages in any of the protocols.

The service consumer uses the XML web service broker to locate the service provider that exposes the XML web service. The XML web service can be found dynamically at run time from a service broker, or it can be hard-coded at design time. Using the dynamic process makes the application dynamically configurable, and allows it to handle load balancing. XML Web Services and the endpoints (the service providers) are found by using the UDDI registry. For a full discussion on how to use UDDI, see Chapter 30.

The service consumer implements a proxy class that is used on the consumer to hide the details of the XML web service. This makes it possible for the developer to use the methods of the XML web service as if they were local methods.

XML Web Service Broker

XML web service brokers (service brokers) are used by service providers to publish the XML Web Services in the UDDI registry. (For a refresher on UDDI see Chapter 25.) The service broker provides the following:

- Contact information for the XML web service.
- Text description for the XML web service.
- Classification of the XML web service.
- Links to documentation about the XML web service.
- The location of the endpoints of the XML web service, stored as URLs.

The service consumer uses the service broker to search for an XML web service and then discovers the information that is needed to bind to that XML web service.

The method used by the service broker to make XML web service information available to service consumers uses the UDDI, which is a distributed registry. It allows service providers to publish their XML Web Services, and service consumers to find information about those published services. UDDI consists of three parts—business addresses, a list of categories, and technical information. Any XML web service can be described using these three parts.

XML Web Services Programming Model

The programming model used to build XML Web Services is based on some key features.

- **Stateless**   The XML web service is stateless. By not storing information between invocations, the service becomes more scalable, even if the burden on the developer to design the stateless component can be quite high.

- **Web protocols**   XML Web Services are totally programmed around the standard web protocols—HTTP, XML, SOAP, and UDDI.

- **Loosely coupled**   By avoiding shared storage and data, XML Web Services makes the distributed application more resistant to service failures or to services being unavailable.

- **Data types**   The data type used with XML Web Services is XML. XML is used in all areas of XML Web Services. For a refresher on XML, see Chapter 25.

 EXAM TIP   *Loosely coupled* is a key term that usually points to the right answer. Making components loosely coupled makes the component scalable, which is usually the optimum goal.

Building an XML Web Service

You now have the background information about XML Web Services. The next step is the fun part of building some XML Web Services and then consuming them. Although we'll be focusing on the use of C# .NET for our examples, XML Web Services can be built using any of the .NET languages. An XML web service is an ASP.NET project saved with the file extension .asmx, and where the methods have been marked to be published as web methods.

An XML web service is made up of four separate parts:

- The processing directive
- The namespaces
- The public class
- Methods that are web-callable

In the next sections, we will look at how to create an XML web service, as well as identify the parts of the project. We will create an XML web service that will convert between metric and imperial measurements.

Creating the Project

Start the example by creating a new Visual C# project in Visual Studio .NET. Select the ASP.NET Web Service template, call the project `CImperial`, and locate it on the `localhost` server, as shown in Figure 28-3. Click OK, and the project will be created as shown in Figure 28-4.

The first thing you need to do is rename the project files to reflect your names rather than use the default names created by the New Project Wizard. Change the name of the `Service1.asmx` file to `Imperial.asmx`, as shown in Figure 28-5. The note in the middle of the display prompts you to drag objects from the Toolbox or the Project Explorer onto the view, for the object to be part of the service. You can also click on the Imperial.asmx.cs tab to see the source code for the project, as in Figure 28-6.

The source code module has some items added by default, as shown in the following code segment. The following is the complete code generated by the wizard, and we have inserted some explanations to highlight the features.

```csharp
using System;
using System.Collections;
using System.ComponentModel;
using System.Data;
using System.Diagnostics;
using System.Web;
using System.Web.Services;
```

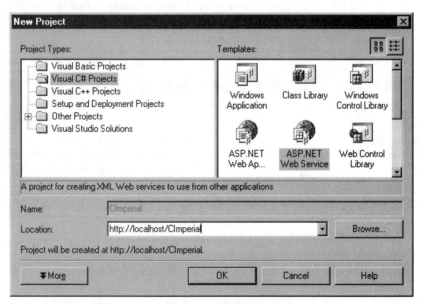

Figure 28-3   The start of the `CImperial` XML web service project

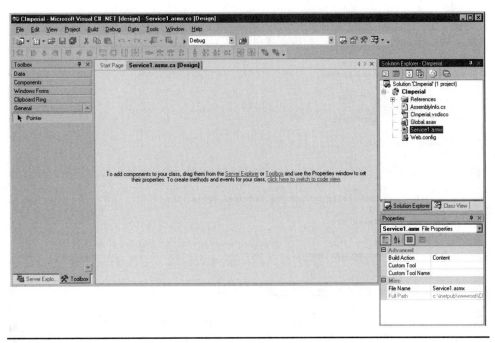

Figure 28-4   The initial display of the project

Figure 28-5
The Solution
Explorer with
the renamed file

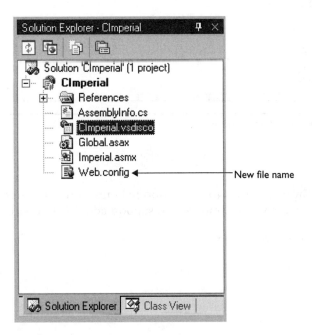

Figure 28-6   The code module

The namespaces that are imported must contain `System.Web.Services`. The other namespaces are imported to support additional services.

```
namespace CImperial
{
```

The preceding line declares that this component is in the CImperial namespace.

```
/// <summary>
/// Summary description for Service1.
/// </summary>
public class Service1 : System.Web.Services.WebService
{
```

The preceding segment declares the public class Service1 and inherits from System.Web.Services.WebService. This makes the class an implementation of an XML web service.

```
public Service1()
{
    //CODEGEN: This call is required by the ASP.NET Web Services Designer
    InitializeComponent();
}
```

The preceding constructor calls InitializeComponent() to perform any custom initialization. The default implementation of InitializeComponent() is an empty body.

```
#region Component Designer generated code

//Required by the Web Services Designer
private IContainer components = null;
```

The preceding line declares a private member of type IContainer to hold references to any components that are added to the XML web service, and it initializes the member to null.

```
/// <summary>
/// Required method for Designer support - do not modify
/// the contents of this method with the code editor.
/// </summary>
private void InitializeComponent()
{
}
```

The preceding initialization function is used by the Visual Studio .NET designer to initialize any components that are added to the XML web service project.

```
/// <summary>
/// Clean up any resources being used.
/// </summary>
protected override void Dispose( bool disposing )
{
    if(disposing && components != null)
    {
        components.Dispose();
```

```
      }
      base.Dispose(disposing);
   }
   #endregion
```

The preceding code is the clean-up code that will iterate through the IComponent member, calling the Dispose() method on all components that have been added to the project. Finally the base class's Dispose() method is called.

```
      // WEB SERVICE EXAMPLE
      // The HelloWorld() example service returns the string Hello World
      // To build, uncomment the following lines then save and build the project
      // To test this web service, press F5
      //       [WebMethod]
      //       public string HelloWorld()
      //       {
      //            return "Hello World";
      //       }
   }
}
```

The preceding code is the last part of the generated code. It is a sample declaration of a web method that will return the string "Hello World" to the caller of the method. The [WebMethod] attribute marks the public HelloWorld() method to be published and callable.

We will enable the sample service, by removing the comments as is seen in the following code segment, to see the XML web service in action.

```
...
      // WEB SERVICE EXAMPLE
      // The HelloWorld() example service returns the string Hello World
      // To build, uncomment the following lines then save and build the project
      // To test this web service, press F5
      [WebMethod]
      public string HelloWorld()
      {
         return "Hello World";
      }
...
```

Once you are done, save the project, and press F5 to build and run the XML web service. The result is that your web browser will start up and display the information page about the XML web service, as shown in Figure 28-7. The note about the default namespace is important, as it makes sure you use your namespace rather than the http://tempuri.org/ namespace that Microsoft has designated as the testing namespace for XML Web Services.

Service1

The following operations are supported. For a formal definition, please review the <u>Service Description</u>.

- <u>HelloWorld</u>

This web service is using http://tempuri.org/ as its default namespace.

Recommendation: Change the default namespace before the XML Web service is made public.

Each XML Web service needs a unique namespace in order for client applications to distinguish it from other services on the Web. http://tempuri.org/ is available for XML Web services that are under development, but published XML Web services should use a more permanent namespace.

Your XML Web service should be identified by a namespace that you control. For example, you can use your company's Internet domain name as part of the namespace. Although many XML Web service namespaces look like URLs, they need not point to actual resources on the Web. (XML Web service namespaces are URIs.)

For XML Web services creating using ASP.NET, the default namespace can be changed using the WebService attribute's Namespace property. The WebService attribute is an attribute applied to the class that contains the XML Web service methods. Below is a code example that sets the namespace to "http://microsoft.com/webservices/":

C#

```
[WebService(Namespace="http://microsoft.com/webservices/")]
public class MyWebService {
    // implementation
}
```

Visual Basic.NET

```
<WebService(Namespace:="http://microsoft.com/webservices/")> Public Class MyWebService
    ' implementation
End Class
```

For more details on XML namespaces, see the W3C recommendation on <u>Namespaces in XML</u>.

For more details on WSDL, see the <u>WSDL Specification</u>.

For more details on URIs, see <u>RFC 2396</u>.

Figure 28-7   The service information page

The name of the only declared web method is listed at the top of the page—click the HelloWorld link to review the SOAP request and response headers that are used to call the web method, as shown in Figure 28-8.

 EXAM TIP   The Service help pages are great for getting the WSDL document (the WSDL document will be explained in the "WSDL" section of this chapter).

Click Invoke to see the XML document that represents the return value from the web method (see Figure 28-9).

Service1

Click here for a complete list of operations.

HelloWorld

Test

To test the operation using the HTTP GET protocol, click the 'Invoke' button.

Invoke

SOAP

The following is a sample SOAP request and response. The **placeholders** shown need to be replaced with actual values.

```
POST /CImperial/Imperial.asmx HTTP/1.1
Host: localhost
Content-Type: text/xml; charset=utf-8
Content-Length: length
SOAPAction: "http://tempuri.org/HelloWorld"

<?xml version="1.0" encoding="utf-8"?>
<soap:Envelope xmlns:xsi="http://www.w3.org/2001/XMLSchema-instance" xmlns:xsd="http://www.w3.org/200
  <soap:Body>
    <HelloWorld xmlns="http://tempuri.org/" />
  </soap:Body>
</soap:Envelope>
```

```
HTTP/1.1 200 OK
Content-Type: text/xml; charset=utf-8
Content-Length: length

<?xml version="1.0" encoding="utf-8"?>
<soap:Envelope xmlns:xsi="http://www.w3.org/2001/XMLSchema-instance" xmlns:xsd="http://www.w3.org/200
  <soap:Body>
    <HelloWorldResponse xmlns="http://tempuri.org/">
      <HelloWorldResult>string</HelloWorldResult>
    </HelloWorldResponse>
  </soap:Body>
</soap:Envelope>
```

Figure 28-8   The SOAP request and response headers

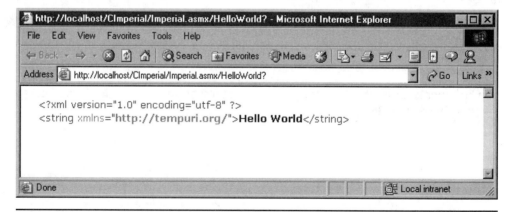

Figure 28-9   The return data from the web method

The default behavior when you call an XML web service directly from a browser is for the .NET Framework to render the service as an information page, listing all the web methods that are defined in the service. This Service page forms the basis for unit testing of the XML web service. For more information on unit testing and debugging of XML Web Services see Chapter 25.

The first thing you need to do with the XML web service is to change the namespace from http://tempuri.org/ to http://xxx.yyy/. You would replace the URI with one for your organization to ensure that you have a unique namespace. Adding the attribute shown in bold in the following listing to the class definition will change the namespace of the XML web service.

```
...
[WebService(Namespace="http://xxx.yyy/")]
public class Service1 : System.Web.Services.WebService
{
...
}
```

Figure 28-10 shows the display that results when the revised project is executed by pressing F5.

Implementing the Web Methods

Now we need to define methods that are callable as web methods. We will continue the metric and imperial conversion XML web service from the last section. In order to make a method available to be called, it must be exposed as a web method. The following code segment exposes the Ckm() and Cmi() methods:

```
[WebMethod]
public double Ckm(double mi)
{ ... }

[WebMethod]
public double Cmi(double km)
{ ... }
```

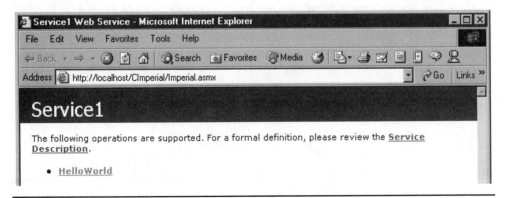

Figure 28-10   The project after the namespace has been set

The methods must be public in scope and marked with the [WebMethod] attribute to be available to service consumers.

To start implementing the conversion service, create the following web methods. The conversions are: 1 mi = 1.609344 km, and 1 km = 0.621371 mi. Comment out the HelloWorld() web method used in the previous section, and add the following definitions to the Imperial.asmx.cs source file.

```
[WebMethod]
public double Ckm(double mi)
{
    return(1.609344 * mi);
}

[WebMethod]
public double Cmi(double km)
{
    return(0.621371 * km);
}
```

Save and execute the XML web service by pressing F5. The resulting display should be as shown in Figure 28-11. Select the Ckm conversion function, and a page requesting the value of the parameter will be displayed, as shown in Figure 28-12. Enter the parameter value (60 miles in this example), and click Invoke to display the resulting calculation, as shown in Figure 28-13.

Perform a test of both methods using a range of values to ensure that the conversion methods work.

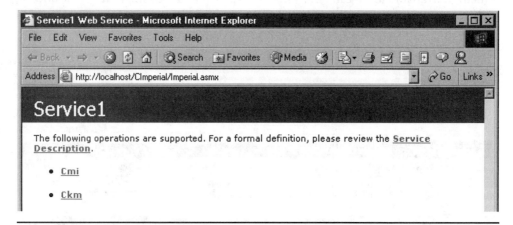

Figure 28-11   The conversion service

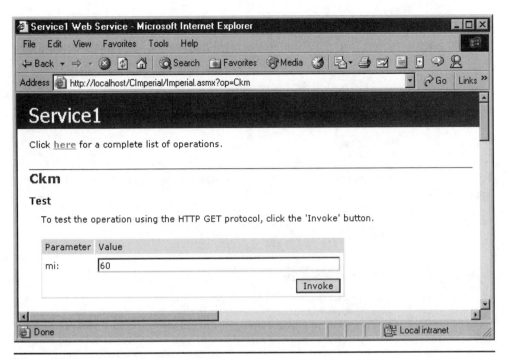

Figure 28-12 Entering the parameter

Figure 28-13 The returned XML result

Setting the Web Method Attributes

The [WebMethod] attribute you used in the previous section has a number of properties that are used to customize the way the WebMethod operates. Table 28-1 describes those properties.

To use the properties with the [WebMethod] attribute, you include the properties in a bracketed list as part of the attribute. The following example sets the CacheDuration to 600 seconds:

```
[WebMethod(CacheDuration = 600)]
```

To add additional parameters, use a comma to separate the properties, as in the following example:

```
[WebMethod(CacheDuration = 600, Description="This is a test")]
```

Property	Description
BufferResponse	The BufferResponse property controls how the response from the WebMethod is returned to the client. If the property is set to True (the default setting), ASP.NET will buffer the entire response before returning anything to the client. This type of buffering is very efficient. If the BufferResponse property is set to False, ASP.NET will send the response in 16KB packets.
CacheDuration	The CacheDuration property controls the lifetime of the cached response. The default setting is 0, which means that caching is disabled for results. The property is in seconds with 0 turning it off, and any other value indicating the amount of time the result should be cached.
Description	This property supplies the description of the WebMethod that will be supplied on the XML web service Help page.
EnableSession	When the EnableSession property is set to True, the WebMethod can use the Session object to maintain state between calls. The default setting is False.
MessageName	You can uniquely identify an overloaded WebMethod by using the MessageName as an alias. The default value of the MessageName property is the name of the WebMethod, and changing the property will publish the new name.
TransactionOption	This property enables the XML web service method to participate as the root object in a transaction using the Microsoft Distributed Transaction Coordinator (MS DTC).

Table 28-1   Attributes for the [WebMethod] Attribute

You can use these attribute properties to modify how the conversion XML web service is defined. To start, replace the two web methods you defined earlier with the following definitions:

```
[WebMethod(CacheDuration = 3,
     Description="This is the miles to km int conversion",
     MessageName = "CkmInt")]
public int Ckm(int mi)
{
   // This is the integer version
   return((1609344 * mi)/1000000);
}
[WebMethod(CacheDuration = 3,
     Description="This is the miles to km double conversion",
     MessageName = "CkmDbl")]
public double Ckm(double mi)
{
   // This is the double version
   return(1.609344 * mi);
}
[WebMethod(CacheDuration = 3,
     Description="This is the miles to km int conversion",
     MessageName = "CmiInt")]
public int Cmi(int km)
{
   // The is the int version
   return((621371 * km)/1000000);
}
[WebMethod(CacheDuration = 3,
     Description="This is the miles to km double conversion",
     MessageName = "CmiDbl")]
public double Cmi(double km)
{
   return(0.621371 * km);
}
```

The use of the `Description` and `MessageName` properties in the preceding code illustrates how you can overload methods in an XML web service.

Save and execute the project by pressing F5. The result should look like what is shown in Figure 28-14. Test the web methods to ensure that they truly work as overloaded functions and that the conversion works.

The Project Files

The different files that are included in the Solution Explorer are part of the project and perform important tasks during the design-time and runtime phases of the XML web service. These files are listed in Table 28-2.

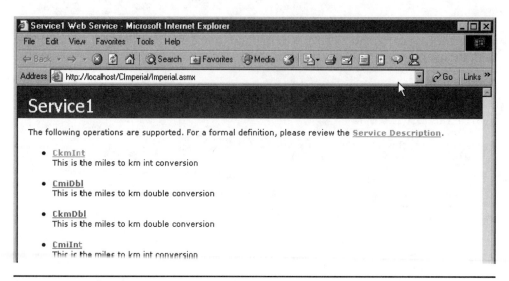

Figure 28-14 The enhanced conversion service

File	Description
Global.asmx	This optional file is located in the root directory of the web application and is used to configure handlers for events raised by the ASP.NET application or session objects. The Global.asmx file cannot be returned to a client browser because the .NET Framework is configured to reject any request for the file. Should a new version of the Global.asmx file be saved into the root directory of the application, the Global.asmx is recompiled when all current connections are closed.
Web.config	This is the configuration file for the XML web service. By using this file, you can configure all aspects of the service, including security. For more information about the Web.config file, see Chapter 30.
.vsdisco file	This is the dynamic discovery document that is used to publish the XML web service. To use dynamic discovery, publish the .vsdisco file rather than the XML web service.
AssemblyInfo.cs	This file contains project information and will be compiled into the XML web service assembly.
/bin folder	This folder off the root of the application is where the compile output of the application will be stored. The /bin folder is also important in that any assembly added to it will be available to the application without any registration.

Table 28-2 Files Used by an XML Web Service

EXAM TIP The /bin directory is very important. Any assemblies copied into the /bin directory are available to the application without any registration.

XML Web Service Consumers

We will now look at how you can create an application that will consume an XML web service. There are a number of different steps, and we will look at them in turn. First, we will revisit the Web Services Description Language (WSDL) and the structure of a WSDL document. Then we will look at the XML web service discovery process. We will also look at the XML web service proxy and how it is generated using wsdl.exe, and we will then implement the consumer using Visual Studio .NET and C# .NET.

WSDL

The Web Services Description Language (WSDL) is an XML grammar that describes an XML web service by defining the messages it accepts and sends. The WSDL document forms a contract between the service provider and the service consumer.

The WSDL document is a list of definitions—indeed the root element of the WSDL document is named <definitions>. Table 28-3 describes the elements that must be present in the <definitions> element.

The best way to see WSDL in action is to look at an XML web service and then describe it using WSDL. The following code has been tagged with attributes and defines a storage-only class (Weather) that has been marked with the [XmlRoot] attribute to be called "forecast". Each of the data members is marked with the [XmlElement] attribute, identifying them as public entities.

```
[XmlRoot("forecast")]
public class Weather
{
    [XmlAttribute("city"]
    public string City;
    [XmlElement("state"]
    public string State;
    [XmlElement("country"]
    public string Country;
    [XmlElement("windspeed"]
    public decimal WindSpeed;
    [XmlElement("winddirection"]
    public string WindDirection;
    [XmlElement("temperature"]
    public decimal Temperature;
    [XmlElement("airpressure"]
    public decimal AirPressure;
    [XmlElement("sky"]
    public string Sky;
}
```

PART V

```
public class WeatherForecast
{
    [WebMethod]
    public Weather GetForecast(string city)
    {
        Weather w = new Weather();
        w.City = "Mimico";
        w.State = "Ontario";
        w.Country = "Canada";
        w.WindSpeed = 5.0;
        w.WindDirection = "NNW";
        w.Temperature = 33.0;
        w.AirPressure = 960.4;
        w.Sky = "Partly cloudy";
        return w;
    }
}
```

Given the C# source code with XML web service attributes we can now start building the WSDL document. The first step is to define the data types that are used in the messages the XML web service supports. This is done by describing them using the Extensible Schema Definition Language (XSD). The namespaces used in this example are s (which is xmlns:s=http://www.w3.org/2001/XMLSchema), and s0, which refers to the namespace of the [WebService]. The data type definition for the Weather class would be as follows:

```
<s:complexType name="Weather">
  <s:sequence>
    <s:element minOccurs="1" maxOccurs="1" name="state" type="s:string" />
    <s:element minOccurs="1" maxOccurs="1" name="country" type="s:string" />
    <s:element minOccurs="1" maxOccurs="1" name="windspeed" type="s:decimal" />
    <s:element minOccurs="1" maxOccurs="1" name="winddirection" type="s:string" />
    <s:element minOccurs="1" maxOccurs="1" name="temperature" type="s:decimal" />
    <s:element minOccurs="1" maxOccurs="1" name="airpressure" type="s:decimal" />
    <s:element minOccurs="1" maxOccurs="1" name="sky" type="s:string" />
  </s:sequence>
  <s:attribute name="city" type="s:string" />
</s:complexType>
```

Element	Description
type	Defines the data types that are used to exchange messages.
message	Describes the messages that are exchanged.
portType	Lists a set of operations and the messages for those operations.
binding	Describes the protocol binding for service operations.
service	Groups ports to provide the web service.

Table 28-3   Some of the Elements in an WSDL Documents

The preceding XSD document represents the following XML document:

```xml
<?xml version="1.0" encoding="utf-8"?>
<forecast city="Mimico">
   <state>Ontario</state>
   <country>Canada</country>
   <windspeed>5.0</windspeed>
   <winddirection>NNW</winddirection>
   <temperature>33.0</temperature>
   <airpressure)960.4</airpressure>
   <sky>Partly Cloudy</sky>
</forecast>
```

Once the data types are defined, you need to define the structure of the messages that are exchanged. In this example, the GetForecast() method is the only WebMethod defined, so inbound messages will have the same name as the method, while outbound messages will have the same name as the method with the word "Response" appended. The following XML segment would be nested inside the type element, and it defines the two messages for our example:

```xml
<s:element name="GetForecast">
   <s:complexType>
      <s:sequence>
         <s:element minOccurs="1" maxOccurs="1" name="city"
                    nillable="true" type="s:string" />
      </s:sequence>
   </s:complexType>
</s:element>
<s:element name="GetForecastResponse">
   <s:complexType>
      <s:sequence>
         <s:element minOccurs="1" maxOccurs="1" name="forecast"
                    nillable="true" type="s0:Weather" />
      </s:sequence>
   </s:complexType>
</s:element>
```

The next step in building the WSDL document is to define the message elements based on the structure just defined. When the message element is defined, it will have one or more part child elements. The part child element is similar to a parameter in a method call. The definition of a request message has all the in and inout parameters, while the response message contains all out and inout parameters as well as the return value. The following code segment defines the request and response messages:

```xml
<message name="GetForecastIN">
   <part name="parameters" element="s0:GetForecast" />
</message>
<message name="GetForecastOut">
   <part name="parameters" element="s0:GetForecastResponse" />
</message>
```

PART V

Now you can start putting the pieces together by declaring the portType element that will define the XML web service and the messages that the service handles. In other words, you define the endpoints for the service. The following lines perform that operation:

```
<portType name"WeatherService">
   <operation name="GetForecast">
      <input message="s0:GetForcastIn" />
      <output message="s0:GetForecastOut" />
   </operation>
</portType>
```

The preceding definition declares the logical endpoints of the service. The next step is to specify how you can bind to the port where the GetForecast operation is available. That is done using the binding element, as in the following code segment:

```
<binding name="WeatherService" type="s0:WeatherService">
   <soap:binding transport-http://schemas.xmlsoap.org/soap/http
                  style="document" />
   <operation name="GetForecast">
     <soap:operation soapAction="http://xxx.yyy/GetForecast" style="document" />
     <input>
       <soap:body use="literal" />
       </input>
     <output>
       <soap:body use="literal" />
     </output>
   </operation>
</binding>
```

The final step you need to take to create the WSDL document is to specify the protocol endpoints that are used to connect to the XML web service. To do this, define the service element as in the following code lines:

```
<service name="WeatherService">
   <port name="WeatherService" binding="s0:WeatherService">
      <soap:address location="http://localhost/Weather/Forecast.asmx" />
   </port>
</service>
```

NOTE The complete code for the preceding WSDL document is available in the Chapter 28 folder on the accompanying CD.

There may seem to be a lot of work involved in producing the WSDL document, but even that can be automated. By opening the XML web service in a browser and selecting Service Description, the entire WSDL file is made available. The exam will not test you on how to create the file automatically though—you will just need to know about the parts that make up the WSDL document.

EXAM TIP The parts of the WSDL document are `type`, `message`, `portType`, `binding`, and `service`. Remember that the order is important.

Discovering XML Web Services

As you saw in the previous section, the WSDL document describes all the aspects of how a consumer should communicate (exchange messages) with an XML web service. In order to use an XML web service, the consumer must be able to find the WSDL document that defines the service. XML web service discovery is the process that a consumer goes through to find an XML web service and learn how to communicate with it.

Earlier in this chapter, you were introduced to the three nodes that make up the architecture of an XML web service—the service provider, service consumer, and service broker. It is the role of the service broker to help service consumers find the description of the XML web service and assist in learning about the service. If the service isn't published through a service broker, you need a method to discover the XML web services that are available at an endpoint. To that end, there is `disco`, a discovery tool that enumerates the XML Web Services that are available at a particular endpoint.

You can make the discovery information available either statically through a `.disco` document, or dynamically which means the discovery document is generated at run time.

Static Discovery

The static discovery is based on a discovery file that is made available to the consumer. The file usually has the extension `.disco`, but that is not enforced. The static discovery file is an XML document that contains the references to the entry points where discovery and contract information can be found.

The following is an example of a static discovery document in which you can see the two main elements: `discoveryRef`, which supplies additional information, and `contractRef`, which points to the document that can supply the contract information.

```
<?xml version="1.0"?>
<discovery xmlns:xsi="http://www.w3.org/2000/10/XMLSchema-instance"
           xmlns:xsd="http://www.w3.org/2000/10/XMLSchema/"
           xmlns="http://schemas.xmlsoap.org/disco/">
   <discoveryRef ref="http://localhost/WeatherService/Weather.disco"/>
   <contractRef ref="http://localhost/WeatherService/Weather.asmx?wsdl"
                docRef="http://localhost/WeatherService/Weather.asmx"
                xmlns="http://schemas.xmlsoap.org/disco/scl/"/>
</discovery>
```

Note the parameter that is passed to the `contractRef` element (`Weather.asmx?wsdl`) that will retrieve the contract information from the XML web service. The `contractRef` can also be a separate XML file that defines the contract.

Dynamic Discovery

Dynamic discovery is not enabled by default. It must be turned on either in the `ma-chine.config` file (which is system-wide) or in the `web.config` application file. Dynamic discovery is enabled by removing the comment from the `.vsdisco` `httpHandler` element, as shown in the following code segment from the `machine .config` file:

```
<httpHandlers>
<!--
    <add verb="*" path="*.vsdisco"
        type="System.Web.Services.Discovery.DiscoveryRequestHandler,
            System.Web.Services, Version=1.0.3300.0, Culture=neutral,
            PublicKeyToken=b03f5f7f11d50a3a"
        validate="false"/>
-->
```

Once the dynamic discovery is enabled, a file named `<XML Web Service name> .vsdisco` must be placed in the root of the application. If Visual Studio .NET is used to create the XML web service, a default `<XML Web Service name>.vsdisco` is placed in the root of the application.

EXAM TIP It is illegal for you to place a `.vsdisco` and a `.disco` file in the same directory.

The following is an example of the file that Visual Studio .NET generated for the `WeatherService`. The file is called `WeatherService.vsdisco`.

```
<?xml version="1.0" encoding="utf-8" ?>
<dynamicDiscovery xmlns="urn:schemas-dynamicdiscovery:disco.2000-03-17">
    <exclude path="_vti_cnf" />
    <exclude path="_vti_pvt" />
    <exclude path="_vti_log" />
    <exclude path="_vti_script" />
    <exclude path="_vti_txt" />
    <exclude path="Web References" />
</dynamicDiscovery>
```

The default is to exclude the private directories from the discovery process. The dynamic discovery process is based on the `.vsdisco` extension being mapped to the `Aspnet_isapi.dll` that performs the discovery. The discovery process searches the folders for files with the extension `.asmx`, `.vsdisco`, and `.disco`—the discovery process ends if one of these extensions cannot be found.

EXAM TIP Enabling dynamic discovery on production servers will expose information about your XML Web Services to anyone on the network, so you should only use dynamic discovery for development environments.

Proxies for XML Web Services

The consumer of an XML web service must be able to properly assemble the messages that are sent to the services, as well as understand how to disassemble the return messages. When you consume XML Web Services, you do so through a proxy class that performs the work of taking your method calls and packaging them up into messages, and vice versa with return messages.

The tool you use to create the proxy is `wsdl.exe`, along with the WSDL document that describes the service. The `wsdl.exe` utility tool has many command-line switches. To see a complete listing, execute this command:

```
wsdl /?
```

In order to generate the proxy, you will need to run the following command:

```
>wsdl /l:cs /o:Wproxy.cs http://localhost/Weather.asmx?WSDL /n:WeatherService
```

This command produces a C# language source file (the `/l:cs` part of the command) in the current directory, and calls the file `Wproxy.cs` (the `/o` part). The information is gleaned from the `Weather.asmx` XML web service in the root of the `localhost`, and the namespace used is `WeatherService`.

The resulting source file needs to be compiled, and the following command performs the compilation:

```
>csc /out:/bin/Wproxy.dll /t:library /r:system.web.dll, system.dll,
system.xml.dll, system.web.services.dll, system.data.dll Wproxy.cs
```

The command compiles and builds a library (`/t:library`), which is placed in the /bin directory and is called `Wproxy.dll`. All the namespaces that are listed after the `/r` command-line switch are the namespaces that will be imported. Finally, the name of the source file is listed.

Building an XML Web Service Consumer

In this section we will consume the XML web service. We will look at two examples to highlight how the service is consumed. The first example will use a console application to consume the imperial to metric converter service created earlier in the chapter. The second will use a Windows Form to do the same.

The procedure outlined in this section can be used to consume XML Web Services with Web Forms or other web services. Irrespective of the consumer application, the steps involved in consuming the XML web service is the same:

1. Create a proxy class for the XML web service.

2. Reference the proxy class in the consumer's code.

PART V

3. Instantiate the proxy in the consumer's code.

4. Call an XML web service method through the instance of the proxy class.

Consuming a Web Service with a Console Application

In this example, we will build a console application that uses the imperial to metric conversion XML web service.

To begin, create a Visual C# project using the Console Application template and call the application mikm, as shown in Figure 28-15.

Add a reference by right-clicking the References node in the Solution Explorer and selecting Add Web Reference. In the Add Web Reference dialog box, enter **http://localhost/CImperial/Imperial.asmx** in the address field, as shown in Figure 28-16, and press ENTER. The Service help page will be displayed in the dialog box.

Click the Add Reference button to add the web reference, and as you add the reference, the proxy class is automatically generated by Visual Studio .NET. Expand the Web References node in the Solution Explorer as shown in Figure 28-17. The node named localhost contains all the references found on the local server. Because the name localhost can be confusing, rename the node to Converter.

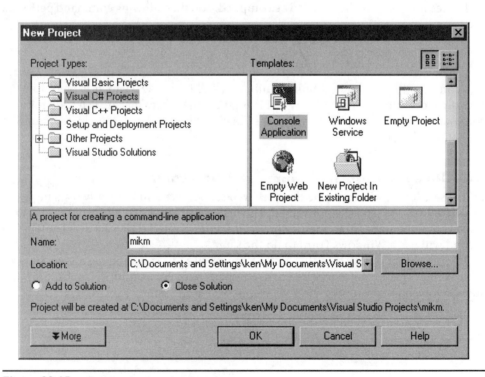

Figure 28-15 Creating the console consumer

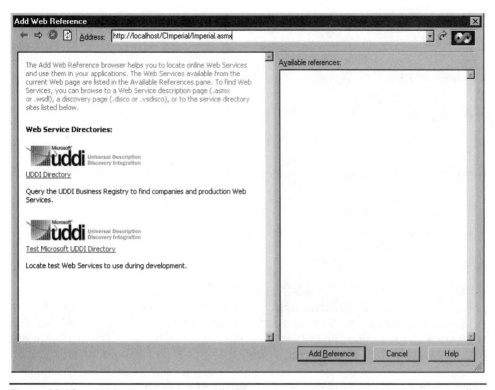

Figure 28-16   The Add Web Reference dialog box

Figure 28-17
The Solution
Explorer showing
the references

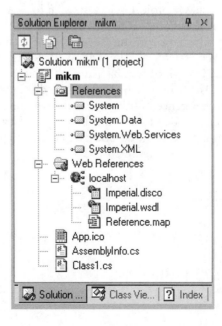

Now you can create the consumer. Enter the following code in the `Class1.cs` source file:

```
using System;
namespace mikm
{
    /// <summary>
    /// Summary description for Class1.
    /// </summary>
    class Class1
    {
        /// <summary>
        /// The main entry point for the application.
        /// </summary>
        [STAThread]
        static void Main(string[] args)
        {
            mikm.Converter.Service1 k = new mikm.Converter.Service1();
            Console.WriteLine(k.Cmi(100));
        }
    }
}
```

In the preceding code, the referenced XML web service is used by declaring a reference (k) to `mikm.Converter.Service1` and then calling the `WebMethod` (`Cmi`) on that reference. Run the application by pressing CTRL-F5 (this way the console will prompt you to press "any key" before closing the console).

Consuming a Web Service with a Windows Form

In this next example, we will consume the same XML web service using a Windows Form.

Start a new Visual C# project, select the Windows Application template, and call the project `Wkimi`, as shown in Figure 28-18.

Add a reference by right-clicking the `References` node in the Solution Explorer and selecting Add Web Reference. The Add Web Reference dialog box will open. Enter **http://localhost/CImperial/Imperial.asmx** in the address field, as shown in Figure 28-19, and press ENTER. The Service help page will be displayed in the dialog box.

Click the Add Reference button to add the web reference, and as you add the reference, the proxy class will automatically be generated by Visual Studio .NET. Expand the `Web References` node in the Solution Explorer, and rename the `localhost` node to `Converter`, as shown in Figure 28-20.

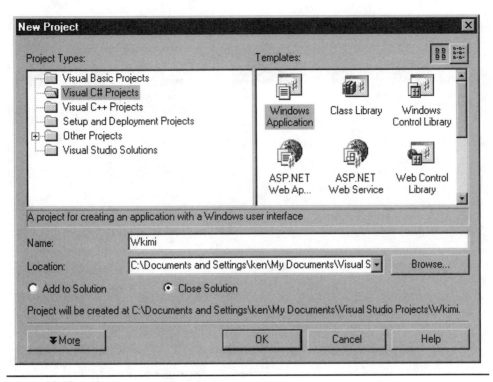

Figure 28-18   Creating the Windows Form

Add two text boxes and a button to the form, and implement the following code in the Button click event.

```
private void button1_Click(object sender, System.EventArgs e)
{
    Wkimi.Converter.Service1 k = new Wkimi.Converter.Service1();
    int i, m;
    m = Int32.Parse(textBox1.Text);
    i = k.Ckm(m);
    textBox2.Text=i.ToString();
}
```

Save and execute the application by pressing the F5 key. Then test it by entering values in textBox1 and clicking the button. Make sure the conversion works.

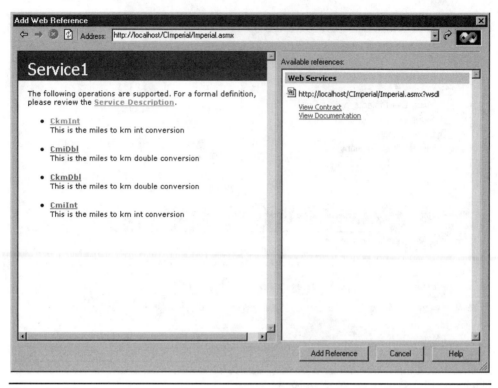

Figure 28-19   Entering the new address in the Address field.

Figure 28-20
The Solution
Explorer with
the renamed
web reference

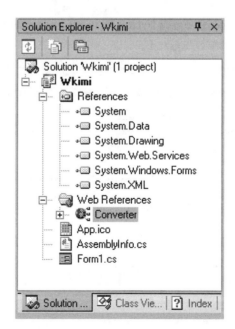

Asynchronous Web Methods

Asynchronous method calls enable components to work together on a problem while being totally disconnected from each other—this is called *asynchronous programming,* or *loose binding.*

The asynchronous process is started by the calling component informing the called component where to send back a message (a callback) when the asynchronous process is complete. The called component starts the processing while the caller continues with other tasks, rather than waiting for the called component to finish. When the called component is finished, it sends a message to the caller by calling the callback. The end result of this type of processing is that there are very few times when the system is blocked and the user needs to wait. For a discussion on callbacks see Chapter 4.

Consider a software component that retrieves information for a sales report from a database. The average time needed to retrieve the information is 20 seconds. A synchronous version of the application would call the software component and wait for the component to return the data. The client would be blocked until the data was returned. Changing the model to an asynchronous communications model will leave the client able to do other things while the data is being retrieved.

There are a number of scenarios in the real world where waiting times are involved—file and database access, network I/O, Web access, and so on. You can take advantage of asynchronous solutions in your software to keep users productive.

The object model of the .NET Framework provides a uniform environment for asynchronous calls across the .NET Framework. A couple of methods are included in classes to provide built-in support for asynchronous calls. For example, the `Stream` class (`System.IO.Stream`) provides the `Read()` method for synchronous calls and the `BeginRead()` and `EndRead()` pair of methods for asynchronous access.

In Chapter 4 you were introduced to delegates—classes that encapsulate function pointers. The asynchronous method call is based on the use of delegates to encapsulate references to callback methods. The methods for creating asynchronous calls use an `AsyncCallback` delegate and two methods `Beginxxx()` and `Endxxx()` of the proxy class. The xxx in the `Beginxxx()` and `Endxxx()` refers to the method name. For example, the `GetForecast()` method would have a `BeginGetForecast()` and an `EndGetForecast()`.

The following procedure describes how the asynchronous call is performed:

1. Instantiate an `AsyncCallback` delegate.

2. Call a `Beginxxx()` method of the proxy, and pass a reference to the proxy.

3. When the callback is called, use the `IAsyncResult` parameter that is passed in order to access the proxy.

4. Call `Endxxx()` to complete the asynchronous call.

The following code expands the functionality of the console consumer used in the previous section. Change the `Class1.cs` source file to the following.

```
using System;
namespace mikm
{
  /// <summary>
  /// Summary description for Class1.
  /// </summary>
  class Class1
  {
    /// <summary>
    /// The main entry point for the application.
    /// </summary>
    [STAThread]
    static void Main(string[] args)
    {
      mikm.Converter.Service1 k = new mikm.Converter.Service1();
      AsyncCallback callback;
      callback = new AsyncCallback(Class1.Callback);
      k.BeginCmi(100,callback,k);
    }
    static void Callback(IAsyncResult ar)
    {
      mikm.Converter.Service1 k = (mikm.Converter.Service1) ar.AsyncState;
      int i = k.EndCmi(ar);
      Console.WriteLine(i);
    }
  }
}
```

Run the application by pressing CTRL-F5 (this way the console will prompt you to press "any key" before closing the console).

 EXAM TIP   The Beginxxx() method is called to start the asynchronous process. The callback method calls the Endxxx() method to end the call and retrieve the return data.

SOAP Extensions

The .NET Framework includes ways and means for us to process the raw SOAP messages before they are deserialized into objects within the Framework or after they are serialized before they are sent on to the consumer. This functionality is included in the SOAP extensions, and they allow us to work with the data outside of the SOAP environment. In order to take advantage of the SOAP extensions, you need to derive one class from System.Web.Services.Protocol.SoapExtension and one class from System.Web.Services.Protocol.SoapExtensionAttribute.

One common reason for using SOAP extensions is to be able to encrypt and decrypt the SOAP headers for transmission. For a full discussion on encryption and SOAP extensions, see Chapter 30.

In order to understand how you can get hold of the raw SOAP messages, you need to understand how the .NET Framework routes SOAP messages. The Framework uses event stages to decide on the routing—when a SOAP message comes in, the server determines which method it will route to, and then it checks to see if there are any extensions, and if so invokes the extensions with the event stage BeforeSerialize.

When the extension returns, the server deserializes the SOAP stream and invokes the methods with the `AfterDeserialize` stage.

Summary

In this chapter, you have met up with one of the .NET distributed components—the XML web service—and you have learned how to create a web service and how to consume it. In terms of the exam, this chapter forms the basis of a handful of the questions, but the concept of how to build XML Web Services and how to consume them is central in the majority of the exam questions.

You also learned about the WSDL document that forms the contract for the XML Web Services and about the five parts that make up the WSDL document: `type`, `message`, `portType`, `binding`, and `service`.

When connecting from a consumer to the XML web service, you need to create a proxy class to encapsulate the web service. The tool that performs that task is `wsdl .exe`, which we also looked at in this chapter. Visual Studio .NET created the proxy when you set a web reference to the service.

SOAP extensions are used to provide raw access to the SOAP stream before it is deserialized.

Test Questions

1. You have found that you need to use SOAP extensions to gain access to the SOAP messages before they have been deserialized. What namespaces must be imported? Select all that apply.

   A. `System.Web.Services.Protocol.SoapExtension`

   B. `System.Web.Services.Protocol.Soap.Extension`

   C. `System.Web.Services.Protocol.Soap,ExtensionAttribute`

   D. `System.Web.Services.Protocol.SoapExtensionAttribute`

2. Your manager has asked you about interoperability between XML Web Services and an existing CORBA environment. What wire protocol will you tell your manager about that will interoperate with CORBA?

   A. RPC

   B. COM+

   C. SOAP

   D. DCOM

3. When discussing the XML Web Services architecture, which sentence best describes the service broker node?

   A. Broadcasts the available services.

   B. Advertises the available services in Active Directory.

    C. Advertises the services that are registered in the Registry.

    D. Assists the consumer to find the provider that supplies a particular web service.

4. You have developed an XML web service that calculates an index to describe the current state of the air in your city. You have coded the following web methods, but when you compile the class, you receive error messages. What code will you change to successfully compile your project?

```
[WebMethod]
public double GetIndex(int x, double y, char a)
{ … }
[WebMethod]
public double GetIndex(int x, int y, char a)
{ … }
```

    A. Add the `System.Web.Service.Overload` namespace to the project.

    B. Add unique `MessageName` properties to the two `WebMethod` attributes.

    C. Change the return data type of the two overloaded methods to make them different.

    D. Change the name of the two web methods to be unique.

5. You want to ensure that your web method uses the cache for results, so you change the web method attribute to `[WebMethod(BufferResponse = true)]`. When you investigate, you find that your web method still is not using the cache. What is the most efficient way of ensuring that your web method uses the cache?

    A. Add `CacheTime=300` to the `WebMethod` attribute.

    B. Add `Cache=true` to the `WebMethod` attribute.

    C. Add `EnableCache=true` to the `WebMethod` attribute.

    D. Add `CacheDuration=300` as a parameter to the `WebMethod` attribute.

6. What is the name of the root element in a WSDL document?

    A. definition

    B. wsdl_root

    C. xml_root

    D. root

7. You need to configure dynamic discovery for your XML web service. What two steps must be performed to enable dynamic discovery? Select two answers.

    A. Provide a `.vsdisco` file in the root folder of the application.

    B. Provide a `.disco` file in the root folder of the application.

    C. Uncomment the `.vsdisco` `httpHandler` entry in the `machine.config` file.

    D. Uncomment the `.dyndisco` `httpHandler` in the `machine.config` file.

8. What sentence best describes loosely coupled components?

   A. Both components use a common event model to communicate.

   B. Both components use public variables and methods to communicate.

   C. Both components use only public methods to communicate.

   D. Both components use asynchronous methods to communicate.

9. You need to build a proxy class for an XML web service. What tool will you use? Select all that apply.

   A. cdc.exe

   B. wsdl.exe

   C. proxy.exe

   D. disco.exe

10. When you create an XML web service, it is stored in a source file. What is the extension of that source file?

    A. .xmls

    B. .asxm

    C. .asmx

    D. .asxml

11. By adding the [WebService(Namespace="http://xxx.yyy")] attribute in front of the class that defines the XML web service, you modify a namespace. What is that namespace?

    A. The namespace of the XML web service.

    B. The default namespace of the SOAP messages.

    C. The namespace of the ASP.NET server.

    D. The default URL that all redirections will go to.

12. By setting the EnableSession property to True, you have access to what resources?

    A. Nothing. You need to create the session first.

    B. Session variables.

    C. Application variables.

    D. Local variables stored in the Web Method session.

13. The XML web service broker stores information about the XML web services that have published their services to the broker. What structure does the service broker store the information in?

    A. Broker registry.

    B. Windows Registry.

      C. UDDI registry.

      D. XML document.

  14. True or false? XML documents contain the data model of the data they contain.

      A. True

      B. False

  15. After creating a proxy class, you compile it. What type of file will the proxy be compiled to?

      A. `.dll`

      B. `.asmx`

      C. `.aspx`

      D. `.proxy`

Test Answers

  1. **A and D.** The other namespaces do not exist.

  2. **C.** RPC is Windows only, COM+ is not a protocol—it is an environment, and DCOM is the same as RPC.

  3. **D.**

  4. **B.** The namespace in A does not exist, C is syntactically wrong, and D would break the design of the overloaded methods.

  5. **D.** The other properties do not exist.

  6. **A.**

  7. **A and C.**

  8. **D.** By using asynchronous method calls, the two components are truly loosely coupled. Answer C could be a good answer as well, but the question said "best describes." A and B are examples of how not to build component models.

  9. **B.**

  10. **C.**

  11. **A.**

  12. **B.**

  13. **C.**

  14. **A.**

  15. **A.**

Data Again

In this chapter, you will

- Create and manipulate `DataSet` objects
- Access and manipulate data from a Microsoft SQL Server database
- Create and manipulate XML data

The data-driven application is the most common type of application that you will be working with, and this importance is echoed in the XML Web Services exam. In this chapter, we will round out our coverage of data technologies by looking at how you can implement XML web services that both expose and consume data.

The move to use XML documents both as the source and the client storage of data means that we need to look at how you can create an XML document from an existing ADO.NET `DataSet` and directly from Microsoft SQL Server.

This chapter will mostly consist of exercises that will show the code and techniques needed to understand the questions on the exam. For a review of the basics of ADO.NET and the SQL language, see Chapter 10.

ADO.NET and XML Web Services

The emergence of ADO.NET with the .NET Framework has made the use of disconnected data environments an almost automatic choice. The use of disconnected environments makes applications more scalable and more responsive for the end user. When you develop XML web services that use data, you will almost certainly take advantage of the disconnected nature of the `DataSet` object in ADO.NET.

Before we look at the `DataSet` object, though, we need to revisit the objects in ADO.NET and see how they relate to each other.

The ADO Objects Revisited

The objects in ADO.NET are divided into two major classes: the `DataSet` classes and the .NET data provider classes:

- A DataSet class manages data storage and management in a disconnected in-memory cache. The DataSet class is totally independent of the underlying data source.

- A .NET data provider class is specific to the type of data source used. The functionality of the .NET data provider classes includes the ability to connect to, retrieve data from, modify data in, and update data sources.

DataSet Classes

A DataSet object can have multiple tables associated with it. The tables are accessed through a Tables property that refers to a collection of DataTable objects that are in the DataSet. If the tables have relationships between them, those relationships are available through the Relations property, which refers to a collection of DataRelation objects in the DataSet.

By using the DataRelation object, you can join two tables together to programmatically read the data in a parent/child relationship.

.NET Data Providers

The ADO.NET classes contain .NET data providers that encapsulate the connection to a data source, as well as the functionality to read, change, and update data in the data source. The .NET data providers are designed to be lightweight and provide a minimal abstraction layer between the data source and your code. Microsoft supplies three .NET data providers, for SQL Server, OLE DB, and ODBC providers. The objects that form the .NET data providers are XxxConnection, XxxCommand, XxxDataReader, and XxxDataAdapter objects. These objects are named with a prefix (shown as Xxx to indicate the generic name) that indicates what database technology they are used with, as shown in Table 29-1.

 EXAM TIP Remember what provider works with what database—this is knowledge that will be tested in the exam.

Some of these .NET data provider objects have child objects associated with them. For example, the XxxConnection object has an XxxTransaction object and an XxxError object that expose underlying functionality.

Generic Object Name	Specific Object Names
XxxConnection	SqlConnection, OleDbConnection
XxxCommand	SqlCommand, OleDbCommand
XxxDataReader	SqlDataReader, OleDbDataReader
XxxDataAdapter	SqlDataAdapter, OleDbDataAdapter

Table 29-1 Names of .NET Data Provider Objects

The `XxxDataAdapter` lets you can manage the disconnected side of the ADO.NET environment by acting as the manager of the `XxxConnection` and `DataSet` objects. You can use the `XxxDataAdapter` to populate the `DataSet` and to update the data source with any changes that have been made to the `DataSet`.

One important point that cannot be mentioned often enough is that the SQL Server provider (`SqlConnection`, `SqlCommand`, `SqlDataReader`, and `SqlDataAdapter`) only works with Microsoft SQL Server version 7 or higher. You can also use the OLE DB providers with the SQL Servers if you want, and that can be a very good technique when you want to be able to use the same code to access different data sources and to just change the connection string.

Connection Strings

In order to create a connection to a data source, you need to create a connection string that provides the `XxxConnection` object with information about the database, authentication account, password, and connection options. The connection string you build will define the context of the connection.

The parameters of the connection string will differ somewhat depending on the data provider—they are listed in Table 29-2.

The connection string can be built manually by entering the parameters by hand, or you can use Visual Studio .NET to build the string for you. Either way, the type of ADO.NET provider is the important part.

 EXAM TIP Remember that a connection string with a Provider parameter is not for use with the `SqlConnection` object.

Parameter	Description
Provider	The OLE DB provider to use. This parameter is only used with the OLE DB .NET data provider.
Initial Catalog	The name of the database to connect to.
Data Source	The name (or address) of the database server to connect to.
User ID	The username if connecting using SQL Server Authentication.
Password	The password to use if connecting using SQL Server Authentication.
Trusted Connection	This can be True or False. It specifies whether the connection will be encrypted.
Persist Security Information	The setting that specifies whether sensitive security information is to be re-sent if a connection is reopened. The default is False, and changing this property to True can be a security risk.

Table 29-2 Connection String Parameters

DataSets

The `DataSet` object in ADO.NET represents data in a local in-memory cache and provides the functions for accessing the data regardless of where the data originated. It is a disconnected representation of the data, and it does not have to be connected to the data source for the data to be available.

The data in a `DataSet` is organized much as data is represented in a relational database. The `DataSet` uses the `DataTable` collection to represent the tables—a `DataTable` represents one table of in-memory data, and it uses the `DataColumn` collection to represent the columns of the `DataTable`. The `DataSet` presents a relational view of the data, and the data can optionally be represented in XML format. We will look at the XML representation later in this chapter.

DataSet Schemas

The terms "schema" and "data model" are used interchangeably to describe how the `DataSet` is built, that is, how the data is separated into tables. The schema ensures that the data in the `DataSet` is presented in a normalized fashion. The process of designing the schema is called *data modeling*, a mathematical process that takes any data and breaks it into entities (tables) in such a way that the data is only stored once in the schema. The end result of the data-modeling design is that the database is normalized.

The exam will not test you on your data-modeling skills; rather, the questions will focus on the implementation of the schema and the use of the `DataSet`. We will follow this plan by looking at the different objects and at how they are used with the `DataSet`.

Database Objects

The basic objects we need to work with are the `DataSet`, `DataTable`, and `DataColumn` objects. Using these three objects, you can implement any schema. Let's start by looking at where the `DataSet` fits into the scheme of things. Figure 29-1 shows the relationship between the database and the `DataSet` object. The `DataSet` itself can be seen in Figure 29-2, where the relationships between the objects are shown.

When you model (design the schema for) a `DataSet`, you can use constraints to guarantee that the data that is inserted into or deleted from a `DataTable` meets the business rules for that data. There are two types of constraints available: a `UniqueConstraint`

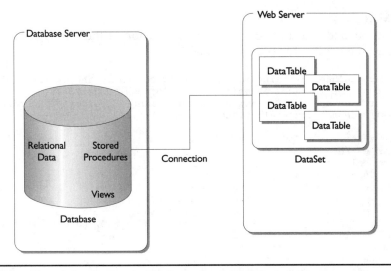

Figure 29-1   The relationship between the database and the `DataSet` object

ensures that the data entered into a `DataColumn` of a `DataTable` is unique, and the `ForeignKeyConstraint` verifies that data entered in the `DataColumn` already exists in a referenced `DataColumn`.

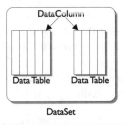

Figure 29-2   The relationships between the `DataSet` objects

Constraints

Constraints are added to the `Constraints` collection of the `DataTable` object, as you can see in the following code segment:

```
// Create an UniqueConstraint on the OrderID column on the Orders table
DataColumn dcOrderID = ds.Tables["Orders"].Columns["OrderID"];
UniqueConstraint ucOrderID = new UniqueConstraint("UC_OrderID",dcOrderID);
ds.Tables["Orders"].Constraints.Add(ucOrderID);

// Create a ForeignKeyConstraint
DataColumn parentCol;
DataColumn childCol;
ForeignKeyConstraint dsFKC;
// Set parent and child column variables.
parentCol = ds.Tables["Orders"].Columns["OrderID"];
childCol = ds.Tables["Orders"].Columns["OrderID"];
dsFKC = new ForeignKeyConstraint("OrderIDFKConstraint", parentCol, childCol);
// Set null values when a value is deleted.
dsFKC.DeleteRule = Rule.SetNull;
dsFKC.UpdateRule = Rule.Cascade;
dsFKC.AcceptRejectRule = AcceptRejectRule.Cascade;
// Add the constraint, and set EnforceConstraints to true.
ds.Tables["Order Details"].Constraints.Add(dsFKC)
ds.EnforceConstraints = True
```

The constraints fill the same function as do their database counterparts—if one of the constraints is violated, the operation will throw an exception that can be caught using a `try... catch` construction.

The Data Model

When you implement a schema, you need to create the `DataSet` object and then add `DataTable` objects to it. Finally, the `DataColumn` objects are added to the `DataTable`. The first thing you need before you create the `DataSet` is a data model (schema) to implement. Figure 29-3 shows the data model for the `DataSet` we will work with in the next section. In this `DataSet`, we have removed the relationships between the tables to make the model easier to read.

The four tables contain the core data that describe a customer order. Each table has columns with properties like name, data type, and length, and we will use these values when we build the objects.

Building a DataSet

In this section, we will build a `DataSet` object that reflects the data model (schema) in Figure 29-3. Start by creating a new Visual C# project in Visual Studio .NET, and select the ASP.NET Web Service template. Name the project `DataSet1`, and locate it on the `localhost` server, as shown in the following illustration.

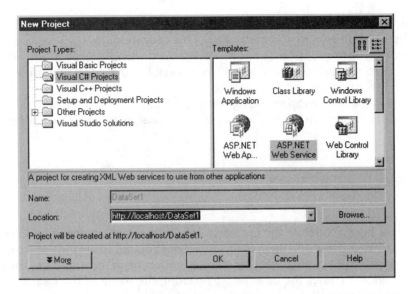

Once the project is created, open the code module for the XML web service. You will need to add some code to the code module that will create the `DataSet`.

Order Details *

Column Name	Data Type	Length	Allow Nulls
OrderID	int	4	
ProductID	int	4	
UnitPrice	money	8	
Quantity	smallint	2	
Discount	real	4	

Customers *

Column Name	Data Type	Length	Allow Nulls
CustomerID	nchar	5	
CompanyName	nvarchar	40	
ContactName	nvarchar	30	✓
ContactTitle	nvarchar	30	✓
Address	nvarchar	60	✓
City	nvarchar	15	✓
Region	nvarchar	15	✓
PostalCode	nvarchar	10	✓
Country	nvarchar	15	✓
Phone	nvarchar	24	✓
Fax	nvarchar	24	✓

Products *

Column Name	Data Type	Length	Allow Nulls
ProductID	int	4	
ProductName	nvarchar	40	
SupplierID	int	4	✓
CategoryID	int	4	✓
QuantityPerUnit	nvarchar	20	✓
UnitPrice	money	8	✓
UnitsInStock	smallint	2	✓
UnitsOnOrder	smallint	2	✓
ReorderLevel	smallint	2	✓
Discontinued	bit	1	

Orders *

Column Name	Data Type	Length	Allow Nulls
OrderID	int	4	
CustomerID	nchar	5	✓
EmployeeID	int	4	✓
OrderDate	datetime	8	✓
RequiredDate	datetime	8	✓
ShippedDate	datetime	8	✓
ShipVia	int	4	✓
Freight	money	8	✓
ShipName	nvarchar	40	✓
ShipAddress	nvarchar	60	✓
ShipCity	nvarchar	15	✓
ShipRegion	nvarchar	15	✓

Figure 29-3   The data model

The first thing that needs to be checked is that the System.Data namespace is included in the list of namespaces at the start of the code module—System.Data is the namespace needed to support DataSet objects. You will also need to add additional namespaces to support specific ADO.NET providers, but that can wait until you set up the database connection.

Next, declare a private variable to represent the DataSet—call the variable ds. Then create a public method in the Service1 class with a signature as shown here:

```
...
DataSet ds;
...
public void makeDataSet()
{
}
```

Now you have a variable for the DataSet, so you can go ahead and create the DataTable objects and add them to the DataSet. You can create the DataTable objects by using the Add() method of the Tables collection in the DataSet. The following code segment creates the DataSet by passing the name of the DataSet to the constructor, and then creates the four DataTable objects.

```
public void makeDataSet()
{
    ds = new DataSet("OrderSet");
    DataTable dtOrderDetails = ds.Tables.Add("Order Details");
    DataTable dtCustomers = ds.Tables.Add("Customers");
    DataTable dtProducts = ds.Tables.Add("Products");
    DataTable dtOrders = ds.Tables.Add("Orders");
}
```

The next step is to add the columns to the DataTable objects. The technique for this is similar to adding the DataTable objects to the DataSet—the DataTable object has a Columns collection, and you can use the Add() method to add the columns to the DataTable. The following code line shows a Column object being added to a DataTable object:

```
DataColumn colODOrderID = dtOrderDetails.Columns.Add("OrderID", typeof(Int32));
```

The data type that is used for the dtOrderID column must be a valid data type in the .NET Framework. You need to use the typeof() method to pass the data type rather than just using the data type itself.

Adding the remaining columns to the DataTable objects results in the following code listing. Please note the .NET Framework data types and how they map to the Microsoft SQL Server data types:

```
public void makeDataSet()
{
    ds = new DataSet("OrderSet");
    DataTable dtOrderDetails = ds.Tables.Add("Order Details");
    DataTable dtCustomers = ds.Tables.Add("Customers");
    DataTable dtProducts = ds.Tables.Add("Products");
```

```
DataTable dtOrders = ds.Tables.Add("Orders");
DataColumn colODOrderID =
      dtOrderDetails.Columns.Add("OrderID", typeof(Int32));
DataColumn colODProductID =
      dtOrderDetails.Columns.Add("ProductID", typeof(Int32));
DataColumn colUnitPrice =
      dtOrderDetails.Columns.Add("UnitPrice", typeof(Double));
DataColumn colQuantity =
      dtOrderDetails.Columns.Add("Quantity", typeof(Double));
DataColumn colDiscount =
      dtOrderDetails.Columns.Add("Discount", typeof(Double));

DataColumn colCustomerID =
      dtCustomers.Columns.Add("CustomerID", typeof(String));
DataColumn colCompanyName =
      dtCustomers.Columns.Add("CompanyName", typeof(String));
DataColumn colContactName =
      dtCustomers.Columns.Add("ContactName", typeof(String));
DataColumn colContactTitle =
      dtCustomers.Columns.Add("ContactTitle", typeof(String));
DataColumn colAddress =
      dtCustomers.Columns.Add("Address", typeof(String));
DataColumn colCity =
      dtCustomers.Columns.Add("City", typeof(String));
DataColumn colRegion =
      dtCustomers.Columns.Add("Region", typeof(String));
DataColumn colPostalCode =
      dtCustomers.Columns.Add("OrderID", typeof(String));
DataColumn colCountry =
      dtCustomers.Columns.Add("Country", typeof(String));
DataColumn colPhone =
      dtCustomers.Columns.Add("Phone", typeof(String));
DataColumn colFax =
      dtCustomers.Columns.Add("Fax", typeof(String));

DataColumn colProductID =
      dtProducts.Columns.Add("ProductID", typeof(Int32));
DataColumn colProductName =
      dtProducts.Columns.Add("ProductName", typeof(String));
DataColumn colSupplierID =
      dtProducts.Columns.Add("SupplierID", typeof(Int32));
DataColumn colCategoryID =
      dtProducts.Columns.Add("CategoryID", typeof(Int32));
DataColumn colQuantityPerUnit =
      dtProducts.Columns.Add("QuantityPerUnit", typeof(String));
DataColumn colPUnitPrice =
      dtProducts.Columns.Add("UnitPrice", typeof(Double));
DataColumn colUnitsInStock =
      dtProducts.Columns.Add("UnitsInStock", typeof(Int32));
DataColumn colUnitsOnOrder =
      dtProducts.Columns.Add("UnitsOnOrder", typeof(Int32));
DataColumn colReorderLevel =
     dtProducts.Columns.Add("ReorderLevel", typeof(Int32));
DataColumn colDiscontinued =
      dtProducts.Columns.Add("Discontinued", typeof(Boolean));

DataColumn colOrderID =
      dtOrders.Columns.Add("OrderID", typeof(Int32));
DataColumn colOCustomerID =
```

```
        dtOrders.Columns.Add("CustomerID", typeof(String));
    DataColumn colEmployeeID =
        dtOrders.Columns.Add("EmployeeID", typeof(Int32));
    DataColumn colOrderDate =
        dtOrders.Columns.Add("OrderDate", typeof(DateTime));
    DataColumn colRequiredDate =
        dtOrders.Columns.Add("RequiredDate", typeof(DateTime));
    DataColumn colShippedDate =
        dtOrders.Columns.Add("ShippedDate", typeof(DateTime));
    DataColumn colShipVia =

        dtOrders.Columns.Add("ShipVia", typeof(Int32));
    DataColumn colFreight =
        dtOrders.Columns.Add("Freight", typeof(Double));
    DataColumn colShipName =
        dtOrders.Columns.Add("ShipName", typeof(String));
    DataColumn colShipAddress =
        dtOrders.Columns.Add("ShipAddress", typeof(String));
    DataColumn colShipCity =
        dtOrders.Columns.Add("ShipCity", typeof(String));
    DataColumn colShipRegion =
        dtOrders.Columns.Add("ShipRegion", typeof(String));
}
```

Now we need to look at a concept that you'll need before you complete this example later in the chapter. The `DataTable` objects in the `DataSet` are related to each other, and you can implement that relationship by using a couple of objects available in the `DataSet` object.

DataSet Relationships

The relationship between tables in a schema is modeled using primary key and foreign key constraints that are combined using a `DataRelation` object. Let's start with a refresher of the relationship terminology.

Using Primary and Foreign Key Constraints

The *primary key* is a structure in a table that can consist of one or more columns that are guaranteed not to have any duplications. The primary key is usually implemented as a unique index. One common candidate for a primary key is a column that represents the ID of the data stored in the table, such as an OrderID. The primary key is used to ensure the uniqueness of the data stored in the rows of that table.

The *foreign key* is a constraint on a table that references one or more columns in that table to a primary key on a different table in the database. The reference is such that no entry of data is allowed in the table if there is no corresponding entry in the primary key column of the other table. For example, you could not enter data into the Orders Details table for an order that had not been entered into the Orders table first (the OrderID must already be inserted in the Orders table).

In the context of foreign keys, the table that has the primary-key constraint is called the *parent table*, and the table that has the foreign-key constraint is called the *child table*. The relationship between the tables is a one-to-many relationship, where the parent table represents the "one" side and the child table represents the "many" side. Figure 29-4 shows the relationships in the `DataSet` we have been building.

The foreign key constraint can be used to restrict what actions can be performed on the two tables that are connected through this relationship of primary key and foreign key. There are two operations that have actions defined for the relationship—`Delete` and `Update`. The `Delete` operation has a `DeleteRule` property in the foreign key constraint, and the `Update` operation has an `UpdateRule` property. These properties can be set to one of the four `Rule` values:

- Cascade—When a value in the primary key changes, the corresponding action is performed in the foreign key. This is the default behavior.

- SetNull—Sets the value in the foreign key to `DBNull`.

- SetDefault—Sets the value in the foreign key to the default value for the column(s).

- None—Performs no action, but it raises an exception so you can customize the processing.

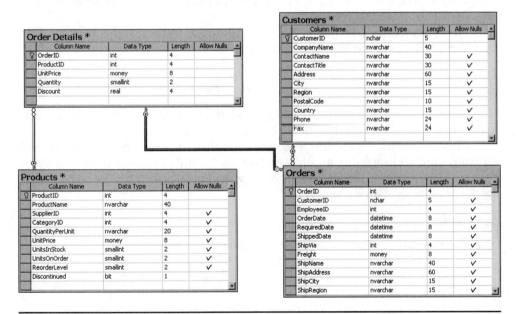

Figure 29-4 The `DataSet` with relationships

EXAM TIP Remember that the primary key is the *one* (unique) side of the relationship, and the foreign key is the *many* side.

To set the specific action for the foreign key constraint, you use code similar to the following code segment:

```
ForeignKeyConstraint dsFKC;
// Set parent and child column variables.
parentCol = ds.Tables["Orders"].Columns["OrderID"];
childCol = ds.Tables["Orders"].Columns["OrderID"];
dsFKC = New ForeignKeyConstraint("OrderIDFKConstraint", parentCol, childCol);
// Set null values when a value is deleted.
dsFKC.DeleteRule = Rule.SetNull;
dsFKC.UpdateRule = Rule.Cascade;
```

Navigating Related Data

The `DataSet` object represents data in tables and columns, but does not provide the functionality to retrieve and work with data using relationships—the `DataRelation` object performs that task, as well as enforcing referential constraints.

The `DataRelation` object is the final object for us to look at in the `DataSet`. It is used to define the relationship between two tables in a `DataSet`. The typical relationship is that two tables are linked by one column in each table that represents the same data, such as an `OrderID` column.

To create a `DataRelation` object, you add it to the `Relations` collection of the `DataSet` object, as in the following code segment:

```
ds.Relations.Add("FK_CustOrder", dtCustomers.Columns["CustomerID"],
                 dtOrders.Columns["CustomerID"]);
```

The `DataRelation` object was added by providing the primary and foreign key constraints to the `Add()` method of the `Relations` collection.

The benefit of creating the `DataRelation` is that you can now navigate the parent/child structure programmatically—without the `DataRelation` object, that would not have been possible. The following code segment iterates through the `DataSet` using the `DataRelation` we just created.

```
foreach(DataRow drCustomer in ds.Tables["Customer"].Row)
{
    foreach(DataRow drOrder in drCustomer.GetChildRows{
                              dataset.Relations["PersonPet"])
    {
        // Process the data in the row
    }
}
```

Adding Constraints and Working with Data

Let's go back to the example we started earlier in the chapter. We'll add data to the `DataSet` and retrieve the data through the XML web service help application. If you closed the project earlier, open the DataSet1 project now.

Constraint	On Object	Constraint Name
UniqueConstraint	dtProducts.Columns["ProductID"]	ucProdID
UniqueConstraint	dtCustomers.Columns["CustomerID"]	ucCustID
UniqueConstraint	dtOrders.Columns["OrderID"]	ucOrdID
ForeignKeyConstraint	dtOrderDetails.Columns["ProductID"] to dtProducts.Columns["ProductID"]	fcProdID
ForeignKeyConstraint	dtOrderDetails.Columns["OrderID"] to dtOrders.Columns["OrderID"]	fcOrdID
ForeignKeyConstraint	dtOrders.Columns["CustomerID"] to dtCustomers.Columns["CustomerID"]	fcCustId
DataRelation	ucCust to fcCust	
DataRelation	ucOrdID to fcOrdID	
DataRelation	ucProdID to fcProdID	

Table 29-3   The Constraints for the DataSet1 Project

You first need to add some constraints and one relation in order to relate the four DataTable objects in the DataSet. The constraints are listed in Table 29-3.

The code that adds these constraints should be added to the end of the makeDataSet() method. It should look like the following code.

```
public void makeDataSet()
{
// add the constraints to the dataset
   UniqueConstraint ucProdID = new UniqueConstraint(
        "UC_ProdID",dtProducts.Columns["ProductID"]);
   dtProducts.Constraints.Add(ucProdID);
   UniqueConstraint ucCustID = new UniqueConstraint(
        "UC_CustID",dtCustomers.Columns["CustomerID"]);
   dtCustomers.Constraints.Add(ucCustID);
   UniqueConstraint ucOrdID = new UniqueConstraint("
        UC_OrdID",dtOrders.Columns["OrderID"]);
   dtOrders.Constraints.Add(ucOrdID);
   DataColumn cCol = dtOrderDetails.Columns["ProductID"];
   DataColumn pCol = dtProducts.Columns["ProductID"];
   ForeignKeyConstraint fcProdID = new ForeignKeyConstraint(
        "FK_ProdID", pCol, cCol);
   dtOrderDetails.Constraints.Add(fcProdID);
   cCol = dtOrderDetails.Columns["OrderID"];
   pCol = dtOrders.Columns["OrderID"];
   ForeignKeyConstraint fcOrdID = new ForeignKeyConstraint(
        "FK_OrdID", pCol, cCol);
   dtOrderDetails.Constraints.Add(fcOrdID);
   cCol = dtOrders.Columns["CustomerID"];
   pCol = dtCustomers.Columns["CustomerID"];
   ForeignKeyConstraint fcCustID = new ForeignKeyConstraint(
        "FK_CustID", pCol, cCol);
   dtOrders.Constraints.Add(fcCustID);
   ds.Relations.Add("FK_Cust", dtCustomers.Columns["CustomerID"],
                       dtOrders.Columns["CustomerID"]));
```

```
    ds.Relations.Add("FK_Ord", dtOrders.Columns["OrderID"],
                            dtOrderDetails.Columns["OrderID"]);
    ds.Relations.Add("FK_Prod", dtProducts.Columns["ProductID"],
                            dtOrderDetails.Columns["ProductID"]);
}
```

Once you have defined the schema (data model) for the DataSet, you need to enter some data. For this example, we will only enter some rows for each DataTable so that we have some data to test with. The following list shows the data we will enter into the Customers DataTable.

- CustomerID: 42
- CompanyName: Merl & Son, International Winery
- ContactName: Merl
- ContactTitle: Chief Bottle Washer and CEO
- Address: Storgatan 12
- City: Stockholm
- Region:
- PostalCode: SE-110 15
- Country: Sweden
- Phone: +46 08 113 45
- Fax: +46 08 113 46

We will also add some other customers to our DataSet—you can pick random information for this example.

You can insert information into a DataTable with one of two methods. The first method uses the DataRow object and an index into the DataRow to identify the DataColumn. The following code segment will insert some columns into a row; the new row is created by the utility method NewRow(), which is part of the DataTable.

```
DataRow drCustomer = dtCustomers.NewRow()
drCustomer[0] = 42;
drCustomer[1] = "Merl & Son, International Winery";
...
drCustomer[10] = "+46 08 113 46";
```

The index of the DataRow object can also be used with the DataColumn name, as in the following line of code:

```
drCustomer["City"] = "Stockholm";
```

After the data is added to the DataRow object, the DataRow must be added to the DataTable object's Rows collection, as shown in this code segment:

```
dtCustomers.Rows.Add(drCustomer);
```

The second method of inserting data is by using the Add() method of the Rows collection of the DataTable object. In this method, you create a new object that will represent the entire row, and it is initialized by passing a comma-delimited list of data values, as shown in the following code segment:

```
DataTable dtCustomers = ds.Tables["Customers"];
dtCustomers.Rows.Add(new Object[] {42, "Merl & Son, International Winery",
    "Merl", "Chief Bottle Washer and CEO", "Storgatan 12",
    "Stockholm", "", "SE-110 15", "Sweden",
    "+46 08 113 45", "+46 08 113 46" });
```

 NOTE You can also load data from an XML document into the DataSet, and we will look at that topic in the "XML Data" section later in this chapter.

Now you know how to add data to populate the DataSet in the DataSet1 project. You need to create a new method in the Service1 class with the following signature:

```
public void populateDataSet();
```

Implement the populateDataSet() method to add some customers to the DataSet (ds), as in the previous code segment, and feel free to add more customers.

Once you have populated the Customers table, you will need to populate the Products table—use the data in Table 29-4 to populate the DataSet. The columns that are not listed should be set to 0 (zero) for numeric data types and "" (empty string) for string types. This code also goes in the populateDataSet() method.

The resulting code that is added to the end of the populateDataSet() method should look like this:

```
DataTable dtProducts = ds.Tables["Products"];
dtProducts.Rows.Add(new Object[] {42, "Universal Answer", 0, 0,
                                  "", 1242.34, 1, 0, 0, 0});
dtProducts.Rows.Add(new Object[] {12, "Whitby Herring", 0, 0,
                                  "", 4.12, 150, 0, 0, 0});
dtProducts.Rows.Add(new Object[] {7, "Mimico Tuna", 0, 0,
                                  "", 42.12, 65, 0, 0, 0});
```

Now that you have customers and products entered, you can create orders for those customers. The first step is to define the order that will be inserted in the Orders DataTable. The data in Table 29-5 should be inserted, again using 0 (zero) for numeric values and empty strings for string values for columns that are not in the table.

ProductID	ProductName	UnitPrice	UnitsInStock
42	Universal answer	1242.34	1
12	Whitby herring	4.12	150
7	Mimico tuna	42.12	65

Table 29-4   The Data for the Product DataTable

OrderID	CustomerID	OrderDate	RequiredDate	ShippedDate
1	42	Today's date	5 days	Today's date

Table 29-5   The Order Data for the Orders `DataTable`

The code that inserts the data in the Orders `DataTable` should look like this:

```
DataTable dtOrders = ds.Tables["Orders"];
...
DateTime dtNow = DateTime.Today;
dtOrders.Rows.Add(new Object[] {1, 42, 0, dtNow , dtNow.AddDays(5),
                                dtNow, 0, 0.0, "", "", "", ""});
```

The final step in populating the `DataSet` is to add the details of the order to the Order Details `DataTable`. The data is in Table 29-6.

The code should be similar to this code segment.

```
DataTable dtOrderDetails = ds.Tables["Order Details"];
...
dtOrderDetails.Rows.Add(new Object[] {1, 42, 4200.00, 1, 0.00});
dtOrderDetails.Rows.Add(new Object[] {1, 12, 6.00, 40, 0.00});
dtOrderDetails.Rows.Add(new Object[] {1, 7, 73.05, 6, 0.00});
```

That is it. The XML web service is almost ready. All that is left is to create the web method and call your processing methods to generate the `DataSet`. Enter the following code in the `Service1` class:

```
[WebMethod]
public DataSet GetData()
{
    makeDataSet();
    populateDataSet();
    return ds;
}
```

Save and execute the XML web service by pressing F5. The resulting window is shown in Figure 29-5.

OrderID	ProductID	UnitPrice	Quantity	Discount
1	42	4200.00	1	0.00
1	12	6.00	40	0.00
1	7	73.05	6	0.00

Table 29-6   The Data for the Order Details `DataTable`

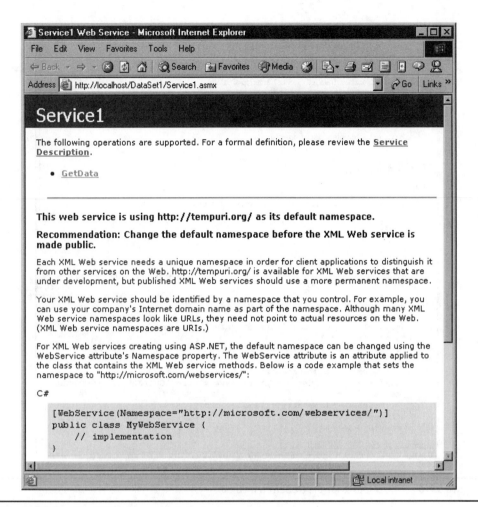

Figure 29-5   The XML web service help display

Click the GetData link to get the display shown in Figure 29-6. In this display, you can see the SOAP code that will call the XML web service, along with your one control labeled Invoke.

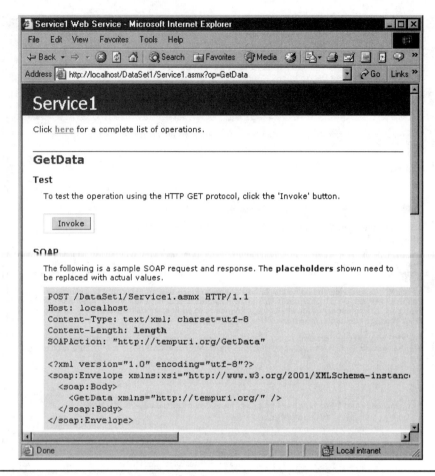

Figure 29-6   The test page for the `GetData` method

Click the Invoke button to execute the web method. The result is shown in Figure 29-7, and the return data is in XML, as expected.

Figure 29-7 The XML data that is returned by the GetData web method

We have now looked at the code that makes it possible to work with DataSet objects to send data between XML web services and consumers of those services. We also saw how to work with the data programmatically. The next step is to look at how you can work with XML documents.

XML Data

XML (Extensible Markup Language) is another acronym you will have seen used throughout this book. XML was discussed in Chapters 8 and 25, so we will not detail the XML rules here. The purpose of this section is to show you how you can work with data in XML format programmatically by using the Document Object Model (DOM) for XML. This will include looking at the `XmlReader` object and the operations that can be performed with it.

Microsoft incorporated XML support into SQL Server 2000, and the exam will surely include questions on the extensions to the Transact-SQL language, so we have included information on that extension in this section as well.

 EXAM TIP Remember the six rules of well-formed XML—(1) there can be only one root element, and all elements require (2) matching opening and closing elements that are (3) case sensitive and must be (4) nested properly. Attributes must have their (5) values enclosed in quotes and (6) cannot be repeated.

Document Object Model (DOM)

XML is increasingly used to move data between processes, and, as such, it is a very powerful language that simplifies the data exchange in a heterogeneous environment. It allows the sender and receiver of the data to operate on the data in a programmatic way. The object model that has become the standard (endorsed by the W3C) is the Document Object Model (DOM) that is the standard API for XML, and there is a second API that can be used to access XML documents called Simple API for XML (SAX). DOM uses an object model to operate on the data in the XML document, while SAX uses an event-driven API to work with the data. The standard is DOM, and that is what is tested in the exam, but that does not mean SAX can be ignored as a technology.

The standard way of accessing XML documents is through the DOM, and that is what the exam will test you on; the remainder of this chapter will work with the DOM.

Let's have a look at the object model of DOM. In the true sense of the word, everything in DOM is a *node*. When you explore the objects, you will find that everything is a node in a b-tree, where the document is the root.

The XML document is parsed into a DOM tree when the document is read by the parser. Once the parser has loaded the document, it is available for you to manipulate. The tree structure of the DOM can be seen in Figure 29-8.

The XML document that was used in Figure 29-8 is as follows:

```
<?xml version="1.0"?>
<booklist>
    <book language="en">
        <isbn>0072224436</isbn>
    </book>
    <book>
...
</booklist>
```

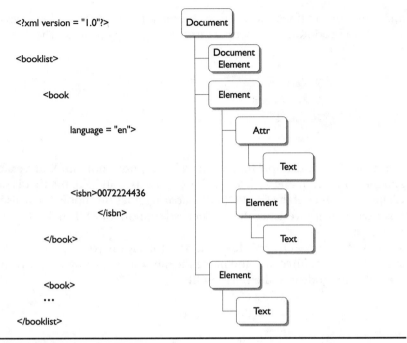

Figure 29-8   The tree structure of DOM

The following objects are in the DOM:

- **Document object**   This is the topmost node of the DOM. This node contains the entire content of the XML document.

- **Element objects**   This node represents the elements in the XML document. The root element <booklist> is an element object, as are the <book> and <isbn> elements.

- **Attr objects**   This node represents the attributes of the document, such as the language attribute.

- **Text object**   This node represents the textual value stored in an element or attribute.

The DOM exposes a number of collections that make it easy to work with multiple elements or attributes at the same time.

Every object in the DOM is a node that defines some properties that are available when you work with the document. For example, the navigation properties firstChild, lastChild, nextSibling, and previousSibling let you move through the node tree. Each node also has properties that you can query to find the type and name of the node: `nodeType` returns a number that defines what the node is, whereas the `nodeName` property returns the name of the node. The different node types are as follows:

1	Element node
2	Attribute node
3	Text node
9	Document node

Let's look at an example that will read in the public domain XML version of Macbeth and then print it on the console. This example uses an XML file that is provided in the Chapter 29 folder of the CD-ROM that accompanies this book. We'll also use the `System.Xml` namespace, since that is where all support for XML in the .NET Framework comes from.

Copy the `Macbeth.xml` file to a new folder, on your C: drive. Create a new C# source file in that directory, and name the file `Dom.cs`, using your favorite editor, enter the following code into the `Dom.cs` file.

```
// Dom.cs
using System;
using System.IO;
using System.Xml;

public class Dom
{
    public static void Main(string[] args)
    {
        string XmlFileName = "Macbeth.xml";
        Dom myDom = new Dom();
        myDom.ParseTree(XmlFileName);
    }
    public void ParseTree(string XmlFileName)
    {
        // use a try/catch block to ensure we handle any errors
        try
        {
            Console.WriteLine("\nLoading the {0} file, please wait", XmlFileName);
            XmlDocument myDoc = new XmlDocument();
            myDoc.Load(XmlFileName);
            // after we have loaded the file display the content
            Console.WriteLine("/nDisplaying the content of the {0} file",
                                                            XmlFileName);
            XmlNode node = myDoc;
            // go through and display all the nodes in the document
            PrintNodes(Console.Out, node);
        } catch (Exception e)
        {
            Console.WriteLine("Exception: {0}", e.ToString());
        }
    }
    public void PrintNodes(TextWriter cOut, XmlNode node)
```

```
{
    try
    {
        PrintNodeInfo(cOut, node);
        if (node.HasChildNodes)
        {
            PrintNodes(cOut, node.FirstChild);
        }
        if (node.NextSibling != null)
        {
            PrintNodes(cOut, node.NextSibling);
        }
    } catch (Exception e)
    {
        Console.WriteLine("Exception: {0}", e.ToString());
    }
}
public void PrintNodeInfo(TextWriter cOut, XmlNode node)
{
    cOut.Write ("{0} [{1}] = {2} ", node.NodeType, node.Name, node.Value);
    int Attributes = 0;
    if (node.Attributes != null)
    {
        Attributes = node.Attributes.Count;
    }
    for (int i = 0; i < Attributes; i++)
    {
        cOut.Write("{0} [{1}] = {2} ", "Attr", node.Attributes[i].Name,
                                          node.Attributes[i].Value);
    }
    cOut.Write('\n');
}
}
```

This program makes use of the XML document, and it traverses the tree, printing information about the nodes as they are found. In order to compile the program, you need to execute the command-line C# compiler as follows:

```
F:\xml>csc Dom.cs
Microsoft (R) Visual C# .NET Compiler version 7.00.9466
for Microsoft (R) .NET Framework version 1.0.3705
Copyright (C) Microsoft Corporation 2001. All rights reserved.

F:\xml>
```

When the program is executed, it will print all the nodes in the XML document. A partial listing is shown here:

```
F:\xml>Dom
Loading the Macbeth.xml file, please wait
Displaying the content of the Macbeth.xml file
Document [#document] =
XmlDeclaration [xml] = version="1.0"
Element [PLAY] =
Element [TITLE] =
Text [#text] = The Tragedy of Macbeth
```

```
Element [fm] =
Element [p] =
Text [#text] = Text placed in the public domain by Moby Lexical Tools, 1992.
Element [p] =
Text [#text] = SGML markup by Jon Bosak, 1992-1994.
...
Element [LINE] =
Text [#text] = Took off her life; this, and what needful else
Element [LINE] =
Text [#text] = That calls upon us, by the grace of Grace,
Element [LINE] =
Text [#text] = We will perform in measure, time and place:
Element [LINE] =
Text [#text] = So, thanks to all at once and to each one,
Element [LINE] =
Text [#text] = Whom we invite to see us crown'd at Scone.
Element [STAGEDIR] =
Text [#text] = Flourish. Exeunt
```

In this example, we used the Load() method of the XmlDocument object to read the document into the DOM. Next, we will look at how to work with the XmlReader and XmlWriter classes.

XmlReader

With the XmlReader class, you can process the XML document using techniques similar to the ones available in the Simple API for XML (SAX) packages.

The XmlReader class is an abstract base class that provides the ability to read and parse an XML file in a forward-only, read-only, non-cached manner for a number of classes that inherit from it. The following classes are derived from the XmlReader class:

- **XmlTextReader**   Reads character streams. This class has no support for schemas.

- **XmlNodeReader**   Parses XML DOM trees. This class has no support for schemas.

- **XmlValidatingReader**   Provides a fully compliant validating XML parser with schema support.

 EXAM TIP   The XmlReader class is the base class for a number of specialized readers.

To show the XmlReader in action, we will build a program that is based on the XmlTextReader class. This example will read, parse, and display an XML file.

Create a C# source file in the same directory that contains the Macbeth.xml file, and name it XmlReader.cs. Using your favorite editor, enter the following code into the XmlReader.cs file.

```
// XmlReader.cs
using System;
```

```
using System.IO;
using System.Xml;

public class ReadXml
{
    public static void Main(string[] argh)
    {
        StreamReader stream = null;
        try
        {
            string XmlFileName = "Employees.xml";
            if (argh.Length > 0)
            {
                XmlFileName = argh[0];
            }
            Console.WriteLine("Reading XML ...");
            stream = new StreamReader(XmlFileName);
            XmlTextReader reader = new XmlTextReader(stream);
            reader.WhitespaceHandling = WhitespaceHandling.None;
            ReadXml.ReadIt(reader);
        }
        catch (Exception e)
        {
            Console.WriteLine("Exception: {0}", e.ToString());
        }
        finally
        {
            if (stream != null)
                stream.Close();
        }
    }
    public static void ReadIt(XmlTextReader r)
    {
        int i = 0;
        try
        {
            while (r.Read())
            {
                i++;
                Console.Write("Read[{0,3}]:", i);
                PrintInfo(Console.Out, r);
            }
        }
        catch (Exception e)
        {
            Console.WriteLine("Exception: {0}", e.ToString());
        }
    }
    public static void PrintInfo(TextWriter cOut, XmlReader r)
    {
        if (r.HasValue)
        {
            cOut.Write("{0} [{1}] = {2} ", r.NodeType, r.Name, r.Value);
        }
        else
        {
            cOut.Write("{0} [{1}] ", r.NodeType, r.Name);
        }
        if (r.HasAttributes)
```

```
    {
        while (r.MoveToNextAttribute())
        {
            cOut.Write("{0} [{1}] = {2} ", r.NodeType, r.Name, r.Value);
        }
    }
    cOut.Write("\n");
  }
}
```

The bold line in the preceding code specifies the handling of whitespace in the XML document. The WhitespaceHandling parameter is set to WhitespaceHandling.None, which ignores any whitespace.

To compile the program, use the command-line compiler csc. The XML file that is hard-coded in the program is Employees.xml, and it contains the following data:

```
<?xml version="1.0"?>
<employees>
    <employee>
        <name>John Smith</name>
        <salary>54000</salary>
    </employee>
    <employee>
        <name>Robert Jones</name>
        <salary>61000</salary>
    </employee>
    <employee>
        <name>Sue Brown</name>
        <salary>65000</salary>
    </employee>
</employees>
```

When you run the program, the output produced shows the document parsed into its nodes, as can be seen here:

```
F:\xml>xmlreader
Reading XML ...
Read[  1]:XmlDeclaration [xml] = version="1.0" Attribute [version] = 1.0
Read[  2]:Element [employees]
Read[  3]:Element [employee]
Read[  4]:Element [name]
Read[  5]:Text [] = John Smith
Read[  6]:EndElement [name]
Read[  7]:Element [salary]
Read[  8]:Text [] = 54000
Read[  9]:EndElement [salary]
Read[ 10]:EndElement [employee]
Read[ 11]:Element [employee]
Read[ 12]:Element [name]
Read[ 13]:Text [] = Robert Jones
Read[ 14]:EndElement [name]
Read[ 15]:Element [salary]
Read[ 16]:Text [] = 61000
Read[ 17]:EndElement [salary]
Read[ 18]:EndElement [employee]
Read[ 19]:Element [employee]
```

```
Read[ 20]:Element [name]
Read[ 21]:Text [] = Sue Brown
Read[ 22]:EndElement [name]
Read[ 23]:Element [salary]
Read[ 24]:Text [] = 65000
Read[ 25]:EndElement [salary]
Read[ 26]:EndElement [employee]
Read[ 27]:EndElement [employees]
```

In this output, the whitespace was ignored. The default whitespace handling is to re-turn all whitespace. To experiment with the whitespace handling, change the bold line in the earlier program code to read as follows:

```
reader.WhitespaceHandling = WhitespaceHandling.All;
```

After compiling the program again, you can execute it, and you will get output as follows:

```
F:\xml>xmlreader
Reading XML ...
Read[  1]:XmlDeclaration [xml] = version="1.0" Attribute [version] = 1.0
Read[  2]:Whitespace [] =


Read[  3]:Element [employees]
Read[  4]:Whitespace [] =

Read[  5]:Element [employee]
Read[  6]:Whitespace [] =

...
Read[ 35]:Element [salary]
Read[ 36]:Text [] = 65000
Read[ 37]:EndElement [salary]
Read[ 38]:Whitespace [] =

Read[ 39]:EndElement [employee]
Read[ 40]:Whitespace [] =

Read[ 41]:EndElement [employees]
```

The whitespace in the XML document is now returned, as well as the nodes.

The XmlTextReader is one of the objects that are used to parse XML documents and programmatically work with them. Once you have an XML document loaded, you can process the data in the nodes by using C#, or you can take advantage of the transfor-mations that can be performed. The next section will explore XML and transformations.

Transformations and XML

Using Extensible Stylesheet Language (XSL), you can transform the contents of an XML document into any other character-based format that is, itself, a well- formed XML doc-ument. For example, you can transform an XML document to HTML for display in a browser, or you can transform the XML document to meet the formatting required by some other service. For a refresher on XSL, see Chapter 25.

XSL support in the .NET Framework is found in the `System.Xml.Xsl` namespace. The `XslTransform` class in that namespace supports XML documents using XSL style sheets. The process of transforming an XML document starts with an instance of the `XslTransform` class: the XSL style sheet is read into the `XslTransform` object through the `Load()` method. Then the `Transform()` method is called with an `XPathDocument` as input, and the output can be a writer, a stream, or an `XmlReader`. The `XPathDocument` is constructed from an XML document.

As an example, we will transform an XML document with employee information into an HTML table (the XML and XSL files are in the Chapter 29 folder on the accompanying CD-ROM). The XML document `Empl.xml` follows:

```
<?xml version="1.0" ?>
<empls>
    <employee id="42">
        <name>John Smith</name>
        <salary payperiod="Monthly">62000</salary>
        <department>Development
            <title>Sr. Developer</title>
        </department>
    </employee>
    <employee id="43">
        <name>George Brown</name>
        <salary payperiod="weekly">53000</salary>
        <department>Customer Support
            <title>Customer care specialist</title>
        </department>
    </employee>
    <employee id="44">
        <name>Linda Philips</name>
        <salary payperiod="bi-weekly">52000</salary>
        <department>Development
            <title>Tester</title>
        </department>
    </employee>
    <employee id="45">
        <name>Guy Jones</name>
        <salary payperiod="monthly">72000</salary>
        <department>Accounting
            <title>Bean Counter</title>
        </department>
    </employee>
</empls>
```

The transformation will be performed by the following XSL style sheet, `Empl.xsl`:

```
<xsl:stylesheet xmlns:xsl="http://www.w3.org/1999/XSL/Transform" version="1.0">
    <xsl:template match="/">
        <HTML>
        <TABLE border="1">
        <xsl:for-each select="empls/employee">
            <xsl:sort select="name"/>
            <TR VALIGN="top">
                <TD>
```

```
            <xsl:value-of select="name" />
        </TD>
        <TD>
            <xsl:value-of select="@id" />
        </TD>
        <TD>
            <xsl:value-of select="salary" />
        </TD>
        <TD>
            <xsl:value-of select="department" />
        </TD>
        <TD>
            <xsl:value-of select="department/title" />
        </TD>
      </TR>
    </xsl:for-each>
    </TABLE>
    </HTML>
  </xsl:template>
</xsl:stylesheet>
```

In order to transform the XML document, you need to write a command-line program. Create a folder on your hard drive, and copy the XML and XSL files from the Chapter 29 folder on the CD-ROM to the folder. Then create a C# source file in the same directory, and name the file `Trans.cs`. Using your favorite editor, enter the following code:

```
// Trans.cs
using System;
using System.IO;
using System.Xml;
using System.Xml.XPath;
using System.Xml.Xsl;

public class Trans
{
    public static void Main()
    {
        String xmlFile = "Empl.xml";
        String xslFile = "Empl.xsl";
        String transOut = "Empl.htm";

        try
        {
            XslTransform xslt = new XslTransform();
            xslt.Load(xslFile);
            XPathDocument xpathDoc = new XPathDocument(xmlFile);
            XmlTextWriter xOut = new XmlTextWriter(transOut, null);
            xOut.Formatting = Formatting.Indented;
            xslt.Transform(xpathDoc, null, xOut);
            xOut.Close();
        }
        catch (Exception e)
        {
            Console.WriteLine("Exception: {0}", e.ToString());
        }
    }
}
```

When you execute this program, the output is an HTML file (Empl.htm) located in the same directory as the program. The HTML that was generated through this transformation was indented because you specified the formatting in the bold line in the preceding program. The HTML output code looks as follows:

```
<HTML>
  <TABLE border="1">
    <TR VALIGN="top">
      <TD>George Brown</TD>
      <TD>43</TD>
      <TD>53000</TD>
      <TD>Customer Support
                Customer care specialist</TD>
      <TD>Customer care specialist</TD>
    </TR>
    <TR VALIGN="top">
      <TD>Guy Jones</TD>
      <TD>45</TD>
      <TD>72000</TD>
      <TD>Accounting
                Bean Counter</TD>
      <TD>Bean Counter</TD>
    </TR>
    <TR VALIGN="top">
      <TD>John Smith</TD>
      <TD>42</TD>
      <TD>62000</TD>
      <TD>Development
                Sr. Developer</TD>
      <TD>Sr. Developer</TD>
    </TR>
    <TR VALIGN="top">
      <TD>Linda Philips</TD>
      <TD>44</TD>
      <TD>52000</TD>
      <TD>Development
                Tester</TD>
      <TD>Tester</TD>
    </TR>
  </TABLE>
</HTML>
```

When you open the Empl.htm file in a browser, the table is displayed as shown in Figure 29-9.

One issue that remains after you have transformed a document is validation—the process of guaranteeing that a document meets the rules. That's our next topic.

Validating XML

XML documents are designed to be passed between different services and processes, some of which are supplied by other entities and run on computers that you have no control over. This global reach means that you will need a way to guarantee that the doc-

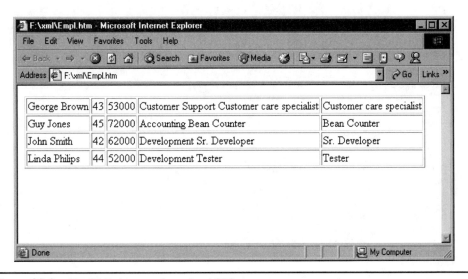

Figure 29-9   The XML data transformed to HTML

ument you just received from one of your vendors is correct in format. This is the process of validation. A valid XML document must meet the six rules for an XML document, and it must be validated against a schema. The schema is the definition of the elements, the attributes, the order of the nodes, the valid data types, the ranges of values, and how the nodes relate to each other.

The support for validation is provided through the XmlValidatingReader class that is created from an XmlReader—the XmlValidatingReader has a ValidationType property that controls how an XML document is to be validated. The possible values for the ValidationType property are

- Auto—Senses the type (DTD or XML schema) of validation automatically
- DTD—Forces DTD validation
- Schema—Forces schema validation
- None—Performs no validation

The first of the two types of validation is Document Type Definition (DTD), and it is the original standard for validation formats. DTD has been considered a legacy type since the XML schema was turned into a standard. The XmlValidatingReader class uses the ValidationEventHandler() callback method that is called when a validation error has been found.

In order to explore validation, we will write an example that uses a DTD to validate an XML document (both of which are found in the Chapter 29 folder on the accompanying CD-ROM). The XML document is the `Emplo.xml` file shown here:

```
<?xml version="1.0"?>
<!DOCTYPE emplo SYSTEM "Emplo.dtd">
<emplo>
    <employee>
        <fullname>Gregory Small</fullname>
        <remuneration>23500</remuneration>
        <title>Programmer</title>
        <location>Halifax</location>
    </employee>
    <employee>
        <fullname>Marg Simpson</fullname>
        <remuneration>51000</remuneration>
        <title>Tester</title>
        <location>Vancouver</location>
    </employee>
    <employee>
        <fullname>Patrik Soames</fullname>
        <remuneration>45000</remuneration>
        <title>System Architect</title>
        <location>Ottawa</location>
    </employee>
    <employee>
        <fullname>John Smith</fullname>
        <remuneration>112000</remuneration>
        <title>Project Manager</title>
        <location>Toronto</location>
    </employee>
</emplo>
```

The DTD file is `Emplo.dtd`:

```
<!ELEMENT emplo (employee*)>
<!ELEMENT employee (fullname, remuneration, title, location)>
<!ELEMENT fullname (#PCDATA)>
<!ELEMENT remuneration (#PCDATA)>
<!ELEMENT title (#PCDATA)>
<!ELEMENT location (#PCDATA)>
```

To build the example, you will need to create a folder on your hard drive, and copy the `Empl.xml` and `Emplo.dtd` to that folder. Then create a C# source file in the same folder, and name it `Valid.cs`. Using your editor, enter the following code in the `Valid.cs` source file.

```
// Valid.cs
using System;
using System.IO;
using System.Xml;
using System.Xml.Schema;

public class Valid
{
    private Boolean bOut;
    XmlValidatingReader reader;
```

```
    public static void Main(String[] argh)
    {
        Valid val = new Valid();
        val.ValidateIt("Emplo.xml");
    }

    public void ValidateIt(String xmlFile)
    {
        bOut = true;
        try
        {
            Console.WriteLine("\nXML file: {0} is validating", xmlFile);
            reader = new XmlValidatingReader(new XmlTextReader(xmlFile));
            reader.ValidationType = ValidationType.DTD;
            // register the delegate for the event
            reader.ValidationEventHandler += new ValidationEventHandler
                                                            (this.ValHand);
            Console.WriteLine("Validating using DTD");
            XmlDataDocument doc = new XmlDataDocument();
            doc.Load(reader);
            Console.WriteLine(
                    "Validation finished.\nThe outcome of the validation was a {0}",
                                        (bOut ? "success" : "failure"));
        }
        // invalid XML exception
        catch (XmlException e)
        {
            Console.WriteLine("Exception: {0}", e.ToString());
        }
        // all other exceptions
        catch (Exception e)
        {
            Console.WriteLine("Exception: {0}", e.ToString());
        }
    }
    public void ValHand(object sender, ValidationEventArgs args)
    {
        bOut = false;
        Console.Write("\nValidation error: {0}", args.Message);
        // get a reference to the XmlTextReader
        XmlTextReader x = (XmlTextReader)reader.Reader;
        // print out the line with the error
        Console.WriteLine("\nLine({0}) Character {1}",
                                        x.LineNumber, x.LinePosition);
    }
}
```

To compile the program, you need to execute the command-line C# compiler, like this:

```
csc Valid.cs
```

After you execute the program, the output should look like the following.

```
F:\xml>valid

XML file: Emplo.xml is validating
Validating using DTD
Validation finished.
```

The outcome of the validation was a success. Break the schema of the XML file by deleting the `<location>` element from one of the employees, and rerun the `Valid.exe` program. The result should be similar to the following, depending on which line you deleted.

```
F:\xml>valid

XML file: Emplo.xml is validating
Validating using DTD

Validation error: Element 'employee' has invalid child element 'title'.
Expected: 'remuneration'. An error occurred at file:///F:/xml/Emplo.xml(13, 4).
Line(13) Character 4
Validation finished.
The outcome of the validation was a failure
```

XML is a very big topic, and it is used in every aspect of the .NET Framework. Expect to see multiple questions in the exam that present information in XML format.

Microsoft SQL Server and XML Support

When Microsoft SQL Server 2000 was released, there was almost no XML support built into any of the database products available. Microsoft included rudimentary XML support for SQL Server in the .NET Framework once the Framework was released.

The .NET SQL provider contains support for retrieving an XML stream from Microsoft SQL Server 2000. The `SqlCommand` object has the `ExecuteXmlReader()` method, which returns an `XmlReader` object populated with the result of the SQL statement specified for the `SqlCommand`.

The following code segment illustrates the use of the `ExecuteXmlReader()` method:

```
...
using System.Data.SqlClient;
using System.Xml;
...
SqlCommand xmlCm = new SqlCommand(
                    "SELECT * FROM Customers FOR XML AUTO, ELEMENTS",
                    dbCon);
XmlReader reader = xmlCm.ExecuteXmlReader();
```

The `FOR XML` clause specifies that the `SELECT` statement will return XML. The `AUTO` mode returns query results as nested XML elements, and the `ELEMENTS` option maps columns as elements rather than as attributes.

Summary

This ends our visit to the land of data. The code you have worked with in this chapter is the type you will see in real-world applications that are built to give the developer full control of the process. This chapter looked at a number of special areas of the ADO.NET environment, especially the `DataSet` object and the use of XML.

In the XML Web Services exam, there will be many questions that present similar code, and you must understand how to read that code to be able to answer the questions. The questions may be on totally different topics from the ADO.NET `DataSet` code that was presented here.

The programmatic manipulation of XML documents through the DOM or through `XmlReader` objects is another skill that will be tested directly or indirectly.

We cannot emphasize enough the importance of understanding and having a working knowledge of the contents of Chapters 10, 16, 20, and this chapter.

Test Questions

1. What namespace must be used in order to use the DOM for XML support?

   A. System.Data.Xml

   B. System.Xml

   C. System.Xml.DOM

   D. System.DOM

2. You need to be able to retrieve data from a `DataSet` object that has four `DataTable` objects. There are currently `UniqueConstraint` and `ForeignKeyConstraint` objects on the `DataTable` objects to enforce the data rules. You find that you can retrieve data from the individual `DataTable` objects, but you are not able to retrieve data from the combination of `DataTable` objects in a parent/child manner. What should you do to be able to retrieve the data in a parent/child manner?

   A. Set the `EnforceParentChild` parameter of the `DataSet` to True.

   B. Set the `EnforceRelation` parameter of the `Relations` collection to True.

   C. Add `DataRelation` objects to the `Relations` collection to make the `DataSet` present the data in a parent/child manner.

   D. Add a primary key and a foreign key to each of the `DataTable` objects that should present the data in a parent/child manner.

3. You need to retrieve data from a Microsoft SQL Server 2000. Currently, you are using an `OleDbConnection` object to connect to the database server. You need to be able to retrieve the data from the database server in XML format. Which approach would be the most efficient? Select all that apply. Each answer constitutes part of the whole answer.

   A. Change to the SQL .NET provider.

   B. Use the `ExecuteXmlReader()` method of the `XxxCommand` object.

   C. Use the DOM to create the XML document.

   D. Use the `XmlDocument.Load()` method to create the XML document.

4. True or False. XML Transformations can be used to create a form letter.

A. True.

B. False.

5. You have been given a project that loads data into a `DataTable`, and you find that the project will not compile. You localize the problem to the statements that load the data into the `DataTable`, as shown in this code segment:

```
DataTable dtProducts = ds.Tables["Products"];
dtProducts.Rows.Add(new RowSet{42,
                    "Universal Answer", 0, 0, "", 1242.34, 1, 0, 0, 0});
dtProducts.Rows.Add(new RowSet{12,
                    "Whitby Herring", 0, 0, "", 4.12, 150, 0, 0, 0});
dtProducts.Rows.Add(new RowSet{7,
                    "Mimico Tuna", 0, 0, "", 42.12, 65, 0, 0, 0});
```

What is the most efficient way of making the project compile?

A. Replace the curly braces `{}` with square brackets `[]`.

B. Remove the new keyword from the `Add()` method.

C. Replace the reference to `RowSet` in the `Add()` method with `Object[]`.

D. Change the `Add()` method to the `Load()` method.

6. You are parsing an XML document using an `XmlReader`. You find that the resulting node tree is very large compared to the number of elements and attributes in the XML document. Why would the result of the parsing produce a large node tree?

A. The `WhitespaceHandling` parameter is set to `WhitespaceHandling.All`.

B. The `WhitespaceHandling` parameter is set to `WhitespaceHandling.None`.

C. The `WhitespaceHandling` parameter is set to `WhitespaceHandling.Auto`.

D. The `WhitespaceHandling` parameter is set to `WhitespaceHandling.Special`.

7. Which of the following classes supports XML schemas? Select all that apply.

A. `XmlReader`

B. `XmlDocument`

C. `XmlValidatingReader`

D. `XmlNodeReader`

8. You are developing an application that will connect to a Microsoft SQL Server 6.5, and you need to select the appropriate ADO.NET connection object for this database server. What ADO.NET connection object is the most appropriate?

A. `XxxConnection`

B. `SqlConnection`

C. `OleDbConnection`

D. `OdbcConnection`

9. What makes an XML document valid? Select two answers.

A. The XML document only uses elements from the XML standard.

B. The XML document is parsed successfully with a schema or DTD attached.

C. The XML document meets the six rules for XML.

D. The XML document meets the golden XML rule.

10. What is the result when the following XML document is parsed?

```
<?xml version="1.0"?>
<towns>
   <town>
      <name>Mimico</town>
   </town>
   <town>
      <name>Whitby</town>
   </name>
</towns>
```

A. It will parse successfully.

B. An XmlException will be thrown.

C. An Exception will be thrown.

D. A syntax error will be reported.

11. Given the following code segment, what will happen if the call to doc.Load(reader) throws an XmlException?

```
try
{
   Console.WriteLine("\nXML file: {0} is validating", xmlFile);
   reader = new XmlValidatingReader(new XmlTextReader(xmlFile));
   reader.ValidationType = ValidationType.DTD;
   // register the delegate for the event
   reader.ValidationEventHandler += new ValidationEventHandler
                                        (this.ValHand);
   Console.WriteLine("Validating using DTD");
   XmlDataDocument doc = new XmlDataDocument();
   doc.Load(reader);    // Line with XmlException
}
catch (Exception e)
{
   Console.WriteLine("Exception: {0}", e.ToString());
}
catch (XmlException e)
{
   Console.WriteLine("XmlException: {0}", e.ToString());
}
```

A. The line "XmlException: ..." is printed to the console.

B. The line "Exception:..." is printed to the console.

C. The program will terminate with a general failure.

D. The program will continue without any extra output.

12. What is the correct way to create a `DataTable` in a `DataSet`? Select all that apply. Each answer constitutes one part of the answer.

   A. `DataTable dtOrders = new DataTable("Orders");`

   B. `DataTable dtOrders = DataTable("Orders");`

   C. `DataTable dtOrders;`

   D. `ds.Tables.Add("Orders");`

13. Where do you add `Constraint` objects?

   A. To the `Constraint` collection of the `DataTable` object.

   B. To the `Constraint` collection of the `DataColumns` object.

   C. To the `Constraint` collection of the `DataSet` object.

   D. To the `Constraint` collection of the `DataRelation` object.

14. When you build the schema of a `DataSet`, you need to model the data types of the data that will reside in the `DataColumn` objects. What data type would you use to represent a date?

   A. date

   B. day

   C. System.DateTime

   D. variant

15. True or False. HTML must be well formed to be used with XML.

   A. True.

   B. False.

Test Answers

1. B.

2. C. The `DataSet` must have a `DataRelation` object for each pair of `DataTable` objects that should present their data in a parent/child manner.

3. A and B. Only the SQL .NET provider has support for XML from the server, and the `ExecuteXmlReader()` method makes that XML available.

4. B. False, the resulting document must be a well-formed XML document.

5. C. You must use an `Object` array.

6. A.

7. C.

8. C. The `SqlConnection` works only with Microsoft SQL Server 7.0 or higher.

9. B and C.

10. B.

11. B. The first `catch` block that matches the exception will execute.

12. D. You add the `DataTable` to the `DataSet`.

13. A.

14. C.

15. A.

Deployment and Security

In this chapter, you will

- Deploy an XML web service
- Secure an XML web service
- Access unmanaged code using InterOp

The deployment of an XML web service consists of two actions—the physical movement of the XML web service to the production server and the discovery configuration. The configuration of the discovery, whether static or dynamic, is the more important because the discovery configuration will determine how clients find out about the XML web service and how they access it. In this chapter, you will learn how to publish an XML web service to a UDDI registry (dynamic discovery) and to configure the XML web service to use static discovery.

This chapter will also address the related topic of how to call unmanaged native code libraries through the InterOp functions and how to ensure these libraries are available when the XML web service is deployed.

Deploying an XML Web Service

When you are getting ready to deploy an XML web service, you need to decide how the XML web service will be published. The XML web service can be published to a UDDI registry that will act as the broker that clients can use to dynamically locate your service, or it can be published statically, meaning that clients must know exactly where the service is located in order to access it. We will now look at how to publish an XML web service to a UDDI registry.

UDDI Registry

The UDDI (Universal Description, Discovery, and Integration) registry performs the role of an XML web service broker, which makes it possible for potential consumers to find an XML web service. To learn more about the structure of UDDI see Chapter 25.

The UDDI API specification defines functions that access the UDDI registries. There are two types of API defined:

- The Publisher API, which is used to publish information to a UDDI registry.
- The Inquiry API, which is used to read information from a UDDI registry.

In addition to these standard APIs, Microsoft has released a UDDI SDK. These APIs define a large number of Simple Object Access Protocol (SOAP) messages that are used to communicate with a UDDI registry.

To include support for the Publisher and Inquiry APIs the following namespaces must be imported in to the C# program, these are the namespaces that support UDDI in the .NET Framework:

```
using Microsoft.Uddi;
using Microsoft.Uddi.Api;
using Microsoft.Uddi.Business;
using Microsoft.Uddi.ServiceType;
using Microsoft.Uddi.Binding;
using Microsoft.Uddi.Service;
using Microsoft.Uddi.Authentication;
```

We will look at how you can use the Publisher and Inquiry APIs in the following sections.

The Publisher API

Through the Publisher API you can gain authorized access to the UDDI registry and publish information by adding and deleting elements. You need to be both authenticated (identified) and authorized (given access) to be able to modify information in the UDDI registry, and you must first get an authorization token by calling get_authToken(). This token is then added as a parameter to subsequent calls. Once you are finished with the Publisher API, you will need to destroy the token by calling discard_authToken().

 EXAM TIP Call get_authToken() to get an authorization token, and release the token by calling discard_authToken().

The methods used to add and edit elements in the UDDI registry belong in the save_xxx() family of methods that operates on the main UDDI types, where xxx is replaced by the UDDI data-type:

- save_business()
- save_service()
- save_binding()
- save_tModel()

The methods used to delete elements in the UDDI registry use these `delete_xxx()` methods:

- `delete_business()`
- `delete_service()`
- `delete_binding()`
- `delete_tModel()`

Once the elements are added, you will need to define the relationships between business entities. The following methods perform those actions:

- `add_publisherAssertions()`
- `get_assertionStatusReport()`
- `get_publisherAssertions()`
- `delete_publisherAssertions()`

We will call these methods as if they are local to us. The methods, however, are operations that can be invoked from UDDI by using SOAP.

You will have to decide whether we will use a commercial UDDI registry or a private registry solution. A commercial UDDI registry is run by a company like Microsoft as a for-profit operation, while a private solution is a UDDI registry that is implemented in a company for internal use. We will explore the private solutions in this book, as that is what is tested in the exam.

There are three ways to publish an XML web service as a private registry solutions.

- **Private UDDI registry** The UDDI specification was designed to be a public, replicated repository—there were no provisions made for private UDDI registries. There is currently work in progress to include private UDDI registries.
  The advantage of implementing a private UDDI registry is that when the UDDI specification is changed to include private registries, you are ready for that.
  The disadvantage is that to implement the private UDDI registry, you will have to correctly implement the full UDDI specification.

- **Private publish/discover architecture** You can implement only a minor part of the UDDI specification to build an architecture that is tailored to your environment.
  The advantage is that you can build a custom implementation and do not need to wait for the UDDI specification to be updated.
  The disadvantage is that the implementation is customized, and it is not compatible with the standard.

- **Hard-code endpoints** The simplest private solution is to hard-code the endpoints of the XML web service. This solution does not require UDDI. The location of the XML web service is the endpoint, and hard-coding the endpoint makes the address static for the client.

The advantage is that you don't have to search for the XML web service, and the solution can be very quickly implemented.

The disadvantage is that you need to change your applications if the XML web service needs to be moved to a different location.

In the following example, we will publish an XML web service to a UDDI registry. The first thing you need to define are the keys for your source and destination:

```
static string tModelKeySource = "uuid:535C20ED-1288-4e6a-8BA4-94BAE8A2E7A4";
static string tModelKeyDest = "uuid:A2567465-CB09-4418-A438-5570EF4D4248";
```

These keys are defined as `static` to ensure they will never change.

Now you need to register the business entity. To do this, define the following `PubBus()` method:

```
private BusinessDetail PubBus(string name, string description, Contact contact)
{
    Publish.AuthenticationMode = AuthenticationMode.UddiAuthentication;
    Publish.Url = "http://abc.abc/";
    Publish.HttpClient.Credentials = new NetworkCredential
                            ("ken","password","KENSNABBEN");

    BusinessEntity bEntity = new BusinessEntity();
    bEntity.Name = name;    // name = the business entity
    bEntity.Descriptions.Add("en",description);
                        // description = the long name of the business
    bEntity.Contacts.Add(contact);

    Microsoft.Uddi.SaveBusiness sBusiness = new SaveBusiness();
    sBusiness.BusinessEntities.Add(businessEntity);
    BusinessDetail bd = sBusiness.Send();
    return bd;
}
```

You can call the `PubBus()` method by passing it the name, description, and contact information for the business entity.

```
BusinessDetail bd;
Contact con = new Contact();
con.PersonName = "John Smith";
con.Emails.Add("john.smith@abc.abc");
con.Descriptions.Add("en","Web Site Administrator");
bd = PubBus("ABC Corp","The ABC Corporation Service", con);
```

Once the business is registered, you can proceed to publish the service, as in the following function.

```
private ServiceDetail PubService()
{
    // assign the Service name
    string serviceName = "ABC conversions";
    // retrieve the business key
    string businessKey = bd.BusinessEntities[0].BusinessKey;
```

```
    // get the tModelKey
    string tModelKey = tModelKeySource;
    // make the URL dependent on the server we are running on.
    string urlAccess = string.Format
                ("http://{0}/acb/ABC.asmx",Environment.MachineName)
    // define the descriptions
    string bindingDescription = "ASP.NET service";
    string tModelDescription = "ABC web service";
    Publish.AuthenticationMode = AuthenticationMode.UddiAuthentication;
    Publish.Url = "http://abc.abc/";
    // authenticate
    Publish.HttpClient.Credentials = new NetworkCredential
                        ("Ken","password","KENSNABBEN");

    BindingTemplate bTemp = new BindingTemplate();
    bTemp.Descriptions.Add(bindingDescription);

    AccessPoint aPoint = new AccessPoint(URLTypeEnum.Http,urlAccess);
    bTemp.AccessPoint = accessPoint;

    TModelInstanceInfo tMInstInfo = new TModelInstanceInfo();
    tMInstInfo.TModelKey = tModelKey;
    tMInstInfo.Descriptions.Add(tModelDescription);

    bTemp.TModelInstanceDetail.TModelInstanceInfos.Add(tMInstInfo);

    BusinessService bService = new BusinessService();
    bService.BusinessKey = businessKey;
    bService.Name = serviceName;
    bService.BindingTemplates.Add(bTemp);

    SaveService sService = new SaveService();
    sService.BusinessServices.Add(bService);
    ServiceDetail sd = sService.Send();
    return sd;
}
```

What makes this code portable is that the URL for the service is built by getting the server name from the `Environment.MachineName` property.

Once the service is published, you can proceed to use UDDI to find the service from the client.

The Inquiry API

You can use the Inquiry API to locate and enumerate the data in a UDDI registry. The API defines methods for finding data in the UDDI registry. The following `find_xxx()` methods support the main UDDI types.

- `find_service()`
- `find_business()`
- `find_relatedBusinesses()`
- `find_binding()`
- `find_tModel()`

The UDDI registry uses a key that is a Universally Unique Identifier (UUID)—this key is used to communicate with the client. For example the find_business() method returns a UUID key that is used as a parameter to the find_service() method call to find a service exposed by a specific business.

SOAP messages are used to encapsulate the find_xxx() methods, as you can see in the following code segment, which shows a search for a business entity named ABC:

```
<?xml version="1.0" encoding="UTF-8" ?>
<Envelope xmlns="http://schemas.xmlsoap.org/soap/envelope/">
    <body>
        <find_business generic="1.0" xmlns="urn:uddi-org:api">
            <name>ABC</name>
        </find_business>
    </body>
</Envelope>
```

You can also use the find_relatedBusinesses() method to locate businesses that have relationships with a given business.

In order to get more information about a specific element, you use the get_xxx() methods:

- get_businessDetail()
- get_businessDetailExt()
- get_serviceDetail()
- get_bindingDetail()
- get_tModelDetail()

Let's look at how you can locate and use an XML web service. There are four steps involved:

1. Use find_business() to locate the business that publishes XML web services.
2. Retrieve service information for the services published by that business.
3. Retrieve the binding template for a service.
4. Access the XML web service using the binding information.

The following code segment shows how to find a business:

```
FindBusiness fBus = new FindBusiness();
fBus.Name = "ABC";
BusinessList bList = fBus.Send();
```

Once you have located the business, you need to navigate the list that the business returns in order to retrieve binding information and the binding template. This is shown in the following code segment:

```
foreach(BusinessInfo bInfo in bList.BusinessInfos)
{
    foreach(ServiceInfo sInfo in bInfo.ServiceInfos)
    {
```

```
        FindBinding fBinding = new FindBinding();
        fBinding.ServiceKey = sInfo.ServiceKey;
        BindingDetail bDetail = fBinding.Send();
        foreach(BindingTemplate bTemp in bDetail.BindingTemplates)
        {
            if (bTemp.TModelInstanceDetail.TModelInstanceInfos[0].TModelKey ==
                tModelKey)
            {
                sURL = bTemp.AccessPoint.Text;
                goto gotIt;
            }
        }
    }
gotIt:
}
```

Now that you have located the binding information, all you need to do is set the URL property of the XML web service proxy and invoke the XML web service methods. This is shown in the following code segment:

```
XWService xws = new XWService();
xws.URL = sURL;
XmlNode amount = xws.getAmount("checking");
```

The preceding example demonstrates the four steps involved in finding and using an XML web service through a UDDI registry.

The Microsoft UDDI SDK

Microsoft has published the UDDI SDK to make using the UDDI APIs easier. The UDDI SDK provides managed wrappers for the UDDI data structures and APIs. The wrappers are in the `Microsoft.UDDI` namespace and are represented as .NET classes. The `Send()` method performs the action of the class.

Deployment

The physical deployment of an XML web service involves copying the folder of the XML web service to the production server. The copy can be as simple as using the XCOPY deployment, or using a Setup Project with the service. The key in any deployment is that the registration of the service is performed properly, as you saw in the previous sections.

Securing an XML Web Service

We need to consider security for XML web services just as we do for any other software product on a network. There are three aspects of security: authentication, authorization, and secure communication.

Authentication

Authentication is the process of verifying that the client is truly who he or she claims to be—this is done by collecting credentials (name and password) from the user. The credentials are validated against an authority like a database—if the credentials are valid, the client is an authenticated identity.

PART V

The Internet Information Service (IIS) offers three security mechanisms:

- **Basic authentication**   The basic authentication method is widely used. It is a standard method for collecting name and password information from the consumer. The basic authentication method is part of the HTTP specification and is a standard that is widely supported by browsers. It transmits the security credentials in clear text, resulting in a possible security breach unless the transmission channel is encrypted using Secure Sockets Layer (SSL).

- **Digest authentication**   The W3C has introduced digest authentication as a replacement for the basic authentication. In digest authentication, a binary hash is built from the name, password, requested resource, HTTP method, and some random values generated from the server.
  To generate a hash, the browser applies an algorithm that is considered one-way, meaning that there is there is no known way of getting back to the clear text from the binary hash.
  Digest authentication is supported in HTTP 1.1.

- **Integrated Windows authentication**   This authentication is based on the consumer having a Windows account that can be used for authentication. The strength of integrated Windows authentication is that the username and password are not sent across the network. Rather, a hash of the credentials is used. In addition, the method can make use of the Kerberos v5 protocol to take advantage of the secret-key cryptography provided in Active Directory and Kerberos v5. The biggest problem with integrated Windows authentication is that the server and client must have network communication over TCP/IP ports for the authentication—these ports are normally never left open on any devices that are used on the Internet because of the risk of intrusion into the system from Internet hackers.

Because you can create custom SOAP headers, you can also add your own authentication mechanism instead of using the built-in solutions. An XML web service consumer can add credentials to the SOAP header that are then retrieved by the XML web service, which can use the credentials to authenticate the consumer. For a refresher on SOAP, see Chapter 25.

The authorization configuration is performed on IIS because IIS is the service that the consumer will interact with to get access to an XML web service.

IIS Authentication

In order to configure authentication for an XML web service, you need to configure IIS through the Internet Services Manager. To start the Internet Services Manager, select Start | Programs | Administrative Tools | Internet Services Manager.

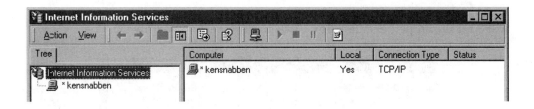

 EXAM TIP Remember that the authentication method for Windows authentication is set in IIS.

Expand the server in the Tree view, and then the Default Web Site, and you will see several entries, as shown in Figure 30-1.

Figure 30-1
The expanded
content of the
default web site

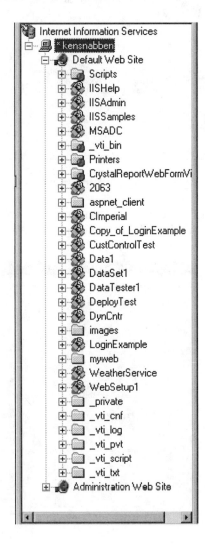

PART V

Select the web site you want to configure, right-click on it, and select Properties. This will open the Properties dialog box. Click on the Directory Security tab.

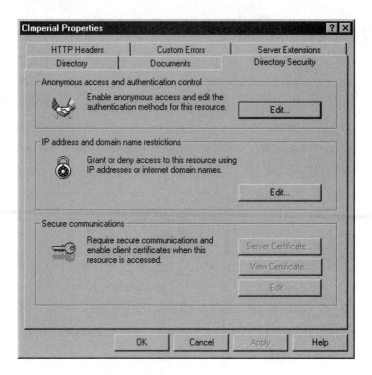

Security settings are configured under the Anonymous Access and Authorization Control section. Click the Edit button to open the Authentication Methods dialog box.

You can configure authentication in this dialog box. The default setting is that anonymous access is permitted. The proxy account that is configured for the anonymous can be changed in the Anonymous User Account dialog box shown in the following illustration—that you reach by clicking Edit; this account must be given the most restrictive access to the site possible.

If you configure Basic Authentication in the Authentication Methods dialog box, you must make sure that the accounts that will access the XML web service are given permission to log on to the web server that is hosting the XML web service. If you configure Digest Authentication for Windows Domain Servers, the domain controls must have a clear-text copy of the account's password to be used when comparing against the hash the consumer sends in. You will be requested to agree to the clear-text passwords when you select digest authentication, as shown here.

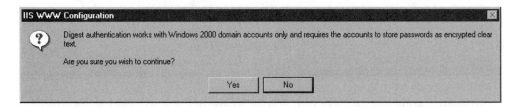

If you configure integrated Windows authentication, the user will not be prompted for credentials unless the integrated Windows authentication fails.

 EXAM TIP Integrated Windows authentication can not pass a firewall unless the administrator opens additional ports. It is highly unlikely that the administrator will do so because of the security risk involved.

Once the IIS configuration is complete, the XML web service must be configured to use the required authentication. This is done by editing the Web.config file that is located in the root directory for the XML web service. To enable the Windows-based authentication method (basic, digest, or integrated Windows) that was configured with IIS, add the following to the `Web.config` file:

```
<configure>
   <system.web>
      <authentication mode = "Windows" />
   </system.web>
</configure>
```

To access the user credentials, you can use the `Context` object as in this demo web method from Visual Studio .NET:

```
[WebMethod]
public string HelloWorld()
{
    return "Hello World " + Context.User.Identity.Name;
}
```

The result of this web method is seen in the illustration here.

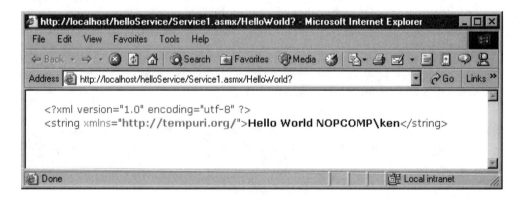

When you consume an XML web service by using the `wsdl` tool or by adding a web reference in Visual Studio .NET, the proxy class will inherit from the `SoapHttpClientProtocol` class. Through this class you have access to the `Credentials` property that is used to read or set security credentials. In order to control the authentication process, you can use the `NetworkCredential` class as shown in the following code segment.

```
WService ws = new WService();   // instantiate the XML Web Service proxy
// get a NetworkCredential object
ICredentials cred = new NetworkCredential("Ken", "password", "nop.com");
// configure the client credentials
ws.Credentials = cred;
string s;
try
{
```

```
    s = ws.HelloWorld();
} catch
{
    Console.WriteLine("Authentication Failed!");
}
```

 EXAM TIP Use the `NetworkCredential` class to specify the authentication when calling an XML web service.

The Windows authentication methods work well in intranets, but because of the additional ports that need to be opened to communicate through a firewall, these methods are not used on the Internet. The next section will deal with SOAP headers and how to customize them for authentication.

Custom SOAP Headers

For authenticating users on the Internet, you will most likely want to use a database that stores the account information of authorized users; your authentication implementation then passes these credentials from the user to the XML web service so the service can authenticate the user.

The SOAP header is a convenient area where additional information can be passed between the consumer and server. When you want to pass usernames and passwords in the SOAP header, you need to be concerned about the security of the information, and the best solution is to use strong encryption on the header only.

To customize the SOAP headers, you need to derive a class from `SoapHeader` as in the following code segment.

```
using System.Web.Services;
using System.Web.Services.Protocols;
public class AuthenticationHeader : SoapHeader
{
    // declare storage for username and password
    public string username;
    public string password;
}
// declare the XML Web Service
public class HelloService : WebService
{
    // declare a reference to the header
    public AuthenticationHeader m_header;
    [WebMethod]
    [SoapHeader("m_header", Required=false)]
    public string HelloWorld()
    {

    }
}
```

As you are implementing a custom authentication method, you need to turn off the authentication in the XML web service's `Web.config` file, as shown in the following code segment. Otherwise, the settings in the Web.config file would override the custom authentication.

```
<configuration>
    <system.web>
        <authentication mode = "None" />
    </system.web>
</configuration>
```

Authentication ensures that we know the identity of the entity that is accessing the service. The other side of the coin is *authorization*—ensuring that the entity has been granted the right to perform the actions requested. Authorization is our next topic.

Authorization

The three players in the authorization game are ASP.NET, the .NET Framework, and the Windows operating system. These three provide many techniques that combine to build a secure environment. When an XML web service consumer wants to access a resource, the effective permissions for that resource is the combination of the authenticated consumer's Windows permissions, the assembly's declarative access security, and the role-based security for the XML web service:

- The Windows operating system's security is based on the ability of the administrator to control the access to resources. All resources in the Windows operating system have Discretionary Access Control Lists (DACLs) associated with them. Only administrators can modify these DACLs to control the access for the users (consumers).

- Code-access security, or the assembly's declarative access security, is the programmatic method of ensuring that a user is authenticated before giving access to resources or running specific code.

- Role-based security groups users into roles that give identical access to users with similar needs. When the user is added to a role, it is not the user's credentials that are used but the role's. Using role-based security makes the administration of security easier.

Authorization can also be controlled as part of the XML Web Services URI namespace by modifying the <authorization> section of the Web.config file that is located in the root of the application. The statements in the <authorization> section take this form:

```
<[allow|deny] [users] [roles] [verbs] />
```

The following examples highlight the use of this element:

```
<configuration>
    <system.web>
        <authorization>
            <allow users="MIMICO\Dan"/>
```

```
            <deny users="MIMICO\Des"/>
            <deny users="?"/>
            <allow roles="service"/>
        </authorization>
    </system.web>
</configuration>
```

The `users="?"` part in the preceding code matches the anonymous user that is the default web user.

The new concept that has been introduced into software engineering over the last number of years is role-based security—in the next section we will look at how to configure roles and authorization.

Role-Based Security

Role-based security was introduced in Microsoft Transaction Server (MTS) and moved into the COM+ services. By using roles, you define what jobs or tasks the user performs rather than who the user is. For example, in a database application there are entry clerks who will perform data entry, and they will be given insert permission. Another role is the analyst, who requires read-only access to the data. Another role refers to the administration of the data, and the users in this role are given full control over the database.

The .NET Framework added to this task-oriented role environment by adding two new concepts: *principals* and *identities*. The principal represents the security context that the code is running under, and the identity encapsulates information about the user and the entity that has been authenticated.

The .NET Framework has four classes that are used to encapsulate the identities:

- `WindowsIdentity`
- `FormsIdentity`
- `GenericIdentity`
- `PassportIdentity`

XML web services can only work with the `WindowsIdentity` and `GenericIdentity` classes. The `WindowsIdentity` class is based on the Windows authentication methods, and it can impersonate a user other than the one that is connected to the current thread. This ability makes it possible to access resources on behalf of a user. The `GenericIdentity` class represents the user that has been authenticated through a custom authentication method.

There are two principals used in role-based security:

- `WindowsPrincipal`
- `GenericPrincipal`

The `WindowsPrincipal` class represents the Windows users and the roles those users belong to. The `GenericPrincipal` represents an identity and a list of roles that the identity belongs to.

Through the `WindowsIdentity` and `WindowsPrincipal` objects, you have access to information on the consumer through the `Context.User` object. For example, to find out whether a user is in a specific role, you can use the `IsInRole()` method as shown in the following code segment:

```
if (Context.User.IsInRole("BUILTIN\\Developers"))
{   }
```

This segment tested to see if the currently authenticated user belongs in the Windows group called Developers on the local server. However, it's probably better style to use the `WindowsBuiltInRole` enumeration rather than hard-code the role.

In this next example, the same test is performed, but we use the enumeration instead:

```
if (Context.User.IsInRole(WindowsBuiltInRole.Developers))
{   }
```

The use of authentication and authorization gives us the ability to control who can access our XML web services. The problem is that the data, and possibly the authentication credentials, can be stolen in transit if the communication is in clear text. Encryption is one way to help secure that information, and in the next section we will explore encryption.

Secure Communication

You can encrypt messages as they are sent between the XML web service and the consumer of the service. Encryption takes a lot of resources and is considered an expensive operation, so we need to pick the right level of encryption. There are several strategies:

- **Encrypt the whole message**   This is the sledgehammer method, as it is very unlikely that all messages require encryption. It is easy to implement this method, but it makes a high demand on the computers involved in the communication.

- **Encrypt only the body of the message**   This puts slightly less load on the servers than encrypting the whole message, but it is still probably more than is needed.

- **Encrypt only the header of the message**   SOAP headers contain authentication information, so it is a good thing to encrypt them. The load on the servers that this involves is rather light.

- **Encrypt only some select messages**   From the system's point-of-view, this is the best trade-off—it puts a light load on the servers, and it offers security only when it is needed. The other side of the coin is that the developer will need to spend more time developing the processing for this model, creating an algorithm that decides what messages to encrypt.

- **No encryption**   You must ask yourself if you really need to encrypt any traffic, and if the answer is no, then don't encrypt.

- **Partition the XML web service**   If you find that part of your XML web service requires encryption while another part doesn't, you can build two XML web services—one for secure communication and one for open communication. This is a very functional solution.

There are a number of options that can be used to encrypt the traffic between the XML web service and the consumer. Here are two of those options:

- **Secure Sockets Layer (SSL)** Using SSL for the communication is an easy way to configure encryption. With SSL, the entire message is encrypted.
- **Custom SOAP extensions** Using custom SOAP extensions gives you (the developer) full control over how the messages are encrypted and what messages are encrypted.

Now that we have identified the options, we will look at how to implement SSL and custom SOAP extensions.

Implementing SSL

SSL is based on *security certificates*. A security certificate is a binary structure that has been issued by a trusted certificate authority (CA). The standard certificates are called X.509 certificates, after the standard number.

You need to request a certificate from a CA, who will verify that you are who you claim to be by verifying names, addresses, and so on. The certificate is created by the CA signing the certificate with its *private key*.

Private keys are binary numbers that are prime numbers. The private key is called *private* because it is stored in such a fashion that it cannot be accessed by anyone but the owner of the key. Anything signed with a private key can be verified to have been signed with that key by using the public key that corresponds to the private key. This pair of keys makes up the basis for most encryption in the public sphere today.

The fact that you can verify that the certificate was signed by the CA means that you can trust the certificate without having to contact the CA every time, and by proxy the entity that the certificate was made out for can also be trusted to be who he or she claims to be.

In order to enable SSL in IIS, you need to open the properties for the web site that requires SSL, as shown in Figure 30-2. In the Directory Security tab, click the Server Certificate button to manage the certificates for the server. Adding the certificate received from the CA enables SSL for that web site. In order to be able to use certificates for virtual sites, the default web site must have a certificate first.

One problem with SSL is that it provides all-or-nothing encryption. You do not have the control to encrypt only some messages, or just the headers. For this type of control, you need to use the custom SOAP header extensions.

Using Custom SOAP Extensions

SOAP extensions allow you to get to the raw SOAP envelope before or after the serialization of the data. By working with the raw data, you can control how it is encrypted during transmission. To create the extensions, you need to create a class that inherits from the `System.Web.Services.Protocols.SoapExtensions` class.

PART V

Figure 30-2
The Web Site
Properties dialog
box, Directory
Security

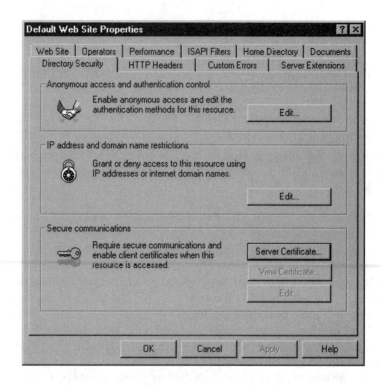

The encryption support comes from the DESCryptoServiceProvider class. This class that provides access to the cryptographic service provider (CSP) that provides Data Encryption Standard (DES) support. The following code segment shows how to use the class.

```
ICryptoTransform cryptographer;
ICryptoTransform decryptographer;
cryptographer = des.CreateEncryptor(key, IV);
decryptograph = des.CreateDecryptor(key, IV);

CryptoStream cStream;
cStream = new CryptoStream(message, cryptographer, CryptoStreamMode.Write);
// perform some interesting processing here
cStream = new CryptoStream(message, decrytpographer, CryptoStreamMode.Read);
```

To encrypt and decrypt messages, you need to apply the custom attributes that reference the SOAP extensions.

Access Unmanaged Code Using InterOp

The distributed environment that has been, and still is, the leading distributed environment for Microsoft systems is the COM environment. Even though XML web services are cast to be the replacement of COM components, that will not happen overnight.

You can expect to incorporate COM components from existing systems into your designs. There are some issues with the COM components though. The first is that they are native code for the platform, and they are executing in their own unmanaged process spaces. In order to be able to communicate between the managed code in our XML web service and the unmanaged code in the COM component, you need to marshal the method call and the data between the two environments. This is InterOp, or more correctly COM InterOp.

There is also an issue with deployment. COM components must be registered in the Registry database in order for client software to be able to locate them. During deployment, the component must either be deployed with the XML web service, or the Registry database on the production server must be updated with the Registry setting for the COM component. The utility that is used to register COM components is `regsvr32.exe`. Let's look at how you can incorporate COM components in your XML web service.

Using a COM Component

In order for C# code to reference and access a COM component, you will need to include a wrapper class also called a proxy for the COM component. This wrapper class encapsulates the COM objects and the interfaces in C# classes. The wrapper class is technically called the Runtime Callable Wrapper (RCW), and it is the part that makes the component self-describing. It wraps the COM component in a layer of XML called the manifest, so the component looks like a .NET assembly to the application.

The utility tool that actually performs the proxy creation is the Type Library Importer (`tlbimp.exe`), and it is included with the .NET SDK. You can execute `tlbimp.exe` manually to control the generation of the .NET proxy. If you execute the `tlbimp.exe` utility with the `/?` command-line switch, it will give you a brief help display.

EXAM TIP Use the `tlbimp.exe` utility to generate the proxy for a COM component.

Even though it looks like we have hidden the COM component (with all its problems) behind the RCW, that is not the case. The COM component is still the part that needs to perform the work. COM components that are used by .NET applications still have to be deployed in the same careful and meticulous way as always. They must even be registered using the `regsvr32.exe` utility as follows:

```
regsvr32 tconv.dll
```

EXAM TIP The `regsvr32.exe` utility is only used to register COM components in the Registry.

`tlbimp.exe` converts the COM component's internal objects as follows:

- COM CoClasses are converted to C# classes.
- COM structs are converted to C# structs.

EXAM TIP   COM components used by .NET applications must be registered in the Windows Registry.

Once you have built the RCW, you can proceed to use the COM component in the XML web service. The following example highlights the technique:

```
// Create the COM object
//
// the RCW must be included in the build
//
// the COM components RCW is in TempConv.dll
// the CoClass is named Conv
class Application
{
    public static int Main()
    {
        // This line will call CoCreateInstance(...)
        TempConv.Conv tc = new TempConv.Conv();
        //
        // query QueryInterface for the IConvert interface
        // by using explicit cast to the interface
        //
        TempConv.IConv ic = (TempConv.IConv)tc;
        //
        // call the CtoF() method on the interface
        //
        double ft = ic.CtoF(33);
        return 0;
    }
}
```

In order to call `QueryInterface`, you explicitly cast the reference to the interface, and then you call the methods of the interface as if they were normal methods of the object.

EXAM TIP   There is no `QueryInterface` through InterOp—you use casting instead.

Summary

In this chapter, you have learned how to publish an XML web service and how to finally deploy the XML web service. The focus is on the publishing—the physical movement of the files that make up the service is secondary.

The UDDI APIs are the key to making an XML web service available to your customers. It is also the key for the consumers of the XML web service who must query for and locate a service to bind to.

The security aspects of authentication and authorization were looked at, as well as how to secure the network traffic using SSL or custom SOAP extensions. The all-or-nothing nature of SSL was explored.

The final issue in this chapter was the COM InterOp, and how to make COM components available to your XML web service.

The exam will test your knowledge in the InterOp and how to find the XML Web Service, expect code segments in the exam that uses a number of areas of knowledge to test these topics.

Test Questions

1. You need to create a UDDI registry for your company. What are your options regarding private UDDI registries?

   A. Use the Private UDDI SDK from Microsoft.

   B. Implement your own private UDDI registry by implementing the entire UDDI specification.

   C. Implement a custom publish/discover architecture.

   D. Hard-code the endpoints.

2. You are developing an XML web application that will be published to a public UDDI registry. You need to create the business detail for your company, and part of the business detail object is the `Contact` object. Which code segment correctly builds a `Contact` object?

   A. Is it this code?

```
Contact con = new Contact();
con.PersonName = "Robert Burns";
con.Emails.Add("robert.burns@haggis.sc");
con.Descriptions.Add("en", "Sales Manager");
```

   B. Is it this code?

```
Contact con = new Contact();
con.PersonName = "Robert Burns";
con.Descriptions.Add("en", "Sales Manager");
```

   C. Is it this code?

```
Contact con = new Contact();
con.Descriptions.Add("en", "Sales Manager");
```

   D. Or, is it this code?

```
Contact con = new Contact();
con.PersonName = "Robert Burns";
con.Emails.Add("robert.burns@haggis.sc");
con.Descriptions.Add("Sales Manager");
```

3. You are writing the code that will publish an XML web service to a UDDI registry. You need to complete the following line of code:

```
Publish.HttpClient.Credentials = <<< Insert code here >>>;
```

   What code must you replace `<<< Insert code here >>>` with?

   A. new `AccessPoint(Http, Access)`

   B. new `UDDICredential(sn, sp, sv)`

   C. new `NetworkCredential(sn, sp, sv)`

   D. `"Provider=UDDI;UserID=sa;password;"`

4. You are developing an XML web service that will consume an XML web service. You have received the following code from one of your coworkers who worked on a similar project before.

```
...
FindBusiness fBus = new FindBusiness();
fBus.Name = "ABC";
<<< INSERT CODE HERE >>>;
foreach(BusinessInfo bInfo in bList.BusinessInfos)
{
    foreach(ServiceInfo sInfo in bInfo.ServiceInfos)
    {
        FindBinding fBinding = new FindBinding();
        fBinding.ServiceKey = sInfo.ServiceKey;
        BindingDetail bDetail = fBinding.Send();
        foreach(BindingTemplate bTemp in bDetail.BindingTemplates)
        {
            if (bTemp.TModelInstanceDetail.TModelInstanceInfos[0].TModelKey ==
                tModelKey)
            {
                string sURL = bTemp.AccessPoint.Text;
                goto gotIt;
            }
        }
    }
}
gotIt:
}
XWService xws = new XWService();
<<< INSERT CODE HERE >>>;
XmlNode amount = xws.getAmount("checking");
...
```

What code segment must you replace <<< INSERT CODE HERE >>> with? Select two code segments.

A. xws.URL = sURL;

B. bService.BusinessKey = businessKey

C. BusinessList bList = bService.BusinessKey.Send()

D. BusinessList bList = fBus.Send();

E. BusinessList.URL = sUrl

F. xws = sUrl

5. You are configuring security for an XML web service. The authentication should use the user's login credentials from their workstations. What steps do you have to perform to configure the security? Select all correct answers. Each answer makes up part of the solution.

A. Configure integrated Windows authentication in IIS.

B. Include <authentication mode="Integrated" /> in the Web.config file in the root of the XML web service.

C. Include <authentication mode="NTLM" /> in the Web.config file in the root of the XML web service.

   D. Include `<authentication mode="SSL" />` in the `Web.config` file in the root of the XML web service.

   E. Include `<authentication mode="Windows" />` in the `Web.config` file in the root of the XML web service.

   F. Disallow anonymous access in IIS.

6. You have received an XML web service that was designed by another developer at your company. You need to be able to access the login name of the user who is using the XML web service. You have verified that the XML web service is correctly configured for authentication—you need to assign the login name of the user to the string `strUser`. What code segment correctly assigns the login name of the user to `strUser`?

   A. `strUser = Context.User.Name;`

   B. `strUser = Identity.Name;`

   C. `strUser = User.Identity.Name;`

   D. `strUser = Context.User.Identity.Name;`

7. You have located the following lines in the `Web.config` file for the XML web service you are currently working on. What is the function of the lines?

```
<configure>
   <system.web>
      <authentication mode = "Windows" />
   </system.web>
</configuration>
```

   A. The authentication mode is set to Windows NT authentication.

   B. The authentication mode is set to integrated Windows.

   C. The authentication mode is set to what IIS is set to.

   D. The authentication mode is set to Windows 2000 Active Directory.

8. You are investigating the XML web service shown in this code segment:

```
WService ws = new WService();   // instantiate the XML Web Service proxy
// get a NetworkCredential object
ICredentials cred = new NetworkCredential("Ken", "password", "nop.com");
// configure the client credentials
ws.Credentials = cred;
string s;
```

   You need to assign the return value from the XML web service to the string `s`. Which code segment correctly assigns the return value to `s`?

   A. Is it this segment?

```
s = HelloWorld();
```

B. Is it this segment?

```
try
{
   s = ws.HelloWorld();
} catch
{
   Console.WriteLine("Authentication Failed!");
}
```

C. Is it this segment?

```
s = ws.cred.HelloWorld();
```

D. Or, is it this segment?

```
s = ws.HelloWorld();
```

9. You are developing an XML web service that will use custom SOAP headers, and you need to correctly define the SOAP header. In the following code you need to insert code at the marks.

```
using System.Web.Services;
using System.Web.Services.Protocols;
<<< Insert code here >>>
{
   // declare storage for username and password
   public string username;
   public string password;
}
// declare the XML Web Service
<<< Insert code here >>>
{
   // declare a reference to the header
   public AuthenticationHeader m_header;
   [WebMethod]
   <<< Insert code here >>>
   public string HelloWorld()
   {
      ...
   }
}
```

Which code segments must replace the lines marked << Insert code here >>>? Select three correct answers.

A. `[SoapHeader()]`

B. `[SoapHeader("m_header", Required=false)]`

C. `public class HelloService : SoapHeader`

D. `public class HelloService : WebService`

E. `public class AuthenticationHeader : WebService`

F. `[SoapHeader(username, password)]`

G. `public class AuthenticationHeader : SoapHeader`

10. You have implemented an XML web service that uses custom SOAP header authentication. When you test the XML web service, you find that the custom SOAP header authentication does not work. What is the most efficient way of making the XML web service use the custom SOAP header authentication?

A. Add or change the `<authentication mode="None"/>` element to the `Web.config` file.

B. Add or change the `<authentication mode="Custom"/>` element to the `Web.config` file.

C. Add or change the `<authentication mode="SOAP"/>` element to the `Web.config` file.

D. Add or change the `<authentication mode="IPP"/>` element to the `Web.config` file.

11. You have configured authorization for the XML web service you are currently developing. The configuration can be seen in the following segment:

```
<configuration>
   <system.web>
     <authorization>
         <allow users="MIMICO\Dan"/>
         <deny users="MIMICO\Des"/>
         <allow users="?"/>
         <allow roles="service"/>
     </authorization>
   </system.web>
</configuration>
```

What users have access to the XML web service? Select all that apply.

A. Des from Mimico

B. Dan from Mimico

C. Andy from Mimico

D. Anonymous users

E. The Service role

12. You need to encrypt the SOAP header. What is the correct method to use?

A. Inherit the web service class from the `SoapHeaderEncrypt` class.

B. Custom SOAP headers.

C. SOAP header extensions.

D. Enable SSL for the XML web service and configure it to encrypt the headers.

13. You need to test whether a consumer of your XML web service is a member of the local serviceadmin role. What is the correct way of testing for role membership?

A. `if (Context.User.IsInRole("BUILTIN\serviceadmin")) { ... }`

B. `if (Context.User.IsInRole("BUILTIN\\serviceadmin")) { ... }`

  C. `if (Context.User.IsInRole("(local)\\serviceadmin") { ... }`

  D. `if (Context.User.IsInRole("(local)\serviceadmin") { ... }`

14. True or false. In order to enable SSL on an XML web service, you need to have a certificate for the IIS default web site.

  A. True

  B. False

15. True or false. A COM component must be registered in the server where the XML web service is located.

  A. True

  B. False

Test Answers

 1. **B.** There is currently no public solution for a private UDDI registry.

 2. **A.** The `PersonName` and at least one e-mail address and description must be included.

 3. **C.**

 4. **A** and **D.**

 5. **A, E,** and **F.** In order to make IIS enforce integrated Windows authentication, you will have to turn off anonymous access.

 6. **D.**

 7. **C.** IIS controls which method of authentication actually is used.

 8. **B.** *Correctly* means that you must handle the credential exception if the access fails.

 9. **B, D,** and **G.**

10. **A.** The authentication mode must be turned off for custom methods to work.

11. **B, D,** and **E.** Des is explicitly denied; Andy is not in the list and if he does not change his login to anonymous, he will not have access.

12. **C.**

13. **B.**

14. **A.**

15. **A.**

PART VI

Appendixes

About the CD-ROM

The CD included with this book contains three practice exams—one each for these exams:

- **Exam 70-315**—Developing and Implementing Web Applications with Microsoft Visual C# .NET and Microsoft Visual Studio .NET

- **Exam 70-316**—Developing and Implementing Windows-Based Applications with Microsoft Visual C# .NET and Microsoft Visual Studio .NET

- **Exam 70-320**—Developing XML Web Services and Server Components with Microsoft Visual C# and the Microsoft .NET Framework

The CD-ROM included with this book comes complete with MasterExam, MasterSim, the electronic version of the book, and Session #1 of LearnKey's online training. The software is easy to install on any Windows 98/NT/2000 computer and must be installed to access the MasterExam and MasterSim features. You may, however, browse the electronic book directly from the CD without installation. To register for LearnKey's online training and a second bonus MasterExam, simply click the Online Training link on the Main Page and follow the directions to the free online registration.

System Requirements

Software requires Windows 98 or higher and Internet Explorer 5.0 or higher and 20MB of hard disk space for full installation. The electronic book requires Adobe Acrobat Reader. To access the online training from LearnKey, you must have RealPlayer Basic 8 or the Real1 plug-in, which will be automatically installed when you launch the online training.

LearnKey Online Training

The LearnKey Online Training link will allow you to access online training from Osborne.Onlineexpert.com. The first session of this course is provided at no charge.

Additional sessions for this course and other courses may be purchased directly from www.LearnKey.com or by calling 800-865-0165.

The first time that you run the training, you will required to register with the online product. Follow the instructions for a first-time user. Please make sure to use a valid e-mail address.

Prior to running the online training, you will need to add the Real plug-in and the RealCBT plug-in to your system. This will automatically be facilitated when you run the training the first time.

Installing and Running MasterExam and MasterSim

If your computer's CD-ROM drive is configured to auto-run, the CD-ROM will automatically start up when you insert the disk. From the opening screen, you may install MasterExam or MasterSim by clicking the MasterExam or MasterSim buttons. This will begin the installation process and create a program group named LearnKey. To run MasterExam or MasterSim select Start | Programs | LearnKey. If the auto-run feature did not launch your CD, browse to the CD and double-click the RunInstall icon.

MasterExam

MasterExam provides you with a simulation of the actual exam. The number of questions, the type of questions, and the time allowed are intended to be an accurate representation of the exam environment. You have the option to take an open-book exam, including hints, references, and answers, a closed-book exam, or the timed MasterExam simulation.

When you launch the MasterExam simulation, a digital clock will appear in the top center of your screen. The clock will continue to count down to zero unless you choose to end the exam before the time expires.

MasterSim

MasterSim is a set of interactive labs that will provide you with a wide variety of tasks that allow you to experience the software environment even if the software is not installed. Once you have installed MasterSim, you can access it quickly through this CD launch page or you can access it through Start | Programs | LearnKey.

Electronic Book

The entire contents of the Study Guide are provided in PDF. Adobe's Acrobat Reader has been included on the CD.

Help

A help file is provided and can be accessed by clicking the Help button on the main page in the lower-left corner. Individual help features are also available through MasterExam, MasterSim, and LearnKey's online training.

Removing Installation(s)

MasterExam and MasterSim are installed on your hard drive. For *best* results for removal of programs, use the Start | Programs | LearnKey | Uninstall options to remove MasterExam or MasterSim.

If you want to remove the RealPlayer, use the Add/Remove Programs icon from your Control Panel. You may also remove the LearnKey training program from this location.

Technical Support

For questions regarding the technical content of the electronic book or MasterExam, please visit www.osborne.com or e-mail customer.service@mcgraw-hill.com. For customers outside the 50 United States, e-mail international_cs@mcgraw-hill.com.

LearnKey Technical Support

For technical problems with the software (installation, operation, removing installations), and for questions regarding LearnKey online training and MasterSim content, please visit www.learnkey.com or email techsupport@learnkey.com.

The New Microsoft Developer Tracks

So you want to be a Microsoft Certified Solution Developer (MCSD)? You have come to the right place. We will look at the tracks you can take in the new program and focus on the C# track, since it is the subject of this book. In this appendix, you will also find valuable information about taking the exam, how to study for the exam, and what to do the day of the exam.

What Is an MCSD for Microsoft .NET?

A Microsoft Certified Solution Developer (MCSD) is an individual who has taken and passed a series of Microsoft developer exams, thereby demonstrating competence in the skill level determined by Microsoft. The certification that you receive as a result (MCSD) is a recognized industry certification and can open doors for you (if you are newer to the field) or assist with advancement in your current employment. If you already have an MCSD credential, you are not required to update your status to the .NET platform; however, it is advisable to do so. Since .NET development is so radically different from earlier versions (for example, Visual C++ 6.0, Visual Basic 6.0, and so forth), it is a good idea to upgrade your skills.

In order to become an MCSD under the .NET platform, you must pass four required (core) exams and one elective exam. Let's look at the core exams:

- **Exam 70-300—Analyzing Requirements and Defining .NET Solution Architectures** At the time of writing, the objectives of this exam have not been released. It can be assumed, however, that this exam will replace Exam 70-100, "Analyzing Requirements and Defining Solution Architectures," whereby a successful candidate will be able to analyze business requirements within given scenarios and provide the solution architecture that optimizes business results.

- **Exam 70-305 or Exam 70-315—Developing and Implementing Web Applications with Microsoft Visual Basic .NET (70-305) or Microsoft Visual C# .NET and Microsoft Visual Studio .NET (70-315)** If you are a Visual Basic developer, you will want to follow the Visual Basic .NET track and take exam 70-305. However, the fact that you are reading this book suggests that you have decided to follow the Visual C# .NET track and will take exam 70-315. The 70-315 exam will test your ability to work with Web Forms, ASP.NET, and the Microsoft .NET Framework. The exam objectives are covered in this book in Part III. In order to be successful on Exam 70-315, you should be proficient in the topics covered in Parts I, II, and III of this book.

- **Exam 70-306 or Exam 70-316—Developing and Implementing Windows Applications with Microsoft Visual Basic .NET (70-306) or Microsoft Visual C# .NET and Microsoft Visual Studio .NET (70-316)** If you are a Visual Basic developer, you will want to follow the Visual Basic .NET track and take exam 70-306. However, as suggested previously, you are probably here to take the Visual C# .NET exam—70-316. This exam will test your ability to work with Windows-based applications using Windows Forms and the Microsoft .NET Framework. The exam objectives are covered in Part IV of this book. Be sure that you have closely met the objectives of Parts I, II, and IV of this book before you take the exam.

- **Exam 70-310 or Exam 70-320—Developing XML Web Services and Server Components with Microsoft Visual Basic .NET (70-310) or Microsoft Visual C# .NET and the Microsoft Visual .NET Framework (70-320)** A Visual Basic developer will probably follow the Visual Basic .NET track and take exam 70-310. However, you will be interested in Exam 70-320, which works with Microsoft Visual C# .NET. This exam will test your ability to work with middle-tier components, server components, and XML web services by using Visual Studio .NET and the Microsoft .NET Framework. The exam objectives are covered in Part V of this book. If you work through Parts I, II, and V of this book, you should be ready to take exam 70-320.

In order to complete the requirements for an MCSD under the .NET Framework, you must take one elective exam. You can choose from any of the following exams:

- **Exam 70-229—Designing and Implementing Databases with Microsoft SQL Server 2000 Enterprise Edition** This exam will measure your ability to design and implement database solutions by using Microsoft SQL Server 2000 Enterprise Edition.

- **Exam 70-230—Designing and Implementing Solutions with Microsoft BizTalk Server 2000 Enterprise Edition** This exam will measure your ability to implement, administer, and troubleshoot information systems that incorporate Microsoft BizTalk Server 2000. You will also be tested on your ability to analyze, design, build, and implement integrated business process solutions by using Microsoft BizTalk Server 2000.

- **Exam 70-234—Designing and Implementing Solutions with Microsoft Commerce Server 2000**   This exam will measure your ability to design and implement solutions by using Microsoft Commerce Server 2000.

Microsoft suggests that candidates for any of these exams (and in particular, for the MCSD designation) have at least two years of experience in developing and maintaining solutions and applications.

What Is an MCAD for Microsoft .NET?

There is a second certification that candidates can take that is a modified subset of the MCSD. It is called MCAD (Microsoft Certified Application Developer). If you are a programmer/analyst or a application/software developer, this may be the right certification for you. Microsoft has split the two levels of the software development cycle into the two different certifications. If you are involved in analyzing and developing software, you may want to investigate the MCSD. However, if your role is to develop, test, deploy, and maintain software, the MCAD is right for you.

The MCAD certification requires that you take two core exams and one elective exam. You can choose one of the following core exams:

- Exam 70-305—Developing and Implementing Web Applications with Microsoft Visual Basic .NET and Microsoft Visual Studio .NET

- Exam 70-306—Developing and Implementing Windows-Based Applications with Microsoft Visual Basic .NET and Microsoft Visual Studio .NET

- Exam 70-315—Developing and Implementing Web Applications with Microsoft C# .NET and Microsoft Visual Studio .NET

- Exam 70-316—Developing and Implementing Windows-Based Applications with Microsoft Visual C# .NET and Microsoft Visual Studio .NET

The second core exam can be selected from the following list:

- Exam 70-310—Developing XML Web Services and Server Components with Microsoft Visual Basic .NET and the Microsoft .NET Framework

- Exam 70-320—Developing XML Web Services and Server Components with Microsoft Visual C# .NET and the Microsoft .NET Framework

The elective exam can be chosen from this list:

- Exam 70-229—Designing and Implementing Databases with Microsoft SQL Server 2000 Enterprise Edition

- Exam 70-230—Designing and Implementing Solutions with Microsoft BizTalk Server 2000 Enterprise Edition

- Exam 70-234—Designing and Implementing Solutions with Microsoft Commerce Server 2000

- Exam 70-305, 70-306, 70-315, or 70-316—any of these exams can be used for the elective as long as it is not also used for the core exam.

How to Prepare for Microsoft Exams

If you have read the recommended parts of this book and have worked your way successfully through the questions at the end of each chapter and the sample exams on the CD that comes with this book, you are almost ready for the Microsoft exams. We say "almost" because you must be prepared for the types of questions that you will see on the Microsoft exam. Although the exams on the CD have attempted to simulate real exams, we are bound by non-disclosure agreements not to divulge the questions on the exam. However, let's take a moment to look at the format of the questions.

What the Questions Might Look Like

Be prepared for questions that will tax your patience at reading. As one of their favorite tricks, Microsoft will present you with a long and complicated scenario. Your task is to work your way through the obfuscation of extra, non-significant details and find the crux of the question. What is it that they want you to do? Look at the following example:

Sample Exam Question

"You are the project leader of a major software-development project for ABC Corporation. Your team has presented you with a series of needs analyses, group reports, and user-requirement documents. You have analyzed all the relevant material and are now in the process of interviewing the management groups for information regarding the user-interface requirements. After a discussion with the accounting department, you become aware of a significant change to the initial design of the project. The accounts payable users need a user interface that will allow them to interact with suppliers in an online fashion and they need to be able to transfer information, such as purchase orders, back and forth. The user interface needs to be displayed in a web browser and connect to the Microsoft SQL Server 2000 database. The database will contain the information necessary to connect to the supplier's database, and the middle-tier components will accomplish the task of making the connection. Which of the following technologies must be used to satisfy the account payable users' request?

    A. Windows Form application

    B. Web Form application

    C. XML web service

    D. .NET remoting"

Although this is a fictitious example, you can see how the extraneous information in the question can sideline your thoughts. Take the time to read the question thoroughly and then look for the "hidden" question that is being asked of you. Sometimes, it helps to read the answers first and then read the question. It can help you focus on the real intent of the question.

The exam can contain a number of different question types. You may find questions that ask for a single, keyed-in response. The bulk of the questions will be presented to you in multiple choice format. However, you may find questions that present very large scenarios, have exhibits that you must open, or ask you to move objects around a screen in order to present the answer. Be prepared for any type of question.

You will also find that Microsoft presents you with a lot of code. The only way to become comfortable with this is to spend time working with the code of Visual C# .NET. You must be able to quickly, under time pressure, assess the validity of code, choose the most appropriate code, or find errors in code segments. Be sure that you have had the experience necessary to accomplish this.

The Logistics of the Exam

Where you take the exam and how you find out your score are probably questions on your mind if you have never taken a Microsoft exam before. Here are some helpful hints for you when preparing for the actual day of your exam.

Registering for the Exam

As we write this, there are two organizations that deliver tests for Microsoft:

- **Prometric (http://www.prometric.com)** In order to schedule your test, you can either call their test hotline or register online at http://www.2test.com.

- **VUE (http://www.vue.com)** You can register for your exam online through VUE's web site.

Both of these places will let you know the closest test center location for you. Once you register with them, you will be given a time and location for the exam. You will need to have two pieces of ID ready to present at the test center (one must be a photo ID).

The Day of the Exam

Be sure to arrive at the exam at least 20 minutes in advance of your booked time. You will need that time to relax and calm yourself (in addition to providing the necessary information to the test center—IDs, signing-in, and so on). It is advisable to not cram information into your head minutes before the exam. You will need to have a cool head to read through the questions and not panic. The following tips may help you when taking the exam:

- *Read every question thoroughly.* Don't leave anything out.

- *Answer every question.* A missed question is a missed mark, and there is no penalty for an incorrect answer.

- *Watch the clock.* You will be given a timed period in which to take the exam. Be sure that you have judged the questions accurately and don't find yourself with ten questions and five minutes remaining.

- *Most of Microsoft's exams allow you to mark a question and return to it later.* Take advantage of this. You can undermine your own confidence by spending a long time on a question whose answer eludes you. Mark it and return to it later.

- *Don't panic.* If you have studied hard and have been successful going through the questions in this book, you are probably more than ready to take the exam. Many very qualified individuals have fallen prey to panic when taking exams. Take a deep breath and relax—you know your stuff. Now show Microsoft that you know it.

How Will You Find Out if You Were Successful?

There's no long wait for finding out your results. As soon as you are confident that you have completed all of the questions and reviewed any troubling questions, you will be asked if you are finished. As soon as you click Finish or End Test (or whatever the button says), you will wait a few seconds (a few agonizing seconds) and then your result will be displayed. You will be informed of either a pass or a failure. Microsoft will not divulge to you the questions that you got wrong or the questions that you got right. You will not know your personal area of difficulty. Microsoft does this to protect the integrity of their exams and to ensure that when you are successful, your credentials mean something significant.

What to Do if You Were Not Successful?

No one wants to fail a test. But rest assured that even the gurus who take an exam a month fail at some time. You may not have read a couple of questions correctly. In your excitement, you may have clicked on the wrong answers for a few questions. Don't despair! You simply take your time and retake the exam when you are ready. You may find, especially if it is your first exam, that you do not pass the first time. Most of that may be due to your inexperience at taking Microsoft exams and not your inexperience with the actual product. Take your time to review the material and go through the questions in the chapters and on the CD again. You will be successful the next time!!

Exam Objectives

Each chapter in the three parts of the book that deal specifically with the exams begin with the objectives that will be covered in that chapter. In this section, we will list the objectives of each of the three exams.

Exam 70-315

At the time of writing, Exam 70-315, "Developing and Implementing Web Applications with Microsoft Visual C# .NET and Visual Studio .NET," included the following objectives:

Objective	See Chapter(s)...
Creating User Services.	11, 12, 15
Create ASP.NET pages.	11, 12
Add web server controls, HTML server controls, user controls, and HTML code to ASP.NET pages.	11, 12, 14, 15
Implement navigation for the user interface.	12
Validate user input.	12
Implement error handling in the user interface.	15
Implement online user assistance.	15
Incorporate existing code into ASP.NET pages.	12
Display and update data.	10, 16
Instantiate and invoke Web Services or components.	13
Implement globalization.	7
Handle events.	4, 11, 12, 13
Implement accessibility features.	15
Use and edit intrinsic objects.	11, 12
Creating and Managing Components and .NET Assemblies.	6, 7, 17
Create and modify a .NET assembly.	6
Create web custom controls and web user controls.	14
Consuming and Manipulating Data.	10, 16
Access and manipulate data from a Microsoft SQL Server database by creating and using ad hoc queries and stored procedures.	10
Access and manipulate data from a data store. Data stores include relational databases, XML documents, and flat files. Methods include XML techniques and ADO.NET.	10, 16
Handle data errors.	16
Testing and Debugging.	9, 17
Create a unit test plan.	9
Implement tracing.	9, 17
Debug, rework, and resolve defects in code.	9, 17

PART VI

Objective	See Chapter(s)...
Deploying a Web Application.	17
Plan the deployment of a web application.	17
Create a setup program that installs a web application and allows for the application to be uninstalled.	17
Deploy a web application.	17
Add assemblies to the Global Assembly Cache.	17
Maintaining and Supporting a Web Application.	17
Optimize the performance of a web application.	17
Diagnose and resolve errors and issues.	17
Configuring and Securing a Web Application.	17
Configure a web application.	17
Configure security for a web application.	17
Configure authorization.	17
Configure and implement caching.	17
Configure and implement session state in various topologies, such as a web garden and a web farm.	17
Install and configure server services.	17

For the most up-to-date listing of exam objectives, visit Microsoft's web site at http://www.microsoft.com/traincert/exams/70-315.asp.

Exam 70-316

At the time of writing, Exam 70-316, "Developing and Implementing Windows-Based Applications with Microsoft Visual C# .NET and Visual Studio .NET," included the following objectives:

Objective	See Chapter(s)...
Creating User Services.	
Create a Windows Form by using the Windows Forms Designer.	18
Add controls to a Windows Form.	18, 19
Implement navigation for the user interface.	18, 19
Validate user input.	19
Implement error handling in the user interface.	19
Implement online user assistance.	24
Display and update data.	10, 20
Instantiate and invoke web services or components.	21

Objective	See Chapter(s)...
Creating User Services.	
Implement globalization.	7, 24
Create, implement, and handle events.	18, 19
Implement print capability.	24
Implement accessibility features.	24
Creating and Managing Components and .NET Assemblies.	
Create and modify a .NET assembly.	6, 24
Create a Windows control.	22
Consuming and Manipulating Data.	
Access and manipulate data from a Microsoft SQL Server database by creating and using ad hoc queries and stored procedures.	10, 20
Access and manipulate data from a data store. Data stores include relational databases, XML documents, and flat files. Methods include XML techniques and ADO.NET.	10, 20
Handle data errors.	10, 20
Testing and Debugging.	
Create a unit test plan.	9
Implement tracing.	9, 24
Debug, rework, and resolve defects in code.	9
Deploying a Windows-Based Application.	
Plan the deployment of a Windows-based application.	23
Create a setup program that installs an application and allows for the application to be uninstalled.	23
Deploy a Windows-based application.	23
Add assemblies to the Global Assembly Cache.	6, 23
Verify security policies for a deployed application.	23
Maintaining and Supporting a Windows-Based Application.	
Optimize the performance of a Windows-based application.	24
Diagnose and resolve errors and issues.	24
Configuring and Securing a Windows-Based Application.	
Configure a Windows-based application.	24
Configure security for a Windows-based application.	24
Configure authorization.	24
Implement identity management.	24

For the most up-to-date listing of exam objectives, visit Microsoft's web site at http://www.microsoft.com/traincert/exams/70-316.asp.

PART VI

Exam 70-320

At the time of writing, Exam 70-320, "Developing XML Web Services and Server Components with Microsoft Visual C# .NET and the Microsoft .NET Framework," included the following objectives:

Objective	See Chapter(s)...
Creating and Managing Microsoft Windows Services, Serviced Components, .NET Remoting Objects, and XML Web Services.	
Create and manipulate a Windows service.	26
Create and consume a serviced component.	26
Create and consume a .NET remoting object.	27
Create and consume an XML web service.	25, 28
Implement security for a Windows service, a serviced component, a .NET remoting object, and an XML web service.	30
Access unmanaged code from a Windows service, a serviced component, a .NET remoting object, and an XML web service.	30
Consuming and Manipulating Data.	
Access and manipulate data from a Microsoft SQL Server database by creating and using ad hoc queries and stored procedures.	10, 29
Create and manipulate DataSets.	10, 29
Access and manipulate XML data.	29
Testing and Debugging.	
Create a unit test plan.	9
Implement tracing.	9
Instrument and debug a Windows service, a serviced component, a .NET remoting object, and an XML web service.	30
Use interactive debugging.	30
Log test results.	30
Deploying Windows Services, Serviced Components, .NET Remoting Objects, and XML Web Services.	
Plan the deployment of and deploy a Windows service, a serviced component, a .NET remoting object, and an XML web service.	30
Create a setup program that installs a Windows service, a serviced component, a .NET remoting object, and an XML web service.	30
Publish an XML web service.	30
Configure client computers and servers to use a Windows service, a serviced component, a .NET remoting object, and an XML web service.	26, 27, 28
Implement versioning.	6, 30
Plan, configure, and deploy side-by-side deployments and applications.	30
Configure security for a Windows service, a serviced component, a .NET remoting object, and an XML web service.	30

For the most up-to-date listing of exam objectives, visit Microsoft's web site at http://www.microsoft.com/traincert/exams/70-320.asp.

Summary

This appendix has presented the exams that are covered in this book as well as some advice for taking the exams. We wish you the best of luck and hope this book has been helpful in preparing you for the exam. Be sure to review the CD that comes with this book—there are a lot of helpful tools for studying and preparing for the exams. Good luck on your quest to become a Microsoft Certified Solution Developer!

Command-Line Syntax

In addition to the compilers for C# (csc.exe), C++ (cl.exe), and VB .NET (vbc.exe) the Microsoft .NET Framework SDK adds a number of tools designed to make it easier for you to create, deploy, and manage applications and components that target the .NET Framework. This appendix will introduce these tools and will also detail the command-line usages of csc.exe.

Command Utilities

In order to be able to run these command-line utilities, you must configure the environment properly. The Visual Studio .NET installation includes a command file (VCVARS32.bat) that configures the command environment properly. The command file is installed in the \bin directory of your installation (the default is c:\Program Files\Microsoft Visual Studio.NET\vc7\bin). The command file is configured during the installation of Visual Studio to correspond to your computer's set-up. Do not replace a missing or damaged VCVARS32.bat file with a VCVARS32.bat from another machine. Rerun setup to replace the missing file.

To run VCVARS32.BAT you can execute it from the path or you can use the shortcut. Select Start | Programs | Microsoft Visual Studio .NET | Visual Studio .NET Tools | Visual Studio .NET Command Prompt.

TIP We recommend that you create a shortcut to the .NET command prompt on your desktop and in the Windows taskbar.

The .NET Framework SDK tools are grouped according to use:

- Debugging tools (see Table C-1)
- Configuration and deployment tools (see Table C-2)
- Security tools (see Table C-3)
- General tools (see Table C-4)

Debugging Tools

Tool	Description
Microsoft CLR Debugger (DbgCLR.exe)	Provides debugging services with a graphical interface to help application developers find and fix bugs in programs that target the runtime.
Runtime Debugger (Cordbg.exe)	Provides command-line debugging services using the Common Language Runtime Debug API. It is used to find and fix bugs in programs that target the runtime.

Table C-1   The .NET Framework SDK Debugging Tools

Configuration and Deployment Tools

Tool	Description
Assembly Cache Viewer (Shfusion.dll)	Lets you to view and manipulate the contents of the Global Assembly Cache using Windows Explorer.
Assembly Linker (Al.exe)	Allows you to use either resource files or Microsoft Intermediate Language (MSIL) files to generate a file with an assembly manifest.
Assembly Registration tool (Regasm.exe)	Registers .NET Framework classes to the Registry, which allows COM clients to create .NET Framework classes transparently.
Assembly Binding Log Viewer (Fuslogvw.exe)	Displays log-file information for failed assembly binding. This information can help you diagnose the reasons the .NET Framework has problems locating an assembly at run time.
Global Assembly Cache tool (Gacutil.exe)	This tool allows you to view and manipulate the contents of the Global Assembly Cache and download cache. You can use Gacutil.exe in build scripts, makefile files, and batch files.
Installer tool (Installutil.exe)	Allows you to install and uninstall server resources by executing the installer components of a specified assembly.
Isolated Storage tool (Storeadm.exe)	Displays and manages all existing stores for the currently logged-on user.
Native Image Generator (Ngen.exe)	Lets you create a native image from a managed assembly and install the image in the native image cache on the local computer.

Table C-2   The .NET Framework SDK Configuration and Deployment Tools

Tool	Description
.NET Framework Configuration tool (`Mscorcfg.msc`)	Provides a graphical interface for managing .NET Framework security policy and applications that use remoting services. This tool also allows you to manage and configure assemblies in the Global Assembly Cache.
.NET Services Installation tool (`Regsvcs.exe`)	Allows you to add managed classes to Windows 2000 Component Services (COM+) by loading and registering the assembly and generating, registering, and installing the type library into an existing COM+ 1.0 application.
Soapsuds tool (`Soapsuds.exe`)	Lets you compile client applications that communicate with XML Web Services. The technique used is called *remoting*.
Type Library Exporter (`Tlbexp.exe`)	Generates a type library from a Common Language Runtime assembly.
Type Library Importer (`Tlbimp.exe`)	Converts the type definitions found within a COM type library into equivalent definitions in managed metadata format.
Web Services Description Language tool (`Wsdl.exe`)	Generates the code for XML Web Services and XML web service clients, XML Schema Definition (XSD) schema files, and the `.disco` discovery documents from WSDL (Web Services Description Language) contract files.
Web Services Discovery tool (`Disco.exe`)	Allows you to discover the URLs of XML Web Services located on a web server.
XML Schema Definition Tool (`Xsd.exe`)	Generates XML schemas that follow the XSD language proposed by the World Wide Web Consortium (W3C). This tool generates Common Language Runtime classes and `DataSet` classes from an XSD schema file.

Table C-2   The .NET Framework SDK Configuration and Deployment Tools *(continued)*

Security Tools

Tool	Description
Certificate Creation tool (`Makecert.exe`)	Creates X.509 certificates for testing purposes only.
Certificate Manager tool (`Certmgr.exe`)	Manages certificates, certificate trust lists (CTLs), and certificate revocation lists (CRLs).
Certificate Verification tool (`Chktrust.exe`)	Verifies the validity of a file signed with an X.509 certificate.

Table C-3   The .NET Framework SDK Security Tools

Tool	Description
Code Access Security Policy tool (Caspol.exe)	Allows you to examine and modify security policies for the machine, user, and enterprise-level code access.
File Signing tool (Signcode.exe)	Signs a Portable Executable (PE) file with an Authenticode digital signature.
Permissions View tool (Permview.exe)	Allows you to view the minimal, optional, and refused permission sets requested by an assembly. You can also use this tool to display the declarative security used by an assembly.
PEVerify tool (PEverify.exe)	Conducts MSIL type-safety verification checks and metadata validation checks on an assembly.
Secutil tool (Secutil.exe)	Extracts public-key information or Authenticode publisher certificates from an assembly. The output is formatted so it can be incorporated into code.
Set Registry tool (Setreg.exe)	Allows you to change the Registry settings for the Software Publishing State keys.
Software Publisher Certificate Test tool (Cert2spc.exe)	Tests a Software Publisher's Certificate (SPC), or creates an SPC from one or more X.509 certificates.
Strong Name tool (Sn.exe)	Allows you to create assemblies with strong names.

Table C-3   The .NET Framework SDK Security Tools *(continued)*

General Tools

Tool	Description
Common Language Runtime Minidump tool (Mscordmp.exe)	Creates a file containing a core dump of information that can be useful when analyzing system issues in the runtime.
License Compiler (Lc.exe)	Allows you to create a .licenses file that can be embedded in a Common Language Runtime executable. It reads text files that contain licensing information.
Management Strongly Typed Class Generator (Mgmtclassgen.exe)	Allows you to quickly generate an early-bound class for a specified Windows Management Instrumentation (WMI) class.
MSIL Assembler (Ilasm.exe)	Generates a PE file from Microsoft Intermediate Language (MSIL).
MSIL Disassembler (Ildasm.exe)	Produces a MSIL source file from a Portable Executable (PE) file.

Table C-4   The .NET Framework SDK General Tools

Tool	Description
Resource File Generator tool (`Resgen.exe`)	Converts text files and `.resx` (XML-based resource format) files to .NET Common Language Runtime binary `.resources` files that can be embedded in a runtime binary executable or compiled into satellite assemblies.
Windows Forms ActiveX Control Importer (`Aximp.exe`)	Converts type definitions in a COM type library for an ActiveX control into a Windows Forms control.
Windows Forms Class Viewer (`Wincv.exe`)	Finds managed classes matching a specified search pattern, and displays information about those classes using the Reflection API.
Windows Forms Resource Editor (`Winres.exe`)	Allows you to quickly and easily localize the Windows Forms forms in your application using a GUI tool.

Table C-4   The .NET Framework SDK General Tools *(continued)*

C# Compiler (csc.exe)

In order to compile and run a C# program, you will need to have the .NET Framework installed on your computer. Microsoft has made the .NET Framework available as a free upgrade, and you can either download it from http://msdn.microsoft.com (approximately 130MB) or order a CD with the .NET Framework.

After installation, the C# compiler is available from the command prompt to create Portable Executable (PE) files from your source files (see the previous "Command Utilities" section for information on how to set up the environment for use with command-line tools).

Using the C# Compiler (`csc.exe`) is rather complicated because it has a large family of command-line options that control the behavior of the compiler. The next section will give you an overview of most of the command-line switches that are available.

csc Command-Line Syntax

In Table C-5, you can see all the command-line switches understood by the C# compiler. To get an instant listing of the command-line switches, you only need to execute the `csc.exe` program with the `/help` switch to produce the following listing:

```
C:\>csc /help
Microsoft (R) Visual C# .NET Compiler version 7.00.9466
for Microsoft (R) .NET Framework version 1.0.3705
Copyright (C) Microsoft Corporation 2001. All rights reserved.
            Visual C# .NET Compiler Options
                    - OUTPUT FILES -
/out:<file>             Output file name (default: base name of file with main
                        class or first file)
/target:exe             Build a console executable (default) (Short form:
                        /t:exe)
...
```

PART VI

Option	Description
@	Specify a response file.
/?	List compiler options to `stdout`.
/addmodule	Specify one or more modules to be part of this assembly.
/baseaddress	Specify the preferred base address at which to load a DLL.
/bugreport	Create a file that contains information that makes it easy to report a bug.
/checked	Specify whether integer arithmetic that overflows the bounds of the data type will cause an exception at run time.
/codepage	Specify the code page to use for all source-code files in the compilation.
/debug	Emit debugging information.
/define	Define preprocessor symbols.
/doc	Process documentation comments to an XML file.
/filealign	Specify the size of sections in the output file.
/fullpaths	Specify the absolute path to the file in compiler output.
/help	List compiler options to `stdout`.
/incremental	Enable incremental compilation of source-code files.
/lib	Specify the location of assemblies referenced via `/reference`.
/linkresource	Create a link to a managed resource.
/main	Specify the location of the `Main()` method.
/nologo	Suppress compiler banner information.
/nostdlib	Do not import standard library (`mscorlib.dll`).
/noconfig	Do not compile with the global or local versions of `csc.rsp`.
/nowarn	Suppress the compiler's ability to generate specified warnings.
/optimize	Enable or disable optimizations.
/out	Specify output file.
/recurse	Search subdirectories for source files to compile.
/reference	Import metadata from a file that contains an assembly.
/resource	Embed a .NET Framework resource into the output file.
/target	Specify the format of the output file using one of four options: `/target:exe` `/target:library` `/target:module` `/target:winexe`
/unsafe	Compile code that uses the `unsafe` keyword.
/utf8output	Display compiler output using UTF-8 encoding.
/warn	Set warning level.
/warnaserror	Promote warnings to errors.
/win32icon	Insert an `.ico` file into the output file.
/win32res	Insert a Win32 resource into the output file.

Table C-5   The `csc.exe` Command-Line Switches

Examples

The C# compiler commands can be typed in at the command-line prompt or as part of command files used to build the application. The following examples are executed from the command prompt:

- Compiles `File.cs` producing `File.exe`:

  ```
  csc File.cs
  ```

- Compiles `File.cs` producing `File.dll`:

  ```
  csc /target:library File.cs
  ```

- Compiles `File.cs` and creates `Hence.exe`:

  ```
  csc /out:Hence.exe File.cs
  ```

- Compiles all of the C# files in the current directory, with optimizations on and defines the DEBUG symbol. The output is `File2.exe`:

  ```
  csc /define:DEBUG /optimize /out:File2.exe *.cs
  ```

- Compiles all of the C# files in the current directory, producing a debug version of `File2.dll`. No logo and no warnings are displayed:

  ```
  csc /target:library /out:File2.dll /warn:0 /nologo /debug *.cs
  ```

- Compiles all of the C# files in the current directory to `Thusly.hence` (a DLL):

  ```
  csc /target:library /out:Thusly.hence *.cs
  ```

The .NET Class Library

The .NET Framework includes an extensive collection of prebuilt class files. These have been grouped together in meaningful namespaces and published to the .NET Class Library. It would fill the entire book if we were to cover every class and namespace here. However, that is not our purpose. What we will attempt to do is document some of the more common and possibly more useful classes in the library.

Keep in mind that any class you select from the class library can be used in any of the .NET programming languages, so, in effect, this appendix is pertinent to all of the languages included in .NET, such as Visual Basic .NET, JScript .NET, and so on.

Accessing Classes from the .NET Class Library

The .NET Class Library is broken down into namespaces which, as we have seen, are a convenient way to group together classes with a common or related background. Figure D-1 illustrates a very small piece of the .NET Class Library. When you look at this diagram,

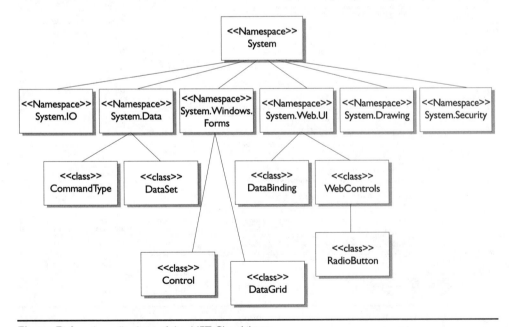

Figure D-1 A small subset of the .NET Class Library

keep in mind that we have only shown 6 of the approximately 84 namespaces, and under each namespace only two of hundreds of the underlying classes. If this has given you a sense of the magnitude of this library, remember that you can add to it as well. We are only looking at Microsoft's structure in these instances—third-party namespaces will expand the library even further.

Every namespace that you explore within the class library contains classes, structures, enums, delegates, and interfaces (not necessary all of them) that you can use in your programs. As discussed before, to use a namespace, code a line like the following at the beginning of your program:

```
using System;
```

This code tells the compiler that you may be using one or more of the different types in the System namespace.

There are many ways to access the documentation for .NET Library types. We will talk about two of the ways. First, within the Visual Studio .NET development environment is a large documentation and help subsystem. Figure D-2 shows the root of the .NET Class Library help structure. The best way to find it is by typing **Class Library** in the Look For

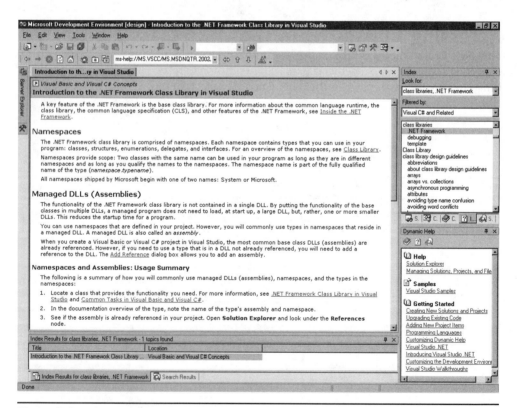

Figure D-2   Documentation for the .NET Class Library

field (a search tool). When you do this, you will see the introduction page, and you can begin locating valuable information by clicking on the Class Library hyperlink. That link will direct you to a page that has links to every namespace in the .NET library, as shown in Figure D-3.

 TIP You can add the web page to your list of favorites by selecting View | Other Windows and Favorites from the menus. If you are anything like us, you will find this page extremely helpful as you become familiar with the classes available to you.

By selecting one of the namespaces shown in Figure D-3, you will find that you are able to see all of the classes within that namespace.

There is another way to find help on the .NET Class Library, and that is by using Microsoft's MSDN web site at http://msdn.microsoft.com. Currently, the page that you saw in Figure D-2 is also on Microsoft's site (see Figure D-4).

Whichever method you choose when accessing the documentation, you will find that Microsoft has spent a fair bit of time in making sure that the information is available to you and is easily readable.

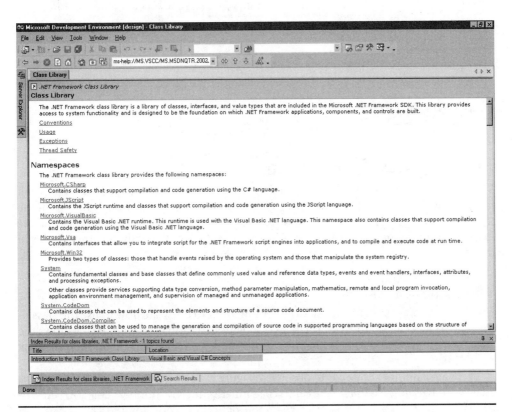

Figure D-3 The .NET Class Library namespaces

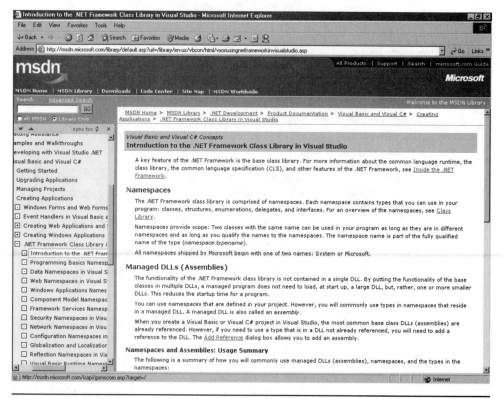

Figure D-4   The .NET Class Library documentation on the Internet

The System Namespace

Microsoft has grouped together a collection of classes that will help you with common tasks. Table D-1 gives you an example of some of the classes that you might find in the System namespace. Remember that this is just a short list of common classes available in the System namespace. Take some time to become familiar with the other classes in the library.

The Math Class

There are a lot of classes to choose from, but in order to illustrate how to use the class library, we have selected the Math class as our demonstration class. Figure D-5 shows the page you will receive if you choose the System link from Figure D-3 and then click the Math link.

There are a number of things to observe in Figure D-5. Notice that the inheritance hierarchy is in the top-left corner—the Math class inherits directly from System.Object. In the large, gray-shaded area you can see the definition code for the class—public sealed class Math. This means that you cannot create any children of the Math class.

Class Name	Purpose
ApplicationException	A parent class for non-terminating program errors.
Array	Methods for creating, searching, and sorting arrays.
Console	Standard input, output, and error streams. These are used for console applications.
GC	A class for controlling the system garbage collector.
Math	Methods for common mathematical functions. See the "The Math Class" section that follows for more details.
Object	The parent class of every class.
OperatingSystem	A class that provides information about the operating system—version and the like.
String	An immutable set of characters.
SystemException	The base class for predefined exceptions.
UInt32	A structure that represents 32-bit unsigned integers.

Table D-1   A Short List of the Types of Classes in the System Namespace

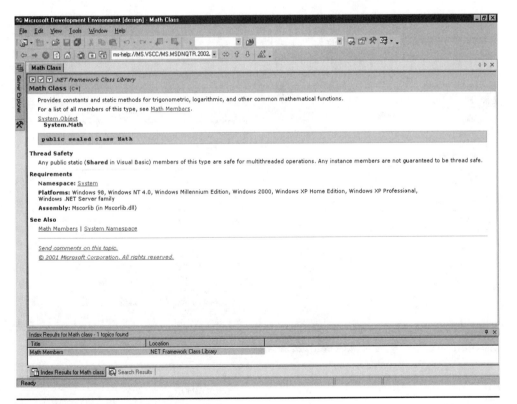

Figure D-5   The Math class documentation

This summary page also shows you how safe the code is to use in multithreaded operations. Notice, as well, that the platforms are listed on this page, along with the assembly in which the class is found (in this case `Mscorlib.dll`).

If you are interested in checking out the properties and methods that are available for use in this class, click the Math Members link. You will see a screen that looks like the one in Figure D-6.

There are two fields, `E` and `PI`, that are listed, along with their purpose. As you can see from the list, there are many public methods in the `Math` class. We will select one, the `Round()` method, in order to dig deeper into this documentation. The `Round()` method is used to return the integer nearest to the number given, following the rules of rounding. For example, the following code segment returns 12.

```
using System;
class Rounding
{
    public static void Main()
    {
        Console.WriteLine (Math.Round(12.42));
    }
}
```

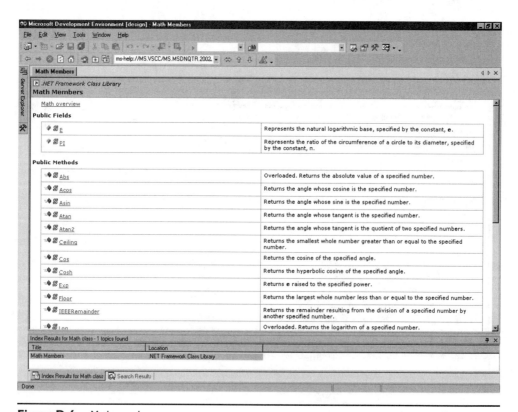

Figure D-6   Math members

In order to select the documentation for the Round() method, simply click on the method in the window shown in Figure D-6, and you will see the screen in Figure D-7.

This method is overloaded four times in order to give you an opportunity to pass it different sets of parameters. In our previous example, we simply sent the method a double value (12.42). However, you could send a decimal and an int, as well as a double and an int. This again demonstrates the power of overloading methods—you don't have to remember four different method names.

Notice the signature of all the methods. They are all static methods. This means that you do not need an instance of the class in order to call the methods. As a matter of fact, if you examine the code from our example, you will notice that we simply called the method directly from the class name itself:

```
Console.WriteLine (Math.Round(12.42));
```

Most of the utility methods in the System class will operate in a similar fashion.

If you wish to dig deeper into the documentation, you can select any of the links for the overloaded methods. We chose the first one to demonstrate:

```
public static decimal Round(decimal);
```

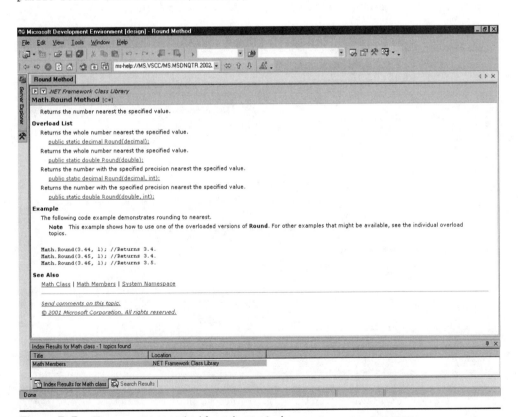

Figure D-7   The Round( ) method from the Math class

As Figure D-8 shows, by selecting the link, you receive valuable information detailing the method. Even though we have chosen to look at a relatively easy concept, rounding, you can imagine that if you needed to find out about a method you knew nothing about, the documentation presented here would be worth its weight in gold.

A Final Note on the System Namespace

Microsoft has attempted to alleviate some of the confusion that can arise when there are so many different namespaces and classes from which to choose. By using the System namespace and then further subdividing it, you really have one focused area in which to start your search. You will find that there are a few other top-level namespaces, such as Microsoft.Csharp, Microsoft.Jscript, Microsoft.VisualBasic, and so on, that are used to describe classes pertinent to the individual languages. However, you will probably spend most of your time in the System namespace.

Although this is not specific to the System namespace, there is another area of the documentation that may be of interest to you. It is possible to view the namespace hierarchy in order to see which classes are base classes and which are derived classes. Figure D-9 illustrates the System namespace inheritance scheme. You will find a link on each of the namespace home pages that will take you to <<namespace>> hierarchy.

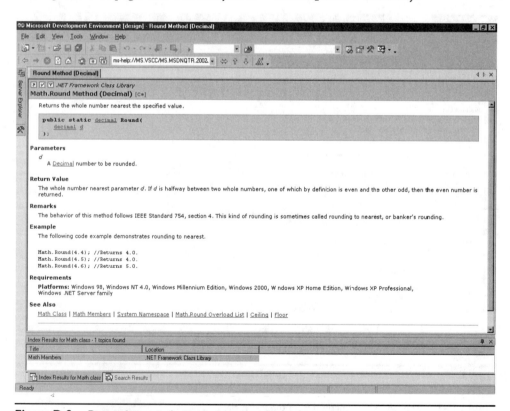

Figure D-8   Digging deeper in the Math documentation

Figure D-9   The System namespace inheritance hierarchy

Useful System Namespaces

We will now take a brief look at some of the namespaces that might be pertinent to you on the Microsoft exams, in particular, System.Data, System.Web.UI, and System.Windows.Forms. You saw System.Data in Chapter 10, and the other two were discussed in Parts III and IV on Web and Windows development.

System.Data Namespace

You will find in the System.Data namespace a lot of classes that make up part of the ADO.NET structure. This allows you to manipulate data from many different sources. ADO follows a concept of universal data access and provides tools to access, update, and connect to data in any location. For more information on ADO.NET, please review Chapter 10 on basic data access. Table D-2 lists some of the classes found in this namespace.

There are many classes, interfaces, delegates, and enumerations available within the System.Data namespace. For example, in the following list, you will see the inheritance structure of the classes in the System.Data namespace. You can use this as a reference

Class	Purpose
Constraint	Simulates a constraint on one or more DataColumn objects
DataColumn	Represents the field level from a table
DataException	Represents an exception that is thrown from ADO.NET components
DataRelation	Represents the relationship between two DataTable objects
DataRow	Same as DataColumn, except it represents a row of data
DataSet	Represents the powerful, internal cache of data returned
DataTable	Represents one table of in-memory data

Table D-2   Sample classes from the System.Data namespace

to the classes that are available in the namespace. Although this is a long list, for the purposes of the three Microsoft exams, you should become familiar with this namespace.

```
System.Object
    System.Attribute
        System.ComponentModel.DescriptionAttribute
            System.Data.DataSysDescriptionAttribute
    System.Collections.Hashtable
        System.Data.PropertyCollection
    System.ComponentModel.MarshalByValueComponent
        System.Data.DataColumn
        System.Data.DataSet
            ---- System.ComponentModel.IListSource,
                 System.ComponentModel.ISupportInitialize,
                 System.Runtime.Serialization.ISerializable
        System.Data.DataTable
            ---- System.ComponentModel.IListSource,
                 System.ComponentModel.ISupportInitialize,
                 System.Runtime.Serialization.ISerializable
        System.Data.DataView
            ---- System.ComponentModel.IBindingList,
                 System.Collections.IList,
                 System.Collections.ICollection,
                 System.Collections.IEnumerable,
                 System.ComponentModel.ITypedList,
                 System.ComponentModel.ISupportInitialize
        System.Data.DataViewManager
            ---- System.ComponentModel.IBindingList,
                 System.Collections.IList,
                 System.Collections.ICollection,
                 System.Collections.IEnumerable,
                 System.ComponentModel.ITypedList
    System.Data.Constraint
        System.Data.ForeignKeyConstraint
        System.Data.UniqueConstraint
    System.Data.DataRelation
    System.Data.DataRow
    System.Data.DataRowView
        ---- System.ComponentModel.ICustomTypeDescriptor,
             System.ComponentModel.IEditableObject,
             System.ComponentModel.IDataErrorInfo
    System.Data.DataViewSetting
```

```
        System.Data.DataViewSettingCollection
        ---- System.Collections.ICollection,
             System.Collections.IEnumerable
    System.Data.InternalDataCollectionBase
        System.Data.ConstraintCollection
        System.Data.DataColumnCollection
        System.Data.DataRelationCollection
        System.Data.DataRowCollection
        System.Data.DataTableCollection
    System.Data.TypedDataSetGenerator
    System.Delegate
        System.MulticastDelegate
            System.Data.DataColumnChangeEventHandler
            System.Data.DataRowChangeEventHandler
            System.Data.FillErrorEventHandler
            System.Data.MergeFailedEventHandler
            System.Data.StateChangeEventHandler
    System.EventArgs
        System.Data.DataColumnChangeEventArgs
        System.Data.DataRowChangeEventArgs
        System.Data.FillErrorEventArgs
        System.Data.MergeFailedEventArgs
        System.Data.StateChangeEventArgs
    System.Exception
        System.SystemException
            System.Data.DataException
                System.Data.ConstraintException
                System.Data.DeletedRowInaccessibleException
                System.Data.DuplicateNameException
                System.Data.InRowChangingEventException
                System.Data.InvalidConstraintException
                System.Data.InvalidExpressionException
                    System.Data.EvaluateException
                    System.Data.SyntaxErrorException
                System.Data.MissingPrimaryKeyException
                System.Data.NoNullAllowedException
                System.Data.ReadOnlyException
                System.Data.RowNotInTableException
                System.Data.StrongTypingException
                System.Data.TypedDataSetGeneratorException
                System.Data.VersionNotFoundException
            System.Data.DBConcurrencyException
    System.ValueType
        System.Enum
            System.Data.AcceptRejectRule
            System.Data.CommandBehavior
            System.Data.CommandType
            System.Data.ConnectionState
            System.Data.DataRowAction
            System.Data.DataRowState
            System.Data.DataRowVersion
            System.Data.DataViewRowState
            System.Data.DbType
            System.Data.IsolationLevel
            System.Data.MappingType
            System.Data.MissingMappingAction
            System.Data.MissingSchemaAction
            System.Data.ParameterDirection
            System.Data.PropertyAttributes
```

```
System.Data.Rule
System.Data.SchemaType
System.Data.SqlDbType
System.Data.StatementType
System.Data.UpdateRowSource
System.Data.UpdateStatus
System.Data.XmlReadMode
System.Data.XmlWriteMode
```

 TIP You would be wise to investigate this namespace thoroughly before writing the Microsoft exams. Although you will find the testing more specific to data access within the Web or Windows Forms, you will still need to have a good understanding of ADO.NET, the architecture for which the `System.Data` namespace was built.

System.Web.UI Namespace

Just as the classes for ADO.NET were encapsulated inside of the `System.Data` namespace, you will find the classes and interfaces for ASP.NET server controls and pages inside the `System.Web.UI` namespace. These classes will allow you to create the user interface components for your web applications. You will discover classes that provide server controls, user controls, data binding, web page state management, and a lot more here. Table D-3 lists a few of the classes to be found in `System.Web.UI`.

The use of this namespace is discussed in an entire part of this book, Part III. You will need to understand it for the web application exam.

The System.Windows.Forms Namespace

The `System.Windows.Forms` namespace is a very large namespace that is used for creating Windows-based applications. In order to take advantage of the power of the

Class	Purpose
Control	Contains properties, methods, and events that are shared by all ASP.NET server controls
DataBinding	Creates data-binding expressions at design time within Visual Studio .NET
HtmlTextWriter	Writes a sequential series of HTML-specific characters and text on a Web Forms page
Page	Represents an `.aspx` file
StateBag	Represents the state of server controls in terms of their view state
UserControl	Represents the `.ascx` file when it is called from an `.aspx` file

Table D-3   Some of the Classes Within the `System.Web.UI` Namespace

Windows operating system, many classes have been prebuilt to represent components in the Windows interface. You will find the following types of classes in this namespace:

- **Controls**   You will find text boxes, combo boxes, labels, lists, buttons, and the like in this grouping.

- **Control, User Control, and Form**   `Control` is base class for all the controls on a Windows form. The form allows you to create dialog boxes, windows, and so on, and the user control is there so that you can create custom controls that are made up of other controls.

- **Common dialog boxes**   If you want to represent the common file-open, file-print, font, and other dialog boxes, you will find a lot of useful classes in this section of the namespace.

- **Components**   You will find menus, help, tool tips, and the like here.

As we mentioned, this is a very large namespace, and as such, is better viewed within the documentation. Part IV of this book explores several of the classes found in the `System.Windows.Forms` namespace. As with `System.Web.UI`, you will need to know these classes for the exam, so we have devoted a full part of the book to them.

Summary

This has been a brief introduction to the .NET Class Library. Hopefully you now have an appreciation for the amount of work that has been done by the developers of the library, to help you spend more time on your business problems. We recommend that you dig around the documentation a bit in order to become more familiar with the classes in the different namespaces.

Glossary

We have included this glossary because we really understand that some of the acronyms, terms, and .NET-speak can be very overwhelming. It's a good idea to make sure that this handy list rolls off your tongue before you go into the exam. You will find that some questions will incorporate as many terms as possible just to confuse the issue. You can also use this glossary as a reference when you are working through the book. Enjoy!

A

abstract class   A **class** that cannot be **instantiated**. An abstract class contains at least one **abstract method**. It operates as a **base class** from which other classes **inherit**.

abstract method   A method in an **abstract class** that has no implementation. It acts as a template. Concrete classes that inherit from the abstract class must implement any abstract methods.

abstraction   An object-oriented design concept that, when employed, means the design focus is on the essential attributes of an **object**, and the inner workings are hidden. Abstraction means that a complex object can be reduced to its simplest terms.

access modifiers   Modifiers that define the visibility level of **classes** and class members. Examples of access modifiers include *public*, *protected*, *private*, and so on.

ACID   A term that represents atomicity, consistency, isolation, and durability. Atomicity is an all-or-nothing term for transaction processing; consistency means that transactions leave a database in a consistent state and don't break any constraint rules; isolation means that a transaction is not affected by other transactions; and durability means that transactions are protected against hardware and software failures.

activation   The process of creating a remote **object** on a **server** and obtaining a reference to the **proxy** of the object.

Active Server Pages (ASP)   A Microsoft technology for creating web pages that have dynamic content, meaning that inside the web page are server-side code segments.

ActiveX control   A component that uses **COM** technology. As such, it implements the IUnknown **interface**.

ActiveX Data Objects (ADO)   A language-neutral object model of **COM** components that describes **objects** used for accessing data.

ADO.NET   A language-neutral object model that uses the **.NET Framework** to describe **objects** used for accessing data.

alias   A name given to identify resources on an intranet or on the Internet. A **Web Form**, an HTML page, and so forth, can all be given alias names that can be used programmatically.

application domain   A unit of isolation for an application. The **Common Language Runtime** allows one process to be divided into many application domains.

Application Program Interface (API)   A set of routines, protocols, and tools for building software applications.

ASP.NET   A web development platform that allows developers to build enterprise applications using the **.NET Framework** and a web object model.

assembly   A logical unit of .NET components. Assemblies can be made up of many files, and they contain **metadata** information used by the runtime environment. When you use assemblies, you do not need to install the component into the system Registry.

assembly cache   A storage area for side-by-side **assemblies**. The **Global Assembly Cache** contains assemblies that will be shared among many different applications. The download cache stores code downloaded from the Internet.

asynchronous methods   Methods that do not require the application to wait for their completion before another method call is made.

attribute   A description within an XML element that provides extra information for the element.

authentication   The process of identifying an individual for security reasons. Authentication deals with *who the individual is* and not *what the individual can do*. Also see authorization.

authorization   The process of giving individuals permissions to access **objects**. Authorization deals with *what the individual can do* instead of *who the individual is*. Also see authentication.

B

base class   The **class** from which another class inherits. At the top of the **inheritance** structure is the base class, `Object`, from which every other class inherits.

boxing   The ability to call on methods of primitive types. For example, you can convert a **value-type variable** to a **reference-type variable** using boxing.

breakpoint A debugging location in a program that will cause the program to temporarily suspend execution. The developer can then query variable values, test code, watch the call stack, and so forth.

C

caching Storing frequently requested documents in the memory of a **server** or a **client** machine. This process speeds up the retrieval of web documents.

callback The address that an **event** source calls when an event happens.

cascading style sheet (CSS) A mechanism for adding styling to web documents, such as fonts, colors, and so forth. A style sheet contains the rules for transforming the web document.

casting The process of converting one **object** type to another, compatible object type.

certificate A digital attachment to a message. The certificate contains security information about the provider of the message, such as who they are and if they can be trusted.

channel An **object** that is responsible for the actual wire transmission of a remote request.

class A definition or blueprint of an **object**. A class file contains a class description, along with the members of the class (methods, fields, and so forth). Classes are the foundation of **object-oriented programming**.

client The requestor of the services of a remote **object**.

client-activated object (CAO) A remote object that is activated by a client application.

CLR See Common Language Runtime.

CLS See Common Language Specification.

codebehind A class that is accessed by an .aspx file. It is a separate file from the .aspx file.

COM See Component Object Model.

Common Language Runtime (CLR) The runtime environment that supplies services for .NET code, such as object lifetime, debugging, and code-access security.

Common Language Specifications (CLS) The minimum requirements that a .NET language must support. In order to create components that are accessible from every .NET implementation, the code must follow the CLS.

PART VI

Common Type System (CTS)   Defines a set of rules that all .NET language compilers must follow. These rules specify information about reference and value types.

Component Object Model (COM)   Microsoft's framework for developing components that will interact using standard **interfaces**.

connection pooling   The ability of a database provider to create a pool of connections that a new connection request can utilize.

console application   A template for a solution that will run within the context of a console.

constructor   A pseudo-method that is called when the new keyword is used to create an **object**. Code placed within a constructor will execute exactly once when the object is created.

CSS   See **cascading style sheet**.

CTS   See Common Type System.

custom control   A control that is created by someone other than the .NET Framework. A custom control can be created from scratch or can use controls already in existence and build upon their functionality.

D

data binding   The ability to tie data source information to a control or **object**.

data consumer   A component that is capable of displaying data.

data provider   The source of the data. A data provider is required to gain access to a database. Common data providers include *OleDbProvider*, *SqlProvider*, and so forth.

DCOM   See Distributed Component Object Model.

delegate   A reference type that is similar to a C++ function pointer. If you want to pass a method to another method, you need a delegate.

deployment   The process of distributing an application to another computer, an intranet, the Internet, and or elsewhere.

derived class   The class that is created by **inheriting** from a **base class**. All classes derive from the Object class.

Discovery of Web Services (DISCO)   The process of using a URL to find the location of a web service. Not only can the location be found, but information about the service can be retrieved through the discovery process. Information such as how to interact with the service can be retrieved.

distributed application   An application that has components that are not local to each other. An example of a distributed application is a 3-tier model application, whereby the user interface is located on one computer, the business logic resides in a middle-tier server, and the back-end database is found elsewhere.

Distributed Component Object Model (DCOM)   Microsoft's object model that defines the interaction of components that are remote to each other.

dynamic-link library (DLL)   A library of executable functions or **classes**. A DLL can be used by many applications at one time.

dock   A window that floats on top of other windows or snaps to the side of another window.

document type definition (DTD)   A document that states which tags and **attributes** are used to describe the elements in an XML file.

E

encapsulation   The process of combining members, such as methods and fields, to create a single **object**. The ability to hide the data and methods from the user of the class is also a part of encapsulation.

enumeration   A **value type** that provides alternative names for the values of a primitive type.

event   An action that may be caused by user intervention or the underlying system and that can be detected by a program. Actions include clicking the mouse button, clicking a Windows button, and so forth.

exception   A condition that causes a program to halt or terminate abnormally. Exceptions include dividing by zero, attempting to access a nonexistent file, and so forth.

exception handling   The process of ensuring that program **exceptions** do not cause the application to terminate. Acceptable exceptions, such as a database being unavailable, can be caught and dealt with through exception handling.

Extensible Markup Language (XML)   A specification that allows for the definition of data using customized tags and elements.

Extensible Stylesheet Language (XSL)   A specification that looks like a template for XML documents. Similar to **cascading style sheets**.

Extensible Stylesheet Language Transformations (XSLT)   A language used in XSL that can convert XML documents into other XML documents.

PART VI

F

formatter   An **object** responsible for converting a method request into a transmission-capable message and vice versa.

G

GAC   See Global Assembly Cache.

garbage collection   The process by which **object** references that have been set to NULL are removed from memory. In effect, the actual object is destroyed.

Global Assembly Cache (GAC)   The code **cache** that stores **assemblies** that will be shared among multiple applications. Any assembly that is stored in the GAC must have a **strong name**.

globalization   The process of creating software that can be used by multiple **locales** and cultures.

globally unique identifier (GUID)   A unique number used to identify a component, application, file, user, and so forth. GUIDs are also used in the Windows Registry to identify **DLLs**.

H

heap   A memory location reserved for **objects** of undefined size (all objects). A **reference-type variable** contains the address of an object located in the heap.

Hypertext Transfer Protocol (HTTP)   The protocol of the Web. It defines how messages are formatted and carried over the internetwork. HTTP commands can be sent to a web server to request a certain page.

I

impersonation   Execution of **ASP.NET** code—authenticated and authorized client.

inheritance   The technique of creating a **class** file that derives from a parent class file. All methods and data of the parent are inherited by the child class.

instantiation   The process of creating a new **object** instance. The **constructor** of the class file is called first, and then the **object** instance is built.

interface   A **class** file that creates a contract. Other classes that implement the **interface** are obligated under the contract to implement the public methods of the interface.

J

just-in-time (JIT) compilation   The process by which **Microsoft Intermediate Language** is converted into machine code when the code is run.

L

lifetime   The amount of time that an **object** is allocated in memory.

locale   The language, character, date/time, and currency rules that are specific to a given country.

localization   The process of creating **resources** that are specific to a **locale**.

M

managed code   Code that supplies **metadata** that is read by the runtime and provides information about memory management, code access, security, and so forth. Any code that is created using **Microsoft Intermediate Language** is executed as managed code.

metadata   Information that describes the underlying data. Simply put, it is data about data. Metadata can supply information to the runtime about security, binding, debugging, and the like.

Microsoft Intermediate Language (MSIL)   The language created when a program is compiled using the .NET Framework. It is one step away from being native code (code specific to the application platform).

N

namespace   A logical grouping of related **classes**. By using namespaces, you can group together classes and types that are logically bound to each other. The namespace then provides a means of locating the class through its hierarchical name.

native code   The code that is created when MSIL code is compiled to be machine-specific.

.NET Framework   The platform for building and deploying .NET applications. These applications include Web services, **Windows forms**, **Web forms**, **console applications**, and so forth.

.NET Framework class library   A collection of prebuilt **classes** that can be used by any application. These classes provide the developer with reusable components.

O

object   The instantiated representation of a **class** file. A single class file is the template for one or more objects to be created.

object-oriented programming (OOP)   The art of using **objects** in the programming environment to represent real-life entities or functionality.

overloading   The process by which a method can have many definitions. For example, the `ToString()` method of the `Object` **class** has many overloaded implementations. The distinguishing factor of an overloaded method is its parameter list.

override   The ability to change the functionality of a parent **class** method. Child classes inherit a method from the parent and can change or add to the functionality of that method by overriding the parent method.

P

platform invoke   The ability of a **managed code** segment to call an unmanaged code segment.

polymorphism   Meaning many forms. The technique of creating **object** relationships such that a method called on a parent object reference will invoke the method of the actual object, which could be a child object.

port   An endpoint to a logical connection. Well known ports are numbered in the range of 0 to 1024. New applications can use port numbers greater than 1024.

principal   A security context that represents the identity and role of the user.

private assembly   An **assembly** that is only accessible to programs within the same directory.

proxy   An **object** that represents a remote object. A client calls the methods of the remote object, and the proxy object intercepts the method call and passes it to the **remoting** infrastructure.

R

Rapid Application Development (RAD)   A programming environment that allows the developer to quickly build applications. Several tools are included in the development environment that abstract the complexity of certain operations, such as building graphical user interfaces.

reference-type variables   A variable that provides a handle or reference to an actual **object**. Object method calls are all done through reference variables. Dare we call them pointers? See also **value-type variables**.

reflection   A runtime process by which information can be determined about **assemblies** and the types of **objects** they contain.

remoting   A communication process and architecture that defines the methods by which a client **object** can make calls to a remote object.

resource files   Any file (not an executable file) that contains information that will be used by an application. Resource files can contain **locale**-specific information, images, and so forth.

role   A named set of **principals** that operate under the same security rules.

S

satellite assembly   An **assembly** that holds only **resource files**.

serialization   The process of creating a storable form of an **object's** data (or state).

server   A component that provides services to a **client's** request.

server-activated object   A remote **server object** that is activated through its own code. Server-activated objects can be in one of two modes: *SingleCall* (which creates a single instance for each client) or *Singleton* (which creates a single instance for all clients).

server control   An element that can be placed on an **ASP.NET** page or a **Web Form**.

serviced component   A **class** that can be hosted by a COM+ application and that can use COM+ services.

session state   The data that is unique to an **object**. Session state specifies the information that an object knows for the life of its session.

shared assembly   An **assembly** that can be shared by multiple applications. Shared assemblies are installed in the **GAC** and have **strong names**.

side-by-side deployment   The ability to have multiple versions of a component installed. In order to support applications that require earlier versions of a component, side-by-side deployment allows backward compatibility with no versioning headaches.

Simple Object Access Protocol (SOAP)   An **XML**-based protocol for exchanging information over a network.

SOAP extensions   Algorithms that allow developers to alter a **SOAP** message that is sent to and from an **XML web service** or **client**. This provides for the ability to alter the functionality of the web service—an example would be adding an encryption algorithm to the service.

stored procedure   A set of instructions that are stored on the database **server**. A user program can call a stored procedure, and it will execute from compiled instructions on the server.

strong name   A name that includes a text name, a version number, and optional culture information for an **assembly**. Included in the name is a public key and a digital signature. Assemblies that are intended for shared access must be given strong names.

T

template   A declarative page fragment used to provide a visual interface for a templated ASP.NET server **control**.

trace listener   An **object** that collects trace messages from an application. The listener object then directs the message to the appropriate output.

trace switch   An **object** in the application's code that can control the **tracing** conducted at runtime. By using trace switches, you can programmatically turn off tracing, configure the level of tracing, and determine the output for the tracing messages.

tracing   The mechanism by which runtime messages regarding the execution of an application can be generated.

U

UDDI   See Universal Description, Discovery, and Integration.

unboxing   The conversion of a **reference type** to a **value type**.

Universal Description, Discovery, and Integration (UDDI)   A mechanism by which web services are published and advertised. **Client** applications can also use UDDI to locate web services and information about the services.

unit test plan   The process of creating units of code and testing their functionality outside of the "big picture." Stub programs are created to simulate the outside activity.

unmanaged code   Code that is created without the **CLR** requirements. Since the requirements are not met, the code can still run in the runtime environment but cannot take advantage of runtime services such as **garbage collection**, security, and the like.

V

value-type variables   Data types that describe primitive data types: integers, floating-point numbers, and so forth. Value types can be converted to **object** references by using **boxing**. See also **reference-type variables**.

W

Web Forms   A framework that supports server-side controls and renders HTML on web browsers.

Web Services Description Language (WSDL)   An XML-based language that describes the services offered by a **server**.

Windows Forms   A framework that supports .NET components on a **Windows form**.

Windows Service   A component that runs in the background of a Windows session. The service is always running and can answer **client** requests at any time.

WSDL   See Web Services Description Language.

X

XML   See Extensible Markup Language.

XML Web Service   An HTTP-, XML-, and SOAP-based programming model that provides distributed component access over standard protocols.

XSL   See Extensible Stylesheet Language.

XSLT   See Extensible Stylesheet Language Transformations.

INDEX

References to figures and illustrations are in italics.

/ (forward slashes), 190

A

INTERNATIONAL CONTACT INFORMATION

AUSTRALIA
McGraw-Hill Book Company Australia Pty. Ltd.
TEL +61-2-9415-9899
FAX +61-2-9415-5687
http://www.mcgraw-hill.com.au
books-it_sydney@mcgraw-hill.com

CANADA
McGraw-Hill Ryerson Ltd.
TEL +905-430-5000
FAX +905-430-5020
http://www.mcgrawhill.ca

**GREECE, MIDDLE EAST,
NORTHERN AFRICA**
McGraw-Hill Hellas
TEL +30-1-656-0990-3-4
FAX +30-1-654-5525

MEXICO (Also serving Latin America)
McGraw-Hill Interamericana Editores S.A. de C.V.
TEL +525-117-1583
FAX +525-117-1589
http://www.mcgraw-hill.com.mx
fernando_castellanos@mcgraw-hill.com

SINGAPORE (Serving Asia)
McGraw-Hill Book Company
TEL +65-863-1580
FAX +65-862-3354
http://www.mcgraw-hill.com.sg
mghasia@mcgraw-hill.com

SOUTH AFRICA
McGraw-Hill South Africa
TEL +27-11-622-7512
FAX +27-11-622-9045
robyn_swanepoel@mcgraw-hill.com

**UNITED KINGDOM & EUROPE
(Excluding Southern Europe)**
McGraw-Hill Education Europe
TEL +44-1-628-502500
FAX +44-1-628-770224
http://www.mcgraw-hill.co.uk
computing_neurope@mcgraw-hill.com

ALL OTHER INQUIRIES Contact:
Osborne/McGraw-Hill
TEL +1-510-549-6600
FAX +1-510-883-7600
http://www.osborne.com
omg_international@mcgraw-hill.com